## Praise of Richard Lloyd Dewey's
## *Porter Rockwell: A Biography*

"Riveting reading, solidly researched."
—Gannett Newspapers (*USA Today*, etc.)

"Dramatic and convincing."
—*West Coast Review of Books*

"Superlative work."
—James A. Cox, *Midwest Book Review*

"The writing is slick and the pace is fast.
Dewey has done his homework."
—*Deseret News*

"The best book of several written on Porter Rockwell."
—Duaine Hiatt, *This People Magazine*

"Masterfully written, fully documented."
—Dr. Fred R. Gowans, Professor of History,
    Brigham Young University

"Remarkable book . . . engaging . . . exciting."
—Dr. John A. Schultz, Professor of History,
    University of Southern California

"Rockwell's life was an extraordinary mix of faith
and firepower. Well-researched."
—Dr. Walter Nugent, Professor of History,
    Notre Dame University

# JOSEPH SMITH

## AND THE LATTER-DAY SAINTS

VOLUME 1

BOOKS BY RICHARD LLOYD DEWEY:

*Porter Rockwell: A Biography* (1986, Revised 9th Edition 2006)

*Rockwell: U. S. Marshal* (1987)

*The Porter Rockwell Chronicles, Vol. 1* (1999)
*The Porter Rockwell Chronicles, Vol. 2* (2000)
*The Porter Rockwell Chronicles, Vol. 3* (2001)
*The Porter Rockwell Chronicles, Vol. 4* (2002)

*Hubener vs. Hitler* (2003, Revised 2nd edition 2004)

*Joseph Smith: A Biography* (2005)

BOOKS WITH FOREWORDS BY RICHARD LLOYD DEWEY:

*History of Joseph Smith by His Mother, Lucy Mack Smith:*
*The Unabridged, Original Version,*
compiled by R. Vernon Ingleton (2005, 2006)

*Life of Joseph Smith the Prophet,*
by George Q. Cannon (2005)

*Autobiography of Parley P. Pratt* (2005)

# JOSEPH SMITH

## AND THE LATTER-DAY SAINTS

A BIOGRAPHY IN THREE VOLUMES

VOLUME 1

## Richard Lloyd Dewey

STRATFORD
BOOKS

Santa Monica, California | Provo, Utah

2014

*Joseph Smith and the Latter-day Saints, Volume 1*

By Richard Lloyd Dewey

Stratford Books, Inc.
Stratfordbooks@yahoo.com

Cover photo: Stan MacBean from Photographic Solutions
Joseph Smith portrait: © David Lindsley. Used by permission.

First Edition: December 2014

Printed on acid-free paper in accordance with standards set by the American Library Association

Printed in the United States of America

*To Christian Miles Dewey,*
*a hard-working, faithful son*
*whose family looks up to him*
*for making the right*
*sacrifices*

JOSEPH SMITH

From the portrait *Brother Joseph* by David Lindsley.
Used by permission. © David Lindsley.

*"It ain't ignorance causes so much trouble;
it's folks knowing so much that ain't so."*

**JOSH BILLINGS**
(Henry Wheeler Shaw)

Nineteenth-century lecturer,
writer and folk humorist

As currently planned, Volumes 2 and 3
should be released in coming alternate years.
Also, the index and bibliography may be included
in the final volume.

# FOREWORD

If Joseph Smith was anything, he was bold. Some would say audacious.

For starters, this resident of upstate New York in the early 1800s claimed to have been visited by God and angels.

Then he published a 588-page book that he claimed he translated, using sacred seer stones, from writings by a series of ancient American prophets spanning a thousand years. How this unlearned backwoods young man, who could barely even write basic English sentences, could have written this book—or how anyone, for that matter, could have made it up *and written it so rapidly* (See Appendix G of this book for *how rapidly*)—has remained an inexplicable mystery to those who cannot bring themselves to believe that there was anything divine or supernatural involved.

No sooner had he published the book, than he set up a church that eventually adopted the name of the Church of Jesus Christ of Latter-day Saints ("LDS," or "Mormon") and sent out missionaries throughout the United States and later into Canada and England to spread the word that God was ushering in the final dispensation through revelations to a modern prophet (Joseph himself), preparatory to Christ's future Second Coming and Millennial reign.

Not satisfied with introducing a new book of additional scripture, he next set himself to the task of revising and correcting that venerable book, the Bible, and later publishing numerous revelations that he claimed to be receiving from Jesus Christ, restoring lost truths and imparting new doctrines and instructions. Somewhere along the line Joseph also purchased Egyptian mummies and eventually "translated" some of the accompanying papyri, which he claimed had been penned by none other than the Old Testament prophet Abraham.

He directed his followers to build the city of Zion on the very edge of the American frontier, in Missouri. When mobs of unbelieving locals chased them out, Joseph Smith, while languishing in jail on unsubstantiated charges, advised his followers to regroup in Illinois. There they quickly turned a tract of marsh land on the banks of the Mississippi into a thriving community of stylish brick homes with magnificent gardens and orchards on remarkably spacious lots that rivaled Chicago as the largest city in the state, described by contemporary visitors as being the most beautiful frontier city in America. At his urging they began building a magnificent temple—the most imposing edifice west of the Atlantic coast—that Joseph himself did not live to see completed.

At the height of his career, he headed a large militia and had missionaries stumping for him all over the country in his run for president of the United States, but his life was abruptly cut short when he was assassinated by an anti-Mormon mob in Carthage, Illinois, at the young age of 38.

Americans in Joseph Smith's day were no more inclined to believe his claims than they are today. Christians generally assumed that the need for prophets had ceased with the coming of Christ some 18 centuries earlier, and it was already becoming socially acceptable to question whether there had ever been such a thing as a genuine prophet—a human through whom God made known His will to the rest of humanity.

Joseph and the missionaries that he sent out were usually met with extreme skepticism and often violent persecution. But there was something about him and the book he published that quickly attracted large numbers of devoted followers.

*Richard Lloyd Dewey* | JOSEPH SMITH AND THE LATTER-DAY SAINTS, VOLUME 1

With his followers also came enemies. His chief antagonists appeared early and in several varieties. Protestant Christian ministers were alarmed to see many of their best congregants flocking to the Mormons, and were determined to put him down. Newspaper editors soon discovered that Joseph and the Mormons made good copy. They eagerly spread tales of him and his followers, whom they assumed to be deluded fanatics, not caring to check their facts so long as the stories helped sell papers. Once Joseph had his church up and running, there was a steady supply of disaffected followers who were either excommunicated or left the church over personality clashes, power struggles, or unwillingness to embrace the new revelations that kept coming. These dissidents found a receptive audience among unbelievers for their complaints against Joseph, which allegations quickly made their way through the rumor mill, into the newspapers, and across the country and beyond. Later, when communities of Latter-day Saints, as they called themselves, grew large enough to create a voting bloc that could swing elections, politicians took up the cry against those uncontrollable Mormons.

And so the battle lines were drawn by the four major camps of his day—ministers, editors, dissidents, and, politicians— powerful enemies who took on Joseph at every turn and churned the tide of public opinion against him. Those battle lines have remained to this day, with public perception still being antagonistic, as a rule, toward him and the church he founded, and with its members still harboring a lingering sensitivity to the persecutions that drove the early Latter-day Saints as many as five times from their homes and eventually beyond the boundaries of the United States at that time, with hundreds perishing on the western prairies, as they escaped to the Rocky Mountains under the direction of Joseph's successor Brigham Young.

The result of all this is that it seems almost impossible for anyone to write objectively about Joseph Smith. Non-LDS writers naturally assume that Joseph was deluded, deceived, a fraud, or mentally off. So they draw upon the wealth of materials written by his detractors and thus tend to cast him in the worst possible light. LDS writers, on the other hand, are noticeably resistant to writing anything that would give readers pause to question whether Joseph Smith was indeed a prophet of God. Come to think of it, that really is the crux of the matter: whether he was or wasn't. So both camps tend to be driven to write what the other side calls propaganda, fearing perhaps that to do otherwise would call into question their own beliefs, one way or the other.

If Joseph Smith was the conniving charlatan and con man that his detractors make him out to be, he's not worthy of attention other than as a cautionary example of how such characters operate, or to protect succeeding generations from being duped by his fraudulent claims. But if, on the other hand, he actually did see and converse with heavenly beings, then what they imparted to him would be more than a little significant.

Joseph is no longer around for people to make their assessments based on personal observation, interaction, or the "vibe" they pick up from him. But many of his contemporaries left accounts of their interactions with and observations of him, and he left a considerable body of his own writings—both of which make up the bulk of this book.

In it, Richard Lloyd Dewey lays out the facts relative to Joseph Smith—not just the ones that thrill believers or the ones that fill detractors with indignation, but *all* the relevant facts necessary to flesh out the complete picture of the man. You see, writers about Joseph Smith typically leave out a lot of significant details regarding his life. Dewey supplies those details—details that are critical to assessing whether Joseph Smith truly was what he claimed to be.

Self-proclaimed prophets come along every generation. As a society we usually disregard them because we've learned that whatever following they gather almost invariably falls apart rather quickly once they disgrace themselves, or withers into obscurity after the death of the charismatic leader. That's what Joseph Smith's foes assumed would happen with his followers, either when they came to their senses or he was killed.

But it didn't. Instead, the church that he established has continued to grow worldwide to where it is now the fourth-largest Christian denomination in the United States and, in the estimation of non-LDS author and award-winning social scientist Mark Koltko-Rivera, Ph.D., appears poised to become the next major world religion. How does one account for that? Was it just some strange sociological phenomenon? Was it merely his martyrdom that kept the church going and attracted converts after his death? Did the Church of Jesus Christ of Latter-day Saints simply luck out with a string of capable leaders as his successors? Just what is it that continues to make Mormonism a vibrant force?

Mr. Dewey has done a masterful job of depicting Joseph Smith's followers from the very beginning of the movement. Latter-day Saint readers will be delighted to discover in these pages the personalities behind so many of the names that appear in the *Doctrine and Covenants* and church history. Drawing as he does on eyewitness accounts, the author also vividly and brilliantly portrays the excitement, wonder, and fervor that impelled thousands to forsake "respectable society" and suffer ostracism, persecution, and privation to follow Joseph wherever he went or to venture to far-flung locales at his bidding. He has captured the essence of what made Mormonism a phenomenon that continued to rile American society for decades after Joseph's martyrdom. He brings to life the interpersonal dynamics that played such a pivotal role in Joseph Smith's life and the history of the church that he founded.

It's an amazing tale, told from the perspective of one who, as a young man living in the Southern United States and close to graduating from school, set out to investigate Joseph Smith's claims from scratch, completely unbiased. The author had been raised in another faith—he had been an altar boy, in fact, a rather devout one at that—till he began questioning. He became convinced there was something to this Joseph Smith fellow. After graduating from college, his subsequent researches, first in writing his best-selling biography of Porter Rockwell (colorful western gunslinger), and then another 11 years preparing this biography of the Mormon prophet, have only served to strengthen that conviction.

From the time of Joseph Smith's first vision, there was never a dull moment in Joseph's life. It was filled with action and passion, triumphs and suffering, both the most exquisite and sublime joys and the most heart-wrenching trials, until the day of his violent death. Richard Lloyd Dewey does the story justice with a riveting narrative that reads more like a novel than a historical tome.

Thoroughly researched, this 3-volume biography (of which you are holding the first volume) goes far beyond the single-volume biography of Joseph Smith that the author published in 2005. In fact, it is probably the most detailed, comprehensive biography of the Mormon prophet to date. Dewey carefully documents his sources and keeps commentary to a minimum. After all, the facts speak forcefully for themselves and generally require little explanation. His writing is engaging and exciting, never dull and academic. He succeeds admirably in letting the reader get to know Joseph on a new level—a *personal* one.

Dewey has a knack for exploring and answering all the questions that naturally come to mind in reviewing Joseph Smith's story—hence the numerous appendices and additional details given in the endnotes. One appendix alone (Appendix U) contains the best, thorough yet concise, historical run-down you are likely to ever encounter, of the departure by mainstream Christianity from Jesus Christ's original doctrine and priesthood between the time of Christ's apostles and Joseph Smith's day. This period, the "Great Apostasy," made Joseph Smith's mission and the restoration of the gospel of Jesus Christ to the earth necessary, as Latter-day Saints see it. Other appendices relate in some detail the efforts of the Great Reformers who paved the way to make Joseph's mission even possible.

This is the biography of Joseph Smith that should have been written decades ago—but couldn't have, considering the lingering prejudices and limited access to information that prevailed in the pre-Internet era. Dewey captures all the grandeur and pathos of Joseph Smith's tumultuous, agonizing, glorious life. It's an amazing, stirring story. Read on and decide for yourself: was Joseph Smith the charlatan most assumed he was, or the genuine modern prophet he claimed to be?

VANCE L. HAWKINS
Historical research consultant

# PREFACE

JUST 83 days before his death, Joseph Smith declared, "You don't know me; you never knew my heart. No man knows my history. I cannot tell it; I shall never undertake it. I don't blame anyone for not believing my history. If I had not experienced what I have I would not have believed it myself. . . . When I am called by the trump of the archangel and weighed in the balance, you will all know me then."[1]

There's good reason for Joseph starting and stopping his history 11 different times. It was complicated. Hard to write. Filled with heartaches. He found writing a "little, narrow prison, almost as it were total darkness of paper, pen, and ink," and English "a crooked, broken, scattered and imperfect language."[2] He was more comfortable with verbal communication, at which he became masterful by the end of his career. So he preferred to dictate to scribes many of his journal entries (as detailed in Appendix A: "A History of Joseph's Histories"). Nevertheless, despite his many efforts over the years to write or dictate his story, he lamented that he never recorded enough of it, particularly of the early years.

This book attempts to fill in the gaps.

Why did I write it?

In the 1980s I became fascinated by his childhood friend, Porter Rockwell, a well-known gunfighter and U.S. deputy marshal, and wrote a biography about him, searching out every piece of information I could find. In researching that I became more and more intrigued by Joseph Smith. And knew I had to write a book about him.

This is what I found.

Joseph Smith is likely misunderstood more than any religious figure in American history. Mainly from books that have defamed him over the past nearly 2 centuries. Ironically, hard news reporters over the decades have actually improved their objectivity about him. But others, certain very bright authors, have perpetuated old myths.

If only a fraction of their writings were true, the church Joseph founded should quickly have gone as extinct as Jonestown. As columnist Tom Anderson once wrote regarding certain intellectuals, "It's not that they're ignorant. It's just that they know so much that isn't true."[3] (Anderson was rephrasing a quip by nineteenth-century folk humorist Josh Billings, which appears at the beginning of this book.) Many, nevertheless, have likely written from a sincere desire to relate the truth, believing and quoting the anti-Joseph sources.

This book takes a look at him from an honest viewpoint as well, but from that of a believer, yet one who looked at Joseph initially from another culture, another faith.

The challenge for millions, with respect to Joseph Smith, has been what to believe.

Because of misinformed yet often well-intentioned writers, some pretty interesting myths have been perpetuated. Others have passed by word of mouth.

A quick look at a few:

In Europe I've personally heard more than one person repeat with conviction a rumor that dates back over a century—that a tunnel exists under the ocean between England and the United States. Latter-day Saint missionaries kidnap young women and send them through this tunnel to America, where they are forced into polygamy.

Another persistent myth is that Mormons still practice polygamy. Well, they can if they want their names immediately removed from church rolls. It's simply not allowed in the organization. Hasn't been for over a hundred years. (Break-off "fundamentalist" groups do but they are far from mainstream Mormonism and are comparatively small in number.) Many book, newspaper, and TV reports still blur the distinction between the LDS church and break-off groups, leaving a fuzzy impression for millions that the church itself still practices plural marriage.

One of the more amusing myths, still encountered to this day, believe it or not, is that Mormons have horns. Children in European nations several decades ago asked young missionaries regularly if they could see their horns. Missionaries would sometimes respond in jest, "Wait till the sun goes down. But it's not like what you've heard. We're not devils. We're *werewolves*." Kids got the humor, thinking the missionaries cool.

Another rumor bandied about Europe, which I've personally heard, is: "Kidnapped girls are forced into the Salt Lake Temple by their captors who want to marry them, only to be chased up the stairs to the roof. Their options are to give in and get married or jump off the roof into the Great Salt Lake, and swim away." (Quite a feat, that, as the Great Salt Lake is a good 15 miles from the temple.[4])

In many ways the myths have gone from bad to worse to head for the hills. But just in case you're wondering if anyone buys outlandish myths these days, including ones not involving Latter-day Saints, consider this:

Public Policy Polling, sponsored by Fordham University and rated one of the most accurate of the 28 major political polls, conducted a poll in 2013 showing that 4 percent of the registered voters in the United States (over 5.2 million people) believe that shape-shifting reptilian humanoids have invaded earth and live in underground bases, waiting to emerge and take over the world. They are half-breed reptilian descendants from an inter-galactic breeding expedition 7,000 years ago between male aliens from the constellation Draco and Earthian women. And they now control most of the world's leaders, including former President George W. Bush and Queen Elizabeth II. Double that number of believers to include unregistered voters, then add another 7% who responded "not sure"—and their unregistered voter counterparts—and you have perhaps 24 million people in the U.S. alone (plus millions more around the globe) believing in or open to the idea of this absurd theory. Its chief promulgator, a Brit, has followers in 47 countries.[5]

The upside to this poll is that only a small percentage of civilized society will believe the crazy stuff, perhaps because of advancements in education, but enough people are open to nonsensical myths to make our planet an interesting place.

More myths about Mormons . . .

They have a weird lifestyle. Homespun clothes. No electricity, dancing, or cars.

As a young teen visiting my grandparents' in Miami, I saw a family wading in the ocean, all dressed in black, the women in long skirts and the men with long beards. I said to my parents, "Who are those people?"

My mother repled, "They're Mormons."

I believed her for years.

The thing about clothes, electricity, dancing, and cars comes from people commonly confusing the Mormons with the Amish. True, Mormons dress more modestly than most in society, but are generally in style. And as for dancing, it has been a mainstay in LDS recreation, including church-owned college dance teams winning numerous national championships from hip-hop to ballroom.[6]

More significantly, the LDS faithful embrace technological advancements. Utah is one of the leading high-tech centers in the world and Latter-day Saints include a host of successful scientists, surgeons, and researchers, including the inventor of television[7] and one of the first NASA physicist/astronauts.

Don L. Lind, active in his LDS faith, was among the first astronauts in the 1960s, whom I saw at church functions in Huntsville, Alabama, home of NASA's Marshall Space Flight Center, where the pioneers of the U.S. space program gathered (including a number of Latter-day Saint scientists).

The researchers included non-Mormon notables such as Wernher von Braun, first director of the center. After developing Germany's rockets in World War II he had sought out and surrendered to the Americans, wishing to help a country that "uses the Bible," and not the Soviet Union, then became the man most responsible for America successfully launching into space and reaching the moon. (He was also featured as the long-distance, bigger-than-life inspiration and mentor for the young rocket-building protagonist in one of my favorite movies, *October Sky*, based on a true story.) A NASA website pays him tribute as "without a doubt the greatest rocket scientist in history."[8]

Von Braun actually befriended my parents. As a teen-ager I remember him and his family at our home, including Thanksgiving dinner, after having met us through my mother's morning television show. (A side note here is that my parents were "no respectors of persons," befriending and inviting home-less people over for meals as well, including someone who be-came my personal friend, an older African-American gentleman with whom I fished on the wide Tennessee River in my idyllic childhood, reminiscent in some respects to Huck Finn—from my favorite American novel—especially in regards to roaming, rowing, and exploring the river wilderness with nearly absolute freedom, year in and year out, and making unusual friends). The example of my parents taught me not only to value those from all walks of life equally, but it opened my eyes to certain people with character traits of accomplishment coupled with modesty—and taking the time to help people like that kid in *October Sky*. Not only von Braun and my parents, but others whom I've observed have displayed those traits extraordinarily well, including some rather remarkable Latter-day Saints.

Which brings us to the next major myth: that Mormons are "unaccomplished."

I recall an old *Frazier* episode of a well-meaning but com-pletely incompetent acquaintance of Frazier—a rather funny episode, actually, in which a Mormon becomes his agent and inadvertently sabotages his chances for getting gigs, until his former agent, the conniving and manipulative Phoebe, is able to win Frazier back, convincing him he needs someone "com-petent" this time, despite her shenanigans and dishonesty. The Mormon guy, stereotypically, happened to be a scoutmaster and sang in the Tabernacle Choir, but was a "nice guy" incapable of functioning in a competitive business world. The writers of the series clearly mirrored the myth believed by some of society (and they also justified in a Hollywood-humorous way the theme that the ends—achieving success—justify the means).

By contrast, from what my parents made me aware of in my childhood are traits I have observed since in a number of Latter-day Saints—from space scientists to CEOs—who have achieved success, with great competence, but honestly and quietly. Since most don't wear their success on their sleeves, one often does not hear of their accomplishments unless outsiders broadcast them. Without that publicity, most Mormons have simply gone about their lives, while much of the world generally believes the ongoing myth about them being "unaccomplished."

A first cousin to that myth is that Mormons are "uneducated."

Giving the lie to that is a recent report from Forbes magazine: 2 of Utah's largest cities (Salt Lake City and Provo) rank in the top third of the "most educated cities in the United States," with one city (Provo) in the Top 4, among the largest 150 metropolitan areas.[9] Many top educators are Latter-day Saints as well.

Another myth—Mormons are like a middle-Eastern sect.

Once I sat with a family interested in learning about the LDS faith from a pair of Mormon missionaries. I heard the wife ask, "Do you meditate? Chant? Stare off into space and stuff?"

A missionary responded, "Yes, just this morning I stared at the toaster for 5 minutes, chanting over and over, "How could I have burned the toast again? How could I have burned the toast again?"

Though bizarrely sarcastic he made a point they thought was funny, and next time they likely won't confuse Mormons with middle-Eastern religions.

Easily a Top Five myth is that Latter-day Saints worship Joseph Smith. Truth is, they have never—not even in his lifetime—considered him to be any sort of divinity or anything other than mortal (nor do they see him as a perfect mortal), and they certainly have never worshipped him. They simply revere him for the faithful role they see him playing in obeying the directions he claimed to receive directly from heaven to restore Christ's gospel to the world.

Another myth is that Latter-day Saints replaced the Bible. Not by a long shot. They see the Bible as the first witness to Jesus Christ. And they also embrace, as a second witness of Christ, Joseph's translated book of ancient American scripture, the *Book of Mormon*. Not in place of the Bible, but alongside it, as additional scripture. Along with revelations received by Joseph and his prophet successors. (The reason is this—Latter-day Saints believe, as Joseph Smith put it, "in all that God has revealed, all that He does now reveal, and . . . that He will yet reveal many great and important things pertaining to the Kingdom of God."[10]) Some detractors acknowledge Latter-day Saints believe the Bible but claim they ignore it. Simply untrue. The LDS Sunday School program worldwide spends an equal amount of course study time and materials on the Bible, for one entire year on the Old Testament, one year on the New Testament, one year on the *Book of Mormon*, and one year on new revelations—the *Doctrine and Covenants*. Then they keep rotating that schedule for all their Sunday School classes and at-home reading assignments. Same with the worldwide Seminary and Institute programs for hundreds of thousands of high school and college students respectively, who attend an hour a day before school or "release-time" attendance for their open periods during regular school hours.

But some of Joseph's detractors are so adamant that the Bible is the only possible scripture that they will try anything to keep people from even looking at the *Book of Mormon*— including scare tactics. Perhaps the most popular one of all is an oft-quoted verse about "not adding to the Bible." Using it, detractors quote the Apostle John: "If any man shall add unto these things, God shall add unto him the plagues that are written in this book." (Revelation 22:18) Sounds scary, right? Who wants to get hit with plagues? However, the Apostle John is not talking about adding to the Bible—in fact the compilation of books known as the Bible didn't even exist at the time John wrote this, nor would it for another 2 centuries. (See Appendix P:

"Who Compiled the Bible and When?") Instead, he is talking about not adding to "this book" of Revelation. In fact, the verse actually spells out exactly what portion in the book of Revelation should not be added to—only a specific prophecy.[11]

Those who don't know any better believe the scripture-twisters. I have included 5 appendices in this biography that analyze the history of the Bible and how it came about—including numerous bumps in the road over the centuries as it was translated, compiled, and published. You might, in fact, be astonished by its history.

Another myth: Joseph Smith was a racist. Not only did he write against slavery but he accepted African-Americans into his home with open arms as free people to live with him. (Likely less than 1% of activist abolitionists ever did that.) Many opinion-makers have rarely reported the real side of him, instead they have set up a straw man, claiming he was something he wasn't, so detractors could beat up the publicly displayed scarecrow.

This book, by the way, has no connection to the LDS church, nor to any organization or educational institution—it is entirely of my own authorship and responsibility and is the result of my research, with help from others, based on what I consider essential facts.

But myths by detractors have been slung across the earth's orbit for 2 centuries, and they disregard essential facts.If NASA engineers disregard essential facts they could put a missile probe meant for Mars on a trajectory entirely missing the planet, only to head into endless space. Similarly, I believe opinion makers have launched a craft about Joseph that has been off course for so long that what is left of him is a revisionist caricature, one that has completely missed the mark.

I further believe those who don't have the facts and present misinformation should be given a break. If they don't know any better, they don't know any better. (Likewise, if they believe I don't have my facts straight, hopefully they can disagree with tolerance.)

On a radio talk show once, taking calls about my Porter Rockwell biography, I fielded a question of sorts from an older lady claiming she absolutely knew Joseph Smith ordered Porter Rockwell to drown little old ladies in the Mississippi River. When I asked her how she knew, her logic was interesting: "Because my grandmother told me and she lived in Illinois." "Ah, the secret's out," I said. I seriously then told her that simply wasn't Porter's modus operandi—it did not jibe with the facts. A skilled gunman and defender of the folks he was. But a murderer he was not—especially of little old ladies.

She didn't buy it. My explanation didn't fit her treasured, anti-Mormon family sentiments. She proceeded to rip into me for defending Porter—and got pretty vindictive.(The talk show host, no particular friend to Mormons himself, took my side and argued against her. He even cancelled his guests for the next hour to keep me on, intrigued by and open-minded to this story of a long-haired gunfighter who protected Joseph Smith and the Latter-day Saints.) The bottom line was, this caller made it clear she had no tolerance for Mormons.

As for myth-induced intolerance, at one time the LDS church stopped sending missionaries to certain southeastern states, where I was raised, because of beatings and lynchings from the outrageous myths that stirred people to anger. But times have changed. The LDS church now thrives there. Yet while the animosity has disappeared, much misinformation hasn't. Rumors abound everywhere. Fortunately, tolerance began to increase with the generation of my parents, who incidentally never really learned much about Latter-day Saints, yet were never ones to put down another's religion.

Few people do, I believe, until they are stirred up by inflammatory books and lectures from people who have an agenda.

Many of those making a ruckus about the Mormons are ex-Mormons who search for reasons to justify their move out of the church, focusing on the naysaying sources to convince themselves they have done the right thing. Others are folks with a political agenda against the church, disagreeing with its stance on social issues, who thus seek to defame its founder. And, finally, some are religious leaders of other faiths who take up the hue and cry of their predecessors from almost 2 centuries ago, often with honorable motives to protect their flocks from the "misguided Mormons," although some have less honorable intentions—feeling the heat of competition—with perhaps fear of losing congregational members who contribute to their livelihood. (There also seems to have been a fair number of bruised egos over the years who've seen pairs of young missionaries convert their sheep right out from under them.)

I'll never forget the visit from my priest when I was investigating Mormonism. I genuinely liked this fellow whom I had known nearly all my life, yet he struck me as possibly being under the spell of all 3 motives. That was a very hard day for me, as his visit was the last-ditch effort by family and friends to keep me from breaking with multi-generational traditions (despite their respect and newly found admiration for Mormons). All I had to go on was what I knew deep down was true.

In short, many innocent folks inquiring about Joseph have been misled by the many detractors of Joseph Smith, historical and modern.

For example, one of my favorite book reviewers described Joseph recently as a man "impossible to like." (The fellow is still one of my favorite book reviewers, incidentally.)

What?

If he knew what I knew, he would find Joseph actually more than likable—probably downright admirable. Not a perfect fellow, that Joseph. But he was remarkable in how he dealt with opposition, sacrificed personal comforts to help others, and made positive contributions on a host of issues, with or without his claimed contributions of bringing crucial ordinances to the earth, such as sealing husbands and wives together in marriage for eternity if they choose (instead of being married for this life only—"till death do you part").

However, that reviewer apparently believed what he had read in a recent book he reviewed, that puts Joseph in a dark light.

Few and far between are the biographies that present him in a fair light, which include hard-to-avoid facts.

Patriot and future president John Adams in 1770 decided to defend a highly unpopular group of defendants—the British soldiers who fired upon the mob at the Boston Massacre. A move as unpopular as it could get. He even did it pro bono. He knew it would rankle to the core his fellow patriots. But he knew the Brits were innocent of murder. They had acted in self-defence to quell a raging Colonial mob. In Adams's sterling defensive argument he coined a term for the ages:

"Facts are stubborn things."[12]

This book focuses on the facts, including ones a lot of people, both among believers and disbelievers in Joseph Smith, would like to ignore.

Two sides for two centuries have addressed what they see as facts. From two diametrically opposite viewpoints.

On one side, Joseph's enemies have written the vast majority of books about him, and they have continually made a case against him with the grievances of detractors. That antagonistic side has become the dominant, one-sided view of him by the public at large.

Hopefully the open-minded will at least consider the other side—here presented from a different angle by one who has seen Joseph's story from 2 sides, and now presents some of those "stubborn facts."

Please take the journey back with me a couple hundred years and learn for yourself what I have learned . . .

J OSEPH Smith has a history unparalleled in inspiration, intrigue, and mystery. By the 21st century his followers went on to establish the 4th-largest Christian denomination in the United States,[1] with even more members outside the U.S., with the worldwide name of *The Church of Jesus Christ of Latter-day Saints.*

Growing up in Sharon, Vermont, and then upstate New York, Joseph blended in well with neighbors. But when events of religious significance began unfolding, he became a target of unusual interest, with enemies claiming his family members were less than upstanding. Ironically, before his "divine call," his family name was connected with an unusually solid reputation. His ancestors were stalwarts of their communities, and his own parents even made substantial sacrifices to repay debts. Other books devote entire chapters to his ancestry, but this biography focuses on Joseph himself and those closest to him who had a significant influence on his life.

The first recorded event to affect his family occurred when a certain business venture went awry. His father was a partner in a small merchandise store at Randolph, Vermont, which engaged in a modest amount of exporting overseas.[2] And from that single venture the Smiths were left "in indigent circumstances."[3]

The poignancy of the account holds significance to anyone who has been dealt an unfair business blow. Before Joseph was born, his father, Joseph senior, invested heavily in ginseng, which is grown wild in Vermont, in order to sell to China.

The Chinese valued the root for its purported ability to create virility in men, to prolong life, and to fight the plague raging there, according to Joseph's mother, Lucy Mack Smith,[4] so they paid top dollar for it. Joseph senior secured as much as he could from local farmers and crystallized it. A turn in his family's fortunes came when he turned down a cash offer from a man named Stevens, a few miles south in Royalton, who offered him $3,000 for his entire inventory—67% of its full value. Joseph senior made the most momentous financial mistake of his life, which would affect them for decades—he turned it down, feeling he could get the full price if he sold it himself to China.[5]

Thinking he could make another $1,500, he took his lot of ginseng to New York City and there arranged for it to be shipped to China on consignment, trusting others to deliver it there, to make the sale, and to return with the cash and pay him.

The Royalton merchant, Stevens, who had made him the $3,000 offer, sent young Stevens, his son, to sail on the same ship as Joseph's ginseng, and assigned him to make the sale for Joseph.

When the son returned, he presented Joseph with only a small chest of tea, claiming it was a bad market. In reality the market had remained stable for ginseng, and Chinese consumers demanded even more product. The proof in this came when Joseph senior's brother-in-law, Stephen Mack, presently caught the young Mr. Stevens crystallizing ginseng. Putting 2 and 2 together, he realized a bad market would not induce the young man into such an enterprise. Stephens in fact had hired 8 or 10 workers. Suspicious, Mack found him one day a bit soused—and began firing questions. Stephens, feeling no pain, admitted he had made a small fortune off Joseph senior's ginseng in China, leaving the Smiths high and dry. He even showed Mack a trunk with a large amount of silver and gold. Later when stone-cold sober, he realized his little show-and-tell had put him in a predicament and hightailed it out of the country. Mack raced to tell Joseph senior about it but, by the time Smith came to Stephens to collect his money, Stephens had given him—and the United States of America—the slip. Joseph senior followed him to Canada, but in vain.[6]

Completing his financial Armageddon, the goods in Joseph senior's store became due. He owed a Boston distributor $1,800. Fortunately, he had $2,000 coming to him from customers. Unfortunately, they refused to pay. If he had collected commodities from his customers in place of cash—which they had agreed to—he could have sold off the commodities to pay his Boston distributor, but his customers left him on a limb.[7]

In order to make that $1,800 payment to his distributor, he did the honorable thing, but it wiped out his family financially. He sold the farm. All he got, however, was $800 of its $1,500 value. In addition, Lucy put up her $1,000 cash wedding present. The debt was now paid but they were flat broke. They were, says Lucy, "free from embarrassment of debt but not from the embarrassment of poverty."[8] They could no longer work their own farm, but would have to work on others' as "tenant farmers" (considered by many as "lower-class" citizens), doing day labor.


Without a farm now they moved to Royalton for a few months, then to Sharon, Vermont, where they rented Lucy's father's farm in the hills above White River. Although it was poor land, they worked it hard, and it was here that Joseph was born on December 23, 1805,[9] under the heritage of sacrifice and toil.

The doctor who brought him into the world was Joseph Adam Denison of Bethel, Vermont, 12 miles northwest of Sharon.[10]

Joseph was born 2½ years after his sister Sophronia (1803), and 5 and 6 years after his 2 brothers, Hyrum (1800) and Alvin (1799) at Tunbridge on the farm they had lost.

Children and adults alike worked feverishly to eke out a living.

Within 2 years of tenant farming, by 1805, things had gotten a bit better for the Smiths. Joseph senior had taken up teaching in the winter in Sharon, Vermont while farming in the warmer months, renting one of his father's farms. His wife Lucy reported their condition as "gradually improving, until we found ourselves quite comfortable again."[11]

Lucy does not delineate why they moved again, but they did—likely because, as in so many places, the land in Sharon at some point began to not pull enough revenue, even with the added teaching income. So, once again, hoping as always to find more suitable land that might produce better crops, they moved to another farm.

This time to Tunbridge, where Joseph's brother Samuel Harrison (1807) was born 2 years after Joseph. Almost immediately they moved yet again, to nearby Royalton, Vermont. Two other brothers were born there—Ephraim in 1810 (who died 11 days later) and William in 1811. All 3 of these last boys shared the same birthday—March 13.[12] For a 14-year stint they moved every 2 years.

(This was a similar scenario to their parents—Lucy's and Joseph senior's—who had started out in old cities along the coast. For Lucy's family it was Lyme, Connecticut, and for Joseph senior's it was Topsfield, Massachusetts, from which they had become "pioneers" by moving westward to smaller villages, never settling in any one very long—until Joseph senior's father, Asael Smith, did eventually stop and stay in Tunbridge, Vermont, for many years, where he met Lucy Mack Smith, Joseph's mother.)

The first 8 years after losing their farm, from 1803–1811, all their moves had taken place in less than 6 miles to 3 nearby villages—Tunbridge, Royalton, and Sharon, Vermont.

In 1811, when Joseph was 5½, he began school on Dewey Hill in Royalton, taught by Deacon Jonathon Finney.

What Joseph Jr. did not learn from his school he might have learned from his part-time schoolteacher father.

The parents knew that, in order to get ahead and secure a future for their children and themselves in retirement, they would need to own property again. That was the simple fact of early American life.

So they continued to work hard at home. They secured 100 pounds of candles, allowing them to have enough light to work at nights and turn 200 yards of cloth into family clothing.[13]

Later in 1811, the family moved away from their 6-mile radius of small Vermont towns to the next state over—New Hampshire. This was a bigger undertaking, simply because of the length of the move over rugged, primitive roads 20 miles away. They settled in the town of Lebanon, New Hampshire.[14] In Lucy Mack Smith's account, *The History of Joseph Smith by His Mother: the Unabridged Original Version* (Stratford Books, 2nd edition 2007, eBook edition 2012), she reports that their lives improved, especially in the realm of education, as they found good schools for the children, having been deprived of schooling due to their circumstances before then.[15]

Probably in the late summer before fall harvest, Hyrum, age 11, attended Moor's Charity School in Hanover, in association with Dartmouth College.[16] Alvin and Sophronia, 13 and 8, went to common (elementary) school. Joseph Jr., who was still 5½, attended a common school nearby, and his 2 younger brothers, Samuel and William, 3 years and 6 months, respectively, remained at home. (The following year, 1812, Katharine would be born.)

Just when things were again improving for the Smith family, the next great blow occurred—a plague hit them[17]—right before Joseph's 8th birthday, the winter of 1812–1813.

Thousands in the area were killed by this disease, and the Smiths were all struck with it as well. One after another was taken down, as the parents watched helplessly. Their children's skin looked horrid, they became delirious, all contracted high fevers, and their tongues turned black. And there was no cure for it.

Little Sophronia was hit hardest—for 90 days—until she was left limp and still, and given up for dead by doctors. According to Lucy's account, through the prayers of her and her husband, a miracle occurred. As she was wrapping the dead girl in a blanket, she hugged the body closely and paced the floor, only to hear the child start sobbing and breathing again. To their amazement the fever was gone. This incident convinced Lucy that God lived, that He took a personal interest in people, and that He actually answered prayers.[18]

But young Joseph was struck with his own nightmare.

JOSEPH'S fever left after two weeks, and a resulting sore formed in his armpit.

Typical of abusive and just plain bad medical practices of the day, a Dr. Parker treated him with a hot shovel and bone liniment, despite Joseph insisting he had not injured his shoulder.[1] Later they would learn the pain had come not from a sprain, as the doctor insisted, but from a large abscess between his breast and shoulder. When it was lanced, the pain left that area, says Lucy, quoting Joseph, and "shot like lightning" down his side into the marrow of the bone of his leg.[2] This, says Joseph, went to his left ankle and shin,[3] which, adds Lucy, discharged a quart of infectious matter.[4]

His mother recounts him saying, "Oh, Father! The pain is so severe how can I bear it!"[5] His leg soon began to swell and, says Lucy, he "continued to suffer the greatest agony for the space of two weeks longer."[6] Lucy carried him in her arms much of the time to help alleviate the suffering, upon which she was taken ill due to her anxiety. Hyrum then stayed with him constantly, rubbing his leg to attempt to comfort him—the first recorded incident of Hyrum's closeness to him.

According to Lucy, after another week, "we thought it advisable to send again for the surgeon." Apparently it was now Dr. Stone. "He made an incision of eight inches on the front side of the leg, between the knee and ankle. This relieved the pain in a great measure"[7]—but only until the wound began to heal. Then the pain became as violent as ever,[8] as the infection attacked the bone. Joseph had, by today's definition, osteomyelitis, a bacteria-caused, acute bone or bone marrow infection. The wound itself began healing but became infected, so the doctor made a bigger incision, all the way to the bone.[9]

"It commenced healing the second time," says Lucy, "and as soon as it began to heal, it also began to swell again, which swelling continued to rise till we deemed it wisdom to call a council of surgeons."[10]

Lucy reports 7 men[11] riding up to the house (Joseph recalls 11.)[12] The third operation would be very dramatic. The decision was made to amputate.

When they entered the room where Joseph lay, one of the doctors, likely Stone, told Joseph: "My poor boy, we have come again."[13]

According to Joseph, when the doctors announced they would amputate, he refused to let them:

"Young as I was, I utterly refused to give my assent to the operation, but consented to their trying an experiment by removing a large portion of the bone from my left leg."[14]

Lucy recounts the scene a bit differently—that as they came to the door, she called them aside and asked them their plan. When they told her they'd amputate, it hit her like "a thunderbolt."[15] She appealed to Dr. Stone, the "principal surgeon,"[16] to try one more time to save the leg. She urged him to cut "around the bone" and take out only the diseased part.[17] They consulted among themselves and agreed to her suggestion.

Amputation may have been the doctor's foremost recommendation because of its simplicity.[18]

This council consisted of Dr. Stone and several others: Nathan Smith and Cyrus Perkins of Dartmouth Medical College plus 4 to 8 others—likely "residents" (similar to apprentices in other professions, these were graduates of medical school but not yet fully licensed physicians, working under the tutelage of doctors for 1 to 3 years, similar to today's system).

Despite the pain, Joseph was fortunate to receive the services of a doctor who had discovered a revolutionary technique of bone surgery, far ahead of his time, by experimenting on typhoid patients suffering from bone infection. Nathan Smith was a renowned surgeon from Dartmouth College at Hanover and, without his attending to Joseph during the operation, the boy would likely have lost his leg—and perhaps his life.

The doctors were surprised at the boy's resoluteness. Especially when he disobeyed their new orders—he flat out refused to be bound. He told them he needed only his father to hold him. He also turned down liquor to soften the pain.

Lucy says he made a final request: "Looking up into my face, his eyes swimming in tears, he continued, 'Now, Mother, promise me that you will not stay, will you? The Lord will help me, and I shall get through with it. So leave me and go away off till they get through with it.'"[19] He so much did not wish to distress her that even while facing impending, traumatic pain he was thinking more of her than himself—highly unusual even for adults—but he was 10. In making this decision, he recalled the example of his parents, remembering them praying over his sister. Because of that, he felt God would assist him. Abiding by his wishes Lucy went several hundred yards away, in order to not hear him.[20]

The operation, she says, consisted of first boring holes into both sides of the bone and breaking off 2 large pieces with forceps. (Joseph recalls 1.) At the first 2 pieces of bone that were broken off, his screams pierced the air across the fields to her. She could not hold herself back and commenced running to the house. She recalls Joseph seeing her and reacting. "Oh, Mother, go back, go back; I do not want you to come in. I will try to tough it out if you will go away."[21]

Next, says Lucy, "When the third piece was broken away, I burst into the room again—and oh, my God! What a spectacle for a mother's eye!"[22]

The wound was torn open, blood still gushing from it, and his bed was soaked in red. "Joseph was pale as a corpse." Worse, "large drops of sweat were rolling down his face, whilst upon every feature "was depicted the utmost agony."[23] She was then forced from the room, not allowed to return until all the blood was washed away.

The operation was a success, but over time he lost much weight, such that, says Joseph, "my mother could carry me with ease."[24] In time, "additional pieces of bone afterwards worked out before my leg healed."[25] He also had to use crutches for at least 3 years, and would later say that when he was 12, it was extremely painful for him to walk long distances, which exhausted him.[26] Thereafter, he would retain a slight limp the rest of his life.

About 2 years later he was sent to his uncle Jesse at Salem, confident the "sea breezes" would enhance the healing process.[27] There he stayed for an unknown length of time, but likely was initiated into the world of, or at least saw from a distance, the riches and sophistication of high society—with its art, literature, clothing, furnishings, and foods, which he would later appreciate. No more is known of Joseph's early years except that he recovered completely and was tall for his age. He was also redheaded as a lad and retained some of that color through his life.

At the end of the day, typhoid fever had wrecked the Smith's financial situation. One year of battling the disease left them with medical bills they could not pay, in addition to many missed days of work. Further, the parents were drained of all energy, left totally exhausted.[28]

After 3 torturous years in New Hampshire, in 1814 they moved back to Vermont, this time to the town of Norwich, near the other 3 where they had lived, and began sharecropping for Esquire Moredock.

Then came their next setback: their first year's crops failed. So they picked fruit from their orchard[29] and sold it, while also possibly working in town.

"The crops the second year were as the year before—a perfect failure," says Lucy. "Mr. Smith now determined to plant once more,"[30] and if that failed, his plan was to move to New York.

The next year their crops did indeed fail. The reason—an "untimely frost," she says.[31] On June 8, 1816, snow fell hard across New England, in part causing a famine. And this famine was caused by the summer staying dry and cold. Farmers even had to import corn to feed their animals at the exorbitant price of $3 per pound ($96.47 in today's currency). And that was the proverbial straw.

Lucy states, "This was enough; my husband was now altogether decided upon going to New York."[32] Thousands of Vermont residents fled along with them; so many, in fact, that 64 years later their county would, remarkably, have 3,000 less people than the year they left. (Economically, so many left that it would take all the way until the early 1900s for the state to recover.) Yet, ironically before the famine, their village of Tunbridge had looked highly promising, with unprecedented growth, the population having skyrocketed between the years 1790 and 1810.

The weird weather conditions that caused this growth-stunting famine were in not only North America but northern Europe as well, rooted in the explosion of a volcano known as Tamboro in Sumbawa, an island off Indonesia, in 1815.[33]

Fortuitously, it sent the Smiths packing, and they would end up at the perfect location where Joseph Jr. could receive the future spiritual treasure that awaited him, a book engraved on golden plates buried by ancients. And from that resulted a publishing phenomenon in 75 languages and 150 million copies, ranking in the top 4 most-printed books in world history, in free market economies, per below:

1. The Bible (over 2.5 billion).
2. Qur'an (800–900 million; Muslim scripture, in Arabic).
3. *A Tale of Two Cities* (200 million) by Charles Dickens.
4. The *Book of Mormon* (*over* 150 million), translated by Joseph Smith.
5. (tie) *Scouting for Boys: A Handbook for Instruction in Good Citizenship* (150 million) by Robert Baden-Powell.
5. (tie) *The Lord of the Rings* (150 million, combining copies in the series) by J. R. R. Tolkein.[34]

(The producer of this list, for the *Southern Review of Books*, provides this description for the *Book of Mormon*: "multiple authors, translated by Joseph Smith, Jr. Religious text published in 1830, over 150 million copies worldwide.")

Indirectly, a volcano precipitated the discovery.

Had not the famine occurred, they may have remained in Vermont, but the ginseng debacle that had caused them to lose their farm, in conjunction with bad crops at all the following farms they rented, coupled with typhoid fever that decimated them financially, so weakened their situation that the effects of the famine proved to be the final blow.

What drove them specifically to New York were the accounts they heard of a remarkable place—a newly settled community in western New York where wheat "was raised in abundance" from easily tilled, soft-soiled land,[35] with people buying large plots of land on long-term credit—their only hope of ever pulling out of their financial morass. They learned of this promised land from Vermont newspapers, which advertised great opportunities in the west country of New York for only $2–3 per acre ($64–$96 in today's money).

In the summer of 1816 Joseph senior launched an expedition to Palmyra, New York, 300 miles away, to explore the possibilities of moving there and improving their lives. He liked what he saw.

So, when young Joseph was 10, the family packed up again and took flight to greener pastures.

Their destination: Palmyra, New York, where Joseph Jr. would receive life-altering experiences that would spin his entire family's life in a new direction and even turn their whole community upside down.

And from it Joseph would change the lives of millions.

CHAPTER 3

THE Smiths' move to Palmyra was fraught with drama.

First, Joseph's father hired a driver named Caleb Howard to take him alone to Palmyra. Lucy paints the poignant scene:

"My sons Alvin and Hyrum followed their father some distance with a heavy heart."[1]

Upon arriving, Joseph senior treated a complete stranger once again as he had with the ginseng fiasco—as he himself expected to be treated—and he paid Howard in advance to move the family.

Howard did in fact show up for them, but just as Lucy and her children were about to ride away, several creditors appeared on the scene, demanding more money from Lucy—even though they had been carefully paid in full. Lucy felt 2 pressures, causing her to consider double-paying these men—first, "I concluded it would be more to our advantage to pay their unjust claims than to hazard a lawsuit,"[2] which would necessitate their return in the dead of winter from 300 miles away, likely leaving their children and property in New York. And, with not being able to afford attorneys against these creditors, they could come up on the short end of a legal stick, leaving them completely penniless and stranded, away from children and home.

Secondly, Lucy realized she could not afford to pay the driver Howard to wait, as the teams were "waiting on expense."[3] Howard in fact may have been putting pressure on her to hurry, demanding more money if they did not leave immediately. So, considering these pressures, she paid the creditors the $150 they demanded.

Two neighbors however saw the injustice and volunteered to retrieve witnesses to recover her money, but she refused. The clock was ticking and Howard was likely still pressuring her to leave. The 2 neighbors then offered to raise the funds from other neighbors, but Lucy proudly turned down that help as well. (For neighbors to have been so willing to help, Lucy and others in the family likely warranted a certain degree of respect. As in her next place of residence, where she provided free service as a country doctor, she probably showed the same exemplary friendship in Vermont to people who needed help, and thus had people practically lining up to help her in return.)

Joseph was turning 11 in the winter of 1816–1817, when the family of 7 children, from ages 4 to 17, finally embarked on their journey with Lucy and her mother Lydia and "a great quantity of woolen clothing for my children."[4]

When they left, they bid farewell to all their family and familiar areas in which they had been raised, and launched forth into a new adventure almost 300 miles away in Palmyra.

On the trip their wagon overturned.[5] Lydia received fairly serious injuries, enough to cause her death 2 years later, in 1818.[6] She was left off at Royalton, Vermont, near her son Daniel Mack's residence, which had been Lydia's destination.

Lucy states in her rough draft: "Here I was to take leave of my affectionate mother, to whom I was indebted for all the religious instructions, as well as most of the educational privileges which I had ever received. The parting hour came; my mother wept over me long and bitterly. She told me that it was not probable she should ever behold my face again."[7]

Another disaster that impeded their progress to Palmyra was Caleb Howard, whose impatience escalated into full-scale abuse of the children, particularly young Joseph.[8]

Howard spent the money Joseph's father had advanced him, mostly at inns along the way, drinking and gambling. Perhaps not entirely sober, he was irresponsible with their goods and, more importantly, with his passengers. He insisted some of the Smith children travel with a family named Gates heading their direction. The reason: Howard liked 2 of Gates' daughters and had them sit up front on his buckboard. Not having room for the 10-year-old Joseph with his lame leg, he split up the Smith family by tossing Joseph and his crutches off the buckboard and, according to Joseph, "made me travel in my weak state through the snow 40 miles per day for several days, during which time I suffered the most excruciating weariness and pain . . . and thus he [Howard] continued to do day after day through the journey, and when my brothers remonstrated with Mr. Howard for his treatment to me, he would knock them down with the butt of his whip."[9]

According to Lucy's rough draft manuscript of her history, it was actually Caleb Howard's cousin—also named Howard—who took the family, although Caleb himself had been the driver for Joseph senior days previously.[10]

Whichever Mr. Howard it was, when they arrived at Utica, New York, he threw the Smith family goods "out of the wagon," says Joseph, "into the street, and attempted to run away with the horses and wagon, but my mother seized the horses by the reign and, calling witnesses, forbid his taking them away, as they were her property."[11] Lucy's version is similar to Joseph's but states she told off Howard "in the presence of a large company of travelers" in the barroom.[12] She further says the tavern was 20 miles west of Utica,[13] so they were essentially being abandoned in the middle of nowhere.[14]

Because of the public denunciation, she was able to keep the wagon and retrieve her property scattered in the street. She also fired Howard on the spot.

The next leg of their journey to Palmyra was even worse for Joseph:

"On our way from Utica, I was left to ride on the last sleigh in the company, (the Gates family were in sleighs) but . . . I was knocked down by the driver, one of Gates's sons, and left to wallow in my blood until a stranger came along, picked me up, and carried me to the Town of Palmyra."[15] Lucy indicates she took charge of their wagon for the Palmyra trip. Likely, she and the older children drove the family wagon filled with goods to Palmyra, while the younger ones rode behind them in sleighs, Joseph being assigned to the last one, with Lucy unaware of Joseph's fate until Joseph's rescuer caught up to them. One can imagine the horror his family felt when they saw him later in his bloodied condition with the stranger.

That the stranger then traveled with them is indicated by the fact he drove Joseph all the way to Palmyra, as well as the fact Joseph stopped with his family along the way at inns to sleep, so the stranger must have stayed at the same locations. Lucy obviously welcomed this good Samaritan, who now traveled with her family.

Meanwhile, she must have faced unimaginable stress, not only seeing Joseph beaten and bloodied, but attempting to house her family every night with no money, since Howard had spent all their funds the first leg of the trip from Lebanon, New Hampshire to Utica, New York. Because of this, says Joseph, "My mother was compelled to pay our landlords' bills from Utica to Palmyra in bits of cloth, clothing, etc."[16] Thus, being destitute from the fraudulent creditors, the Smiths were out of money and had to trade all their goods and even their clothing to survive the journey. They made their last payment to an innkeeper with Sophronia's eardrops.[17]

All that hard work to make the children's clothing, along with the entire inventory of extra cloth she had bought, was now gone. For a proud, self-reliant woman there was additional pain—one can only imagine how Lucy felt not being capable of paying innkeepers on the journey, having to practically beg them to take pieces of cloth in lieu of cash.

When they arrived in Palmyra they had only 2 cents.[18]

But, "notwithstanding our misfortunes and the embarrassments,"[19] Lucy was grateful they could all be reunited again. And Joseph Jr. was among the children who "surrounded their father," when they reunited, states Lucy in her rough draft, "clinging to his neck, covering his face with tears and kisses."[20]

But they had very little clothing to now face the winter cold. Nevertheless, they were together again.

Palmyra was the 6th community in which the Smith family settled and the 8th home they would establish, but once again they were completely broke, yet full of faith.

Upon their arrival in 1816 Palmyra was a rugged little town of only 600 people, nestled in log cabins among a couple stores. A year later the Erie Canal would begin construction right through town,[21] connecting the Great Lakes with New York City, revolutionizing commerce and launching prosperity.

The area had just opened up for white settlement a quarter century earlier, in 1789, under the name "Swift's Landing." The residents changed the name to Palmyra in 1796 to impress, and hopefully recruit, a certain school teacher. By 1800 it had nearly 1,000 residents. Before the Erie Canal was built, Palmyra relied on Canandaigua, a town 12 miles south, as its main neighbor and sister-city for commerce, with both towns being founded at the same time; but the canal's completion put Palmyra into the stratosphere—connecting it to larger metropolitan areas like Albany, Buffalo, and even New York City. Construction on the canal would begin in 1817, with Palmyra's portion being completed 5 years later in 1822. Three years after that (8 years' total construction) the canal would be finished in 1825, tying Buffalo and Albany together, which were 363 miles apart, with Palmyra between them, leaving Canandaigua in the dust.

The Smiths finally had a dream—of owning land and becoming stable again, as they had been before the ginseng theft. So they had a meeting and decided to buy property. But they realized it would have to be a family effort. "We all now sat down and counseled together," says Lucy. "'How shall we,' said my husband, 'be able to sustain ourselves and have anything left to buy land?'"[22]

They knew they would have to continue working as unsettled laborers for a time.

That time lasted 18 months.

The 3 oldest boys (Hyrum, Alvin, and Joseph) grabbed whatever odd jobs came their way—farming, well-digging, trapping and fishing—while Lucy developed her artistry by painting oil-cloth as table covers to sell. "I furnished all the provisions for the family and, besides this, began to replenish our household furniture in a very short time by my own exertions."[23]

Near the Methodist campgrounds at the edge of town they "opened a 'cake and beer shop,' as described by sign board, doing business on a small scale . . . [making a] scanty but honest living," recalls Pomeroy Tucker, an apprentice at the local print shop.[24]

At their shop, Joseph worked as a clerk, overseeing "merchandise, consisting of ginger-bread, pies, boiled eggs, root beer, and other notices of traffic," which were sold predominantly to young people attending the revivals and other public functions on the campground, states Thomas L. Cook in a Palmyra newspaper years later.[25]

They also sold goods from a handcart in town whenever there was a public event.

For the most part, Lucy's husband worked as a cooper, says son William,[26] a craft he had acquired from his father Asael. One neighbor erroneously thought Lucy's husband and all the boys were coopers.[27] All of these endeavors allowed them to scrape by. The shop was located on Vienna Street as it headed off toward Vienna Township from Palmyra. Nearby was a campground used by the Methodists, where revivals were held. Those attending revivals could buy from the Smiths. (Two centuries later scenes would be cinematically depicted of only several dozen people attending them, but in reality there were huge crowds—on at least one day over 10,000 people poured onto the grounds for a revival.[28])

In addition to coopering, Joseph senior would go on errands for the family in town and, once there, work odd jobs at stores and farms. When local farmers needed extra workers collecting hay, he and his older sons would work as hired hands. They also dug wells and gardened. By now, the older two—Alvin and Hyrum—were big enough to help substantially with the family income. Since wheat prices were high during this period, and would remain so until 1819, farmers could pay the boys more. While the oldest two were at this point their father's best workers, Joseph was coming of age as a laborer and could soon hold his own. William said of his older brother Joseph: "The townspeople knew where they could get a good hand, and they were not particular to take any of the other boys before Joseph either."[29]

As for their working for others a great deal in order to save up money, the head of the house, Joseph senior, was not even living at home when the census taker came in 1819—he was likely living on someone's farm as a hired hand that season.[30]

Lucy herself worked as a community doctor, possibly not for money but simply to help her neighbors, as earlier.

The whole family was industrious, and the local economy was booming. The family dream was coming true—they were to become property owners again.

In the fall of 1817 they finally bought their land—they made a contract for 100 acres 2 miles south of Palmyra at $6–7 per acre.[31]

It was considerably higher than the $2–3 per acre they had heard about for land while in Vermont but, due to the booming Palmyra area, it was not an altogether bad deal.

And with the money they saved they made nearly all the first payment within a year. At that time they paid all they thought was needed, and figured they had claim to the property, so in the winter of 1817–1818 they began building a log house.

Their new home was 2 miles south of Palmyra, just south of the county line, between southern Wayne County (home to Palmyra) and Farmington County (home to Manchester), so they were officially residents of Farmington, New York (renamed Manchester a few years later in 1822).

It was adjacent to the Evertsons' land, on an adjacent parcel owned by a local businessman, Samuel Jennings.[32]

To make the house workable for such a large family, they added a wing of sawed wood slabs, to sleep all 10 of them.[33]

They finished it the fall of 1818. They also "commenced clearing," reports Lucy. "I believe something like 30 acres of land were gotten ready for cultivation the first year."[34] Her son William doubles that number—they cleared 60 acres "of the heaviest timber I ever saw."[35] He says they cleared it mostly with fire.[36] Then they had the daunting task of fencing it and planting an orchard, he adds.[37] It was a large orchard, recalls Lucy.[38] All the acres were cleared by the father and 3 oldest boys, including Joseph Jr., who was added to the mix of adult labor now with Hyrum and Alvin.

They sold their ashes to manufacturing facilities in Palmyra known as "asheries," used to make potash. They also sold their unburned wood in town as firewood. Meanwhile they kept acres of maple trees intact on the land and, in 1819, the spring after they moved onto the farm, they began making maple syrup from 1,200 to 1,500 trees.[39] "To gather the sap and make sugar and molasses [his term for thick maple syrup] from that number of trees was no lazy job," says Joseph's brother William.[40] One season they won the county prize for maple syrup they produced[41]—an arduous task of hammering a spike into a tree, attaching a bucket under the hole to collect the sap that would ooze out, and boiling it down into syrup at the ratio of 33 gallons of sap for every gallon of finished syrup. The result was a sweet, delicious, healthful commodity. From that they would also make the granular-like sugar, which they also made the spring after they arrived.[42] And the Smith family had its hands full, averaging 1,000 pounds of maple sugar per year, says Lucy in her rough draft.[43]

Unlike their rented Vermont farm, this soil was indeed fertile.

Meanwhile, in 1817, when Joseph was 11, a new family arrived from Belcher, Massachusetts, and planted themselves just 1 mile away.[44] As their nearest neighbor, the family of Orin and Sarah Rockwell became close friends with the Smiths.[45] Their 4-year-old son, Orrin Porter Rockwell (whose first name was spelled differently than his father's and who would generally go by just "Porter") attached himself to young Joseph. They likely fished, played, and performed chores together, with Porter considering Joseph his closest friend the rest of his life.

Despite the hope the Erie Canal brought, an economic nightmare hit the region—in fact, the entire nation. And the Smiths once again suffered along with everyone else. How they handled it showed yet again their particular brand of resourcefulness, revealing to young Joseph both the resilience his family possessed and the inner strengths he needed to develop—which someday would be summoned in order to survive a deluge of personal attacks.

C H A P T E R 4

THE nation's economic woes were tied to the country's struggle to recover after the War of 1812. First came the Panic of 1819, when Joseph Jr. was 13. Farmers began selling their lands. And then came the resulting depression. Many had to just walk away from all they owned.

The typical 2-year plan for farming followed by families generally was to grow corn for animals and people—this was the 1st year's crop. Then they would grow wheat the 2nd year, hoping for a small surplus to sell for cash. Unfortunately for the Smiths, their timing was poor but unavoidable, because when they were ready to grow wheat, it dropped in price by nearly half, due to the depression.[1]

Thus, when they did harvest their first wheat crop in 1821, they made very little money.

To make more, all the family pitched in and, according to Joseph Jr.:

"It required the exertions of all that were able to render any assistance for the support of the family. Therefore we were deprived of the benefit of an education.

"Suffice it to say, I was merely instructed in reading, writing, and the ground rules of arithmetic, which constituted my whole literary acquirements."[2]

His common school attendance was hit and miss. He possibly attended school a short while in Palmyra. But they continued reading the Bible and learning from their parents in a home school, struggling through intense poverty and barely surviving.

Dr. John Stafford, a neighbor who lived a mile away, says of Joseph Jr. that he was "a real clever, jovial boy. . . . The old woman [Lucy] had a great deal of faith that their children were going to do something great."[3]

Of their education he reports, "Joe [senior] was quite illiterate. After they began to have school at their house, he improved greatly."[4] Thus, the father learned much from the home schooling, along with the children, apparently after his work each day, and, if this was the case, his role since the beginning may have been more as a supervisor of studies, learning as they learned, rather than as a traditional educator.

Stafford also reports that at their home school they studied the Bible.[5] Years later his interviewers would ask, "Who was their teacher?" to which he answered, "They did not have any teacher; they taught themselves."[6] An illiterate but learning father would certainly fit that paradigm.

The children working and missing common school as much as they did was not entirely socially acceptable to the higher echelon of town society. Lucy and Joseph senior were both socially conscious and likely felt the pains of ostracism from them, especially if any was directed toward their children. Lucy seemed especially vulnerable to worrying about appearances regarding her small but growing farm. Once she faced the embarrassment of ladies' comments at a tea party. Attending were wives of wealthy merchants and the minister. One commented disparagingly of her log house, saying, "She deserves a better fate." Another made a two-edged compliment, saying Lucy was so kind to everyone that she ought to have the best of everything. She did not take the comments well and got riled up. Defending herself aggressively, she apparently scolded them, pointing out that the minister's son was always at the bar and the gambling house, while she and her family, owed no one, which merchants invariably do.[7] She would not hold back from stating her mind about insults, intended or not.

———————

Lucy adds that at the end of the second year, "when the time for making the second [mortgage] payment drew nigh, Alvin went from home to get work in order to raise the money and, after much hardship and fatigue, returned with the required amount."[8] Later the other boys would do the same, as they could make more money by living on the premises of those who hired them, saving travel time.

"This payment being made, we felt relieved, as this was the only thing that troubled us; for we had a snug little house, neatly furnished, and the means of living comfortably. It was now only two years since we entered Palmyra almost destitute of money, property, or acquaintance. The hand of friendship was extended on every side."[9]

In her rough draft she adds:

"We had every reason to believe that we had many good and affectionate friends, for never have I seen more kindness or attention shown to any person or family than we received from those around us.

"Again we began to rejoice in our prosperity, and our hearts glowed with gratitude to God for the manifestations of his favor that surrounded us."[10]

"The following spring we commenced making preparations for building another house, one that would be more comfortable for persons in advanced life."[11]


Lucy meanwhile believed her husband was receiving inspired visions which had begun in Vermont as early as 1811. This helped prepare her to accept her son Joseph's later accounts. It was now 1816 and Joseph was 10 years old. The 1st of his father's dreams, among 7 different ones he received (5 of which Lucy recorded)[12] convinced his wife that the local preachers had no special knowledge of heavenly things. (Asael, Joseph senior's father, had held a similar conviction.)

It was a dramatically visual dream. He traveled in a dreary field drenched in death-like silence. He "could see nothing save dead fallen timber" with "not a vestige of life," says Lucy. The spirit who was with him defined the field as the world in regards to true religion, a dead world hostile toward understanding. He traveled to a box, opened it, and began eating its contents, which the spirit told him would make him wise. Just then, he was surrounded by beasts bellowing, tearing the earth, and coming closer from every direction, "so close upon me that I was compelled to drop the box and fly for my life. . . . I awoke trembling."[13]

A 2nd dream has similarities to "Lehi's dream," recorded in the book that would be translated by her son Joseph. The dream has Joseph senior being led to a tree bearing white fruit and bringing his family to it. Near the tree was a large building of prideful people pointing at them with scorn. In the dream the spirit told Joseph senior that the fruit was the love of God and that the building was Babylon.[14] (While detractors would claim Joseph's translated account was influenced by his father's dream, supporters maintain the same instruction can be given to different men in different generations from the same divine source.)

The Smith parents were concerned about bringing up their children right, setting examples of honesty, thrift, and sobriety. Certainly their debt-payment sacrifices were a highlight. Believing that hymns were a form of music combined with prayer, the children were taught to sing hymns in an unusual fashion—on their knees. They also heard their parents pray for their offspring to be protected from sin.[15] The prayers were lengthy, and while at least William, who would later often be at odds with his family, did not care for the large amount of parental instruction, he seemed to appreciate his mother's efforts, labeling her "a very pious woman and much interested in the welfare of her children, both here and hereafter." As such, he says she "made use of every means which her parental love could suggest, to get us engaged in seeking for our soul's salvation."[16]

Lucy says she taught her children to walk "in the love of God," and that "never was there a more obedient family."[17]

They were looked upon as a reliable family. Their neighbor, Orlando Saunders, recalls, "I knew all of the Smith family well. They have all worked for me many a day. They were very good people." When asked if he knew Joseph, Saunders replied, "Oh, just as well as one could, very well. He has worked for me many a time, and been about my place a great deal. . . . and he was a good worker."[18] Their reputation was exemplary—none could outwork them—and they consistently showed their Christian charity. Saunders adds, "They were the best family in the neighborhood in case of sickness; one was at my house nearly all the time when my father died."[19] He also addressed their integrity: "I always thought them honest. They were owing me some money when they left here. One of them came back in about a year and paid me."[20]

A Mrs. Palmer, whose family farm was near the Smiths', states, "The father of the family was above average in intelligence. I have heard my parents say that he bore the appearance of having descended from royalty." Of Lucy she says: "Children loved to go to her home." Of Joseph Jr.: "My father loved young Joseph Smith and often hired him to work with his boys. I was about six years old when he first came to our home. I remember going into the field on an afternoon to play in the corn rows while my brothers worked. When evening came, I was too tired to walk home and cried because my brothers refused to carry me. Joseph lifted me to his shoulder, and with his arm thrown across my feet to steady me, and my arm about his neck, he carried me to our home."[21] While Mrs. Palmer and her family would never join Joseph's religious persuasion, they were attached to the boy.

Joseph, meanwhile, was formulating thoughts on a rather high plane and seemed to undergo a metamorphosis. He says he became interested in matters of faith "at about the age of 12 years,"[22] which would have been in the last few weeks of 1817 or in early 1818 (about a year after the revivals had swept through). The result of the revival had the Presbyterians becoming the dominant Palmyra religion, which was the same year the Smiths moved to Palmyra. This is significant because of the run-ins the Smiths would have with them. Joseph also states that between ages 12 and 14 he became "seriously impressed with regard to the all important concerns for the welfare of my immortal soul."[23] This led him to begin reading the Bible. He then became concerned about the situation of the world with its "wickedness" and "contentions," along with his own sins and mistakes.[24] This was written in a ledger book on 6 pages during the second half of 1832, the first account of his own religious experiences.

All the while, Lucy said Joseph was "much less inclined to the perusal of books than any of the rest of our children, but far more given to meditation and deep study."[25]

Then, at age 14, he became simultaneously curious about and bothered by the contentions among the local religions. He later writes there was "an unusual excitement" on the subject of religion. He adds that priest and convert alike contended with one another.[26]

Revivals swept the region. While at first intrigued by them (according to Orsamus Turner in Chapter 5), he described them as a "strife of words and a contest about opinions,"[27] creating "stir and division" instead of "good feelings one for another."[28]

He said he marveled that people who professed Christianity did not live or talk according to the way they professed, causing "grief to my soul."[29]

Among those in the forefront of the 1820 religious war were 3 Palmyra churches—all with their own buildings: a Presbyterian church—the only one in the town center; a Baptist church 2 miles west (built in 1808, when 100 people joined during a revival that year); and a 2nd Presbyterian church east of town (built before 1820). (Two more churches would be built within the next 3 years—a Methodist church in 1822 and a Quaker church in 1823.)[30]

---

Joseph had his pick of religions, but events would soon unfold that would lead him down an entirely different path . . .

# CHAPTER 5

YOUNG Joseph's parents waged a mental warfare in their minds regarding which religious path they should choose.

Joseph senior was religious in his own way. He had likely looked at Universalism in 1797 but did not regularly attend any church thereafter.

When still living in Vermont Lucy had at that time attempted to persuade him to join the Methodists, but his father and brother had dissuaded him from it.

When his father Asael came to visit, he threw Thomas Paine's notoriously anti-Christian 1795 book, *Age of Reason*, into Joseph senior's house and ordered him to read it until he believed it, according to Lucy in her rough draft.[1] Asael's Universalist beliefs of a highly benevolent Creator flew in the face of the Methodists' stricter outlook on God—an ironic theme, considering his hostile action. (Paine's book was highly skeptical of Christianity, which coincided with many Universalists' beliefs.)

Now, in Palmyra, Joseph senior seemed willing to attend church on occasion with Lucy. Meanwhile, she had her own concerns. While all the contention caused her to doubt the local churches, she still hoped to find the true church with God's authority.[2]

So she talked with Deacon Davies, who, admirably, was concerned for her worldly comfort, but, to her chagrin, left Christ out of the equation. She returned home disappointed.

She was even more disconcerted with a certain Presbyterian preacher who did not understand the subject on which he spoke. She described his lecture as "emptiness" and "vanity." She left the service, feeling an "aching void."[3]

As a result, she decided for now she could not find the religion she was seeking, so she decided to just read the Bible. A minister of another congregation did baptize her but did not require that she join a church, which she appreciated.[4]

However, in time she would apparently enjoy at least one tent revival meeting (described 4 paragraphs below) and after that a Presbyterian minister's sermons (described in Chapter 7).

Meanwhile, her husband pushed for prayer in the family circle, possibly being influenced by revivals when they hit the community. Several years before moving to New York, in 1810–1811 he became temporarily excited about religion, perhaps influenced by his brother-in-law, Solomon Mack, who was converted at that time. But Joseph senior still could not attach himself to an institution.

All the while the community contentions continued to bother Joseph. The *Palmyra Register* reports revivals spreading throughout the state in 1820.[5] The Philadelphia General Assembly of 1820 for the Presbyterian Church states that 6 extremely active areas for revivals were in New York alone, of the 8 areas in the United States they cited.[6]

Some of these revivals were all-day events, attended by a couple hundred or even several thousand participants coming from miles away, bringing their families and goods in wagons. They cooked out in the open and often stayed several days. They socialized and listened to music. Markets were set up and produce was sold. Alcohol was, too, which may have had some effect on the revivals. Traveling ministers would take turns preaching, sometimes 3 at a time in different parts of camp. Traveling ministers were in fact the norm of the day, even when there were no revivals, and they would preach in cabins and schools and under the stars.

Joseph may have attended out of curiosity, out of respect for his mother, or out of the desire to sell pies, as the family still attempted selling food wherever there were crowds gathered, as did other families imbued with an entrepreneurial nature. Joseph reportedly told an acquaintance, Alexander Neibaur, that he wanted to experience what his mother, his sister, and his brother had at a revival meeting, adding that he "wanted to get religion too, [and] wanted to feel and shout like the rest, but could feel nothing."[7]

Orsamus Turner, one of the two printer's apprentices at the *Palmyra Register* who were acquainted with Joseph, said Joseph caught "a spark of Methodism in the camp meeting away down in the woods on the Vienna road," and that "he was a very passable exhorter in evening meetings,"[8] which may not be true, considering Turner's loose adherence to certain facts.

Another printer's apprentice, with whom Joseph would later work, Pomeroy Tucker, said that Joseph joined the probationary class of the Palmyra Methodist Church.[9] (Joseph in fact admitted he was "somewhat partial to the Methodist sect," with "some desire to be united with them."[10] Nevertheless, he felt he could not find any church as set forth in the New Testament.)

Orsamus Turner also said Joseph attended meetings of a "juvenile debating club" at the Durfee Street schoolhouse, where youth would talk of political and moral ethics—a higher dialogue than one would suspect of farm boys and girls of the day.[11]

Joseph even wondered for a while during this period whether there was a God, according to another friend, Oliver Cowdery,[12] who would get to know him later. So Joseph based his faith in Deity on the sun and the moon "rolling in their majesty through the heavens, and also the stars shining in their courses, and the earth also upon which I stood." In this statement he includes "the beast of the field and the fowls of heaven and the fish of the waters."[13]

Ironically, Joseph's family did not know his spiritual turmoil. For a 3-year period, "from the age of 12 years to 15, I pondered many things in my heart concerning the situation of the world of mankind—the contentions and divisions, the wickedness and abominations, and the darkness which pervaded the minds of mankind. My mind became exceedingly distressed, for I became convicted [convinced] of my sins and, by searching the scriptures, I found that mankind did not come unto the Lord, but that they had apostatized from the true and living faith, and there was no society or denomination that built upon the gospel of Jesus Christ as recorded in the New Testament, and I felt to mourn for my own sins and for the sins of the world."[14] From his pondering he was convinced there indeed had been an apostasy, just as his father's dreams had indicated.

Allen Coates layers a bit of "old time religion" into Joseph's inquiry:

"They were having revival meetings in the Methodist Church and my grandfather invited Joseph Smith, the boy, to go up with him. . . . And Grandfather, a great man, talked religion . . . while he was working, see. And he got the boy interested. And he said, 'Are you ready to go to a meeting with me?' Well, the boy agreed to it right away because everything looked bright in that way to him and he was getting on the road somewhere where he ought to be [getting interested in religion].

"And so they went over to the meeting and he got so interested in it, he caught the spirit some-time."[15]

Coates remarks about Joseph's character and his grandfather's influence on him:

"[Joseph] was a good boy to work. I heard that. Oh yes, there was nothing lazy about him. He was up and coming and looking to get ahead and he got more inspiration from my old grandfather."[16]

Joseph's brother William adds, "There was an unusual revival in the neighborhood. It spread from town to town, from city to city, from county to county, and from state to state. My mother attended those meetings and, being much concerned about the spiritual welfare of the family, she persuaded them to attend the meetings. Finally my mother, one sister, my brothers Samuel and Hyrum became Presbyterians. Joseph and myself did not join; I had not sown all my wild oats. (William was 11; likely his definition of "wild oats" was different than the common connotation of today, of being wildly promiscuous.) At the close of these meetings the different ministers began to beat around to see how many converts they could get to join their respective churches. All said, "Come and join us, we are right."[17]

William Smith draws the battleground map that led to Joseph's confusion amidst this war of ideas:

"There was a joint revival in the neighborhood between the Baptists, Methodists, and Presbyterians, and they had succeeded in stirring up quite a feeling. And after the meeting the question arose which church should have the converts. Rev. Stockton was the president of the meeting and suggested that it was their meeting and under their care, and they had a church there and they ought to join the Presbyterians."[18]

He adds in another interview, "The people in our neighborhood were very much stirred up with regard to religious matters by the preaching of a Mr. [George] Lane, an elder of the Methodist Church, and celebrated throughout the country as a 'great revival preacher.'"[19]

Later William clarifies, "But as Father did not like Rev. Stockton very well, our folks hesitated [joining his congregation], and the next evening a Rev. Mr. Lane of the Methodists preached a sermon on 'what church shall I join?' And the burden of his discourse was to ask God, using as a text, 'If any of you lack wisdom, let him ask of God, who giveth to all men liberally. . . .' And, of course, when Joseph went home and was looking over the text, he was impressed to do just what the preacher had said."[20]


That was the background which led Joseph to search the scriptures for an answer.[21]

Joseph would write:

"In the midst of this war of words, and tumult of opinions, I often said to myself, what is to be done? Who of all these parties are right . . . . I was one day reading the Epistle of James, first chapter and fifth verse, which reads, 'If any of you lack wisdom, let him ask of God that giveth to all men liberally . . . and it shall be given him.'

"Never did any passage of scripture come with more power to the heart of man than this did at this time to mine. It seemed to enter with great force into every feeling of my heart. I reflected on it again and again . . . . At length I came to the conclusion that I must either remain in darkness and confusion or else I must do as James directs . . . .

"I retired to the woods to make the attempt. It was on the morning of a beautiful, clear day, early in the spring . . . . It was the first time in my life that I had made such an attempt, for amidst all my anxieties I had never as yet made the attempt to pray vocally.

"After I had retired to the place where I had previously designed to go, having looked around me, and finding myself alone, I kneeled down and began to offer up the desires of my heart to God.[22]

From his brother's perspective, William states of Joseph, "and going out in the woods with child-like, simple trusting faith, believing that God meant just what he said, he kneeled down and prayed."[23]

Joseph continues: "I had scarcely done so, when immediately I was seized upon by some power which entirely overcame me, and had such astonishing influence over me as to bind my tongue, so that I could not speak."[24]

He then adds a portion not contained in the canonized "Standard Works" of the church. It describes in more detail precisely how his tongue felt: "My tongue seemed to be swollen in my mouth, so that I could not utter." In this same source he adds additional details: that after he heard the sound of someone walking toward him, "I strove again to pray, but could not. The noise of walking seemed to draw nearer. I sprung up on my feet and looked around, but saw no person."[25]

Continuing his main narrative:

"Thick darkness gathered around me, and it seemed to me for a time as if I were doomed to sudden destruction.

"But, exerting all my powers to call upon God to deliver me out of the power of this enemy which had seized upon me, and at the very moment when I was ready to sink into despair and abandon myself to destruction—not to an imaginary ruin, but to the power of some actual being from the unseen world, who had such marvelous power as I had never before felt in any being—just at this moment of great alarm, I saw a pillar of light exactly over my head, above the brightness of the sun, which descended gradually until it fell upon me.

"It no sooner appeared than I found myself delivered from the enemy which held me bound."[26]

Orson Pratt adds that the light "appeared to be approaching him from the heavens. As it came nearer it seemed to grow brighter until it settled upon the tops of the trees. He thought it would consume the leaves of the trees; but it gradually descended and rested upon him."[27]

Joseph's brother William adds: "He saw a pillar of fire descending. Saw it reach the top of the trees. He was overcome, became unconscious, did not know how long he remained in this condition, and when he came to himself, the great light was about him."[28] One can question William's interpretation of Joseph as "unconscious," since William related this point 64 years after the fact.[29]

Charles Lowell Walker reports 73 years after the event, in 1893: "Brother John Alger said while speaking of the Prophet Joseph Smith, that when he, John, was a small boy, he heard the Prophet Joseph relate his vision of seeing the Father and the Son, that God touched his eyes with his finger and said, 'Joseph, this is my Beloved Son, hear Him.' As soon as the Lord had touched his eyes with his finger he immediately saw the Savior."[30]

Walker adds more details of Alger's report: "After meeting, a few of us questioned him about the matter, and he told us at the bottom of the meeting house steps that he was in the house of Father Smith in Kirtland when Joseph made this declaration, and that Joseph while speaking of it put his finger to his right eye, suiting the action with the words so as to illustrate and at the same time impress the occurrence on the minds of those unto whom he was speaking. We enjoyed the conversation very much, as it was something that we had never seen in church history or heard of before."[31]

Joseph continues: "When the light rested upon me I saw two personages, whose brightness and glory defy all description, standing above me in the air. One of them spake unto me calling me by name and said—pointing to the other—"This is my beloved Son, hear him."[32]

J OSEPH continues his narrative . . .

"My object in going to inquire of the Lord was to know which of all the sects was right, that I might know which to join. No sooner, therefore, did I get possession of myself, so as to be able to speak, than I asked the personages who stood above me in the light, which of all the sects was right (for at this time it had never entered into my heart that all were wrong)—and which I should join.

"I was answered that I must join none of them, for they were all wrong, and the personage who addressed me said that all their creeds were an abomination in his sight; that those professors were all corrupt, that 'they draw near to me with their lips but their hearts are far from me; they teach for doctrines the commandments of men: having a form of godliness but they deny the power thereof.'"

". . . And many other things did he say unto me, which I cannot write at this time. When I came to myself again, I found myself lying on my back, looking up into heaven. When the light had departed, I had no strength; but soon recovering in some degree, I went home. And as I leaned up to the fireplace, Mother inquired what the matter was. I replied, 'Never mind, all is well—I am well enough off. . . .'

"It seems as though the adversary was aware, at a very early period of my life, that I was destined to prove a disturber and an annoyer of his kingdom; else why should the powers of darkness combine against me? Why the opposition and persecution that arose against me, almost in my infancy?

"Some few days after I had this vision, I happened to be in company with one of the Methodist preachers, who was very active in the before mentioned religious excitement and, conversing with him on the subject of religion, I took occasion to give him an account of the vision which I had had. I was greatly surprised at his behavior; he treated my communication not only lightly, but with great contempt, saying it was all of the devil, that there were no such things as visions or revelations in these days, that all such things had ceased with the Apostles, and that there should never be any more of them.

"I soon found, however, that my telling the story had excited a great deal of prejudice against me among professors of religion and was the cause of great persecution, which continued to increase; and though I was an obscure boy, only between fourteen and fifteen years of age, and my circumstances in life such as to make a boy of no consequence in the world, yet men of high standing would take notice sufficient to excite the public mind against me, and create a bitter persecution; and this was common along all the sects—all united to persecute me.

"It caused me serious reflection then, and often has since, how very strange it was that an obscure boy, of a little over 14 years of age, and one, too, who was doomed to the necessity of obtaining a scanty maintenance by his daily labor, should be thought a character of sufficient importance to attract the attention of the great ones of the most popular sects of the day, and in a manner to create in them a spirit of the most bitter persecution and reviling. But strange or not, so it was, and it was often the cause of great sorrow to myself.

"However, it was nevertheless a fact that I had beheld a vision. I have thought since, that I felt much like Paul, when he made his defense before King Agrippa and related the account of the vision he had when he saw a light and heard a voice, but still there were but few who believed him; some said he was dishonest, others said he was mad; and he was ridiculed and reviled. But all this did not destroy the reality of his vision. He had seen a vision, he knew he had, and all the persecution under heaven could not make it otherwise; and though they should persecute him unto death, yet he knew, and would know to his latest breath, that he had both seen a light and heard a voice speaking unto him, and all the world could not make him think or believe otherwise.

"So it was with me. I had actually seen a light and, in the midst of that light, I saw two personages, and they did in reality speak to me; and though I was hated and persecuted for saying that I had seen a vision, yet it was true. . . .

"For I had seen a vision; I knew it, and I knew that God knew it, and I could not deny it, neither dared I do it—at least I knew that by so doing I would offend God and come under condemnation.

"I had now got my mind satisfied so far as the sectarian world was concerned—that it was not my duty to join with any of them, but to continue as I was until further directed."[1]

Over the years Joseph would write about his experience on 6 different occasions. All six reflect consistency on the major facts. Where certain details are included in some accounts but not in others, the mosaic is clear: no version takes away from another, and later ones in fact add clarity to the overall picture. One example is Joseph's first account, wherein he states, "I saw the Lord and He spake unto me, saying: 'Joseph, my son, thy sins are forgiven thee . . . . Behold, I am the Lord of glory. I was crucified for the world.'"[2] In this account he does not mention the Father appearing (possibly because the focal point of the message comes from His Son, Jesus Christ). Also, the first account is a brief overview that lacks many details. In another account, an enlightening additional fact given by Joseph is that he saw many angels in addition to the Father and the Son.

While critics pounce on the fact that "not all the information is in every account," and therefore attempt to discredit all his accounts by viewing them as contradictory, believing Latter-day Saints view the accounts as they would view 6 accounts of any event written by an individual on 6 different occasions over a period of several years—some accounts would simply give more details than others. But additional details in and of themselves do not constitute contradictions, unless there are actual, clearly defined contradictions, which these 6 accounts do not contain. Why did the first account not give all the details? Two obvious reasons: (1) Because of the ridicule and reviling that resulted from opening up to one minister, Joseph was obviously deeply pained. He therefore would tell very few people of his experience—his family and only the closest of friends—for many years, and even then he would reveal only partial details in some of the accounts. (2) He was commanded "not to proclaim these things or to mention them," as he informed his parents after another vision.[3] Therefore, Joseph held sacred facts to himself and did not even tell his parents for a time about the First Vision. In fact, he would tell neither of them about his next vision—of the angel Moroni—until specifically commanded by the angel to tell his father.

When he had naively related the account to a Methodist minister, thinking he would receive encouragement, he had immediately learned his lesson—to be discreet. This was another reason to abbreviate future accounts

Years later, in 1832, he would write his first account and, being leery of criticism, would make it a shortened one; then in 1838 he would write the fullest account, which would be published in 1842 and presented to the public, being the opening pages to his own history, which is the canonized version used today. This history he decided to publish only after numerous critics had reported distortions about him. Perhaps that was the reason, perhaps not—that missionaries at that point began to include the First Vision, as it has come to be known, as part of their presentations. Another reason for not focusing on the First Vision may be that the *Book of Mormon* was his focal point as the key to people's conversions. But with time and reflection he added the First Vision to the cornerstone of the church's message.

After Joseph confided to the one minister, many in the community would not even associate with his family, and, later, certain self-proclaimed enemies would claim the family members were of such low class that no one would associate with them. Joseph's brother William states, "We never knew we were bad folks until Joseph told his vision. We were considered respectable till then, but at once people began to circulate falsehoods and stories in wonderful ways."[4]

Thomas H. Taylor, a Palmyra attorney, tried to figure it out: "There was something about him they could not understand; some way he knew more than they did, and it made them mad. . . . The only trouble was they [the Smiths] were ahead of the people; and the people, as in every such case, turned out to abuse them, because they [the Smiths] had the manhood to stand for their own convictions. I have seen such work all through life." When asked by an interviewer, "What did the Smiths do that the people abused them so?" he said, "They did not do anything." The interviewer then asked, "But a good many tell terrible stories, about them being rogues, and liars, and such things. How is that?" Taylor responded, "Oh, they are a set of d––––d liars. I have had a home here, and been here, except when on business, all my life—ever since I came to this country—and I know these fellows. They make these lies on Smith, because they love a lie better than the truth. I can take you to a great many old settlers here who will substantiate what I say, and if you want to go, just come around to my place across the street there, and I'll go with you." When Taylor's interviewers said they would "go see those fellows." Taylor replied, "You will find they don't know anything against those men when you put them down to it. They could never sustain anything against Smith."

He concludes, "I knew them [the Smiths] very well; they were very nice men, too."[5]

A man who would later work on a project involving Joseph, John H. Gilbert, reports succinctly, "Oh, I don't think the Smiths were as bad as people let on for."[6]

Joseph himself said his family received "many persecutions and afflictions" after the First Vision.[7]

But why the opposition? Latter-day Saints believe that with the Restored Gospel of Jesus Christ on the earth, there is an adversarial being, literally Satan, who opposes the work of the Restored Gospel, which had its launch with the First Vision.

So why was Joseph, of all people, chosen to be heaven's mouthpiece? Some have rejected his message because the restoration did not occur through established, educated, diplomaed ministers of religion. As Eliza R. Snow, a confidant to Joseph, analyzes, "He was a mere boy, honest, full of integrity, unacquainted with the trickery, cunning and sophistry employed by politicians and religious hypocrites to accomplish their ends. Like Moses of old, he felt incompetent and unqualified for the task—to stand forth as a religious reformer in a position [that was] the most unpopular."[8]

A deeper analysis comes later from Brigham Young, who says Joseph "was foreordained in eternity to preside over this last dispensation," specifically, "long before the foundations of the earth were laid."[9]

Joseph's family embraced his report of the First Vision, yet his mother, a sister, and at least one brother continued active in the Presbyterian faith another 7 years, until about October 1827. (Presbyterian records indicate their memberships were suspended on March 2, 1830, after 18 months of inactivity.)[10]

Immediately after his experience in the Sacred Grove behind the Smith home, Joseph told his mother, "I have learned for myself that Presbyterianism is not true," but he added that he would not try to prevent her from going to any church she wished to attend.[11]


Joseph was told in an April 1830 revelation that he "received a remission of his sins,"[12] apparently referring to the First Vision. He also said his "soul was filled with love, and for many days I could rejoice with great joy, and the Lord was with me."[13]

Joseph's father seemed the most prepared of all family members, due to his dreams—some occurred before and some after his son's first vision. One or more of them involved the apostasy of the church that Christ established upon the earth. Both the subject matter of his dreams and the fact he felt he had received them from God may have prepared the way for him to accept his son's account.

No more visions came to Joseph for several years. Meanwhile, he grew and became an even harder worker, yet along with his brothers, sisters, and parents, barely stayed above the line of starvation. But now he faced the ridicule, disdain, and open hostility of neighbors scoffing at his story—all because the minister in whom he had confided leaked the news.

As a family the Smiths faced other issues. They were trying to live down their poverty, as well as face the problems of an imperfect father.

Joseph senior admitted he had been "out of the way through wine."[14]

He seemed to appreciate his son Hyrum's not laughing him to scorn, although other people did when he drank too much.[15] Such laughter at their father doubtless caused young Joseph and all his siblings embarrassment.

Joseph senior also confesses letting down his children in another manner: "I have not been diligent in teaching them the commandments of the Lord, but have rather manifested a light and trifling mind."[16]

He had, of course, lost the Vermont farm through the ginseng theft, but still it had been outrageously unwise to not sell it for cash. Soon he would lose this Palmyra farm as well. Perhaps most painful of all to him, points out historian Richard Bushman, was the fact he had no inheritance to leave his wife and children—the goal of most responsible fathers of the time.[17]

Despite the challenges at home, young Joseph faced even more difficult ones in the community. With word out about his vision, he now had to confront, for the first time in his life, elements of anger and harassment.

His mother writes in her *History of Joseph Smith by His Mother: The Unabridged Original Version* (Stratford Books, 2006; eBook, 2012) that Joseph was once crossing his yard, coming home from an errand, when a gunshot fired past him. His family ran outside and searched, but the ambusher was gone, leaving (as they found the next morning) only an imprint in the mud where he had lain under a wagon. But the missed shots had hit their cow, leaving lead in the head and neck, not killing it, however, as it was left still standing.[18]

The Smiths kept themselves busy building their dream home. Over the next 2 years, they built it in the winters and farmed in the summers. According to Lucy, the house was framed first and, at the end of 2 years, they finally had the materials to finish it.

During Joseph's teenage years, meanwhile, he was not involved in any church, "having been forbidden [by Deity] to join any of the religious sects of the day," he writes, adding that he was persecuted by those who should have been his friends. Thus, "I was left to all kinds of temptation and, mingling with all kinds of society, I frequently fell into many foolish errors, and displayed the weakness of youth and the foibles of human nature."[19] He clarifies that he was not guilty of "any great or malignant sins. . . . But I was guilty of levity, and sometimes associated with jovial company, etc."[20]

While being a quiet child in the eyes of his mother, Joseph had another side to him. Around others—perhaps mainly other teens—he had a distinctly gregarious nature. Being naturally friendly made him an easy target for that jovial crowd. His enemies never claimed he was involved in vandalism, sexual promiscuity, or dishonesty during his teens, but his friends claimed he drank. Ezra Pierce describes it as "socially, like everybody else."[21] Neighbor Orlando Saunders said of the community, "Everybody drank them times," adding, "the Smiths with the rest; they never got drunk to my knowledge."[22] Joseph's future boss Josiah Stowell said Joseph drank a glass but, "I never knew him to get drunk."[23] John Stafford reports, "It was common for everybody to drink, and to have drink in the field; one time Joe, while working for someone . . . drank too much boiled cider.

He came in with his shirt torn." An interviewer asked Stafford, "Had he been fighting and drunk?" "No; he had been scuffling with some of the boys. Never saw him fight; have known him to scuffle [fight playfully]; would do a fair day's work if hired out."[24]

But he did apparently have some serious fights, perhaps defending himself against persecution, and at other times for other reasons. Later he states it gave him a sense of shame,[25] especially since his parents had taught him that fighting and quarreling were "beastly" sins.[26] Later, at age 26, he would write that his mistakes "brought a wound upon my soul,"[27] and when he was almost 29, he would write that his vices were of a "light" and "vain" mind, wherein he exhibited "a foolish and trifling conversation."[28] This, he states, was "the worst that my accusers can substantiate against my moral character."[29] Vicious verbal attacks against his family became common. Enemies would drag up every imaginable accusation—some absurd—including a rumor that the Smiths had stolen a sheep. But the victim of the theft exonerated them. An interviewer asked retired physician John Stafford, "You were living at home at the time, and it seems you ought to know if they got a sheep, or stole one, from your father?" Stafford replied, "They never stole one, I am sure."[30]

But Joseph had other imperfections. Even at age 17 Joseph felt weighed down by them, believing his behavior was "not consistent with that character which ought to be maintained by one who was called of God as I had been."[31] Thus one Sunday night while still 17—the night of September 21, 1822, after his family had been "sitting till quite late" talking about the "diversity of churches" and "the many thousand opinions" about scripture"[32]—he felt an overwhelming concern about how he stood in the eyes of God. So, after the others went to sleep, he stayed awake to pray, he reports, "for forgiveness of all my sins and follies."[33] From his bedside, while supplicating the Lord, he felt confident he would receive an answer, and soon a light appeared in his room, which increased until "the room was lighter than at noonday."[34]

He declares, "A personage appeared at my bedside, standing in the air, for his feet did not touch the floor. He had on a loose robe of most exquisite whiteness. . . . His whole person was glorious beyond description.

"I was afraid, but the fear soon left me. He called me by name, and said unto me that he was a messenger sent from the presence of God to me and that his name was Moroni; that God had a work for me to do; and that my name should be had for good and evil among all nations, kindreds, and tongues. . . . He said there was a book deposited, written upon gold plates, giving an account of the former inhabitants of this continent and the sources from whence they sprang. He also said that the fullness of the everlasting Gospel was contained in it, as delivered by the Savior to the ancient inhabitants; also that there were two stones in silver bows—and these stones, fastened to a breastplate, constituted what is called the Urim and Thummim—[and were] deposited with the plates; and the possession and use of these stones were what constituted 'Seers' in ancient or former times; and that God had prepared them for the purpose of translating the book."[35] Joseph further states that Moroni instructed him to show the plates, breastplate, and the Urim and Thummim to no one without permission, or he would be destroyed.[36] Joseph said that as Moroni spoke more, he could see in vision the location of the plates.[37] Lucy recalls the angel also telling him:

"The churches that are now upon the earth are all man-made churches. There is a record for you, Joseph, but you cannot get it until you learn to keep the commandments of God, for it is not to get gain. But it is to bring forth that light and intelligence which has long been lost in the earth. Now Joseph, beware, or when you go to get the plates, your mind will be filled with darkness, and all manner of evil will rush into your mind to prevent you from keeping the commandments of God, that you may not succeed in doing his work."[38]

The light then gathered around the angel until the room was dark, except for a pillar of light, which rose skyward. Moroni ascended within the pillar until he was gone. Lying there and thinking about what he had seen, Joseph again observed a conduit of light growing brighter. Moroni reappeared and stated the same things as earlier, but this time he added that the sword, famine, and pestilence would be coming in Joseph's generation. Then Moroni disappeared as before, but came a third time and repeated again what he had said, this time adding that Satan would try tempting him to obtain the plates for money, due to his family's extreme poverty.

Joseph writes that the next morning he arose exhausted, and went to work in the fields but was too tired to be of any use. Alvin, his oldest brother, asked him to keep up with the work, so Joseph went to work again. But after a short time, he stopped. Since he was a hard worker, his father thought it strange. Figuring he was sick, he told his son to return home to be doctored.

"On coming to a beautiful green, under an apple tree," states Lucy, "he stopped and lay down, for he was so weak he could proceed no further."[39]

T HE next thing Joseph realized was this: Moroni was standing in the air—surrounded by light—even though it was daylight. And chastising him:

"Why did you not tell your father that which I commanded you to tell him?"

"I was afraid my father would not believe me," replied Joseph.

"He will believe every word you say to him," responded Moroni.[1]

Joseph's father heard him, believed him, and told him to do everything the angel had instructed.[2] Possibly because of his own dreams, Joseph's father was thoroughly supportive. In fact, all those dreams he had had in recent years would suddenly make sense. They had been building up to this.

Joseph went straight to the hill where the plates were buried. He had "no trouble" finding it, says Joseph Knight, a frequent guest to the home and close family friend. "For it appeared plain as though he was acquainted with the place—it was so plain in the vision that he had of the place."[3]

Joseph would later learn the ancient name for the site—Cumorah—from the translated plates, but would actually hear the name Cumorah before then, in late May 1829, while traveling with associates, as described in Chapter 19, when a white-bearded older gentleman would come to the wagon in which he and friends were traveling, and mention the name.[4]

The hill itself was almost 4 miles south of Palmyra on the road to Canandaigua, just south of Manchester. The hill, "of considerable size and the most elevated of any in the neighborhood," writes Joseph,[5] was on the east side of the road. He climbed the high hill and, nearly at the top, on the west side, he found the place he had seen in vision. There, he spotted a large stone that was partly buried. It was "thick and rounding in the middle, on the upper side," says Joseph, "and thinner towards the edges, so that the middle part of it was visible above the ground, but the edges all round were covered with earth."[6] After brushing the dirt from the edges with his hands, he obtained a lever, "which I got fixed under the edge of the stone." He then used "a little exertion" to raise it up. "I looked, and there indeed did I behold the plates!"[7]

They were resting in a stone box that had been cemented together, along with the breastplate and Urim and Thummim.

The stone box sat on 4 pillars of cement, according to Lucy in her rough draft.[8] The flat side faced in and the rounded sides faced out.

Lucy states that the visit was not over. "While Joseph remained here the angel showed him, by contrast, the difference between good and evil, and likewise the consequences of both obedience and disobedience to the commandments of God."[9] She does not go into any detail of what that meant.

Knight reports Joseph asking the angel about the plates: "When can I have it?"

"The answer," says Knight, "was 'the 22nd day of September next, if you bring the right person with you.'

"Joseph says, 'Who is the right person?'

"The answer was, 'Your oldest brother.'"[10]

"The time for bringing them forth had not yet arrived," says Joseph himself, "neither would it, until four years from that time; but he told me that I should come to that place precisely in one year from that time, and that he would there meet with me, and that I should continue to do so until the time should come for obtaining the plates."[11]

Note that *the angel did not say* it would be 4 years till he got the plates; he merely said to return in 1 year. It was Joseph who later said in retrospect that it would be 4 years afterward that he would receive the plates. At the time, Joseph actually thought he would receive them each year that he went. So, his target date as a 17-year-old for obtaining the plates was 1 year later—in September 1824, when he would be 18. Only in time would he learn how long it would actually take—4 years.

On this topic Lucy adds, "The angel told him at the interview mentioned last [at the apple tree when he was told to tell his father of the plates] that he could not take them from the place wherein they were deposited until he had learned to keep the commandments of God—not only till he was willing, but able, to do it."[12] (Again, in his mind, that was in just a year.)

That evening he decided to trust those closest to him. He recounted these experiences to his family.[13] They not only believed, but, according to Joseph's brother William, were all "melted to tears, and believed all he said."[14]

The next night he told them not to relate any of these experiences outside the family circle because, when wicked men would hear of these things, they would try to take their lives.[15] Many a person had been and would be killed for treasure of any kind, especially gold.

Furthermore, since Joseph had been "burned" by telling the Presbyterian minister about the First Vision (his seeing the Father and the Son 3½ years previously), he did not wish to divulge the angel's visit either, generally keeping his cards close—until 1831 when he would begin telling others outside his circle of family and friends.

Lucy chronicles:

"From this time forth Joseph continued to receive instructions from the Lord, and we continued to get the children together every evening for the purpose of listening . . . all seated in a circle, father, mother, sons and daughters, and giving the most profound attention to a boy, 18 years of age [actually 17], who had never read the Bible through in his life."[16]

This period of time in which Joseph waited to receive the plates is described by Lucy:

"The sweetest union and happiness pervaded our house, and tranquility reigned in our midst.

"During our evening conversations Joseph would occasionally give us some of the most amusing recitals that could be imagined. He would describe the ancient inhabitants of this continent, their dress, mode of traveling and the animals upon which they rode; their cities, their buildings with every particular; their mode of warfare, and also their religious worship. This he would do with as much ease, seemingly, as if he had spent his whole life with them."[17] On at least one occasion his family heard him relate the angel's visit.[18]

The drudgery of daily farm work was eased by the focus it gave them—with the anticipation of evening conversations. Lucy says her family had "something upon which we could stay our minds."[19]

Wandle Mace records Lucy adding more on this: "During the day our sons would endeavor to get through their work as early as possible and say, 'Mother, have supper early, so we can have a long evening to listen to Joseph.'"

Mace adds that Joseph related to them the ancients' "implements of husbandry." Then, very significantly, he quotes Lucy saying exactly where Joseph learned all this: ". . . many things *he had seen in vision.*"

He then quotes her conclusion: "Truly ours was a happy family, although persecuted by preachers."[20]

Significantly, Joseph was receiving visions about the people he would soon be translating about. Mace also states, "She [Lucy] told how their family would all be seated around the room while they all listened to Joseph with the greatest interest as he taught them the pure principles of the gospel as revealed to him by the angels, and of his glorious vision of the Father and the son."[21]

The friends to whom he related these things were few. Joseph Knight junior states that Joseph related his account to both him and his father, Knight senior, as well, adding, "My father and I believed what he told us. I think we were the first after his father's family."[22]

Wandle Mace adds, "Oh, how many happy hours I have spent with these good old folks. They were as honest and true as it was possible for mortals to be; and they exemplify the words of the Apostle who said, 'All that will live godly in Christ Jesus shall suffer persecution'" (2 Tim. 3:12).[23]

The Smiths' trusted neighbors, the Rockwells, were also enraptured by young Joseph's stories. According to Elizabeth Roundy, to whom Rockwell would later relate his childhood experience, "Joseph Smith's father and mother used to come to his father's house and tell his parents of the wonderful things that were being revealed to their son Joseph. He said he used to watch for their coming and plead with his mother to let him stay up to keep the pine torch burning, as that was the only means they used to illuminate their dwelling."[24]

Although Porter was 7½ years younger, it was during this several-year period that he and Joseph cemented a lifelong friendship—one of undeviating loyalty to one another that would serve Joseph well in later years. Their camaraderie had already taken a big step forward when Porter broke his leg at age 10 in 1823. A Palmyra doctor had tried straightening it but managed to leave him with one leg shorter than the other, resulting in Porter, like Joseph, having a telltale limp that would last a lifetime.[25] This, no doubt, provided their neighbors a chuckle or two, seeing the two lads walking together down rural roads and village streets the same odd way.

The two families remained friends as well. (A third of a century later, a newcomer to the scene, Parley P. Pratt, would report first meeting Porter's mother in the fall of 1830 at Hyrum Smith's home.[26]) The families would intertwine and interact for years.

For some reason, Joseph would make one or more trips to the hill after his first failed attempt to receive the plates, according to his brother William Smith and their mother Lucy,[27] despite his believing he could not receive them for another year. Perhaps while there he would attempt to better camouflage the stone box, or would merely sit on a log and stare at the site with hope. Or there, perhaps, is where he received his visions of the ancients (as mentioned by Mace). Parenthetically, the hill, he would later learn, was a significant spot in the history of the people as described within the plates.

Meanwhile, during this period, the family built their house. The frame had been raised in November 1822, but much work still needed to be done. Alvin was in charge of construction and selflessly wanted a place for his parents to feel settled. Lucy reports him saying, "I am going to have a nice pleasant room for Father and Mother to sit in and everything arranged for their comfort, and they shall not work any more as they have done."[28] Ironically, despite his lofty desires, the exact opposite would plague them the rest of their lives.

Only 2 months after Joseph's first visit to the Hill Cumorah, on November 15, 1823, Alvin became severely ill. With their own doctor away, another, named Greenwood, prescribed calomel as his medicine. Alvin at first refused to take it, but finally gave in after much persuasion.[29] Soon he realized the substance was stuck in his abdomen, and he could not recover from it. He called in each member of his family to say goodbye and asked the next 2 oldest, Hyrum and Sophronia, to make certain the house was finished for their parents and to take care of them in their old age. "Be kind to them and remember what they have done for us,"[30] he admonished them. He called Joseph in alone and requested him to follow through as commanded by Moroni and make certain he obtained the buried plates. Four days later he faced his final hour. The poignancy is painted by Lucy, speaking of her youngest daughter, also named Lucy:

"We took hold of her to take her away, but she clinched him with such a strong grasp that it was with difficulty we succeeded in disengaging her hands.

"As I turned with the child to leave him, he said, 'Father, Mother, brothers and sisters, farewell! I can now breathe out my life as calmly as a clock.' Saying this, he immediately closed his eyes in death.

"The child still cried to go back to Alvin. One present observed to the child, 'Alvin is gone; an angel has taken his spirit to heaven.' Hearing this, the child renewed her cries and, as I bent over his corpse with her in my arms, she again threw her arms around him and kissed him repeatedly.

"And until the body was taken from the house, she continued to cry and to manifest such mingled feelings of both terror and affection at the scene before her as are seldom witnessed."[31]

The autopsy showed the calomel was wedged in his upper bowel, surrounded by gangrene.[32]

The hardship on the family could not be measured, nor could it be for his fiancée, who "never recovered her wonted animation and good spirits," reports Lucy in her rough draft.[33] In her 1853 published book she adds, "We were for a time almost swallowed up in grief, so much so that it seemed impossible for us to interest ourselves at all about the concerns of life."[34]

One neighbor stated that Alvin was the main worker of the family farm.[35] Lucy adds that, because of his innate goodness, the entire neighborhood mourned his death. Joseph states that Alvin was the "noblest" of the family and that he had "no guile."[36] He was also an example of justice and boldness to Joseph. Once he and Joseph had attended a fighting match between 2 Irishmen. One was winning and decided to gouge out the eyes of the other. So, Alvin jumped in, "took him by his collar and breeches and threw him over the ring,"[37] saving the other man's eyesight. Young Joseph would later say of Alvin, "I remember well the pangs of sorrow that swelled my youthful bosom and almost burst my tender heart when he died."[38]

Ten months after Alvin's death—a year after Joseph's first visit to the Hill Cumorah—Joseph tried obtaining the plates for the first time. But because his oldest brother was dead, "he was disappointed and did not know what to do," writes friend Joseph Knight. "But when the 22nd day of September [1824] came, he went to the place,"[39] thus returning to the hill.

Lucy states that as he reached into the box and lifted the plates, the thought hit him that "probably there was something else in the box besides the plates, which would be of some pecuniary advantage to him."[40] At that moment he took them out, relates Joseph Knight Sr.,[41] "and laid them down," says Lucy,[42] "by his side," adds Knight,[43] "very carefully," recounts Lucy,[44] "thinking," continues Knight, "there might be something else here.

Lucy explains another reason why he laid the plates down: "for the purpose of covering the box, lest someone might happen to pass that way and get whatever there might be remaining in it."[45] Knight says that in laying the plates down, he disobeyed. "But he was told to take the book and go right away."[46] (Lucy clarifies he was told this a year earlier, when the angel visited him at the apple tree.[47])

She then explains what happened next: "After covering it, he turned round to take the record again, but behold it was gone, and where, he knew not.[48]

Knight adds: "And he was astonished that the book was gone. He thought he would look in the place again and see if it had not got back again. He had heard people tell of such things. And he opened the box and, behold, the Book [plates] was there. He took hold of it to take it out again and, behold, he could not stir [move] the Book any more than he could the mountain. He exclaimed, 'Why can't I stir [move] this Book?'"[49]

Joseph himself writes, "I cried unto the Lord in the agony of my soul—why can I not obtain them?"[50]

Lucy details it more deeply: "He was much alarmed. He kneeled down and asked the Lord why the record had been taken from him; upon which the angel of the Lord appeared to him and told him that he had not done as he had been commanded, for in a former revelation he had been commanded not to lay the plates down or put them for a moment out of his hands, until he got into the house and deposited them in a chest or trunk having a good lock and key; and, contrary to this, he had laid them down with the view of securing some fancied or imaginary treasure that remained."[51]

Lucy states he then had "further conversation with the angel." After which, "Joseph was permitted to raise the stone again, when he beheld the plates as he had done before. He immediately reached forth his hand to take them, but instead of getting them, as he anticipated, he was hurled back upon the ground with great violence."[52] (Oliver states he was physically shocked.[53]) "When he recovered," concludes Lucy, "the angel was gone."[54]

Joseph himself writes *why* he could not take the plates—he had been "tempted of the adversary and sought the plates to obtain riches and kept not the commandment that I should have an eye single to the glory of God."[55]

Later, his friend Oliver Cowdery would explain this more, saying Joseph knew the plates could "relieve his family from want." There was also the wealth factor: he could use the treasure to "raise him above a level with the common earthly fortunes of his fellow man"[56]—in other words, the plates could make him rich.

Apparently, Joseph Smith was merely summarizing the event, while Knight, Lucy, and Oliver add numerous more details.

Knight actually adds facts little known even to most Latter-day Saints. Sometime before departing, the angel told Joseph "he could not have it now," with similar wording of a year earlier—but with a surprise ending (here italicized): "But the 22nd day of September next he might have the Book if he brought with him the right person. Joseph says, 'Who is the right person?' The answer was, "You will know." *Then he looked in his glass and found it was Emma Hale, daughter of old Mr. Hale of Pennsylvania, a girl that he had seen before, for he had been down there before with me.*"[57] A year earlier, of course, he was told to bring his oldest brother, who had since died, so now he had new instructions—to bring a certain girl.

Lucy wraps up his heartbreaking failure to obtain the plates. After a year of hope and enthralling family and friends about his visions, he now had to return home without the one thing he was living for: "And he arose and returned to the house, weeping for grief and disappointment."[58]

Lucy picks up the account when Joseph arrived home, after failing to get the plates for the second time:

"As he was aware that we would expect him to bring the plates home with him, he was greatly troubled, fearing that we might doubt his having seen them. As soon as he entered the house, my husband asked him if he had obtained the plates.

"The answer was, 'No, Father, I could not get them.'

"His father then said, 'Did you see them?'

"'Yes,' replied Joseph, 'I saw them, but could not take them.'

"'I would have taken them,' rejoined his father, with much earnestness, 'if I had been in your place.'

"'Why,' returned Joseph in quite a subdued tone, 'you do not know what you said. I could not get them, for the angel of the Lord would not let me.'"[59]

Now it became a family effort—not just a solo endeavor by Joseph—to prepare for the reception of the plates. Lucy reports it:

"Joseph then related the circumstance in full, which gave us much uneasiness, as we were afraid that he might utterly fail of obtaining the record through some neglect on his part. We therefore doubled our diligence in prayer and supplication to God."[60] Thus, it became the family's business to not see their brother and son fail.

Joseph now knew he would have to cleanse his heart of wanting financial gain from *any* contents of the stone box—not just the plates. He had been told by the angel to come back a year later. But it would now take 3 more visits—and 3 more years—before he would learn from Moroni if he was ready for the plates.


Meanwhile, the family had been torn over whether to attend local churches.

In 1824 a revival came to town. Lucy details the outcome:

"Shortly after the death of Alvin [who had died in November 1823], a man commenced laboring in the neighborhood to effect a union of the different churches, in order that all might be agreed and thus worship God with one heart and with one mind.

"This seemed about right to me, and I felt much inclined to join with them; in fact, the most of the family appeared quite disposed to unite with their numbers; but Joseph, from the first, utterly refused even to attend their meetings, saying, 'Mother, I do not wish to prevent your going to meeting, or any of the rest of the family's; or your joining any church you please; but do not ask me to join them. I can take my Bible and go into the woods and learn more in two hours than you can learn at meeting in two years, if you should go all the time.'

"To gratify me, my husband attended some two or three meetings but peremptorily refused going anymore, either for my gratification or any other person's.

"During this excitement Joseph would say it would do us no injury to join them, that if we did we should not continue with them long, for we were mistaken in them and did not know the wickedness of their hearts. One day he said that he would give us an example and that we might set it down as a prophecy, namely: 'You look at Deacon Jessup,' said he, 'and you hear him talk very piously. Well, you think he is a very good man. Now suppose that one of his poor neighbors should owe him the value of a cow and that this poor man had eight little children; moreover, that he should be taken sick and die, leaving his wife with one cow, but destitute of every other means of supporting herself and family—now I tell you that Deacon Jessup, religious as he is, would not scruple to take the last cow from the poor widow and orphans in order to secure the debt, not withstanding he himself has an abundance of everything.'

"At that time this seemed impossible to us, yet one year had scarcely expired when we saw Joseph's prophecy[61] literally fulfilled.[62]

Meanwhile, Lucy joined the Presbyterians with 3 of her children—Hyrum, Samuel, and Sophronia. One unstated reason may have been convenience—it was the only church right in town with a meetinghouse.[63]

The reason her husband had completely stopped attending goes back not only to his dreams but to his own upbringing, as well as a remarkable gaffe by their Palmyra minister:

First, his upbringing. Joseph senior's grandfather Samuel had been a Congregationalist, successful businessman, property owner, and town leader. But his son Asael broke away from the traditional mold, becoming a Universalist.[64] This likely had an affect on his son, Joseph senior, in not toeing the traditionalist line.

Second, Joseph senior's own dreams caused him to break even farther away from the mainstream, the dreams which had begun in 1811.

Third, and the crowning point, was when their minister, Reverend Benjamin Stockton, began teaching that Alvin had gone to hell because he had not attended church.[65] That did not sit particularly well with Joseph senior, causing him to never grace their halls with his presence again.

His attitudes may have had an effect on son Joseph Jr.

But Joseph Jr. was figuring out a lot more on his own. Especially when he saw how the community was now treating his family.

Alvin's death brought unexpected drama.

Besides Reverend Stockton's claim that Alvin had gone to hell, accusations arose designed to hurt the family—one or more persons claimed Alvin's buried body had been mutilated. Gossip spread like a winter sleet storm and it was the talk of the town. To find out if this were true, Joseph senior and a group of friends realized the grizzly necessity of digging up the grave and inspecting the corpse, now 10 months old—which they did—and found the rumors false. To set the record straight, they advertised in the *Wayne Sentinel* for 2 weeks, beginning with that day—September 25, 1824—declaring that no one had touched the body and asking the rumors to cease.[66] The accusations then spun into a bizarre theatre of the absurd. A rumormonger claimed that Alvin's body had actually been exhumed and taken by his brother Joseph Jr. in order to obtain the plates. Word had gotten out that Alvin was supposed to accompany Joseph to the plates[67] (of course alive, rather than dead), but the rumors would not stop and now slid into dark, ridiculous realms.[68]


More drama ensued: the family was targeted by the town for a social boycott. This was doubtless even more painful to Lucy, as it would be for any mother . . .

# CHAPTER 8

MRS. Palmer of Palmyra had a bittersweet view of Joseph:

"One of our church leaders came to my father to remonstrate against his allowing such close friendship between his family and the 'Smith Boy,' as he called him.

"My father defended his own position by saying that Joseph was the best help he had ever found. He told the churchman that he always fixed the time of hoeing his large field to that when he could secure the services of Joseph Smith, because of the influence that boy had over the wild boys of the neighborhood, and explained that when these boys or young men worked by themselves, much time would be spent in arguing and quarreling, which often ended in a ring fight. But when Joseph Smith worked with them, the work went steadily forward, and he got the full worth of the wages he paid."[1] (Joseph Knight junior similarly states, "My father said that Joseph was the best hand he ever hired.")[2]

Mrs. Palmer resumes her account:

"I remember the churchman saying, in a very solemn and impressive tone, that the very influence the boy carried was the danger they feared for the coming generation, that not only the young men, but all who came in contact with him would follow him, and he must be put down."

Later, after he obtained the plates, she wrote this report, which includes the following:

"Not until Joseph had had a second vision and begun to write a book which drew many of the best and brightest people of the churches away, did my parents come to a realization of the fact that their friend, the churchman, had told them the truth. Then my family cut off their friendship for all the Smiths.

"My parents then lent all the aid they could in helping to crush Joseph Smith; but it was too late. He had run his course too long. He could not be put down.

"There was never a truer, purer, nobler boy than Joseph Smith," Palmer concludes, before what she termed "superstition" led him astray.[3]

The drama against Joseph evolved into mild "hazing." Thomas H. Taylor reports, "Rascals at one trip took Joseph Smith and ducked him in the pond that you see over there."[4]

Then came another form, as the opposition heightened.


The Erie Canal was coming on strong. While Palmyra's portion was done 3 years earlier (as described in Chapter 3), the final third, the western portion, was now completed (in 1825), whereupon the governor, DeWitt Clinton, celebrated his 7 years of work by taking a barrel of water from Lake Erie to the Atlantic, where he poured it on November 4, 1825, after a 9-day journey. Thus, the completed canal could now bring even greater prosperity to the region—more so than when only Palmyra's middle portion was finished.

Meanwhile, Palmyra had mushroomed from a promising village with a few cabins and a couple stores when the Smiths arrived to a regular little town of brick homes, a hotel, and a tavern, plus 10 gristmills, 17 sawmills, 6 distilleries, and an ironworks. Manchester, where the Smiths lived just south of Palmyra, also had a wool mill dating back to 1813, which now could produce finer wool for finer clothes. By late 1825, after the complete canal had been opened a short time, Palmyra boasted of having dry good stores, a dancing school, and 2 millinery shops. Right along the canal is where commerce boomed and farmers brought their produce for shipment.

A bugle would announce the arrival of a barge, the largest of which could carry up to 75 tons—far superior to and faster than wagons, which had been the only hauling method before 1825. Thus, shipping costs were reduced to a fraction and the area's economy blossomed. It was much easier now for people to move West and develop the country as well, with a way to sell their goods all the way back to the East Coast.

Thus, the Smiths seemed to be primed like everyone else to benefit from the economic windfall. But their financial well-being was about to be pulled right out from under them . . . as the result of enemies.


The Smiths' home had been finished in 1823, when Joseph was 17.

In 1825, when they were putting the finishing touches on it, Russell Stoddard, a carpenter they had hired, rode up to the house with 2 others. He offered to buy the place. Lucy was not interested—they were just months away from their last payment on the farm. With Joseph senior gone Lucy and Hyrum talked to the men alone and told them their farm was not for sale. So Stoddard informed them they had to leave—because he now actually owned the deed![5] Stoddard and company had gone to the Smiths' sales agent a few miles south in Canandaigua and lied, saying Joseph senior and Joseph junior had deserted the family and that Hyrum was destroying the farm—ruining the land by chopping down the maple trees and burning the fences.[6]

The agent believed Stoddard and gave him the deed to the property upon receipt of the last month's payment.

So Stoddard, now holding the title, demanded the Smith family walk away from their farm immediately—the farm for which they had worked so hard. Hyrum and his mother begged to let them stay longer, as they had no place to sleep, but Stoddard would not relent.

Hyrum immediately galloped off to a family friend, Gain C. Robinson, who was outraged by the event and went to bat for the Smiths. Within 2 hours he collected 60 signatures from their neighbors, attesting to their good character and industry, and presented it to Hyrum, who charged off to see the land agent.[7]

Because of this, the agent sided with the Smiths, but he announced it was too late—he had given Stoddard the deed. Nevertheless, the agent was furious, and sent for Stoddard and his group. They refused to come. That made the agent even angrier, and he threatened them with a warrant. Under this pressure they acquiesced.

In a private meeting Stoddard bragged to the agent he had the deed. "Oh, no matter about Smith—he has gold plates, gold bibles, he is rich; he don't want anything."[8] The agent castigated them, and convinced them to give the Smiths a chance to pay him $1,000 for the deed—but they had just 2 days. Hyrum needed his father—and they were in a race against time. But he had no idea how to reach him. The land agent came up with a strategy. He told Hyrum to send out letters addressed to his father at public houses—hotels and taverns—on the roads he traveled.

Within hours his father happened to see a letter and raced home with Joseph Jr.

There, they talked it over and realized they were against a brick wall. They had no money and no options but to comply or leave the farm. Being broke, they had only one way out— they would have to find an investor to buy the farm and rent it back to them. Time was running out. Stoddard would soon take possession of the farm if they didn't act fast.

Panicking, Lucy found a Quaker gentleman willing to help, but when she arrived to see him, he had just spent his last $1,500 on another deal 30 minutes earlier. Now, with only 24 hours left before Stoddard would take possession of the farm, she traveled alone, night approaching, for 10 miles on a road through a dense forest.

Arriving home, she learned that the old Quaker gentleman had found another Quaker friend named Lemuel Durfee, who was willing to buy the farm and rent it to them. Now very late in the evening, Joseph senior hastened to find him 4 miles away, and he arrived just before daylight. Seeming to be open-minded over the idea of the deal, the older man nevertheless wished for his son, the sheriff, to accompany them all to the agent.

So Joseph senior had to go find Durfee's son, the sheriff, 3 miles further down the road. Time was running even shorter now, and the deadline was approaching.

Joseph found the sheriff and accompanied him back to his father, Lemuel Durfee. Immediately they all rode off to Canandaigua to see the agent, with time now running out.

Lucy reports:

"The anxiety of mind that I suffered that day can more easily be imagined than described. I now looked upon the proceeds of our industry, which smiled around us on every hand, with a kind of yearning attachment that I never before had experienced."[9]

At 9:30 P.M. Joseph senior and the two Durfees finally arrived at the agent in Canandaigua. There at the meeting were Stoddard and company, who, predictably put up a fuss. They tried to fight the deal on a technicality—they claimed it was past 10:00 P.M. but eventually capitulated on that point and gave up the deed to the younger Mr. Durfee for a total of $1,135. Lucy's rough draft reveals the bittersweet deal they struck: They could stay on their farm, and have a place to make a living on land they had cleared and a house they had built, but it was no longer theirs. They would get to use it for 1 year. But if they kept it up well (as determined by the new landlord), they could stay as long as they wished. However—and this was a particularly painful point to the Smith family—they would have to give up young Samuel as an indentured servant for 6 months. In early 19th-century New England it was a mild form of slavery. The parents would essentially lose the lad for half a year, and, being an extremely tight-knit family, their trepidation was nearly tangible.

With the con artist Stoddard out of the way, they leased the farm for 3 years, until December 30, 1828. Then they decided to move to a larger house just south and across the road. Although the new house was larger, Lucy was still attached to the first because of Alvin's work on it, wanting to settle his parents there—so she viewed losing the house a true tragedy.

Ever since Joseph's report to the minister about his First Vision, the entire family had become the target of escalating harassment. And enemies would now practically come out of the woodwork to find other angles from which to attack them. . .

Including what happened next . . .

CHAPTER 9

WHEN Joseph was still 19, in October 1825, he was approached by a wealthy farmer from South Bainbridge, New York. This gentleman, Josiah Stowell, wanted to find a lost silver mine in the Susquehanna Valley. Stowell had already paid for some excavation work there, based on an old document he had obtained that described a silver mine existing nearby, one that had been discovered and explored by Spaniards. He also had heard that Joseph possessed a certain talent for finding ancient treasure, based on a certain "seer stone" Joseph purportedly possessed (Chapter 17 has more details).

When Stowell recruited Joseph he was convinced of his powers. The reason: upon visiting with Joseph in Manchester, he saw the lad look through a stone and describe "Stowell's house and outhouses" precisely. Since Stowell had failed to find gold with other diggers, he was convinced he must try talking Joseph into helping him.

So he made Joseph an offer.

Joseph at first refused it. He even "endeavored to divert him from his vain pursuit," reports Lucy.[1] However, Joseph finally acquiesced when Stowell offered him high wages, which turned out to be not that much—$14 per month[2]—but Joseph thought he would be paid more when presented the job. (Based on 12-hour workdays, 6 days per week, which was common for the period, that works out to $1.92 per hour in today's money).

———Joseph, his father, and several neighbors began the journey
with Stowell to the site of the buried treasure.

That same month—October 1825—Joseph senior and junior
went just south of the New York border to dig for the mine. This
group of "money-diggers," as they came to be called, comprised
Joseph junior, Joseph senior, Hyrum, George Proper, Samuel
Lawrence, Josiah Stowell, and Alva Beaman.[3]

Several of the group had begun months earlier—in the early
summer of 1825—but they failed to find the purported mine. So
during this late October journey Stowell recruited Joseph and his
father more heavily, and they signed an agreement November 1,
contracting to receive ⅔₁ of the ore, coins, and bars or ingots of
gold or silver bars they hoped to find underground. The treasure
site was at Harmony, Pennsylvania, 26 miles downriver from
Stowell's New York farm. At some point Joseph was warned by
the angel to stay away from the money-digging crowd because
of their evil doings. Finally, after about 2 weeks, Joseph talked
Stowell into stopping. In the middle of November, the group
broke up. But not before a life-altering occurrence.

When Joseph and his father first arrived in Pennsylvania
they boarded with the Hale family of Harmony. (They probably
arrived about November 1, as Isaac Hale signed the agreement
papers that day, being the legal witness for the paperwork.)

The Hales were unusually charitable people, opening their
home to traveling ministers and leaving food on the doorsteps
of needy families, generally after hunting trips. (On these, the
father, Isaac Hale, would salt the meat and give much of it away.)

Isaac was born in Connecticut in 1762 and had moved to
Harmony about 1790. He had bought land and was well established. Besides being a well-known hunter, he was the type of
solid citizen one would want as a witness to the legal papers,
so Stowell recruited him. This allowed Joseph to meet Hale's
family. And his lovely daughter, Emma Hale. And because of
that, Isaac wished he had never witnessed the legal papers . . .
nor that his daughter and Joseph had ever laid eyes on one
another . . .

Emma Hale was the 7th of 9 children. Born July 10, 1804, she taught school, says Emily Coburn,[4] had dark hair, and charmed people with her large, hazel eyes.

Joseph was smitten by her.

He, meanwhile, was a handsome[5] and intriguing lad—tall and muscular, with a "large full chest,"[6] broad shoulders,[7] blue eyes,[8] and auburn hair. Some described his hair as reddish, particularly when he was younger. Bathsheba W. Smith describes it as "golden brown and very pretty,"[9] while James Palmer labels it "a flaxen color."[10] Governor Thomas Ford would say he was "uncommonly well muscled."[11] He had long legs[12] and was described as quite handsome,[13] with a voice that was "low and soft"[14]—but it could project well to large groups of people.[15]

While common belief is that he stood 6 feet tall (the standard even-number expression for tall people of the day—also the figure reported by one of his uncles[16]—he apparently grew to between 6'2" and 6'3", according to those who saw him in adulthood. The average height of men in the U.S. from Northern European descent was quite a bit shorter—at 5 feet 5.5 inches just a few years earlier (in the 1700s), compared to today's 5 feet 9.2 inches.[17] To the average American male looking up to him today, Joseph would have been comparable to a man about 6 feet 7 inches.[18] (See Appendix B: "The Height of Men through History" for more details.)

By 1842, at age 36, he would weigh 212 pounds,[19] but when he courted Emma at 19 he was likely well under 200 and rather lean.

He also had an attractive smile, and smiled often, according to a later writer for the St. Louis *Weekly Gazette*.[20]

His friends described him in other ways. David Whitmer states, "He was a very humble and meek man."[21] Eliza R. Snow adds, "He was humble as a little child."[22] His expression was "mild and almost childlike," writes Emmeline Blanche Wells.[23] He bore "an unconscious smile," reports Parley P. Pratt, adding that he was "affable, beaming with intelligence and benevolence, mingled with a look of interest."[24] That look, he says, included a "serene and steady, penetrating glance."[25] According to John W. Hess, "there was something heavenly and angelic in his looks that I never witnessed in the countenance of any other person."[26] Bathsheba W. Smith describes it as "the most heavenly countenance."[27]

He "had a very pleasant disposition and always seemed to be happy," states Elias Cox,[28] while Joseph described himself as "playful and cheerful."[29] Mercy R. Thompson says he was "always cheerful" and "always had a smile for his friends."[30] Bathsheba W. Smith adds that he was "genial, affable, and kind."[31] William Taylor echoes them, stating he was "always the most companionable and lovable of men—cheerful and jovial."[32] Jacob Jones says he was "always jovial," adding that he "could crack a joke."[33]

He was also a practical joker with his "most familiar friends,"[34] according to George Q. Cannon's magazine, the *Juvenile Instructor.* (Cannon as a teen knew him well, and wrote the only biography of him ever written from interviews with his personal friends—*Life of Joseph Smith the Prophet*, by George Q. Cannon, Stratford Books, 2005; eBook, 2012) That side of Joseph's humor was described by friends. For example, friend Benjamin Johnson held 9 silver dollars in his hand. Joseph hit Johnson's hand from underneath and the coins scattered everywhere. The two men playfully wrestled.[35] Journals are replete with accounts of his playful nature.

Newel Knight, knowing Joseph since a boy, writes, "In all his boyish sports and amusements, I never knew any one to gain advantage over him, and yet he was always kind and kept the goodwill of his playmates."[36] He was consistently considerate of others and, according to the future first governor of California, Peter Burnett, he "would not oppose you abruptly, but had due deference to your feelings."[37] Wandle Mace reports, "He had a free and easy manner, not the least affectation."[38] Mercy B. Thompson similarly states, "There was not the slightest appearance of ostentation . . . on his part. He was as free and sociable as though we had all been his own brothers and sisters or members of one family." She further describes him as "unassuming as a child."[39]

He may have looked young for his age at 19, when he met and showed interest in Emma, which perhaps may have been somewhat embarrassing for her, because when he was in his thirties he was described as "young looking" for his age."[40] Yet it may have bothered Emma even more that he was a year and a half younger than she—a social stigma that couples often hid. But the interest he took in others, combined with his warmth, charm, cheery disposition, and smile, no doubt melted her, and soon they were courting.

"My folks were bitterly opposed to him," Emma would tell their oldest living son.[41] And the reasons would unfold. Emma's father, Isaac Hale, first became opposed to the digging project, losing faith in it, and thereafter looked down on the treasure-digging boarders, of which Joseph was a part.

Isaac further claimed Joseph was "very saucy, and insolent to his father,"[42] although no where in Smith family records nor others' numerous accounts and journals was that ever indicated. Perhaps Isaac saw a riff between them on one occasion and was quick to judge the young man. Other, deeper reasons would unpeel in time.

In contrast to Isaac Hale, Joseph's wealthy boss, Josiah Stowell, even before his later religious conversion, consistently viewed young Joseph with respect, and would until his dying day—this despite the fact they never found any treasure. (Previous to this of course, Stowell had hoped Joseph possessed a gift for "divining"—using a rod or some other means to search for treasure by holding it over the ground until it would "dip" where the treasure supposedly lay.) But Joseph's method was different. Emma's father, Issac Hale, claims Joseph would look into a stone in a hat, covering his face with it.[43]

Once Isaac recalled Joseph stating a large treasure was near them, but as the diggers came closer to it, he could no longer see it.[44]

Perhaps the cynical Hale had doubts, but the possibility exists that Joseph did see other treasure, as well, which he could not obtain. For example, in 1877 Brigham Young wrote that Porter Rockwell was "an eyewitness to some powers of removing the treasures of the earth. He was with certain parties [presumably Joseph] that lived nearby where the plates were found that contain the records of the *Book of Mormon*. There were a great many treasures hid up by the Nephites. Porter was with them one night where there were treasures, and they could find them easy enough, but could not obtain them. . . . It was told to me by Porter . . . he is a man that does not lie."[45] Similarly, Martin Harris, another early friend to Joseph, later reported he accompanied 2 acquaintances, all taking "some tools to go to the hill and hunt for some more boxes, or gold or something, and indeed we found a stone box. We got excited about it and dug quite carefully around it, and we were ready to take it up, but behold, by some unseen power, it slipped back into the hill. We stood there and looked at it and one of us took a crowbar and tried to drive it through the lid and hold it, but the [crow]bar glanced off and broke off one corner of the box."[46]

Lucy and Joseph report that it was Joseph himself who told Stowell to give up treasure-hunting. In mid-November, perhaps November 17, 1825, after a month of searching, they all did give up.[47] But repercussions came from this event that would haunt the Smith family for decades.

His enemies would now begin declaring that he was a "money digger" and could not be trusted. Despite the commonality of the trade, and the fact divining was to many a respected and standard method for finding wells by America's early settlers, some looked down on Joseph for his participation.

Many influential men of wealth, besides Josiah Stowell, were "money diggers" as well. It was practiced among many respected Christians and community leaders. Stowell had actually been "educated in the spirit of orthodox Puritanism, and was officially connected with the first Presbyterian Church of the town," says Bainbridge physician W. D. Purple, who knew him, adding that Stowell was "a very industrious exemplary man."[48]

That others were commonly engaged in treasure "digging" is substantiated by Porter Rockwell's sister years later, after growing up in Manchester, but not part of the their faith: "There was considerable digging for money in our neighborhood by men, women, and children."[49] In 1825 the *Wayne Sentinel* at Palmyra reprinted an article from the Windsor, Vermont *Journal* that stated, "respectable men" believed treasure was in the Green Mountains and had dug for it for years.[50]

Nevertheless, enemies to Joseph years later would try to emphasize Joseph's "money digging" in order to discredit his later work in translating the *Book of Mormon*, which in itself seemed to be "buried treasure" at which cynics would scoff. Because Joseph also used a seer stone in translating most of that book—as well as receiving a number of his revelations later used in the *Doctrine and Covenants*—enemies for years would try to tie him into the myths that unfortunately surrounded the activities of many rodsmen and money diggers. (See Appendix C: "Money-diggers and Rodsmen" for more details.)

Joseph likely was subject to superstitions as well as to misunderstanding certain Bible doctrines until he would receive more information—the restored gospel—several years later.

While Latter-day Saints believe that "the adversary," Satan, can counterfeit true spiritual gifts, some believe there may be some validity to the early American claim that "divining rods" were indeed "divine." Oliver Cowdery possessed a "rod of nature" that Joseph stated in the *Book of Commandments* was "the work of God."[51] And Joseph's "seer stone" had other miraculous powers, say Latter-day Saints, while other, similar stones apparently possessed powers that were not of a divine origin.


Joseph's father and neighbors that were part of the silver mine project returned home, while Joseph stayed on Stowell's farm. He worked for Stowell as a farmhand and attended Emma Hale's school when he could in order to study reading, writing, and a little more about Emma.

ESPITE Isaac Hale's rising opposition, Joseph sought
to court his daughter. He rode to nearby Harmony as often as
he could. Fortunately for the young suitor, his own family did
not need his services on their farm as much now—they had
a good crop, higher prices, and a sufficient crew of labor. The
Erie Canal was producing exponentially higher revenues and
the local economy, including the population, was booming. So
Joseph was free to stay and court Emma.

He meanwhile was working hard just to survive. Stowell
hired him to work on his farm and maybe in his mills—but it
was quite a commute for Joseph—26 miles north.

When he was not working for Stowell, he was hired by
Joseph Knight Sr. of Colesville, New York—a bit closer to the
Pennsylvania border. Although no one knows what Joseph's employment consisted of there, Knight owned a farm in Colesville,
a gristmill, and a wool carding plant on which Joseph may
have worked machinery.[1] He possibly alternated employment
between both gentlemen, because Knight and Stowell lived near
each other—Knight's farm in Colesville was 3½ miles south of
Stowell's farm near South Bainbridge—both in New York.

Because of Joseph proving his trustworthiness in working
for both men, they lent the Smith family money against the
next year's wheat crop.[2]

In 1826, just months after looking for silver for Stowell, Joseph went to school in Chenango County and perhaps in Broome County, New York,[3] at the age of 20, for a period of several months at most.


Even with all the ridicule and harassment over the First Vision he had received in Palmyra, he never made an avowed enemy in his life. Until now. Nor had he ever appeared in court, nor had most young men his age. But that was about to change. A self-declared enemy now decided to take him on.

A member of his boss's family named Peter Bridgeman claimed Joseph was an imposter. He also labeled him disorderly. And then dragged him to court.

Joseph went to trial in Bainbridge, New York, on March 20, 1826, at the age of 20, and was tried by Albert Neely, a justice of the peace. Because Peter Bridgeman had pushed the trial forward with such obsessive zeal, the justice apparently viewed his case as somewhere between borderline and absolute absurdity, since so many respectable citizens utilized the services of diviners for both treasure hunting and water searching. Perhaps the judge saw the irony of Joseph being one of the few, if not the only, to ever have any charges brought against him for it. Ironically, in at least 3 of the several reports of this trial still in existence, Joseph actually testified against himself, revealing his activities with full disclosure. Technically a rarely enforced law about "glass-looking" had been broken. So Joseph was charged with a misdemeanor as a "glass looker" and possibly had to pay one court expense—but the only one—the judge's trial costs of $2.68.

Ironically Joseph had apparently given up his divining activities before the trial anyway, so it is likely that Bridgeman was out to get him for some other reason. Perhaps he felt protective of his uncle, Josiah Stowell, not realizing Stowell had been the aggressive party, not the one being cheated as Bridgeman likely supposed (especially at $14 per month).

One A. W. Benton wrote of Joseph: "The public had him arrested" (in truth it was one person) "as a disorderly person, tried and condemned before a court of justice" (strangely strong language, since he was immediately released with no reported fine or sentence), "but because he was a minor, because they hoped he might reform, he was designedly allowed to escape."[4] In reality he was simply released, and even "honorably acquitted," with no action required. His accuser was later labeled an "officious person" by a friend of Joseph.[5]

Joseph continued working and living on Josiah Stowell's farm while courting Emma for several months. At her home her brother Alva, especially, and other brothers, pestered Joseph unmercifully, perhaps about the First Vision or glass looking or both. During a fishing excursion, the brothers so hassled Joseph that he tossed away his coat and challenged them to a fight, an example of his quick temper when harassed.

In November, still 1826, Joseph left the Stowells because Josiah Stowell "could not pay him for his work very well," states Joseph Knight Sr.[6] He went to live with and work for Knight in Colesville,[7] saving money for his future. That future, young Joseph quickly realized, should include Emma Hale. Knight lent him a horse and sleigh to make visits to her.

The next thing Joseph did was return home and tell his parents about Emma.

"Joseph called my husband and myself aside," recalls Lucy, "and said, 'I have been very lonely ever since Alvin died, and I have concluded to get married; and if you have no objections to my uniting myself in marriage with Miss Emma Hale, she would be my choice in preference to any other woman I have ever seen.' We were pleased with his choice and not only consented to his marrying her, but requested him to bring her home with him and live with us."[8] Remarkably, they had not even met her, but held strong respect for Joseph's judgment.

Over the years Joseph had seen numerous girls about the villages—at school, stores, and while working the retail booths at the county events and revivals, where thousands of people would gather, including numerous young people who attended the revivals. He also had been in the company of two of Stowell's daughters,[9] but Emma was his choice for a lifelong companion.

According to Lucy, Joseph wished to marry Emma in December 1826, just over a month after he met her (around November 1, 1826). His mother began rearranging the house to receive Emma.[10] (In fact, she was doing that when the aforementioned Stoddard demanded that the Smith family vacate,[11] as detailed earlier.)

Upon learning of his plans to marry Emma, generous family friend Martin Harris (who had hired Joseph years before as a boy) gave Joseph a fine wedding gift—a new suit.

Much better dressed now, Joseph approached Emma's father and asked for his daughter's hand in marriage . . .

E MMA'S father flat out refused to give his consent for their marriage. As he put it, Joseph was "a stranger, and followed a business that I could not approve."[1] That "business" was the 2-week treasure hunting stint that Isaac could not get unstuck from his emotional craw.

At least that was Isaac's official excuse for opposing the marriage. The real reason, thought Joseph, was religious. Isaac was a dyed-in-the-wool Methodist.

But Joseph's relationship with Emma took a turn upward when Emma visited the Stowells in Bainbridge, and in walked Joseph. During their visit—whether a short or long one is not recorded—he proposed to her. Stowell encouraged her to accept, knowing Joseph's qualities.

And apparently right there, she agreed to marry him.

So the young couple hatched a plan. They decided to elope. On a Sunday January morning,[2] the 21-year-old Joseph took off riding with the 22-year-old Emma while Isaac was at church. Neighbors W. H. Hine and his spouse saw them tearing past their house on an old horse, with Emma riding behind Joseph,[3] just like in the storybooks. They galloped to South Bainbridge and were married by Squire Tarble at his home.

Fifty-two years later Emma would recall it less romantically, even clinically, but understandably so, since she was being interviewed by her son in the presence of her second husband:

"I had no intention of marrying when I left home; but, during my visit at Stowell's, your father visited me there. My folks were bitterly opposed to him, and, being importuned by your father, aided by Mr. Stowell, who urged me to marry him, and preferring to marry him to any other man I knew, I consented. We went to Squire Tarble's and were married."[4] From this more clinical assessment of their history, they eloped in one of two ways: (1) they rode off right then and there from the Stowells' to Squire Zechariah Tarble, or (2) they went their separate ways and, later during a church service when her family was gone, Joseph rode up to her home to get her, as described by the W. H. Hine account above, wherein they rode off to Squire Tarble's to be married.[5]

Her father, Isaac Hale, says Joseph carried Emma off.[6]

In whichever case, they married at Tarble's house in South Bainbridge on January 18, 1827.[7]

After the ceremony they left for Joseph's homestead in Manchester. There, Joseph's parents welcomed her as their own daughter, and they lived with them while Joseph farmed through the next season.

Some months later, Emma decided she wanted her belongings, since she had taken off with only the clothes on her back, so she wrote her father, asking for her other clothes, furniture, and cows, and he consented.

In August 1827, 7 months after they were married, Joseph rode to get them.

At Harmony, he found her father madder than a homeless hornet—Joseph had "stolen" his daughter, and Isaac tearfully told him so. Hale vowed he would rather see her dead than married to Joseph. Joseph tried allaying his fears, and informed Isaac he was done with treasure-hunting. He also promised him that he "expected to work hard for a living, and was willing to do so."[8]

Isaac claims Joseph agreed he would now give up "glass looking" for treasure (which he had anyway), and would move with Emma back to Harmony in the coming months. Additionally, said Isaac, Joseph consented to look for new employment.[9]

That softened Isaac's heart, and he would even help Joseph get started in business.[10]

Her brother Alva also shook hands with Joseph, agreeing to bury their differences. Alva's change of heart was apparently sincere. He later committed to helping Joseph move from Palmyra to Harmony—a daunting, several-day task on rough roads. For now, Joseph returned to Manchester with Emma's belongings.

On the way, he told Peter Ingersoll, whom he had hired to help load and transport Emma's property, that he planned to make good on his promise to his father-in-law, but he feared the peer pressure of returning to treasure hunting. "It will be hard for me," said Joseph, "for they will all oppose, as they want me to look in the stone for them to dig money."[11] Ingersoll says Joseph was right: "They urged him, day after day, to resume his old practice of looking in the stone."[12]

Once back in Manchester, Joseph had a remarkable experience. On September 21, 1827, his father sent him on a business errand to Manchester and expected him home by 6 P.M.

When the day ended, with night falling, he was still not back. All began to wonder. Anxious, his parents waited and worried.

The tradition among Latter-day Saints is that Joseph, 4 years earlier, had been told by the angel that he would receive the plates in 4 years, period. And to check back to the site every year for instruction. This is based on some people's interpretation of Joseph's own history contained in the *History of the Church*,[13] adopted into the Pearl of great Price. But Joseph may have simplified the events, since he hated writing anyway, and merely given us the bottom line. According to Joseph Knight junior, who was staying there as a guest, and from Lucy's comments, it was considerably more dramatic, with nothing cut and dry. Apparently Joseph thought each year he would receive the plates—and even on the 4th year they felt it was predicated on obedience, so his receiving the plates was not a sure thing.

In this more dramatic version, Joseph told Knight that the angel said if he would do what was right, "according to the will of God, he might obtain the plates the 22nd day of September next, "and if not, he never would have them."[14] He was speaking of the very next day! Simply put, Joseph would either receive the plates within 24 hours—or never. For years he knew it would be on a September 21–22, but this "now or never" news came as a surprise. The pressure was on, with Joseph left wondering if he was worthy. So the night before the 22nd, Joseph still may not have known if he would get the plates.

But that was not his only worry. He knew that if he did get the plates, people would be waiting in the wings to waylay him. Word had leaked out about a September date 2 to 3 years earlier when his father had told their friend Martin Harris in confidence about the plates (and ordered him to tell no one), but Martin had[15]—possibly to his wife, who managed to attract trouble like a magnet—so rumors had been spreading.

"We always had a peculiar anxiety about him whenever he was absent," writes Lucy in her rough draft, "for it seemed as though something was always taking place to jeopardize his life."[16]

Finally, Joseph, exhausted, entered and collapsed into a chair, "pale as ashes."[17] Joseph senior questioned his son why he was late and what was wrong.

Silence.

His father threw other questions at him but he ignored them.

Lucy said nothing.

She later describes the scene: "The fact was, I had learned to be a little cautious about matters with regard to Joseph, for I was accustomed to see him look as he did on that occasion, and I could not easily mistake the cause thereof."[18]

His father said, "Joseph, why are you so late? Has anything happened to you?"

Lucy reports, "Presently he smiled and said in a calm tone, 'I have taken the severest chastisement that I have ever had in my life.'"[19]

Lucy says his father got angry, fearing that some neighbor had confronted him, but Joseph explained what had happened.

On the road near the hill, the angel had visited him. The message had been bittersweet. Moroni told him he was neglecting the work of God. But there was a flip side: He could now obtain the gold plates!

He detailed the angel's reprimand: "I had not been engaged enough in the work of the Lord; that the time had come for the record to be brought forth, and that I must be up and doing, and set myself about the things which God had commanded me to do. . . . I now know the course that I am to pursue, so all will be well."[20]

Joseph thus expressed confidence he could pull it off. No longer did he view the plates as earthly treasure to help his family but as a gift from God to assist mankind.

So now it was time to get the plates. Joseph told only Emma and his mother exactly when he was going to the hill to get the plates. Not even his father knew. One plausible reason was this: his family would have insisted on going along to protect him, because of so many threats in the air, but he wanted to keep a low profile. So he took only his wife. (Earlier, of course, he had received instructions—even when he was single—to bring Emma, so there was no question about her going.)

Still, he feared a surprise attack. Specifically by Samuel Lawrence, a neighbor who had searched for treasure with him. "Joseph was some afraid of him, that he might be a trouble to him," records Joseph Knight.[21] Thus, he got his father to spy out the Lawrence home "to see if there was any signs of his going away that night. He told his father to stay till near dark, and if he saw any signs of his going, "You tell if I find him there [at the hill] I will thrash the stumps with him.'"[22]

But at his neighbor's farm over the hill Joseph senior did not see Sam Lawrence. So after dark he returned home.

Meanwhile, Joseph Knight Sr. found young Joseph making preparations to go to the hill. He did not exactly know when he was going, nor that he would be taking Knight's horse and buggy. Joseph's plan to use the rig was likely to throw off would-be pursuers who would be on the lookout for the Smith family's rig. He kept his trip to the hill as a surprise from Knight, probably because Knight would have insisted on going to protect him, which would have only drawn attention. Joseph knew one thing only—he had to sneak out before dawn of September 22 for it still to be the evening of September 21, the target night declared by Moroni.

So he left for the Hill Cumorah at midnight. Before leaving, he asked his mother if she had a chest, lock, and key. Frustrated, Lucy told him no. Joseph calmed her. "I can do very well for the present without it—be calm—all is right."[23] At this point, Lucy obviously knew what he was up to. Within minutes Emma walked through the room wearing a bonnet and riding apparel. When she and Joseph went outside, they climbed atop Knight's wagon and rode away.[24]

That morning, after sunrise, Joseph senior sauntered in and sat at the breakfast table. First thing he did was ask for Joseph. Lucy tried to change the subject, but he wouldn't let go. "I must have Joseph sit down here and eat with me."

Lucy retorted, "Well now, Mr. Smith, do let him eat with his wife this morning; he almost always takes breakfast with you."[25] Lucy was covering for Joseph, but their dialogue also reveals the unique closeness between father and son.

Minutes later Joseph Knight entered, complaining about the missing horse.

"Never mind the horse," said Lucy. "Mr. Knight doesn't know all the nooks and corners in the pastures; I will call William; he will bring the horse immediately."[26] Another cover-up.

Knight then began looking for his wagon, and found that it, too, was missing. Knight now feared both were stolen,[27] not knowing Joseph had borrowed them.

After breakfast, Joseph and Emma returned home. With no fanfare, they simply walked into the house. Knight at that point became aware of the fact they had been gone, and, more important, realized what had taken place, now seeing his buggy and horse resting outside.

Lucy began trembling, she writes. She feared they had not been obedient enough over the past year and had lost the opportunity to receive the plates. She left the room. Sensitive to her feelings, Joseph followed her. "Do not be uneasy, Mother; all is right."[28]

At that point he showed her the covered Urim and Thummim. "See here, I have got a key."[29] She did not know Joseph's meaning, but it was to help translate the plates. He then handed her the items covered with a silk handkerchief,[30] which, she says, consisted of two 3-cornered diamonds set in glass like eyeglass lenses, and that the two lenses were set in silver bows connected like old-fashioned spectacles.[31] "He took them again and left me but said nothing respecting the record," states Lucy.[32]

Joseph sat down to breakfast and did not say a word about the plates. But soon he felt too excited to keep it a secret. He decided to announce the discovery. Surprisingly, his emphasis was more on the Urim and Thummim than the plates.

After breakfast, Joseph called Knight to join him in another room. "He set his foot on the bed," writes Knight, "and leaned his head on his hand and says, 'Well, I am disappointed.'

"'Well,' say I, 'I am sorry.'

"'Well,' says he, 'I am greatly disappointed; it is 10 times better than I expected.'

"Then he went on to tell the length and width and thickness of the plates and, said he, 'They appear to be gold.' But he seemed to think more of the glasses or the Urim and Thummim than he did of the plates, for, says he, 'I can see anything; they are marvelous.'"[33]

Joseph also said he was to possess the plates until the messenger came for them again.

But he had not brought the plates home. Rather, he had hid them in an old birch log, says Lucy,[34] or a hollow oak tree top, according to Martin Harris 32 years later,[35] who adds that Joseph cut off some bark and carved out the interior, then rested the plates inside and replaced the bark.[36] Lucy says that the log was decayed,[37] making it easier for him to dig out a cavity to hide the plates, and that the bark was still intact, which enhanced the camouflage. The hole he dug in the log was just large enough to fit the plates, and then he covered it with "some old stuff that happened to lie nearby,"[38] she says, likely dead woodland matter—broken twigs and old leaves.

Joseph's first item of business was to get a box made. Lucy sent him to a cabinetmaker, one who had made furniture for his sister Sophronia. Lucy told him to promise the furniture maker half produce and half cash—the same arrangement Sophronia had secured. Joseph would have the box within a couple days, but he knew he had no way of paying for it then— nor immediately—and not even half down, because, as Lucy says, "There was not a shilling in the house."[39] So, although worried, they proceeded on faith.

On the following day, someone came to Joseph and told him he was needed to perform labor for a Mrs. Wells on a well at Macedon, New York, 5 miles west and slightly north of Palmyra[40]—so he left immediately. This work paid for the chest. In Lucy's rough draft she labels it a "provision of Providence."[41] Adding to the small miracle, not only had this lady never asked for Joseph's assistance before,[42] but no one had ever even heard of her.


But then Hades broke loose—all because of the Martin Harris leak:[43]

The day after Joseph left to work on the well, a neighbor came knocking, pumping Joseph's father for information. Within hours Joseph senior learned that 10 or 12 men working with Willard Chase were plotting to steal the plates. They had even sent for a conjurer 60–70 miles away to help locate the hiding spot.[44]

Brigham Young later illuminates the scene. He describes him as a "fortune-teller—a necromancer, an astrologer, a soothsayer [who] possessed as much talent as any man that walked on the American soil, and was one of the wickedest men I ever saw."[45] Brigham would not meet Joseph for another 5 years, but since 1817, the year Brigham turned 16, he had lived in central New York (Auburn and Port Byron) where, in one of these two towns, he evidently had known the fortune-teller and could make this assessment.

The next morning Joseph's father decided to spy again on the intruders. He climbed over the hill east of his property and walked down to the Lawrence farm. What he discovered shook him.

When the older gentleman arrived, men were in the back yard talking. He told them he was there on "an errand," and they sent him inside the house. Entering the rear door, he left it "a little ajar in order to overhear their conversation," reports Lucy.[46] They stood in the yard near the door and were devising plans to steal the plates, he reported, which they called "Joe Smith's gold bible."[47]

The conjurer had traveled all the previous day and night, but Lucy notes he still found the energy to be extremely animated. Mrs. Laurence became uneasy and stepped out another back door "and called to her husband in a suppressed tone, but loud enough to be heard distinctly by Mr. Smith, 'Sam, Sam, you are cutting your own throat.'" Sam Lawrence did not reply, but the conjurer yelled to her, "I am not afraid of anybody—we will have them plates in spite of Joe Smith or all the devils in Hell!"[48]

When the woman returned inside, she evidently walked to the room where Joseph senior was eavesdropping. She had not known he was even on the property. He put down a newspaper he had been holding and casually remarked, "I believe I have not time to finish reading the paper now."[49] He sauntered out of the house and returned home. She was likely left aghast, wondering how much he had overheard.

When Joseph senior arrived home he asked Emma if Joseph had taken the plates from their place of deposit, or if she was able to tell him where they were. She answered no to both questions. Joseph senior then announced to the others present what he had seen and heard over the hill.[50]

Emma, having remarkable faith, said she did not know what to do, but surmised that if Joseph was supposed to get the record, he would, and that his enemies could not stop him.

His father offered this insight: "Yes, he will if he is watchful and obedient, but remember that for a small thing Esau lost his birthright and blessing. It may be so with Joseph."[51] After all, Joseph was just out of his teens and by his own admission had already been chastised by the angel for negligence. So now they began worrying. Emma decided to ride off to find him at his well-digging job in Macedon—except she had no horse. So Joseph senior ordered his son William to round up a stray. Within the hour Emma was galloping off to find Joseph.[52] When she arrived at Macedon she told him of the plot to steal the plates.

Immediately, he borrowed a horse and galloped out of Macedon and 5 miles east to Palmyra, with Emma riding at his side on her horse. Through the streets of Palmyra they rode and another 2 miles south to Manchester. Jumping off his steed, he found his father pacing around outside, distraught. He assured his father the plates were safe. Lucy recounts the dialogue from Joseph:

"Father, there is no danger—all is perfectly safe—there is no cause of alarm."[53] Joseph felt confident he could assure him of this because, before coming home, he had looked into the Urim and Thummim and had seen that the plates were untouched.[54]

Despite the plates being safely hidden in the woods, he decided now to bring them home. Ironically, they would be less secure, but at least be under everyone's watchful eye. Next, Joseph instructed Hyrum to find a chest with "a good lock and key" and have it ready when he returned with the plates.[55] This was likely the chest that was to be built by the cabinet maker.[56]

So Joseph went to get the plates. But this time he was alone, dressed in his frock—a long, loose coat worn by craftsmen—which he had worn to dig the well.

Lucy states that once he arrived at the plates' hiding place, he wrapped them in his frock and placed them under his arm.

Fearing attack on the wide-open road, he traveled through thick trees. Traveling some distance, he came to a log. He managed to jump over it, says Lucy, although he likely climbed over it, since the plates weighed 40 to 50 lbs., estimates Martin

Harris.[57] (Willard Chase reports Joseph saying the plates weighed 40–60 lbs.;[58] Joseph's brother William puts them at 60.)[59]

But then—from either the conjurer's "talents" or simply from a rather amazing coincidence—others spotted Joseph in the forest,[60] carrying the gold plates.

As Joseph maneuvered over the log, a man sprang from behind and clubbed him. The weapon was a gun.

Joseph turned and knocked him flat, then bolted off with the plates. A half mile further he was again attacked—the same way. He knocked this attacker down also, and resumed his run.

The leader of the group trying to get the plates from Joseph was actually the conjurer.

Brigham Young gives his backstory, along with how evil transcended the previous world into this one, reaching its tentacles through time and space to try to snare Joseph.

"In regard to the battle in heaven . . . I do not think it lasted long; for when Lucifer, the Son of the Morning, claimed the privilege of having the control of this earth and redeeming it, a contention rose; but I do not think it took long to cast down one-third of the hosts of heaven, as it is written in the Bible. But let me tell you that it was one-third part of the spirits who were prepared to take tabernacles [physical bodies] upon this earth, and who rebelled against the other two-thirds of the heavenly host, and they were cast down to this world . . . to this terra firma that you and I walk upon, and whose atmosphere we breathe, and they have been opposed to him from that day to this, with Lucifer at their head, He is their great General—Lucifer, the Son of the morning. He was once a brilliant and influential character in heaven, and we will know more about him hereafter.

"Do you not think that those spirits knew when Joseph Smith got the plates? Yes, just as well as you know that I am talking to you now. They were there at the time, and millions and millions of them opposed Joseph in getting the plates; and not only they opposed him, but also me in the flesh. I never heard such oaths fall from the lips of any man as I heard uttered by a man who was called a fortune-teller, and who knew where those plates were hid. He went three times in one summer to get them—the same summer in which Joseph did get them. Baptist, Presbyterian, and Methodist priests and deacons sent for him to tell where those plates were, and to get them out of the hill where they were deposited, and he had not returned to his home from the last trip he made for them more than a week or 10 days before Joseph got them. Joseph was what we call an ignorant boy; but this fortune-teller, whose name I do not remember, was a man of profound learning.

"He had put himself in possession of all the learning in the States—had been to France, Germany, Italy, and through the world—had been educated for a priest, and turned out to be a devil. . . . He could preach as well as the best of them, and I never heard a man swear as he did. He could tell that those plates were there, and that they were a treasure whose value to the people could not be told, for that I myself heard him say. Those spirits driven from heaven were with him and with others who tried to prevent Joseph's getting the plates; but he did get and secrete them, though he had to knock down two or three men, as he was going home, who were waylaying him to kill him."[1]

Before reaching home he was assaulted again—this time taking a hard hit with a gun.[2] When he hit the man back, "he dislocated his thumb, which, however, he did not notice until he came within sight of the house," says Lucy. Then "he threw himself down in the corner of the fence in order to recover his breath. As soon as he was able, he arose and came to the house. He was still altogether speechless from fright and the fatigue of running."[3]

After resting inside a few moments, he ordered his young brother Carlos to retrieve his father and two friends—Knight and Stowell—to find the men outside who had chased him, in case they were lurking about to launch another attack. The two searched, according to his request, but found no one.

Then he sent Carlos to fetch Hyrum and bring him home. Hyrum was at a neighbor's house having tea with 2 in-laws. Lucy recounts:

"Just as Hyrum was raising a cup to his mouth, Carlos touched his shoulder.

"Without waiting to hear one word from the child, he dropped the cup, sprang from the table, caught the chest, turned it upside down and, emptying its contents on the floor, left the house instantly with the chest on his shoulder."[4] This may or may not have been the same chest that Lucy advised them to have built by Sophronia's cabinetmaker.

His wife's sisters "were greatly astonished at his singular behavior and declared to his wife . . . he was certainly crazy." In response, Hyrum's wife laughed and replied, "It is just like him to fly off in a tangent when he thinks of anything in that way."[5] Little did they know, Hyrum was taking the chest in order to protect what he figured was God's most important treasure for man on planet Earth.

Receiving the chest, Joseph locked up the plates. He then "threw himself upon the bed," says Lucy.[6] After resting a moment, he went to the kitchen, where he told his father everything that had transpired. Listening in were Josiah Stowell and Joseph Knight Sr. Other friends and neighbors soon formed about him and listened.

News of the plates spread like wildfire. Everyone wanted to know something, says Lucy, about "the strange circumstance which had taken place."[7] Then he showed them his thumb, saying, "I must stop talking, Father, and get you to put my thumb in place, for it is very painful."[8] Noteworthy are his first 2 concerns—even over his immediate physical pain—first, his exhaustion that led him to the bed, and second, his willingness to share the information of what had just happened.

Thereafter, he "related to our guests," says Lucy in her rough draft, "the whole history of the record."[9] These were not just any guests, but those to whom Joseph would be willing to relate so much delicate information—the more open-minded people. She concludes, "They listened and believed all that was told them."[10]

According to his brother William, their father then wished to see the plates. "What, Joseph, can we not see them?" he asked.

Joseph responded, "No. I was disobedient the first time, but I intend to be faithful this time, for I was forbidden to show them until they are translated."[11]

While no one was yet allowed to actually see them, reports family friend Joseph Knight,[12] Smith family members were permitted to handle them as long as the plates were covered with a cloth. William Smith describes them as thin metal sheets that could be turned like book pages. He adds that they were an alloy of gold and copper, much heavier than stone.[13]

Further, he states, "I could tell they were plates of some kind and that they were fastened together by rings running through the back."[14] He concurs with his mother on their size, he says, "as described in Mother's history,"[15] stating that while the plates were wrapped in Joseph's frock, "Father and my brother Samuel saw them as I did, while in the frock. So did Hyrum and others of the family."[16] In later years, when William was asked by an interviewer if he wanted to remove the cloth and see the plates, he replied, "No, for Father had just asked if he might not be permitted to do so, and Joseph, putting his hand on them, said: 'No, I am instructed not to show them to anyone. If I do, I will transgress and lose them again.' Besides, we did not care to have him break the commandments and suffer as he did before."[17] In saying "lose them again" he is possibly referring to Joseph not being worthy to receive them each of the first 3 years he attempted to obtain the plates, as explained in this endnote.[18]

Edmund Clarke Briggs was William's interviewer in 1891, asking him the question, "Did you not doubt Joseph's testimony sometimes?" William replied, "No. We all had the most implicit confidence in what he said. He was a truthful boy. Father and mother believed him, why should not the children? I suppose if he had told crooked stories about other things, we might have doubted his word about the plates, but Joseph was a truthful boy. That father and mother believed his report and suffered persecution for that belief shows that he was truthful. No, we never doubted his word for one minute."[19]

While Emma also did not actually see the plates, she says she felt them, and adds that they were usually kept secure in a red morocco trunk, perhaps the same one that Hyrum had brought over. Later, when Emma and Joseph were living alone in Harmony, Pennsylvania, on property owned by Emma's parents, "the plates often lay on the table without any attempt at concealment, wrapped in a small linen table cloth which I had given him to fold them in," reports Emma many years later. "I felt of the plates, as they lay on the table, tracing their outline and shape. They seemed to be pliable like thick paper, and would rustle with a metallic sound when the edges were moved by the thumb, as one does sometimes thumb the edges of a book."[20] This last comment of hers is similar to William's description. Emma further states, rather matter-of-factly, "I moved them from place to place on the table, as it was necessary in doing my work."[21]


Joseph remained on the farm now, wishing to be near the plates while he worked the fields. Soon after receiving the plates, says Lucy:

"He came in from work one afternoon and, after remaining a short time, he put on his coat and left the house. . . . When he returned he requested me to come downstairs. I told him that I could not leave my work just then, yet upon his urgent request I finally concluded to go down and see what he wanted, upon which he handed me the breastplate spoken of in his history.

"It was wrapped in a thin muslin handkerchief, so thin that I could see the glistening metal and ascertain its proportions without any difficulty."[22]

Describing the breastplate's shape, Lucy adds, "It was concave on one side and convex on the other, and extended from the neck downwards as far as the center of the stomach of a man of extraordinary size. It had four straps of the same material for the purpose of fastening it to the breast, two of which ran back to go over the shoulders, and the other two were designed to fasten to the hips. They were just the width of two of my fingers (for I measured them), and they had holes in the end of them to be convenient to fastening."[23] Joseph then placed the breastplate in the cherry wood chest with the Urim and Thummim.[24]

Martin describes the Urim and Thummim as 2" in diameter, perfectly round, and ⅝" thick at the center, thinning at the edges.[25]

Lucy states of the Urim and Thummim, "It was by this that the angel showed him many things which he saw in vision; by which he could also ascertain at any time the approach of danger, either to himself or the record."[26] On account of this "he always kept the Urim and Thummim about his person."[27]

Soon, he was made aware of danger to the plates, apparently through the Urim and Thummim.

Says Lucy:

"Joseph came to the house in great haste and inquired if there had been a company of men about.

"I told him not a single individual had come to the house since he left.

"He then said that a mob would be there that night, if they did not come before that time, to search for the record, and that it must be removed immediately."[28]

The same night "a man by the name of Beaman came in from the village of Livonia," reports Lucy, "a man in whom we reposed much confidence and who was well worthy of the same. Joseph told him his apprehensions of a mob being there that night and that they must prepare themselves to drive them away; but that the first thing to be attended to was to secure the record and breastplate."[29]

According to Joseph Bates Noble, who would befriend Beaman's daughter Mary when she would later teach school, Beaman then helped Joseph hide the plates.[30] He was actually "permitted to handle the plates with a thin cloth covering them."[31]

At this point, Joseph removed hearthstones in the west room and buried the chest inside the hearth.[32] Then he raced to relay the stones. Just as he and others had put the stones back, a "large company of men, well armed," says Lucy,[33] charged the house, likely led by either Sally or her brother Willard Chase.

Joseph surprised them—he "threw open the doors" and, reports Lucy, "hallooed as if he had a legion at hand, in the meantime giving the word of command with great emphasis; while all the male portion of the family, from the father down to little Carlos [aged 11], ran out of the house with such fury upon the mob that it struck them with terror and dismay, and they fled before the little Spartan band into the woods, where they dispersed themselves to their several homes."[34] He had likely learned this trick from grandfather Mack,[35] via Lucy.

With the word out, neighbors harassed the Smiths. Incessant questions. Demands to see the plates. Sneaking around the property. New overt attempts to steal them.

Living under the cloud of this nightmare, the Smiths would endure more attacks on their farm. They seemed to all feel the pressure of protecting the plates.

Joseph Knight Sr. says Joseph told the neighbors he could not show them under any circumstances, "but many insisted and offered money and property to see them."[36]

The angel, according to Lucy, told Joseph, "You will have to be watchful and faithful to your trust, or you will be overpowered by wicked men, for they will lay every plan and scheme that is possible to get it away from you, and if you do not take heed continually, they will succeed."[37]

Brigham explains who the wicked were: "When Joseph obtained the treasure, the priests, the deacons, and religionists of every grade went hand in hand with the fortune-teller and with every wicked person to get it out of his hands and, to accomplish this, a part of them came out and persecuted him."[38]

Word spread as far as Fayette, 27 miles east, about the plates' existence. David Whitmer notes: "Before I knew Joseph, I had heard about him and the plates from persons who declared they knew he had them, and swore they would get them from him."[39]

Some of those after the plates were Joseph's former partners. Martin Harris explains their interesting logic: "The money-diggers claimed that they had as much right to the plates as Joseph had, as they were [had been at one time] in company together [searching for Stowell's silver mine]."[40]

Following this same line of logic, feeling justified in their strange request, 2 men came to Joseph's house one day to persuade him to give them a "share" of the plates. One was the rodsman from Livonia, Alva Beaman—the same who had won their confidence and helped Joseph hide the plates. The other was Samuel Lawrence, the neighbor over the hill, who had plotted earlier to steal them.

A witness to this scene was Joseph Knight Sr., still visiting the Smiths. He says of Beaman and Lawrence, "They proposed to go shares with him and tried every way to bargain with him. But could not. Then Beaman took out his rods and held them up and they pointed down to the hearth where the plates were hid. 'There,' says Beaman, 'it is under that hearth.'"[41]

(Lucy says Beaman had earlier seen Joseph plant the plates beneath the hearth.[42] So this dramatic moment was not all that dramatic.) Joseph Knight relates it in such a way that Beaman was not present when the plates were hidden under the hearth, and thus his use of the rods to find the plates was effective.[43] Knight further labels him "a great rodsman."[44] Beaman would later see the folly of his activities in trying to take the plates, as he and his wife would faithfully follow Joseph the remainder of their lives.[45] (See more details about Beaman in the endnote.)

But for now, Joseph forced Beaman and Lawrence outside. Since he knew they knew where the plates were, he moved the artifacts once again after they left. He wrapped them in clothes and carried them to his father's cooper shop[46] "across the road." There, he laid them "in a quantity of flax, in the shop loft," says Lucy.[47] Then he nailed up the empty box, tore up the shop floor, and placed the box under it as a decoy. Lucy says he received "an intimation"—presumably from the Urim and Thummim—that a mob was approaching.[48]

The nightmare was just beginning.[49]

When evening came, Willard Chase and his sister Sally Chase came with a mob to search the Smiths' property.[50] Beaman may or may not have been part of the mob, but a year later was part of another mob—an angry one that Sally's brother Willard was part of (as shown in the following chapter), so it is possible that Beaman and Willard Chase were close enough acquaintances for Beaman to share what he knew about the plates' presence under the hearth. In any case Sally had in the past "found a green looking glass, through which," says Lucy, "she could see many very wonderful things."[51] Porter Rockwell's sister later reported Sally being hired by people who sought her services, as she could find anything lost, stolen, or hidden.[52] Retired physician John Stafford reports what he had heard: "The neighbors used to claim Sally Chase could look at a stone she had and see money. Willard Chase used to dig when she found where the money was. Don't know as anybody ever found any money."[53]

Lucy adds of Sally:

"She said that she saw the precise place where 'Joe Smith kept his gold bible hid' and, obedient to her directions, the mob gathered their forces and laid siege to the cooper's shop."[54] She describes what happened next:

"As soon as night came, the mob came also and commenced ransacking the place. They rummaged round the house and all over the premises," but did not come into the farm house.[55] Nevertheless, "they still went from place to place by her direction," determined to get the plates.[56] "After making satisfactory search they went away."[57]

Interestingly, Sally Chase led the mob everywhere on the premises except the farm house where she likely had been tipped off by Beaman about the plates' location under the hearth. Perhaps she guessed that Joseph would have taken the plates out of the hearth and even out of the house, and/or perhaps she thought her looking glass was telling her it was elsewhere.

The next morning the Smiths entered the shop and found the floor torn up and the empty cherry wood chest smashed.[58]

Immediately, Joseph ran up the ladder to the loft. There he found the plates safely buried in the flax.[59]

Whether there was any validity to Sally's "magic" or not, Lucy does not seem to question it,[60] but it failed the mob in the end.[61]

But the mobs were not finished with them . . .

O VER a year later David Whitmer would come across a small, angry mob of young Palmyra men—some of the same from before. They claimed Joseph "had promised to share with them."[1]

Among them, once again, were Alva Beaman and Willard Chase. Beaman may have actually been the one to build the box that held the plates, although Willard Chase takes credit for that[2]—Chase in fact claims he was justified in partial ownership of the plates because of the box he supposedly built(!)

As stated, apparently the agreement to share earlier treasures gave them justification to mob Joseph to get their shares of the artifacts he now had, given to him by the angel.

Joseph, of course, could have told them to take it up with the angel, but instead, more diplomatically, ignored them.

Because they and Joseph had signed the old silver mine agreement of Stowell's, they figured it should extend somehow to Joseph's plates. Two years later. In a different state. With a different treasure.

Obviously, to any sane mind, there was no reason Joseph should share the plates with neighborhood scoundrels, given Moroni's warning for 4 consecutive years.

However, rather than the alleged "shares" being the main problem now facing the Smiths, Joseph Knight Sr. indicates the real problem was a group of people who "persecuted and abused" Joseph's family for simply not showing them the plates.[3]

While some neighbors looked upon the plates as a hoax, others believed their existence because of the honesty of the family. Among those was longtime Palmyra resident Thomas H. Taylor, who said he knew the Smiths very well and figured Joseph had in fact received the plates out of the hill. "Why not he find something as well as anybody else? Right over here in Illinois and Ohio, in mounds there, they have discovered copper plates since." He states he never saw Joseph's later translated work after it was published, and did not know anything about it, nor care, but believed Joseph's claim. He says the Smiths "were good, honest men."[4]

According to the future governor of New York, DeWitt Clinton, artifacts made of copper were also discovered in the western region of New York, as close as nearby Canandaigua, one village south of Manchester,[5] where they lived.

Before the translation was complete and the book was published, word did get out that the plates contained more than their intrinsic worth—that they actually had been discovered through nontraditional means and were "an ancient record, of a religious and divine nature and origin" (as published in the June 26, 1829, issue of the *Wayne Sentinel*).[6] Two Rochester newspapers also published statements in 1829 that the plates contained more than their mere material value: The Rochester *Advertiser and Telegraph* reports the plates were supposed to have teachings "far superior to the book of life,"[7] while the Rochester *Gem* states it claimed to be "an ancient record of divine origin."[8]

Even long before the newspaper accounts, public awareness had begun growing exponentially, causing increasing curiosity over its newly perceived value as an ancient record—rather than its mere market value in its weight of gold. This gave young Joseph entirely too much publicity, making it obvious that he could in no way translate the plates in peace—unless he and Emma moved.

But he needed money for that, and he knew only Martin Harris had that money. So he prevailed upon his mother to invite Harris to their farm for a visit.

"This indeed was an errand that I much disliked," says Lucy, "as Mr. Harris's wife was a very peculiar woman, one that was naturally of a very jealous disposition; besides this, she was rather dull of hearing and, when anything was said that she did not hear distinctly, she suspected that it was some secret which was designedly kept from her."[9]

Lucy made the trek alone to Martin's farm 1½ miles north of Palmyra (3 miles north of Manchester, where the Smiths lived), and she arrived as Martin was putting in a new hearth. She chatted with Martin's wife, also named Lucy but more frequently called "Aunt Dolly."[10] When Lucy told Dolly about the plates, she was hooked. So hooked, in fact, she offered Lucy money just to see them. According to Dolly 3 years later, she demanded that Lucy take her money, but only if Dolly could help in translating the plates. Lucy sidestepped the request. She turned to Martin and invited him to pay them a visit in Manchester[11]—the reason for Lucy's being there. According to Lucy, she turned the money down flat—a $200 offer from Dolly[12] and $75 more from Dolly's sister,[13]—for a combined total equivalent to $12,087 in today's currency, a hefty amount for the Smiths, particularly in light of their financial circumstances.

Joseph would soon learn how quickly a friendly acquaintance can mutate into an enemy. If Dolly was offended at her offer being turned down, she was doubly offended at not being invited to visit the Smiths along with her husband—but that did not stop her.

Days later, in Manchester, Lucy Mack Smith opened the door to greet Martin, only to find his determined wife standing there. Martin would not show up for several days, fighting his own demons of doubt. Meanwhile it did not take long for his wife's obdurate nature to unleash itself. Almost immediately she begged to see the plates. That not working, she attempted bribery again—this time directing it at Joseph. But Joseph told her he was forbidden to show them to anyone—his standard answer.

Immediately she began hounding him, asking if the story of the plates was true and declaring that if he really had the plates, she would both see them and help him publish them. "He told her she was mistaken—that she could not see them," reports Lucy.[14] Dolly might have offered to be Martin's liaison to Joseph, because Joseph then commented that he would deal with Martin directly. "This highly displeased Mrs. Harris, for she considered herself altogether superior to her husband."[15]

She then accused him. "Now, Joseph, are you not telling me a lie?"[16]

Next, she demanded a witness—to speak to someone who had actually seen the plates. If he would only present her with one, she said, she would help with the translation.[17] (As if Joseph wanted her around for that.) "This closed the evening's conversations," says Lucy,[18] with an obvious answer from Joseph.

That night Dolly dreamed of the plates. Reports Lucy: She even dreamed that an angel told her "she had disputed the servant of the Lord and said his word was not to be believed and had also asked him many improper questions—she had done that which was not right in the sight of God."[19] In other words, she was royally told off. But this only caused her to awake the next morning more excited than ever. And even more determined to help him. So this time she offered Joseph a loan—not a bribe—of $28.[20]

Joseph refused, of course, but needed flour so they could eat, so he went away for a few days to work. Before leaving, according to Martin years later, Dolly and her daughter were allowed to lift the plates in the box[21] (although obviously the plates remained covered). Dolly and the daughter then left for home, as Joseph headed to his new job.

At the Smith home several days later, Martin arrived while Joseph was still away. But he seemed a different man. Consumed with skepticism. Overcome by doubt. Demanding proof. So he interviewed the Smiths. "I talked with them separately, that I might get the truth of the matter," he writes, then when Joseph returned he interviewed him as well, and compared his statements with theirs, seeking to unearth a contradiction.[22]

Joseph startled him. He told him this: the angel had told him that Martin should now assist in the translation.[23] Martin replied, "If it is the devil's work, I will have nothing to do with it, but if it is the Lord's, you can have all the money necessary to bring it before the world. You must not blame me for not taking your word."[24]

Martin was then allowed to lift the box of plates. He went immediately home. He ran to his bedroom and prayed. He says the answer was at that moment manifested by God, declaring that "it was His work, and that it was designed to bring in the fullness of His gospel to the gentiles. . . . He showed this to me by the still small voice spoken in the soul."[25]

Next, Martin heard Joseph was in danger—a mob planned to tar and feather him if he would not show them the plates. Joseph's anxiety heightened. He desired to move to Harmony, reports Lucy, so they sent word to Emma's family there,[26] announcing the time had arrived, as Joseph had earlier received Isaac Hale's consent to move there.

Emma's brother Alva soon arrived[27] and likely helped them pack. Before leaving town, Joseph and Alva went to a public house to transact business. There, Martin stepped up and presented Joseph with $50, doubtless as the sum to which Joseph Knight refers: "He obtained fifty dollars in money and hired a man to move him and his wife to Pennsylvania to her father's, his wife being unwell and wanted to go to her father's."[28]—a second reason to move to Harmony, aside from the danger to them and the plates.

In presenting this money Martin said, "I give it to the Lord for His own work."[29]

Despite Martin's generosity, Joseph wished to sign a note and call it a loan. However, Martin refused and flat out gifted it to him.[30]

Martin, as much as he had created problems for Joseph by leaking word out about the plates, now became an important benefactor. Two other times he had helped him—giving him money for his wedding suit and hiring him when he was only 10 years old for 50 cents a day, wherein Joseph had proven he was an honest, hard worker—so now Joseph's good reputation was paying off.

Martin had a varied religious background. He had joined at least 5 churches and knew the Bible backward and forward. His wife Dolly was a Quaker; at one time he had been as well. He sported a distinguished look with side whiskers, owned 240 acres, grew wheat, and owned a factory for making flannel cloth, as well as owning other businesses. Civically, he was the overseer of highways, a school commissioner, and was known to be honorable. Slowly he became more and more involved with Joseph.

The 23-year-old Joseph also received assistance from 14½-year-old Porter Rockwell, his neighbor. Although his own family was like most—eking out an existence off the land—Porter was so convinced of Joseph's account of the angel that "he went after his day's work was done," he told a friend years later, "and picked berries by moonlight and in the early morning, and sold the berries and gave Joseph the money to help with the printing. He also gathered wood [and] hauled it to town and sold it and used the means for the same purpose."[31] This friend of Rockwell's, Elizabeth Roundy, adds: "No man loved Joseph the prophet more than O. P. Rockwell. He was not one having the advantage of education but his heart was devoted to the cause of truth. He would not have hesitated to have given his life for Joseph at any time."[32] (See the author's work, *Porter Rockwell: A Biography*, Paramount Books, New York, 9th Revised Edition, 2006; eBook, 2013.) While the printing costs were far greater than a young farm lad could help much with, Porter's modest financial assistance was appreciated and possibly used for moving expenses so Joseph could translate the plates.

Joseph's adventure was not over. A mob of 50 men across town asked Dr. Alexander McIntyre to lead them in an attack on Joseph's farm, so they could steal the "gold bible."

McIntyre refused, courageously standing up for Joseph and ordering them "to go home and mind their own business."[33] Lucy reports, "After this, a quarrel arose among them respecting who should be captain, and it ran so high that it broke up the expedition."[34]

Soon Martin heard more of their plots, so he told Joseph to get out of town 2 days earlier than planned.[35]

Immediately Joseph put the metal plates and breastplate into a box,[36] which he nailed shut. He then placed the box in the bottom of a 40-gallon barrel, ⅓ full of beans. He loaded the barrel on the back of a wagon.

With Emma, he took off on a crisp Saturday night in December 1827.[37] It was a 4-day, 128-mile journey to Harmony, and the trip was not without hardships. They faced freezing winter cold, and Emma was pregnant.

When they arrived at Harmony, the Hale family heartily welcomed Emma and helped them unload. While doing so, her family discovered the small box in the bean barrel but did not believe Joseph and Emma's claim—that it held gold plates. Her father Isaac later said the box was the size of those used for window glass—10 by 12 inches.[38]

He describes the event further: "I was allowed to feel the weight of the box, and they gave me to understand that the book of plates was then in the box—into which, however, I was not allowed to look." This angered him, and he castigated Joseph: "If there was anything in my house . . . which I could not be allowed to see, he must take it away."[39]

So he did. Joseph hid the plates in the nearby forest. His hiding of the plates was not over. According to Joseph Knight, when word got out, obviously from Emma's family, "the people began to tease him to see the book and to offer him money and property, and they crowded so hard that he had to hide it in the mountain."[40] Thus, he may have moved them from the forest to a mountain, if Knight's description of the location is accurate.

Still, he and Emma were allowed to live on their property. (Two years and 8 months later, upon Joseph's final payment in August 1830, her parents would transfer to Joseph this section of land for $200.[41] Additionally, Emma owned 6 other acres somewhere on the property, perhaps next to where they lived.)

Soon after arriving they moved to her oldest brother Jesse's house,[42] where Jesse had lived before moving to Illinois. It was a maple-floored, 2-room house on 13½ acres overlooking the Susquehanna River. Perhaps most pleasing to Joseph was the privacy—150 yards from her parents. The upstairs loft was partitioned off and made into a room with an east-facing window, where he could enjoy each breaking day with a bright dawn.

Downstairs was a combined living room and kitchen, a fireplace, and, around the corner, a bedroom.

In the upstairs loft, immediately after settling in, Joseph began translating what would become the published plates. In this loft he would in fact translate many of the plates. On this land was also a barn, says Joseph Knight.[43]

Joseph and Emma would live there 2⅔ years. The initial period Joseph translated was from December 1827 to February 1828—2 months, with few days for actual writing. Emma was his first scribe, and then her brother Reuben[44] for a very short while, in order to finish the first 116 pages of manuscript.

When Joseph began translating, he first became acquainted with the characters. According to Lucy, "The first step that he was instructed to take in regard to this work was to make a facsimile of some of the characters, which were called reformed Egyptian, and to send them to some of the most learned men of this generation and ask them for the translation."[45] However, as he refined his process, he apparently transcribed directly from the plates. Another distinguishing factor between his earlier months of translating vs. his later ones is the tools he used. His first translation tool was the Urim and Thummim, which he used for the first part of the book (the part that Martin Harris would lose, says Emma.[46]) "After that he used a small stone," she says, "not exactly black, but was rather a dark color."[47] This was a "seer stone." (The seer stones actually have a fascinating history, showing they could apparently be used for good or bad, believed Joseph and many of his contemporaries. See Appendix D: "Seer Stones and Joseph Smith," for more details.)

Joseph Knight reports the process in detail: "Now the way he translated was he put the Urim and Thummim into his hat and darkened his eyes, then he would take a sentence and it would appear in bright Roman letters. Then he would tell the writer, and he would write it. Then that would go away. The next sentence would come, and so on. But if it was not spelled right it would not go away till it was right, so we see it was marvelous. Thus was the whole translated."[48] When he later used the seer stone he may not have used the hat.

Those who actually watched Joseph translate—Oliver Cowdery, Martin Harris, Joseph Knight, and David Whitmer—believed he was *transcribing*.[49]

According to one scholarly analysis cited by Richard Bushman of the method used—from studying the flow of dictation—Joseph would see 20–30 words at a time. He would say them aloud to his scribe and then pause, apparently waiting for the next 20–30 words to appear.[50] (The present author, however, has a different take on why 20–30 words were written at a time, based on the new writing instrument Oliver used [described in Chapter 23]: Oliver's pen simply ran out of ink after every 20–30 words, Joseph's style of dictation notwithstanding.)

From that same study—and this aspect of the analysis is likely accurate—it appears Joseph spelled out the harder-to-pronounce names.[51]

The conclusion of the study also seems accurate—Joseph apparently transcribed the book from what he read in the interpreters, rather than composing it.[52]

Those closest to Joseph claim he had no source material from which to write—no background research, no plot outlines, no manuals of grammar, no maps or history books or studies of Hebrew culture. Only the plates.

Emma later informed her oldest son: "In writing for J. Smith, I frequently wrote day after day, often sitting at the table close by him, he sitting with his face buried in his hat, with the stone in it and dictating hour after hour, with nothing between us."[53] She then adds: "No man could have dictated the writing of the manuscript unless he was inspired. . . . When returning after meals or after interruptions, he would at once begin where he had left off, without either seeing the manuscript or having any portion of it read to him. It would have been improbable that a learned man could do this; and for one so ignorant and unlearned as he was, it was simply impossible."[54]

She said in the same interview, "Joseph Smith could neither write nor dictate a coherent and well-worded letter, let alone dictating a book like the *Book of Mormon*."[55] Emma saw his every move, living in a primitive house with him. Because of these tight quarters, she felt qualified to attest to Joseph's claims: "He had neither manuscript nor book to read from. If he had had anything of the kind, he could not have concealed it from me."[56]

The remarkably short time in which he wrapped up translating the book is especially impressive (as detailed in Chapter 23).

The only description given by Joseph Smith himself of the process by which he translated the record was: "by the gift and power of God."[57]—a declaration bold and simple.

He and Emma struggled to survive their second married winter. Noteworthy is their relationship: Except for trying times covered in Volume 3, they apparently got along well. When her son asked 52 years later, "Were you in the habit of quarreling?" She replied, "No. There was no necessity of any quarreling. He knew that I wished for nothing but what was right; and, as he wished for nothing else, we did not disagree. He usually gave some heed unto what I had to say."[58]

Trying to translate became frustrating. "Now he could not translate but little," explains friend Joseph Knight Sr., "being poor and nobody to write for him but his wife. And she would not do much and take care of her house, and he being poor and no means to live, but work."[59] He had another frustration: "His wife's father and family were all against him and would not help him,"[60] except her brother Reuben. Thus, their truce had never taken full affect, despite Joseph's concessions to Isaac. Therefore, he needed someone to write the words as he dictated, but since he had to work to stay alive, the plates just sat there. Although Emma was consumed with housework, she did transcribe when she could, which, she stated, was, "day after day."[61] But that time each day was limited, and the days she could help were in streaks, with some days and weeks affording her no time at all to help.

Emma's family, though not willing to help, were civil, although they covered it with a veneer of iciness. The bottom line is Joseph needed help from somewhere.

Therefore, says Joseph Knight, "He and his wife came up to see me the first of the winter 1828 [probably December 1827] and told me his case." Unfortunately, the news Knight gave them was grim.

"I was not in easy circumstances and I did not know what it might amount to, and my wife and family [were] all against me about helping him. But I let him have some little provisions and some few things out of the store—a pair of shoes and 3 dollars in money to help him a little."[62] ($3 in late 1827 was equivalent to $132 in today's currency, so it was still a generous gift from someone low on cash.)

Doubtless pleased they could receive any help, Joseph and Emma returned to Harmony.

In January 1828, says Knight, "his father and Samuel [his brother] came from Manchester to my house when I was busy drawing lumber. I told him they had traveled far enough. I would go with my sleigh and take them down tomorrow."[63]

Knight thus took Joseph's father and brother Samuel to Harmony for a visit. Once there, says Knight, the next morning, "I gave the old man a half a dollar and Joseph a little money to buy paper to translate, I having but little with me."[64]

Joseph Knight's folksy, clean recollection of his next trip south reveals how his wife switched from enemy to convert:

Two months later in March, he began preparations to visit Joseph again. "The sleighing being good, I told my wife, 'I must go down and see Joseph again.'

"'Why do you go soon, for?' said she.

"Says I, 'Come go and see.'

"And she went with me. Next morning we went down and found them well and were glad to see us. Joseph talked with us about his translating and some revelations he had received, and from that time my wife began to believe and continued a full believer until she died."[65]

That same early winter of 1828, Martin received a vision he knew was from God. Joseph writes: "Because of his faith and his righteous deed [helping pay for Joseph's move to Harmony] the Lord appeared unto him in a vision and showed unto him His marvelous work, which he was about to do."[66]

Martin immediately planned a trip to Harmony, but when his wife Dolly learned of it, she made up her mind to go with him.

Well aware of her ability to create problems, he gave her the slip. He headed south to Harmony alone, taking only Joseph's brother Hyrum.[67]


When Martin arrived at Harmony in early winter 1827–1828, he announced to Joseph his vision, which also included the following—"that he must go to New York City with some of the characters."[68] (The trip had previous planning, according to Lucy,[69] but now it had the impetus of Martin's vision.)

Joseph adds, "So we proceeded to copy some of them, and he took his journey to the Eastern cities and to the learned."[70]

While he was gone to New York City, Dolly came to Lucy Mack Smith, asking where Martin was, whereupon Lucy told her he had gone East to visit linguists.

"On hearing this she became highly exasperated and charged me with planning the whole affair."

Lucy was not to be trifled with—the feisty Dolly had met her match: Lucy lit into her. "I protested against it, asserting that I had nothing to do with the plan." She explained why: she was consumed with simply running the home.

So Dolly attacked her on another issue. She claimed the Smiths were out to get her money. She then issued a veiled threat—she said she "knew how to take care of it."

This fired up Lucy even more. "'Now, stop,' said I. 'Do you not know that we have never asked you for money or property?'"

Dolly agreed, but "went home in a great rage,"[71] determined to have revenge. Somebody had to pay for Martin's deserting her and shooting off to New York City on an exciting adventure while leaving her at home. Somebody would pay. Anybody.

ARTIN Harris strongly felt that Joseph's work was true. But his own reputation was on the line. So he worked hard to get the transcription validated. He may have had 2 other motives for getting involved. He went to the home of John A. Clark, an Episcopalian priest in Palmyra.

Clark perceived that Martin's interest in the plates was twofold—to clarify controversial points of religious doctrine and to make money from the venture. Clark would write about it, adding that Martin visited him "much in earnest."[1] As a reflection of his visitor's enthusiasm it was possibly meant to be a subtle slight against Martin for being overly anxious—not an attractive trait in scholarly society.

Next Martin went to Luther Bradish, an assemblyman in Albany, the capital of New York. Bradish had visited Egypt and, to some extent, studied antiquities. Perhaps because of that, Martin wished to meet him—1 of the 5 noted scholars of the day with knowledge of Egyptian characters. To do this he needed a "letter of introduction," a standard formality of the times. To obtain one, he went to a man named "Mitchell,"[2] likely Samuel Latham Mitchill, a doctor, professor, congressman, classicist, and vice president of Rutgers Medical College in New York City, in the hopes of gaining access to 1 of the 5. The 5 scholars included 1 from Columbia, 2 from Harvard, and 2 from Yale.[3]

Of these 5, only 1 was available at the time—Charles Anthon of Columbia College in New York City. Mitchill granted Martin Harris his "letter of introduction." So off he went to the big city in the early spring of 1828.[4]

Anthon had taught Greek and Latin for 8 years, had never married, and was 41. He lived on campus in lower Manhattan and was considered somewhat of a grouch. After the 2 men visited, Martin Harris came back with this report, as published in the *History of the Church*:

"When Martin showed the characters and the translation to Anthon, he declared the translation correct, 'more so than any he had before seen translated from the Egyptian.'"[5]

Martin then showed him more characters, those not yet translated. Anthon said they were "Egyptian, Chaldaic, Assyric, and Arabic," and wrote him a certificate verifying that. But as Martin walked away, Anthon asked where he had found the characters. Martin told him they were from plates an angel of God had revealed. Anthon asked to see the certificate back. He tore it in pieces. To his chagrined visitor, Anthon declared there was no such thing now as angels ministering to people. So he offered to translate the plates himself. Then he arrogantly added he would only do so if they were brought to him. Martin told him that he could not, that part of the plates were sealed, and that in any case he was forbidden to bring them. Anthon responded, "I cannot read a sealed book."[6]

Joseph Knight adds more details: "And he [Anthon] wrote a very good piece to Joseph and said if he would send the original he would translate it. But at last Martin told him that he could not have the original for it was commanded not to be shone. And he [Anthon] was mad and said, 'What does this mean,' and he tore the paper that he wrote all to pieces and stamped it under his feet and says, 'Bring me the original or I will not translate it.' Mr. Harris, seeing he was in a passion, he said, 'Well, I will go home and see, and if they can be had I will write to you immediately.' So he came home and told how it was and they went to him no more."[7]

Interesting is Knight's emphasis on Anthon: "he was mad," and "tore the paper that he wrote all to pieces," and "stamped it under his feet," and "Mr. Harris, seeing he was in a passion . . ."

What appears as Anthon's academia-inspired arrogance actually proved to be a fulfillment of Bible prophecy, according to Joseph,[8] which he says was recorded in Isaiah of the Old Testament thousands of years earlier:

"And the vision of all is become unto you as the words of a book that is sealed, which men deliver to one that is learned, saying, read this, I pray thee, and he saith, I cannot; for it is sealed."[9]

(Martin later said he did not know of the Isaiah prophecy before he went to New York City,[10] nor did Joseph, according to Orson Pratt.)[11]

Martin Harris then went back to Dr. Mitchill, who, according to Martin, agreed with Anthon's initial written verification.

Nevertheless, Harris may have been confused in his account, or Anthon may have overstepped his bounds and exaggerated his abilities. The reason is: the characters in the "Anthon Transcript" were not able to be deciphered—by any man living on earth at that time, learned or unlearned.

Not yet anyway. Not until ancient Egyptian translations could take place, which was several years away. This would occur when a series of scholars would discover how to decipher hieroglyphics. The key discovery in that was the Rosetta Stone—a ¾-ton black, granite-like stone, approximately 4 × 2 feet and 11 inches thick, that was inscribed in 196 B.C. with text written by Egyptian priests praising a 13-year-old pharaoh (See Appendix E, "The Rosetta Stone: Unusual History of an Unusual Stone.")

The stone was discovered July 15, 1799, by Pierre Bouchards, a French army officer, along the Nile River, while his men were expanding Ft. Julien, an old Turkish fort, to protect them from invasion by the British.

Its journey and how it had gotten there were bizarre:

Mysteriously, the Rosetta stone had disappeared for 1,400 years. Over time, it had made its way to the location of the fort, where it had become just another rock used for construction by the Egyptians themselves at least 400 years before it was discovered by the French.

Unknown to many historians, the Rosetta Stone then became the focus of an adventure akin to, although perhaps less dramatic than, modern-day, iconic 20th- and 21st-century cinematic adventures like *Raiders of the Lost Ark* and *National Treasure* depicting archeologists scrambling to obtain possession of "historical objects."

When the British attacked Egypt, the French marched north to the Mediterranean to fight the enemy, hauling the stone with them. But the British won. So the French retreated, taking the stone with them again, this time to Alexandria. There they hid it in a warehouse, covering it with carpets.

Now, all across Europe, scholars and even generals became aware of it, and they knew that for the purpose of unearthing Egypt's ancient mysteries this one stone gave them their best shot, as it was apparent that this stone had the same text inscribed on it in 3 different languages or writing systems— Greek, Demotic, and hieroglyphics. Greek the scholars knew, but the 2 ancient Egyptian scripts had long been a mystery.

Napoleon himself, upon seeing the 3 languages carved on the stone, knew he had his own national treasure.

And now the adventure of protecting it made for high drama. The eventual checkmate came when, once conquered, the French refused to surrender it.

So, a French scholar, seeing the impasse, lead British scholars down an alley to the warehouse where the stone was hidden. He warned the British to take it quickly and keep it out of sight, or French soldiers would steal it. Then, a British colonel hauled it away in the darkness of night on his armored carriage and sailed it to England 3 years after its discovery, in February 1802.[12]

Once in London, the stone frustrated both French and British scholars who sought to unravel its mystery. No one could. So they made copies of the stone and sent them to other scholars across Europe.

These scholars chipped away at it for years, knowing that whoever could figure it out would become world famous.

But the stone still remained a mystery.

Until Jean Francois Champollion worked his magic.

Champollion knew 2 languages necessary to crack the code—Greek and Coptic (an early Egyptian language). He used Coptic to help decipher the 2 Egyptian scripts carved in the stone—Demotic (used earlier than Coptic), and hieroglyphics (the earliest of all).

Champollion first published his Egyptian grammar in 1836 and his Egyptian dictionary in 1841 (13 years after Martin Harris visited Charles Anthon).

Ironically, Anthon would have needed both books to translate Egyptian correctly, but had neither. Nevertheless, he was most likely one of the world's leading experts on ancient Egypt and its language until Champollion made the historic breakthrough.

Had Anthon's inflated ego not interfered, he may have assisted Martin with his 1828 verification, but in the end, it could have backfired on Joseph: Anthon's overstepping his abilities might have revealed his analysis was built, essentially, on a house of cards.

Six years after their 1828 visit, Anthon wrote a letter describing his encounter with Martin, and 7 years after that he wrote a second letter—both refuting most of what Martin claimed. (However, Anthon recklessly contradicted himself—in the 1834 letter he claimed he refused to give Martin a written opinion,[13] but in the 1841 letter he stated he actually did give the opinion "without any hesitation" in order to expose the deception.[14])

People who knew Martin vouched for his integrity, and Joseph readily accepted his report. Anthon, however, denigrated Harris's character, calling him "a plain and apparently simple-hearted farmer" in his second letter. Anthon made another glaring mistake: he claimed Martin had said he had been asked to contribute toward publishing the book, and planned to sell his farm, so he had come to New York for a second opinion.

However, in 1828 when Martin visited Anthon, Martin had not even been approached yet by Joseph about the book's printing. Anthon would have merely read of these incidents long after the plates were published. Another mistake by Anthon is that when he describes the characters in his 1841 letter to Reverend John A. Clark, he does so inaccurately, because they do not even come close to matching the characters Martin took to Anthon. Anthon claims in the second letter that he told Martin the characters were a conglomeration imitating various alphabets. He says they came from Greek and Hebrew and were in a "rude delineation of a circle," similar to the Mexican calendar, and that "the paper contained anything else but 'Egyptian hieroglyphics.'"[15] While Anthon could not have translated hieroglyphics as early as 1828, he should have at least known what they looked like. Either Anthon's selective memory came into play, or he felt jilted when Martin declined to let him "translate," and wished to condemn that which he could not fully be a part of.

In that second letter, 13 years after Anthon had met Martin, Anthon adds with a dig that "the countryman" Martin Harris later came back and tried to give him a printed copy of the "golden Bible."[16]

Probably the most accurate statement Anthon made was his declaration to Martin that the characters looked "very remarkable, but he could not decide what language they belonged to."[17]

Reportedly, Anthon made a similar statement, as told by Martin to Charles Butler, a banker in Geneva, New York, when Martin applied for a loan. Butler later stated that Martin told him Anthon's claim—the characters were "very curious, but [he] admitted that he could not decipher them."[18]

John H. Gilbert, later a typesetter for printing the contents of Joseph's plates, said that Martin returned from his trip to New York feeling "Joseph was a little smarter than Professor Anthon."[19]

As to whatever became of the transcript that Martin took to Anthon, it may have ended up in the possession of David Whitmer. In any case, a copy that Whitmer had was later given to the Reorganized Church of Jesus Christ of Latter Day Saints (later renamed Community of Christ) by his descendants in 1903.

An intriguing footnote to all this took place 16 years after Martin's visit to Anthon. A small, eastern-states Latter-day Saint newspaper in New York City, titled *The Prophet*, edited by Samuel Brannan, published 3 lines of characters, which it claimed were from Martin's transcript that he took to Anthon. Dated December 21, 1844, the newspaper states, "The following is a correct copy of the characters taken from the plates which the *Book of Mormon* was translated from: the same that was taken to Professor Mitchell, and afterwards to Professor Anthon of New York, by Martin Harris."[20] (See this endnote for a description of this eastern newspaper and an introduction to its fascinating editor, Samuel Brannan.) These 3 lines likely had their roots in a black and gold placard of that same year, which has the same characters and nearly the same description. The publisher of the placard is a mystery. Since then, no definite determination has been made to ascertain whether or not the characters are Egyptian. The book from which the plates were transcribed is the *Book of Mormon*, not written in true Egyptian, but a "reformed" Egyptian, according to Joseph Knight,[21] close friend of Joseph Smith, who heard descriptions and information about the plates from Joseph himself. The book itself states it was written in that language.[22]

Martin's New York City adventure was over. Whatever his frustrations, he had accomplished his main mission and now returned to Palmyra satisfied that the characters were genuine. Yet his desire to help Joseph was just beginning. And it did not go without opposition.

When Martin returned home, reports Lucy, "his wife's anger kindled afresh at his presence, insomuch that she prepared a separate bed and room for him, which room she refused to enter."[23]

Then her anger took a new turn. Her daughter Lucy, named after her, was romantically pursued by a young Mr. Dikes. Martin was highly in favor of Dikes, but Dolly opposed him until "a scheme entered her brain," reports Joseph's mother.[24] Dolly told Dikes that if he would somehow get the Egyptian characters from Martin, and procure a room in Palmyra to transcribe them and bring her the transcript, she would consent to his marrying her daughter.

Dikes, likely knowing what a hellion this woman could be if she opposed the marriage, agreed. He succeeded, and received the girl as his "promised reward."[25]

Dolly was just beginning her manipulative conquests. To this day, however, the whereabouts of her pirated copy remains a mystery.

Martin now made plans for a second trip to Harmony—this time to write for Joseph as a scribe. He had not seen Joseph since visiting Anthon and was anxious now to assist with the translation.

Dolly, of course, demanded to go with him. Martin agreed, but only under the stipulation that he would bring her back in 1 or 2 weeks, upon which he would return to Joseph alone to continue the work. She agreed.

"But Mr. Harris little suspected what he had to encounter by this move," reports Lucy,[26] in her inimitable tongue-in-cheek tone.

On their journey, Dolly tested Martin's diminishing patience. Occasionally he would pull out the characters to show people, only to discover Dolly taking out of her own pocket an exact copy, bragging that "Joe Smith" was not the only one with the characters.[27]

As soon as Martin and Dolly arrived in Harmony, she informed Joseph "that her object in coming was to see the plates," says Lucy, "and that she would never leave until she had accomplished it."[28]

Brazenly, Dolly ransacked Joseph and Emma's home—"every nook and corner about the house—chests, trunks, cupboards,"[29] But she could not find the plates. So the next day she went out in the snow and began digging up the ground. About 2 P.M. she "came in rather ill-natured." Strangely, she asked if snakes lived in that country in the winter. Emma told her no. Dolly replied, "I have been walking round in the woods to look at the situation of your place [spying] and, as I turned round to come home, a tremendous black snake stuck up his head before me and commenced hissing at me."[30] It had, in fact, shaken her so badly that the next day "she left the house and took lodging during her stay in Pennsylvania with a neighbor" of the Hales, states Lucy.[31]

The aforementioned mountain near them where Joseph hid the plates, according to Joseph Knight, may have simply been an elevated part of this forest to begin with, or perhaps he simply defined the whole area as a "mountain." Indeed, the township is about 1,000 feet above sea level; thus, the plates may have only been buried once. (But if the plates were buried twice, and indeed were moved to a more elevated spot, it could have occurred after this time, since Dolly almost discovered them in the nearby "forest.")

The next day Dolly told the Hales' neighbor more details— that when she found the spot where the plates were apparently buried, she stooped down to scoop away the snow and leaves, until the black snake "gave her a terrible fright." So she ran "with all possible speed" to the house. To the neighbor she described the reptile as "horrible."[32]

CHAPTER 15

THE snake did its job, apparently. Dolly gave up hunting for the plates.

But matters only got worse. Over the next 2 weeks she played the role of itinerant "busybody."

"She did all that lay in her power to injure Joseph in the estimation of his neighbors," reports Lucy, "telling them that he was a grand imposter," with "a design upon her husband's property."[1]

Meanwhile, Martin faithfully performed as Joseph's scribe, putting up with his wife's shenanigans.

Joseph and Emma tolerated her as well.

At one point Martin was apparently influenced by her unwavering negativity. One day, just to prove to himself that Joseph was not a fraud, he substituted another stone for the seer stone, wondering if Joseph would continue translating. Joseph immediately announced he could not translate—everything appeared dark. Martin was satisfied.

A great relief came to them all when Dolly Harris headed home. But the damage had been done. The Harmony neighbors were all alerted and fully suspicious. Worse, they were completely antagonistic toward Joseph. Obviously, so were the Hales. Now more than ever.

Even if Martin's report 31 years later were accurate—that Dolly had handled the plates earlier (while they were covered)—

she was unsatisfied, perhaps not wanting to just know of their existence but, like Professor Anthon, demanding to control the situation and, falling short of that, becoming antagonistic toward the whole thing.


The ride home allowed Dolly to stew like a madwoman. With renewed vigor to sway Martin.

Probably not the most joyful of journeys in Martin's life, he heard her incessant demands that he stop associating with Joseph. Further, "She endeavored to dissuade her husband from taking any further part in the publication of the record,"[2] says Lucy.

But Martin paid her no attention. He returned to help Joseph, as promised,[3] which proved, probably, to be 9 glorious weeks away from her.


Left alone in New York, Dolly poured scalding water onto Joseph's reputation. Vilifying him to the Palmyra townspeople, she went from "place to place and from house to house telling her grievances," says Lucy, declaring that "Joseph Smith was practicing a deception upon the people, which was about to strip her of all that she possessed."[4]

Earnest in her concerns, she "carried away her furniture, linen, and bedding, also other moveable articles, until she nearly stripped the premises of everything that could conduce either to comfort or convenience, depositing them with those of her friends and acquaintances in whom she reposed sufficient confidence to assure her of their future safety."[5] Demanding that her furniture be distributed until they were safe, she complained to her neighbors until she got her way, no matter how much it inconvenienced them, as houses were small and space was at a premium.

———————

Martin stayed with Joseph from April 12 to June 14, 1828— the second phase of translating—and the two worked hard. (Knowing what awaited Martin at home, likely he wished he could have stayed longer.)

On June 14, 1828, Martin completed his work as scribe, finishing 116 pages on foolscap paper, and prepared to leave for Palmyra.

He pleaded with Joseph that he might show the 116 pages to several of his family members—his wife, his wife's sister, his brother, and his parents—but when Joseph inquired of the Lord, he was told no. Martin did not like that answer and pleaded with Joseph to ask again. Again the answer was no. Martin prevailed upon him to ask one more time. When Joseph did so, says Joseph, the Lord told him to go ahead. But as part of the deal, Martin was told he could show them to only 5 individuals—his wife, her sister Abigail Cobb, his brother Preserved, and to his parents—and he had to covenant with the Lord to obey this counsel. Elated, Martin left with the 116 pages.

The next day Joseph and Emma's first child, Alvin, was born[6]—but lived only a few hours. The boy's grave site would be visible from Joseph's translating room.

Emma then lay in bed for 2 weeks, close to death. Joseph was consumed by his cares for her and thought of nothing else. For a third week he watched her recover, and then realized he had something else to worry about—the 116-page manuscript. He had not heard from Martin since his departure 3 weeks earlier.

Soon Emma, too, became worried about it. She requested Joseph to return to Palmyra and recover the manuscript.

Now consumed with concern, he struck out on the seemingly endless 4-day journey, so overwhelmed with worry that he could neither eat nor sleep.[7]

---

In her rough draft Lucy outlines Joseph's 2 fears—of never again "touching a finger to the work," and invoking "the hot displeasure of the Almighty" against him, having "regarded man more than his Maker."[8]

While he hurried home on a stagecoach, a stranger saw his consternation, and when Joseph had to make the last 20 miles on foot, the stranger insisted on helping him. He found Joseph so exhausted from worry that he led him the last 4 miles by the arm. Even so, "he would fall asleep as he was walking along, every few minutes," the man would tell Lucy.[9] They finally arrived before dawn. Soon the stranger took breakfast with them and left.

After Joseph ate a little, he immediately sent for Martin, and they all waited impatiently for him to arrive. Lucy illustrates the horrific scene:

"We supposed that Mr. Harris would be there as soon as it was ready, to eat with us, for he generally came in such haste when he was sent for. It was now near six o'clock [A.M.] and he lived three miles distant. At eight o'clock we set the victuals on the table, as we were expecting him every moment. We waited till 9, and he came not—till 10, and he was not there; till 11, still he did not make his appearance."[10]

One can only imagine Joseph's worry and the stress overpowering him. He had actually fallen asleep while walking his last 20 miles of a 135-mile journey. Even the first 115 miles had been a slow, exhausting, agonizingly bumpy stage coach ride on rough roads. Lucy describes the emotionally torturous wait they had for Martin to show.

"But at half past 12 we saw him walking with a slow and measured tread towards the house, his eyes fixed thoughtfully upon the ground. On coming to the gate he stopped instead of passing through, and got upon the fence and sat there some time with his hat drawn over his eyes. At length he entered the house. Soon after which, we sat down to the table, Mr. Harris with the rest. He took up his knife and fork as if he were going to use them, but immediately dropped them. Hyrum, observing this, said, 'Martin, why do you not eat; are you sick?' Upon which, Mr. Harris pressed his hands upon his temples and cried out in a tone of deep anguish, 'Oh, I have lost my soul! I have lost my soul!"

"Joseph," says Lucy, "who had not expressed his fears till now, sprang from the table, exclaiming, 'Martin, have you lost that manuscript? Have you broken your oath and brought down condemnation upon my head as well as your own?'

"'Yes, it is gone,' replied Martin, 'and I know not where.'"[11]

Martin had shown the 116 pages to his wife Dolly and his family, to whom he was given permission.

"His wife was so pleased with it that she gave him the privilege of locking it up in her own set of drawers, which was a special favor, for she had never before this allowed him even the privilege of looking into them," reports Lucy[12]—based on his report to her.

One day he and Dolly took a 10–15 mile trip to visit a relative of hers, and he returned home alone. Once there, he dove into a discussion with a friend who expressed great interest in the 116 pages.

"The man's curiosity was much excited," says Lucy, "and as might be expected, he earnestly desired to see the manuscript. Martin was so anxious to gratify his friend that, although it was contrary to his obligation, he went to the drawer to get the manuscript, but the key was gone. He sought for it some time, but could not find it."[13] So, he broke open his wife's bureau, injuring it "considerably," grabbed the manuscript, and waived it in front of his friend's face. Then he moved it to his own set of drawers. Soon, "he showed it to any good friend that happened to call on him."[14]

Dolly returned and saw her bureau marred. "Her irascible temper was excited to the utmost pitch, and an intolerable storm ensued."[15] She became violent. The atmosphere in Martin's home was thus when Joseph returned from Harmony to New York. "Because of this," states Lucy in her rough draft, "she was accused of having taken the transcripts by stealth and having secreted them."[16]

Lucy analyzes Martin's state of mind. "Having once made a sacrifice of his conscience, Mr. Harris no longer regarded its scruples; so he continued to exhibit the writings until a short time before Joseph arrived, to anyone whom he regarded as prudent enough to keep the secret, except our family, but we were not allowed to set our eyes upon them."[17]

Thereafter he seemed to take it for granted, "and thought but little about the manuscript,"[18] not bothering to show it to anyone. At that point, the Smiths came calling. The gravity of the situation apparently dawned on him when he opened the bureau—and it was gone. Suddenly realizing the importance of his earlier directive, he tore apart the house—but to no avail. "He asked his wife where it was," reports Lucy. "She solemnly averred that she did not know anything respecting it."[19] It was only now that he felt guilty about his neglect and unauthorized showings.

At the Smith home Joseph fell into a pit of spiritual anguish. According to his mother, he exclaimed, "Oh, my God! All is lost. All is lost! What shall I do? I have sinned—it is I who tempted the wrath of God. I should have been satisfied with the first answer which I received from the Lord; for he told me that it was not safe to let the writing go out of my possession."[20] He paced the floor crying. He turned to Martin and demanded he look again, but Martin assured him he had searched everywhere, even ripping open the beds and pillows looking for it. Joseph replied, "Then must I return [to my wife] with such a tale as this? I dare not do it, lest I should kill her at once.[21] (See endnote for a clarification.) And how shall I appear before the Lord? Of what rebuke am I not worthy?"[22]

Lucy writes of her own anguish:

"What could I say to comfort him when he saw all the family in the same situation of mind as himself; for sobs and groans and the most bitter lamentations filled the house.

"However, Joseph was more distressed than the rest, as he better understood the consequences of disobedience. And over what would seem to others to be a very trifling neglect of duty, he continued pacing back and forth, meantime weeping and grieving like a tender infant until about sunset when, by persuasion, he took a little nourishment." This anguish was piled onto his already exhausted emotional and physical state.

"The next morning we set out for home. We parted with heavy hearts, for it now appeared that all which we had so fondly anticipated and which had been the source of so much secret gratification had in a moment fled and fled forever."[23]

WHILE Dolly Harris claimed she did not take the manuscript, the Smiths and Martin believed otherwise. One Palmyra citizen claims Dolly stole it while Martin slept, then afterwards burned it, not telling anyone of her deed until several years after the contents of the plates were published.[1] Emma's family knew another person, Mrs. McKune, who reported to them that Dolly burned part of the manuscript but kept part of it to discredit Joseph.[2] The manner in which she could discredit Joseph was carefully calculated: if he published the book, she would bring to light the original copy, with alterations, and point out the wording discrepancies.

That Dolly did not completely destroy the 116 pages is consistent with a revelation Joseph received, stating, "Satan has put it into their hearts to alter the words which you have caused to be written."[3] Dead-on with the scriptural prophecy is Lucy's assessment: "The manuscript has never been found; and there is no doubt but Mrs. Harris took it from the drawer with the view of retaining it until another translation should be given, then to alter the original translation for the purpose of showing a discrepancy between them and thus make the whole appear to be a deception."[4]

In the case of the 116-page manuscript, the Lord had a backup plan, Latter-day Saints believe, which outwitted her. Joseph was not to again translate the stolen parts, but rather translate other plates he had. These gave an account written by the ancient prophet Nephi for the same events, but from a different perspective, one of a primarily religious history rather than a "largely secular history" (which the lost manuscript contained), thus making the "new version" of the translated work even more valuable to readers.[5]

When Joseph returned to Harmony, he was so wrought with grief, taking blame for the lost manuscript, that he could only find solace in working on the farm.

According to Lucy, Martin suffered also, "temporally as well as spiritually." The same day he reported the lost manuscript to Joseph, "a dense fog spread itself over his fields and blighted his wheat while in the blow, so that he lost about two-thirds of his crop, whilst those fields which lay only on the opposite side of the road received no injury whatsoever."[6]

By now Martin likely had second thoughts about having married his first cousin when she was 15. Being 10 years older than Dolly, perhaps his wisest domestic decision would be to permanently separate from her (quite possibly a mutual decision), less than 3 years later, in April 1831, a rare event for the times.[7] (Dolly would die in 1836, and Martin would remarry a stalwart woman who would not only share his faith but would outshine him in faithfulness.)

Meanwhile, Joseph continued his penitence. He writes: "As I was pouring out my soul in supplication to . . . be forgiven of all that I had done contrary to his will, an angel stood before me and answered me."[8] He was told by the angel, in essence, he had put himself on the line by trusting Martin with so much responsibility, and that he would have to suffer the consequences by giving up the Urim and Thummim.

"This I did as I was directed and, as I handed them to him, he remarked, 'If you are very humble and penitent, it may be you will receive them again; if so, it will be on the 22nd of next September."[9] No mention was made of giving up the plates.

Much to his relief, he was then told in a revelation, "Thou art still chosen and art again called to the work."[10]

Joseph later states, "On the 22nd of September I had the joy and satisfaction of again receiving the Urim and Thummim."[11]

That same fall of 1828, Joseph senior wrote his own father and brothers that his son Joseph had, over the years, been receiving visions.

Joseph senior's brothers all scoffed at the news that their nephew was a visionary, but their father Asael believed it, feeling a branch of the family would someday be raised up to greatly affect mankind for the better. In the excellent work by George Q. Cannon, the only biography of Joseph written from interviews with his personal friends (*Life of Joseph Smith the Prophet*, Stratford Books, 2005; eBook, 2012) Cannon states that Joseph's grandfather Asael in fact believed that one of his seed would "promulgate a work to revolutionize the world of religious faith."[12] Young Joseph then wrote a letter to at least one of his father's brothers, including a warning to the wicked of the earth. That uncle (and at least one of his sons) immediately had a change of heart and believed it, saying, "Joseph wrote like a prophet."[13] (Three of Joseph's 4 living Smith uncles would eventually believe.)

Joseph continued farm work under the strain of renewed criticism from Emma's father: Isaac Hale felt his son-in-law had wasted his time with the seer stone and the Urim and Thummim, and should've been outside simply tilling the land. During this depressing period of being banned from translating, and putting up with the undercurrents of disapproval, Joseph and Emma visited her parents' Methodist congregation—likely a conciliatory gesture toward his in-laws—as his brother-in-law was a Methodist "class leader" in Harmony, preaching as a lay minister.

Joseph possibly asked to join the class. However, Emma's cousin, Joseph Lewis, steamed with anger when he discovered Joseph's name on the roll—and objected to having a "practicing necromancer" in the class. He demanded Joseph to remove his name or repent. One can imagine the ripples of conflict this caused in the clan, as some of the Hales likely hoped to reform the deluded Joseph and their beloved cousin and sister, Emma. So Joseph apparently stopped going—after all, he was only attending to keep the peace anyway, and it was backfiring. However, his name would not be not be crossed off the class rolls for another 6 months,[14] although apparently he did not attend.

Ironically, Joseph was in large part dependent on his father-in-law, and lived under that burden while his wife recovered from ill health once again. Dealing with Emma's sickness, he performed her all-consuming household chores that engulfed every family—making soap, preparing meals, repairing posses-sions, sewing torn clothes, making new clothes, and laundering by hand—as well as his own farming tasks. This burden was nothing compared to the twofold stress of being dependent and looked down upon by his in-laws, while simultaneously feeling crushed by the guilt of losing the manuscript.

New conflicting emotions gnawed at him, including, certainly, a sense of failure. All in all, he was stuck. It was possibly because of these burdens he did not write to his parents for 2 months.

Worried, his parents set out to visit him in February 1829. Lucy writes of a small miracle—that Joseph actually sensed their impending arrival. He even told Emma when they were approaching, although he could not see them. He was so convinced of his premonition that he left Emma to go down the road, and there, amazingly, he found his parents ¾ of a mile away.[15]

To Lucy's relief, she states that when they saw him he still had his pleasant expression, and they were especially grateful to hear the plates and translating tools were safe. Lucy reports they were on Emma's bureau in a red morocco trunk.[16]

Lucy and Joseph senior now met Emma's parents for the first time. Lucy describes them as "an intelligent and highly respectable family. They were pleasantly situated and lived in good style on an extensive and well-cultivated farm."[17] She further states, "The time on our visit with them we passed very agreeably and returned home relieved of a burden which was almost insupportable, and our own present joy far overbalanced all our former grief."[18]

Finally, after 8 months of no translating, in February 1829 Joseph received a revelation stating he could begin again. (But, except for sporadic help from Emma, 2 more months would pass before he would resume translating consistently.) He also received a revelation for his father stating that "a marvelous work" was about to come forth to the world, and that if his father desired to be a part of it, he was now "called to the work."[19]

Emma, somewhat recovered from the physical and emotional strains of the past 10 months, began again acting as scribe for Joseph, whenever she could break away from heavy household duties. Lucy states that when Joseph wanted the work to progress faster than what his wife could contribute, he began praying to the Lord to send him a scribe.[20]

Martin, meanwhile, thought he should perhaps help financially. Unfortunately, he shared that idea with his wife, who once again began hounding him, calling him crazy, predicting he would ruin his family and himself if he financed the "golden bible." As a consequence, Martin was not sure if he should get involved in printing the book, but was intrigued by the idea. Even haunted by it. Eventually he felt compelled to visit Joseph.

The following month, March 1829, Martin took a trip to Harmony. When he saw Joseph he stated that he would feel more secure if there were a witness. As a result, he asked that any third party be permitted to see the plates—echoing Dolly's demand a year and a half earlier, likely influenced by her doubts.

Later that month Joseph told Martin some startling news— that the Lord gave him a revelation stating there would be not just one, but three, witnesses, and if Martin would humble himself and admit his mistakes he would be one of them. Further, Martin could afterward declare to the world that he had actually seen the plates! Because of his propensity for needling Joseph, the revelation added, "You [Joseph] shall say unto him that he shall do no more, nor trouble me any more concerning this matter."[21] The revelation finally directed Joseph to cease translating for a time, until "I will provide means whereby thou mayest accomplish the thing which I have commanded thee."[22]

That revelation would soon be fulfilled when one Oliver Cowdery came knocking at his door . . .

OLIVER Cowdery was 22, a year younger than Joseph. He was a single man and the son of a follower of Nathaniel Wood. The religious leader and rodsman Woods hailed from Oliver's hometown of Wells, Vermont, just 50 miles from Joseph's birthplace. Oliver's family had migrated south, as the Smiths had, and at about the same time.

Oliver worked as a store clerk, a blacksmith, and then a school teacher. He had moved to New York City, wanting to financially assist his parents,[1] and then to Palmyra. As fate would have it, he was not even supposed to teach there—his brother Lyman was, who had applied to Hyrum Smith, one of the trustees (considered one of the most responsible positions in the community). But Lyman Cowdery had backed out of his contract, leaving the path open for Oliver to replace him.[2] In Palmyra he boarded with various families, the tradition of school teachers, and soon learned of Joseph's claims through his 24-year-old friend, David Whitmer. He was, in fact, distantly related to Joseph: he and Lucy were 3rd cousins.[3]

When he finally boarded with the Smiths, he asked Joseph senior about the plates. "For a considerable length of time [he] did not succeed in soliciting any information," writes Lucy.[4] "At last, however, he gained my husband's confidence," and because of that he learned "a sketch of the facts" about the plates.[5]

He then told Lucy's husband that he was "highly delighted" with what he had heard, and that he "had been in a deep study upon the subject all day."

The next day it stormed. All day in fact. So after school he stayed with another neighbor closer to the school. The day after that, he said to Lucy's husband that their last conversation "seems working in my very bones, and I cannot for a moment get it out of my mind."[6]

Oliver then told Joseph's parents, "My plan is this: My term of school will be out in March, and I want Hyrum, as he is one of the trustees, to manage to have my school money ready for me as soon as the school closes, that I may be able to set off for Pennsylvania immediately. Samuel, I understand, is going down to Pennsylvania to spend the spring with Joseph. I shall make my arrangements to be ready to accompany him thither by the time he [Samuel] recovers his health."[7] He then surprised and delighted them with this declaration:

"I have made it a subject of prayer, and I firmly believe that it is the will of the Lord that I should go. If there is a work for me to do in this thing, I am determined to attend to it."[8] But it was not yet spring and school was not yet out. Also, he was under contract to continue teaching. Nevertheless, continues Lucy:

"From this time, Oliver was so completely absorbed in the subject of the record that it seemed impossible for him to think or converse about anything else."[9] She then explains her family's problems and how they affected Oliver:

"We began to make preparations to remove our family and effects to the log house we had formerly lived in but which Hyrum now occupied. We now felt more keenly than ever the injustice of the measure which had placed a landlord over us on our own premises and who was about to eject us from them. . . .

"This I thought would be a good occasion for bringing to Oliver's mind the cause of all our present privations, as well as the misfortunes which he himself was liable to if he should turn his back upon the world and set out in the service of God. . . ."[10]

"'Now, Oliver,' said I . . . 'In consequence of these things, Oliver, we cannot make you comfortable any longer, and you will be under the necessity of taking boarding somewhere else. For we shall have to crowd ourselves together in a log house where we shall have none of the conveniences that we have here.'"[11]

He replied that he did not wish to leave her and her husband, apparently attached to them.[12]

In March Joseph's brother Samuel likely dreaded the idea of moving back to his family's old cramped quarters, and continued his plans to visit Joseph for the spring and probably to assist him in planting crops.

School finally ended and Oliver was free to go with him.

So they set out for Pennsylvania[13] to see Joseph.

On their way, they stopped at Fayette and visited Oliver's friend, David Whitmer. Oliver told him he would write him as soon as he got to know Joseph and could come up with an opinion.[14] Perhaps the main reason he stopped there was to see David's sister, Elizabeth Ann, although she was only 14½ at the time. Yet, it was not an uncommon age for the day to begin serious courtships.

Lucy continues with Cowdery's chronicle:

"The weather, for some time previous, had been very wet and disagreeable—raining, freezing and thawing alternatively, which had rendered the roads almost impassable, particularly in the middle of the day. Notwithstanding, Mr. Cowdery was not to be deterred—either by wind or weather—and they persevered until they arrived at Joseph's house, although one of Oliver's toes was frozen, and he, as well as Samuel, suffered much on the road from fatigue." On April 5, 1829, they arrived in Harmony, where Oliver met Joseph the first time.

As for Joseph, says Lucy, "Although he had never seen Mr. Cowdery before, he knew that the Lord was able to fulfill all his promises."[15]

Joseph finally had his full-time scribe.

"They sat down and conversed together till late," she adds. "During the evening Joseph told Oliver his history."[16]

The next day Oliver was a witness to Joseph's purchase agreement with Isaac Hale, buying land from Emma's father.[17]

And the day after that, April 7, 1829, they commenced the work of translation.

"Day after day," says Oliver, "I continued uninterrupted to write from his mouth as he translated with the Urim and Thummim."[18] He and Joseph worked in the same room, with no physical barriers between them. In speaking with her son, Emma adds, "Oliver Cowdery and your father wrote in the room where I was at work."[19]

This was different than when Martin Harris had taken dictation with a blanket between them.[20] Oliver transcribed,[21] as Emma had,[22] with the plates out of view, by being wrapped in a linen cloth on the table,[23] as stated in Chapter 12. Later, in Fayette, New York, Oliver's future wife, Elizabeth Ann, would become an eyewitness to the same process, saying Joseph "never had a curtain drawn between him and his scribe."[24]

Joseph's translation work consisted of looking into the seer stone, described by Joseph Knight[25] in Chapter 13.

But Joseph would use other stones for other purposes.

While Emma described his translation stone as almost black, a white stone also existed, so he had at least 2, possibly 3.

The 1st—likely the white one—appeared in 1822 a half mile from his farm when he was digging for a well with Willard Chase. Lucy reports that with it he could see things "invisible to the natural eye."[26] Chase also spoke of it, though he is not an entirely reliable source, since he claimed the plates were in part his, and he helped to lead the attacks on the Smith farm to steal them. As such, he claimed in 1833 that he was the one who discovered the stone and that Joseph took it. He also claimed he was still trying to get it back as late as 1830.[27] He may have exaggerated his part in finding the stone, but if one gives him the benefit of the doubt, he may have seen the stone first, or simultaneously with Joseph, but Joseph took possession of it and, according to Joseph, it was heaven's gift to him, since he would receive revelations through it. Later, Emma's brother, Alva Hale, said Joseph told him in Harmony that the "gift in seeing with a stone" was a "gift from God."[28] He knew conclusively the stone was for him.

This or another stone was described by Wilford Woodruff in 1888 as being "found by revelation some 30 feet under the earth (ground), and carried by him through life."[29] (Wilford placed such importance upon it that he actually dedicated it in 1888 at Manti, Utah, upon a temple altar.[30])

As for the white stone, a court convened in 1826 about Joseph's treasure hunting, instigated by enemies who wished to discredit him, since much of society and even some laws looked down on treasure seeking. There, a court witness said Joseph "pretended" to read from a book using a white stone.[31] The part of the witness's statement about the color of the stone may be accurate, despite the context of him trying to discredit Joseph.

In 1841 Joseph showed the white stone in Nauvoo to the Council of the Twelve, reports Brigham Young.[32]

The darker seer stone that Joseph used for translating the plates apparently came into his possession after the Urim and Thummim were taken by the angel, after Martin lost the 116 pages.[33]

A 3rd stone may have cropped up—the one used for treasure hunting. That stone may have worked for some things but not treasure hunting, since they found no treasure. Alva Hale, Emma's brother, living in her father's Harmony household, claims Joseph told him the "gift in seeing with a stone" was "a gift from God,"[34] but that he had been deceived in treasure seeking, and did not intend to deceive anyone else. Joseph's metamorphosis from avid treasure hunter—or at least willing—to trying to avoid treasure hunting altogether, apparently began when he realized he himself had been deceived. He also supposedly said, "'Peeping' was all d------d nonsense," according to Alva Hale, Emma's brother.[35]

Evidence shows that before 1823, soon after finding the stone, he was at the forefront of treasure-seeking, but apparently his conscience began bothering him, realizing he was using the stone for inappropriate purposes. After 1823 he continued to hunt treasure sporadically, and probably for very short periods, either with or without the stone, but no longer as an instigator, and staying in the background (as described in Appendix F: "Treasure-hunting and Joseph Smith").

Joseph's background with treasure hunting may or may not have been known by Oliver Cowdery. But his new associate would soon see him dealing firsthand with seer stones.

Meanwhile, Oliver continued his translation work by taking direct dictation from Joseph.

As to what Oliver transcribed, it appears that he picked up right where others had left off 14 months earlier—at the start of Mosiah, according to scholar Dean C. Jesse, who analyzed Oliver's handwriting.[36] Then they went through all the rest of the book to the end, then backtracked and translated 1 Nephi up to Mosiah. (The author believes they possibly launched their teamwork at Words of Mormon, which is 2 pages prior to Mosiah. If Oliver truly did start right at Mosiah, then Joseph must have received assistance from his other scribes, starting 2 pages earlier, before Oliver arrived.)

A telltale sign is that a gaping hole appears at Mosiah—it lacks Mormon's standard style of introducing each book found in all his other abridged books.

In Harmony Joseph had received a revelation in May 1829 directing him to go to the "plates of Nephi" (the "small" plates),[37] which would cover the first 400 years. These small plates of Nephi would act as the replacement portion for the missing 116 pages.[38]

How he would do it is this: upon finishing the translation of Mormon's abridgment of the "large" plates (from Mosiah to Mormon, Chapter 7) and Moroni's addenda (the last 2 chapters of Mormon plus the books of Ether and Moroni), he and Oliver would start on the small plates of Nephi, which begin at 1 Nephi 1:1—"Having been born of goodly parents"—and end at Omni, just before Words of Mormon.

According to those who knew Joseph, for him to have undertaken the gargantuan task of writing the book from the plates, with all its complexities and interweaving plots, without a single inconsistency, seems quite impossible, especially for a semi-literate farm boy.

At times Joseph and Oliver talked about the account they were translating. During their first month together, in April, they disagreed over a fairly bizarre theory—of John the Apostle being allowed by God to live on earth through the centuries. They agreed to use the interpreters to learn the answer. From this they learned that God had indeed kept John on the earth to live until the Second Coming.[39] It was this same John who viewed the future history of the world and recorded from it the book of Revelation in the New Testament.

"These days," says Oliver 5 years later, "were never to be forgotten. To sit under the sound of a voice, dictated by the *inspiration* of heaven, awakened the utmost gratitude of this bosom!"[40]

While obviously thankful for Oliver's help, Joseph still suffered from poverty. Because of this, their translating had interruptions. One day they walked 26 miles to Colesville, hoping Joseph Knight Sr. could help them—but he was gone! They trudged back to Harmony and began knocking on doors for work. No luck. Not many days later, failing to find work, they went home, obviously discouraged, only to find a cache of survival foods.

Joseph Knight Sr. had heard of their hardships and once again had come to the rescue. He had brought Joseph and Oliver lined writing paper, 9 or 10 bushels of grain, 5 or 6 bushels of potatoes, a pound of tea, and a barrel of mackerel.[41] It was a miraculous mission of mercy.

Upon returning and seeing the food and goods, they rejoiced—and certainly Emma and Samuel along with them.[42]

Knight summarizes, simply, "And they were glad, for they were out."[43]

Oliver wrote David Whitmer, who was still waiting for his opinion about Joseph and his revolutionary religious ideas.

Oliver told him that Joseph did indeed have the record of ancient people, and it contained their revealed truths.

That same month, April 1829, Joseph received for Oliver a revelation through the Urim and Thummim. In it Oliver was directed to "stand by" Joseph "faithfully, in whatsoever difficult circumstances he be for the word's sake," and to "admonish him in his faults" and "receive admonition of him," to "be patient, be sober, be temperate."

Then came the clincher that convinced Oliver: "Behold I am Jesus Christ, the Son of God. . . . If you desire a further witness, cast your mind upon the night that you cried unto me in your heart, that you might know concerning the truth of these things. Did I not speak peace to your mind concerning the matter? What greater witness can you have than from God?"[44]

Oliver confided to Joseph his secret—that he had actually "cried" unto God in his heart while in the Smiths' Manchester home one night in bed, praying to know the truth about the plates. The Lord had given him the witness so described in the revelation—of speaking peace to his mind concerning the matter—and Oliver had told no one of it.

David Whitmer, Oliver's friend in Fayette, records:

"When Oliver Cowdery went to Pennsylvania, he promised to write me what he should learn about these matters, which he did. He wrote me that Joseph had told him his (Oliver's) secret thoughts, and all he had meditated about going to see him, which no man on earth knew, as he supposed, but himself, and so he stopped to write for Joseph."[45] Oliver wrote David a second letter, including a few lines of what had been translated.[46]

In the same revelation, Oliver was reminded of a second witness he had received—that while in Manchester he had asked God if he should go to Harmony to help Joseph. On that occasion God had answered his prayer as well. "If it had not been so," the revelation now told him, "thou wouldst not have come to the place where thou art at this time."[47]

Oliver was thoroughly convinced.

In an earlier revelation for Oliver—his first, actually—Joseph had told him the Lord was granting him a gift to translate, if Oliver so desired. Certainly Joseph could have used his assistance, but when Oliver sat down to translate, nothing happened.

So Joseph received another revelation explaining why: "You have not understood; you have supposed that I would give it unto you, when you took no thought save it was to ask me. But behold, I say unto you, that you must study it out in your mind; then you must ask me if it be right, and if it is right I will cause that your bosom shall burn within you."[48] This simple declaration would be used by Latter-day Saints as a guide to understanding how prayers are generally answered in their daily lives.

Before now, Oliver had thought God would simply give him translated words—but it required mental effort. Joseph then informed him the Lord was releasing him from translating, but that he should continue to act as scribe. Nevertheless a lesson had been learned.


Over the next few weeks, Joseph and Oliver wished to tackle theological questions. And they wanted answers. They discussed the "authority" to baptize, feeling no one could just go out and baptize another without divine authorization.

Oliver states it was "easily to be seen that amid the great strife and noise concerning religion, none had authority from God to administer the ordinances of the gospel."[49] Their concern grew, and Joseph states that on May 15, 1829, they became so concerned over it that they put down their translating tools and walked to a sugar grove on the hillside.[50] A sugar grove, in fact, would have been a grove of maple trees.

To their surprise, part way through their prayer, "on a sudden, as from the midst of eternity," reports Oliver, "the voice of the Redeemer spake peace unto us, while the veil was parted and the angel of God came down clothed with glory."[51] He also describes the angel descending, saying he was "in a cloud of light."[52]

THIS messenger, on May 15, 1829, announced himself as John the Baptist.

He said he was sent to the 2 young men by Jesus' earthly apostles, Peter, James, and John, who held the higher—Melchizedek—priesthood, which Joseph and Oliver would later receive from those apostles themselves, now immortal beings.

Both of these priesthoods and the authority to administer them in their respective ordinances, including baptizing and giving others the gift of the Holy Ghost, he explained, had been lost from the earth for centuries, shortly after Christ's death when the apostles were killed.

Then he conferred the lesser—or Aaronic—priesthood on each man, reports Oliver Cowdery in a letter 17 years later.[1]

He did this by laying his hands on both, saying, "Upon you my fellow servants, in the name of Messiah I confer the Priesthood of Aaron, which holds the keys of ministering of angels, and of the Gospel of repentance, and of baptism by immersion for the remission of sins."[2]

He also said this priesthood should remain on the earth as long as the earth would stand, according to Reuben Miller, who recorded in his journal what he heard Joseph say.[3]

John the Baptist next told Joseph to baptize Oliver and vice versa. So the 2 men left the hill and went down to the Susquehanna River, about ¼ mile from the house.

"Immediately upon our coming up out of the water," says Joseph, "after we had been baptized, we experienced great and glorious blessings from our heavenly father."[4] wherein they not only rejoiced, but prophesied many things to come.[5] Oliver excitedly exclaimed, "What joy! What wonder! What amazement!" He then says of John the Baptist: "His voice, though mild, pierced to the center, and his words, 'I am thy fellow servant' dispelled every fear. . . . What joy filled our hearts. . . . The assurance that we were in the presence of an angel . . . and the truth unsullied as it flowed from a pure personage, dictated by the will of God is to me past description."[6] Oliver also says they heard the voice of Jesus.[7]

Joseph would write more simply and straightforwardly of their indescribable joy: "We were filled with the Holy Ghost, and rejoiced in the God of our salvation."[8]

As they returned to the house, they overheard Joseph's brother Samuel praying aloud in the woods, although his intention was to pray alone, in secret. Impressed by what Joseph overheard, he felt his younger brother was ready for baptism. He walked up to him and confided about their experience moments earlier, adding that they now had the authority to act in God's name. They invited him to be baptized and he accepted.

They went straight to the water and baptized Samuel.[9]

Traditionally, baptism by a person holding the proper authority, Latter-day Saints believe, results in an epiphany of purity, feeling cleansed from one's past sins. One new blessing Joseph and Oliver felt from their baptisms was that they understood the scriptures in a new and better way. "Our minds being now enlightened," explains Joseph, "we began to have the scriptures laid open to our understandings, and the true meaning and intention of their more mysterious passages revealed unto us, in a manner which we never could attain to previously, nor ever before had thought of."[10]

Joseph and Oliver kept the experience to themselves and to trusted family members only, after Joseph had learned the hard way.

Meanwhile, Samuel would live only a few more years, during which he would become one of the first missionaries, one of the eight witnesses to the plates [discussed later], and would actually die for the restored gospel.


The next significant event in Joseph's history was his receiving the higher priesthood.

He and Oliver were now visited by 3 ancient apostles described in the New Testament of the King James Bible—Peter, James, and John—who laid their hands on the heads of the 2 mortals and conferred the "Melchizedek Priesthood." This gave Joseph and Oliver the authority to act in God's name—to heal the sick, cast out devils, establish congregations, and conduct meetings.

As for exactly when it happened, there is no actual record, but it likely occurred in the next 2 weeks—the second half of May, 1829, according to scholar Larry C. Porter.[11] B. H. Roberts, an early 20th-century official church historian, believes it occurred sometime between May 15, 1829, and August 1830, with greater likelihood of it taking place by April 6, 1830, and most likely long before that—by June 30, 1829.[12]

Certainly it occurred before April 6, 1830, because of events that would transpire on that day in which the priesthood was involved.

As for the 2 men receiving the Melchizedek Priesthood, Oliver says that the apostle Peter was the one who actually conferred it upon them. He also states that both he and Joseph were then allowed to "look down through time and witness the effects these two [priesthoods] must produce."[13]

Similar to their recent experience with John the Baptist, Joseph and Oliver kept this event to themselves and trusted family.[14]


Joseph received more exciting news—that a "great and marvelous work" was about to come into the world.[15] Knowing what it entailed, he was perhaps impatient to share it with family members, but could not, since he was in Harmony and they were in Manchester.

However, Hyrum soon came to Harmony for a visit. Jumping in his face with the news, Joseph told him all about it, and Hyrum caught his contagious enthusiasm, even requesting a revelation for himself. Through the Urim and Thummim he was told to "seek to bring forth and establish the cause of Zion. . . . If you desire, you shall be the means of doing much good in this generation."[16] Thrilled with the revelation, Hyrum gladly accepted the call.

Just as the heavens seemed to be opening, plans were being laid elsewhere to shut the lid on the work.

Joseph was about to face a new form of opposition. And, in this arena, his enemies would hound him endlessly—wasting not only his time but nearly all his money in order to defend himself from allegations thrown at him, which were designed to put him in prison and stop him from his work—all told, hurling 48 different legal battles his way.

Now came legal battle number 1—and it sprang from his old friend Dolly Harris. The woman simply could not let go of her revenge. Possibly she felt wronged or sidestepped for Joseph wishing to ally himself with only her husband. Perhaps she felt burned because he had declined her offer of money. Or scorned because he refused to work with her.

But what riled her up now was this:

When Samuel returned to his New York home from Harmony, he brought news of Joseph having Oliver on board, with both men making big strides with the translation. This excited Martin Harris, who determined to go down to Pennsylvania himself to see the progress.[17] He knew he had stopped the work cold by losing the first 116 pages, so he felt relieved it was not only back on track but going full speed. To the extent he was excited about it, Dolly was angry.

As she saw her husband preparing for the trip south, she determined to stop him.

"To this end," says Lucy, "she undertook to prove that Joseph never had the record that he professed to have."[18] Accordingly, she mounted her horse and, similar to earlier at Harmony, "flew from house to house through the neighborhood" to stir up bad feelings against Joseph.[19] But this time she took it a step further. She resolved to create a new set of problems—the worst yet—by using arrest warrants to fight him.

"Having ascertained the number and strength of her adherents, she entered a complaint against Joseph before a certain magistrate of Lyons."[20] She even got a county official ready to ride off to Pennsylvania to arrest Joseph in the event she won her court battle.

To accomplish her designs she made an affidavit of many claims against Joseph and even gave names to the court officer of all they should subpoena. Among them was her husband, a principal witness in the case.

On the day of the trial, says Lucy, neighbors came and told her that the witnesses had gone to Lyons to obtain a verdict against Joseph. "This very naturally gave me great anxiety," admits Lucy in her rough draft.[21] Immediately after their friends and allies left, Hyrum came in, and she asked him what could be done.

"'Why, Mother,' said he," reports Lucy, "'we can do nothing except to look to the Lord: in him is all help and strength; he can deliver from every trouble.'

"Seeing such confidence in my son strengthened me in this hour of trial. Not being accustomed to lawsuits of this character, I trembled for the issue, for this was the first time a suit had ever been preferred before a court against any of my family. I retired to a secluded place and poured out my whole soul in entreaties to God for the safety of my son and continued my supplication for some time; at length the Spirit fell upon me so powerfully that every foreboding of ill was entirely removed from my mind, and a voice spoke to me, saying, 'Not one hair of his head shall be harmed.' I was satisfied.

"I arose and repaired to the house. I had never before in my life experienced such happy moments. I sat down and began to read, but my feelings were too intense to allow me to do so.

"My daughter-in-law Jerusha came into the room soon after this, and when she turned her eyes upon me, she stopped short and exclaimed, 'Why, Mother! What is the matter? I never saw you look so strangely in my life.'

"I told her that I had never felt so happy before in my life, that my heart was so light and my mind so completely at rest that it did not appear possible to me that I should ever have any more trouble while I should exist.[22] I then informed her, in relation to the witness which I had received from the Lord, that Joseph's enemies would have no power over him. I had received a promise that he would be protected. Overpowered by the strength of my feelings, I burst into tears."[23] Such intimate expressions of faith and trials are contained primarily in her rough draft (best seen in *History of Joseph Smith by His Mother, Lucy Mack Smith* [Stratford Books, 2006; eBook, 2012]—the best by far of all published versions, which also includes the first printed, unabridged 1853 edition and all notes by church historians since, all compiled masterfully by R. Vernon Ingleton).

Meanwhile the trial went in this manner:

"The witnesses being duly sworn—the first arose and testified that Joseph Smith told him that the box, which he had, contained nothing but sand; and he, Joseph Smith, said it was gold, to deceive the people.

"Second witness swore that Joseph Smith had told him that it was nothing but a box of lead, and he was determined to use it as he saw fit.

"Third witness declared that he once inquired of Joseph Smith what he had in that box, and Joseph Smith told him that there was nothing at all in the box, saying that he had made fools of the whole of them, and all he wanted was to get Martin Harris's money away from him, and that he (witness) was knowing to the fact that Joseph Smith had, by his persuasion, already got two or three hundred dollars.

"Next came Mrs. Harris's affidavit, in which she stated that she believed the chief object which Joseph Smith had in view was to defraud her husband out of all his property, and that she did not believe that Joseph Smith had ever been in possession of the gold plates, which he talked so much about.

"The magistrate then forbade the introduction of any more witnesses until Martin Harris should be sworn. Martin, being called upon, testified with boldness, decision and energy, to a few simple facts. When he arose he raised his hand to heaven and said, 'I can swear that Joseph Smith never has got one dollar from me by persuasion, since God made [created] me. I did once, of my own free will and accord, put fifty dollars into his hands in the presence of many witnesses for the purpose of doing the work of the Lord. This I can pointedly prove; and I can tell you, furthermore, that I have never seen in Joseph Smith a disposition to take any man's money without giving him a reasonable compensation for the same in return. And as to the plates which he professes to have, gentlemen, if you do not believe it, but continue to resist the truth, it will one day be the means of damning your souls.'

"After hearing this testimony the magistrate told them they need not call any more witnesses but ordered them to bring him what had been written of the testimony already given. This he tore in pieces before their eyes and told them to go home about their business and trouble him no more with such ridiculous folly."[24]

In the meantime, according to Lucy's rough draft, Joseph was 150 miles away in Harmony (from the magistrate in Lyons) and knew nothing of the matter "except for an intimation that was given through the Urim and Thummim."[25]

As for Joseph's arrests overall, church historian George A. Smith states, "He was never found guilty but once. On a certain occasion he was brought before a magistrate in the state of New York and charged with having cast out devils; the magistrate, after hearing the witnesses, decided that he was guilty, but as the statutes of New York did not provide a punishment for casting out devils, he was acquitted."[26]

———————

Conditions improved. Joseph Knight Sr. came to see Joseph on several occasions during this time with more wagonloads of provisions, bringing his son, Knight junior, from their home in Colesville, New York.

Knight junior, as stated earlier, said that his father declared that Joseph Smith Jr. was the best farmhand he ever had, adding he was "a boy of truth."[27] In addition to his father knowing Joseph Smith in his younger years, Knight junior had also worked with young Joseph on the farm years earlier and had become well acquainted with him. Before Joseph's move to Harmony, both Knight senior and junior had believed him when he had told them of his First Vision, but 2 of Knight junior's older brothers had not.[28]

In Joseph's hour of need for sustenance while he continued the work, another family came to the rescue as well . . .

In late May 1829 the following happened: According to Lucy, as Joseph was translating the plates through the Urim and Thummim, "he received, instead of words of the book, a commandment to write a letter to a man by the name of David Whitmer"[29]—Oliver Cowdery's aforementioned friend.

The revelation boldly requested of this man, whom Joseph had never seen, to come to Pennsylvania and take him and Oliver to the Whitmers' home in Fayette, New York, because his life was in danger.[30] Harmony was 135 miles away—and it was a tough trip over rough roads. . . . a lot to ask of a total stranger.[31]

David Whitmer recalls the incident 54 years later and, just as with Lucy's account, makes no mention that Joseph's request was by revelation. Although Joseph felt it was from God, he apparently exercised diplomacy and merely asked for David's help by way of a personal request.

David makes no mention that Joseph ever said it was by revelation: "Soon after this, Joseph sent for me to come to Harmony to get him and Oliver and bring them to my father's house."[32] That was all.

But the amazing events that followed left an indelible impression on him . . .

WHEN David Whitmer received the bold letter from Joseph Smith, he was stunned. He showed it to all family members, asking what he should do.

Lucy chronicles the event: David was told by his father he could not leave to help Joseph. The reason—they had as much wheat sown upon the ground as they could harrow for at least 2 days.[1]

David reflects: "I did not know what to do, I was pressed with my work. I had some 20 acres to plow, so I concluded I would finish plowing and then go."[2]

He continues: "I got up one morning to go to work as usual and, on going to the field, found between five and seven acres of my ground had been plowed during the night. I don't know who did it; but it was done just as I would have done it myself, and the plow was left standing in the furrow."[3]

Lucy relates what happened next:

"David went to the field and found that he had two heavy days' work before him. He then said to himself that if he should be enabled, by any means, to do this work sooner than the same had ever been done on the farm before, he would receive it as an evidence that it was the will of God that he should do all in his power to assist Joseph Smith in the work in which he was engaged.

"He then fastened his horses to the harrow and, instead of dividing the field into what is, by farmers, usually termed lands, he drove round the whole of it, continuing thus till noon when, on stopping for dinner, he looked around and discovered, to his surprise, that he had harrowed in full half the wheat.

"After dinner he went on as before, and by evening he finished the whole two days' work.[4]

"His father, on going into the field the same evening, saw what had been done, and he exclaimed, 'There must be an overruling hand in this, and I think you had better go down to Pennsylvania as soon as your plaster of paris is spread, and bring up the man of God with his scribe.' To this also David agreed."[5]

"The next morning David took a wooden measure under his arm and went out to spread the plaster, which he had left two days previous in heaps near his sister's house, but on coming to the place he discovered that it was gone! Every vestige of it was gone from the spot where he left it.[6] He then ran to his sister and inquired of her if she knew what had become of it.

"Being surprised, she said, 'Why do you ask me? Was it not all spread yesterday?'

"'Not to my knowledge,' answered David.

"'I am astonished at that,' replied his sister, 'for the children came to me in the forenoon and begged of me to go out and see the men sow plaster in the field, saying that they never saw anybody sow plaster so fast in their lives. I accordingly went and saw three men at work in the field, as the children said, but supposing that you had hired some help on account of your hurry, I went immediately into the house and gave the subject no further attention.'

"David made considerable inquiry in regard to the matter, both among his relatives and neighbors, but was not able to learn who had done it. He related the circumstance to his father, who was quite as much at a loss to determine how the thing was brought about.

"However the family was convinced that there was an exertion of supernatural power connected with this strange occurrence, and all hands went about preparing David for his journey."[7]

"David immediately set out for Pennsylvania and arrived there in two days without injuring his horses in the least, though the distance was one hundred thirty-five miles."[8]

David reports:

"I was a little over two and a half days going, and traveled over 40 miles the first day, and met them on the third day. . . . Oliver told me they knew just when I started, where I put up at night and even the name on the sign board of the hotel where I stayed each night, for he had asked Joseph to look at the seer stone, that he did so and told him all these particulars of my journey. Oliver asked me, when I first met [up with] them, when I left home, where I stayed on the road, and the names of the persons at hotels.

"I could not tell the names but, as we returned, I pointed out the several houses where I had stopped, when he took out his book and found them to correspond even to the names on the sign boards, all of which he had written before we met. As had been told him by the prophet, and which agreed in every particular."[9]

Another report of his is similar, but in it he mentions an additional small miracle, italicized below:

"When I arrived at Harmony, *Joseph and Oliver were coming toward me, and met me some distance from the house.*

"*Oliver told me that Joseph had informed him* when I started from home, where I had stopped the first night, how I read the sign at the tavern, where I stopped the next night, etc., and *that I would be there that day before dinner.*

"*And this was why they had come out to meet me; all of which was exactly as Joseph had told Oliver, at which I was greatly astonished.*"[10]

Lucy continues: "When he arrived, he was under the necessity of introducing himself to Joseph, as this was the first time that they had ever met."[11]

Young David Whitmer then formally invited Joseph to move to his father's home in Fayette, New York, where Joseph would have free food and a room, along with having David's brothers to serve as scribes.

David also said the people in his neighborhood were anxious to hear Joseph's message.

Hoping to end the incredible loneliness he had endured since a boy of 14—having few believers in his work—Joseph exulted in the idea of widening his circle. He joyously accepted David's offer.

Before leaving, Joseph "inquired of the Lord to know in what manner he should carry the plates," says Lucy. "The answer was that he should commit them into the hands of an angel for safety and, after arriving at Mr. Whitmer's, the angel would meet him in the garden and deliver them up again into his hands."[12] This angel may not have been Moroni, as some Latter-day Saints assume from tradition, but someone different, as explained below, and whom Oliver and David were about to meet on their journey north.

Joseph and Oliver climbed aboard the Whitmer wagon "without delay"[13] and rolled northward to their new home, leaving Emma in Harmony to take charge of affairs while Joseph was gone (or possibly going with them, as analyzed in Endnote 19).

David continues:

"When I was returning to Fayette with Joseph and Oliver, all of us riding in the wagon, Oliver and I on an old-fashioned, wooden, spring seat and Joseph behind us; while traveling along in a clear open place, a very pleasant, nice-looking old man suddenly appeared by the side of our wagon and saluted us with, 'Good morning, it is very warm,' at the same time wiping his face or forehead with his hand.

"We returned the salutation and, by a sign from Joseph, I invited him to ride if he was going our way. "But he said very pleasantly, 'No, I am going to Cumorah.' This name was something new to me, I did not know what Cumorah meant. We all gazed at him and at each other, and as I looked around inquiringly of Joseph, the old man instantly disappeared, so that I did not see him again."[14]

A similar report with additional details was given by Edward Stevenson in his journal: David Whitmer related to him that he and Oliver were riding with Joseph on a wagon when they saw "an aged man about 5 feet 10, heavy set and on his back an old fashioned army knapsack strapped over his shoulders and something square in it, and he walked alongside of the wagon and wiped the sweat off his face, smiling very pleasant. David asked him to ride and he replied, 'I am going across to the Hill Cumorah.'"[15] (See this endnote for additional information about this incident plus a third account, along with analysis.)

Cumorah was the hill where Joseph had obtained the plates, but the name of it was not known till the plates were about half translated, which was some days away. (See Appendix G: "A New, Surprising Time Line for Translating the Plates" for an analysis of how these 2 accounts provide an important key to understanding that Joseph and Oliver still had at least 45% of the plates left to translate, which they would finish the following month—June 1829. The analysis also shows an argument for the translation being accomplished in far fewer days than heretofore believed.)

In the plates, toward the end, a prophet-general describes his final battle and what he did with the plates, wherein the hill is first named.

"And it came to pass that when we had gathered in all our people in one to the land of Cumorah, behold, I, Mormon, began to be old; and knowing it to be the last struggle of my people, and having been commanded of the Lord that I should not suffer the records which had been handed down by our fathers, which were sacred, to fall into the hands of the Lamanites, (for the Lamanites would destroy them) therefore I made this record out of the plates of Nephi, and hid up in the hill Cumorah all the records which had been entrusted to me by the hand of the Lord, save it were these few plates which I gave unto my son Moroni."[16]

The translated work from the plates, logically, would be named the *Book of Mormon*. So many of the threads within the plates' narratives begin coming together at this point, that when translating, Joseph doubtless saw the treasure he really had.

Interviewing David Whitmer years later, Joseph Fielding Smith asked about the old man who had met them on their way to Fayette: "Did you notice his appearance?"

David replied:

"I should think I did. He was, I should think, about 5 feet 8 or 9 inches tall and heavy set, about such a man as James Vancleave there, but heavier; his face was as large, he was dressed in a suit of brown woolen clothes, his hair and beard were white, like Brother Pratt's, but his beard was not so heavy. I also remember that he had on his back a sort of knapsack with something in [it], shaped like a book. It was the messenger who had the plates, who had taken them from Joseph just prior to our starting from Harmony.

"Soon after our arrival home, I saw something which led me to the belief that the plates were placed or concealed in my father's barn. I frankly asked Joseph if my supposition was right, he told me it was.

"Some time after this, my mother [Mary Elsa Whitmer] was going to milk the cows, when she was met out near the yard by the same old man (judging by her description of him) who said to her: 'You have been very faithful and diligent in your labors, but you are tired because of the increase in your toil; it is proper therefore that you should receive a witness that your faith may be strengthened.'

"Thereupon he showed her the plates.

"My father and mother had a large family of their own; the addition to it, therefore, of Joseph, his wife Emma, and Oliver very greatly increased the toil and anxiety of my mother. And although she had never complained, she had sometimes felt that her labor was too much, or at least she was perhaps beginning to feel so.

"This circumstance, however, completely removed all such feelings and nerved her up for her increased responsibilities."[17] Lucy wraps up the narrative: "On arriving at Waterloo [actually Fayette], Joseph received the record according to promise [in the Whitmers' garden, from the hands of the "very pleasant, nice-looking old man," the angel]. The next day he and Oliver resumed the work of translation, which they continued without further interruption until the whole work was accomplished."[18]

The Whitmer brothers did indeed assist as scribes, as David promised—including one named Christian, recalls David,[19] but mostly John, according to Joseph,[20] who proved at the time to be the most helpful of the 8 Whitmer children, states Joseph, "in writing during the remainder of the work."[21] (Over the long run, 2 of the Whitmer boys would prove the most faithful—as covered in Volume 2—Christian being one of them, Peter Jr. the other.[22]) Oliver nevertheless took most of the dictations. David reports, "It was a laborious work, for the weather was very warm, and the days were long, and they worked from morning till night."[23]

The Whitmer boys' parents had moved there from Pennsylvania in about 1809 and bought a farm. They were Pennsylvania Germans who had joined the German Reformed Church. The father of the family, Peter senior, was a responsible citizen—a school trustee and overseer of highways, both elected offices.[24]

Now in Fayette, Joseph translated fairly quickly, but not without obstacles. The main problem, he admitted to David, was that sometimes he "found he was spiritually blind and could not translate. He told us that his mind dwelt too much on earthly things, and various causes would make him incapable of proceeding with the translation."[25] For example, says David, after Emma came up to visit:

"One morning when he was getting ready to continue the translation, something went wrong about the house and he was put out about it. Something that Emma, his wife, had done. Oliver and I went upstairs, and Joseph came up soon after to continue the translation, but he could not do anything. He could not translate a single syllable.

"He went downstairs, out into the orchard, and made supplication to the Lord; was gone about an hour; came back to the house, asked Emma's forgiveness, and then came upstairs where we were, and then the translation went on all right. He could do nothing save he was humble and faithful."[26]

David's promise to Joseph came true—many in Fayette were showing interest in Joseph's work. Upon his arrival, they even invited him to speak in their homes, urging their friends to listen. Many believed, and some were willing to embrace the teachings.

Oliver Cowdery continued helping Joseph as his scribe, with less pressure on him now, since he had the help of 3 Whitmer brothers. This, of course, freed up Oliver to court their sister more aggressively.

Then Martin Harris arrived in June 1829 from Palmyra. At some point, Joseph's excitement at seeing him turned into dismay—immediately he began asking for a revelation about seeing the gold plates. As if that weren't enough of a distraction, 2 others joined in—Oliver Cowdery and David Whitmer—all 3 trying to convince Joseph to let them see the plates. Martin had learned 3 months earlier that he was to be one of them, but now he began to hound him.

No one knows the precise day the translation of the plates was completed. Interviewing David Whitmer 52 years later, the *Kansas City Star* reported that about July 1 it was completed,[27] but Lucy puts it just before the Three Witnesses saw the plates, which was mid-June.[28] Based on her track record of memory accuracy, and the fact she wrote her book 15 years after the event compared to Whitmer's interview of 52 years afterward, her recollection of the facts is probably more accurate. Nevertheless, because she was not infallible with her dates, the possibility does exist that Whitmer was correct regarding the "around July 1" date.)

Joseph immediately sent a messenger to his parents with the news of the completed translation, and requested they join him in Fayette.[29]

Lucy elucidates on the remarkable miracle that followed:

"The same evening we conveyed this intelligence to Martin Harris, for we loved the man, although his weakness had cost us much trouble. Hearing this, he greatly rejoiced and determined to go straightway to Waterloo [actually Fayette] to congratulate Joseph upon his success.

"Accordingly, the next morning we all set off together and, before sunset, met Joseph and Oliver at Mr. Whitmer's.

"The evening was spent in reading the manuscript, and it would be superfluous for me to say . . . we rejoiced exceedingly.

"The next morning after attending to the usual [daily Smith family] services, namely, reading, singing, and praying, Joseph arose from his knees and, approaching Martin Harris with a solemnity that thrills through my veins to this day when it occurs to my recollection, said, 'Martin Harris, you have got to humble yourself before your God this day, that you may obtain a forgiveness of your sins. If you do, it is the will of God that you should look upon the plates in company with Oliver Cowdery and David Whitmer.'"[30]

Joseph and Oliver walked across a field to David Whitmer, who was plowing. They informed him the day had arrived. David tied his plow horses to a fence and waited for Martin to join them.

When Martin arrived, the 4 men walked into the woods near the Whitmers' house,[31] sat on a log, and discussed the plates, then began to pray—first Joseph, then the others. Nothing happened. They prayed once more. Again nothing. Finally Martin arose and left them, saying later, "I knew it was me that was keeping the angel from appearing."[32]

When he left the group, says Joseph, "We knelt down again, and had not been many minutes engaged in prayer, when presently we beheld a light above us."[33] (Interestingly, it took "minutes"—which, to those of the men unschooled in regular, lengthy prayer may have found this an interminably long period of time to be praying—yet the rewards were remarkable . . .)

David Whitmer fills in the details: "All at once, a light came down from above us and encircled us for quite a little distance around; and the angel stood before us. He was dressed in white and spoke and called me by name and said, 'Blessed is he that keepeth His commandments.' . . . A table was set before us and, on it, the records were placed. . . . While we were viewing them, the voice of God spoke out of heaven, saying that the Book was true and the translation correct."[34]

Oliver states, "I beheld with my eyes, and handled with my hands the gold plates from which it was translated."[35]

Joseph describes the moment:

"In his hands he held the plates which we had been praying for these to have a view of. He turned over the leaves one by one, so that we could see them, and discern the engravings thereon distinctly.

"He then addressed himself to David Whitmer, and said, 'David, blessed is the Lord, and he that keeps his command-ments;' when, immediately afterwards, we heard a voice from out of the bright light above us, saying, 'These plates have been revealed by the power of God, and they have been translated by the power of God.'" Joseph's report is similar to David Whitmer's account of the angel's words: "The translation of them which you have is correct, and I command you to bear record of what you now see and hear."[36]

Also on the table, adds David, were other objects:

"We not only saw the plates of the *Book of Mormon* but also the brass plates, the plates of the Book of Ether, the plates containing the records of the wickedness and secret combinations of the people of the world down to the time of their being engraved, and many other plates.

"The fact is, it was just as though Joseph, Oliver and I were sitting just here on a log, when we were overshadowed by a light. It was not like the light of the sun nor like that of a fire, but more glorious and beautiful.

"It extended away round us, I cannot tell how far, but in the midst of this light, about as far off as he sits," (David Whitmer, in his interview, pointed to John C. Whitmer, sitting a few feet from him) "there appeared as it were, a table with many records or plates upon it, besides the plates of the *Book of Mormon*, also the Sword of Laban [owned by a character whose account was described in the plates], the Directors—i.e., the ball which Lehi had [this was a compass used to help the ancient prophet Lehi cross the ocean to the New World]—and the Interpreters [that is, the translating tools—the Urim and Thummim].

"I saw them just as plain as I see this bed (striking the bed beside him with his hand), and I heard the voice of the Lord, as distinctly as I ever heard anything in my life, declaring that the records of the plates of the *Book of Mormon* were translated by the gift and power of God."

At this point in his interview, David Whitmer was asked by Orson Pratt: "Did you see the angel at this time?"

David responded: "Yes, he stood before us. Our testimony as recorded in the *Book of Mormon* is strictly and absolutely true, just as it is there written."[37]

(David Whitmer never did indicate if the angel who showed them the plates was the same one he saw on the roadside, saluting them on their trip from Harmony, or another.)

Joseph here picks up the narrative:

"I now left David and Oliver, and went in pursuit of Martin Harris, whom I found at a considerable distance, fervently engaged in prayer. He soon told me, however, that he had not yet prevailed with the Lord."[38]

Martin Harris continues his account of hoping to see the plates: "In my desperation I asked the Prophet seer to kneel down with me and to pray for me also that I may also see the plates, and we did kneel down and pray. Immediately, the angel stood before me and said, 'Look' and when I glanced at the angel, I fell, but I stood on my feet and saw the angel turn the leaves of gold and I said, 'It is enough, my Lord and my God.' I then heard the voice of God say, 'The book is true and translated correctly.'"[1] (To clarify, the voice was separate than the angel, as the angel was clearly a messenger—and not God.)

Joseph Smith reports it from his view: when Martin received a vision he said, "'Tis enough, 'tis enough; mine eyes have beheld.' He jumped up, rejoicing, shouting, 'Hosanna,' and he blessed God."[2]

An interesting detail is added in this account by Joseph—the fact that Joseph, while seeing the vision, was uncertain Martin was seeing the exact same thing, because of the way Joseph states it: "The same vision was opened to our view, at least it was again opened to me, and I once more beheld and heard the same things; whilst at the same moment, Martin Harris cried out, apparently in ecstasy of joy."[3]

The result of this miracle was a great relief to Joseph.

Lucy and her husband were visiting the Whitmers when the 4 men returned home, so Lucy saw the aftermath firsthand:

"When they returned to the house, it was between three and four o'clock P.M. Mrs. Whitmer, Mr. Smith and myself were sitting in a bedroom at the time. On coming in, Joseph threw himself down beside me and exclaimed, 'Father, Mother, you do not know how happy I am; the Lord has now caused the plates to be shown to three more besides myself. They have seen an angel who has testified to them, and they will have to bear witness to the truth of what I have said, for now they know for themselves that I do not go about to deceive the people, and I feel as if I was relieved of a dreadful burden which was almost too heavy for me to bear, and it rejoices my soul that I am not any longer to be entirely alone in the world.'

"Upon this Martin Harris came in. He seemed almost overcome with joy and testified boldly to what he had both seen and heard.

"And so did David and Oliver, adding that no tongue could express the joy of their hearts and the greatness of the things which they had both seen and heard."[4]

In the house they immediately signed an affidavit stating what they had all seen:

"We, through the grace of God the Father, and our Lord Jesus Christ, have seen the plates. . . . And we also know that they have been translated by the gift and power of God, for his voice hath declared it unto us; wherefore we know of a surety that the work is true. . . .

"And we declare, with words of soberness, that an angel of God came down from heaven, and he brought and laid before our eyes, that we beheld and saw the plates and the engravings thereon. . . ."

"The voice of the Lord commanded us that we should bear record of it."

Oliver Cowdery
David Whitmer
Martin Harris[5]

Lucy records in her rough draft that Martin was still reeling, almost overcome with joy.[6]

Martin then gave his own testimony: "I have now seen an angel from heaven . . . . I have also looked upon the plates and handled them with my hands, and can testify of the same to the whole world. But I have received for myself a witness that words cannot express, that no tongue can describe; and I bless God in the sincerity of my soul that he has condescended to make me—even me—a witness of the greatness of his work and designs in behalf of the children of men."[7]

None of the Three Witnesses would ever retract or deny their testimony of seeing the plates, although each would go through a trial of faith on other issues. (For a summary of their future and their testimonies, see Appendix H: "What Happened to the Three Witnesses?")

The next day Joseph's parents returned to their home in Manchester, a cheerful, happy company," records Lucy in understated tones.[8]

Two important tasks remained for Joseph and Oliver—to return the plates to a designated place and to publish the book.

Before tackling the publishing problem, they obediently took the plates to the Hill Cumorah, where Joseph had learned he would have to go when he received them. Brigham Young describes what happened next:

"Oliver says that when Joseph and Oliver went there, the hill opened, and they walked into a cave in which there was a large and spacious room. He says he did not think, at the time, whether they had the light of the sun or artificial light, but that it was just as light as day. They laid the plates on a table; it was a large table that stood in the room. Under this table there was a pile of plates as much as 2 feet high, and there were altogether in this room more plates than probably many wagon loads; they were piled up in the corners and along the walls. The first time they went there the sword of Laban hung upon the wall; but when they went again it had been taken down and laid upon the table across the gold plates; it was unsheathed, and on it was written these words: 'This sword will never be sheathed again until the kingdoms of this world become the kingdom of our God and his Christ' [the millennial reign of Christ after His Second Coming]."[9]

In a few days, Joseph, Oliver, and the Whitmers went to Lucy's home to fulfill the second task—to "make us a visit and make some arrangements about getting the book printed."[10]

This group of visitors would also witness a miracle. They would come to be known as the Eight Witnesses. Except for Mary Elsa Whitmer, who was also apparently allowed to see the plates (Chapter 19) they would be the next, and last, people to view them. Four of them were her sons—Peter Whitmer Jr., Jacob, John, and Christian. Another was her son-in-law, Hiram Page. Also among the group would be Joseph's father and 2 of his brothers—Hyrum and Samuel.[11] As with the Three, these witnesses would likewise never deny their testimony of seeing the plates.

(Although Mary Elsa Whitmer was shown the plates as a reward for her faith, she evidently was given no assignment or responsibility regarding them—only the 11 designated witnesses were called as special witnesses.)

Joseph took this group of 8 men near to or in the Sacred Grove itself, where Joseph had his First Vision, "a little grove, a place where the family was in the habit of offering up their secret devotions to God," says Lucy. "They went to this place because it had been revealed to Joseph that the plates would be carried thither by one of the ancient Nephites."[12]

And there Joseph—rather than the angel who appeared to the first three witnesses—showed the plates to the eight: "We did handle [them] with our hands. And we also saw the engravings thereon, all of which has the appearance of ancient work. And . . . we have seen and hefted . . . And we lie not, God bearing witness of it."[13] This was the signed statement of the "Eight Witnesses."

Like the Three Witnesses now, their reputations were on the line. They knew what they were declaring would not be popular. But they were answering to a higher power than the general public.

Perhaps the 56 signers of the Declaration of Independence and Martin Luther with his "95 Theses" at Wittenberg felt a similar responsibility—they knew what was true and had to declare it, no matter the cost.

In signing the document, doubtless all eight breathed in the solemn moment, knowing what they might be sacrificing in terms of public acceptance, prestige and power.

This declaration would be published along with a statement from the Three Witnesses about a year later, in the first edition of the translated plates. Every edition since has included the testimony of both the Three and the Eight Witnesses.

This translated and published book would be the *Book of Mormon*, named after the prophet who abridged the plates and passed them on to his son, Moroni, according to the record itself, (as mentioned in Chapter 19). Moroni lived on the American continent and buried the plates in 421 A.D.

Lucy finishes her account of this event: "After these witnesses returned to the house, the angel again made his appearance to Joseph, at which time Joseph delivered up the plates into the angel's hands."[14] While no specific mention is made as to which angel this was, Lucy does give a clue, saying, "the angel again"—which would be the same as the one the Three Witnesses saw, which again may or may not be the one whom David Whitmer and Oliver Cowdery had seen saluting them on their journey north from the side of the road from Harmony, whom the Whitmer boys' mother had also been visited by.

Later, John Whitmer, of the Eight Witnesses, wrote a separate, personal testimony of the event: "I have most assuredly seen the plates from whence the *Book of Mormon* is translated and that I have handled these plates, and know of a surety that Joseph Smith Jr. has translated the *Book of Mormon* by the gift and power of God."[15]

Hiram Page, another of the Eight Witnesses, also made a separate statement: "To say that a man of Joseph's ability, who at that time did not know how to pronounce the word Nephi, could write a book of six hundred pages, as correct as the *Book of Mormon*, without supernatural power . . . it would be treating the God of heaven with contempt to deny these testimonies."[16]

Since by now they would have received the Melchizedek Priesthood (just days earlier, in fact), they wondered when they would receive an actual office in that priesthood.

Joseph and Oliver had "for some time made this a subject of humble prayer," says Joseph, who, with the others, finally got together in the "chamber of Mr. Whitmer's house" to turn their prayers up a notch, to "seek of the Lord what we now so earnestly desired."

Then, to their "unspeakable satisfaction," says Joseph, revealing the result of praying so earnestly, their prayers were answered: "for we had not long been engaged in solemn and fervent prayer, when the word of the Lord came unto us in the chamber, commanding us that I should ordain Oliver Cowdery to be an Elder in the Church of Jesus Christ, and that he also should ordain me to the same office, and then to ordain others as it should be made known unto us from time to time."[17] But not yet. The time was not right—it would be a while before they would actually ordain each other as elders.

With the manuscript finished, Joseph knew he had to immediately get it published. But he did not know of the adventure before him . . .

T HE first step in printing the *Book of Mormon* was to find a printer willing to print it.

Not an easy task.

Lucy states in her rough draft that on a Monday, 4 days after the Eight Witnesses viewed the plates, "the whole company from Waterloo [actually Fayette] went to Palmyra" to find a printer.[1] First they approached Egbert B. Grandin, who was also part-time publisher of the *Wayne Sentinel* newspaper. Grandin knew the locals would boycott the book, so he turned it down.

Next, they checked out those in surrounding towns, including all 8 newspaper presses in Rochester.[2] They twice appealed to Thurlow Weed, printer and publisher of the anti-Masonic *Enquirer*, but he turned them down flat. Then they tried Elihu F. Marshall, publisher of another Rochester newspaper. And he was the first to agree to print it. Before Joseph and Martin signed the contract, however, they made one last attempt to convince Grandin, perhaps because he was much closer and therefore easier to work with in delivering manuscript portions, picking up proofs, etc., and/or perhaps his personality was more suitable—possibly lower key or less skeptical or seemed more flexible—and they sensed he'd be better to work with. Any number of intangibles make up a group decision in choosing a printer, and theirs was indeed a monumental decision. But they made it. They wanted him.

They assured Grandin that despite Palmyra citizens' efforts to squash the book's publication, it could not be stopped. Grandin thought about it and some of his friends convinced him to just do it.[3] Soon, he, Joseph, and Martin set up a meeting to sign the agreement.

Before Joseph went to Palmyra to sign it, says Lucy, "Dr. McIntyre came in and informed us that 40 men were collected in the capacity of a mob with the view of waylaying Joseph on his way thither; that they requested him (Dr. McIntyre) as they had done once before, to take command of the company; and that upon his refusing to do so, one Mr. Huzzy, a hatter of Palmyra, proffered his services and was chosen as their leader.

"On hearing this, I besought Joseph not to go; but he smiled at my fears, saying, 'Never mind, Mother, just put your trust in God and nothing will hurt me today.'

"In a short time he set out for Palmyra. On his way thither lay a heavy strip of timber, about half a mile in width and, beyond it, on the right side of the road lay a field belonging to David Jackways. When he [Joseph] came to this field, he found the mob seated on the string of fence running along the road. Coming to Mr. Huzzy first, he took off his hat and, good-naturedly saying, 'Good morning, Mr. Huzzy,' passed on to the next [man], whom he saluted in like manner, and the next, and so on till he came to the last.

"This struck them with confusion and, while they were pondering in amazement, he passed on, leaving them perched upon the fence like so many roosting chickens, and arrived at Palmyra without being molested.

"Here he met Mr. Grandin, and writings were drawn up between them to this effect—that half of the price for printing was to be paid by Martin Harris and the residue by my two sons Joseph and Hyrum. These writings were afterwards signed by all the parties concerned.

"When Joseph returned from Palmyra, he said, 'Well, Mother, the Lord has been on my side today; the devil has not overpowered me in any of my proceedings.'"[4]

He told his mother the mob went home, and, "I'll warrant you they wish they had stayed there in the first place. "Mother, there is a God in heaven and I know it."[5]

So Grandin was Joseph's man.

But Grandin soon threw a wrench in the works: he demanded a guarantee—before he would even start setting type—of $3,000. (In today's money that comes to $129,580, or $43.19 per copy,[6] considerably higher than manufacturing costs by 21st-century standards; in fact, the cost was closer to full retail price in today's money than to manufacturer's cost. However, the price being charged was fair, as books at that time were very high-priced due to slower pre-press, printing, and binding technology.)

Martin Harris was the man Joseph needed. Joseph knew it and soon Martin realized it. His wife Dolly suspected it and opposed him all the way—so when it was time to recommit the mortgage for the purpose of the book payment, she fought so vehemently that Martin backed away from his promise.

Instead he sought to get a loan to pay Grandin. This was not a secure deal for Joseph, since obviously the books would have been used for collateral, and Grandin could have taken possession of not only Harris's half but Joseph's half of the books in the event Martin defaulted on the loan. And that, obviously, could thoroughly hamper missionary work with no books for Joseph to use, if Martin reneged.

But Martin was determined, and rode off to a Geneva, New York, bank. There, the banker was impressed with Martin's business reputation and the fact that the Presbyterian minister in Palmyra had recommended him, but when he learned what the loan was for, he turned Martin down.

Hyrum Smith was so thoroughly disgusted with Martin's cowardice to not follow through on the original plan—of using the mortgage for only paying off the books—that he told Joseph to simply find another source. One option, Hyrum heard, was selling the Canadian copyright to raise money. Whereupon, Joseph sent Oliver Cowdery and Hiram Page to Toronto to make the attempt.

Joseph had felt that sending the small delegation was the result of revelation. But the 2 men could find no one interested in the Canadian copyright. Cowdery and Page returned to New York empty-handed. They went straight to the Whitmer homestead, explained to Joseph their failure, and wanted an explanation. All, including Joseph and the now gathering Whitmer clan, were dumbfounded. All they could do was stare at Joseph, waiting for a response. Joseph, apparently humble enough to admit he did not know, left the group. He pulled out the seer stone and inquired. He returned to them with the answer, according to David Whitmer, which he immediately told them—that some revelations were from God, others are "of man," and others are "of the devil."[7]

David Whitmer later synthesized what he had learned with this statement: "When a man enquires of the Lord concerning a matter, if he is deceived by his own carnal desires, and is in error, he will receive an answer according to his erring heart, but it will not be a revelation from the Lord."[8] He summarizes that the Toronto experience is a case in point, and that "they all should have profited."[9] David Whitmer and Hiram Page eventually felt the reason for the failure was Joseph being pressured to seek it in the first place, essentially "demanding" an answer of God, when such an answer was not naturally forthcoming.[10]

Meanwhile, the Smith family fully supported Joseph.


The future governor of Utah, Stephen Harding, graduated from college and came home to Palmyra. Having learned about Joseph's unusual but widely heralded book, he went straight to see him at the print shop to learn more. Although Harding was perceived as just another young man in town, Joseph graciously invited him to his home. There, Oliver read portions of the manuscript to him, and Harding was generously fed with fresh raspberries, bread, and milk by Lucy Mack Smith, who stayed up late with him to talk further, after all had gone to bed. (This was in fact a typical display of warmth the Smith family afforded strangers. Incidentally, Steven Harding would never become part of their fold.[11] See endnote for more information about Harding.)

Meanwhile, Martin Harris finally decided to pull through for Joseph.

On August 25, 1829, he mortgaged his farm for $3,000 and committed to pay Grandin the entire amount within a year and a half. Grandin could now sell Martin's farm if he defaulted, so with that backup, Grandin began production on the book.

One good thing came from Martin's lost 116 page manuscript: Joseph learned to always make a backup, and not put so much trust in his fellowman. So he assigned Oliver to make a copy for the printer, and kept the original for himself. This he locked away and kept guarded 24 hours a day by his family. Meanwhile, Oliver and others delivered only a few pages at a time to the printer, as needed, with all such deliveries accompanied by a bodyguard. Additionally, Joseph was given in revelation 3 more instructions:

(1) Peter Whitmer Jr. was designated as that bodyguard for Oliver's trips to the printer when no one else could go, (2) Peter was also to stay at the Smith family house to guard the writings, and (3) the writings were to be guarded at all times.[12]

The manuscript copy itself was kept by Oliver the rest of his life. On his deathbed he gave it to David Whitmer.[13] (Additional information reveals David's determination to keep it among friends and family. See Appendix I, "David Whitmer: Keeping the Manuscript.") It was the only copy with the printer's marks, including lines close together, written in ink on both sides of each sheet of unruled foolscap paper, and about 500 pages (250 sheets total).

According to one of the typesetters, it came "on foolscap paper, closely written and legible, but not a punctuation mark from beginning to end."[14]

So the printing process was finally launched. Oliver took the first 24 pages to Grandin in mid-August 1829 and occasionally used a typesetting stick to help set type, although Grandin's typesetter claimed Oliver set only 10 or 12 pages.[15]

Oliver, nevertheless, was proud of his printing contribution: "It may look rather strange to you," he wrote Joseph, "that I have so soon become a printer."[16]

Since both Stephen Harding[17] and Pomeroy Tucker[18] report seeing Joseph at Grandin's print shop after printing work began on the book, it appears that Joseph hung around for at least some time before returning home to Harmony. When the first proof sheet of the title page rolled off the press, the printer held it up for Joseph, Oliver, and Martin Harris to gaze upon with awe, realizing it was the "dawning of a new gospel dispensation."[19]

About 6 weeks after printing began, Joseph returned to Emma on October 4, 1829, according to a letter he wrote Oliver.[20] Lucy indicates he may have left for Harmony right after securing the book deal with Grandin—in late June or July[21]—but her meaning may not be clear or she may be in error.

Joseph knew he had left the manuscript and its copy in safe hands with his family and friends.

However, the harder they tried to keep the manuscript safe, the more opposition they faced.

Lucy states, "The clouds of persecution again began to gather. The rabble and a party of restless religionists began to counsel together."[22]

One day, as Oliver and a Mr. Robinson were printing the book, they suspected others in the adjoining room were plotting something. Lucy details the scene:

"Mr. Robinson, being curious to know what they were doing in the next room, applied his ear to a hole in the partition wall and, by this means, overheard several persons expressing their fears in reference to the *Book of Mormon*. One said it was 'destined to break down everything before it if there is not a stop put to it; and that it was likely to injure the prospects of their ministers, and then inquired whether they should endure it.

"'No, no,' was the unanimous reply.

"It was then asked, 'How shall we prevent the printing of this book?'

"Upon which it was resolved by the meeting that three of their company should be appointed to go to the house of Mr.

Smith on the following Tuesday or Wednesday, while the men were gone to their work, and request Mrs. Smith to read the manuscript to them; that after she had done reading it, two of the company should endeavor to divert her attention from it to some other object, while the third, seizing the opportunity, should snatch it from the drawer, or wherever it should be kept, and commit it immediately to the flames.

"'Again,' said the speaker, 'suppose we fail in this and the book is printed in defiance of all that we can do to the contrary. What means shall we then adopt? Shall we buy their books and allow our families to read them?'

"They all responded, 'No.'

"They then entered into a solemn covenant, binding themselves by tremendous oaths[23] that they would never purchase even a single copy of the work or permit one member of their families to buy or read one, that they might thus avert the awful calamity which threatened them." (Speculation as to the meaning of "awful calamity" could range from the influence they feared the book might have on leading people away from their churches, to a much darker scenario—i.e., taking an oath of some sort to seek vengeance on any of their group who might break the covenant. Lucy's choice of words—"binding themselves by tremendous oaths"—leaves open speculation.)

"Oliver Cowdery came home that evening," continues Lucy, "and, after relating the whole affair with much solemnity, he said, 'Mother, what shall I do with the manuscript? Where shall I put it to keep it away from them?"

"'Oliver,' said I, 'I do not think the matter so serious after all, for there is a watch kept constantly about the house, and I need not take out the manuscript to read it to them unless I choose, and for its present safety I can have it deposited in a chest under the head of my bed in such a way that it never will be disturbed.'

"I then placed it in a chest, which was so high that when placed under the bed the whole weight of the bedstead rested upon the lid. Having made this arrangement, we felt quite at rest, and that night the family retired to rest at the usual hour, all save Peter Whitmer who spent the night on guard."[24]

Four days later, says Lucy, and "soon after my husband left the house to go to his work, those three delegates appointed by the council came to accomplish the work assigned them. Soon after they entered, one of them began thus:

"'Mrs. Smith, we hear that you have a gold bible; we have come to see if you will be so kind as to show it to us?'

"'No, gentlemen,' said I, 'we have no gold bible, but we have a translation of some gold plates, which have been brought forth for the purpose of making known to the world the plainness of the gospel, and also to give a history of the people which formerly inhabited this continent.'

"I then proceeded to relate the substance of what is contained in the *Book of Mormon*, dwelling particularly upon the principles of religion therein contained. I endeavored to show them the similarity between these principles and the simplicity of the gospel taught by Jesus Christ in the New Testament.

"'Notwithstanding all this,' said I, 'the different denominations are very much opposed to us. The Universalists are alarmed lest their religion should suffer loss, the Presbyterians tremble for their salaries, the Methodists also come and they rage, for they worship a God without body or parts, and they know that our faith comes in contact with this principle.'

"After hearing me through, the gentlemen said, 'Can we see the manuscript then?'

"'No, sir,' replied I, 'you cannot see it. We have done exhibiting the manuscript. I have told you what it contains and that must suffice.'

"He made no reply to this but said, 'Mrs. Smith, you and the most of your children have belonged to our church for some length of time, and we respect you very highly. You say a great deal about the *Book of Mormon*, which your son has found, and you believe much of what he tells you, yet we cannot bear the thoughts of losing you, and they do wish—I wish—that if you do believe those things, you would not say anything more upon the subject; I do wish you would not.'

"'Deacon Beckwith,' said I, 'if you should stick my flesh full of faggots and even burn me at the stake, I would declare, as long as God should give me breath, that Joseph has got [received] that record and that I know it to be true.'

"At this he observed to his companions, 'You see it is of no use to say anything more to her, for we cannot change her mind.' Then turning to me, he said, 'Mrs. Smith, I see that it is not possible to persuade you out of your belief, therefore I deem it unnecessary to say anything more upon the subject.'

"'No, sir,' said I, 'it is not worth your while.'

"He then bade me farewell and went out to see Hyrum."[25]

Similar conversation. Same results. But the dialogue took a different turn. Hyrum said, "Will you, Deacon Beckwith, take one of the books, when they are printed, and read it, asking God to give you an evidence that you may know whether it is true?"

Beckwith replied, "I think it beneath me to take so much trouble; however, if you will promise that you will confess to me that Joseph never had the plates, I will ask for a witness whether the book is true."[26]

Ridiculous request. End of conversation.

They next went to Samuel, who quoted them Isaiah 56:9–11, referring to them as "greedy dogs," never having enough, and as "shepherds that cannot understand," with every one out for his own gain.[27]

Having been chewed out, the 3 religionists left. A church court, to no one's surprise, suspended Lucy, Samuel, and Hyrum and censured them, also banning them from communion.[28]

As Hyrum may have felt, no love was lost.

With all their precautions, however, an enemy did manage to get ahold of the manuscript . . .

Writing under the remarkably absurd pen name of Obadiah Dogberry, one Abner Cole somehow acquired a few pages of the manuscript by stealth. For one who wrote using such a whimsical pseudonym, his intentions were more than a little ominous.

He possibly stole it from the print shop, with or without Grandin's help, but proceeded to set type on the press that he rented from Grandin during off hours. Cole was a former justice of the peace, was known as a town "busybody," and had decidedly anti-Joseph views. He determined to print portions of the *Book of Mormon* to make it book look bad—printing a few pages, making derogatory remarks, and even changing the wording to make it look outrageous and licentious.

It so happens that Hyrum Smith felt "very uneasy" at home about the work at the printing office, and dashed off with Oliver to investigate.[1] Since it was Sunday, they were surprised to see activity in the shop. They went upstairs, found Cole, and asked him what in the world he was doing. "Cole replied that he could not have the press in the daytime during the week and was obligated to do his printing at night and on Sundays," says Lucy.[2]

Suspicious, Hyrum looked around and discovered something startling—a prospectus of Cole's small weekly newspaper— which included an advertisement that claimed parts of the *Book of Mormon* would be printed in the next issue! The reason, Cole stated, was to allow subscribers access to the book without paying for it.

Cole had tossed in vulgar writing between verses, trying to pass it off as part of the translation,[3] in order to turn off potential buyers of the book.

To seal the deal, he threw in copious amounts of negative editorializing, including declarations such as "priestcraft is short-lived."

Hyrum confronted him on the spot.

Lucy reports the scene:

"Mr. Cole, what right have you to print the *Book of Mormon* in this manner?"

"It is none of your business," said Cole. "I have hired the press and will print what I please, so help yourself."

"Mr. Cole, that manuscript is sacred, and I forbid your printing any more of it."

"Smith, I don't care a d——— for you; that d——— gold bible is going into my paper in spite of all you can do."[4]

Cole kept right on printing, completely unintimidated.

While his paper was officially called *The Reflector*, and began publishing weekly in September 1829, Lucy says it was named *Dogberry Paper on Winter Hill*—perhaps that was a subtitle, editor's column, or special section of *The Reflector*—and she adds, "He had already issued six or eight numbers and, by taking them 10 or 20 miles into the country, had managed to keep them out of our sight."[5]

Hyrum was flabbergasted—he rushed home to tell his father all about it.

Joseph senior, equally shocked, galloped off to tell Joseph Jr. all the way in Harmony.[6]

Joseph, despite his generally mild manner, was well aware of one of his faults: His not-backing-down nature could, upon provocation, quickly degenerate into fisticuffs.

Together, Joseph and his father launched the long haul to Manchester, literally dancing with death in the bitter winter cold. Once reviving himself at home, Joseph dashed off to the

Palmyra printing office, where he caught Cole right in the act of printing the manuscript.

Joseph pulled no punches and demanded him to stop. Surprisingly, Cole wanted to fight right on the spot. Usually Joseph was up for such a challenge, but this time used his mind and a stratagem.

Lucy describes the scene:

When Joseph walked in on him, he spoke politely. "How do you do, Mr. Cole, you seem hard at work."

Cole responded, "How do you do, Mr. Smith?"

"Mr. Cole, that book and the right to publish it belong to me."

Cole threw down his coat, rolled up his sleeves, and came toward Joseph, smacking his fists together. Cole said, "Do you want to fight, sir? Do you want to fight? I will publish just what I please."

Joseph reported to his mother that Cole's grotesque appearance and behavior were so ridiculous that, rather than getting angry, he actually smiled at him.

"Now, Mr. Cole, you had better keep your coat on—it is cold, and I am not going to fight you."

Cole did not back down. "Sir, if you think you are the best man, just pull off your coat and try it."

"There is law," responded Joseph, "and you will find that out, if you do not understand it. But I shall not fight you, sir."[7]

Cole cooled down and finally agreed to arbitration. He lost and was told to stop.

He didn't.

He printed excerpts from the manuscript twice more in *The Reflector*, January 13 and 22, 1830.[8] But that was finally the end of it.

Yet Cole had done his damage.


Between Abner Cole, Dolly Harris, and the local ministers, little wonder that half the community was in an uproar over Joseph and the plates.

In Palmyra, true to the ministers' threats, groups of people were becoming upset that the book was even getting printed.

Soon a large meeting was held. Most citizens promised not to buy the book.

During the fall and winter, says Lucy, "We held no meetings because of the plotting schemes."[9] One can assume she was speaking of gatherings that included friends, wherein Joseph would speak of his experiences, or perhaps she was referring to informal prayer meetings with family and friends.

Grandin was pressured to stop printing. The citizens told him the Smiths had lost their farm and would not be able to pay him except by the sale of books. And since no one would buy them, Grandin would never be paid. So Grandin told Martin Harris he needed a payment before he would continue. Martin balked.

Harmony was an ironic name for the town in which Joseph lived. Costing Joseph more time and money, he once again mounted up and rode off to Palmyra to settle the printing conflict. His first step was seeing Martin to urge him to make the necessary payment to Grandin.

But predictably, Martin's wife Dolly intervened. She told Martin she would have no part of it. And it was Martin who had to live with Dolly and her daily tantrums—not Joseph.

To Martin's credit, he had the faith to accept Joseph's calling to get the book published. And he complied by selling part of his farm to a neighbor[10]—over shrieks from his wife echoing across the meadow.

So Grandin began printing again.

As for the publishing date of the *Book of Mormon*, the *Wayne Sentinel*, Grandin's paper, announced on March 19, 1830, that it would be completed and ready in the coming week.[11] This puts the completion date likely between March 21 and March 26, 1830. On March 26 the *Wayne Sentinel* made the official announcement and also published the title page: "The above work, containing about 600 pages, large Duodecimo, is now for sale, wholesale and retail, at the Palmyra Bookstore, by Howard & Grandin."[12]

The books probably started coming off the press that day. All 5,000 copies would be bound in beautiful brown leather.

The first edition ended up being bound in calfskin, not sheepskin (as most have erroneously asserted, because of the binder's newspaper announcement months earlier advertising for 600 sheepskins, apparently for binding the *Book of Mormon*).[13] (Evidence indicates this from a DNA study—see the above-referenced endnote for details—and from the author's interviews with specialty bookbinders, who have bound with both sheepskin and calfskin, knowing the 2 leathers' characteristics.)

Despite the binder's advertisement, the switch was made—perhaps because the binder could not find a large enough quantity of sheepskins, or possibly because he found lower pricing or better availability of calfskins. Parenthetically, in some cases books were not bound with one contiguous piece; rather, patches of calfskin were used to cover missing sections. It is possible that an oil-soaking technique was used to give the covers of some copies a marbled color and added texture. Further noteworthy is the little-known fact it took 21 months to bind all 5,000 copies—from March 1830 to December 14, 1831.[14]

Finally, after all the work of receiving and hiding the plates, the persecutions, the time-preventing obstacles to translating (such as sickness, farm work, traveling and looking for work), the attempts by neighbors to grab the plates, the plot by religionists to burn the manuscript, the shenanigans of "Obadiah Dogberry," the mob meetings, the slander and manuscript theft by Dolly Harris, the gossip by neighbors, and the financial nightmare that Joseph had faced trying to get the plates published—all while struggling to simply survive—Joseph surely smiled, watching the first Smythe-sewn copies coming from the binders and all neatly boxed up.

But within days, Martin began panicking. The book was selling poorly at the bookstore—the only one in town, downstairs from Grandin's print shop. So Martin found himself each day on a street corner hawking it to neighbors. Whether he was tossed out there on his ear by Dolly to get their money back, or was simply selling on his own accord, he was discovering the book, to his chagrin, was basically a bomb.

That same spring Joseph came to Manchester on a trip from Harmony with Joseph Knight Sr., when they spotted someone down the road. Joseph Knight details it:

"When we got near to his [Joseph's] father's we saw a man some 80 rods before us run across the street with a bundle in his hand.

"'There,' says Joseph, 'there is Martin going to cross the road with something in his hand.'

"Says I, 'How could you know him so far?

"Says he, 'I believe it is him,' and when we came up it was Martin with a bunch of Mormon Books.

"He came to us and after compliments he says, 'The books will not sell, for nobody wants them.'

"Joseph says, 'I think they will sell well.'

Perhaps unknowingly, it was a historic understatement by Joseph. Martin had no idea of the future salability of the book, and his fear of losing money caused him to quickly lose sight of the powerful testimony he had received at the hands of an angel. He was now obsessing over lost money and even wanted out of the printing debt balance. Brazenly, he asked Joseph for different instructions from God.

"I want a commandment."

"Fulfill what you have got," said Joseph, according to Knight, who adds that Joseph was frustrated with Martin, since he had received enough revelations about the book.

"I must have a commandment," demanded Martin 3 or 4 times.

Martin traveled with them to the Smith home and spent the night, sleeping "in a bed on the floor with me," says Knight.

"In the morning he got up and said he must have a commandment to Joseph and went home."[15]

The next morning he demanded again that revelation from Joseph.[16]

And he got it. That afternoon Joseph and Oliver received a revelation together. In it, Martin was told not to covet his own property but to "impart it freely to the printing," and to "pay the printer's debt—release thyself from bondage."[17]

Martin did some soul-searching, and the timing couldn't have been better: Grandin had decided to stop making more books, likely seeing the book sales bombing. Not only was Martin Harris not taking more copies from Grandin to sell, but Grandin's own shop was hardly selling any—obviously due to the boycott. So Grandin in March 1830 stopped the project.

Unlike modern printing, all 5,000 copies did not come off the press in one day. They came off in increments. Thus, Grandin could stop the process anytime he wanted—and he did.

He brought either printing or binding or both to a halt, until Martin would give him more assurances he would get paid.

So together Martin and Joseph marched into Grandin's shop and assuaged his fears.[18] Martin assured Grandin he would sell his farm to pay the bill—not just wait for a "fire sale" down the road on the mortgaged land.

He had mortgaged his entire farm of 240 acres on August 5, 1829, and the terms were this: Grandin could sell as many acres as needed to pay the $3,000 bill for printing and binding. Should he default, Grandin could sell the whole 240 acres at public auction and allow Martin to keep everything above $3,000.[19] However, Grandin apparently feared that the auctioned land would not cover the full $3,000—especially if it were auctioned like a fire sale, with no ready-made buyers. He had likely counted on book sales paying the bill, hoping to not auction off the mortgaged farm. But the boycott obviously caused him to panic.

Martin Harris kept his word and sold some of his land. Thus, a foreclosure sale would never take place—it was not needed. To pay the bill Martin would sell 151 of his 240 acres[20]—not at public auction, but rather in a private sale directly from Martin to a man named Thomas Lakey. Those 151 acres were purchased by Lakey on April 1, 1831 (2 months past the 18-month mortgage due date of February 5, 1831).[21]

Lakey had to pay for it in gold, perhaps because Grandin demanded that form of payment. Incidentally, he was only the middleman, as the real purchaser was John Graves, who came from England with his wife and daughter in 1831. Among the party was a Mrs. Granger, who brought with her the $3,000 in gold, wrapped in a belt around her waist. With that gold, Graves paid Lakey, who passed the gold on to Grandin to pay for the book's printing.[22] Thus, Martin paid Grandin in full.[23] (Martin did have the security of a contract he had signed with Joseph on January 16, 1830[24]—giving him equal rights with Joseph—and this allowed him to take and sell as many copies as needed to cover the cost of printing. But since they did not sell, it was up to Joseph to somehow repay him.)

Meanwhile, Martin kept flogging the book on the streets to the very townspeople committed to boycott it. He did sell a few, at $1.25 each—merely a trickle toward his $3,000 investment.[25] In 1830 $1.25 equaled $57.99 in today's money, so the books were pricey, as all books were until printing methods improved. Thus, the high price could have contributed to buyer resistance.)

Eventually Martin did get all his money back to cover the sold land—repaid by Joseph himself.

Little did he know, but the very copies he held on the street corner would someday sell for upwards of a quarter million dollars each by the early 21st century to first-edition collectors, and over 150 million copies would be in print in 108 languages by then as well. But for now he sold what he could, one by one, with a heavy heart.

Then came another barrage against Joseph: the beginning of full frontal assaults by regional newspapers . . .

ITHIN days, regional New York newspapers launched an attack against Joseph. With snowballing effect, they began soaking up whatever news they could about him from each other, reprinting "facts" without even questioning their sources, sensationalizing and fictionalizing additional pieces along the way.

In a colorful display of what came to be termed *yellow journalism* years later, they sought to create storms of discontent and simultaneously sell newspapers. (See Appendix J: "Yellow Journalism and the New York Press" for comparisons to the later New York City newspapers.)

The newspapers of western New York began the onslaught against Joseph in this manner:

The *Palmyra Freeman* printed an article, followed by Rochester newspapers in late August and early September. The Rochester *Gem, Daily Rochester Advertiser, Rochester Republican*, and *Horn of the Green Mountains* all headlined their articles, "Fanaticism" and "Blasphemy," labeling Joseph and his followers "Salem Witchcraftism." (Ironically, this was accurate from another angle—society would gang up against Joseph's people, just as the women in Salem had been ganged up against, due to rumor and innuendo.) At its best, it was yellow journalism 68 years early, writing anything to sell newspapers; at its worst, it was a premeditated character assassination of

Joseph. These papers threw labels at him faster than he could blink: "charlatan," "fraud," "imposter," ad infinitum.

Most of their attacks were based on the *Book of Mormon*. And from their articles it was obvious they had never read it and knew nothing about it. But that did not get in the way of wanting to sell papers.

Joseph and his mother would write of this period but make no mention of these articles, either unfazed by them or choosing to take the high road.


Benjamin Franklin, only 15 years before Joseph's birth, had pioneered public libraries.[1] Almost immediately they had swept the nation—even to small frontier towns like Palmyra and Manchester. But the inventory at such places was limited.

Rumors then and later would claim Joseph gained important information for his book from the Manchester library, yet such books available then were sparse on details of the ancient world.

Also, there is no evidence Joseph even went to the Manchester library, 5 miles from his home. Had he been inclined to go to one, it would have been to the much closer Palmyra library, just 2 miles away.

Scholar Hugh Nibley writes: "Wilford Poulson has compiled a bibliography of works available in libraries in Palmyra [and vicinity] in Joseph Smith's time; from it, we can see what books Joseph Smith could have read, but it is very doubtful that he read many, because he was very busy. He was very hard-pressed by poverty; what could he have had at his disposal? Very little. Allowing the maximum, if he'd spent *all* his free time studying, and had people going around the countryside bringing these books to him, he still couldn't have had much to go on."[2]

More than likely, he never gave the local libraries a second glance. Why? It simply wasn't his nature. He didn't like to read. He had less interest in books than his siblings, says his mother.[3] And his friends never wrote of him reading—never saw him with a book. No one ever reported seeing him at a library. Not once. Just not that type of boy.

In Palmyra were several bookstores, and the first local book auction was held in 1819,[4] but the Smiths were too poor to buy books.

Some of Joseph's enemies would come up with wild guesses—that Joseph "could have been told" or "possibly overheard" talk of ancient culture and geography that would account for his later writings.

A thin argument at best, it is negated by the sheer depth, complexity, and detail that Joseph would include in his translated writings, when he would dictate his own epic religious history of ancient America—which the aggregate amount of overheard conversations from locals would have affected at most a fraction of a percent had he in fact not translated the entire record by divine means. But he and those closest to him maintained that he did. The reason he could have been influenced by others so little (or not at all) is this: readers of those books had, as Nibley points out, not much to go on. Joseph would write far more details than anything available—by several thousand-fold. Similarly, the sheer volume of new theology in his writings, which his followers would claim was complementary to the Bible, was found in no other books. Certainly it was not the stuff of overheard conversations by backwoods farm boys. Or even top-flight theologians of the day. The doctrines were revolutionary and packed with detail. As were the accounts he gave of the ancients themselves—their travels, customs, conspiracies, and conflicts.

Adding to the unlikelihood that his peers provided details for his book is the fact that he kept "light-hearted" company as a teen, including ruffians, but certainly not bookwormish sorts—those who could recite what they might have learned on the geography of the Arabian peninsula or the latest theories on ancient civilizations (which was sparse in detail anyway). Being more of a typical farm boy at that age, Joseph probably would not have had the patience for such company and, in the unlikely event he did have an acquaintance bold enough to insist he and his companions listen to such academic expostulations,

Joseph, like any normal lad, would more than likely have fled the scene, anxious to get away from such nerdy kids.


The *Book of Mormon* itself has a number of intriguing aspects:

The short time spent translating it was especially impressive, given that it took probably 4 normal work weeks (spread over a 9–11 week period) to create a 584-page book loaded with depth and complexities. (As first referenced in Chapter 19, see Appendix G: "A New, Surprising Time Line for Translating the Plates.")

By understanding the writing tools they used, an even greater respect is generated for the translating/dictating team of Joseph and Oliver, especially given their time restraints.

First, the metal pen and ink system of writing allowed for absolutely no time for rough drafts—not even one.

When understanding the process of writing with a metal pen (technically a "dip pen with a metal nib"), one can appreciate how remarkably difficult it was to finish even that one draft.

Second, while people normally handwrite several pages for each printed page (because a book's type font and leading—the distance between lines vertically—are typically so much smaller than they are in handwriting), Oliver actually had to write smaller than the average printed page. The reason is, they barely had enough paper to pull off a single draft. A total of 250 sheets were covered in Oliver's tiny penmanship that placed 16.8% more words on each handwritten page than was on the finished book's average printed page (584 printed pages compared to 500 front-and-back handwritten pages). Thus, they worked under not only tight time constraints but paper constraints as well, so the writing had to go directly from the source to finished draft. Period.

Third, there was not a moment to spare for rewriting, and indeed they claimed there was none, as similarly witnessed by Emma in Chapter 13, wherein she states:

"No man could have dictated the writing of the manuscript unless he was inspired. . . . When returning after meals or after interruptions, he would at once begin where he had left off, without either seeing the manuscript or having any portion of it read to him. It would have been improbable that a learned man could do this; and for one so ignorant and unlearned as he was, it was simply impossible."[5]

Putting her claim into even clearer perspective, a stack of drafts are generally necessary for a work that is even a fraction of the complexity of this, even for the best of writers who are experienced, literate, and brilliant craftsmen with words—even those extremely rare writers, if they exist, who might be versed so well in the latest archaeology, languages, Hebrew culture, and Bible doctrine and citations, that they could write free of any resource material, yet weave intricate plots with numerous, new proper nouns and then come back later to some of the same names and locations as they would reoccur, without rereading any earlier portions, without skipping a beat, and without a single mistake. As Emma implies, it was remarkable that even after a meal or a night's sleep Joseph could return to the story with no cues of what he had last dictated and without a single reminder of the numerous names, plots, and narrative twists from earlier that applied to what he was about to write.

In summary, there was no getting up to speed and no stack of drafts. Just one draft. Without looking back. In merely 4 weeks of actual work.

More background on Oliver's pen: The metal-nibbed pen was the next generation up from the goose feather quill pen. First developed in the 1600s, it was made available by 1663 and probably first advertised in 1792 in the *London Times*, but it was not mass-produced nor sold at an affordable price for people like Oliver Cowdery until John Mitchell of Birmingham, England developed the manufacturing process in 1822, just 7 years before Oliver began working with Joseph. (Had the time line been minutely different in the evolution of writing instruments, and had the mass-produced metal pen not been available for a mere 8 more years (which is less than 1/700,000th of the 6,000 year history of writing Instruments), it would have taken far longer to have taken the dictation, plodding along with a goose feather at 2 to 3 words at a time, tapping the quill, redipping it in the inkwell, slowly and smoothly stroking the ink on paper so it would not smear illegibly, adding sand to each sheet of paper to soak up the ink blotches, then blowing it off each sheet. (This quill pen process was the primary method used the previous 12 centuries, since 600 A.D. until the 1822 breakthrough, and it represented a good portion of that 6,000 year history of writing instruments.) So the timing couldn't have been better.

This new invention of a mass-produced metal pen allowed Oliver to write 2 or 3 sentences at a time before dipping it in an inkwell and starting the process over again. So the new writing tool, though spectacular compared to the centuries-old quill pen process, was still mind-stretchingly tedious.

Other interesting facts about the *Book of Mormon*:

The book has 337 proper names, 188 of them original, including unheard-of animal types and numerous localities[6]— with no inconsistencies spread over hundreds of pages, including a vast new vocabulary for a young man who hated writing and rarely even read. The book also describes a very detailed system of weights and measures that were unheard of in modern times,[7] and a number system based on 8 rather than 10—all highly revolutionary concepts for a mostly illiterate farm boy.

The book describes the landscape of 2 civilizations. It details armies with their strategies and battles. The compiler of the plates, Mormon, was a field general, so he describes military tactics, battle plans and even armaments.

The book lists newly named animals and gives a description of trade and architecture. It describes the people and the prophets. Doctrine is given that clarifies doctrines of the Bible, with numerous prophecies, lectures, and stories of faith, including individuals and nations rising and falling.

The book follows 3 groups of people to America, covering mostly from 600 B.C. to 421 A.D.

As with the Bible, it is divided into books—15 in all, named after the main author of each.[8] They are taken from 3 sets of plates, which the ancient authors engraved. Two of the sets are described in Appendix G; the 3rd contained a history of an earlier civilization that left the Old World and settled in the New World many hundreds of years earlier (given as the book of Ether in the *Book of Mormon*).


The chief story starts in Jerusalem. Lehi is a prophet and predicts the city's downfall. He is warned to leave the city with his and one other family. They first go to the Arabian peninsula and are told that God has a new home for them.

They wander for 8 years until they are commanded to build a ship along the seashore. Some of Lehi's children obey, led by Nephi, and some rebel, led by Laman. After a drawn-out voyage, consisting of numerous trials—in many ways a microcosm of a person's life, in fact—they arrive at the shores of the Promised Land, on the American continent. The sons who rebel chase off the others, the believers.

So the believers are constantly in fear of attack. From this family division, 2 separate nations are born—the Nephites and the Lamanites—who would almost always be at each other's throats. For centuries.

(The descendants of 2 of his sons become the "Lamanites," who are the darker-skinned Native American people, while the descendants of the other sons and their friends, the "Nephites," become those who retain a "fairer" skin.)

Through all their battles and contentions, intrigues and conflict, assassinations and all-out war, are the teachings of the Nephite prophets, who admonish the people to keep the commandments in order to be protected from the ever-attacking Lamanites.

After a millennium, the rebellious branch, the Lamanites, prevail, as the Nephite civilization disintegrates through un-righteousness and bloodshed.

The last 2 living prophets are Mormon and Moroni. As stated earlier, Mormon abridges metal plates from the records of centuries, and leaves them with his son Moroni. Then, Moroni inscribes final words on the plates and buries them, likely as the last living Nephite. It is this same individual who visited Joseph as an angel 1,402 years later and lead him to the plates.

As to the scope and location of the events described in the book, the story does not purport to be the record of the only people in the Western Hemisphere; indeed, the Bering Strait migrations, which indicate Native Americans may have had their origins in Asia and migrated down from Alaska, or other theories of origins, may be accurate, but the *Book of Mormon* tells the story of only this particular group of settlers from the Old World, which became extensive, numbering in the millions at one point, and which may have spread itself over much of North and South America, or perhaps mainly in certain parts of eastern North America, as one prevalent theory suggests.

The book abounds with geographical references, sometimes very detailed, without contradicting itself. But as these references are merely incidental to the narrative, they do not need to be, nor are they, specific enough to enable modern readers to figure out precisely where the events took place.

What is known for certain is the following: the last battles were fought in Ohio and New York, and the Nephite armies were spread to the west, at least as far as the Rocky Mountains, and to the east all the way to the Atlantic Ocean, according to a revelation Joseph received[9] (covered in Volume 2 of this biography).

Scholars meanwhile are gathering all the evidence they can, even based on DNA analysis. Interestingly, Joseph wrote a newspaper editor saying, "The *Book of Mormon* is a record of the forefathers of our western tribes of Indians.[10] The term "western" in his day generally referred to the Midwest. However, "the narrow neck of land" described in the *Book of Mormon* could be Central America—or, according to some—an area in the Great Lakes.

Apparently at least some *Book of Mormon* history took place in South America, because numerous drawings of ancients in caves there indicate both a white and darker skinned people living and fighting amongst themselves. These drawings, in fact, are what inspired noted Norwegian explorer Thor Heyerdahl to launch an expedition and write of it, which became a best-selling book in the late 1960s—*Kon Tiki*.[11]

Before Heyerdahl's discovery in Latin American caves, in 1946 British writer Harold T. Wilkins reported of a vanished white race that had occupied the whole of South America in ancient times, stating it had been "living in lost cities, amidst the crumbling ruins of once splendid palaces and temples in South America."[12]

Also, in 1874, historian Hubert Howe Bancroft wrote there were "numerous vague traditions of settlements or notions of white men, who lived apart from the other people of the country and were possessed of an advanced civilization."[13]

Both of these early accounts correlate with Heyerdahl's discovery of cave paintings showing the 2 races in early South America before the white race was driven away.

The reason for Heyerdahl's scientific expedition was this— the cave drawings showed the darker skinned people driving off the whiter skinned people. He theorized they went west across the Pacific from South America on rafts, inspiring him and his crew to build a crude raft to replicate their journey. Thus, with a small crew, he set sail across the Pacific himself, disproving the accepted theories of scientists who claimed ocean currents could not possibly have taken people across the Pacific. (There is one similar account within the *Book of Mormon* that tells of a "curious" explorer named Hagoth who led people in large ships to sea, who never were heard of again; some Latter-day Saints believe that modern revelation has stated those people landed in certain Polynesian Islands, and that some of today's people in the South Pacific have as their ancestors those South American/Lamanite adventurers.)

In terms of importance, however, the location of the events in the *Book of Mormon* takes a distant backseat to the historical and theological contents within the book itself.

After more than a century of digging and exploring, archae-ologists have been unsuccessful in either proving or disproving the *Book of Mormon*. Both proponents and opponents can argue forever and one side cannot conclusively refute the other side's arguments. Pro and con cases can be made regarding empirical evidence, and no definitive case can be agreed upon by scientists. Therefore, Latter-day Saints rely on a tool that no one can refute: the promise of receiving an answer as to the truthfulness of the book through prayer—in other words, *spiritual* evidence.

Although they do not rely on physical evidence to prove the book's veracity, Latter-day Saints are mildly encouraged by the growing body of "coincidences" that serve as evidence to buttress the conviction they have arrived at by other means.

For example, historian Richard Bushman points out that researchers have unearthed positive evidences to the *Book of Mormon*, including dozens of details in ancient American antiquities, which describe cultural norms of ancient Israel— the original home to *Book of Mormon* prophets—ranging from their daily lives to coronation rituals.

Many of these details were not known at the time of Joseph's dictation of the plates, even to the most serious scholars. Of further significance, some passages are written in the poetic Hebrew form called *chiasmus*, where a group of sentences reverse at midpoint, then repeat themselves in reverse order.[14] These details were not discovered until well after Joseph's translation,[15] and certainly would not have been known by Joseph when he dictated from plates.

Other details include the olive orchard parable in the 5th chapter of the book of Jacob, which displays a remarkable (and accurate) understanding of olive tree horticulture.[16]

The *Book of Mormon* itself says that it was engraved on the golden plates in "reformed Egyptian." It turns out that the use of Egyptian characters to write in another language was common in the Middle East at the time of Lehi, the founder of the colony that is the subject of the majority of the *Book of Mormon*. This "reformed Egyptian" would compare to Meroitic, which also used Egyptian characters to write another language's words.[17]

Joseph Smith could not have anticipated the future debate he would spark about the mention of horses in the *Book of Mormon*. Horses are mentioned in the book, yet for 170 years critics of the *Book of Mormon* claimed no horses could have existed since no horse bones had been discovered. Apologists argued the parallel problem dealing with the history of the Huns: no evidence of horses has been found by archaeologists for areas occupied by the Huns, who used horses extensively.[18] However, skeptical archaeologists saw only what was in front of their faces and would not buy the parallel. Then, ancient horse bones were indeed discovered—on the Yucatan Peninsula in Mexico.

Nor could Joseph, in his nonexistent geographical studies, have known about Oman—the small oasis at the Gulf of Arabia—where Lehi's journey would have taken them after traveling down the Arabian peninsula. Oman was plentiful with food, in the midst of a desert. In the *Book of Mormon* is the name "Nahom," where Lehi presumably stopped in modern-day Oman. A site there has since been discovered with the name "Nhm,"[19] strikingly similar to "Nahom."

Another item Joseph did not know about was how kings bestowed their powers to their sons—through the ritual of the crown—which is described in detail in the *Book of Mormon*. Dozens of details in the book reflect ancient Hebrew color and culture, much of it unknown even to scholars when Joseph was dictating.[20]

Non-Mormon scholars, including Krister Stendahl and James H. Charlesworth, have picked up on authentic details of Middle Eastern origins within the *Book of Mormon* text.[21]

Another, Cyrus Gordon, has found details of culture from the Eastern Hemisphere at sites in the Western Hemisphere.[22]

Jonathan Edwards Jr. has also drawn parallels of similarity between the Hebrew and Mohican languages and cultural practices.[23]

Richard Bushman points out that early American notables such as Roger Williams and William Penn, among others, spoke or even wrote treatises about the Israelite connection with the American Indians.[24]

Ancient Americans, according to the *Book of Mormon*, received a visit from the resurrected Savior, Jesus Christ, shortly after His death in Jerusalem.

Centuries later, legends of the Savior's visit survived, passed down from generation to generation in the Americas and the islands of the sea.[25]

So, when white explorers arrived in the New World, natives enthusiastically and reverently greeted them as the returning great white god.

Well known are reports of the Spanish conquistadors.

When Francisco Pizarro first encountered the Inca people high in the mountains of southeastern Peru in 1533, he and his men were greeted as "Viracochas" (deity) because they possessed lighter skin, like their God, Viracocha,[26] who centuries earlier had promised to return. Other Spanish chroniclers, including Juan de Betanzos, describe Viracocha as a "White God" with a beard.[27] Pedro Sarmiento de Gamboa notes Viracocha as being a "man of medium height, white, and dressed in a white robe like an alb, secured round the waist, and that he carried a staff and a book in his hands."[28]

Another figure of Inca folklore in the southeast Peruvian valley of Cusco was Manco Capac,[29] whose existence is clouded by mystery but is mentioned in written chronicles as a bearded white man.[30]

Further east, in Brazil, the great white god was known as Sume. Another legend labels him as Payetome. Both identify him as a white man.[31]

Going north to Chile, we encounter legends of a great white god known as El Apostol de Chilenos, who visited that people.[32]

In nearby Columbia lived the Muyscas. There, a great white god named Bochica visited them from the east—a bearded man with long robes.[33]

Going even further north to Mexico, Spanish explorer Hernan Cortes discovered another civilization, the Aztecs. In 1519 he was greeted as the great white god Quetzalcoatl. Cortes wrote letters to Charles V of Spain, describing the Aztecs' gullibility when their king, Montezuma II, offered his throne to Cortés.

The Aztecs lived in Chihuahua Valley of central Mexico in the 1300s–1500s. The name of their god was represented by a feathered, flying serpent, symbolic of a Creator Deity who had created mankind. The snake itself was symbolic of the vast sky above. Apart from the symbolisms, in some legends Quetzalcoatl was described as white and bearded. He had reportedly come from the sky and promised to return.

With regard to Quetzalcoatl, 19th-century Latter-day Saint leader John Taylor writes:

"The story of the life of the Mexican divinity, Quetzalcoatl, closely resembles that of the Savior, so closely indeed that we can come to no other conclusion than that Quetzalcoatl and Christ are the same being."[34]

President John Taylor's assessment seems highly plausible when considering the Aztec king's welcoming speech to the bearded, white Spanish conquistador, wherein thousands of Aztecs bowed before the Spaniard. At that point Montezuma II addressed Cortes with humility, revealing an understanding of specific *Book of Mormon* teachings that had been handed down:

"You have graciously arrived [for the Second Coming], you have known pain [the Crucifixion and Atonement], you have known weariness [a difficult ministry plus betrayal], now come on earth, take your rest, enter into your palace, rest your limbs; may our lords come on earth [for the launch of the Millennium]."[35]

Some scholars independent of Christian theology believe the Aztecs fell to the Spaniards without a fight because they truly believed in the returning Quetzalcoatl,[36] making them vulnerable to the conquistadors.

The earlier Toltecs (same location in Mexico as the Aztecs but 5 centuries earlier) had accounts of Kate-Zahl, a great white god with gray-green eyes and golden sandals. He taught the people a gospel of peace with 12 disciples (just like Christ when He arrived in ancient America, according to the *Book of Mormon*). The accounts of Kate-Zahl were written by one researcher, L. Taylor Hansen, who notes that the research and resulting book had "grown from a beginning of little knowledge and amused indifference, to a larger knowledge marked by skepticism and finally into a greater knowledge of developing amazement, legend by legend."[37]

The Mayans called the great white god Kukulkan, who was similar to Quetzalcoatl—a feathered serpent, symbolically, whom some believe was a bearded white man. The Mayans lived in Central America—Guatemala, Belize, western Honduras, northern El Salvador, and southern Mexico—from about 1800 B.C. to the classic period of 250–900 A.D., when they numbered in the millions, building pyramids and exploring science, surviving all the way to modern times.[38]

In the Caribbean islands, the Taino or Locono natives, as they should have been termed (but were named Arawaks by the Spaniards), thought Christopher Columbus was a "great white god." In 1493 he wrote King Ferdinand of Spain, reporting his reception by the natives in "the first island which I found." (This island he named San Salvador and is 1 of about 11 plausible islands researchers have identified as the first island he visited in the Western Hemisphere.[39])

Columbus did not try to impress anyone with a great white god theory. No Franciscans were involved in putting their angle on his report, as modern secularists have accused later Franciscans of doing. (Appendix K: "Attacking the Great White God" discusses how most scholars are skeptical, as secular-progressives notably are, wishing to dismiss "great white gods" in general and especially any notions that point to the possibility of an actual deity that visited ancient Americans, wanting to chalk it all up as myth. The only alternative is to accept the plausibility that a Christ figure or other supernatural being appeared to the ancients in America.)

The following words were written by Columbus himself long before there was an alleged Franciscan agenda. He simply presented a candid report on how he was received by the natives: "Those I bring with me [Arawak natives[40]] are still of the opinion that I come from Heaven. . . . Others went running from house to house, and to the neighboring towns, with loud cries of 'Come! Come! See the men from Heaven!' So all came, men and women alike, when their minds were set at rest concerning us, not one, small or great, remaining behind, and they all brought something to eat and drink, which they gave with extraordinary affection."[41]

Christopher Columbus, an Italian by birth with expedition funding from Spain, was the first of the "great white gods" coming from Europe in the 15th and 16th centuries, and he did not even know it.

At the other end of the Caribbean Sea, south and west of the Bahamas, are 36 Caribbean island groups known as the Lesser Antilles.[42] Another tribe lived there—a ferocious one— the Caribs. These natives had the same legends—of a white bearded man, one they called Tamu or Zune, who had come from the East and later disappeared in an "easterly direction," writes Colonel A. Braghine in his 1940 book, *The Shadow of Atlantis*.[43] (Incidentally, when the Spaniards saw the Caribs' bodies covered in red dye, *roucou*, they thought it was their natural skin color, which inspired the nickname "red-skins.")

The Aztecs and Mayans had degenerated from their fore-fathers' Christian beliefs, claim *Book of Mormon* proponents, to the point of practicing human sacrifice, while the Caribs of the Caribbean had apparently degenerated into cannibalism in one form or another.[44] But the legend of the great white god persisted among them. (See the previous endnote for a discussion of the Caribs-as-cannibals controversy.)

In North America, mostly in Arizona and New Mexico, the most fascinating account of all took place among the Hopi tribe. Their legends are replete with the great white god Pahana—a benevolent, bearded white man who anciently visited them, taught them to live peacefully with one another, and left to the east, promising he would one day return.

In 1540 when the Spaniards first made contact with them, the Hopi thought this might be the returning Pahana.[45]

Tribal tradition states that upon Pahana's return, the Hopi priest was to give a distinct handshake to Pahana, who would reciprocate with the same grip. But when the Spanish leader shook hands with the Hopi leader, he mistook the Hopi's intention and thought he was begging, so he gave him a coin. The Hopi immediately knew this great white god was not only clueless but could be trouble,[46] which the Spaniards proved to be.

Another report verifies the above in every particular, adding more details: The Spanish leader was Pedro de Tovar. When he saw the Hopi's Bear Clan leader extend his hand forward with his palm up in order to shake hands, Tovar interpreted it as "begging," when it was in fact to form the *nakwatch*, the ancient symbol of brotherhood. Tovar then curtly commanded one of his men to drop a gift into the Hopi's hand.[47] After this incident, the Hopi escorted the Spanish to Oraibi, fed and housed them, and explained "the ancient agreement" to them, which included a prophecy and directive that the 2 groups were to reconcile, correct each other's laws, live side by side, and share in common all the land's riches, then join in one religion, which would establish the truth of life as one brotherhood. These ideas flew over the Spaniards' heads, and they left, wanting only gold.[48] But these concepts contain rather remarkable parallels to the *Book of Mormon*'s prophecies of the Latter Days.

Another account states that the Hopi were certain that the Spanish conquistador was not the Pahana because of something even more telling than the botched handshake: the Spaniards decided to show their power and destroy a Hopi village—not exactly a sign of benevolence from their Creator.

This in fact made the Hopi people hopping mad. But the Spaniards soon learned they should not have messed with them. In this rather remarkable debacle, the Spaniards attacked the Hopi, turned them into slaves, and forced them to turn their crops over to them, while teaching them "Christianity." Not a good idea.

In 1680 the Hopi decided they were fed up. They attacked their oppressors and went on a rampage—killed all the soldiers, priests, and monks in sight and tore down the churches.

The Spaniards then had the gall to try again. In the late 1600s they regained military control but never again had much influence over the tribe.[49] They did, however, make some Catholic converts in one village named Awatovi. This so enraged the other Hopi that they attacked their own people: in 1700 they raided Awatovi and killed most of the convert males, removed the women and children to other Hopi villages, and burned the village to the ground.[50]

When the Spanish were not trying to enslave and force religion on them, the Hopi actually got along rather well with the Spaniards.[51]

The Hopi never gave up their hope for Pahana's return. They considered him not only the great white God but their "Lost White Brother." Various versions of the legend exist, but most include other parallels to the *Book of Mormon* and the book of Revelation in the Bible: he is their Elder Brother (which the Savior, Jesus Christ, is to Latter-day Saints and other Christians) who promised to return again, wherein the wicked will be destroyed (the Second Coming), after which will be a new age of peace (the millennial reign of Jesus Christ), and the Fifth World will be ushered in (life after Final Judgment). The legend also includes Pahana bringing a missing portion of a Hopi stone considered sacred (the Savior is to reveal all missing scripture at or after His Second Coming), and he will appear from the sky wearing red (Jesus will wear red at His Second Coming—Revelation 9:13)].[52] Hopi are also buried facing eastward, expecting to meet Pahana when he comes from the east,[53] a tradition in many Christian circles including Latter-day Saints.

Because Hopi art includes a plumed serpent, their symbolisms apparently parallel the Aztec and Mayan accounts of Quetzalcoatl and Kukulkan.

While some Native American tribes in North and South America have their origins in Asian peoples who came across the Bering Strait (such as the Eskimos) and mostly filtered down through the Western Hemisphere, *Book of Mormon* proponents believe that the ancestry of certain other tribes, including the Hopi, tie directly to the civilizations reported in the *Book of Mormon*.

A later missionary who attempted to communicate with the Hopi, despite the tribe's nightmarish history with Christian missionaries, was Jacob Hamblin, an early Mormon settler in Utah and lands south.

When Jacob came along 188 years after the Hopi's initial overthrow of the Spaniards, he learned they had a definite distaste for religious white people. They had not forgotten the white race who had forced them into slave labor and Catholicism. So Hamblin was perhaps the first white Christian missionary in 2 centuries to confront them face to face—and it happened one day when, brazenly, he went walking right into their village . . . unarmed.

But what he was armed with was a conviction that the *Book of Mormon* told the history of the Hopi's ancient ancestors. Hamblin became an iconic figure in the West, refusing to ever carry a weapon while traveling through lands of the most hostile Native Americans—simply because he was determined to never take the life of a native.[54]

As such, he was considered the supreme peacemaker. On this day that he arrived at the Hopi village (and all the other days of his life), he was never harmed (although his life was indeed threatened numerous times by warring tribes who captured and threatened him with torture and death.) Among the Hopi and others, Hamblin won their respect and trust. And his courage and message resonated with them. He first visited the Hopi in 1858, then, just 17 years later they allowed him to build a Latter-day Saint church on their land. (For more about his unusual and at times thrilling life's story, see *Jacob Hamblin: His Life in His Own Words, an account by Hamblin himself with foreword by Richard Lloyd Dewey*, Stratford Books, 2001/2012, softcover and eBook. Both editions have been re-typeset for easier reading.)

Other North American tribes had a great white god. The Yakima tribe of the Pacific Northwest had Tlazoma (also known as Tacoma), whom they revered so greatly that they renamed their highest mountain, Tacoma, in honor of his coming—which is Washington state's Mt. Rainier, as renamed by the whites).

An important researcher of the Mexican Toltecs recalls her unusual travels in northern Canada among the various tribes:

"I . . . took a grand circle tour of the far north, ending up with a thousand miles by dog-team. During this never-to-be-forgotten year, I had contact with many tribes and once more the recurring White Prophet Legend."[55]

Meanwhile, the worst outcome of all for a white explorer was that of British Captain James Cook. In the Hawaiian Islands he was treated as the returning great white god Kona, whose return the natives had long anticipated. However, upon figuring out that Cook's men were mere mortals, the natives commenced a bloodbath. (See Appendix L: "The Great White God Who Fell from Grace.")

By contrast, the Spanish conquistadors on the American mainland generally found few natives fighting back, so they took full advantage of the natives' expectations that this was their returning god.

According to the Bible (John 10:16), Jesus Christ taught his disciples: "And other sheep I have, which are not of this fold: them also I must bring, and they shall hear my voice."[56] The *Book of Mormon* testifies that those other sheep included people in the Western Hemisphere and the islands of the sea, whom He visited after His resurrection.

Nineteenth-century historian Hubert Howe Bancroft wrote a complete history of North America in numerous volumes. Of the various tribes' great white god he writes: "They are all described as white, bearded men, generally clad in long robes."[57] Some scholars have been intrigued by the natives' dealings with "the white god." Among them, Robert F. Marx has written extensively about these legends, coming to the conclusion that they "figure in almost every indigenous culture in the Americas."[58]

Interestingly, Catholic Franciscans of the 16th century, including Francisco Hernandez de Cordoba, discovered elements of Christianity in pre-Columbian religions. He was a chaplain sent by Bartolome de Las Casas, Bishop of Yucatan, to the Mayas where the Spaniards had not yet visited. Las Casas describes a letter Hernandez wrote him after one year there: a Mayan chief told Hernandes that they believed in God who lived in heaven, and that there was a Father, Son, and Holy Ghost. The

Father was called Izona, who had created men and all things. The Son was Bacab, born from a virgin named Chibirias, and the Holy Ghost was Echuah.[59]

Another Franciscan of the 16th century was Toribio de Benavente "Motolinia." He also discovered elements of Christianity in the pre-Columbian religions and thus believed that an early Christian had evangelized the Americas(!) He assumed it was St. Thomas of the New Testament, who, according to legend, had traveled off on a distant mission, "beyond the Ganges"—a 1,600-mile river cutting across northeast India, running parallel to and south of the China border. It was seen as the gateway to the far, far East and beyond. However, *Book of Mormon* proponents would argue that rather than Thomas preaching beyond the Ganges all the way to the Americas, it was the Savior Himself who evangelized the New World when He appeared to these tribes' ancestors after His resurrection.[60]

Author Tony Decker has an excellent book treating doctrinal and scriptural reasoning for taking the book seriously— *Why I Believe the Book of Mormon (and Why Anybody Can)* (2007)—while researchers Harold Brown and Bruce W. Warren, teamed with author Blaine M. Yorgason, present hundreds of archaeological discoveries in their reasoning for considering the book from a different angle, in *New Evidences of Christ in Ancient America* (1999).

Far outreaching the interesting asides and facts from growing research is the Latter-day Saints' belief that faith is required, as well as a testimony from the Spirit of God, to fully appreciate the *Book of Mormon* and to know that it is true.


The *Book of Mormon* mentions several sets of plates. They can be summarized thus:

The 1st set are the plates of Nephi. This consists of 2 sections of records—a nonreligious history in one and a religious record in the other. The 1st one is large, the 2nd one small.

The 2nd set are the plates of Mormon. On this the ancient prophet Mormon abridged the plates of Nephi and added a commentary (hence the name of the overall book), followed by his son Moroni, who continued the commentary.

Third, and finally, are the plates of Ether, which Moroni also abridged. This is a chronicle of the Jaredite group, who came to America many generations before the Nephite civilization, at the time the Tower of Babel was abandoned and the population was scattered. The tower is mentioned in Genesis, Chapter 11, of the Old Testament.[61]

Ten key points and teachings in the *Book of Mormon* are the following:

1.   The book is a second witness of Jesus Christ. The title page states the purpose of the book is to convince "Jew and Gentile that Jesus is the Christ, the Eternal God."

2.   America, the promised land, is choice above all other lands.

3.   The people will not be protected unless they keep the commandments of God.

4.   Churches will become man-made and contentious with one another (which many of Joseph's converts would find a true doctrine, wanting to be free from the verbal attacks of pastor versus pastor).

5.   The Nephites of ancient America would, in their pride, build up churches that would deny the miracles of God and rely on their own wisdom.

6.   The hand of God the Father was paramount in establishing the United States. The book contains a prophecy that a new country would break away from its mother country (England) and be set up as a free people by the hand of God the Father himself, in order that the restored church could later be established and thrive in a free country. Latter-day Saints heartily embrace the "history of miracles" when viewing the Revolutionary War, wherein a ragtag army, according to George Washington himself, received miracle after miracle to defeat the greatest military in the world—the highly financed, well-trained, seemingly invincible British army and navy.

7.   Governments in general should be established by law—
not men—and be determined by the voice of the people and
their representatives, which is the outline of a republic, such
as the one governed by the U.S. Constitution and the one that
flourished among the Nephites in the 1st century B.C. in ancient
America.

8.   Christ made reference in the New Testament of the King
James Bible to "other sheep, which are not of this fold." These
were, the Saints believe, the Nephites in ancient America, to
whom he later appeared after His resurrection.

9.   A utopian society existed for 200 years after Christ visited
the Americas. The Nephites and Lamanites lived in peace, in
which there was one harmonious church with no poor among
them. As 4 Nephi 16 summarizes, "Surely there could not be a
happier people among all the people who had been created by
the hand of God."[62]

10. However, that happiness was short-lived. Materialism
and pride crept in among these ancient Americans, then class
distinction arose, and finally warfare. The Lamanites and
Nephites were separated into tribes again after the government
broke down. Then the Lamanites swept over the unrighteous
Nephites, and the only survivor among them was Moroni, who
made his way to the Hill Cumorah and buried the abridged
plates, which his father had given him, as stated earlier. Moroni
would, centuries later, appear as an angel and guide Joseph
Smith to receive and translate the same plates.

---

Mormon himself, the ancient compiler from whom the *Book of Mormon* takes its name, writes:

"And behold, I do make the record on plates which I have made with mine own hands.

"And behold, I am called Mormon, being called after the land of Mormon. . . .

"Behold, I am a disciple of Jesus Christ, the Son of God. I have been called of him to declare his word among his people, that they might have everlasting life. . . .

"Therefore I do make my record from the accounts which have been given by those who were before me, until the commencement of my day.

"And then I do make a record of the things which I have seen with mine own eyes.

"And I know the record which I make to be a just and a true record."[63]

Among the tens of thousands of possible accounts he could have included in the *Book of Mormon*, he explains why he included the specific historical accounts that he used in his abridgement—the reason he hand-picked these specific stories and doctrine and not the tends of thousands of others that he could have. Specifically, he tells us how he knows which ones would be best for readers of the book in the latter days:

"Behold I speak unto you as if ye were present, and yet ye are not. But behold Jesus Christ hath shown you unto me, and I know your doing."[64]

After leaving the abridged records to his son, Moroni adds a few of his own words, which include this statement from the final chapter of the book:

"And when ye shall receive these things, I would exhort you that ye would ask God, the Eternal Father, in the name of Christ, if these things are not true; and if ye shall ask with a sincere heart, with real intent, having faith in Christ, he will manifest the truth of it unto you by the power of the Holy Ghost" (Moroni 10:4).[65]

He concludes with the final sentence of the *Book of Mormon*: "And now I bid unto all, farewell. I soon go to rest in the paradise of God, until my spirit and body shall again reunite, and I am brought forth triumphant through the air, to meet you before the pleasing bar of the great Jehovah, the Eternal Judge of both quick and dead. Amen."[66]

Despite organized opposition to the *Book of Mormon*, believers in it became missionaries and took the book to nearby states and to Canada, finding hundreds of people who would read and pray about it. Numerous converts would attest in their recorded journals to a common thread leading to their conversions—that after first reading it, they would ask God if the book was true; then they would receive manifestations, through strong feelings in their hearts, that it indeed was true. This, Joseph asserted, was the Holy Ghost testifying to them of its truthfulness. And these conversions took place despite never-ending attempts by ministers to dissuade their congregations from reading it. Many others were converted because they refused to have anything to do with the existing churches, which were contending with one another. Still others were seemingly "prepared" for Joseph—waiting for the primitive church to be restored, complete with the gifts of healing and the authority for baptizing, etc.

Aside from the press, in the forefront of those leading attacks on the book were Protestant pastors. One interesting case was that of Alexander Campbell, founder of the large and growing Campbellite church, who, apparently intrigued with the *Book of Mormon*, found 20 specific religious issues addressed by the book. Still, he denounced it (although in less vitriolic terms than other church leaders . . . that is, until numerous Ohio members of his congregations later began joining Joseph's group, causing him to go through the roof). (This interesting conflict is covered in Chapter 32.)

Others studied the missionaries' messages long and hard— Brigham Young for 2 years and Anson Call for 6 months. (Call was determined, actually, to prove the book false. But after months of prayer and study, he and Brigham both became convinced it was true.)

Newel Knight believed from reading the Bible that there had been a great apostasy from Christ's original church many centuries earlier. When he heard Joseph speak, he felt he was honest. Then he believed Joseph when he announced fairly earthshaking news—that the original Church of Christ was about to be restored to the earth.

It would have, he said, the same authority to act in God's name as the original church that fell away from the earth. Thus, felt Knight, it was a restoration of the church from the time of Christ—not a reformation or breakaway church from the Roman Catholic Church, which Lutherans, Anglicans, Methodists, and other churches were, as they protested the practices and teachings of the Roman Catholic Church; hence, were Protestants.

Knight was also convinced that the *Book of Mormon* was a completion of the word of God, which, added alongside the Bible, made a more complete set of scriptures.[67]

Enemies would criticize the book, and for decades their various theories would be popular. But in time these critics would fall to the wayside, as believers would shed light on them and dispel their arguments. (For a review of some of the most popular ones, see Appendix M: "Theories Attacking the *Book of Mormon*.")

What Knight and others highly anticipated came about just 11 days after the *Book of Mormon* was first announced for sale:

"A marvelous work and a wonder" was launched—the most significant event since the Atonement and resurrection of Jesus Christ, say the believers, who defined that the "marvelous work" was the restored Church of Jesus Christ to the earth . . . with Joseph as the key instrument in making it all happen . . .

# CHAPTER 24

A T the Peter Whitmer home in Fayette, New York, it happened.[1]

On April 6, 1830, neighbors, friends, and the only 3 who had thus far been baptized met for their first-ever organized church meeting.

Complete with prayer, blessings, confirmations, and the sacrament, they organized America's newest church. Its name: the Church of Christ.

Eight years later it would be renamed the Church of Jesus Christ of Latter-day Saints. The term "saints" meant mere disciples or members, which, Joseph would define, was used in New Testament times, rather than the more commonly used definition in later centuries—that of persons with revered religious status.

Joseph knew a day of organization for the restored church would be coming. Over a year earlier, in March 1829—even before Oliver had arrived on the scene—a revelation had announced, "I will establish my church, like unto the church which was taught by my disciples in the days of old."[2]

Of this April 6 meeting, Joseph's draft history states, "We met together (being six in number) besides a number who were believing."[3]

Those listed in the legal papers were Joseph, Oliver, Hyrum, Samuel, and 2 Whitmers—Peter Jr. and David. David said 40 or 50 others also attended,[4] a larger number than most Latter-day Saints have come to accept through paintings, etc. So the 40–50 onlookers were not mere curiosity seekers—they were actual believers.

According to David Lewis, who attended the meeting at the tender age of 11: "The size of the house where the church was organized was, I should judge, about 14' by 16'. It had no floor except dirt. The village was a very small one, just a little place; I think it was on level ground." He says it was at Fayette "where the church was first organized."[5] The size of the home where they organized was larger, but perhaps the room from which he watched was 14' by 16'. Parenthetically, he notes that at age 11, "I used to often go over to see Joseph."

According to Joseph's writings, the meeting opened with prayer.[6] Then Joseph asked if they accepted him and Oliver as teachers. He also asked if they wanted to be organized. The vote was unanimous. Joseph ordained Oliver elder, and vice versa.[7]

Both men blessed bread and shared it with the men there, and then the same with wine. Women did not participate in the sacrament but would be given equal opportunity soon. (One possible reason for not including them was perhaps a literal interpretation of biblical scripture that often referred to men partaking of the sacrament. But the Saints would soon come to believe that it meant men and women—or, mankind in general. However, early America did not have such a definition at that time.

Oliver and Joseph then laid hands on many to confirm them "members of the Church of Christ" and give them the gift of the Holy Ghost. "The Holy Ghost was poured out upon us to a very great degree—some prophesied, whilst we all praised the Lord, and rejoiced exceedingly," states Joseph.[8] Joseph Knight writes, "They all kneeled down and prayed and Joseph gave them instructions how to build up the church and exhorted them to be faithful in all things, for this is the work of God."[9]

Joseph and Oliver ordained some of them to priesthood offices, as the Spirit manifested. Four others were ordained elders—Hyrum, Samuel, David, and Peter Jr. It was a "happy time, spent in witnessing and feeling for ourselves the powers and blessings of the Holy Ghost," records Joseph.[10] While no mention is made of anyone giving a lecture at this organizational meeting, Joseph had given lectures in Manchester, states Lucy.[11] Oliver also had experience speaking before groups, since he taught groups of children. He would, in fact, give the first public sermon in the church 5 days later at the Whitmer house,[12] according to Joseph's draft history.)

Before the meeting had begun, some members expressed that they wanted a leader. Then they asked Joseph to ask the Lord about it. When the meeting ended, he received a revelation that told them Joseph should guide them, as a calling from God, which defined him as "a seer, a translator, a prophet, an Apostle of Jesus Christ, an elder of the church through the will of God the Father, and the grace of your Lord Jesus Christ."[13] (The endnote explains his "growing" into the calling.)

They also learned they should keep a "record."[14]

Six were baptized that day, and 8 a week later at Seneca Lake, which bordered Fayette to the west. In all, 23 were baptized that first month—April 1830—the first being Joseph's family and friends.

Those baptized at this first meeting included Porter Rockwell and four of his family—his mother, 1 brother and 2 sisters—as well as Martin Harris. Joseph's parents also joined. Since his father had refused to join any church, and his mother had always wanted to belong somewhere, they were finally united in a faith

From the shore of Seneca Lake, Joseph watched his father get baptized, then as he emerged from the water, Joseph took him by the hand and cried out, "Oh! My God! Have I lived to see my own father baptized into the true church of Jesus Christ!"[15] Lucy says he covered his face in his father's chest and wept aloud for joy.[16]

According to Lucy, Joseph's father was baptized in the morning,[17] but Joseph Jr.[18] and Joseph Knight record it occurring in the afternoon.[19] with Knight adding that "it was in a small stream."[20]

Joseph Knight Sr. adds that "Joseph was filled with [the] Spirit to a great degree to see his father [baptized] and Mr. Harris that he had been with so much, he burst out with grief [sobbing] and joy and seemed as though the world could not hold him. He went out into the lot and appeared to want to get out of sight of everybody and would sob and cry and seemed to be so full that he could not live. Oliver and I went after him and came to him, and after a while he came in. But he was the most wrought upon that I ever saw any man. But his joy seemed to be full. I think he saw the great work he had begun and was desirous to carry it out."[21] As for his witnessing his friends' baptisms, Knight explains: "They went forward and was baptized, being the first I saw baptized in the new and everlasting covenant. I had some thoughts to go forward, but I had not read the *Book of Mormon* and I wanted to examine a little more, I being a Restorationer and had not examined so much as I wanted to. But I should've felt better if I had a gone forward. But I went home and was baptized in June with my wife and family."[22]

Six revelations were given to Joseph that day in Manchester, during or after the organizational meeting, and all 6 revelations were later included in the *Book of Commandments* in 6 sections (and the later *Doctrine and Covenants* in 2 sections—D&C 23 and 21). (The "D&C" would later replace the *Book of Commandments* and combine sections from it according to subject matter, etc.)

In just 2 months they would see another breakthrough: in June 1830 they would learn that twelve apostles would at some point be ordained, because of a revelation given them.[23]

For the young lad David Lewis who had attended the first meeting, his simple account of faith was extraordinary:

"I was baptized on my 12th birthday which was May 5, 1830 just 29 days after the organization of the Church. Before leaving home for the purpose of being baptized I promised my mother that I would come right home as soon as the ceremony was performed.

"After the ceremony there was quite a severe thunderstorm. . . .

"Joseph said, 'You better stay till the rain is over.'

"I said, 'I have to go, Joseph, and I must go to keep my promise with my mother.'

"Joseph then shook hands with me and asked the Lord to bless me, and he promised me that the Lord would be with me, and would take me safely home to my mother.

"On the way home I ran up against a big elm tree. I was frightened and thought I was lost. I cried in my fright, but soon I thought of the Prophet's words, that the Lord would guide me home in safety to my mother.

"I thereupon knelt down and asked the Lord to take me safely to my home and to be a lamp to my feet and a guide to my pathway.

"Suddenly a light appeared which resembled the light of a coal oil lamp. I started for home and the light went ahead of me directly on the path where I walked. This light kept moving before me until I reached my home. My mother who was looking out for me saw it also and it lit up her window with its rays. It went around the back door of the house and stopped there.

"My mother opened the door and, just as soon as the door was opened, the light went out.

"I afterwards told Joseph about the light guiding me home. He said, 'David, I knew that you would get lost in the woods, and that the Lord would guide you home.'"[24]

Among the adults as well, miracles would soon be a major portion of their experience. A significant difference between their beliefs and the mainstream churches was that miracles and revelations were not done away, were not fulfilled in the Bible, as most mainstreamers believed.

Another big difference was this new church's having no paid clergy, following New Testament protocol.

Another, certainly, was the modern-day calling of a prophet.

After Joseph set up the church in April, he told David Whitmer he was "through with the work" God had given him, except to preach the gospel.[25] He would tell others the same thing. (Then, ironically, other revelations would come, often launching him in bold new directions.)[26]

The first missionaries would soon disperse among the population, telling people about revelation being restored.

But they would usually not tell them who the prophet was. As late as 1833 Joseph would emphasize revelation rather than himself as the focal point.[27] He modestly took a back seat to the message of the Restoration.

Five days after the eventful April 6 meeting, Oliver Cowdery gave the first "church talk"—a public address in church—at the Whitmers'. A large crowd heard him, and 5 more were baptized, including Hiram Page. More days passed and Oliver baptized another 7.

Soon there were 3 branches of the fledgling church—in Manchester where Joseph lived, in Colesville, and in Fayette— all small western New York towns. Their mission and message was a polarizing one. Many of those who did not embrace it actually found excuses to oppose it. Mobs began gathering at the new church's meetings and throwing stones, sticks, and dirt at them, according to Joseph's brother William.[28] Joseph's sister Katherine adds that rocks and sticks were thrown at their home.[29]

The pious opposed them, and forged an unlikely alliance with the roughnecks. Heretofore, pastors had showered their attention on the bar stool crowd, preaching hellfire and damnation and rousting them out of their cots on Sunday mornings so they could have extra souls to save. Certainly among many were those good-hearted ministers who sought to lift the alcohol-addicted to a more responsible lifestyle. But in general the western New York world now seemed upside down: the pastors and the roughnecks finally had a common enemy—the new church. Pastors preached against them while the roughnecks physically harassed them. Tea parties were better attended now, with women hashing over the latest gossip about the Smiths. To some extent all this opposition backfired, as many in the community became curious at all the commotion and began investigating the group. Joseph was confident the honest in heart would accept the message once they heard it. And many were joining.

To make that happen he worked harder than ever to spread his story.


On one trip he went to Colesville to visit the Knight family.

There, an extremely unusual incident occurred. After holding several meetings in the village, he saw the first miracle of the church performed. Newel Knight, not yet a member, and his wife Sally, were attending a meeting when Joseph asked Newel to pray. Newel declined, saying he would rather pray alone in the woods.

Evidently they spent the night there. Then, when he was alone the next morning, as he tried to pray privately the next morning, he could not. On his way home with his wife, she became upset over how he looked. She sent someone to get Joseph.

Seeing him, Joseph observed he was "suffering very much in his mind, and his body [was] acted upon in a very strange manner. His visage and limbs distorted and twisted in every shape and appearance possible to imagine, and finally he was caught up off the floor of the apartment and tossed about most fearfully."[30]

Eight or nine neighbors and relatives watched,[31] astonished. Then Newel begged Joseph to help him—to cast out the devil. Joseph replied, "If you know that I can, it shall be done."[32] Joseph used the newly restored priesthood from God and exorcised the devil, after which Newel said aloud that he saw the devil leave.[33]

Once freed, Newel Knight reports, "the visions of heaven were opened to my view."[34] When he returned to consciousness, others laid him on his bed.[35]

Most of the company at the scene were so convinced, they were baptized. Needless to say, word of this event spread like a forest fire. And the next month Newel himself was baptized by David Whitmer.[36] (This endnote includes a brief explanation of the exorcism.)

June 9, 1830, the first general conference (in today's terminology) was held, and all church members attended. Afterward, semiannual conferences would be the mainstay as prescribed by the Articles and Covenants—Joseph's recorded revelations.

Members now numbered 30, of whom 5 were the Rockwell family (although Porter's father would hold off another 2 years). Seven attending were elders. Also attending this conference were, once again, many visitors. During the meeting Newel Knight had a vision. Joseph records that during the meeting Newel "saw Heaven opened, and beheld the Lord Jesus Christ seated at the right hand of the Majesty on High."[37]

In that meeting the Articles and Covenants were read and "received by unanimous voice of the whole congregation."[38] The leaders confirmed newly baptized members, ordained priests, and issued licenses.[39] Joseph and Oliver signed the first 2 certificates as First and Second Elders. Joseph read Ezekiel 14, prayed, and exhorted. The minutes indicate that all the men present gave a prayer, if one reads the minutes literally. (It states prayer was given "by all the brethren present,"[40] although whoever recorded it may have meant that the prayer was given by one person for all those present.) And the meeting was dismissed by Oliver.

Not included in the minutes were the miracles.

Joseph recalls that "the Holy Ghost was poured out upon us in a miraculous manner; many of our number prophesied, whist others had the heavens opened to their view,"[41] similar to Newel Knight. Some lay on beds, they were so overcome.

Joseph reports that the apostles of old saw the same things.[42]

After conference Joseph returned to Harmony, where he would begin work on another scripture—a monumental project—as outlined in Chapter 26, one year after he had completed translation of the *Book of Mormon*. Shortly after arriving there he left for New York with Emma and 3 others.

Meanwhile, an unusual incident occurred in Colesville, New York.

Local Presbyterian minister John Sherer, of the largest local church, went to Newel and Sally Knight to visit Sally's sister Emily. He figured her to be a member of his church and was there to dissuade her from becoming interested in the new congregation. But Emily would not budge. So the reverend resorted to stratagem—he thought he could change her mind if he could just get her out of the Knight home where there was such a "bad influence" on her.

So he told her a little white lie—that a brother of hers was waiting outside to take her home. When she went outside, Sherer grabbed her by the arm and tried to force her to leave with him, but he was soon overwhelmed by not only Emily but her older sister Sally, who came flying out of the house.

The good reverend was not yet finished and would try another trick up his sleeve later that week.

The next unusual incident also occurred in Colesville.

Joseph had first gone to Manchester, where his parents lived, then came back to Colesville with Emma, Oliver, David, and John Whitmer to visit Joseph Knight Sr. At this point, Joseph Knight had a number of villagers ready for baptism.

On June 26, 1830, a Saturday afternoon in Colesville, the believers made a dam at a small stream to make a pond for baptizing, but that night, reports Newel Knight, "a mob collected and tore away the dam."[43]

The Sunday meeting continued nevertheless, complete with visitors—including those who had torn down the dam. When the church service ended, they harangued against the new church and started a loud commotion.

Suddenly Reverend Sherer appeared, this time with a letter from Emily's father giving him power of attorney. Either he was truly concerned for her soul, or unable to lose a battle, or was possibly a tad obsessive. In any case, with his newfound authority to control Emily, he forced her to go with him. The church members watched in dismay as he yanked her away from their meeting.

Despite the high drama, Emily soon got out of his grasp and was eventually baptized into the new church.[44]

Sherer did not remain voiceless over his defeat. He wrote to the leaders of the American Home Missionary Society, complaining about his loss and whining that about 20 others had joined Joseph's group in Colesville alone.

So pastors were now doubly incensed. Not only were Joseph's followers still around, after all the pastors' public preaching against them, but they were in fact multiplying—defecting from the pastors' own congregations.

The drama of the broken dam was not over. The next day, June 28, early Monday morning, the New Believers rebuilt the dam and that afternoon began depleting even more from the pastors' congregations, to their utmost dismay. Those baptized included 13 of the Knights,[45] plus Emma Smith and Levi Hall. Concerned neighbors received word of it, which spread quickly through the village, and soon a mob gathered. They heckled the believers, laughing and asking if they were washing sheep.

As the newly baptized "sheep" walked to Joseph Knight's home, the Knights' neighbors continued mocking them. Later that day, 50 mobbers surrounded their home,[46] no longer mocking, but threatening them. Joseph Smith writes they were "raging with anger," and were planning "to commit violence upon us."[47]

Joseph and his group left the senior Knight's home for his son Newel's home, apparently sneaking away, as the mob did not go with them. However, the mob "soon found where they had gone," says Newel, and came to his home.[48]

Once there, Joseph planned to confirm the new members in a sacred ordinance involving the laying on of hands, as in New Testament times. But before he could, Constable Ebenezer Hatch from South Bainbridge came to the door. And at that moment Emma realized she was living through perhaps the most bittersweet day of her life—she had just been baptized and now was witnessing her husband being arrested and dragged away by a constable for the first time.

Lucy states that they actually "dragged him from the desk [or pulpit], as he was about taking his text to preach."[49]

N ow came the second wave of attackers armed with arrest warrants—the first having been 13 months earlier via Dolly Harris.

Now, however, it came from a different person, for a different reason.

Four years earlier Joseph had not been arrested but a court had convened to target him. The reason: treasure hunting, as described in Chapter 10.

Now, a new complaint was brought against him by A. W. Benton, whom Knight described as a "catspaw" of a band of vagabonds.[1] Benton was a doctor who was apparently attempting to retry the 1826 case, claiming that anyone looking for treasure was "disorderly." It was this same Benton who was still upset that Joseph had more or less prevailed at his first court 4 years earlier without even attending it.

Joseph Knight says Benton brought charges against Joseph Smith now for "pretending to see underground—a little clause they found in the New York laws against such things."[2]

Joseph Smith himself said it was for "setting the country in an uproar by preaching the *Book of Mormon*."[3]

Both men were right.

Benton later let the cat out of the bag when he wrote a letter in the *Evangelical Magazine and Gospel Advocate*, admitting his charges had been leveled against Joseph "in order to check the progress of delusion and open the eyes and understandings of those who blindly followed him"—in other words, it was religious persecution.

More cats crawled out in the same letter, with Benton writing, "The *Book of Mormon* was brought to light by the same magic power by which he pretended to . . . discover hidden treasure."[4] He did not confess his part in the scheme but it was obvious that he was the one leveling the legal charges at Joseph.

His strategy was clearly designed to tie in treasure hunting to the *Book of Mormon*, in order to detract from its credibility, similar to Joseph's first trial 4 years earlier.

So Joseph, under arrest for the second time ever, was now riding off to trial at South Bainbridge.

On his journey, Constable Ebenezer Hatch told Joseph that "the plan of those who had got out the warrant for his arrest was to get him into the hands of the mob who were now lying in ambush," according to Newel Knight, who was present at the trial.[5] Hatch admitted he was dead set against it because he was discovering that Joseph was not the kind of person he had been led to believe.[6]

Not far from the house their wagon was overtaken by the mob. The loud, boisterous attackers expected the sheriff to give up his prisoner, awaiting a signal from him. But to their surprise, he "gave the horse the whip," reports Newel, and bolted away from them, escaping with Joseph,[7] to protect him.

But then a wagon wheel came off, and the mob closed the distance. Furiously fixing it to the wagon, the sheriff whipped it on and again gave the mob the slip.[8]

Arriving at South Bainbridge, they made their way quickly to a tavern for safety. Joseph Knight states, "I harnessed my horses and we all went up to the village. But it was so late they could not try him that night and it was put off till morning. I asked Joseph if [he] wanted counsel. He said he thought he should. I went that night and saw Mr. James Davidson, a man I was acquainted with."[9]

Rooms above taverns were the standard for hotels, so they rented one.

The constable had Joseph sleep on the bed, while he slept on the floor with his feet propped against the door and a loaded musket beside him.[10]

Before trial the next day Davidson saw the mob and panicked. Joseph Knight details the conversation: "Mr. Davidson said it looked like a squally day; he thought we had better have John Reid, a pretty good speaker, near by. I told him we would, so I employed them both." The two farmers both knew the law well but were not lawyers.[11]

The two helped Joseph prepare for court, and in the process they became convinced of his innocence. At court they claimed he was "well known for truth and uprightness; that he moved in the first circles of community, and he was often spoken of as a young man of intelligence and good morals."[12] Joseph Knight would pay the consequences for helping Joseph—that very night a mob attacked his farm, overturning some wagons, sinking others in a stream, and blockading his home.[13] Before this night he had been well respected and even beloved by fellow villagers as honest and helpful. But now, to many, he was the enemy.

At 10 A.M. on June 29, 1830, Joseph Smith's trial began before "a crowded multitude of spectators," says Knight's son.[14]

Presiding at the court was Joseph Chamberlain of Chenango County, who served as justice of the peace. About 500 people attended.[15] Chamberlain first heard 2 prosecutors—Burch and Seymour.[16]

Many spoke against Joseph, repeating the rumors they had heard, but none had firsthand knowledge.

Oddly, they once again called Joseph's old boss Josiah Stowell to the stand and questioned him about a horse he had sold Joseph on credit. He said the note he had with Joseph was as good as gold, and that he would sell another to him on credit that very day if asked. The prosecutor then tried to coerce Stowell into agreeing with a popular story about Joseph. The story was this: Joseph had claimed an angel told Stowell to give one of his horses to him. Stowell flatly denied it.

In those treasure-hunting days, Stowell said Joseph was "a fine, likely [likeable] young man, and at that time did not profess religion. He was not a profane man although I did once in a while hear him swear. He never gambled to my knowledge."[17] As stated in Chapter 6, Stowell also declared, "I never knew him to get drunk."[18] Stowell then detailed why he had hired Joseph: he had confidence the young man could help find the treasure. He had also persuaded Joseph to search for the treasure—not the other way around.

Stowell's 2 daughters were then called. They had known Joseph before he was married, when Joseph had lived in their home. The prosecution hoped the girls would demean his character, but they crushed the prosecution by speaking of Joseph in glowing terms—he had always exhibited perfect public and private moral behavior.[19]

The prosecution was stymied. They had run out of arguments.

Joseph, in fact, seemed above reproach. But then the prosecution figured they had worked too hard to simply let him get away. So they tried another angle—they dragged up rumors about Joseph in Broome County. But his defense team countered, arguing that that was another county.[20] Just when it seemed cornered, the prosecution conjured up another way to keep the trial going, hoping to buy time for a warrant to be brought from Broome County. So they called bogus witnesses and grandstanded with endless speeches. Bizarre, off-the-subject, and senseless testimonies dragged on, and Joseph was not allowed to eat, even though there were meal breaks.

Justice Chamberlain finally acquitted Joseph at midnight,[21] labeling Reid a man of "discernment."[22] Reid also felt the judge was "competent" and "discerning," and that narrow-minded religionists were the ones bringing the charges.[23]

Reid would remain Joseph's friend for life, although never accepting his faith. He had protected Joseph well. Joseph Knight summarizes: "But they could find no thing against him, therefore he was dismissed.[24]

However, immediately upon stepping outside, Joseph was arrested again.

The man arresting him now was the constable from Broome County, who threw insults and abuse at him. Knowing Joseph was thirsty and exhausted, he felt it his duty to punish him, and drove him after midnight for perhaps 3 hours without food, rest, or water on a hard wagon 15 miles to Broome County for another trial for the exact same crimes.

This constable took him first to a tavern, where, in the middle of the night, a mob awaited and "used every means to abuse, ridicule, and insult him. They spat upon him, pointed their fingers at him, saying, 'Prophesy, prophesy!'" reports Newel Knight, an eyewitness.[25] Being only a short distance from his wife, Joseph requested to pay bail in order to be with her, but was denied. He then asked for food and was given bread crusts and water.

In their room the constable forced Joseph to lie next to the wall, adding awkward discomfiture by lying beside him with one arm over him, to prevent his escape.[26]

Meanwhile, says Joseph Knight, "I hired both these lawyers [again] and took them down home with me that night."[27]

It was now June 30, 1830, and Joseph was taken that morning to the site of his new trial in Colesville. There, his 2 new farmer friends arrived to defend him once again. The same prosecutors also came riding into town. And at court they presented their case once more. This time 3 judges presided, probably at the home of one of the judges, as court was often held in a judge's living room.

Unlike the previous court, these judges were prejudiced against him. And as the proceeding launched, the prosecution ramped up the same old money-digging claims.

The same witnesses as before were called, and their lies and contradictions were so obvious that even these justices had to reject most of their testimonies. Newel Knight adds, "All they could do was to tell some things that they had heard somebody else say about him."[28]

One of the prosecutors, a determined soul named Seymour, summoned Newel Knight to the stand. He tried to trap him. To Newel he asked, "Have you not had the devil cast out of you?"

"Yes, sir."

"And had not Joseph Smith some hand in it being done?"

"Yes, sir."

"And did he not cast him out of you?"

"No, sir. It was done by the power of God, and Joseph Smith was the instrument in the hands of God on this occasion. He commanded him to come out of me in the name of Jesus Christ."[29]

The prosecution demanded to know what the devil looked like, wanting to discredit him by making him look foolish. Newel was told by one of the judges he did not need to reply to that, but he volunteered to if Seymour would agree to answer a question. Seymour agreed. Newel asked, "Do you, Mr. Seymour, understand the things of the spirit?"

"No, I do not pretend to such big things."

"Well then, it would be of no use to tell you what the devil looked like, for it was a spiritual sight . . . and of course you would not understand it."

Newel got him on that one. He later writes, "The lawyer dropped his head, while the loud laugh of the audience proclaimed his discomfiture."[30]

Not to be outdone, the prosecutors sent out for all the drunks they could find who were willing to testify against Joseph, likely for the bribe of a drink. These new "witnesses" filled the stands with more hours of testimony, adding to the hearsay the court had already entertained.

The court went all night. Bogus witnesses came and went till 2 A.M., and the prosecutors argued the case till 4.

Seymour, who "seemed to be a more zealous Presbyterian," states Newel Knight,[31] spewed "a long and violent harangue" in his summation, also bringing up the old money digging charges. Joseph's defense shot down the arguments point by point, proving the intent of the prosecution was to hound Joseph, not to serve justice.

Newel Knight concludes of Joseph's defenders: "They spoke like men inspired of God."[32] He goes so far as to say, "Those who were arrayed against Joseph trembled under the sound of their voices." He says they were "able to put to silence their opponents and convince the court that Joseph Smith Jr. was innocent."[33]

Background to this scene is related by Reid:

"I was so busy at that time, when Mr. Smith sent for me, that it was almost impossible for me to attend the case and, never having seen Mr. Smith, I determined to decline going. But soon after coming to this conclusion, I thought I heard someone say to me, 'You *must* go and deliver the Lord's anointed!' [his emphasis.] Supposing that it was the man [Joseph's messenger] who came after me, I replied, 'The Lord's anointed? What do you mean by the Lord's anointed?'

"He was surprised at being accosted in this manner and replied, 'What do you mean, sir? I said nothing about the Lord's anointed.' I was convinced that he told the truth, for these few words filled my mind with peculiar feelings such as I had never before experienced; and I immediately hastened to the place of trial.

"Whilst I was engaged in this case, these emotions increased and, when I came to speak upon it, I was inspired to an eloquence which was altogether new to me and which was overpowering and irresistible. I succeeded, as I expected, in obtaining the prisoner's discharge."[34]

A horrible moment for the prosecution came when a noted instigator of the trial, Presbyterian leader Cyrus McMaster, actually shot his case in the foot when he told Joseph openly he considered him guilty "without judge or jury."[35]

A. W. Benton, who had obtained the first warrant for Joseph's arrest, added to the absurdity, shooting their case in the other foot by admitting his intent was to awaken Joseph's followers to his supposed delusion, which, of course, was not even a legal issue.[36]

One of the 3 prosecutors, Mr. Seymour, realized the case was closed. Those wanting to harm Joseph the most had sabotaged the case beyond repair. So Seymour did all that was left that he could do: he directed "a long and violent harangue . . . against me," says Joseph,[37] to placate his fellow prosecutor as well as the mob of persecutors.

Then the judge acquitted him. "They could find nothing against him, therefore he was dismissed," says Joseph Knight.[38] Even the courtroom full of people seemed convinced he was innocent.

Newel Knight states that the constable "came forward and apologized and asked his forgiveness for the ill-treatment he had given him," then warned him that a mob outside planned to "tar and feather him, and ride him on a rail, and further, that if Joseph wished, he would lead him out another way, so that he could escape in safety."[39]

But Joseph didn't take him up on it. Meanwhile, Oliver Cowdery was present, and either a new charge against Joseph or one also involving Oliver was suddenly brought forward. Addison Everett describes what happened next:

"When they were at the justice's house for trial in the evening, all were waiting for Mr. Reid, Joseph's lawyer. And, while waiting, the justice asked Joseph some questions, among which was this:

"'What was the first miracle Jesus performed?'

"Joseph replied, 'He made this world, and what followed we are not told.'

"Mr. Reid came in and said he wanted to speak to his clients in private and that the law allowed him that privilege, he believed.

"The judge pointed to a door to a room in the back part of the house and told them to step in there. As soon as they got into the room, the lawyer said there was a mob outside in front of the house, 'and if they get hold of you they will perhaps do you bodily injury; and I think the best way for you to get out of this is to get right out there,' pointing to the window and hoisting it."[40]

Reid left the courtroom with Joseph and Oliver, according to both Addison Everett[41] and John Reid,[42] and helped them escape. (Reid's offer to assist Joseph and Oliver was similar to the constable's "come with me to escape," and Joseph and Oliver took him up on it.)[43] (One can speculate as to why Joseph did not leave earlier that day with the constable, but perhaps he did not feel the timing was right, or, possibly, Oliver had not been implicated yet and Joseph sensed he might be, or, if Oliver had been implicated already, it is possible the constable was not willing to help Oliver escape with Joseph, and thus Joseph did not want to leave without him. The facts are unclear, and Joseph's delay in leaving are up for conjecture.)

While the 2 men, Joseph and Oliver, escaped out back, Reid then visited the mob of 500.[44] Many were inside the house but obviously most spilled outside. Reid's purpose was to buy time for Joseph and Oliver to escape out back. Reid reports: "The most of them being fond of liquor, I invited them into another room to drink and thus succeeded in attracting their attention, until Mr. Smith was beyond their reach. I knew not where he went, but I was satisfied that he was out of their hands."[45]

Newel Knight picks up the narrative: "They left without taking any refreshment, the mob closely pursuing them, and it was ofttimes as much as Joseph and Oliver could do to escape them."[46]

At some point after the mob gulped down their drinks, they discovered the prisoners had flown the coop. And took out after them.

Addison Everett picks up the narrative:

"They got into the wood in going a few rods from the house—it was night and they traveled through brush and water and mud, fell over logs, etc., until Oliver was exhausted; then Joseph helped him along through the mud and water, almost carrying him.

"They traveled all night, and just at the break of day, Oliver gave out entirely and exclaimed, 'O Lord! Brother Joseph, how long have we got to endure this thing?' They sat down on a log to rest, and Joseph said that at that very time Peter, James and John came to them and ordained them to the Apostleship.

"They had 16 or 17 miles to travel to get back to Mr. Hales, his father-in-law's, but Oliver did not complain any more of fatigue."[47]

A year after Everett wrote this account to Oliver Boardman Huntington, he would write LDS church president Joseph Fielding Smith a letter, presented here with spelling and punctuation corrected. It contains most of the same facts as his account to Huntington, yet has 9 interesting additions (all numbered, italicized and bold-faced by the author):

"And they wandered in [1] *a dense Forest* all night and often times in mud and water [2] ***up to their knees***. And Brother Oliver got quite exhausted [3] *in the after part of the night*, and [4] ***Brother Joseph had to put his arm around him*** and almost carry him. And just as the day broke in the east, Brother Oliver gave out entirely and he, [5] ***Brother Joseph, leaned him against an oak tree just out side a field fence***, Brother Oliver Crying out, 'How long, O Lord, oh, how long, Brother Joseph, have we got to suffer these things?' Just this moment Peter, James, and John came to them and ordained them to the holy apostleship and [6] ***gave them the keys of the Dispensation of the Fullness of Times***. And they had some 16 or 17 miles to go to reach our place of residence, and [7] **Brother Oliver could** [then] ***travel as well as I could***. Now, as to time and place, [8] ***I heard the name of the banks of the Susquehanna River spoken***. But where it was placed, I cannot tell. [9] ***No doubt the oak tree and the field fence were adjacent to the river***. As to time, I cannot be very explicit."[48] (Additional examination is given to this letter in Appendix N: "Analyzing Addison Everett's 1881 Letter about Joseph Smith's Escape.")

This dramatic event is mentioned by Erastus Snow, who said it happened to Joseph and Oliver "at a period when they were being pursued by their enemies, and they had to travel all night, and in the dawn of the coming day, when they were weary and worn, who should appear to them but Peter, James, and John, for the purpose of conferring upon them the Apostleship, the keys of which they themselves had held while upon the earth, which had been bestowed upon them by the Savior."[49]

The date this angelic visit most likely occurred was July 2, 1830, based on the known date of June 28, when Joseph was taken to trial at South Bainbridge,[50] then calculating from that the other days at the second trial in Colesville, and their escape.

Apparently, there were 2 visits from Peter, James, and John to Joseph and Oliver—the 1st being over a year earlier, in the second half of May 1829, when only the *Melchizedek Priesthood* was given the 2 men—and the 2nd, when the *apostleship* was conferred on the 2 men. (Erastus Snow, in fact, only mentions the apostleship being conferred on this particular visit. Also of note, Joseph and Oliver already held the higher [Melchizedek] Priesthood when they conducted the first church meeting 3 months earlier on April 6, 1830, and ordained each other elders within that priesthood.[51])

Back to the story of Joseph and Oliver's escape:

After their angelic encounter, Joseph and Oliver fled through the dawn without stopping . . .

THE *History of the Church* quotes Joseph: "Meantime, and notwithstanding all the rage of our enemies, we had much consolation, and many things occurred to strengthen our faith and cheer our hearts."[1] Certainly the angels' visitation bringing the holy apostleship would have accomplished that, despite the fact they were running for their lives.

After the angels visited them, Joseph and Oliver arrived at the house of his wife's sister, where Emma awaited them.[2] Meanwhile, Joseph had eaten only "a crust of bread for two days," says Lucy, while Emma "had suffered great anxiety about him since his first arrest,"[3] of the back-to-back arrests days earlier. Certainly the relief was almost overpowering to Emma. From Emma's sister's home they hastened to Harmony, arriving the day after escaping[4]—which was later the same day as the ordination—about July 2, 1830. This was the "16 or 17 miles" journey "to get back to Mr. Hales" that Addison Everett reports.[5]

It was just the beginning of fights and flights with courts and mobs. It was also the start of Joseph's seeing his supporters targeted:

The night of the first trial in South Bainbridge, mobs attacked the Knights for helping Joseph. "Our wagons were turned over and wood piled on them, and some sunk in the water," reports Knight's son, Joseph junior. "Rails were piled against our doors, and chains sunk in the stream, and a great deal of mischief done."[6]

But his supporters' sacrifice had worked. Joseph was now free. And his first item of business was to return to Colesville and complete the confirmations from which he had been interrupted by the constables.

So, days later, in early July 1830 still, he and Oliver left Harmony and stealthily made their way back to Colesville to finish their task.

As soon as they arrived, the mob gathered again at the Knights. So Joseph and Oliver had to sneak out the back entrance—just before holding a meeting, and even before they could eat.[7]

After escaping the mob, Joseph says they traveled hard, "except a short time, during which we were forced to rest ourselves under a large tree by the way side, sleeping and watching alternately."[8]

They returned to Harmony again, obviously frustrated.


Safely in Pennsylvania, they launched an eventful course that would affect millions over the next 2 centuries—compiling and copying the revelations that Joseph would receive. Over much of that month, in fact, they would compile and copy all the revelations they had thus far obtained—the current revelations of *Doctrine and Covenants* 24, 25, and 26—and thus set the stage for recording future revelations.

In coming months Joseph would compile two dozen revelations for the benefit of the church, calling them the *Articles and Covenants*. No other churches claimed both to receive and save written revelations, so Joseph was in a new league. (See Appendix O: "Other Churches' Claims to Revelations.") He had actually begun recording his since 1828, but some were lost. So from this point on he and his associates were careful to compile and save them as best they could.

Meanwhile, Joseph launched a monumental work of some-thing else: in June 1830, one month earlier, he had begun trans-lating sacred writings (first mentioned in Chapter 24).

Now, in July 1830, he was safely back in Harmony, where he would continue making headway on those sacred writings. But it was complex. And it would take 3 years of concerted effort plus another 11 of off-and-on work. This major new undertaking?

Revising the Holy Bible.

Joseph synthesized his feelings on it:

"I believe the Bible, as it ought to be, as it came from the pen of the original writers."[9]

Since Joseph's calling was "a seer, a translator, a prophet."[10] the New Believers did not question his authority to correct the Bible and bring it back to the original.

In the process he read through the entire King James Version, deciding to keep 89% of the verses as is. But the other 11% needed work—they had been corrupted centuries earlier and, "because of the many plain and precious things which have been taken out of the book, which were plain unto the understanding of the children of men," writes ancient American prophet Nephi about the Bible, "an exceeding great many do stumble, yea, insomuch that Satan hath great power over them." (1 Nephi 13:29).[11] (Nephi is actually quoting an angel describing the future Christian world, while Nephi sees the future in a vision.)[12]

When one understands the history of the Bible, its flaws become eye-poppingly obvious.

The original Bible manuscripts written in Greek by the apostles and prophets are called autographs and did not survive. (See the objective, scholarly work, *Manuscripts and the Text of the New Testament*, by Keith Elliott and Ian Moir, from academic London publisher Continuum International.)[13] Some say these autographs ended up in thousands of fragmented documents and either disappeared or dissolved into dust.

So the later Bible compilers were dependent on copies of copies that had been tampered with, resulting in several hundred important verses that were confusing, contradictory, or incomplete.

Which leads to a second problem.

According to another study, when the scribes wrote the copies of original manuscripts, they added notes in the margins of the pages (known by scholars as *marginal glosses*) to correct their text. This was especially common if a scribe accidently left out a line or a word. In the margins they also made comments about the text. Unfortunately, when later scribes copied the copies from earlier generations, *they were often not certain if a marginal gloss was meant to be a commentary about the text or a correction to the text itself.* To make matters worse, different regions produced different versions of what had originally been the same text, each with its own set of additions and deleted words, lines, and in some cases more.[14]

In short, the scribes had passed around their copies of manuscripts, complete with changes, like a gigantic, open-ended chain letter—and many a scribe could add his 2 cents to what verses meant. Then the next scribe would add those notes to the manuscript, not knowing if they were corrections or commentary. These scribal changes included deletions of what they did not understand or perhaps what they disagreed with—in some cases entire chapters. Even entire books from the Bible were removed (as discussed further below).

Desiderius Erasmus of Rotterdam, a brilliant Roman Catholic priest by appointment but a scholar at heart, was trained at Oxford, among the world's finest universities. He knew 8 languages fluently, basing his work out of several cities of Europe through which he would rotate, where, as the greatest authority in 14 centuries, he would make the most impact of any man in history on translating the Bible.

Later editions of Erasmus's Greek New Testament became known as *Textus Receptus*, which means "received text." This became the basis for nearly all major English translations of the New Testament for the next 400 years.

In his monumental research he came to the following 2 conclusions:

(1) The original Greek manuscripts had long since disappeared, and (2) he was appalled by the translators who had messed with the Greek manuscript copies—those which had been passed down through the ages: "It can be clear, as they say, even to a blind man," he says, "that often through the translator's clumsiness or inattention, the Greek has been wrongly rendered; often the true and genuine reading has been corrupted by ignorant scribes, which we see happen every day, or altered by scribes who are half-taught and half-asleep."[15]

Joseph Smith likely never heard of Erasmus, but from revelation he made the same point: "Ignorant translators, careless transcribers . . . have committed many errors."[16] He also added to the mix "designing and corrupt priests."[17]

Joseph also stated how he knew that personally from God: "From *sundry revelations which had been received*, it was apparent that many important points touching the salvation of men had been taken from the Bible or lost before it was compiled."[18]

Mincing no words, Erasmus was equally emphatic about the mess some parts of the Bible had become[19]—in fact somewhat of a quagmire.

The fact that the Bible was still 89% accurate—in regards to the actual verses not needing changing—is somewhat miraculous, given that the Bible was compiled from such imperfect sources, a problem amplified by this analysis found in the often-referred-to *Interpreter's Dictionary of the Bible* from Abingdon Press in Nashville, written to actually prove the validity of the New Testament:

"A study of 150 Greek [manuscripts] of the Gospel of Luke has revealed more than 30,000 different readings.

"It is safe to say that there is not one sentence in the New Testament in which the [manuscript] is wholly uniform."[20]

Early versions on the Latin side were equally confusing. Currently about 8,000 early manuscripts of the Latin *Vulgate* exist—all handwritten, with many added changes along the way, especially with the *marginal glosses* problem stated above.

A whole different story is how today's books of the Bible became accepted. (See Appendix P: "Who Compiled the Bible and When?") Some in the modern Christian world would perhaps find it unusual that the Bible was solidified on the continent of Africa.[21]

Still more problems would unfold when scholars made another discovery: not only were the original manuscripts long since gone, but the manuscripts that translators had been using were not even from *the original 1st century*. They hailed from 3 separate families of manuscripts called "text-types": Alexandrian, Western, and Byzantine, ranging from the 100s to the 1500s, each having its own set of problems and corruptions. (This is explained in Appendix Q: "The Three Families of Bible Manuscripts.")

So Joseph Smith's mandate was simple: he set out to find all the muddied up verses he could and clean them up.

Parenthetically, the revisions Joseph did make (on precisely 10.96% of verses) are far fewer than current well-known and widely accepted revisions of the Bible.

While new versions of the Bible would come out over the ensuing decades, the 2 most notable ones were published by Alexander Campbell, the aforementioned religious leader who crossed paths with the New Believers (referenced in Chapters 23 and 32), whose 4 editions of New Testament translations were published from 1826–1835);[22] and Noah Webster, famous for compiling the dictionary, who revised and published the entire Bible in 1833[23] (mainly correcting the grammar from the King James Version while deleting passages "offensive to women," otherwise keeping the text intact). Other New Testament versions were re-created by John Palfrey,[24] Thomas Belsham,[25] Abner Kneeland,[26] and David Bernard,[27] who rewrote according to their take on Christian theology, with no claim to revelation. And there were other translations—22 total during Joseph's lifetime and 75 during his century of the 1800s. In all, since the 1611 King James Bible, about 322 English translations of the Bible have been published.[28]

But all these versions were made by men making corrections based on best guesses, rewriting for clarity to make it more accessible for general readability or to promote their specific theological points of view.

Even the King James Version was written with a point of view—to support the doctrine of the Church of England. In doing so, while keeping much of the inspiration contained in it, its translators made some glaring mistakes. For example, they misdefined the Greek verb *bapt'ze*, which means to "immerse," because the correct definition would have rendered the church's practice of baptizing by sprinkling an embarrassing inconsistency with the Bible—so they made up an English word, "baptize," which meant nothing, only what the Church defined it to mean—as a practice of sprinkling.[29]

They did the same with the New Testament original Greek word, *ep'skopos*, which means "overseer" and "presiding officer," which the original, humble leaders of New Testament congregations were. However, the King James translators changed it to "bishop," which signified just the opposite—the powerful, wealthy, hard-nosed rulers of the Church of England,[30] who whipped, pilloried, and tortured dissidents, while subjugating the peasants with an iron fist. (Joseph Smith's own ancestor, John Lathrop, suffered abuses from a bishop, splitting his family apart and tossing him in prison before exiling him to America for his independent religious beliefs.)[31] (See this endnote for details about his tormentor.)

The King James translators misused another word, *repent*, following the Catholic definition rather than the true meaning—of "reform," "turn around," or "change one's heart," which the Greek and Hebrew words meant.[32] The result is that the King James translation of the Bible in numerous instances speaks of God repenting, as though He had done something wrong, which is not only highly illogical but rather stupid. Joseph Smith, in his revision or "translation" of the Bible, consistently corrected these passages.

Some of the other 19th-century English translators, mentioned above, were spot-on in their translations when it came to correcting the above terms, all of which Joseph Smith got right.

But other translators were incorrect when they tried to redefine Greek words to fit their dogmas.

Previous to this, in the 1500s, doctrines were taught by the church that were so far removed from the Bible that it incited a revolution of religious thought, called the *Reformation*. (See Appendix R, "Launching the Reformation: Prelude to the Restoration" for more details.) This also resulted in courageous attempts to translate and print new and better Bible versions for the Reformation. (See Appendix T: "English Bibles that Shook the World.") In the forefront of the Reformation was the inspiring priest-turned-Protestant, Martin Luther. (For a review of his courageous life, see Appendix R, "Launching the Reformation: Prelude to the Restoration.")

As Charles Dickens had summarized the landscape of *A Tale of Two Cities* with an iconic opening line, so did the Reformation define the landscape of religious thought, with Reformers paying the price—many being hunted and killed.[33] But in the process they printed and made available more accurate versions of the Bible—all from both Erasmus's work and the invention of the printing press, making it affordable to Everyman, the common folk, giving them access to the Old Testament prophets, the New Testament Apostles, and the basic teachings of Jesus Christ . . . but with caveats, as the "plain and precious things" were still missing. Thus, the Reformation was simultaneously the best of times and the worst of times.[34]

Such was the vista on an improved but still spiritually struggling planet when Joseph Smith was born.

His mission, in part, was to bring back all the original material missing from the Bible, according to the New Believers, and take the heaven-inspired Reformation to the next step—the full *Restoration*, complete with priesthood authority to act in God's name again after 17 centuries, since the original church and priesthood had dissipated into the Dark Ages. (See Appendix U, "Christianity after Christ: 17 Centuries of Conflict.")

Because the Reformation had been a giant leap forward in preparing the world for the Restoration, Latter-day Saints honor the Great Reformers.

(Four decades after this event of Joseph revising the Bible, a successor of his, Wilford Woodruff, would record in his journal a vision he received in the St. George, Utah, temple of the Great Reformers and other great men and women requesting the fullness of the priesthood ordinances to be performed for them. The men included Martin Luther and John Wesley, plus 54 of the 56 signers of the Declaration of Independence, as well as George Washington and most U. S. presidents until then, including Abraham Lincoln. All these men had great integrity, and most sacrificed all they had while in earth life.[35]

Joseph's calling included adding more scripture to clarify and simplify the gospel of Jesus Christ, via the *Book of Mormon*, while correctly revising the Holy Bible.

For Joseph's Bible revisions, his followers believe Joseph worked in a different—and far more accurate—sphere than the translators of all previous Bibles.

They believe Joseph went through the entire text, relying solely on divine inspiration.

In this manner he made both simple word corrections and extensive sentence rewrites and, in some cases, long rewrites.[36]

While Joseph's work is termed the *Joseph Smith Translation* (JST), he did not actually translate anything—he did not go from one language to another or use original manuscripts—rather, he revised the Bible through revelation, and he used no tools such as a seer stone (with which he had translated the *Book of Mormon*). Now, he simply used a large edition of the King James Version.

From what is printed in the flyleaf of the copy he used, we know it was purchased from the Egbert B. Grandin Bookstore in Palmyra (which would sell his *Book of Mormon*). According to researcher Kent P. Jackson, Oliver Cowdery bought the Bible that Joseph and Oliver used.[37]

The date of purchase was October 8, 1829, in which the sum of $3.75 was paid—exactly 3 times what Joseph would sell his *Book of Mormon* for. That $3.75 price calculates to $173.97 in today's currency. The book was 9 by 11 inches and was 2 inches thick, printed in 1828 by H. and E. Phinney company of

Cooperstown, New York. It included the Old Testament, the Apocrypha, and the New Testament.

Joseph made check marks in it, while dictating the changes to 6 successive scribes who recorded them from 1830–1833 in a number of manuscripts, to the tune of 447 manuscript pages on large 8 × 14 inch sheets. Joseph himself would write only 4 of these pages and make corrections on just 7 others.[38] The rest of the writing came through his scribes.[39]

Genesis was the first thing he had started revising the previous month (June 1830). That section alone would take 8 months of the project's 3 years to complete. (He would finish the entire preliminary draft on July 2, 1833.[40] On that day he would write, "We are exceedingly fatigued, owing to a great press of business. We this day finished the translating of the Scriptures, for which we returned gratitude to our Heavenly Father."[41])

According to analysts, "Joseph did not, however, make every change in the King James Version that could have been made." W. Jeffrey Marsh and Thomas E. Sherry write, "His sermons from 1833 to 1844 are filled with numerous interpretations about Bible verses not found in the JST. . . . His wife, Emma, mentioned that Joseph wanted to go through the manuscript one more time and then have it printed."[42]

Nevertheless, as scholar Kent P. Jackson states, Joseph worked on it "until he felt that the translation was as the Lord wanted it to be."[43] Sherry and Marsh agree. "Although the Prophet could have done more, he was divinely directed to publish the translation as it stood." (See D&C 42:56–58)[44]

But despite Joseph's tireless attempts to raise money for its printing and despite the First Presidency's multiple pleadings to the New Believers to provide needed funds to print the Bible in full—and immediately[45]—this Bible never was printed in his lifetime.

Without Joseph's corrections, this is the condition of the King James Version, as it has stood for 5 centuries, writes believing, insightful Bible scholar, Robert J. Matthews: the "text may be generally correct in itself, but many important doctrinal items (resulting from the loss of a single word, a verse, a longer passage, or even whole books in some instances) are now missing."[46]

In regards to entire books missing, references are made within the Bible itself to 14 specific, lost books, with another 3 that are either lost or designated by a different title.[47] (See Appendix V: "The Missing Books of the Bible" for a list of books missing from all Bible versions, including the King James Version.)

Joseph's corrections meanwhile spanned across 51 of the 66 books of the Bible, while he rejected the Song of Solomon for not being inspired scripture.

The 10.96% of the Bible verses Joseph actually revised consisted of 3,410 verses out of the King James Version's 31,102.

The version used today by the Church of Jesus Christ of Latter-day Saints (LDS) is the standard, original King James Version with about 600 of Joseph's revised verses in footnotes plus another 200 in an appendix for the longest verses.[48]

Combined, they consist of approximately 800 of his most important corrected verses, which were first added to the 1979 edition of their King James Bible and all editions since.[49]

Additionally there are 411 verses Joseph revised from the Bible that are neither footnotes nor appendix. These verses were transferred in 1851 to that separate book of scripture called the *Pearl of Great Price*. This book was canonized 3 decades later in 1880, and consists of material apparently cut by ancient scribes from the original book of Genesis in the Old Testament (or was simply *added revelation* from the Lord to Joseph regarding the first few chapters of Genesis), as well as a revised chapter in Matthew of the New Testament. These 411 verses were significant in replacing the more important "plain and precious things" that had been removed.[50]

(Also, in all LDS editions of the King James Bible since 1979 is a 300+ page Topical Guide containing the largest selection of references about Jesus Christ ever published in any Bible.)[51]

Aside from Joseph's revision, his early followers and the LDS Church today place strong emphasis on the King James Version for English readers. According to the First Presidency of the LDS Church in an official statement of August 1992:

"While other Bible versions may be easier to read than the King James Version, in doctrinal matters latter-day revelation supports the King James Version in preference to other English translations."[52]

However, even more accurate than that is Martin Luther's German translation of the Bible, which Latter-day Saints in Germany use today. Of this translation Joseph said: "[I] find it to be the most [nearly] correct translation, and to correspond nearest to the revelations which God has given to me for the past fourteen years."[53]

Joseph's followers and family perceived his unpublished Bible manuscripts as treasure. An anecdotal gem comes from a letter Emma wrote to her son Joseph III in 1867 after giving him the manuscripts: "Now as it regards the [manuscripts] of the new translation, if you wish to keep them you may do so, but if not I would like to have them. I have often thought the reason why our house did not burn down when it has been so often on fire was because of them, and I still feel there is a sacredness attached to them."[54]

The original 477 page manuscript and the marked-up large Bible were later given by Joseph's wife, Emma, to the Reorganized Church of Jesus Christ of Latter-day Saints in 1866.

And in 1867 the revised Bible was finally published by them.[55]

In regards to these manuscript pages, Kent P. Jackson, professor of ancient scripture at Brigham Young University and an editor of Joseph's New Translation texts for over 6 years, states:

"Today, they are carefully preserved in the Library-Archives of the Community of Christ in Independence, Missouri.

"None of those who assisted the Prophet as scribes came west with the Saints, and so from the time of his death, contact between the Church of Jesus Christ of Latter-day Saints and the Bible translation was for the most part severed.

"It was not until the 1960s that the contact was reestablished, when Brigham Young University professor Robert J. Matthews undertook the first serious and systematic study of the original manuscripts."[56]

In another report Peterson writes, "More recent efforts by others, including recent scholarly publications on the JST, build on the foundation established by Professor Matthews. Now, thanks to the cooperation of the Community of Christ in making possible the publication of the manuscripts, the texts are available for continued research and exploration."[57]

Jackson concludes, "In November 2004 the Religious Studies Center at Brigham Young University published a facsimile transcription of all the original manuscripts of the Joseph Smith Translation of the Bible."[58] LDS scholars have pored over them, even magnifying them on large computer screens to analyze the work of Joseph's scribes—to determine for example where one left off and another began.

Finally, there was Joseph's concern with that mysterious section of the Bible termed *Apocrypha.*

This was the section of 14 books typically inserted between the Old and New Testaments in older Protestant Bibles but which is not seen today by Protestants except in handed-down family Bibles. This section, however, is still contained in Catholic Bibles, where it is integrated right in the Old Testament. But the Apocrypha was officially removed by Protestants from all editions of the King James Bible in 1885 after 274 years of being in it, as well as from other Protestant Bibles that had been publishing it for up to 360 years, deleted perhaps because of a notion that it is a Roman Catholic scripture. No mainline Protestant churches have ever issued an official declaration about it or why it was removed.[59]

Joseph received a revelation about this section: "Verily, thus saith the Lord unto you concerning the Apocrypha—there are many things contained therein that are true, and it is mostly translated correctly. There are many things contained therein that are not true, which are interpolations by the hands of men."[60]

(For more details on this unusual scriptural section see Appendix W: "Notes on the Apocrypha.")

Today the Church of Jesus Christ of Latter-day Saints has 4 canonized "Standard Works"—the Holy Bible (King James Version, with Joseph's revisions in footnotes and appendix), the *Book of Mormon* (after numerous editions that include small corrections), the Doctrine & Covenants (mostly Joseph's revelations), and the *Pearl of Great Price* (5 short sections, the lengthiest of which comes from Joseph's revision of the book of Genesis).

The Community of Christ accepts the JST of the Bible and 2 versions of the *Book of Mormon*—the Authorized Edition (based on the printer's copy of the 1830 First Edition combined with the 1837 Second Edition) and a Revised Authorized Edition (in more modern language)—plus their own *Doctrine and Covenants* (with some different sections than in the LDS version).


Returning to our narrative of Joseph's life, it is still early July 1830. Joseph and Oliver had just escaped a mob at Colesville, New York, and, while they were now safely back in Harmony, Pennsylvania, they began compiling all his revelations and simultaneously launching their second month of revising the Bible.

Meanwhile, during the previous week, Joseph's brother had had a remarkable experience up in New York state. "On the 30th of June [1830]," writes Lucy, "Samuel started on the mission to which he had been set apart by Joseph, and in traveling 25 miles, which was his first day's journey, he stopped at a number of places in order to sell his books, but was turned out of doors as he declared his principles. When evening came on, he was faint and almost discouraged, but coming to an inn, which was surrounded with every appearance of plenty, he called to see if the landlord would buy one of his books. On going in, Samuel inquired of him if he did not wish to purchase a history of the origin of the Indians.

"'I do not know,' replied the host. 'How did you get hold of it?'

"'It was translated,' rejoined Samuel, 'by my brother from some gold plates that he found buried in the earth.'

"'You d————— liar!' cried the landlord. 'Get out of my home—you shan't stay one minute with your books.'

"Samuel was sick at heart, for this was the fifth time he had been turned out of doors that day. He left the house and traveled a short distance and washed his feet in a small brook as a testimony against the man. He then proceeded five miles further on his journey, and seeing an apple tree a short distance from the road, he concluded to pass the night under it; and here he lay all night upon the cold, damp ground.

"In the morning he arose from his comfortless bed and, observing a small cottage at no great distance, he drew near, hoping to get a little refreshment. The only inmate was a widow who seemed very poor. He asked her for food, relating the story of his former treatment. She prepared him some victuals and, after eating, he explained to her the history of the *Book of Mormon*. She listened attentively and believed all that he told her. But in consequence of her poverty, she was unable to purchase one of the books. He presented her with one and proceeded to Bloomington, which was eight miles further."[61]

Things changed at Bloomington. A Methodist preacher, John P. Greene, was remarkably accommodating and told Samuel he would take a "subscription paper" on his next circuit. This meant he would assist Samuel by asking people to sign a paper if they wanted to buy the book on Samuel's next trip to the village. Greene actually volunteered to help in this way, even though he personally thought the book was a "nonsensical fable."[62]

Samuel left one of his books with him and returned home.

"At the time appointed, Samuel started again for the Reverend John P. Greene's in order to learn the success which this gentleman had met with in finding sale for the *Book of Mormon*."

Lucy writes that she and her husband accompanied Samuel. They passed the tavern "where Samuel was so abusively treated a fortnight previous. But just before we came to the house, a sign of smallpox intercepted us." They asked a stranger "to what extent this disease prevailed. He answered that the tavern keeper and two of his family had died with it not long since, but he did not know that anyone else had caught the distemper and that it was brought into the neighborhood by a traveler who stopped at the tavern overnight." She opines that "some individuals . . . would . . . sacrifice their soul's salvation rather than give a saint of God a meal of victuals.'

After citing a biblical passage related to such incidents, she continues: "We arrived at Esquire Beaman's In Livonia that night. The next morning Samuel took the road to Mr. Greene's and, finding that he had made no sale of the books, we returned home the following day."[63] The astonishing results of this apparently unsuccessful, if not unimportant, mission would only reveal themselves later (see Chapter 30).

Next, 21 people from one family connection joined and were the core of one entire branch of the church—the Colesville Branch. These were from the marriage of Joseph Knight Sr. and his wife, Polly Peck Knight. Immediate and extended family members were joining—cousins, in-laws, aunts, and uncles.

Two main groups were forming now—those around the Whitmers in Fayette and those around the Knights in Colesville.

But Samuel's unknown coup at Bloomington was just beginning to build steam.

Three months passed. It was now August 1830.

Emma's trials were intense. She had faced life alone most of these last 3 months. Joseph was often gone, getting the *Book of Mormon* published and organizing the church. Sometimes she traveled with him, but additional trials would come her way even when keeping his company. Traveling with him to Colesville on her most recent trip, she had witnessed his 2 arrests, his abuse by one of the constables, and his outrageous court assaults, his escape, and being pursued by ruffians. She had also endured the trial of no steady income from him. Her first major test had been 2 years earlier when her firstborn son had died.

While overall a strong and faithful woman, she complained here and there. Joseph received a revelation for her about complaining, which she accepted, admonishing her: "Murmur [complain] not because of the things which thou has not seen."[64] The revelation also directed her to be a comfort to her husband, "with consoling words in the spirit of meekness,"[65] and to continue as his scribe.[66] (In this capacity, it was likely for revelations and various other documents with which Joseph needed assistance.) She was also commanded to "expound the scriptures and to exhort the church,"[67] as well as "to make a selection of sacred hymns"[68] (which she would in fact complete in 1835, with the first published hymnal) for use in church meetings.

She was also told "thy time shall be given to writing and to learning much."[69] She would accomplish that skillfully, evidenced by letters and legal arguments to the governor of Illinois. The revelation also told her to "lay aside the things of this world and seek for the things of a better,"[70] leading one to believe she either worried about or criticized Joseph for not being a better provider. She was indeed attached to her later property, which would become a crushing blow to Joseph, seeing her choosing that property over accompanying him to safety.

She was further told that Joseph would support her from the church's coffers and that she was an "elect lady,"[71] but was warned, "Cleave unto the covenants which thou hast made,"[72] and "beware of pride."[73] She apparently accepted the revelation, as she agreed to be confirmed into the church not much later in her home in the presence of several friends. (Emma and others were confirmed months after their baptisms.) One of these friends to later be confirmed was John Whitmer, now living with them and assisting Joseph in copying and sorting revelations. The other friends present were Newel and Sally Knight, who had traveled to Harmony for a visit.

Before her confirmation, Joseph received an unusual warning. Newel Knight reports:

"As neither Emma, the wife of Joseph Smith, nor my wife had been confirmed, we concluded to attend to that holy ordinance at this time and also to partake of the sacrament before we should leave for home.

"In order to prepare for this, Brother Joseph set out to procure some wine for the occasion. But he had gone only a short distance, when he was met by a heavenly messenger who informed him that it did not matter what the Saints ate and drank when they partook of the sacrament, but that they should not purchase wine or strong drink from their enemies."[74] Apparently it was for their protection so they would not be poisoned. Then he was given the solution: to only use wine freshly produced by themselves.

So the group made their own wine and partook of the sacrament, after which both Emma and Sally were confirmed in the church.[75]

Meanwhile, in New York, Joseph's father and brothers went out on missions to teach and baptize. They literally went without purse or scrip—poor as church mice. In all, 16 missionaries went the first year, and over triple that—58—the next.[76]

Still August 1830:

Joseph's father and brother Don Carlos, age 14, were sent on one of the first missions—to northern New York state and Canada—and would experience one of the most heartbreaking episodes of life in Joseph's family. This would enable Joseph to not merely observe the emotional distress of new converts, but to feel them firsthand—especially his beloved father's pain . . .

On the journey of Joseph's father and youngest brother, the two stopped at Joseph senior's brothers and sisters at St. Lawrence County.

All accepted or would soon accept the restored gospel except one sister, Susanna, and one brother, Jesse, who now threatened to throw them out of his house. (Another brother, John Smith, wrote of their aggressive sibling: "We had always been accustomed to being treated with much harshness by our brother.")[1]

John Smith recounts Jesse's threat: "If you say another word about that *Book of Mormon*, you shall not stay a minute longer in my house, and if I can't get you out any other way, I will hew you down with my broad axe."[2]

The next day Joseph senior visited his parents. His brother John recounts the scene, as the visit took place at another brother's home, that of Silas Smith:

"They were overjoyed to see Joseph, for he had been absent from them so long that they had been fearful of never beholding his face again in the flesh.

"After the usual salutations, inquiries, and explanations, the subject of the *Book of Mormon* was introduced."[3]

"Father received with gladness that which Joseph communicated and remarked that he had always expected that something would appear to make known the true gospel.

"In a few minutes brother Jesse came in and, on hearing that the subject of our conversation was the *Book of Mormon*, his wrath rose as high as it did the night before.

"'My father's mind,' said Jesse, 'is weak, and I will not have it corrupted with such blasphemous stuff, so just shut up your heads!'

"Brother Joseph reasoned mildly with him, but to no purpose.

"Brother Silas then said, 'Jesse, our brother has come to make us a visit, and I am glad to see him and am willing he should talk as he pleases in my house.'

"Jesse replied in so insulting a manner and continued to talk so abusively that Silas was under the necessity of requesting him to leave the house.

"After this, brother Joseph proceeded in conversation, and Father seemed to be pleased with every word which he said. But I must confess that I was too pious, at that time, to believe one word of it.

"I returned home the next day, leaving Joseph with my father. Soon afterward Jesse came to my house and informed me that all my brothers were coming to make me a visit. 'And as true as you live,' said he, 'they all believe that cursed Mormon book, every word of it, and they are setting a trap for you to make you believe it.'" John sarcastically thanked him, but "told him that I considered myself amply able to judge for myself in matters of religion.

"'I know,' he replied, 'that you are a pretty good judge of such things, but I tell you that they are as wary as the devil.'"

Jesse then devised a plot to protect their sister and sister-in-law, in order to "bar their minds against Joseph's influence."

So they visited their other family members and warned them about Joseph.

"My brothers arrived according to previous arrangement, and Jesse, who came also, was very careful to hear every word which passed among us and would not allow one word to be said about the *Book of Mormon*." His brother Asael was already convinced of Joseph's message and wanted John to hear it as well, so he "took me aside and said, 'Now, John, I want you to have some conversation with Joseph, but if you do, you must cheat it out of Jesse. And if you wish, I can work the card for you.'" In other words, they would sneak around the tyrannical brother.

They did so that night. Asael took some family members away in his carriage, while Silas took the rest.

Asael devised a plan for John to bring out a horse for Joseph to ride. "'But when we are out of sight,'" said Asael to John, "'take the horse back to the stable again and keep Joseph overnight.'

"I did as Asael advised," said John, "and, that evening, Joseph explained to me the principles of Mormonism, the truth of which I have never since denied.

"The next morning we (Joseph and myself) went to our sisters, where we met our brothers, who censured me very sharply for keeping Joseph overnight—Jesse, because he was really displeased; the others, to make a show of disappointment."

When Joseph senior and his son Samuel were about to return home that night, says John, "Joseph gave Jesse his hand in a pleasant, affectionate manner and said, 'Farewell, Brother Jesse!'

"'Farewell, Joe, forever,' replied Jesse, in a surly tone.

"'I am afraid,' returned Joseph in a kind but solemn manner, 'it will be forever, unless you repent.'

"This was too much for even Jesse's obdurate heart. He melted into tears. However, he made no reply, nor ever mentioned the circumstance afterwards."[4]

This dramatic, August 1830 event would leave an indelible mark on young Joseph's heart, seeing the unsolvable conflict among his father, aunts, and uncles, and he would feel compassion for thousands who would experience similar familial conflicts.

Meanwhile, his grandfather would never be baptized, but firmly believed.[5]

(Six years later, Joseph senior would journey to his family again. On that trip, Jesse would go so far as to swear out a complaint against Joseph senior because of his religion, and have the authorities take his horse and wagon. Silas would step in and pay $50 [$1,842 in today's money] so that their brother, Joseph senior, could return home.)[6]

It was this same Jesse, the antagonistic uncle of Joseph Jr., whom young Joseph had stayed with when visiting Salem to recover from his leg operation at about age 8. Nothing is known of this relationship, but Hyrum had made a favorable impression upon this uncle in earlier years. Jesse would later write him, addressing Hyrum as "once as I thought my promising nephew," then chastising him for being part of "a great wickedness, unpardonable."[7]

As Joseph's father had this dramatic visit with his family in St. Lawrence County, Joseph himself decided to travel through the hotbed of his enemies. He felt the need to visit church members in Colesville.

So he planned a visit the second half of August 1830, taking 3 others—his brother Hyrum, David and John Whitmer—and all knew they were risking their lives.

Before leaving they held a prayer for protection. In this they were so specific that they actually asked God to "blind the eyes" of their enemies so they would not be recognized or attacked.[8]

At Colesville, they approached Newel Knight's home. Soon they came upon a large crew of road workers, several of whom were avowed enemies.

Joseph records, "They looked in earnest at us but, not knowing us, we passed on without interruption."[9]

Joseph's group held its meeting that night, having the sacrament and a "happy meeting,"[10]

The next morning they started for home.[11]

Arriving at Harmony, however, Joseph and Emma found life in a turmoil. Despite his high ecclesiastical calling, Joseph knew he was responsible for supporting himself, and the reason was quite plain: a revelation told him to sow his fields.[12] And he obeyed.

But, ironically, plans changed fast. Joseph states:

"A spirit of persecution began again to manifest itself against us in the neighborhood where I now resided, which was commenced by a man of the Methodist persuasion, who professed to be a minister of God. This man had learned that my father-in-law and his family had promised us protection, and were friendly, and inquiring into the work; and knowing that if he could get him turned against me, my friends in that place would be but few. [So] he visited my father-in-law and told him falsehoods concerning me of the most shameful nature, which turned the old gentleman and his family so much against us that they would no longer promise us protection nor believe our doctrines.[13]

Without Isaac's protection, Joseph was a sitting duck. This rumormonger may well have been that same character plaguing them earlier—Methodist leader Nathaniel G. Lewis, Emma's uncle on her mother's side.

At one point, in a milder form of teasing, Lewis inquired if the seer stone could be used by any person to translate. Joseph's answer was yes, so Lewis asked to borrow it.[14]

Joseph was not pleased by this mockery, and likely let it go, but the combined ridicule and harassment from others in the village began to wear on him.[15]

Then the persecutions became hotter. And with his in-laws now unwilling to protect him, he and Emma were literally forced out of Harmony.

For most of the previous $2\frac{2}{3}$ years it had been a decent shelter for them, despite its drawbacks and occasional dangers.[16] Before leaving, however, Joseph felt obligated to pay off her father for the 13 acres he had bought from him. So in late August 1830 he borrowed money from a friend, determined to keep his end of the bargain.[17]

Then another reason for leaving launched itself at Joseph: problems were erupting 28 miles north—problems he had never expected to see. The brand of problems that would vex him the rest of his life.

U P the road in Fayette, New York, the Whitmers and Oliver Cowdery were becoming theological loose cannons. They actually had begun thinking they should be able to correct Joseph's revelations—even without his direction—as well as receive revelations for the entire church.

Oliver was more literate and educated than his comparatively unschooled counterpart. So he criticized a written revelation contained in the Articles and Covenants.

He then decided to edit it. Even change its wording.[1]

Joseph shot back a letter demanding to know "by what authority he took upon him to command me to alter or erase, to add to or diminish from a revelation or commandment from Almighty God?"[2]

But Joseph knew there were deeper undercurrents. He realized Oliver had sent him the letter from the Whitmer farm in Fayette where he was staying. So it was clear that Oliver could be—and actually was—stirring up the pot and consequently creating trouble among the Whitmers. Needing to stop the problem in its tracks, Joseph realized he simply had to go north—another reason to move out of Harmony.

So he and Emma packed up to leave once and for all the last week of August 1830.

Trouble is, Joseph had not even a horse to his name, much less a wagon. But Newel Knight came to the rescue once again.[3]

Newel had gotten wind of the persecutions at Harmony and, on his own accord, had ridden off to Harmony to help them any way he could.[4]

With Knight's help, Joseph locked up his Harmony home with furniture in it, loaded up Knights' wagon, and bade farewell to his in-laws, never again to live near them.

Immediately he raced off to Fayette to quell the uprising.

When Joseph arrived at the Whitmer home, he found that Oliver had convinced the entire clan to his way of thinking. Overlooked by historians is the sheer awkwardness of it all. The family dynamic Joseph had to deal with was this: he and Emma had the remarkably uncomfortable task of living in the same house with the Whitmers and Oliver—sleeping under the same roof and taking their meals at the same table, very possibly struggling with small talk—right where his fold was coming apart at the seams.

Undoubtedly it took an emotional toll on Joseph and Emma, being essentially homeless and once again dependent on others. But this time it was worse—staying with people ready to take over the church and oust him.

The others now in fact were apparently beginning to view Joseph as beneath them, thinking they had all the answers.

When Joseph and Emma arrived at the Whitmers, the family actually congratulated them for escaping, genuinely happy to see them.[5] But from there things went downhill fast.

Oliver was young and impetuous. He not only was smarter than Joseph, but likely felt he had to compete within the pecking order among the group of energetic 20-somethings who comprised the core of New Believers.

Especially, perhaps, for the attentions of one Elizabeth Ann Whitmer. She was now 17 months older than the first time he had ever seen her, when he stayed at her home on his way to meet Joseph the first time (and she was 15 months older since the last time they had seen each other, when Oliver and Joseph stayed at her home to finish the translation). She was slightly over 15½ years old now, and 15½ months away from their marriage.[6]

A year and a half before, when they had met, she was 14. Though awfully young by modern definitions, there may have been a spark of mutual interest, but by now it could have been full-blown. If so, it's not improbable for a young man running on testosterone and an ego to boost to prove his pecking order position to a young woman by standing up to the pack's leader—Joseph. While certainly a speculative scenario, it's not out of the realm of realistic possibility. Elizabeth Ann was the sister to all the boys that Oliver dealt with daily, and at the very least he wanted their respect. Especially since he lived with the family now.

In some measure, one of the Whitmer boys, John, must have already looked up to him, since Oliver was solidly on the ground floor of the Restoration, and John seemed the most dedicated of the Whitmers at this time. It would only have been natural for Oliver to have wanted the other brothers to look up to him as well.

Oliver, of course, may not have had the slightest interest in Elizabeth Ann during this rebellion against Joseph, and perhaps felt no need to garner anyone's respect. Perhaps he was a perfectly secure young man, on solid footing with his place in life and content with his spot on the totem among the Whitmer family and Joseph.

In any case, when Joseph arrived in Fayette, he saw the Whitmers had, as he feared, sided with Oliver in this theological insurrection.

Joseph cornered Oliver and jumped in his face.

He challenged him on how he suddenly had the audacity, much less the authority, to change wording to a revelation.[7] The Whitneys backed up Oliver to a man.

As Joseph heard them out, the Whitmers and Oliver became impassioned with their argument, raising their voices and demanding Joseph see things their way.

Joseph writes how difficult it was to reason with them. It was "with great difficulty and much labor that I prevailed with any of them to reason calmly on the subject."[8]

He finally persuaded Christian Whitmer to his side. Then, with Christian's help, he persuaded the rest of the Whitmer clan—and Oliver himself—to his viewpoint. When push came to shove, Oliver swallowed his pride and acquiesced.[9]

Oliver's soul knew truth when he saw it, and he backed down. This time.[10]


Within days Joseph learned he had another battle on his hands: Hiram Page was using a stone to receive revelations about church government!

Worse, he was presenting them to church members, telling them how to run things.

Even worse, Page was married to the sister of the Whitmer brothers, and had them all convinced the revelations were from God.

Oliver included.[11]

If ever Joseph needed a moment to shake his head in wonder, it was now.

Page had collected a large number of "revelations"—so many, in fact, that they were recorded on "a roll of paper," states Newel Knight.[12]

Not just the Whitmers and Oliver were affected, says Newel, but "many in the church were led astray by them."[13]

Something had to be done. Joseph knew the revelations were false. But he had no idea what to do about it. When Newel came to see him in September before the second general conference, he found Joseph "in great distress of mind." So they both knelt in prayer and asked for help. Sharing the room with him, Newel saw firsthand how Joseph spent "the greater part of the night" praying about the problem.[14]

Several days later, just before conference, Joseph received a revelation. It was the answer. It simply said no one was to receive revelations for the entire church "excepting Joseph Smith, Jun., for he receiveth them even as Moses."[15]

In the same revelation Joseph learned that Page had actually been deceived by Satan, and that the revelations he had written with the stone's help were inspired from the dark side.[16] They were in fact "entirely at variance with the order of God's house, as laid down in the New Testament, as well as in our late revelations."[17]

This was powerful information Joseph needed to share. But he would wait until the right moment. Then, likely to his surprise, he received a revelation for Oliver that, rather than scolding him, gave Oliver a positive directive.[18] This, too, Joseph would wait till the right time before presenting it. And in this revelation, Oliver was compared with Aaron of the Old Testament, the assistant to and chief spokesman for Moses. Also, Oliver was told "to declare faithfully" the revelations.[19] Further, he was directed not to "command him who is at thy head and at the head of the church."[20]

But when should Joseph share these revelations? He would ponder the timing.

Meanwhile, the Articles and Covenants contained a growing body of revelations and also now gave structure—"For all things must be done in order, and by common consent in the church."[21] Thus, no one could any more make claims that their revelations were for all others in the church—it simply wasn't God's way. Only the president could.

There would be splinter groups over the decades ahead, but the church membership in general would stay the course, adhering to this directive.

Then as now, Latter-day Saints believe in individual revelation—but revelation for one's stewardship or assignment only (such as for one's own family, or for his designated group within the church—i.e., a bishop for his congregation or a youth leader for his or her youth group). But for revelations that affect the whole church, only the prophet could or can receive those revelations, according to Latter-day Saint belief. This incident was the first to affect this doctrine.

Ironically, these days with trusted friends Oliver, David Whitmer, and Hiram Page were the first threats to the order of the fledgling new church. And to Joseph's chagrin, they were not backing down.

But he had not yet told anyone of his new revelation. He decided that should happen at general conference on September 26, just days away. And, no doubt, he wondered how it would all go down.

Amazingly, before conference, David Whitmer led them in another dissension.

This was the background:

Joseph had stopped using his seer stone after completing the *Book of Mormon*, and actually gave it away to Oliver.

This one action caused David Whitmer to complain bitterly. He said he could only believe in revelations that Joseph received through a seer stone,[22] which meant, he said, only the revelations through June 1829—when Joseph last used the stone 14 months earlier.

From that point to the present, he could only believe some of Joseph's revelations.

So David drew a line in the sand: he wanted someone—anyone—to be using a stone to receive revelations. And he believed that man may as well be Hiram Page,[23] his brother-in-law, who happened to have a stone. Joseph knew he no longer needed the stone, but when the time was right, he would tell them the truth: they should rely on the Holy Ghost.

David never seemed to grasp this idea fully. And it became the first seed of "apostasy" for him that would later grow and flourish, leading him down deeper paths.

These rifts were the beginning of a new form of opposition Joseph would face—and they would add to the arrests and court battles already beginning. Like his previous challenges, this type would trouble him the remainder of his days: talented, capable, but very proud close associates would question him, would think they could lead better than he, and would eventually oppose him.

But for now, Joseph felt he should not jump into the fray with the family. So he held his peace and waited until later, when he could stand in a formal meeting where the Spirit of God would be strongly present, to come down harder. All in all, Joseph felt he was the shepherd of the new flock, and, as such, was determined to protect it.

But increasing drama ensued when the church's second general conference started on September 26, 1830. With 62 members now in their ranks, Joseph found himself at the center of the expected firestorm.

OLIVER stood at general conference and launched his public vitriolic opposition: he claimed Joseph could not receive commandments for the entire church. He maintained that others, like Hiram Page, had a place in the church because their revelations were just as valid.

Joseph faced it in a rather surprising way: with complete calmness he merely stood, looked over the congregation, and told everyone that Page's revelations were, quite simply, false.

Page and his followers were stunned, stubborn, and would not back down.

But Joseph was not about to back down either. Still, brilliantly, he made only one counterpunch, yet in the same move avoided contention: he only asked for a vote of confidence from the congregation. He also boldly directed Oliver to tell Page he had been deceived. It was Joseph's brilliant moment—but a great gamble—as it could have backfired and divided the church.

But it worked. Calmness spread over the congregation. Joseph proclaimed his new revelation, and even Hiram Page agreed the stone's revelations were false.[1] Then, he and everyone else sustained Joseph as leader and prophet.

Knight summarizes the denouement: "After much labor with these brethren, they were convinced of their error."[2]

Oliver, hearing the revelation about him, also stepped in line.

The remainder of the 3-day conference was smooth sailing. Newel Knight states that God gave Joseph great wisdom and power, and "none who saw him administer righteousness under such trying circumstances could doubt that the Lord was with him."[3]

At this September 1830 conference a total of 3 revelations came forth. Members were confirmed, men were given the priesthood, and church business was conducted. But the most dramatic development of all was the calling of 4 new, bright young missionaries that would spin the church in a whole new direction . . .

Days after general conference Joseph received another revelation, one that would require the first major sacrifice of the new church: he announced it would soon be time for "the gathering."[4] This was an exciting doctrine for some, but terrifying for others.

It meant most or all the members would settle some place together, hopefully at a blessed spot. But as to where, they did not know. After Joseph told them about it, they wondered where they would in fact live next. New York? New England, perhaps. Possibly across the entire country. Many felt unsettled through the fall of 1830.

Concurrent with Joseph's dealing with September's dissonance in Fayette, he and Emma stayed not only at the Whitmers' but visited his own family in Manchester.[5]

While in Manchester, Joseph "received a commandment by revelation" to move his family to Waterloo, New York.[6]

This revelation may have caught them off guard—it said his brother Hyrum and his father were in danger.[7]

Joseph directed Hyrum's family to Colesville and ordered his father to Waterloo immediately, ahead of his family, where "he should find favor in the eyes of the people."[8]

Parenthetically, Hyrum and his wife Jerusha had now been married almost 4 years and had moved in with Newel and Sally Knight at Colesville. From there, Hyrum set out on a mission and proclaimed the gospel almost full time, teaching nearby villagers, where he made several converts.

But their father procrastinated—and paid the price. A dear one.

After spending one night in Manchester with his family, Joseph Jr. moved to Macedon and preached there and at other villages[9]—Colesville, Waterloo, Palmyra, and Manchester.[10] He eventually sent for his goods in Pennsylvania and settled in Fayette,[11] back where he was having problems with the Whitmers and Oliver.

When Joseph received the revelation for his father to leave Manchester, the older gentleman balked. And this was the consequence:

A Quaker gentleman came knocking at the door demanding $14, saying he had bought a note from Joseph senior's creditor. Having less than half that to pay, Joseph senior offered him all the money he possessed, $6, with a promise to pay the rest later. Lucy even offered to pitch in her gold jewelry—but the man refused, saying that unless Joseph senior paid the entire sum immediately, he would go to debtor's prison. He did, however, offer Joseph senior a way out: if he would renounce the *Book of Mormon* and burn his copies, he would forgive Joseph senior the debt. Joseph senior refused, of course, so the constable, standing in the shadows, was given the go-ahead to haul him away. Before leaving, despite his being very ill and faint, they would not let him eat. They also disallowed Lucy time to get someone to accompany him, to help give support in his weakened condition from disease.

Lucy adds, "They drove off with my husband, leaving me alone with my little girl."[12]

More besides Joseph's family were being persecuted on religious grounds.

And the drama was just beginning . . . with the Joseph Smith clan right in the thick of it . . .

C H A P T E R 30

T HE next morning Lucy walked on foot several miles to get help. She needed a friend to urge the sheriff into allowing her sickened husband to be unlocked from his foul-smelling cell and taken into the jail yard for fresh air.[1]

In this state Lucy was especially vulnerable when the following happened:

An impertinent young man came to the door, representing a creditor and demanding immediate payment. She told him she would pay him the next day with corn and beans, which she did, procuring a driver to take it to him.[2]

Alone with her young daughter at home that night, she felt overwhelmed with worry.

"When the night closed in, the darkness was hideous; scarcely any object was discernible. I sat down and began to contemplate the situation of my family and myself.

"My husband, as affectionate a companion and tender father as ever blessed the confidence of a family, was an imprisoned debtor. . . .

"While I was thus meditating, a heavy rap at the door brought me suddenly to my feet. I bade the stranger enter." He demanded to know in a hurried manner where Hyrum was. She announced he was gone. He disbelieved her. A second man entered with a search warrant and told her if she would not surrender him, they would take all his belongings they could find.

"Finding some corn stored in the chamber above the room where Hyrum had lived, they declared their intention of taking it. . . .

"The foremost replied that it was wanted to settle a debt which Hyrum was owing to Dr. McIntyre. I told him that it was paid. He disputed my word and ordered his men to take the corn." (Families commonly stored corn to get them through the winter, just to survive, so it was far more important than even money.)

"As they were going upstairs, I looked out of the window. As far as I could see by the light of two candles and a pair of carriage lamps, the heads of men appeared in every direction, some on foot, some on horseback and the rest in wagons.

"I saw that there was no way but for me to sit quietly down and see my house pillaged . . . [by those] who were united in one purpose, namely, that of destroying us from the face of the earth.

"However, there was one resource, and to that I applied. I went aside and kneeled before the Lord and begged that he would not let my children fall into their hands, and that they might be satisfied with plunder without taking life.

"Just at this instant William bounded into the house. 'Mother,' he cried, 'in the name of God, what is this host of men doing here? Are they robbing or murdering? What are they about?'" (Even as a lad, William was bigger and more powerful than most adults. At this time, in August 1830 he was a month shy of 19½ years of age.)

"I told him, in short, that they had taken his father to prison and had now come after Hyrum. But not finding him, they were plundering the house. Hereupon William seized a large hand-spike, sprang upstairs and, in one instant, cleared the scoundrels out of the chamber. They scampered downstairs; he flew after them and, bounding into the very midst of the crowd, he brandished his handspike in every direction, exclaiming, '. . . I will be the death of every one of you.'

"The lights were immediately extinguished, yet he continued to harangue them boisterously until he discovered that his audience had left him. They seemed to believe what he said and fled in every direction, leaving us again to ourselves." Soon her daughter Sophronia, who was 2½ years older than Joseph, and her husband Calvin Stoddard arrived.

"He had been troubled about us all the afternoon. And finally, about the setting of the sun, he told Sophronia that he would even then start for her father's if she felt inclined to go with him.

"Within an hour after their arrival Samuel came. He was much fatigued, for he had traveled twenty-one miles after sunset. I told him our situation and that I wished him to go early the next morning to Canandaigua and procure his father's release from the dungeon.

"'Well, Mother,' said he, 'I am sick; fix me a bed, that I may lie down and rest myself, or I shall not be able to go, for I have taken a heavy cold, and my bones ache dreadfully.'

"However, by a little nursing and some rest, he was able to set off by sunrise."[3]

After arising, Samuel shot off to Canandaigua. He informed the jailor of his business, found his father starving, and went to get him food, then he stayed with him the entire month, all the while aching with a bad flu. His father had been starved 4 days in a literal dungeon of a cell and fed only a pint of watering broth. But because of his son's interference, his condition improved. He spent the remainder of the month in the cooper's shop of the prison yard.

Each Sunday, meanwhile, Joseph senior taught his fellow prisoners, converting 2 men whom he afterward baptized.[4]

Upon being released, Joseph's father and Samuel came home to Manchester, then moved to Waterloo "after much fatigue," says Lucy.[5]

Samuel presented the following report to Lucy about his mission, probably right after returning home sick, before heading to Canandaigua early the next morning to help his father at the jail. He made the same report to his father, most likely at the jail:

"When I arrived at Mr. Greene's," he said, "Mrs. Greene informed me that her husband was absent from home, that there was no prospect of selling my books and even the one which I had left with them, she expected I would have to take away, as Mr. Greene had no disposition to purchase it, although she had read it herself and was much pleased with it.

"I then talked with her a short time and, binding my knapsack upon my shoulders, rose to depart; but as I bade her farewell, it was impressed upon my mind to leave the book with her. I made her a present of it and told her that the Spirit forbade my taking it away.

"She burst into tears and requested me to pray with her. I did so and left my blessing upon the home, and she afterwards told me that she never saw a man that had such an appearance, nor ever heard such a prayer in her life.

"'My God,' said she, 'it seemed as though the very heavens were rent and the spirit of God was poured down upon us.'

"I afterwards explained to her the most profitable manner of reading the book which I had left with her, which was to ask God, when she read it, for a testimony of the truth of what she had read, and she would receive the Spirit of God, which would enable her to discern the things of God."[6]

When Mr. Greene returned home, his wife requested him to read the book[7] and said this about Samuel: "I do know that he would not tell an untruth for any inducement. I know he must be a good man, if there ever was one."[8]

At first her husband refused to read it, "but finally yielded to her persuasions and took the book," says Lucy.[9]

He did read it, prayed, and asked God if it was true. He received a testimony of it. They were both soon baptized and gave their copy to her brother, Phinehas Young, who, as a pastor, began preaching from it.

Phinehas then handed it to his brother, one Brigham Young, who also read it (and later believed, after a 2-year investigation of the church).

Brigham handed it to his sister, who not only believed it but got it into the hands of her son-in-law, Heber C. Kimball[10]—

who would later be a counselor to Brigham Young in the First Presidency of the church.

Brigham would also convince his brother Joseph Young to cease preaching Methodism and embrace the church.

Upon arriving at Waterloo, Joseph's parents and siblings would realize the wisdom of being directed there. They were welcomed with kindness by their new neighbors, and found the entire town to be a refreshing oasis. Finally they felt free from the angry, hostile communities dotting the region.

"Shortly after arriving there, we were made to realize that the hearts of the people were in the hands of the Lord," says Lucy, "for we had scarcely unpacked our goods, when one of our new neighbors, a Mr. Osgood, came in and invited us to drive our stock and teams to his barnyard and feed them from his barn, free of cost, until we could make further arrangements.

"Many of our neighbors came in and welcomed us to Waterloo. Among them was Mr. Hooper, a tavern keeper, whose wife came with him and brought us a present of some delicate eatables. Such manifestations of kindness as these were shown us from day to day during our continuance in the place. And they were duly appreciated, for we had experienced the opposite so severely that the least show of good feeling gave rise to the liveliest sensations of gratitude.

"Having settled ourselves in this place, we established the practice of spending the evenings in singing and praying.

"The neighbors soon became aware of this, and it caused our house to become a place of evening resort for some dozen or twenty persons. One evening, soon after we commenced singing, a couple of little boys came in, and one of them, stepping softly up to Samuel, whispered, 'Mr. Smith, won't you pray pretty soon? Our mother said we must be home by eight o'clock, and we would like to hear you pray before we go.'"

Samuel made certain it happened. "We closed the evening services with prayer in order that the little boys might be gratified," says Lucy. "After this they were never absent during our evening devotions while we remained in the neighborhood."[11]

Obviously the revelation to move proved to be a remarkable blessing to Joseph's family.

At general conference of September 1830, 4 young men had received a dynamic mandate from Joseph Smith, and in its execution it would parallel the Sons of Mosiah from the *Book of Mormon*—creating for the four an unforgettable, thrilling adventure.

But they would also face blistering weather, bigoted ministers, outrageous government agents, stubborn people to teach, and near starvation. Yet they would have a field day. And would, in fact, bring people into the fold in a way they had never dreamed imaginable . . .

ONE of these amazing new missionaries was not even a member of the church when the month began.

His name was Parley P. Pratt. Characterized by a jutting bulldog jaw and determined eyes, Parley was a masterful writer with little formal education. In his early years he had joined the Baptists. In 1827 at the age of 20 he had married. It was an unusual union for the times—his bride was 10 years his senior—and a widow. Her name: Thankful Halsey. Early in their marriage they moved to a village west of Cleveland. Eighteen months later he was converted by one Sidney Rigdon of the Campbellite faith. Parley showed immediate dedication—he sold his farm and served a church mission. Before leaving, he made up his mind to visit New York relatives. On this journey he heard about the *Book of Mormon.* Intrigued, he sent his wife ahead to her parents in Canaan, New York, so he could be free to visit Joseph Smith.[1] His intention was to confront him in Palmyra and put him in his place.[2]

"As Joseph was about commencing a discourse one Sunday morning," writes Lucy, "Parley P. Pratt came in, very much fatigued. He had heard of us at some considerable distance and had traveled very fast in order to get there by meeting time" and "show us our error."[3]

But when Joseph finished, Pratt stood and told them he agreed with him.

Parley read the *Book of Mormon* and had a remarkable experience as described in the next chapter.

After being baptized and ordained (the day following his first meeting Joseph) he launched a mission for his new faith, starting with his relatives, who also lived at Canaan,[4] even though he was not exactly a seasoned member himself. The only convert he made there was his brother Orson, but it proved significant—both would hold the highest position in the new faith, short of being church president.

Together they would attend the fledgling church's second-ever conference—the September 1830 "general conference."

One concern expressed at this conference was how to handle the mandate given to teach the Lamanites in the West, since it had been stated in the *Book of Mormon* that the Native Americans would someday be taught the pure gospel again. Missionaries of other Christian faiths had attempted it with varying degrees of success, but Joseph's followers felt the harvest was ripe for them especially. The reason: they had both the New Testament and the *Book of Mormon*, which detailed the spiritual history of their ancestors.

At this September 1830 conference Joseph called 4 men as missionaries to the Lamanites.

Parley was one, and their mission became the talk of the town. They were extremely young to be traveling in the untamed wilderness and representing a religion with such relative inexperience.

The young men consisted of Parley P. Pratt, age 22 (just baptized that month), Oliver Cowdery, age 24, Ziba Peterson, about age 20, and Peter Whitmer Jr., age 21.[5]

Two were well educated, but 2 were not—Whitmer was a tailor and Peterson a farmer.

The second problem was, none even had proper clothing for the trip—only tattered and stained work clothes.

So Emma and several other women made them clothes, which, as Lucy explains, "was no easy task, as the most of it had to be manufactured out of the raw material."[6]

Emma, says Lucy, was overworked, yet, "whatever her hands found to do, she did with her might until she went so far beyond her strength that she brought upon herself a heavy fit of sickness, which lasted four weeks."[7]

The amazing Emma always threw herself wholeheartedly into the work of the kingdom.[8]

Parley P. Pratt describes the end results of the clothes made for him and his 3 companions: speaking in third person, he said they were "dressed plainly and comely, very neat in their persons."[9]

So the four launched their mission with high hopes. They planned to not only make Lamanite converts but to spearhead the way west for the entire church, where they assumed was the "gathering place."

The four began walking to Ohio. They moved at such an accelerated clip that they almost matched the speed of those traveling by barge and boat on the same route.[10]

Buffalo would be their last bustling city they would see in months. Scottish traveler James Stuart reports for that year: "There must be about 1,000 strangers constantly in this village, just arrived, all in a bustle."[11] The city Buffalo was a true cross-roads for travelers going various directions—north to Canada, west to Lake Erie, east to New York City, and south on only one road, which allowed travelers to then travel to the west.

Right in their own state, 111 miles west of Waterloo, near Buffalo, they made their very first attempt to teach the Lamanites. The village was on a short detour off the main road going south from Buffalo,[12] and was a branch of the Seneca who had settled there. They were known as the Cattaraugus, which meant "foul-smelling river bank," because where they lived, natural gas bubbled up from the river mud.[13]

Here, the missionaries found themselves head-on with the swirling aftermath of a recent battle of sorts between the younger Christian converts and the older tribal leaders who would not budge from their old ways.[14] The 4 young men spoke to some who could speak English, and then left 2 copies of the

*Book of Mormon*—the first ever to Native Americans. Their visit lasted "a few hours," reports Oliver.[15]

The road leading south from there to Ohio was practically impassable, reports Parley P. Pratt, as, after the October rains had fallen, the road became "one vast scene of mud and mire, so that traveling was now very difficult, if not impracticable."[16] He also described their road as "covered with dense forest, with here and there a small opening made by the [traveling] settlers."[17] Despite its rugged terrain it was a stage route. And it led along an old Native American trade road that had deep ruts in the "highway."[18] Here, they carried heavy bags. They went through Westfield, New York, then Erie, Pennsylvania, on their journey. From there they walked along a ridge on the south side of Lake Erie.

They had made the trip on foot in only 10 days,[19] fueled by youthful energy.

They came to a crossroads where the ridge ended at a dip in the land. The road forward continued on to Euclid and Cleveland. Ziba Peterson and Peter Whitmer Jr. stayed on that road.

But another road branched off to the south. Oliver and Parley decided to take that one.

Their first stop—Mentor, Ohio.

Here, they found one area ready to blossom, with one conversion in particular that would affect the new church for good and bad for generations. This one person would immediately magnify their membership more than ever anticipated—and practically turn the church upside down . . .

S IDNEY Rigdon was 37 and fantastically charismatic. He was also half a lifetime ahead of Joseph and his peers in age. Born February 19, 1793, in central Pennsylvania, he always showed ambition, wanting to accomplish more than what he was dealt in life. In his early childhood he was forced to work on his family farm but always craved something "better"—like attending school, which he could not—so he borrowed books. Fueling his desire was his father's refusing to allow him to even use candles. So he would read in the light of burning hickory bark by the fireplace each night till late. He became a self-taught scholar of history and mastered English grammar along with the Bible. At age 26 he finally got a formal education—mostly, if not purely, religious, studying under a Baptist minister. From that he obtained a license to preach and took off into the countryside, targeting Trumbell County, Ohio, and Pittsburgh, Pennsylvania, from 1819–1824.

Gnawing at him was one particular Baptist doctrine: infant baptism. The Baptists believed infants would be damned if they were not baptized—so he left the church.

In 1820 he married Phebe Brooks. From both the pressures of supporting a wife and his disaffection with the Baptists, he left the ministry to work as a tanner. This lasted 2 years, with Phebe's brother his employer. There, he met the now-famous

Alexander Campbell and Walter Scott, 2 immigrant Scotsmen who lifted his thoughts above the mundane.

Wanting to be part of their cause, he left his tanning job to preach again full time.

First stop: Bainbridge, Ohio. The year: 1826. He baptized 50, and they all banded together as a faithful congregation. Next, several people in Mentor, Ohio, asked him to preach regularly as their own minister and build up a church.

And that he did—with gusto.[1]

Then another congregation in Kirtland.

His goal was to help Campbell and Scott develop the new Disciple faith (also called Campbellites), and his success was extraordinary—due largely to his remarkable public speaking ability.[2] He was able to enrapture audiences. Further, his doctrines resonated with many.

Meanwhile in Mentor, Sidney's growing congregation was so infatuated with him that they offered him a salary. This he turned down—just as the Apostles of old would have, he said. Determined nevertheless, they built him a house at the edge of town.

Sidney held meetings with his new Mentor congregation at "a little log building, the Disciple church,"[3] and also met with another congregation at the barn of Reuben P. Harmon.

Walter Scott, meanwhile, was preaching in New Lisbon, Ohio, and would average 1,000 Disciple converts a year for 30 years. Alexander Campbell was also highly successful and would start one of the large Church of Christ organizations.

A newcomer on the scene was Scottish immigrant and successful textile industrialist Robert Owen, a proponent of communal living. Fellow Scotsman Alexander Campbell was apparently intrigued, since communal living was outlined in Acts of the New Testament. So he considered merging Owen's doctrine into his churches.

But Owen gave a public lecture that was unsettling.

On Independence Day, July 4, 1826, he presented an unusual public lecture, as reported in the *Painesville Telegraph*—yet it was not about the nation's independence—it was about his own style of independence.[4]

This freedom, he proclaimed, was from private property, from "irrational systems of religion," and from "marriage founded on individual property."[5]

Campbell became concerned with Owen's growing secularist sentiments. So he drifted into a wait-and-see mode.[6]

Eventually Owen's anti-religious colors flapped bold and clear, so Campbell decided there was too much of an impasse.[7]

Nevertheless, he did not immediately become an enemy to Owen—he merely decided to pass on the idea of a merger.

A year later—1828—Campbell suddenly saw Sidney Rigdon baptizing numerous people into his Disciples church, with many having ties to the Owenites.[8]

Campbell seemed to panic. But when he got an offer to debate Samuel Underhill, the leader of another communal community, he was pushed to make a choice about communal living and, at that moment, turned completely against it. (He declined the request, but turned around and challenged Robert Owen to a debate.[9])

At this point Campbell went to antagonist mode. Soon, steam began spewing between him and Sidney when Sidney wholeheartedly adopted the communal living platform. He made it clear that he supported those who wanted to start such an order. So, with Sidney's blessing, some of his followers launched one in 1830. (This was 1 of 137 such groups founded between the Revolution and the Civil War,[10] and apparently the 3rd one in the Kirtland area.)

The endorsement for communal living by Sidney caused a near eruption, and the schism between him and Campbell began widening.

Making matters worse, Sidney went to Campbell's yearly church conference in Austintown, Ohio, for an inevitable confrontation. There, Sidney told him his congregation at Kirtland wanted to follow the apostles of the New Testament, requiring "a community of goods."[11] He further stated, "That as they established their order in the model church at Jerusalem, we were bound to imitate their example."[12]

But Campbell would have none of it.

So in August 1830, right there at the national conference, Sidney broke away, antagonism pouring all directions, burning all bridges. He would never again be a Campbellite preacher. Possibly relieved, possibly torn, he took out on his own, maintaining not only his Kirtland congregation but his Mentor group as well.

Meanwhile, just months earlier, Sidney had been preaching the Disciples doctrine in numerous nearby towns, when a curious young man heard him. This was Parley P. Pratt (before he met those of the New York religion). Pratt was converted to the Disciples and launched his own preaching circuit that same summer—1830. He later met Joseph Smith, heard him speak, and was converted. Afterward he read the *Book of Mormon*, and later reported that when he got the book, "I read all day. Eating was a burden. I had no desire for food. Sleep was a burden when the night came. For I preferred reading to sleep. As I read, the Spirit of the Lord was upon me, and I knew and comprehended that the book was true, as plainly and manifestly as a man comprehends and knows that he exists."[13]

It was now October 1830, 2 months after splitting with Campbell, and Sidney was free from all associations.

Thus it was when 2 New York missionaries came knocking at his door. As he opened it, he saw none other than Parley P. Pratt standing there. And this made for a truly unusual scene.

Sidney had just months earlier converted Pratt to the Campbellites, likely very proud to have converted someone who had then spun off to become a preacher. Now, seeing Parley in the doorway, Sidney doubtless wondered if his old convert was there to invite him back to the Campbellites and, while he was at it, demand that he ditch the communal thing. But Pratt surprised him—all he did was hold up a book.

Sidney's wife Phebe and their 10-year-old daughter Athalia were present and reported the scene:[14]

Parley: "Brother Rigdon, here is a book which is a revelation from God." Parley then told him how the book came about.

While Sidney was relieved that he wasn't being reprimanded, he nevertheless was caught more than a little off guard, seeing that his former student was now a missionary for that revolutionary New York sect.

Seeing his mentor taken back, Parley handed him the book.

Sidney responded, "You need not argue the case with me. I have one Bible [about] which I claim to have some knowledge, and which I believe to be a revelation from God. But as to this book, I have some doubts, but you can leave it with me when you go away in the morning, and I will read It, and when you come again I will tell you what I think about it."[15]

But the 2 young missionaries weren't through. They boldly asked Sidney if they could preach to his congregation—a move that took him back even more—and, probably in a state of semi-shock, he consented.

That night a large congregation assembled to hear the New Yorkers preach—young Parley and Oliver. Upon finishing, they invited Sidney to respond. He thoughtfully shuffled to the podium, looked over his flock, and told them, "Brethren, we have listened to strange doctrines tonight, but we are commanded to prove all things and to hold fast to that which is good."[16] He then exhorted his congregation "to do likewise, and give the matter a careful investigation, and not turn against it, without being fully convinced of it being an imposition, lest they should possibly resist the truth."[17] Thus ended a significant day for Sidney—October 29, 1830. And one for the missionaries as well, as it was still their first day in this district of Ohio, after their 10-day trek from New York.

Sidney then asked the two to spend the night. They did, and the next morning they told him they were headed off to

Kirtland, 5 miles away, and would return later. But their journey would take a circuitous route.

As soon as they left, Sidney began reading the book.

"He got so engaged in it," writes his son John, "that it was hard for him to quit long enough to eat his meals. He read it both day and night."[18]

Sidney was especially impressed with doctrines it taught that he already accepted—of a gathering of Christian believers and of the upcoming millennial reign of Jesus Christ after His Second Coming. He absorbed the book for 2 weeks. "At last he had read it through and pondered and thought over it," adds John.[19]

When Parley and Oliver left Mentor, they met up with the other 2 missionaries outside Cleveland. The place was a Shaker village named North Union. Parley writes that hats were "given to each of them by the Shakers at the time they passed through this country, so they wore them."[20] The hats had a low crown and broad brim. The *Painesville Telegraph* reports of the 4 missionaries: "Males among them wear a peculiar kind of hat, [by] which they distinguish themselves,"[21]—the first example of the typically shoddy reporting about the missionaries that would, for better or worse, be harmless and amusing like this, or more malicious, like other reports that would unfold and spread for 2 centuries. (The *Painesville Telegraph* would prove to provide both. It was the closest newspaper to Kirtland, 12 miles away, and would attempt to keep its readers abreast of local news and occasional details related to the New York missionaries.)

Uncertain of how to get to Kirtland from there, the 4 missionaries ran into Isaac Morley's wife, Lucy, and asked her for directions.[22]

At Kirtland the four created quite a stir—many listened and were moved by their words. Especially Sidney's communal society—separate from the Mentor congregation—which tried their hardest to live by New Testament standards. They were open-minded and wanted to hear more.[23]

Others in Kirtland would join in time. But for now, the town of 1,018 people[24] was a tough one, surviving by trading with trappers, and not all were a hundred percent civilized. Yet the 4 young missionaries were fearless. They were not only brash, but upbeat, enthusiastic, and, undeniably, charismatic new converts themselves, who at times were more hopeful than realistic. (Whether or not the four were truly this optimistic, the *Painesville Telegraph* reports that they expected to convert and gather the Indians—which they figured was the main purpose of their mission—and that miracles would be manifest.)[25]

And their fresh, bold energy paid off, preaching only a short time in Ohio before converting a veritable multitude.[26]

The details behind their adventure are eye-opening:

While the missionaries were absent from Sidney, he struck out on his own to tell others what he was learning—with astonishing effect.

The next several days went with lightning speed.

On November 3, four people were baptized at Kirtland, says Pratt.[27]

The next day, November 4, Sidney heard missionaries speak on the property of John Morley. Sidney also performed a marriage that day,[28] then joined the missionaries traveling to the villages.[29] He was, of course, not yet a member of the church himself but could not break away from their company. Their message focused on the *Book of Mormon* and was centered on the Savior's visit to ancient America.[30]

This particular day was significant for another reason—the missionaries began basing their operations out of Morley's farm—sleeping there at night and contacting people door-to-door by day. Morley could provide food, shelter, and contacts for the missionaries, as well as travel directions, and he could even help set up locations for meetings around the county—huge meetings—as well as appointments within individuals' homes. All of which he did. Isaac Morley was not only one of their first contacts but the owner of this large farm, which became the base for numerous conversions. (See Appendix X: "Harvest at the Isaac Morley Farm.")

The following day, November 5, they baptized 17 people just before midnight on the Morley farm.[31]

November 6: another baptism on the Morley farm. That day Sidney gave a sermon that supported the New York missionaries and their message, and actually wept before his congregation, "much affected and shedding tears," according to Walter Scott,[32] seeing Sidney touched by the Spirit of God. Once affected, Sidney Rigdon became a force to be reckoned with . . .

# CHAPTER 33

Alvah Hancock attended the November 6, 1830, meeting and saw Sidney Rigdon with the Spirit of God, crying. Alvah then traveled to Chagrin, Ohio, and visited family members. He asked them if they had heard the news.

"What news?" asked Levi, his brother, who recorded this dialogue.

"'Four men have come and have brought a book with them,'" said Alvah, who then told them the message he heard. "'Do you not recollect of reading what the Savior said, how He had other sheep which were not of His fold at Jerusalem? Well,' said Alvah, 'they were here and He came and taught them the same doctrine that He taught them at Jerusalem. And they baptized for the remission of sins and are building up the church as the Apostles used to do in the days of Christ.'"[1]

Levi describes what he experienced after hearing Alvah's report:

"There seemed to fall on me something pleasant and delightful. It seemed like a wash of something warm took me in the face and ran over my body and gave me those feelings that I cannot describe.

"The first words I said were, 'It is truth. I feel it. I will go and hear myself tomorrow.'"[2]

The next day was November 7. The meeting was 7 miles south in Mayfield, at the farm of John Jackson.[3]

It was eventful.

The road to Mayfield was packed. The sheriff and an attorney were among the throng that made the journey, where they "found the roads crowded with people going in the same direction."[4] All this, of course, was a remarkable contrast to what the 4 missionaries had come from in New York, where only a few dozen had shown interest in Joseph's message.

Levi continues his report. After arriving at the farm, he found a spot on the ground, and "sat with both ears open."[5] One person pulled planks off the house so people outside could better hear what was said inside. Those outside also tossed down saddle blankets and carriage seat covers, or just plopped themselves on the ground.[6]

The crowd became enormous.

After the lecture, Parley invited anyone to respond who wished to. Sidney arose first. Levi summarized his comments: "He should never try to preach again, and confessed he was completely used up." Then, "He advised the people not to contend against what they heard."

Sidney then made a startling confession, recorded by eyewitness Josiah Jones: "Elder Rigdon told us . . . his preaching [before now] had been of no use to us."[7] Parley substantiates what Jones says: "At length Mr. Rigdon and many others became convinced that they had no authority to minister in the ordinances of God, and that they had not been legally baptized and ordained."[8]

Like Sidney, Levi was not a member of the new church, but was intrigued by what he saw and heard. Levi describes what happened next: "After he [Sidney] had spoken, there arose another young man whose countenance bespoke a spirit of peace and love. He said he had been a witness to the things declared and the book was a revelation of truth, however strange it might appear to the people."[9] He was 1 of the 4 missionaries.

Nine people were baptized that night.

Still November 7, the missionaries shot off to Kirtland for a scheduled meeting. Sidney went with them and stated again he lacked authority. And again, he cried while speaking and announced his preaching days were over,[10] even though he obviously loved his work. After the meeting, 19 more people were baptized,[11] all influenced by Sidney.

He returned home to Mentor, likely in a bittersweet state, feeling he had found the truth but now must sacrifice doing what he loved most—public speaking.

The missionaries went to visit him there, keeping their promise of 9 days earlier.

Immediately he questioned them about Joseph and the *Book of Mormon*. He was stunned by what he now heard—Joseph was only 24, with very little education—and that was the clincher. It was impossible for an uneducated youth to have written such a book, he decided, so he was completely convinced the book was from God.

The missionaries then invited him and his wife to attend a service in Kirtland, where several of his converts were being baptized.

The Rigdons agreed, wishing to merely watch. But the power they felt at the service convinced them it was more than simply an event to observe. They decided to be baptized right then and there. So, on November 8, 1830, that very night, Parley P. Pratt, Sidney's former young convert to the Campbellites, turned the tables completely and baptized him.[12]

With renewed passion for life he decided there was still a group that needed preaching to. He returned home to preach and help his beloved Mentor congregation.

Repercussions awaited. He found they were furious over the news and had a face-off at church. They demanded to know where he stood. From his pulpit he boldly declared he knew the New York church was true—and that he was going to teach this new gospel to them.

Went over horridly. They took a stand: they blocked him from his church, never letting him enter it again. They also refused to let his family move into the new house they had built for them.[13]

Sidney would not compromise his newly discovered faith. So his new mantra would be to pursue a life of simplicity and humility.

Deciding once and for all his days of having an influence on others were over, he "quit preaching," reports Reuben P. Harmon, "and went into Mr. Morley's field and went to plowing. Worked at common labor for some time."[14] Harmon adds that, in addition to hearing Sidney say he would never preach again, "I heard him make the remark that he never expected to speak in public again."[15]

Meantime, the missionaries were having a veritable field day. After Sidney came in, their baptisms accelerated. If accurate, the *Painesville Telegraph*'s report a week later of 100 converts so far would not be an exaggeration. In this land of simple farm folk and wilderness seekers, the editor stated that the converts included some "of good repute and intellect."[16]

Parley also defined the landscape of their teaching: "Meetings were convened in different neighborhoods. Thousands flocked about us daily,"[17] which was due in part to the large size of the county—16,000 residents—a sizeable one this far west,[18] but still far enough from the centers of civilization to be considered fringe wilderness.

With Sidney aboard, curiosity about the new church was sweeping the region like a sandstorm. Resident John Corrill writes, "Persons came from all quarters inquiring after the new religion, and individuals from more than three counties away came to hear the good news."[19]

One transplant from New York, Joel Miller, who had grown up where the enormous revivals were famous in western New York, stated he attended a meeting at Morley's farm: "I never saw so many people together before."[20]

Nevertheless, Parley states that these meetings were not their only venue. They also went "visiting from house to house,"[21] which enabled them to share their message to those who did not attend the hugely supported farmland lectures.

Sidney's next step was to start over.

He moved his family to Hiram, Ohio, where he and his wife Phebe joined the 17 or so Kirtland converts from the former communal society. There they formed a branch of the new church, comprising 19, including the Rigdons.[22]

The 4 missionaries, meanwhile, continued teaching and converting. The area was catching a groundswell of activity.

John Murdock was a Disciples preacher. He had heard Oliver and Parley preach in Mayfield. He also had worked closely with Sidney. Noteworthy, he and his wife Julia were related to Alexander Campbell by marriage. Murdock was a dedicated Disciple but had nevertheless spent "many years [in] diligent search and prayer before God to not only know the truth but to also find a people that lived according to truth," he writes.[23]

Then the missionaries met him. They convinced him to see "they not only had the truth," says Murdock, "but also the authority to administer the ordinances of the gospel. I therefore was baptized by Elder Pratt and confirmed a member by Elder Cowdery," on November 5, 1830, in Mayfield.[24]

He continues: "I returned to my family, having been absent four days, carrying with me the *Book of Mormon*. And I read it to them, and they believed it, for I was filled with the Spirit when I read."[25]

Murdock then preached about the *Book of Mormon* in his first public sermon 2 days later—November 7. And that day he baptized 5, including his wife Julia and members of their family. Over the next 2 weeks, even larger groups. Over the next 4 months, "about 70 souls," his journal states.[26]

Meanwhile, new convert Levi Hancock was baptized 8 days after Sidney—on November 16. He then passed through Cleveland, Ohio, and "baptized many," he writes in his journal. "Confirmed forty people at one time after a meeting."[27]

The only tool Hancock, Murdock, and other new converts had, since they were completely inexperienced, was their reliance on the Holy Ghost.

Dr. Samuel Underhill, the aforementioned proponent of communal living, debater of Robert Owen, and leader of the Kendal Community, never joined the faith yet writes this candid, firsthand report of how the missionaries for this new church operated:

"The leaders . . . acknowledge to me that what they relied on most was an internal feeling of certainty which they define [as] 'The Spirit of God bearing witness with their spirits that it was the truth.'"

He adds, "You wonder at the success of the New System of the Mormonites! [a recently coined term] I wonder not at all. It is all explained in a few words! It is not the golden bible, it is not the eloquence of their preachers, it is not the result of studied impositions understandingly pursued. No! no! It is not one or all of these. You ask what then can it be? I'll tell you kind reader what it is. . . . Let me ask you, did you never feel in a religious meeting an unexpected mighty solemn feeling—a kind of vivid flame glowing in every part of your frame? . . .

"Had you felt what I have felt and seen what I have, you need only to be told that these feelings are extensively witnessed among the Mormonites, and there, as everywhere, [is] supposed to be the owning and wonder working display of supernatural power, and the wonder is all solved, and the progress of Mormonites is no longer a mystery."[28]

Underhill thus confesses feeling the Holy Spirit bearing witness to what they were teaching, yet he would not join them, convincing himself that his feelings somehow came internally.

But hundreds of others did respond, feeling the Holy Ghost as their guide, Comforter, and compass.

The lack of educated ministers with diplomas made them stand apart from ministers of other faiths. They felt their unique heavenly tool of the Spirit and the authority of the Priesthood sent to them by heavenly messengers gave them all the power they needed.

Thus, the power of their message lay in its simplicity, they felt, with no need for a trained, paid ministry. But their lack of formal ministerial training was a stumbling block for many they taught—as it would be for numerous others over the next 2 centuries.

Perhaps this aspect is best summed up with a journal entry by an antagonist to Joseph Smith. Nancy Trowle wrote the following when Joseph confirmed a number of Ohioans into the church after they were baptized:

"Being about to leave the place, he turned to some women and children in the room, and lay[ed] his hands upon their heads, that they might receive the Holy Ghost, when 'oh!' cried one [her friend, Bostonian Eliza Marsh] to me, 'What blessings, you do lose! No sooner his hands fell upon my head, than I felt the Holy Ghost—as warm water—go over me!'

Hearing that, Trowle decided to challenge Joseph: "And I turned to Smith, and said, 'Are you not ashamed of such pretensions? You, who are no more than any ignorant plough-boy of our land!' . . .[29]

"He only replied by saying, 'The gift has returned back again, as in former times, to illiterate fishermen.'"[30]

ONVERSIONS by the missionaries now began sweeping across the farm meadows like summer rain.

Parley summarized their success: "In two or three weeks from our arrival in the neighborhood with the news, we had baptized one hundred and twenty-seven souls, and this number soon increased to one thousand."[1] (His number of 127 was only 27 more than the *Telegraph*'s estimation, but the eventual number of 1,000 was over 4 times that of members already in New York. It was possibly beyond their wildest dreams, given the struggle they had seen in the Palmyra area.)

These Ohio numbers comprised true converts, since the missionaries baptized only those from their mid-teens and older, following the tradition of other churches,[2] until more revelation would come one year later—in November 1831—clarifying the minimum age for baptism to be 8.[3]

Believers in the Ohio branches during this period called themselves, "Disciples," since many were used to the term, having converted from the Disciples of Christ. The term "disciples" was also a name used in the *Book of Mormon*.[4] Further, the Saints had a revelation wherein God referred to them as "my disciples,"[5] while Joseph would also call them "disciples" upon his arrival in Ohio.[6] William Lyman Staker points out that Ohio members referred to themselves as "the Family," after the term given Morley's group that converted *en masse* to the Saints.[7]

Outsiders gave them other names, such as "the 'new sect'"[8] and "disciples of the new revelation,"[9] while a few months earlier Abner Cole had printed in his newspaper, *The Reflector*, at Palmyra, New York, the weird term "Gold Bible apostles."[10] (His imagination was remarkable, also giving himself the name Obadiah Dogberry, of course.) The movement itself was briefly called "Joseyism," by Cole's *Reflector*,[11] and "the new revelation," by the *Geauga Gazette*.[12] Church members began dropping the term "Disciples" among themselves, likely due to the confusion with Campbell's church in Ohio, and instead began using the term "saints," as used in the New Testament and the *Book of Mormon*.[13] This term among themselves—along with "Latter-day Saints," which came into being with the church's name change in 1838—would remain in use until today.

But the world at large would soon take up the label given by editor Eber Dudley Howe of the *Painesville Telegraph*, with a January 18, 1831, article labeling them "Mormonites" (and their movement, "Mormonism").[14]

This term was so widely accepted in just five months that the Saints actually referred to themselves with this name by June, 1831, when some were still traveling to Ohio.[15]

Before leaving for Missouri, the young missionaries added a 5th man to their team—a local Ohioan named Frederick G. Williams, a 43-year-old medical doctor[16] so convinced of the divinity of the work that he walked away from both his successful practice and his farm to join the 4 young men half his age.

Isaac Morley was left temporarily in charge of the area branches until help would arrive from New York. He was also twice the age of most of his associates and was "a prominent, well-liked citizen with leadership experience," summarizes Mark L. Staker[17] But he still lacked knowledge of anything church-related, other than what he had felt and read in the *Book of Mormon*.[18]

Sidney Rigdon then received news that made his day—if not his year: he was told that he and John Murdock would assist Isaac Morley in taking charge of all the new converts.

It was his first assignment beyond the plough. No doubt he was incredibly relieved and grateful to be called to a position that would utilize his talents. Soon, something else began gnawing at him: he wanted to meet Joseph Smith firsthand. But the missionaries had placed him and the other two in charge before they left. They all knew it was temporary—they needed a more church-experienced leader for the area. Thus, the missionaries had written Joseph a letter, asking to send an elder to preside. "Accordingly," says Lucy, "Joseph dispatched John Whitmer to take the presidency of the church at Kirtland."[19] He would arrive there between January 11 and 18, 1831, according to the *Painesville Telegraph*,[20] a couple months after the missionaries had departed.[21]

Not waiting for Whitmer, because of their confidence in Isaac and team to lead the new converts, the five marched into the huge Ohio prairie alone.

Destination: Missouri.

The date: on or about November 21, 1830.

The weather: extreme cold settling in.

Travel conditions: They were leaving without so much as taking a mule.

The reason: Animals would have no food on the desolate, wintry prairie.

Results: Each of the five had to carry his own heavy pack.

Thus, they resumed their trek from New York to Missouri, with 1,280 miles still ahead of them and a new missionary now on their team.[22]

Not long after leaving Kirtland, Parley was arrested on bogus charges and dragged before a small town court. His companions, of course, would not leave without him, and awaited the outcome.

"We arrived at that place of trial late in the evening; found false witnesses in attendance and a judge who boasted of his intention to thrust us into prison for the purpose of testing the powers of our apostleship, as he called it, although I was only an elder in the church," says Parley.

"The judge boasting thus and the witnesses being entirely false in their testimony, I concluded to make no defense, but to treat the whole matter with contempt."

The officer holding him prisoner ate breakfast with him the next morning. Then his missionary companions came along, and Parley told them quietly to continue traveling ahead, confident he would catch up.

Soon he stepped outside, accompanied by the officer, and said, "'Mr. Peabody, are you good at a race?'

"'No,' said he [the officer], 'but my big bulldog is . . . and he will take any man down at my bidding.'"

Parley said confidently, "'Well, Mr. Peabody, you compelled me to go a mile, I have gone with you two miles. You have given me an opportunity to preach, sing, and have also entertained me with lodging [at the jail] and breakfast. I must now go on my journey. If you are good at a race, you can accompany me. I thank you for all your kindness—good day, sir.'

"I then started on my journey, while he stood amazed, and not able to step one foot before the other. Seeing this, I halted, turned to him and again invited him to a race. He still stood amazed. I then renewed my exertions and soon increased my speed to something like that of a deer. He did not awake from his astonishment sufficiently to start in pursuit till I had gained perhaps two hundred yards. I had already leaped a fence and was making my way through a field to the forest on the right of the road. He now came hallooing after me and shouting to his dog to seize me.

"The dog, being one of the largest I ever saw, came close on my footsteps with all his fury, the officer behind still in pursuit, clapping his hands and hallooing, 'Stu-boy, Stu-boy—

take him—watch—lay hold of him, I say—down with him,' and pointing his finger in the direction I was running. The dog was fast overtaking me, and in the act of leaping upon me when, quick as lightning, the thought struck me to assist the officer in sending the dog with all fury to the forest a little distance before me. I pointed my finger in that direction, clapped my hands and shouted in imitation of the officer. The dog hastened past me with redoubled speed toward the forest, being urged by the officer and myself and both of us running in the same direction.

"Gaining the forest, I soon lost sight of the officer and dog and have not seen them since."[23]

Parley's account of his missionary journey—and his most remarkable life—are contained in *The Autobiography of Parley P. Pratt* (Stratford Books, 2005; and eBook, Stratford edition, 2012—both unabridged.)


Parley caught up to his companions and they continued their journey to Missouri.

Next stop: the Wyandot tribe near Sandusky, Ohio.

Length of stay: several days.

Mission: hoping to teach the entire tribe.

Results: The inhabitants figured to move west soon and decided they were too busy to listen. At least that was the bottom line.

The details are a bit murkier:

After walking there along Lake Erie, the 5 missionaries were surprised when they discovered the condition of this tribe, as described by English traveler Thomas K. Wharton, who had visited there only 4 months earlier: "All the Indians we saw on this 'Reserve' were well-dressed and mounted," and were "far advanced in civilization," speaking "good English," and being "considerable proprietors of cattle, grain, etc."[24] Unfortunately for the five, the tribe had a "resident missionary amongst them," says Wharton[25] (actually 2 Methodist missionaries,[26] "whose labours are said to be quite encouraging," adds Wharton.[27]

Noteworthy was the tribe's propensity for growing large apple orchards, started for them by John Chapman of "Johnny Appleseed" fame.

Parley was optimistic about the results, saying, "We were well received and had an opportunity of laying before them the record of their forefathers, which we did. They rejoiced in the tidings, bid us God speed and desired us to write them in relation to our success among the tribes further west, that had already removed to the Indian territory, where these expected soon to go."[28] Perhaps the tribesmen were simply wrapping their minds around their own migration, or perhaps they were comfortable in their Christianity and were basically apathetic toward the five. In either case, Parley appreciated their reception and says the five took "an affectionate leave of this people."[29]

They trudged through Florence, Ohio, with Parley perhaps the one most upbeat over the results, while the others may have been disappointed they could not convert the Wyandot tribe—not even one person.

Then onto the scene came Orson Hyde, a Disciple preacher. One man they would not soon forget. A man who would affect Joseph for years . . .

O RSON Hyde had been raised as an orphan in poverty. The reason: his father was away fighting the War of 1812, then his mother died, leaving him to be raised by neighbors. He had walked from his birthplace in Connecticut to Kirtland at age 14, sent by his employer to watch over a property there. Then he had clerked at Whitney and Gilbert's store—an iconic structure in early Kirtland—and then studied grammar under Sidney Rigdon, preparing to become a Campbellite minister, which he now was.

He haughtily rejected the missionaries. He labeled them "mostly illiterate men," hardly worth his time. (Ironically, Parley, Oliver, and Dr. Williams all had considerably more education than he, but they came across less arrogantly perhaps than others; further, because he disagreed with them he figured them "ignorant.")

He bought a book from them, read only part of it, and concluded "it was all fiction." He began preaching against it to Sidney's old Disciple congregations in the area.[1] The irony could not have escaped him—he was preaching in opposition to Sidney now, yet Sidney had earlier converted him to the Disciples. For several months Orson Hyde was the appointed pastor of several branches in 2 counties—Lorain and Huron, Ohio—the fruits of Sidney's previous labors.

Leaving Hyde, the missionaries trudged on to Missouri through agonizingly cold winds and icy blowing snow, the temperatures unmatched in a generation, despite the hottest summer on record for 106 years.[2]

The intense cold was exacerbated by the fresh encounter with Hyde and his icy rejection—after having had so much unexpected success the previous 3 weeks only to be met with a basic flop among the Wyandots, and then an even bigger flop with Hyde. The missionaries had many days now to think about Hyde as they fought forward through incredibly miserable winds.

Little did they know at the time, but Orson Hyde would be a success story few could match. He would meet up again with Sidney and join the Saints one year later—on October 30, 1831. Then would become one of the Twelve Apostles and eventually quorum president. He and 3 others would open up Great Britain to missionary work in 1837–1838 and convert over 1,500 people, laying the groundwork for tens of thousands of more British converts he would help to make in a second mission to them a decade later, with his efforts reverberating into a positive, steady stream of converts for 32 years (1837–1869). Although he was in Great Britain a combined total of less than 3 years, from his and a few others' efforts about 35,300 Brits would emigrate to join the Saints in the United States,[3] while others would remain there to maintain a base of operations that would flourish over the next 175 years.

Due to Hyde and a few other missionaries' efforts, at one point, in 1851, there would be almost 3 times as many Saints in Great Britain as in the church's world headquarters in the United States (33,000 in the U.K., compared to 12,000 in Utah).

However, from 1851 to 1869, all but 9,000 of those still in the U.K. would emigrate to Utah. Thus, for the next 85 years, through about 1955, the numbers in Great Britain would hover at and not increase above 9,000, utilizing only a small handful of chapels, yet would later soar to over 186,000 in 347 congregations, with most in their own chapels.[4]

(In a broader statistic, in the first century after Hyde's appearance with his companions in the U.K., 126,593 baptisms would take place there, with 52,000 of these converts emigrating to the U.S. Over the course of that 100 years, of those who would not emigrate, most would die of sickness or old age. Once in the U.S., most immigrants apparently stayed with the church, despite the intense trials they would suffer, which proved a monument to their faith.)

An interesting historical footnote about these British converts—some directly and some indirectly from Hyde's efforts—was provided by novelist Charles Dickens, who visited an emigrant ship, the *Amazon*, before it set sail from London on June 4, 1863, to see what the much-maligned Latter-day Saints were like, after they had survived a tsunami of anti-Mormon press: "I . . . had come aboard the Emigrant Ship to see what eight hundred Latter-day Saints were like. . . . Nobody is in an ill-temper, no-body is the worse for drink, nobody swears an oath or uses a coarse word, nobody appears depressed, nobody is weeping, and down upon the deck in every corner where it is possible to find a few square feet to kneel, crouch or lie in, people, in every suitable attitude for writing, are writing letters. Now, I have seen emigrant ships before this day in June. And these people are strikingly different from all other people in like circumstances whom I have ever seen, and I wonder aloud, 'What would a stranger suppose these emigrants to be!' . . . I should have said they were in their degree, the pick and flower of England.")[5]

The sailing date for the *Amazon* to America was June 4, 1863, 26 years after Orson Hyde would arrive in Great Britain, but the efforts of his work would be manifest for decades afterward. Those aboard the *Amazon* likely included some he had baptized and their next-generation descendants, as well as others who had come into the church as a result of his groundbreaking work there.

Finally, as discussed in Volume 3 of this work, Hyde would travel to Europe, the Ottoman Empire, and the Middle East. On this journey—one week short of his 10-year anniversary of his baptism—on October 24, 1841, he would prophesy of and dedicate Israel for the return of the Jews. This was a monumental event in the eyes of church leaders, which would come to pass over a century later, in 1948, when Israel would be established as a nation under the influence of God, as Latter-day Saints believe.

Hyde's conversion story was similar to many in New York who toiled to receive a witness from God about Joseph's calling as a prophet. (By way of contrast, many in Ohio seemed so extraordinarily "prepared" to receive the restored gospel that they accepted it immediately. Hyde, in that sense, was more like the New Yorkers—it took him a year to embrace the faith, after he had so rudely rejected the missionaries.)

With thoughts of Hyde's rejection still ironically brewing through their minds, having no idea of the groundwork they had laid by even talking to him, the 5 missionaries trudged on to Missouri, heading south to Cincinnati, where they spent several days. Here they taught many people, says Pratt, but "without much success."[6] Then they boarded a steamer bound for St. Louis. Ice blocked the river and they had to walk the last 200 miles to the city. Before arriving, they preached to large congregations while stranded in Illinois 20 miles outside of St. Louis, due to snow up to 3 feet deep.

Then they took their last 300 miles on foot "through vast prairies and through trackless wilds of snow—no beaten road, houses few and far between, and the bleak northwest wind always blowing in our faces with a keenness that would almost take the skin off the face. We traveled whole days, from morning till night," says Parley.

"This was the first mission performed by the elders of the church in any of the states west of New York, and we were the first members of the same that were ever on this frontier."[7] Attempting to look at the bright side, they saw they were indeed pioneers of their faith so far from home.


Meanwhile, back in Painesville, Ohio, Sidney was distraught over his treatment by professing Christians. On the courthouse steps he preached one final sermon about lack of "charity and brotherly love" from local residents who targeted him for accepting the *Book of Mormon*. His sermon was reported in the *Painesville Telegraph*.[8]

In December 1830, Sidney felt so compelled to meet the young prophet from Palmyra that he could not hold back any longer. So he and another Ohioan, Edward Partridge, began a 300-mile trek to New York. From this, Joseph's life—and that of the church—would never be the same . . .

EDWARD Partridge, another gent of Sidney's age, had been intrigued by the young 20-something missionaries. A financially successful hatter, he was a humble and gentle soul, but had a stubborn streak a mile wide.

His wife, however, was more accepting of the missionaries' message, and before the missionaries left Ohio, Parley baptized her. The complex/skeptical Edward got bold and told Oliver they were imposters. But Oliver countered, saying he was grateful that a God in heaven knew the hearts of all men, intimating that Edward did not know the hearts of men, and that thus, fortunately, Edward was not God.

Perhaps intrigued by this, Edward decided to read the *Book of Mormon*. Still not certain, he wanted to meet the Prophet personally.

Upon arriving in New York, Edward went to Manchester. Unable to find Joseph or his family, he began asking the neighbors about their characters.

These neighbors reported the Smiths as rock solid, with unimpeachable character—until Joseph had "deceived" them with the *Book of Mormon*, of course

When Edward walked across the Smiths' farm and saw the good order and industry it exhibited, he realized what they had sacrificed by leaving such a beautiful place. That was the final monument he needed. He made his decision and was ready to be baptized. So he went searching for the Smiths and hunted them down.

Edward Partridge, along with Sidney Rigdon, arrived in Waterloo on December 10, 1830.[1] They entered Joseph's home while he was preaching a sermon.[2] Doubtless it was an event that Sidney and Edward had been anticipating, as here was the young man at his work—that which had instigated Sidney's complete reversal of occupation from minister to farmer-citizen—and which had turned his whole world upside down. Now Sidney could see Joseph and hear him firsthand for the very first time.

After Joseph's sermon, Edward gave his report to the group of what Joseph's old neighbors in Manchester had just said. He then recounted to everyone the obvious sacrifices Joseph had made. Then, he announced, "Brother Joseph will baptize me."

Joseph shot back, "You are now much fatigued, Brother Partridge, and you had better rest today and be baptized tomorrow."

Edward responded, "I am ready at any time."[3]

He was baptized the next day.[4] His baptism took place in beautiful Seneca Lake, which served as the west town line to Fayette.

This account is revealing in that Joseph did not push him for immediate action, stereotypical of many religionists; rather, he exhibited concern for Partridge's well-being after 325 miles of hard travel (300 from Kirtland to Manchester and another 25 from Manchester to Waterloo). And he exercised patience with the new convert.

Parenthetically, Lucy does not say if Sidney had accompanied Edward to Joseph's deserted Manchester farm, but presumably he had, as the two were traveling together.[4]

Immediately after their baptisms, Joseph received revelations for both men: he announced that Edward, a quiet man, would teach the gospel powerfully, "with the voice of the trump,"[5] and that Sidney would perform great things. Doubtless it was a great relief to Sidney—he could see his life's mission was not relegated to pushing a plow.

---

Meanwhile, the 5-man missionary team was still marching to the western border.

Trekking through endless days of frigid January winds and unceasing wet snowfall, they apparently saw no other humans—certainly a frustration, as they were on fire to meet and convert souls, hoping perhaps above all to wash the memory of Orson Hyde from their minds.

Adding to their dilemma, on the many days that they could not make a camp fire, they ate raw pork and stale corn bread, so frozen that they could only nibble at the edges.[6]

Finally, after several weeks, the five trudged into Independence, Missouri, the far western outpost of America.

Exhausted, they decided among themselves that two would remain in the village to work as tailors,[7] while the other three would head across the border.

The three who left for the border first met with the Shawnees and spent the night with them. Then they crossed the Kansas River to the Delaware Indians.

Outside U.S. borders, the three met the tribe's leader, Chief Anderson, the noted Great-grandfather of the Delawares' 10 tribes. He welcomed them in his tent and fed them corn and beans boiled up together, "which proved to be good eating," says Parley, with the use of a spoon that the three of them shared.[8] Using an interpreter, the chief informed them he had never allowed missionaries to speak to his people, and would stick with this policy.

But the three were, of course, intransigent. They told him they had a message that came from the forefathers of his people. They even explained where his people came from, and that their knowledge was contained in the *Book of Mormon*. The chief was so impressed that he changed his mind. He called a special council of 40 tribal leaders to hear Oliver Cowdery.[9]

After the speech, he agreed the 3 missionaries should stay more days, teach his people, and give out copies of the book to all who would read it.[10]

He himself was thoroughly convinced.

Oliver wrote Joseph, "The principle chief says he believes every word of the Book (of Mormon) and there are many more in the Nation who believe."[11]

Parley reports the tribe actually getting excited over their message, when suddenly their opponents brought it to a screeching halt. These antagonists were the established Christian missionaries, envious of their success and claiming they were disturbing the peace.[12] Chief Anderson would have been influential in numerous Lamanites accepting the restored gospel, but their opponents persuaded the government Indian agents to their side, and stopped the 3 missionaries cold.[13]

At that point the three were ordered out of the territory.

Thus, they returned to Independence and joined the others, distraught. All five began teaching the white settlers there but with limited success. Perhaps resentful at their apparently bigoted opponents, they realized the Lamanites' time for conversion would have to be in the future, when government bureaucrats would not be siding with established religionists.


Back in New York, Joseph took an immediate liking to Sidney Rigdon.

And Sidney's stock skyrocketed.

With Oliver Cowdery gone on a mission to Missouri, Joseph had no "right-hand man." So at this opportune time, Sidney "soon worked himself deep into Brother Joseph's affections," states John Whitmer's brother, David, "and had more influence over him than any other man living," becoming Joseph's chief confidant, his "private counselor, and his most intimate friend and brother for some time after they met."[14] He also states, "Brother Joseph rejoiced, believing that the Lord had sent to him this great and mighty man . . . to help him in the work."[15] They all rejoiced in it at first, says David.[16]

Brilliant and talented, Sidney was the perfect assistant for which Joseph was searching. As his contemporaries believed,

Sidney now had the gift of the Holy Ghost, so his preaching was even more powerful than in Ohio.

Sidney accompanied Joseph on his circuit to visit both members and nonmembers willing to listen in nearby villages. They went down to Broome County, where Joseph Knight records Sidney stayed at his house several days and "preached there several times [to the nonbelievers], and he was too smart for them, therefore they wanted to trouble him."[17]

Intellectually, he was a cut above the farm community to whom he spoke. When he preached in Palmyra, "the people stood, trembling and amazed, so powerful were his words," according to convert Emily Coburn.[18]

So powerful, in fact, that enemies could not handle it and threw threats at both him and Joseph.

At meetings Joseph often let Sidney speak in his place, perhaps out of respect, perhaps out of knowing Sidney was a better orator and his doctrines were the same. Perhaps he knew Sidney had a deep-seated need for public speaking, and Joseph wished to satisfy that need and placate his friend—but it also saved Joseph time and energy to work on other, more important matters.

Although Sidney was 13 years older, he was clearly not Joseph's leader, according to all accounts of those who knew the two. Joseph undeniably viewed the church as his stewardship, being prophet, and did not defer to any man.

Critics nevertheless made claims to discredit him any way they could, including advancing a new theory—that Sidney actually influenced Joseph by "inventing the *Book of Mormon*." (See Appendix M: "Theories Attacking the *Book of Mormon*.")

Unlike Joseph, Sidney's passion for learning went all the way back to his childhood.

By contrast, Joseph had little use for reading or books growing up, but was a deep thinker on occasion.

But Sidney's welcome began wearing thin—at least among the young core of Joseph's closest allies, the Whitmer clan.

The reason: David Whitmer says Sidney encouraged Joseph to go with him to Ohio. So some of the members began to balk.

This idea for the Whitmers was especially difficult, as their farm compound was a base of operations that likely gave them a sense of pride. Traveling elsewhere would put them in the same class as all the other travelers—who had looked to the Whitmers' home as a place of security to which to bring friends for meetings, and as their central spot for camaraderie.

The Whitmers began turning against Sidney.

Fearing the impending "gathering" would be in Ohio, the Whitmers' concerns came to light especially when—without so much as visiting Ohio—on January 2, 1831, Joseph announced he had a revelation stating that the whole church was to move there. The announcement came at the next quarterly conference at Fayette in which they were told, "The enemy in the secret chambers seeketh your lives."[19] David Whitmer, of course, doubted this revelation and all others that no longer came through the seer stone. It had been 22 months since Joseph had given up the stone.

With Sydney now on board, the influence of the Three Witnesses declined markedly, and Whitmer, Cowdery, and Harris all seemed to see themselves being supplanted by the new, charismatic, popular public speaker.

This loss of prestige may have contributed to their later disaffection—a dissonance which would inspire mobs to come against the New Believers (detailed in Volume 2). But for now the directive was to "escape the power of the enemy and be gathered unto me a righteous people, without spot and blameless; wherefore, for this cause, I give unto you the commandment that ye should go to the Ohio."[20] (The key was "without spot and blameless." Time would prove that their failings and shortcomings would open the door for them to be vulnerable to the mobs.)

Meanwhile, some of the less faithful blamed Sidney for influencing Joseph, and others even accused Joseph of inventing the revelation "to deceive the people that in the end he might get gain," according to what John Whitmer said some members believed and expressed.[21]

Others of less faith, including (at times) David Whitmer, thought moving *en masse* to Ohio simply unwise.[22] Leaving his property, while doubting Joseph, did not make sense. Coming into play was the fact he was the son of a well-to-do farmer.

Joseph could see the opposition mounting. It was his 3rd in-house challenge (after the 2 incidents 5 months previously—1st, Oliver editing his revelation; 2nd, Oliver and the Whitmers believing in Hiram Page's stone).

But this new opposition to the gathering was even more difficult, as those with property did not want to leave it.

Nevertheless, Joseph persuaded them it was of God.

Still others agreed to pack up and leave from the get-go, putting the news in a positive light as an adventure and unquestionably the will of God.

Despite the varying reactions, within a few weeks most made the commitment to move. And by the end of January 1831, the first party was ready to head West to Ohio.

Meanwhile, Sidney gave a speech from Waterloo's courthouse steps, warning the local populace to leave. No record exists as to how many, if any, nonbelievers heeded his warning, but apparently he felt it important to make this bold announcement.

The sacrifice was significant for all, having to leave their hard-worked farms, their only property on earth, and sell at greatly reduced prices. In some cases they had to rent them out or simply desert them.

But even after they agreed to leave, Joseph had to urge them to get off their haunches and actually get going.


At Ohio, meanwhile, John Whitmer arrived, sent ahead by Joseph to lead the new Ohio converts[23] and prepare them to receive the influx of immigrating New York Saints.


Back in New York, more drama was unfolding. Joseph Knight was right in the thick of it and recorded it all: "Joseph and Sidney went down to Harmony to settle some business.

And the mob found they were gone, and they found [out] when they were expected back, and we found they had a plan laid to take Joseph and Sidney and me. . . . And the day we expected them [back from Harmony] I sent my son down to meet them and told them of their [the mob's] plan, and they turned across to Cenango Point. And so [we] went to the Lakes. And I loaded up what I could carry and went away that night for the Lakes. I also took my wife and daughter, for we were calculating to go soon, for we, a little before, had a revelation to go to Ohio. So the mob watched all night at the bridge. But behold we all came up missing, and the poor mob lost all their trouble [ended up watching in vain]. Now Joseph and I went right on to Kirtland, Ohio."[24]

This was on or shortly after January 8, 1831, and Emma accompanied them.

Unfortunately, she had been sick for weeks and was pregnant, so the move for her was particularly brutal in the cold winter winds. The journey would be 325 miles, and this would be her 8th move in 4 years of marriage.

Using Joseph Knight's sleigh, with some of their party on horseback, she, her husband, her hired maid, Edward Partridge, Sidney Rigdon, Ezra Thayre, and the ever-faithful Joseph Knight Sr.[25] made the long journey, taking copies of the *Book of Mormon*, literally escaping New York with their lives.

Before leaving Fayette, they made 2 stops, teaching and baptizing at both.[26]

So, the Ohio frontier would be Joseph and Emma's newest home. A home filled with numerous trials and adventures . . .

C H A P T E R 37

I N the spring of 1831 the main flock of New York believers launched final plans to emigrate.

First, they would have to sell their New York farms, herds, equipment, and goods, some at a devastating loss. But they would quickly learn that sacrifice was the order of the day.

In fact, that would be their hue and cry for the next 2 centuries—sacrifice for the Kingdom.

On February 4, 1831, Joseph and company reached Kirtland and made quite a splash. Coming into town on a sleigh, he, Emma, and a servant girl "drove up in front of my husband's store," reports Elizabeth Ann Whitney. Joseph jumped off the sleigh and went inside. "He reached his hand across the counter to my husband and called him by name."

Newel K. Whitney, the owner, was taken back and said, "I could not call you by name as you have mine."

Whitney was even more astonished by Joseph's response: "I am Joseph the Prophet. You have prayed me here; now what do you want of me?" He explained to Whitney that in New York he had seen Whitney in a vision praying for him to come to Kirtland.[1]

Joseph and Emma next went to the home of Whitney's partner, Sidney Gilbert, to stay the night. On the way the wagon overturned and the pregnant Emma was tossed into the snow.

At the Gilberts', Emma did not like the look of the room they were offered, and declined to stay, according to Henry Rollins, whose family was staying at the home.[2] However, the real reason could have been the lack of privacy, since another family was living there as well. Or, possibly, she found one of the families there incompatible with her own.

So they went back to Whitney. (Both the Gilberts and Whitneys ran the general store on Main Street, having launched it exactly 4 years earlier. The Whitneys recently had joined Joseph's faith.

Newel Whitney then generously offered his place to Emma, but his wife's aunt was cold to them because of Joseph's being a "preacher."[3]

Not feeling comfortable there either, the Smiths nevertheless stayed.

Whitney and his wife were gracious hosts and reportedly loved having Joseph and his wife with them. They even gave Joseph and Emma their bedroom, the 9 × 12 foot "east room"[4] off the main entrance, which Joseph and Emma may have partly shared with 2 of the Whitney children, who assisted them.[5] It was the only bedroom on the main floor, so this left Newel, Elizabeth Ann, and at least 3—perhaps all 5—of the children to move to an unfinished open area on the top floor, a true sacrifice by a benevolent family. The invitation ended up lasting several weeks, and the Whitneys treated them with kindness—especially Mrs. Whitney.[6]

They had actually prayed the previous autumn for the Holy Ghost to come into their lives. Then they heard a voice instructing them that the word of God was on its way. Parley P. Pratt and the other 3 missionaries had soon arrived and converted them, baptizing them in November, 3 months previous to Joseph's arrival.

So Joseph and his flock had a bit of a stronghold in Kirtland now from which to work—nearly 100 members, says Lucy;[7]

more, says Parley—plus the party of 6 that Joseph and Emma had brought via sleigh. In 3 months the main exodus of 200-plus members from New York would arrive, but until then—in those first 90 days—the Ohio converts would pour into the church with numbers doubling and doubling again. In fact, converts from Ohio living in Kirtland soon sprouted to 600 the first 90 days that Joseph was in town[8]—a surprising growth spurt that was highly welcomed.

These numbers sprang from the efforts of 9 influential families that immediately joined. Missionaries then brought others from the villages in droves.

One convert, Philo Dibble, was also prepared to receive the New Believers. He was thrilled when he heard that 4 men had come to town with a golden Bible, and that one had seen an angel. While others scorned the missionaries, Philo admitted, "I was glad of it"—because "angels had administered to the children of men again." His wife fought him, but he was converted to the church right when he first heard a sermon.[9]

"When I came out of the water," says Dibble, "I knew that I had been born of water and of the spirit, for my mind was illuminated with the Holy Ghost. . . . While in bed that night I felt what appeared to be a hand upon my left shoulder. And a sensation like fibers of fire immediately enveloped my body. . . . I was enveloped in a heavenly influence and could not sleep for joy."[10]

But this stunning success in the church did not go without opposition. Missionaries were persecuted. John Whitmer on one occasion had priests yell at him, "Delusion, delusion!"[11]

In Cleveland, when John Murdock spoke in the Masonic Hall, he had books and inkstands thrown at him.[12] Some missionaries were so worn out from their missions that they had to return to Kirtland for rest.[13]

But their tireless efforts paid off.

---

Meanwhile, other forces opposing them were gathering and forging public opinion, much of that from the local, regional, and national press.

James Gordon Bennett was the first New York City newspaper writer to cover the church, and actually toured upstate New York in the summer of 1831. (In later years Joseph would become close friends with a newspaper editor from New York City of a similar name—James Arlington Bennett.) James Gordon Bennett made this tour with future president Martin Van Buren, and filed a story with the *Morning Enquirer and Courier* in New York City. Bennett would someday own his own major newspaper—the largest in New York City. (See Appendix J: "Yellow Journalism and the New York Press" for various asides about his paper and the famous "yellow journalism" papers referred to earlier.)

Despite the opposition, Joseph's Ohio base was booming. Hundreds of converts were pouring in. Almost too fast to keep up with.

Knowing he needed to standardize and replicate his teachings for everyone (so they could have uniformity), Joseph set out to disseminate church doctrine by publishing the revelations he had received. This way all members could have access to them.

But the challenge of the Ohio converts was not only receiving the information, but living up to the standards that Joseph taught. While having what they felt was the truth, they still had to battle human weaknesses—pride, envy, and disobedience to God's commandments.

Joseph had struggled in New York with some degree of rebellion from his flock of new converts, but his efforts now—with the Ohio converts—would be like jumping from the frying pan into the fire . . .

THE first of Joseph's Ohio problems were more counterfeit revelations to contend with—similar to Hiram Page's stone in New York. The first of a series of such revelations came from an unexpected source, a member named Sister Hubble who believed she was a prophetess.

Similar to Page, Sister Hubble was issuing these revelations, as well as commandments and, even worse, like Page she was gaining followers. Joseph believed the Lord would set things straight. And it happened via a revelation he received. "This ye shall know assuredly—that there is none other [than the church president] appointed unto you to receive commandments and revelations."[1]

"Revelations," as referred to here, meant those given for the whole church. Church members had the right to receive revelations for themselves and their "stewardships"—within the boundaries of their callings—but it stopped there.

Joseph was further disconcerted by certain strange behavior in his meetings—members going into fits and trances. Much of this was a continuance of their previous churches' culture and the behavior exhibited there. Lucy reports:

"This they supposed to be a display of the power of God. Shortly after Joseph arrived, he called the church together in order to show them the difference between the Spirit of God and the spirit of the devil.

"He said, 'If a man arose in meeting to speak and was seized with a kind of paroxysm that drew his face and limbs in a violent and unnatural manner which made him appear to be in pain, and if he gave utterance to strange sounds which were incomprehensible to his audience, they might rely upon it that he had the spirit of the devil. But on the contrary, when a man speaks by the Spirit of God, he speaks from the abundance of his heart—his mind is filled with intelligence; and even should he be excited, it does not cause him to do anything ridiculous or unseemly.'

"He then called upon one of the brethren to speak, who arose and made the attempt but was immediately seized with a kind of spasm which drew his face, arms and fingers in a most astonishing manner.

"Hyrum, by Joseph's request, laid hands on the man, whereupon he sunk back in a state of complete exhaustion. Joseph then called upon another man to speak, who stood leaning in an open window. This man also attempted to speak but was thrown forward into the house, prostrate, unable to utter a syllable. He was administered to and the same effects followed as in the first instance.

"These, together with a few other examples of the same kind, convinced the brethren of the mistake under which they had been laboring."[2]

Thus, Hyrum exorcised evil spirits that night—a stunning example of what Joseph had been teaching.

Meanwhile, Parley P. Pratt of the bold young missionary force sent to Missouri returned to Ohio. Immediately Joseph gave him an interesting assignment—to exorcise evil spirits throughout the Ohio branches. He accomplished this by using the same priesthood powers that Joseph had used to free Newel Knight when he was overtaken in New York, the same power just used by Hyrum.

Despite the setbacks, Joseph saw tremendous potential in Ohio.

Isaac Morley generously had a cabin built for Joseph and his family—one for which the couple expressed tremendous gratitude. It was, in fact, in answer to a revelation on February 4, 1831, which stated a house would be built for them. As for Joseph's view on living while helping others, he believed in the finer things of living—he did not want to live as a Spartan—but also was generous to a fault and believed in absolute sharing. He often shared—or outright gave—whatever he had to others.

Possessing the heart for it himself, Joseph received a revelation on February 9, 1831, stating that the Saints should now divide their property and live the Law of Consecration, based on the same New Testament teachings in the 2nd chapter of Acts that had so intrigued Isaac Morley and Sidney Rigdon before they had joined the Saints:

"And all that believed were together and had all things in common; and sold their possessions and goods, and parted them to all men, as every man had need.[3] . . .Neither was there any among them that lacked; for as many as were possessors of land or houses sold them, and brought the prices of the things that were sold, and laid them down at the apostles' feet; and distribution was made unto every man according as he had need."[4] Thus, the New York Saints began a new order of living—one practiced 3 times earlier in Kirtland, but this one under the auspices of the restored Priesthood.

In this attempt they would divide up the various jobs, while their temporal leader, Edward Partridge, would be chosen as the "bishop" to oversee all their worldly concerns—buildings, cattle, crops, lands, and all their goods—including helping the sick and aged, supervising new businesses, and building schools and churches. His tasks included the redistribution of all goods and food according to each family's needs, while all surplus would be used to expand the kingdom as he saw fit.

While in the secular tradition it could be considered an early form of communism, it was in Joseph's view the Lord's way of economic prosperity. While Latter-day Saint observers since have viewed Marxist communism as an economic and political system developed by the spiritual adversary as a counterfeit system of the correct one, and ruled by the uninspired judgments of men (and made worse by enforcing it with a police state)—they see the 19th-century Law of Consecration as entirely different. Joseph's group emphasized voluntary compliance, combined with heavenly inspiration to direct it. The only condition for the Lord's law of consecration to work, as Joseph pointed out, was for the New Believers to be humble in their attitude, sharing of their goods, and hardworking in their services.

Partridge, their bishop, was known for honesty, humility, and perseverance when the believers' imperfections soon set in, and it was his task to settle their squabbles. All this was appointed by God, as Joseph proclaimed, to alleviate their poverty, rid themselves of materialism, divide as needed among themselves, and allow Joseph to be free to work on spiritual matters, including his revision of the King James Bible, begun 8 months previously, starting with Genesis (covered in Chapter 26). Joseph, newly arrived in Kirtland, was now, in February 1831, finishing the book of Genesis.[5]


Coequal in Joseph's day-to-day concerns was his family. After "several weeks" living in the Whitneys' small frame house, Joseph and Emma moved in early April[6] from Kirtland to the Morley farm,[7] about 1 mile east of the center of town. Here, on April 30, 1831, Emma gave birth to twins—a boy and a girl—but she had been weakened by her midwinter sickness, the ordeal of traveling, and the wreck in the snow the first day in town. Samuel Whitney recalls she had "hard labor, and the blood went to her head, which became black"[8] (apparently meaning her face turned dark). Joseph then sent for a Doctor Card, who came and bled her.[9] The twins died. They had lived 3 hours.[10]

Joseph had told others to not use this doctor but, according to Whitney, the doctor stated later that Joseph panicked and called for him anyway. The Morleys' daughters kindly nursed Emma back to health, but she was now childless and, after 3 births, was severely saddened.[11]

A neighbor, Julia C. Murdock, delivered twins the very next day, but died 6 hours later. John Murdock, the widower, was overwhelmed. He tried raising the twins for 10 days, while dealing with his other young children, all the while farming. Finding it impossible, he asked for help. Joseph and Emma took in the 2 infants to raise with John's blessing, and named them Julia and Joseph Murdock Smith.

A spectacular miracle would later take place at the Morley farm where Joseph and Emma now lived, as discussed in detail in Volume 2. Also covered in that volume is a violent mob attack on Joseph and Sidney at their next residence.

The peace in Ohio they had ridden into was about to evaporate.

In New York, meanwhile, the main body of believers prepared themselves to leave for Ohio. And this would complete the final chapter for the New York Saints. Their journey to Ohio, in fact, would be a microcosm of the early church in general, with its problems, hopes and dreams . . .

THE 30 Saints in Colesville, New York, were trying to leave. Yet their neighbors continually persecuted them, right up to the last minute. Newel Knight, the leader for the exodus, did his utmost to help his group emigrate as one body.

The Fayette branch of 80, however, met a different fate. Neighbors not of their faith kindly saw them off, waving good-byes and praying for their safety. One man even gave them $17—a generous sum in its day ($761 in today's money). This group set forth on the 3rd or 4th of May, 1831.[1] (Preston Nibley's edition of Lucy's book puts the launch month as February or March, 1831, but he or the editors who stated that are mistaken. A footnote to that effect is in the Stratford Books edition—another reason it is the most accurate, up-to-date, and readable edition.) This group was led by Lucy Mack Smith, Joseph's mother, who received a unanimous vote to lead the 80 members on a 5-day barge journey through the Erie Canal. From a check given by someone to help her family she also dispensed food among the needy.

The exodus to Ohio consisted of 3 main groups:

1. The Colesville group of 30 left first, launching late April and arriving May 1 in Buffalo. But winds blew ice into the harbor, delaying them 11 days before they could leave for Ohio.

2. Next was the Fayette group, leaving days later on May 3 or 4, arriving at Buffalo by May 8. It consisted of 80 people in

2 barges—one with 30, led by Thomas B. Marsh, and a second with 50, led by Lucy Mack Smith, consisting of 20 adults and 30 children. Finally was:

3. The Palmyra group of 50, led by Martin Harris. This group left New York as the Fayette group arrived in Ohio, and was the last group, obviously, to travel there.

When Lucy's barge launched, she boldly gathered the members together and reminded them they were "traveling by the commandment of the Lord as much as father Lehi was when he left Jerusalem."[2] She exhorted them "to be solemn and to lift their hearts to God continually in prayer, that we might be prospered. And for the present, let the sisters take seats on one side of the boat and the brethren on the other."[3]

While they had overall exhibited remarkable faith to leave their property and make the journey, she became disconcerted by their human frailties, watching some spend their last money on clothes and then expect others to give them food, for example. This caused about 20 adults and 30 children to be destitute of food. In her rough draft she seems equally disappointed by those "in better circumstances," who "did not seem to consider that the revelation that they help each other was binding upon them." Consequently, she states, "The burden was thrown entirely upon my shoulders. From this time forward I furnished the whole 50 persons with food from day to day."[4]

She also stamped out bickering and complaining, disciplined the overenthusiastic children, assisted the sick ones, helped care for the babies, and counseled the adults.

Additionally, she took control of certain children when their mothers gave up on them.[5]

She also led them through songs and prayers. The ship's captain loved to hear them sing. He even turned the steering over to his first mate so he could listen. His wife, however, who always traveled along to cook for him, refused to go on the journey because of who these people were.[6]

Lucy states, "At the approach of sunset, we seated ourselves and sang another hymn. The music sounded beautiful upon the water and had a salutary effect upon every heart, filling our souls with love and gratitude to God for his manifold goodness towards us."[7]

Lucy Mack Smith's chief concerns—more than the hardships—were the complaints.

This erupted only part way into their trip. Lucy describes it:

"On getting about halfway to Buffalo, the canal broke. This gave rise to . . . discontentment, which was expressed in terms like the following:

"'Well, the canal is broke now and here we are, and here we are likely to be, for we can go no further. We have left our homes, and here we have no means of getting a living; consequently we shall have to starve.'

"'No, no,' said I, 'you will not starve, brethren, nor anything of that sort; only do be patient and stop your murmuring.'"[8]

The Colesville and Fayette members then rendezvoused in Buffalo. However, storms iced them in at the harbor on Lake Erie, so the trip to Ohio was delayed. The Colesville group had already been detained there a week, so during this time Hyrum and his father left them for Kirtland to meet a deadline.[9]

Lucy displayed remarkable leadership, but because she held prayer in public and told strangers who they were, the Colesville Saints started a second wave of complaining—criticizing her because they expected to be "mobbed before the next morning."[10]

To these critics she said, "Mob it is then. We shall attend to prayer before sunset."[11]

She then searched for a particular boat captain who had bought her brother's steamboat, and she found him. Because of that connection, he made room for her people, a small miracle in itself, even though his boat was full. But they had to settle for deck passage[12] (open to the elements and the cold), to which she consented.

The Fayette branch members would leave their 2 barges and merge as 1 group on the steamboat (while the Colesville Saints remained on their boat). The next day the Fayette group transferred their goods to it, "and by the time that we had fairly settled ourselves, it began to rain. This rendered our situation very uncomfortable, and some of the sisters . . . complained bitterly because we had not hired a house [hotel] till the boat was ready to start. In fact, their case was rather a trying one, for some of them had sick children."[13]

Facing this third wave of complaints, she sent Hiram Page to find a room for the women and sick children, "but [he] returned unsuccessful. At this the sisters renewed their complaints." So, "I set out myself with my son William, although it was still raining very fast, to see if it were possible to procure a shelter for them and their children."[14]

Lucy was soon on shore, facing the seemingly impossible task of finding a room for the women with sick children in a harbor town already booked to the hilt . . .

A T the first tavern at which Lucy and William arrived, the landlord said he could easily make room for Lucy's sick passengers. But a woman who was already renting for the night refused to let them stay. She feared catching sickness from one of the children, even though she would not be in contact with them. An obviously opulent woman, she was booking 2 rooms. So the landlord tried talking her into giving up one of the rooms she had booked, and keep just one large room for herself, but she refused. Lucy did not allow this selfishness, from a woman of means, to discourage her, so she battled through the rains with her son, searching for another room to book.

At one point she recounts how her boldness turned into a blessing—she eventually found a woman on shore ready to rent them a row of rooms for all the women and sick children, simply because Lucy had boldly proclaimed her religion when the lady asked who they were. This woman even wanted to learn about their beliefs.[1] So they had a night out of the rain.

Returning to the boat, Lucy learned the worse news yet: the captain's report said the ice was over 20 feet thick, and they would be caked in at least 2 more weeks.[2]

Hearing this, the strong-willed teenager, Porter Rockwell, left the boat to visit his uncle, presumably near Buffalo, whereupon Porter's mother tried stopping him. But he paid her no attention. Chagrined, she called upon Lucy to help.

"Mother Smith, do get Porter back, for he won't mind anybody but you," she reportedly said.[3]

But Porter would not even mind Lucy this time. Other teens disembarked with Porter, following him. Lucy reprimanded and cajoled them, and they all returned to the barge. All except Porter, who would later meet up with the group in Kirtland.[4] But for the moment, it caused consternation to not only his parents but to Mother Smith as well.

Then there was confusion on the boat. Both men and women began breaking into arguments and lambasting Lucy with a fourth wave of complaints. This, she said, was making the church look bad to hundreds of people on shore and in other barges, watching.[5]

For this, she told her people off royally: "How can you expect the Lord to prosper you when you are continually murmuring against him?"[6]

Adding further distress was the group of teenage girls now flirting with strangers[7]—not a socially acceptable behavior of the times.

Next, she exhorted the people on her barge to have faith that the 20 feet of ice could open up and allow them to resume their journey. "At that instant a noise was heard like bursting thunder. The captain cried, 'Every man to his post.' The ice parted, leaving barely a passage for the boat . . . . We had barely passed through the avenue when the ice closed together again and the Colesville brethren were left in Buffalo unable to follow us."[8]

It was the Colesville group—now left in Buffalo and iced in—that had castigated her for telling others who they were, fearing public opinion, while perhaps lacking the faith of Lucy. (One can understand their sensitivity—it was they who had been persecuted by neighbors in New York, not the Fayette branch members with whom Lucy was traveling. The Fayette members, as stated, had been the group treated like royalty when they left.)

Lucy continues:

"After our miraculous escape from the wharf at Buffalo, we called our company together and had a prayer meeting, in which we offered up our thanks to God for his mercy, which he had manifested towards us in our deliverance. We then sang and commenced praying. But before our meeting was broken up, the captain's mate came to me and said, 'Mrs. Smith, do, for God's sake, have your children stop praying, or we shall all go to hell together; we cannot keep one single man to his post, [and] we should go to the devil, for they are so taken up with your praying.' (He said my 'children' because they all called me 'Mother.') Therefore our meeting was broken up.[9]

"As we were leaving the harbor, one of the bystanders exclaimed, 'There goes the Mormon company! That boat is sunk in the water nine inches deeper than ever it was before and, mark it, she will sink—there is nothing surer.' In fact, they were so sure of it that they went straight to the office and had it published that we were sunk, so that when we arrived at Fairport we read in the papers the news of our own death."[10]

More stormy weather hit them on their journey across Lake Erie. Some members got seasick. Now, dehydrated, they were in dire need of water, but their supply was deleted. So Lucy bought some from the cook—but only for the sick among them, since water was of short supply and expensive.

Then, running out of food, Lucy went ashore again and this time bought bread and molasses for the 30 small children on board whom she still personally kept fed.

Finally they arrived at Fairport, Ohio, May 11. When they disembarked, they barraged her with a fifth and final wave of complaining (even after miraculously being spared from the elements by the woman finding them rooms when all had been sold out, and by the ice breaking up to allow passage for only their barge before closing up again).[11] The women were pouting, and some crying. Several men gathered about Lucy, grumbling that they had no shelter on shore, nor any awaiting in Kirtland; further, they didn't even have transportation to Kirtland, 12 miles overland.

On shore, Lucy was actually fearful about transportation, so she quietly asked a stranger about it. To her great relief, when she turned around, she beheld Samuel and Joseph.

Samuel had been warned in a dream to meet the Fayette flock.[12]

His arrival with Joseph made for perfect timing—Lucy was at the end of her rope and needed a boost at this point, so it was a much-needed miracle.

As soon as Samuel and Joseph saw their mother, they wept. They had heard from another traveler, Solomon Humfry, of the ordeal she had faced on the journey, stating that the fatigue was simply too much for her and that her life was in danger. Joseph now pulled her from the group, finding her perfectly exhausted from taking care of them all.[13]

Solomon Humfry had traveled with Lucy's group on the boat and was perhaps the oldest elder in the church at the time, only 2 months younger than Lucy; thus, he could relate to her better than the others and see how the stresses of the journey were impacting her.

Joseph and Samuel loaded everyone up on the teams they had brought with them, and soon they made their way southwestward to Kirtland.

There all 80 received shelter. And there they rejoiced. Lucy presently had a sweet reunion with her husband at the Morleys' house.

Days later, on May 14, the 2nd group of believers arrived—the 30 from Colesville. Days after that the group of 50 from Palmyra led by Martin Harris arrived. So the New York Saints were now all finally intact and safe at a gathering place, which they had for half a year been anticipating.

Yet there were new miracles and problems awaiting them, the likes of which they would never have dreamed.

Because of the openheartedness of so many Ohioans, there were already by April 1831—the one-year anniversary of the church's organization—about 600 Saints spread throughout Ohio and New York.[14] Now that it was late May, there were even more because of all the conversions taking place.

And within 4 years, Kirtland itself would double to 2,000 total residents, with another 200 in nearby villages and farms. (This was just 300 short of the 2,500 number required to be a "town," but it was still a substantial, vibrant community.)

Perhaps half of this 2,200 number were New Believers, with at least several dozen Saints still in New York, continuing branches of the church there.

But for Joseph and his family, and the vast majority of Saints, persecution was—at least for awhile—behind them, with a thriving community accepting them.

It became a place they could immediately call home.

wo important topics of the young prophet will surface in Volumes 2 and 3 of this biography: prophecies and polygamy.

His people will observe Joseph in action as a prophet, seeing prophecies come to pass as he apparently saw the immediate future of some individuals and the more distant future of others. Some prophecies would assist, encourage, or warn individuals on a personal level, while other prophecies would delineate in remarkable detail specific events that would transpire on the national scene.

Jane Snyder Richards, wife of an apostle, reported: "[He] was able to foretell the mysteries of the future with a marked degree of accuracy, and nearly [with] as much readiness as the ordinary individual could relate the happenings of the past.[1]

Bathsheba W. Smith stated: "I have heard the Prophet Joseph preach many times. I have heard him prophesy, and I never knew but that everything came to pass that he said."[2]

These volumes will also depict Joseph's struggling with the new topic of polygamy—a biblical principle restored and practiced for a time in the church he founded (a principle eventually abandoned starting in 1890), yet one that he personally avoided as long as possible, fearing the wrath of Emma, the bride of his youth. This principle proved to be one of his greatest challenges—a principle he felt was revealed to him by the heavens—but which he had no desire to practice. The faith the Saints showed in attempting to practice this doctrine is remarkable, as one reads their journals and letters, but it was difficult beyond imagination. The persecution they would receive from the outside and pressures from the inside drove them to distraction.

The final 2 volumes will also portray Joseph's people struggling with more new trials, as they gain a foothold on the American religious landscape.

Among their challenges (covered in Volume 2) will be an economic collapse in Kirtland, in which many, especially those of his faith, will blame Joseph, even though it coincides with a national depression. Through both of the final 2 volumes mobs will rage and drive his followers again and again.

As for Joseph's personal friends and acquaintances, many described his strengths and weaknesses. As a result, this 3-volume biography includes all known tidbits of his personalty— ranging from his humor to his anger. The next 2 volumes will show additional personality traits, revealing his uniqueness. Despite his flaws, he was respected and even adored by those who knew him best.

Many sensed an inner power within him, which they said came from the forces of heaven when he labored in his calling as a prophet. While a mere mortal, they believed he was fortified with extra inspiration when doing the work of God. Outside that calling, he was just another fellow, but one who was greatly admired by friends and neighbors, many of whom left interesting observations.

Jane Snyder Richards spoke of his approachable nature to even the poor. "As the leader of his people he was ever active and progressive but always modest and considerate of them and their trying circumstances. Socially he was an ideal of affability and always approachable to the humblest of his acquaintances."[3]

William Farrington Cahoon related: "I have seen the sick healed under his administrations in many instances. I have seen cripples healed immediately and leap for joy."[4]

Joseph's first cousin was Jesse Smith, who wrote, "I am unable to fully describe my sensations when in the presence of this wonderful man. . . . I have never heard any human voice, not even my mother's, that was so attractive to me. Even his bitterest enemies, if they had the privilege of hearing him speak, became mollified, and forgot their anger. . . . His domestic animals seemed to love him. . . . The dog and the horses rejoiced when they saw this man. . . . His children rejoiced when he was present."[5]

General Moses Wilson of the Missouri state militia would ride with Joseph to a trial and record, "He was a very remarkable man. I carried him into my house a prisoner in chains, and in less than two hours my wife loved him better than she did me."[6]

John W. Hess confided of his loyalty to Joseph: "During his short stay, I became very much attached to him, and learned to love him more dearly than any other person I ever met, my father and mother not excepted."[7]

A postscript from Hess sheds more insight: "I used to walk six miles every day to see him during his stay in the Richmond jail, although a boy of about 14 years."[8] Likely the lad was afforded the same respect that Joseph gave adults, or young Hess doubtless would not have felt motivated to keep taking the remarkable 12-mile round-trip journey each day through the dead of winter.

John M. Bernhisel testified: "Having been a boarder in General Smith's family for more than nine months, with abundant opportunities to contemplate his character and observe his conduct, I have concluded . . . He is kind and obliging, generous and benevolent, sociable and cheerful. . . . But it is in the gentle charities of domestic life, as the tender and affectionate husband and parent, the warm and sympathizing friend, that the prominent traits of his character are revealed."[9]

Emma reported that whenever Joseph went to work in the garden there would soon be a small crowd around him that "would tramp the ground down faster than he could hoe it up."[10]

Illinois Governor Thomas Ford stated, "It must not be supposed that the pretended Prophet practiced the tricks of a common imposter; that he was a dark and gloomy person, with a long beard, a grave and severe aspect, and a reserved and saintly carriage of his person; on the contrary, he was full of levity, even to boyish romping."[11]

As early as 1831 Ezra Booth, an enemy of Joseph in Kirtland, would write a revealing letter to Edward Partridge. It was highly critical of Joseph, yet insightful: "Have you not frequently observed in Joseph a want of that sobriety, prudence, and stability which are some of the most prominent traits of the Christian character? Have you not discovered in him a spirit of lightness and levity, a temper of mind easily irritated, and an habitual proneness to jesting and joking?"[12]

George Q. Cannon described similar traits in Joseph, but found them endearing: "He could at other times unbend and be as happy and unconventional as a boy. This was one of the most striking characteristics; and it was sometimes held up to scorn by his traducers."[13]

J. B. Newhall, a traveler and journalist from Massachusetts, reported: "He is a jolly fellow and, according to his view, is one of the last persons on earth whom God would have raised up a prophet or priest. He is so diametrically opposite to that which he ought to be in order to merit the titles or to act in such offices."[14]

Brigham Young testified of Joseph's teachings shortly after his 2-year investigation of the church: "I have never seen him, and do not know his private character. The doctrine he teaches is all I know about the matter—bring anything against that if you can. As to anything else I do not care. If he acts like a devil, he has brought forth a doctrine that will save us, if we will abide it. . . . I never embrace any man in my faith. But the doctrine he has produced will save you and me and the whole world."[15]

Benjamin Johnson, who knew Joseph well, said Joseph "would allow no arrogance. . . . Criticisms even by his associates were rarely acceptable, and contradictions [against him] would rouse in him the lion at once."[16] This was apparently one of the self-criticisms Joseph referred to when he spoke of his own follies.

Peter Burnett, a non-Mormon who later became the first governor of California, wrote of Joseph: "He possessed the most indomitable perseverance . . . and deemed himself born to command, and he did command."[17] Burnett also reported a weakness of Joseph. It involved John McDaniel, another non-Mormon, who doubted Joseph could prophesy. This sparked the church leader's temper to the point of almost instigating a fistfight. Joseph reportedly responded: "Nobody can slander me! If my brethren cannot protect me I will do so myself!"[18]

He was quick to anger over personal attacks, as well as instances in which he heard women insulted. He was quite aware of his weaknesses, and some revelations pointed them out even more clearly. The first was in 1828, in which he was rebuked for allowing himself to be persuaded by Martin Harris to take the *Book of Mormon* manuscript. His weaknesses were referred to in the plural as the revelation stated, "And behold how oft you have transgressed the commandments and laws of God."[19]

A year later, in 1829, another revelation declared, "I command you my servant Joseph to repent and walk more uprightly before me."[20] Four years later another revelation revealed, "Verily, I say unto Joseph Smith, Jr.—you have not kept the commandments and must needs stand rebuked before the Lord."[21] Five years after that, still another revelation indicated that God works through men, as imperfect as they are:

"Unto this end have I raised you up, that I might show forth my wisdom through the weak things of the earth."[22]

(Note that while prophets are men laden with imperfections, their attributes are not "malignant" or grossly sinful—such as emotional, physical, or sexual abuse, stealing, or cheating in its various forms.)

In Ohio on June 6, 1832, Joseph handwrote the following letter to Emma, which not only shows his concern for improvement, but the manner in which he should tackle it—through pondering and prayer in a secret place:

"Dear Wife . . . I have visited a grove which is just back of the town almost every day where I can be secluded from the eyes of any mortal, and there give vent to all the feelings of my heart in meditation and prayer. I have called to mind all the past moments of my life and am left to mourn and shed tears of sorrow for my folly in suffering the adversary of my soul to have so much power over me as he has had in times past. But God is merciful and has forgiven my sins, and I rejoice that he sendeth forth the comforter unto as many as believe and humbleth themselves before him. . . . I will try to be contented with my lot [of imperfection], knowing that God is my friend. In him I shall find comfort. I have given my life into his hands."[23]

This same type of pondering took place again while he wandered the streets of New York City. There, he did not report self-scrutiny, rather, he studied others within the city. From that, his followers learned that a secret wilderness can sometimes be in the midst of a bustling metropolis rather than a secluded forest, so long as one is able to find inner peace.

Others who knew Joseph were specific in their descriptions. John Taylor, a highly intelligent leader, related, "I have traveled hundreds of thousands of miles, been on different continents, and mingled among all classes and creeds of people. Yet I have never met a man so intelligent as he was."[24]

William Clayton, a talented clerk and inventor, described him in a personal letter to a friend: "He [is] a man of sound judgment, and possessed of abundance of intelligence, and while you listen to his conversation, you receive intelligence, which expands your mind and causes your heart to rejoice. He is very familiar. . . . I can converse with him just as easy as I can with you."[25]

Howard Coray wrote: "I sat and listened to his preaching at the stand in Nauvoo a great many times, when I have been completely carried away with his indescribable eloquence—

power of expression—speaking as I have never heard any other man speak."[26]

Benjamin Johnson, cited above, also recorded: "I had great opportunity to scrutinize his life and habits. Such were the social and religious elements of his unselfish nature, that those who knew him best loved him most."[27]

This was a common thread through reports by friends. Lucy Meserve Smith (not related to his mother) echoed, "Indeed, he was loved best by those who were the most acquainted with him."[28]

William Holmes Walker confided, "The more extensive my acquaintance and experience became with him, the more my confidence in him increased."[29]

Benjamin Johnson added: "And to me, who became associated with him personally in his family, who became his confidential friend, his financial agent, his trusted companion and nurse in his sickness—to me, he was the embodiment and perfection of all that I could comprehend in perfect manhood,"[30] notwithstanding his weaknesses which Johnson also occasionally saw.

John W. Hess wrote: "There was something heavenly and angelic in his looks that I never witnessed in the countenance of any other person."[31]

Emmeline Blanche Wells also described his countenance: "His expression was mild and almost childlike in repose, and when addressing the people who loved him—it seemed to adoration—the glory of his countenance was beyond description."[32]

She also examined his remarkable power, which the believers declared was the power of God: "At other times the great power of his manner, more than of his voice (which was sublimely eloquent to me) seemed to shake the place on which we stood and penetrate the inmost soul of his hearers, and I am sure that they would have laid down their lives to defend him. I always listened spellbound to his every utterance—the chosen of God in this last dispensation."[33]

In comparing Joseph to Daniel (the prophet of the Old Testament) and Cyrus the Great (founder of the Persian Empire under the Archaemenid dynasty), Parley P. Pratt wrote, "In short . . . the gifts, wisdom, and devotion of a Daniel were united with the boldness, courage, temperance, perseverance, and generosity of a Cyrus."[34]

Unlike reformers of prior centuries, Joseph declared his revolutionary mission succinctly—"I am a witness that there is a God, for I saw Him in open day, while praying in a silent grove, in the spring of 1820." Edward Stevenson records that Joseph made that statement in a schoolhouse at Pontiac, Michigan, "where people thronged in large numbers, more than could be able to find even standing space, in and around the house," creating a "moving, stirring sensation" through the town. "He further testified that God, the Eternal Father, pointing to a separate personage, in the likeness of Himself, said: 'This is my Beloved Son; here ye Him.' O how these words thrilled my entire system, and filled me with joy unspeakable to behold one who, like Paul the apostle of olden time, could with boldness testify that he had been in the presence of Jesus Christ!"[35]

On another occasion, Joseph made declaration of his revolutionary message, which no Reformer had been able to claim: "I will not tell you much of what the Lord told Paul, or of what He told Peter, but I will tell you what the Lord told me."[36]

Nor did any Reformer ever claim, as Joseph did, that he knew the angels so well that he would recognize them by the sound of their voices, even before he would see their faces.[37] This declaration came from Joseph Smith to Joseph B. Noble one day while they were cutting hay in a field.

Similarly, in a stunning claim, John Taylor stated that Joseph was in communication with "such men, for instance, as Abraham, Isaac, Jacob, Noah, Adam, Seth, Enoch, and Jesus and the Father, and the apostles that lived on this continent as well as those who lived on the Asiatic continent. He seemed to be as familiar with these people as we are with one another."[38]

Edward Stevenson revealed more of Joseph's revolutionary mission. He said that Joseph declared that God had fulfilled the words of John the Revelator, citing John in Revelations: "And I saw another angel fly in the midst of heaven, having the everlasting gospel to preach unto them that dwell on the earth, and to every nation, and kindred, and tongue, and people. Saying with a loud voice, 'Fear God, and give glory to him; for the hour of his judgment is come.'"[39]

Many Latter-day Saints believe that angel was Moroni. Stevenson added, "The angel had done his work; the true Church was set up with, first Apostles, secondarily Prophets, with gifts, etc." Stevenson refers to the church set up in the latter days, just as it was first established in the days of Christ. In fact, he is referring to the New Testament scripture, "And he gave some apostles, and some prophets, and some evangelists, and some pastors and teachers." This scripture is actually a letter from the Apostle Paul, directed to the saints—members of the church—at Ephesus. Paul explains why Christ set up His church:

"For the perfecting of the saints, for the work of the ministry, for the edifying of the body of Christ [the church membership]: Till we all come in the unity of the faith, and of the knowledge of the Son of God, unto a perfect man, unto the measure of the stature of the fullness of Christ: That we henceforth be no more children, tossed to and fro, and carried about with every wind of doctrine, by the sleight of men, and cunning craftiness, whereby they lie in wait to deceive."[40] Paul unveils the importance of Christ's church—as a protection from those lying in wait to deceive.

Edward Stevenson boldly proclaimed Joseph Smith as the instrument through whom Christ worked to re-establish that church, just as it had first been established when the Savior Himself lived upon the earth 18 centuries earlier.

Stevenson then quoted Joseph: "And as a servant of God, I promise you, inasmuch as you will repent and be baptized for the remission of your sins, you shall receive the Holy Ghost, and speak with tongues, and the signs shall follow you, and by this you may test me as a prophet sent of God."[41]


Joseph Smith's life, in its entirety, was to Latter-day Saints one of keen discipleship, unbounded generosity, and charismatic influence, as revealed by his followers in page after page of their journals and letters. His mission and claims were so unique that the missionaries he sent out challenged people to 2 simple steps—to read the *Book of Mormon* and pray about it to learn if it was from God.

Likewise, in the final chapter of that book, an ancient prophet invites the reader to "ask God, the Eternal Father, in the name of Christ, if these things are not true." Then comes that prophet's promise, restated in Chapter 23 of this biography, that, "If ye shall ask with a sincere heart, with real intent, having faith in Christ, he will manifest the truth of it unto you."[42] That ancient prophet was Moroni, the same who released the plates to Joseph 14 centuries later.

Without that challenge, claim Latter-day Saints, the current 15 million members worldwide would not have learned for themselves the truthfulness of the Book of Mormon, nor would they have united their hearts to the latter-day work they say is directed by Jesus Christ Himself and restored through Joseph Smith, His prophet on planet Earth.

# Appendices

# T A B L E  O F
# A P P E N D I C E S

# A History of Joseph's Histories

(REFERRED TO IN THE PREFACE)

With the advent of modern scholarship, at least 11 attempts by Joseph Smith to write his history have come to light.

The 1st is a 6-page history that Joseph wrote on 3 leaves of a ledger book, penned between the summer of 1831 and November 27, 1831. Modern handwriting analysis shows it was written by Frederick G. Williams, a scribe and First Counselor to Joseph before Williams apostatized. (Significantly, within that record is Joseph's earliest known written account of his First Vision. For decades it was assumed his only accounts of the vision were written years later.)

Joseph rarely wrote his own journal. He handwrote only parts during 1832 and 1835. The remainder he dictated, as he records on July 5, 1839: "I was dictating history. I say dictating, for I seldom use the pen myself. I always dictate all my communications, but employ a scribe to write them."[1] Yet he had problems with some scribes, and faced other roadblocks while trying to keep a journal:

"Since I have been engaged in laying the foundation of the Church of Jesus Christ of Latter-day Saints, I have been prevented in various ways from continuing my Journal and the History in a manner satisfactory to myself or in justice to the cause. Long imprisonments, vexatious and long continued lawsuits—the treachery of some of my clerks; the death of others; and the poverty of myself and brethren from continued plunder and driving, have prevented my handing down to posterity a connected memorandum of events desirable to all lovers of truth."[2]

Then came Joseph's 2nd attempt at writing a history. On November 27, 1831 he began writing a daily journal, in addition to launching a ledger book. This was significant because it showed when his first written, 6-page account ended, and it showed when he first attempted keeping, separately, a daily journal and a history of the church. In that history of the church, he had important church-related documents recorded in the letter book. Both the letter book and the journal were later used as the basic sources for the later writing of Joseph's official history, published as *History of the Church of Jesus Christ of Latter-day Saints*, in 7 volumes plus an index (actually, the last volume of this set covers a period of the church's history after his life), and the more recent *Joseph Smith Papers*.

Joseph's 3rd attempt at writing a history came in October 1834, when Oliver Cowdery, editor of the *Messenger and Advocate* newspaper in Kirtland, Ohio, introduced the first published history of the church. This account was in the form of letters between Cowdery and W. W. Phelps. It was to be, according to Cowdery, the "full history of the rise of the Church of the Latter Day Saints and the most interesting parts of its progress to the present time." Cowdery also states how Joseph was to assist them: "With his labor and with authentic documents now in our possession, we hope to render this a pleasing and agreeable narrative."[3]

But this history by Cowdery was a bit overhyped. It was far from being a strong narrative. It was, in fact, merely a series of 8 letters covering random historical events, beginning in the October 1834 issue (which discussed the restoration of the priesthood by heavenly messengers) and ending in the October 1835 issue (with the visitation of Moroni to Joseph).

That newspaper series of 8 letters was transcribed into Joseph's journal in 1835.

The 4th attempt at writing a history of Joseph and the church came from Warren Parrish, another scribe. It is sometimes referred to as the 1835 journal. One day Parrish and Joseph picked up Joseph's "large journal" from Frederick G. Williams. Then, later that same day, Parrish began writing a history of Joseph. Soon, however, he switched his efforts to transcribing the letters between Cowdery and Phelps (which Williams had begun transcribing but had not finished).[4] Parrish only managed to finish transcribing the 8 letters into Joseph's history, then inexplicably he quit his other task of actually writing Joseph's history.

Next came the 5th attempt. Warren A. Cowdery took over on Joseph's 1835 journal, before which he made a bold promise: "Here the reader will observe that the narrative assumes a different form. . . . The writer deemed it proper to give a plain, simple and faithful narrative of every important item in his every day occurrences."[5]

At that point began 142 pages of daily journal entries, recorded in third-person singular, from September 22, 1835, through January 18, 1836. But after 4 months the journal ground to a halt. (Noteworthy, within this journal, on November 9, 1835, was recorded an interview with a Jewish rabbi in which Joseph relates his experience with the First Vision.)[6]

Joseph's 6th attempt at a church and/or personal history was his childhood account dealing with the doctors who wanted to amputate his leg when he was a boy. He wrote it in 1838 or 1839.

A 7th attempt at writing his history took place on April 27, 1838, in which Joseph recounts in his writings of spending the day "writing a history of this church from the earliest period of its existence up to this date,"[7] as well as on May 2, 1838, in which he gives that date as a reference in his "History," and May 1–4, 1838, wherein he states that "the First Presidency were engaged in writing church history."[8]

Joseph's 9th attempt at a history commenced June 11, 1839, when he began dictating to clerk James Mulholland, which lasted 4 ½ months. This was the beginning of the multi-volume manuscript used in B. H. Roberts' *History of the Church of Jesus Christ of Latter-day Saints*, published 63 years later, in 1902. Joseph's 1835 journal was utilized as Book A-1 of the multi-volume manuscript. (The 1838 childhood account was not utilized in the B. H. Roberts publication, however, and was not even published until 132 years after it was written, and 68 years after Roberts' history of the church was published.[9] *BYU Studies*, in summer 1970 was the first to publish this account.)[10]

Meanwhile, the opening pages of the 1838 history (Volume A-1 in the manuscript history), consisted of 59 pages written in April and May 1838, which were all written by others than Mulholland. Beginning possibly as early as September 3, 1838, they were transcribed by Mulholland and positioned by him into the beginning of his 1838–1839 account of Joseph. Mulholland also performed various writing assignments for Joseph, beginning September 3, 1838.

However, while Mulholland actually began writing for Joseph at that time, he would not begin to actually write Joseph's history until 9 months later—June 1839, per above. As for his other writing assignments for Joseph, Mulholland stopped writing during the prophet's imprisonment in Missouri during the winter of 1839, but he resumed on April 22, 1839, when Joseph escaped his captors and arrived in Quincy, Illinois.[11] However, it was June 11, 1839, shortly after they settled in Nauvoo, when Mulholland actually began writing the history. Joseph records, "I commenced dictating my history for my clerk—James Mulholland—to write."[12] This 1839 history has the most detailed First Vision account. Another, later, First Vision account was published in the March 1, 1842, issue of *Times and Seasons* in Nauvoo, Illinois. There, the account runs only ½ page of the 3-page article.

This 8th attempt lasted just 4½ months, because Joseph left for Washington, D.C., to confront the President of the United States, seeking reimbursement for the thousands of homes and farms destroyed by the Missourians. Mulholland had managed to write 59 pages before Joseph left, then he died 6 days later.

Over the next 11 months, 0 pages were written, although Joseph had assigned Dr. Robert Foster to keep tabs on their trip, "but he has failed me," laments Joseph.[13] The prophet returned March 1840, 5 months later, so nothing was written during that trip, nor the 7 months following his return.

Joseph's 9th attempt began October 3, 1840, when his life was chronicled by General Church Clerk Robert B. Thompson, who managed to write 16 pages before dying August 27, 1841.

The 10th attempt came over the next 4 months, when 82 pages were written.

The 11th and last (and most successful) attempt came when Joseph landed a detailed, dedicated scribe, in Willard Richards, who was appointed private secretary to Joseph and General Church Clerk in December 1841. Over the next 36 months he would write about 2,000 pages.[14]

Clearly, Warren Cowdery, James Mulholland, and Willard Richards were the 3 most dedicated scribes to assist Joseph in getting his journal written. Posthumously, B. H. Roberts also made some contributions and changes for the 1902 published version. A comprehensive work that came after this was published by compiler/editor Dean C. Jessee in 2008 as *The Writings of Joseph Smith*. And finally came the stellar collection, the *Joseph Smith Papers*, overseen by Jessee, with volumes divided into various categories—translations, journal, history, and revelations.

A P P E N D I X

# The Height of Men through History

(REFERENCED IN CHAPTER 9)

Appreciating Joseph Smith's stature is best understood when placing it in context with the height of other men of his day, and of man's height generally.[1]

While most people believe modern man from European descent is the tallest group in history, studies show some rather surprising facts:

1. Northern European men were tall in the Medieval Era, from the 800s through the 1000s. The reason for this is they lived healthier, including the eating of greater varieties of foods and especially vegetables, and had nomadic lifestyles, dwelling in small villages, away from cities with their communicable diseases, lack of sanitation, and less healthy foods.

2. Later, by the 1600s and 1700s, American men of Northern European descent dropped in height to an average low of 5 feet 5.5 inches, then began climbing in the 1800s—over 1.5 inches in fact—to 5 feet 7.32 inches by 1850.

3. This remained the average height of European-descended man until the early 1900s, when their height finally surpassed the Medieval Era of 5 feet 8.27 inches.

4. In the 1900s the height of American men continued to increase until about 1980, when it reached a plateau of 5 feet 9.2 inches, where it remains today.

5. The height of American men from North European ancestry was therefore the tallest in world history, until just recently, when it has been surpassed by Scandinavian men.

6. In the late 1800s the tallest men in the world were Native Americans. The 8 tribes included in one study were from the plains, where men averaged 5 feet 7.95 inches. Second tallest in the world in the late 1800s were Australian men at 5 feet 7.72 inches, and third were European-descended American men at 5 feet 7.32 Inches.

7. The reason the height of men decreased from the 1000s to the 1500s, according to a study funded by the National Science Foundation, was because of 3 primary reasons:

a. The Little Ice Age (starting in the 1000s according to some, but around 1250, say others) is when the Atlantic ice pack began to grow. Yet some say the Age began even much later). The Little Ice Age lasted until 1850. During Its 850-year reign, the world saw temperatures drop 2–3 degrees, leaving less land to choose from in raising crops and livestock, a 3–4 week shorter growing season each year for crops, and farmers not being able to plant at higher elevations.

b. Large European cities, the bane of civilization, also came into being in the late Middle Ages—which lasted from 1300 to 1500.

c. The 3rd reason for the height of men dropping was mankind's proliferation of exploration and trade, which spread more disease in the 1500s and 1600s.

8. With the Little Ice Age ending in the mid 1800s, the average height of U.S. man increased due to not only warmer growing conditions but also agricultural improvements.

9. The height of American man peaked in the 1830s but started decreasing again, likely due to the spread of diseases from the invention and expansion of steamboats, canals, and

railroads, even though, ironically, America was more prosperous in this era. With these "drawbacks," the European-descended American man's average height dropped to a new low in 1880. But began increasing again with the advent of water purifying, waste removal, personal hygiene emphasis, and the use of antiseptics. (Civil War Union Army records show the tallest soldiers were from the border states and the Midwest, while the shortest were from the northeast and urban centers—likely due to the same factors shown in studies of Medieval European man—fewer varieties of vegetables to eat in the Northeast and, for cities, not only less vegetable variety but lack of sanitation and a greater spread of disease from increased transportation, all resulting in a lower quality lifestyle than for men from the Midwest and border states.)

10. Because the height of man has a direct correlation on the health of a society, concludes researcher Richard Steckel, the height of Native Americans may indicate they were not sickly victims succumbing to European disease, which is the popular, modern image painted of them. True, they were victims of smallpox and TB, but those epidemics were more than offset by certain positive factors within the North American plain tribes in particular. Due to their culture, no one went hungry or uncared for, and they had a varied diet of plants and buffalo. They were also nomadic enough to not have to deal with sanitation and waste problems, and they would ingeniously split up the tribe when illnesses started. Meanwhile, whites in cities ate an incomplete diet, while their ignorance of antiseptics and sanitation substantially contributed to their diseases, causing their shorter height compared to Native American plains tribes. (Steckel leaves out the fact that rural whites, who faced less health issues than their urban counterparts, comprised a substantially higher percentage of the population than city whites. But even when factoring in rural whites, the overall height of American white men—when combining city and rural whites—was less than that of Native American plains tribes, such was the impact of disease-ridden, less healthy-eating population centers on white men.)

11. Another study reveals that poor families produce shorter offspring. This is likely due to having access to less quality foods and certainly a smaller variety of vegetables to eat. In this project, 10,000 Scottish and English children, ages 5–11 years old, were studied, showing that kids with unemployed fathers were shorter. With this economic disadvantage, children from such families typically lacked the financial ability to sustain comparable prenatal and postnatal care compared to families that had fathers who worked. The result is rather startling—it shows that genetics is not the chief factor of kids' height and health for a civilization; rather, the chief factor is prenatal and postnatal care. (The researcher obviously does not address individual families, where genetics is likely a factor, best illustrated by tall parents often producing taller children.)

12. Dutch men are currently the tallest men In the world—about 2 inches higher than American men, and their countrymen are especially known for pre- and postnatal care.

Interesting side notes to this study are:

1. A Norwegian study revealed taller people live longer, except for exceptionally tall people.

2. The average Japanese man has grown 3.15 inches in the last 50 years, while in 1950 Japan had the shortest population of men within industrialized countries.

APPENDIX C

# Money-diggers and Rodsmen

(REFERENCED IN CHAPTER 9)

Caroline Smith, Porter Rockwell's sister, writes that in Manchester, New York, "There was considerable digging for money in our neighborhood by men, women, and children,"[1] most of whom were not of Joseph's religious persuasion.

On February 16, 1825, the *Wayne Sentinel* reprinted an article from the Windsor, Vermont, *Journal*, which said that respectable citizens had been digging for treasure in the Green Mountains for years.[2] The *Sentinel* also stated that "a respectable gentleman" in Tunbridge, Vermont, had stated he had found a gold chest with the help of a vision and a mineral rod.[3]

On March 2 the same newspaper reported a wood chopper saying he had found gold in the trunk of a tree near Utica, New York.

A woman in New London, Connecticut, used a small, transparent rock, according to an article in the *Lyons Advertiser*, August 29, 1827, saying it had "the power of opening to her view the recesses of the earth," which she used to help 2 men dig for a box of coins stolen from a Spanish galleon, the box having been buried in mud under 6 feet of water near the wharf.[4]

In Wells, Vermont, in about 1800, there was a religious cult that used rods to hunt for buried treasure and find lost objects. Oliver Cowdery's father may have belonged to it.[5]

On February 1, 1831, the *Palmyra Reflector* stated that many people throughout the countryside were seeing visions of treasures in the earth—men and women of all ages.[6]

A P P E  D I X

# Seer Stones and Joseph Smith

(REFERENCED IN CHAPTER 13)

A little-known aspect of early American history is the fairly wide acceptance of not only treasure hunting with special "magical" stones, but the stones themselves—known as seer stones. Joseph Smith owned and used them, but warned that although some stones were inspired by God for man's benefit, others were inspired by a dark spiritual force to accomplish its ends—to ensnare and deceive people who used them.

That seer stones were a gift from God, yet could be converted for improper uses, was reported by Wandle Mace, who said that a pair of stones were given to George A. Smith in Nauvoo by a British convert, claiming the stones had been used by church members in England. George then gave the stones to Joseph, who "pronounced them to be a Urim and Thummim as good as ever was upon the earth but, he said, 'They have been consecrated to devils.'"[1]

Extending this logic, Latter-day Saints could speculate that some stones since the beginning of their use might have been dedicated only to unrighteous purposes, from spiritual forces not of heavenly influences. Or, in this case, Joseph may have meant that at one time they were used for good, but since then "they have been consecrated to devils."

As mentioned in the text (Chapter 28), the Whitmers' brother-in-law, Hiram Page, would use a stone for false revelation. Another incident of false revelation was described even earlier in the text (Chapter 12), when Willard Chase's sister Sally used a "green glass, through which she could see many very wonderful things."[2]

As mentioned in the text, Caroline Rockwell Smith, Porter Rockwell's sister, stated that when they had grown up in Manchester, New York, Sally Chase, a Methodist, had a stone which she would consult in behalf of people who came to her for help in finding lost and stolen items.[3]

Joseph had known Chase through money-digging projects but, in time, reports Martin Harris, Joseph was warned: "The angel told him he must quit the company of the money-diggers— that there were wicked men among them. He must have no more to do with them. He must not lie, nor swear, nor steal."[4] This alludes to the possibility that Chase could have possessed those attributes of lying and stealing; certainly his attempted theft of the plates and his claims to partial ownership of them implicate him.

Joseph may have received his first stone under a tree near Lake Erie, according to W. D. Purple, who evidently overheard discussion of this incident at a court hearing in Bainbridge, New York, in 1826.[5] At this hearing, Joseph was charged with disorderly conduct, but the reality was purely a persecution for religious purposes, as discussed earlier in the text (Chapter 10).

Another stone that Joseph reportedly used was discovered by Willard Chase, according to Willard himself.[6] Pomeroy Tucker claims the stone was actually found in the well of Clark Chase.[7] (Noted LDS Historian B. H. Roberts seems to agree with this claim.[8] However, Martin Harris says the well belonged to Mason Chase.[9] There may have also been a green stone, when Joseph later worked in Susquehanna County, Pennsylvania.[10] The Bainbridge, New York, court record, which discussed Joseph's "money-digging," states: "While at Palmyra he had frequently ascertained . . . where lost property was of various kinds; and that "he has occasionally been in the habit of looking through this stone to find lost property for three years."[11] Martin Harris claimed that on one occasion Joseph used a seer stone, discovering a pin in a pile of shavings with it.[12]

As for the Urim and Thummim, the angel returned them to Joseph on September 22, 1828.[13] However, David Whitmer claims the Urim and Thummim were not returned in September, and that Joseph used a seer stone for the balance of the translation,[14] assuming the seer stone was one and the same as the Urim and Thummim. However, the stone he used for translating may have actually been presented to him after the Urim and Thummim were taken from him, upon losing the 116 lost manuscript pages.[15] Supporting this theory, one witness at the Bainbridge, New York court claimed Joseph said he used a white stone to read from a book.[16]

Joseph Smith's own family may have seen his powers at work when using stones. Perhaps due to this, Joseph Capron states, "the family of Smiths held Joseph Jr. in high estimation on account of some supernatural power, which he was supposed to possess."[17]

A P P E N D I X

# The Rosetta Stone:
# Unusual History of an Unusual Stone

(REFERENCED IN CHAPTER 14)

The Rosetta Stone was discovered on July 15, 1799, by Pierre Francois-Xavier Bouchards. He and his men were not run-of-the-mill soldiers, but army engineers, and he was their officer. According to various accounts, either he or his men found it on the west side of the Nile river, while the French were expanding Ft. Julien, an old Turkish fort. Their efforts were meant to protect French-occupied Egypt from British and Turkish invaders coming down the Nile River from the Mediterranean Sea. In so doing they discovered the stone in one of 3 spots, the real knowledge of which has been muddied by conflicting reports at the time: (1) it was built into the fort as part of a wall, or (2) within the foundation, or (3) it was found out in the open.

French soldiers viewed it as a remarkable prize.

Anciently, the stone had been set up in a temple as an elaborate thank-you gift from the priests to the pharaoh-in-puberty. (He was 13.)

Probably 600 years later, in 392 A.D., the stone was taken from the temple when a Roman emperor ordered all non-Christian temples closed. (And within 100 years of Roman rule, hieroglyphics were no longer understood by anyone.) From 392 A.D. to the 15th century the stone disappeared.

Then it reappeared. But it was seen as valueless by the 15th-century Egyptians, so they used it as just another rock to build a fort, under emperor Quaitbay, 18th Sultan of Egypt, to defend the Nile from invaders of the Ottoman Empire, probably during a threat of invasion between 1485 and 1491 (but definitely during his life, which spanned 1416–1496 A.D.).

At this fort the stone remained in obscurity until French soldiers unearthed it 300 years later in 1799.

So the soldiers hauled it to Cairo for study by French scholars for a year and a half. Significantly, 167 scholars had been brought to Egypt by Napoleon to unearth Egypt's mysteries. They published about the stone within their own newspaper at Cairo, and studied it while their army held the invading British and Turks at bay.

Hearing of the invasion, the French scholars sought to save the stone by playing a gigantic game of keep-away (per Chapter 14).

But the Brits became serious about conquering Egypt. They hauled light canon overland and fired into Ft. Julien's newly rebuilt, unhardened cement walls—and succeeded in collapsing the walls and killing about 30 exposed Frenchmen to sharpshooters. The British now swept past Ft. Julien with nothing to stop them from invading Egypt.

Word of the stone spread like a sandstorm among the British, so their scholars soon jumped into the fray.

They wanted that stone.

The capture by the British came when British General John Hely-Hutchinson conquered the French forces in March 1801, landing at Aboukir Bay, and demanded they give up the stone. French General Jacques-Francois Menou refused to surrender it, claiming it was a "personal belonging."[1] At this impasse, he was betrayed by a countryman who took the Brits down dark alleys to its hiding place (per Chapter 14), or possibly the stone was snatched by British Colonel Tomkyus Hilgrove Turner, who claimed to personally take it from Menou.[2]

After loading it on his armored carriage, Hutchinson placed it on a captured 44-gun French frigate, ironically renamed the *HMS Egyptienne*, whereupon it was escorted to England under the personal watch of Colonel Turner.

The stone then arrived at Portsmouth, in south central England, in February 1802.[3]

In summary, the discovery of the Rosetta Stone was fraught with ironies. First, the stone never would have been discovered had the French not rebuilt the wall of Ft. Julien in 1799, in order to "strengthen" it. But that single act of rebuilding caused the loss of the nation: the unhardened, new cement wall allowed the British to collapse it, per the above-mentioned light cannon fire.

The irony does not stop there. What the French lost by replacing that wall and thus losing the fort and all of Egypt, they gained by discovering the stone—although, ironically, it too ended up in the hands of the British.

In another irony, however, the British now owned a vast array of artifacts over which they could merely scratch their heads—everything was written in a mysterious language and they were completely baffled as to what any of the objects were.

The final ironic twist was that victory in the end would belong to the French, when, 20 years later, one of their countrymen, Champollion, would crack the code on the stone and unlock all those ancient mysteries.

Needless to say, few if any historical objects have been the subject of such international intrigue as the Rosetta Stone.


Details of what happened after the stone arrived in England show another irony—how relationships between countries and their scholars can mellow with the passage of time.

Once the stone arrived in England in 1802, Colonel Turner brought it to King George III, who directed that it be placed at the British Museum. First, however, he allowed it to be presented to the Society of Antiquaries of London, of which Turner was a member. Then it was shown to British scholars on March 11, 1802.[4]

At that point the Society made 4 plaster casts of the carvings, which they gave to universities at Oxford, Cambridge, Edinburgh, and Trinity College of Dublin. Right afterward, curators made prints of the inscriptions and sent them to scholars throughout Europe.[5]

The British Museum has housed the stone ever since 1803, the year after it arrived in London, except for 3 occasions:

1.  In 1834 the stone was transferred to the sculpture gallery, when the floor it had been resting upon was determined to be too weak. (Afterward it was sent back to the original location of the museum, although in a rebuilt structure on the site.)[6]

2.  During the years 1917–1919 it was moved 50 feet underground to the Postal Tube Railway to prevent bomb damage by the Germans.

3.  October 1972 was the 150th anniversary of French scholar Jean Francois Champollion's famous published letter that revealed the secret code to hieroglyphics. On that occasion the Rosetta Stone sat in the Louvre in Paris for one month.

Thus, what would have been inconceivable 150 years earlier became a reality in the world of politics and scholars.

Another interesting fact surfaced after that 1972 diplomatic breakthrough. A discovery was made about the stone itself in 2004. As the British museum was cleaning it, the staff discovered the stone was not made of basalt, as previously thought, but granodiorite (with a high quartz content, like a granite; and a high mafic content, like a diorite.) Intriguingly, they found it to be even a different color. It was now a dark grey to black color with large pink and white crystals!

The stone itself is rather intriguing in other aspects: it is 45" tall at the highest portion on the right side, by 28.5" wide at the widest part near the bottom, by 11" thick. It weighs 1,676 lbs. (176 lbs. heavier than ¾ ton).

On it are written 14 lines of hieroglyphics, 32 lines of demotic (another early Egyptian script) and 54 lines of ancient

Greek, in that order, from top to bottom. The top portion is broken off, and probably held another 14–15 lines of additional hieroglyphics—about 12" worth.[7] This was assessed by scholars studying similar stones since discovered. They also determined that it likely had a rounded top and was originally about 59" high[8] rather than its current 45".


The breakthrough in the "language mystery" came about because there were 2 languages on the stone—Greek and Egyptian.

But Egyptian was written in 2 "scripts"—demotic and hieroglyphics. Demotic was used from 650 B.C. to 452 A.D. and hieroglyphics from 3,400 B.C. to at least 396 A.D. (when an inscription was made on a gate post and later discovered).[9] However, hieroglyphics were used mainly for formal inscriptions, while everyday writing used the "hieratic" script[10] (which was not represented on the Rosetta Stone).

In deciphering hieroglyphics, scholars identified a few phonetic characters in the demotic section. Then they compared them to the Greek writing on the Stone, and figured out that they were proper names. They next compared these proper names to the hieroglyphic section. This process took 21 years, with various French, Scandinavian, German, and British scholars chipping away at the mystery. All, in fact, were part of a giant race. The Stone had received worldwide notoriety, and scholars knew that whoever could crack the code first would achieve worldwide fame, which in fact happened.

Champollion is the French mastermind given the most credit for figuring it out. He used Coptic to help decipher the 2 Egyptian scripts carved in the stone—Demotic (used earlier than Coptic), and hieroglyphics (the earliest of all).

Champollion lived from 1790 to 1832, and was said to have learned enough Greek and Latin by the time he was 9 to read Homer and Virgil. He studied Arabic, Sanskrit, Persian, Ethiopic, Zend, and Pahlevi. At age 16 he wrote a paper on the Coptic language, at age 18 became a professor of history at the

Grenoble lyceum, and by the time he was 19 he worked on a Coptic dictionary. A chair was created especially for him at the College de France. The Coptic language he knew had similarities to Demotic (which was on the stone). Meanwhile, Coptic was in widespread use from just prior to 100 A.D. to 900 A.D., then, to a smaller extent, to the late 1600s, and, to an even smaller extent, from the late 1800s onward, within Coptic Orthodox and Catholic churches in Egypt.

Through this combination of what Champollion had mastered and what other scholars provided him, he was given the most credit for unlocking the final key, although other researchers— especially British scholars—contributed significantly, with some making the argument that they deserved equal if not greater credit.


The inscriptions on the stone provide the last point of interest. The writings comprise an agreement between the Egyptian king and the priests. It was dated March 27, 196 B.C., and details the honors given the king—the 5th ruler of Egypt under the Ptolemaic dynasty. (Greeks were ruling the nation and had been since Alexander the Great conquered it in 332 B.C.) The inscription on the stone praises the king for his generosity, describes the siege of Lycopolis, outlines the king's good deeds for the temple, and finally proclaims its chief purpose—to establish a cult for the king. While the messages themselves were not of earth-shattering value, the fact that they were written in 3 "languages" (actually 2 languages and an additional script), one being hieroglyphics, was. It enabled scholars to compare the languages and decipher hieroglyphics—the ancient, mysterious Egyptian language prevalent in the pyramids of Egypt, which no one had understood for centuries.

The mystery was solved.

# Treasure-hunting and Joseph Smith

(REFERENCED IN CHAPTER 17)

The court record of Bainbridge, New York, covered testimony about Joseph's treasure seeking. It details that he had been treasure hunting the previous three years (from 1822, when he discovered the stone, until the convening of the court in 1825).

Joseph admitted he had helped Josiah Stowell several times during that period, looking for hidden treasure deep in the earth (the "bowels of the earth," says Joseph).[1] The court record states "he had frequently ascertained in that way where lost property was," but that "of late he had pretty much given it up on account of injuring his health, especially his eyes," which "made them sore."[2] The court record further states, "He did not solicit business of this kind, and had always rather declined having anything to do with this business."[3]

Apparently his father and the wealthy Stowell had pressured Joseph to keep at it, despite his reluctance. This concept is supported by neighbor William Stafford, who reports Joseph's father as the aggressive treasure seeker on one occasion, hunting for gold and going back to their farmhouse to ask his son for directions. Joseph Jr. could have joined in the hunt but chose not to.[4]

Joseph did possibly join in with others to some extent as late as the fall of 1826 and winter of 1827,[5] with one much later possible involvement in 1836, looking for hidden silver or gold in Salem, Massachusetts,[6] when his people were desperate for money.

As to finding treasure, it seems that on at least one occasion he did find it, but they believed some supernatural power prevented them from obtaining the treasure, as it would "slip into the earth," away from people's grasp. Jonathan Thompson, who believed in Joseph's treasure-finding abilities, maintained he had a "professed skill" and so told the 1826 Bainbridge, New York, court. He also declared that Joseph led them to a chest, but, "on account of an enchantment, the trunk kept settling away."[7]

# A New, Surprising Time Line
# for Translating the Plates

(REFERENCED IN CHAPTERS 19 AND 23)

Hearing the word *Cumorah* for the first time has dramatic implications on the time line of how long it took Joseph to translate the plates

If one takes David Whitmer's account at face value, it becomes evident he clearly had never heard of the word *Cumorah* until the "very pleasant" man mentioned it on his journey to Fayette, New York, a man they soon would realize was an angel dressed as a mortal in simple working clothes.

In hearing *Cumorah*, David implies that not only he, but Joseph Smith and Oliver Cowdery were perplexed: "We all gazed at him and at each other."[1] Certainly, when they resumed their journey, had Joseph or Oliver been acquainted with the word they would have commented about it—how bizarre that this stranger also knew it.

Based on the author's analysis, the word *Cumorah* would first appear to Joseph and Oliver 55% of the way through translating. This is significant because they did not hear this term before the last 2 days of May 1829 when they were also traveling to Fayette. This further means that less than 55% of the plates had been translated in Harmony the previous 7 weeks since they started working on it together on April 7, 1829.

By a simple calculation this means they would translate 45% or more of the plates in Fayette.

As stated in Chapter 17, they would finish translating "in June 1829—the latter part of the month," according to David Whitmer in one interview,[2] or about July 1, according to him in another,[3] while Lucy places it before the Three Witnesses viewed the plates,[4] which would have been near the middle of June[5]—a remarkably fast-paced feat in any of the 3 scenarios.

Before June 1, while in Harmony, Joseph had been sidetracked by time-consuming efforts of trying to stay alive and traveling. But the work in June would now pick up at triple speed.

In looking at the time line of translation, several historically significant facts need analyzing . . .

First, the background.

Joseph had translated, with help from his wife Emma, her brother Reuben, and Martin Harris, a specific section of plates (the first part of the large plates) that had resulted in the earlier manuscript of 116 pages. In all, Joseph had spent his first 2 months off and on translating that manuscript—from December 1827 to February 1828. One might call that manuscript the *first phase.*

Then came an interim period after the *1st phase* ended in February 1828. During this period of no translating, Martin took the plates to New York City to Professor Anthon, as covered in Chapter 14, whereupon Anthon wrote a certificate of authenticity (then apparently felt his ego bruised when told he could not translate the plates himself, and tore up the certificate).

Next, during this same interim period, on June 14, 1828, Martin took the 116 pages on loan from Joseph and lost them.

Shortly after that, Joseph was reprimanded by the angel. Then he was given a second chance to translate, receiving the Urim and Thummim interpreters 3 months later (per Chapter 16) on September 22, 1828.

However, Joseph would not launch the *2nd phase* of translating for another 6½ months after he received the interpreters back. In all, during this interim period, he did not translate for 14 months—February 1828 till April 6, 1829. Then, on April 7, he began the *2nd phase* of translating—when Oliver Cowdery came to help.

This *2nd phase* of translating consisted of 2 periods: the 7 weeks before they moved from Harmony and the 2–4 weeks after they arrived at Fayette. (The reason they were actually going to Fayette was to finish translating, hoping to encounter fewer interruptions.)

On arriving there, says Lucy, "Joseph received the record according to promise" (from the angel they encountered, per Chapter 19). She then gives a clue that impacts the time line: "The next day he and Oliver resumed the work of translation, which they continued without further interruption until the whole work was accomplished.[6] Thus, a great deal more translating was compacted into the month of June 1829 than any other period.

Oliver worked with Joseph on the entire *2nd phase*—except for a little help that Joseph received from Emma Smith, Christian, and John Whitmer in Fayette, New York.


The crux of the author's analysis is this: The finished book would be 584 pages, as originally published in the first edition. As stated in Chapter 17, the 2 men would possibly start translating at a section of the book called Words of Mormon. (The short, 2-page section or "book" called Words of Mormon starts at page 123 of the first edition.)[7]

Scholar Dean C. Jessee believes they started at Mosiah, 2 pages later. However, per this author's analysis, if Oliver did not start at Words of Mormon, then other scribes did—either before Oliver's involvement (sometime between September 22, 1828, when Joseph received the interpreters, and April 5, 1829, when Oliver arrived), or one of the other scribes assisted Joseph with Words of Mormon after Joseph and Oliver arrived in Fayette.

After leaving Harmony in late May 1829, it likely took 2½ to 3 days to arrive at Fayette, New York, 135 miles away, based on others' journeys. They would start translating the day after they arrived—about June 1 or later. Oliver (with a little help from Emma, Christian, and John Whitmer), would take dictation for what would become the next 406 pages of the printed book until they arrived at the word *Cumorah* (which they would encounter at page 529 of the finished book), then continue another 60 pages (until the end of the book). Then they would wrap-around their translation to the beginning of the plates (starting over with the aforementioned separate set of small plates to replace the missing 116 page manuscript that had been based on the large plates). Here they would pick up their translation at page 5 (the first actual page of the later, printed book). They would continue translating until they would finish the small plates, which is page 151 of the finished book. At that point—page 151—all their translation would be done. Regarding the "small" and "large" plates . . .

During this 2nd phase they translated 2 sections:

(1) the rest of the large plates, on which they were allowed to work on only the "unsealed" portion (the "sealed" portion is to be translated at some future date); and

(2) the replacement section or small plates, which, in a revelation Joseph was told are the "plates of Nephi."[8] These small plates cover the same 400-year historical period that they had earlier translated from the large plates (from which the 116 pages had been translated and lost). However, the small plates' version had more theology.[9] Joseph would translate this replacement section of the 400 year period last.

The net result is that, by translating plates in the above order, they would come across the term *Cumorah* 55% of the way through their translation process. This also means, if David Whitmer's account of the old stranger mentioning Cumorah is accurate, Joseph would translate his final 45% (or more) of the book at Fayette in the month of June 1829.

In summary, the 2 men had engaged in part-time translating in Harmony for 7 weeks, before they launched their late May

1829 trip, netting them 55% or less of the book, meaning they would complete the final 45%+ during the next month—June 1829—with few if any interruptions

If David Whitmer's recollection is accurate as to when the book's translation was complete (late June or "about July 1"), then the time spent translating in Fayette should have been 3 to 4 weeks.

But Lucy, with her remarkable memory, states that the manuscript was completed *before the Three Witnesses' vision*, which Richard Bushman places at mid-June 1829.[10] Since they had started the final 45%+ of translating on June 1, 1829, or later, this means their time spent translating at Fayette, if Lucy is accurate, was 2 weeks, meaning only 4 weeks total time was spent translating the plates.

On the other hand, if David Whitmer is correct about the 3–4 weeks spent translating in Fayette (till late June), a total of 6–8 weeks would have been spent on the plates.

As the facts stack up, the author gives more weight to Lucy's time line, meaning that only 4 weeks actual time was probably spent translating.

Either way, this is a rather revolutionary concept in light of the long-accepted belief that Joseph and Oliver completed the manuscript in 10 weeks. Their accomplishment is now even more amazing when one realizes that they did all this work in 20% to 60% less time than heretofore believed—a total time period of only 4 to 8 weeks.

A P P E N D I X

# What Happened to the Three Witnesses?

(REFERENCED IN CHAPTER 20)

The Three Witnesses never recanted their testimonies about seeing and handling the plates. Nor did they ever claim they were pressured by Joseph into saying anything.

Enemies to the church twisted their statements otherwise. For example, Illinois Governor Thomas Ford later said some of the witnesses told him they never saw any plates in the box, and that Joseph had them pray for 2 hours, reprimanding them as having little faith, until they were able to finally see something.[1] Ford, however, was known for twisting reports to fit his agenda.

Each of the Three Witnesses has an unusual story, unfolding years after seeing and handling the plates. All three would leave the church Joseph was instrumental in founding, but two would return.

The only witness to leave the church and stay away was David Whitmer. Becoming disillusioned with Joseph, he never denied seeing the plates and actually bore testimony to seeing them whenever the opportunity arose. Although Whitmer never became bitter toward Joseph and always proclaimed his love for his friend, his main problem seemed to be one of faith: when he saw Joseph give up the seer stone, he figured Joseph must have lost the powers of prophecy, and thus, Latter-day Saints believe, David's faith weakened. He even decided that Joseph led the church astray, so on April 13, 1838, he was excommunicated for apostasy. He continued to live on his property in Missouri, much to the vexation of neighboring Saints, but fled a couple of months later, in June 1838, when he feared that the Danites—whom Joseph quickly excommunicated for militancy—were including him in their threats. Despite being disaffected from the church—or actually because of that—he became the target of many newspaper writers who sought to interview him. None, however, could draw from him anything but a firm testimony of the plates, which he always declared he saw and felt with his own hands.

In 1882 he wrote a booklet to the Christian world declaring his faith in the *Book of Mormon*. He did denounce Joseph's later stand on polygamy and other matters, but added that that should not dissuade people from the book itself, stating, "How plain and simple is the doctrine of Christ set forth therein."[2] He proclaimed that belief until his death and set the record straight in this booklet on another matter:

"It is recorded in the *American Cyclopaedia* and the *Encyclopedia Britannica* that I, David Whitmer, have denied my testimony as one of the three witnesses to the divinity of the *Book of Mormon*, and that the other two witnesses, Oliver Cowdery and Martin Harris, denied their testimony to that book. I will say once more to all mankind, that I have never at any time denied that testimony or any part thereof. I also testify to the world that neither Oliver Cowdery or Martin Harris ever at any time denied their testimony. They both died reaffirming the truth of the divine authenticity of the *Book of Mormon*."[3]

In another interview Whitmer emphasized his determination, even under pressure, to tell the truth, and on one occasion an apparent miracle resulted:

"I have been visited by thousands of people," he remarked, "believers and nonbelievers, amongst them a governor of this state, gentlemen and lades of all degrees and from many nations, sometimes 15 or 20 in a day, all wanting to know if these things are true. I have been surrounded by hostile mobs, on one occasion numbering four or five hundred, demanding I should deny what is published over my name in the *Book of Mormon*; but the testimony I gave to that mob made them fear and tremble, and I escaped from them. One gentleman, a doctor, an unbeliever, told me afterwards that the bold and fearless testimony borne on that occasion and the fear that seemed to take hold of the mob had made him a believer in the *Book of Mormon*."[4]

Five years later the *Richmond Democrat* reported Whitmer's final moments:

"On Sunday evening at 5:30, January 22, 1888, Mr. Whitmer called his family and some friends to his bedside and . . . then addressed himself to all around his bedside in these words:

"'Now you must all be faithful in Christ. I want to say to you all the Bible and the record of the Nephites, (*Book of Mormon*) is true, so you can say that you have heard me bear my testimony, on my death bed.' . . .

"On Monday last [January 23, 1888] at 10 o'clock A.M., after awakening from a short slumber, he said he had seen beyond the veil and saw Christ on the other side. His friends who were constantly at his bedside claim that he had many manifestations of the truths of the great beyond, and which confirms their faith beyond all shadow of doubt.

"He bore his long illness with great patience and fortitude his faith never for a moment wavering, and when the summons came, he sank peacefully to rest, with a smile on his countenance, just as if he was being lulled to sleep by sweet music. Just before the breath left the body, he opened his eyes, which glistened with the brightness of his early manhood. He then turned them toward heaven, and a wonderful light came over his countenance, which remained several moments, when the eyes gradually closed and David Whitmer was gone to his rest."[5]

(For an in-depth interview, see Appendix I, "David Whitmer: Keeping the Manuscript.")

As another witness who saw and handled the plates, Oliver Cowdery would leave the church as well, excommunicated on April 12, 1838, in Far West, Missouri, for apostasy. Specifically, for opposing a doctrine. It was not considered an offence to disagree with a doctrine, but to actively oppose it was. The doctrine he opposed was plural marriage. His 2nd offence was complaining he was being "controlled" by church leaders in earthly matters. Thereafter, he moved to Ohio and practiced law in the town of Tiffin, as well as the adjoining state of Michigan. He became a Methodist, but even during that time never denied his testimony of the *Book of Mormon.*

While in Michigan, one man confronted him: "Mr. Cowdery, I see your name attached to this book. If you believe it to be true, why are you in Michigan [and not gathered with the Saints in Illinois]?"

Oliver replied, "My name is attached to that book, and what I there have said is true. I did see this [the plates]. I know I saw it. And faith has nothing to do with it, as a perfect knowledge has swallowed up the faith which I had in the work, knowing, as I do, that it is true."[6]

He fell into ill health and moved to Wisconsin, where his brother Lyman was an attorney. Phinehas Young kept up letter-writing with him and, from that, Oliver kept in touch with the Utah church.

Eventually he felt so empty that he decided to return to the main fold, which was in its first year of migrating to the Great Basin—Utah Territory. In preparing for that overland journey, he went to Council Bluffs, Iowa, to join the Saints who were preparing for their exodus west. In 1848, he was rebaptized there at age 42 by church icon Orson Pratt.

His stock among the Saints soared. He told them in Iowa that he had viewed and touched the plates and really had received the priesthood from heavenly authority.[7]

Soon, he moved to Richmond, Missouri, too sick to make the long trek West. There, he visited friend, brother-in-law, and fellow member of the Three Witnesses, David Whitmer.

Oliver was bedridden most of 1849 and passed away on March 3, 1850, at age 49 in David Whitmer's home, 25 years before Whitmer himself, the last of the Three Witnesses.

Eighteen years after Oliver's death, on September 7–8, 1878, 2 visitors from Utah also visited Whitmer at Richmond—Orson Pratt and Joseph Fielding Smith, who wrote the following:

"Upon inquiry, Mr. Whitmer informed us that Oliver Cowdery had told him all about his visiting the Church at Council Bluffs and of his having been rebaptized. He said, 'Oliver died the happiest man I ever saw. After shaking hands with the family and kissing his wife and daughter, he said, "Now I lay me down for the last time, I am going to my Savior," and died immediately, with a smile on his face.'"[8]

Whitmer also adds: "I was present at the death of Oliver Cowdery, and his last words were, 'Brother David, be true to your testimony to the *Book of Mormon*.'"[9]

Phinehas H. Young was with Oliver when he died, and reports: "His last moments were spent in bearing testimony of the truth of the gospel revealed through Joseph Smith, and the power of the holy priesthood, which he had received through his administration."[10]


The third and perhaps most intriguing story is that of Martin Harris.

Four individuals—Reuben Harmon, John Gilbert, Reverend Jesse Townsend, and Stephen Burnett—claimed Martin Harris had told them he never saw the plates with his natural eyes, but with his spiritual eyes—"only in vision," as Burnett states in a letter,[11] which is not the entire story, according to another man who did not stay with the faith, but who remained objective enough on this issue to publish Martin's side of the story: "In regards to my testimony to the visitation of the angel, who declared to us three witnesses that the *Book of Mormon* is true,

I have this to say: Of course we were in the spirit when we had the view, for no man can behold the face of an angel, except in a spiritual view, but we were in the body also, and everything was as natural to us, as it is at any time. Martin Harris, you say, called it 'being in vision.' We read in the Scriptures, Cornelius saw, in a vision, an angel of God. Daniel saw an angel in a vision, also in other places it states they saw an angel in the spirit. A bright light enveloped us where we were that filled at noonday, and there in a vision, or in the spirit, we saw and heard just as it is stated in my testimony in the *Book of Mormon*."[12]

His explanation was consistent with the scriptures, but these enemies tried making an issue of it.

Stephen Burnett adds that Martin later said in the Kirtland Temple that he knew the *Book of Mormon* was true and that he had more than once lifted the plates while they were in a box with only a tablecloth or handkerchief over them. Burnett, nevertheless, desired to focus on what he could criticize in Martin's testimony, and left the faith. Others had no problem with Martin's description that he saw them with "spiritual eyes" and were not in the least bit shaken by his statement. The semantics were not a deal-breaker.

Critics could argue till the cows came home in what manner he saw them, but the bottom line is his declaration of what he actually saw:

"As sure as you see my hand, so sure did I see the angel and the plates,"[13] he told Robert Barter.

He also told visiting Utah missionary David Dille in 1853, "For did I not at one time hold the plates on my knee an hour and a half, whilst in conversation with Joseph, when we went to bury them in the woods, that the enemy might not obtain them? Yes, I did. And as many of the plates as Joseph Smith translated I handled with my hands, plate after plate."[14]

Spiritual eyes or not, say Latter-day Saints, his descriptions of what he saw were pretty straightforward.

He also wrote a testimony to Hanna B. Emerson that put to bed critics' claims that he denied ever seeing the plates: "No man ever heard me in any way deny the truth of the *Book of*

*Mormon* [or] the administration of the angel that showed me the plates."[15]

Despite his testimonies of the *Book of Mormon*, Martin did not remain active in the church. First, he and wife Dolly, ever disagreeing over the *Book of Mormon*, separated. He moved to Kirtland, Ohio, and she refused to go with him. About 5 years later she died—in 1836—and their children moved to Ohio to be near him.

November 1, 1837, he then married another woman, Caroline Young,[16] an active Latter-day Saint 31 years younger than him, when she was 20, and had a second family with her. But from Kirtland he did not go westward with the Saints to Missouri[17] nor later to Nauvoo nor the Utah Territory, not being offered what he felt were proper leadership roles. From 1838, when Joseph left Ohio, to 1870, Martin was withdrawn from the church and even joined a different religious group—actually 7 in all, including the Shakers (a Quaker break-off group) and 6 break-away groups from the Saints.

Before 1842 he affiliated with the church of one dissenter—Warren Parrish—where Martin was considered an important member, until others in the group disavowed the *Book of Mormon*, so Martin left them in 1842.

At this point he was rebaptized into the LDS faith, but soon after apostatized into the Shakers (with its nearest congregation 30 miles west of Kirtland, where he remained active 2 to 3 years), then he joined other breakaway groups from the mainstream LDS church:

First, he associated with James J. Strang in 1846–1847 as a member of his high council, even going on a mission to England with 2 others in the fall of 1846, before being checkmated by Latter-day Saint members there.

This is how it happened:

Martin and his 2 companions brazenly attempted to recruit Orson Hyde's new converts.

And the way they did it was equally bold. They crashed a church conference in Birmingham.

This backfired royally.[18]

According to eyewitness George Mantle, when they asked to speak, the district president "told us that it was Martin Harris, an apostate from the faith, that he had abused him and his brethren coming across the sea, and he would not allow him to speak."[19]

Cyrus Wheelock, another eye-witness, adds in a letter that Martin was "rejected by the unified voice of the conference."[20]

Wheelock also writes in his journal: "He was not to be put off, so he must and would preach and accordingly [left] to the street and commenced holding forth [a lecture] to the annoyance of the people."[21]

Wheelock reports in a letter why the Strangites spoke—"to proclaim the corruption of the Twelve."[22]

Mantle picks up the narrative. "When we came out of the meeting, Martin Harris was beset with a crowd in the street."[23]

Hyde and other leaders knew their flock was potentially vulnerable, with new members who saw the conference as their gathering place for strength amidst the daily grind of life and opposition from co-workers, friends, and family opposed to their new faith.

Wheelock adds, "While thus engaged, two policemen very politely waited upon him, each affectionately taking an arm, and thus the curtain fell and the drama closed to the great amusement of the spectators."[24]

In a letter Wheelock adds that the policemen "led Martin away to the lock-up."[25]

Though described by George Mantle as "an elderly man,"[26] Martin Harris was at this point only 64—which in the 1800s was considered "elderly." He and his 2 Strangite companions next went to Liverpool.

Orson Hyde reports: "They complained very much that they could not get an opportunity to do the work which the Lord sent them to perform. [Local Latter-day Saint leader] Elder Marsden, of this town, handled them so effectively in Birkenhead, and made Strangism look so completely mean, that Martin publicly denied being sent by Strang, or being in any way connected with him. This he did in the presence of many witnesses."[27]

The 2 Strangite missionaries accompanying Martin were Leicester Brooks and William Capner, from Ohio.[28]

After this setback, Martin did not know what to do with himself and soon returned home—his short-lived mission had lasted 6 weeks.

Upon arriving in Kirtland he continued his association with the Strangites, but their main group was disenchanted with his incessant preaching of the *Book of Mormon*. Finally, in Strang's usual, undiplomatic way, he blamed Martin for the England mission failure. Strang, not the most popular of sectarian leaders (although he had a following of 3,000 on Beaver Island in Michigan), proclaimed himself not only "prophet" but, bizarrely, "king," and was murdered by malcontents.

In 1847 Martin teamed up with William E. McLellin, a former Latter-day Saint apostle whom Harris had helped choose in 1835. (The Three Witnesses were given this task but were never apostles themselves.) Martin Harris and William McLellin wanted to organize their own Church of Christ now. The two baptized, confirmed and ordained each other, but faced conflict when McLellin wanted to make David Whitmer the real leader, rather than Martin. Further complications came when McLellin spent too much time away from their home base in Kirtland, leaving Martin and their small flock feeling abandoned. The remaining group held a conference on June 3, 1849, to check into several charges some of them were making against McLellin—abusive language and general abandonment (not being around them) as 2 of their 8 concerns. This resulted in Martin withdrawing membership from McLellin, leaving Martin as the leader by default—and now left to his own limited leadership skills. Presiding over the flock, he soon realized, was not his cup of tea, so he gave up and left the church, not even sticking around to watch it wither away.

Rather, he became a wandering preacher. That same year, 1849, he went to Rochester, New York, to proclaim his work to a local newspaper of being on a mission from God, traversing the countryside and preaching.

In the early 1850s Martin decided to associate himself with Francis Gladden Bishop, who had been excommunicated from the Saints after teaching false revelations at Kirtland in 1851 and announcing he would start his own church. Gladden now appointed Martin as a "special witness" by revelation to him. (Gladden also chose his own wife as the other special witness.) But the partnership died almost as quickly as it started.

In September and October 1857 Martin associated with William Swartzell, who had apostatized at Far West, Missouri, in 1838 and testified against Joseph and Hyrum Smith in court, lying about them and the Saints' role in the Missouri Wars, which helped get the 2 men imprisoned in a filthy dungeon for 6 months (as covered in Volume 2 of this biography).

Finally Martin linked up with Joseph's brother William Smith, whom Martin had also helped select as an apostle years earlier. The two worked together over a 3 or so year period when Smith visited Kirtland a handful of times.

Meanwhile, in 1855 Martin, still a "wandering preacher," wrote a proclamation in mid-May stating that there now existed God's "servant and friend . . . called the messenger of the covenant," and that he was that messenger. He used someone, who claimed to be in contact with the dead, to produce the proclamation, so he may have been involved with the "rappers," a nickname for mediums (those who communicate with spirits on the other side), who were now influencing the weakened, remaining Latter-day Saint faithful in Kirtland, as many if not all were joining in with them, much to the Utah Saints' consternation when they learned of it. Thus, the Kirtland Saints-of-sorts were now following a full-fledged psychic, a woman named Fox.[29]

That same year, October 6, 1855, Martin and William Smith held a "conference" in Kirtland and decided to choose a committee to gather followers in Kansas, or someplace else they could agree upon, and to bring together the scattered dissenters among the various groups who had stayed behind when the main body of Saints went west. They also decided "to agree, if possible, upon the word of God." But they got practically nowhere, and Smith went to Iowa, then returned to marry in

Kirtland in late 1857. Despite Martin's reservations of William Smith's continuing absence (similar to William McLellin's general absence earlier in a different group), Martin and all 6 members of their struggling church chose William Smith as leader, but they could not get along. So Martin drove Smith out of town.

In seeking to discredit Martin Harris as a credible witness to the plates, some historical observers have implied that he suffered from mental aberrations, following one shepherd after another; but the accusation is untrue—he actually struck solid alliances with each and accepted invitations to high leadership positions.

While this in itself may have been an apparent problem of inflated ego, Martin felt shunned by the mainstream church not just once under Joseph (in 1838) but a second time under Brigham (in 1847) when Brigham became church President and left him out of callings to a high position. Martin's logic was a bit shaky on this one—by now he was a bona fide Shaker—not exactly First Presidency material, if that's what he was expecting.

In later years he continued his "calling" as an independent "Mormon Preacher"[30] and self-appointed tour guide of the abandoned Kirtland Temple. Meanwhile his second wife, Caroline Young, niece of Brigham, remained faithful, and held to her yearnings to reunite with the Utah Saints. For 18 years she watched him join one apostate group after another. And countless times she attempted to persuade him to take her and their family to rejoin the Saints. But in his stubborn state he refused to budge. So, in 1856 she made the final, life-altering decision to leave him and head west alone, with all 5 children in tow.

And away she went. Making matters harder, she was pregnant, giving birth in Iowa along the way. (They had 7 children in all, as another one had died at age 10 in Kirtland.) This last child that she bore on the way West was one Martin thought he would never see, but their lives would take an unusual twist.

Having no support from a husband to help her with 6 children across the plains, Caroline took 3 years and a great deal of faith to make it to the Utah Territory. Once there, arriving September 1, 1859, she met a man named John Catley Davis, a convert from England whose wife had died on the plains. She figured to never see Martin again and had no way to get divorce paperwork to him. And she needed a husband to assist in her mere survival with all the children in Utah, so on January 16, 1860, just 4½ months after arriving there, she married Davis. While still technically married to Martin.

In 1862, a missionary from Utah, James McKnight, traveled to England. En route, he stopped at Kirtland and saw Martin, saying that Martin actually "came to see me"—revealing the old gentleman's growing desire to associate with representatives from the mainstream church whenever they came to town. McKnight continues, "Of his property there is little or none left. He has now no home; his son [from his first marriage with Dolly] a worthless scapegoat, with whom he lived, being in prison, and the house [where they both lived] deserted."[31]

Then 7 years later, in October 1869, William H. Homer, a returning missionary to Utah, stopped in Kirtland to see Martin and found him a "poor clad, emaciated little man on whom the winter of life was weighing heavily . . . a pathetic figure."[32]

Martin, not knowing his wife had moved on so completely with her life, yearned for his family and even told Homer that he wished to see them: "I should like to see Caroline and the children. . . . but I cannot, I am too poor."[33] Martin had not seen his wife and kids in 14 years, not realizing Caroline had remarried 9 years and 9 months earlier.

Finally in 1870, poor, broke, and failing in health, Martin was visited by Edward Stevenson, another returning missionary, who took the bull by the horns and got Martin to Utah. (First Stevenson traveled alone to Salt Lake City, raised travel expenses of $200 [$5,505 in today's money] from donating Utah members, went all the way back, past Kirtland, to New York City to pay for Martin's train ticket, then returned to Kirtland and personally escorted the old man from Ohio through Chicago to Utah on the exciting, newly created train service that now connected both coasts.)

Arriving in Ogden by train on August 30, 1870 (not far from where the Transcontinental Railroad connected the continent

15½ months earlier),[34] Martin slipped down to Salt Lake City and reunited with the Saints in full faith, getting rebaptized 6 weeks later on September 17, 1870.

He would live almost another 5 years, his life now invigorated. His first 6 weeks especially were a breath of fresh air, being treated like royalty with party after party, and dinner after dinner with poor pioneers and church dignitaries alike. He stayed at the home of his grand-niece, Irinda Crandall McEwan and her husband of 3 years, 30-year-old Scotsman Joseph Thompson McEwan, who had started the first newspaper in Provo. Here in Salt Lake City, hundreds came to visit Martin, states Irinda.[35] He also attended numerous wards and even spoke in the Salt Lake Tabernacle.

On one occasion, Edward Stevenson and several others, including Brigham Young's first councilor, George A. Smith, drove with Martin to the warm springs outside the city for a hot bath.[36]

As their carriage went up a hill, they pulled the curtains back to reveal a magnificent city below, hosting hundreds of frame houses surrounded by beautiful gardens, nestled among wide, well-kept streets,[37] that featured the magnificent temple and tabernacle—miraculous structures for a distant, western, desert city. Stevenson reports Martin almost reeled from the view:

"Who would have thought," said Martin, "that the *Book of Mormon* would have done all this?"[38] His mind may have flashed back to his awkwardly hawking copies in downtown Palmyra, complaining to Joseph, "Nobody wants them."

Martin's wife Caroline, meanwhile, had troubles with her new marriage—actually one big one. At their home 70 miles south of Salt Lake City, in Payson, she witnessed her husband Davis have a squabble with Brigham Young, her uncle, over a parcel of land, whereupon Davis threatened to leave the church if the dispute did not end in his favor. She was probably fed up with husbands tantrumming and rebelling against church authority—after all, she had felt imprisoned in Kirtland for 18 years after Martin had refused to follow the church to Missouri,

Illinois, and Utah—so she sided with Brigham on this one, and decided to leave Davis, her husband of a decade. (In this 2nd marriage, she had given birth to her 8th child, an infant son that died a couple days after birth, which some speculated caused stress between them, weakening the marriage and preparing her for an early exit at the next stressful turn to come along—the spat with Brigham. The couple, meanwhile, had no other children together, although Davis did have a daughter he had brought to the marriage.)

Caroline had raised this girl, Elizabeth, since she was 10, which likely created further emotional conflict within Caroline when she decided to leave. However, at age 20, the daughter was now old enough to launch her own adult life by now, even though she was still at home, according to the 1870 U.S. census, which also showed Caroline still living with Davis.[39]

Caroline apparently left husband Davis that same year and moved to Salt Lake City.[40]

Family historian Helen Homer Parks writes that Caroline may have felt embarrassed over her 2 failed marriages, not being technically divorced from either husband.[41]

However, she met up with Martin when he stayed his first 6 weeks in Salt Lake City, as Caroline lived near Martin, who was staying at the McEwans' during that time.[42] No word on how the reunion went. But one aspect was marvelous: he got to see his baby girl he had never seen, the one whom Caroline had given birth to coming west—Ida May. At this sweet uniting of father and daughter, Martin expressed great joy in finally meeting her.[43] She was now 14.

In all, his decision to not go west with church and family had caused him great pain—pursuing leadership roles in spurious, dead-end breakaway groups—which cost him years of not being with his children. The result was . . . they grew up without their father, plus he lost his faith-driven wife, Caroline, who, after all, had remained almost 2 decades with him before reaching the breaking point.

But now he was back in the fold.

After 6 weeks visiting many hundreds of Saints in the big city, he moved to a town north of Ogden, Harrisville, and stayed with a nephew about 2 weeks. And then about late October 1870 he moved further north to Cache Valley, where he lived at Smithfield with his oldest son, Martin Jr., and family. There, he reunited with another son living there, Solomon. While this son and his family took care of him, they all moved in 1874 to Clarkston, where Martin made this town his final residence, from October 1874 to July 1875.

Meanwhile, there was the Caroline question. She "discreetly and quietly seclude[d] herself in Smithfield, preferring to live near Martin," says family historian Parks.[44] However, Caroline may have primarily wanted to live near her 2 sons there, but in any case apparently kept a congenial association with Martin,[45] and actually changed her last name back to Harris.

Once he came west, she and Martin did not completely avoid each other, as they had seen each other not only in Salt Lake City but again at their son Martin Jr.'s home in Smithfield.[46]

Caroline was now 56 and Martin 87. Another family historian speculates that Martin was so disappointed in hearing the news of Caroline remarrying and sealing herself and the children to Davis, that he refused to get back with her.[47] Perhaps seeing him in a new light—of once again being entitled to the gift of the Holy Ghost, as Saints believe, and from that possessing a more brightened countenance and peaceful aura about him— she was able to let go of the years of agonizing frustration she had endured in the 21 of their 22 years of marriage that he was broken off from the mainstream church, wherein he was "living in darkness," beginning in 1838, when he refused to follow Joseph to Far West, Missouri. She then, of course, did not see Martin for 11 years, from the time she came west in 1859 until he moved west in 1870—which was 4 years earlier. But by now, in 1874, they had been "divorced" for 15 years. And never got back together, due, apparently, to Martin's attitude about her leaving.

An interesting aside is that 87 years later, on February 20, 1962, William H. Homer, a descendant of the Homer who had visited Martin in Ohio, told his bishop, Ben J. Ravsten, that Martin's children and wife Caroline were now sealed to Martin.[48]

A remarkable legacy Martin left was his litany of testimonies on the *Book of Mormon*. One of them was recorded by Homer's ancestor, William Harrison Homer:

"I saw the plates; I saw the angel; I heard the voice of God. I know that the *Book of Mormon* is true and that Joseph Smith was a true prophet of God." Homer adds, "A divine fire glowed in his eyes. His voice throbbed with the sincerity and the conviction of his message. It was the real Martin Harris whose burning testimony no power on earth could quench. It was the most thrilling moment of my life."

Homer further records Martin saying, "Do I believe it! Do I see the sun shining! Just as surely as the sun is shining on us and gives us light, and the [moon] and stars give us light by night, just as surely as the breath of life sustains us, so surely do I know that Joseph Smith was a true prophet of God."[49]

On the night of July 10, 1875, Martin made a final testimony to witnesses in the room, then peacefully passed away. He was 92.

All three witnesses had personal problems with the direction the church was going or were prideful regarding following a youthful church leader in Joseph Smith, but none retracted his testimony of claiming to see the plates, which they say were shown by an angel to them, and which they handled themselves.

# A P P E N D I X I

# David Whitmer:
# Keeping the Manuscript

(REFERENCED IN CHAPTER 21)

Representatives from the mainstream church in Utah paid a visit to David Whitmer in Richmond, Missouri, during his later years, the results of which were published in December 1878.

The initial greeting and first 2-hour meeting seemed warm, but soon turned icy.

Oliver Cowdery had bequeathed a copy of the original *Book of Mormon* manuscript to Whitmer just before dying. Whitmer meanwhile had started his own breakaway group. Cowdery could have sent the manuscript to Utah, since he had rejoined the mainstream church, but evidently had felt a kinship with his fellow witness to the plates—David Whitmer—a friend since before either of them had even met Joseph Smith almost half a century earlier.

So now Orson Pratt and Joseph F. Smith were in town. These Utah men wanted to take the manuscript to church headquarters to preserve it in a safe shelter at Salt Lake City.

When the 2 sides met, the Utah men wanted just one thing—the manuscript.

The Whitmer party wanted one thing also—for them to leave.

But not before the Whitmer group could vent its frustrations, apparently offended that the Utah delegation had shown up wanting the one possession they most highly prized.

The Utah men began with a good argument. In fact, they probably thought they would succeed—surely the Whitmer party would want the manuscript preserved for generations, and their more established church in Utah had the means to preserve it properly.

But their argument fell on deaf ears. And the Whitmer party's response doubtless floored them. (See items 8, 9, and 12 below).

Prior to this interview—for many years in fact—both sides looked at the other as long lost sheep. But black sheep. They felt the other had strayed from what each thought was the pure doctrine of the church as established by the Savior, through the instrumentality of the Prophet Joseph Smith.

The Whitmer group, at least as recorded, took a posture of defensiveness, with an opaque layer of criticalness, per the conversation recorded below.

Note the answer (item #6) to the 3rd question. David Whitmer subtly tells them off.

Also observe the answer (item #10), as a follow-up to the same question, in which Philander Page essentially attempts to corner them by the way he phrases his rhetorical question.

Finally, notice a response by Whitmer (item #15): the Utah men had asked him "some questions," probably about early church history or the *Book of Mormon* itself. But Whitmer apparently refused to answer them, giving as his response that the information they sought was not for outsiders—only for "the Church" (apparently *his* church), "which the world [specifically you outsiders from Utah], cannot comprehend."

Despite the tension, David Whitmer was, ironically, highly respected by the LDS representatives, given his status as the last living member of the Three Witnesses. It is obvious, in fact, they felt honored to have met him.

After describing where they stayed in Richmond, Missouri, they described meeting Whitmer, age 73, in a barroom of the hotel on September 7, 1878. Their visit is recorded by Orson Pratt and Joseph F. Smith as follows:

"He seemed wonderfully pleased, as well as surprised, at seeing Elder Orson Pratt. Said he would not have known him—he had grown so fat and stout; he remembered him as a slender, bashful, timid boy. After a few moments conversation he excused himself, saying he would return again to see us."

Whitmer seemed intent on not being alone when talking with the Utah men. Perhaps he felt threatened, uncertain of what they wanted, or perhaps letters from Utah church leaders over the years had tipped him off as to their intentions. He returned presently to see them—but this time with a resident of the hotel in tow. Thus, he used a near stranger to run interference for him. Upon seeing the Utah men again, he almost immediately invited them to his office. There, at least 7 other men awaited them. "A couple of hours were very pleasantly passed in conversation, principally on Utah matters, when we parted for dinner, agreeing to meet Mr. Whitmer again at his office at 4:30 P.M."

Once back at his office, the Utah visitors obviously wanted to speak to him privately, "but as the place was too public for private conversation and as it seemed impossible to obtain a private personal interview with David Whitmer by himself, we invited him and such of his friends as he saw proper to fetch along to our room in the hotel."

At that point "Whitmer apologized for not inviting us to his house, as it was 'wash day,' and he and his wife were 'worn out' with the extra labor, exposure, etc., consequent on rebuilding since the cyclone."

Whitmer then came to their hotel room with 6 different men this time, including legal representation—a nephew attorney who was in "lawyer mode," advising him in one instance to not follow a recommendation from someone in the conversation.

Pratt writes, "In the presence of these . . . as noticed in Brother Joseph F. Smith's journal, is the account of the interview."

First they covered some questions about church history (as related earlier in this volume). Then their conversation continued with other questions and answers, as numbered by the author below:

Notice all went well until the Utah men would show their hand and reveal why they were there.

[1] "Elder O. P. [Orson Pratt:] Have you in your possession the original MSS [abbreviation for manuscripts—although there was just one; evidently their term for a manuscript of more than one page was manuscripts] of the *Book of Mormon*?

[2] "[David Whitmer:] I have; they are in O. Cowdery's handwriting. He placed them in my care at his death, and charged me to preserve them as long as I lived; they are safe and well-preserved.

[3] "[Joseph F. Smith:] What will be done with them at your death?

[4] "[David Whitmer:] I will leave them to my nephew, David Whitmer, son of my brother Jacob, and my namesake.

[5] "[Orson Pratt:] Would you not part with them to a purchaser?

[6] "[David Whitmer:] No. Oliver charged me to keep them, and Joseph said my father's house should keep the records. I consider these things sacred, and would not part with nor barter them for money.

[7] "[Joseph F. Smith:] We would not offer you money in the light of bartering for the MSS. [manuscripts], but we would like to see them preserved in some manner where they would be safe from casualties and from the caprices of men, in some institution that will not die as man does.

[8] "[David Whitmer:] That is all right [meaning no]. While camping around here in a tent, all my effects exposed to the weather, everything in the trunk where the MSS. were kept became moldy, etc., but they were preserved, not even being discolored (we supposed his camping in a tent, etc., had reference to his circumstances after the cyclone, in June last).

[9] "[Orson Pratt and Joseph F. Smith:] As he and others affirm, the room in which the MSS. were kept was the only part

of the house which was not demolished, and even the ceiling of that room was but little impaired.

[10] "'Do you think,' said Philander Page, a son of Hiram Page of the Eight Witnesses, 'that the Almighty cannot take care of his own?'

[11] "Next day (Sunday, September 8) Mr. Whitmer invited us to his house. . . . David Whitmer brought out the MSS. of the *Book of Mormon.* We examined them closely and those who knew the handwriting pronounced the whole of them, excepting comparatively few pages, to be in the handwriting of Oliver Cowdery. It was thought that these few pages were in the handwritings of Emma Smith and John and Christian Whitmer.

[12] "We found that the names of the eleven witnesses were, however, subscribed in the handwriting of Oliver Cowdery. When the question was asked Mr. Whitmer if he and the other witnesses did or did not sign the testimonies themselves, Mr. W. replied, "Each signed his own name."

[13] "Then where are the original signatures?"

[14] "[David Whitmer:] I don't know; I suppose Oliver copied them, but this I know is an exact copy.

[15] "Someone suggested that he, being the last one left of the eleven witnesses, ought to certify to this copy.

[16] "Lawyer D. Whitmer (Jacob's son) suggested that he had better reflect about it first and be very cautious.

[17] "[Joseph F. Smith] suggested that perhaps there were two copies of the manuscripts, but Mr. Whitmer replied that, according to the best of his knowledge, there never was but the one copy. Herein, of course, he is evidently uninformed.

[18] "Elder O. Pratt again felt closely after the subject of procuring the MSS., but we found that nothing would move him [Whitmer] on this point. The whole Whitmer family are deeply impressed with the sacredness of this relic. And so thoroughly imbued are they with the idea and faith that it is under the immediate protection of the Almighty that, in their estimation, not only are the MSS. themselves safe from all possible contingencies, but that they are a source of protection

to the place or house in which they may be kept, and, it may be, to those who have possession of them.

[19] "Another reason why they cling to this relic is that David Whitmer has reorganized the 'Church of Christ' with six elders and two priests, after the pattern of the first organization, the two priests as we suppose representing Joseph and Oliver as holding the Aaronic priesthood from the hand of John the Baptist. David and John Whitmer were 2 of these 6 elders, 4 others, viz. John C. Whitmer, W. W. Warner, Philander Page, and John Short, having been ordained by David and John. And as the recent death of John has diminished the number to five elders it would be interesting to know if, according to their strict construction, the vacancy can be filled.

[20] "Their creed is to preach nothing but the Bible and the *Book of Mormon*. Mr. Whitmer and others called on us again in the evening, at the hotel, and conversed, reiterating many things before stated."

[21] "Upon inquiry, Mr. Whitmer informed us that Oliver Cowdery had told him all about his visiting the church at Council Bluffs and of his having been rebaptized. [As also reported in Appendix H: "What Happened to the Three Witnesses?"] He said, 'Oliver died the happiest man I ever saw; after shaking hands with the family and kissing his wife and daughter, he said, 'Now I lay me down for the last time; I am going to my Savior,' and died immediately, with a smile on his face."

In an attempt to enlighten David Whitmer, Orson Pratt and Joseph F. Smith closed their conversation with him in the last conversation any Latter-day Saint leaders would apparently have with him. They recorded their conversation as follows:

[22] "In response to some questions, Mr. Whitmer said: 'Many things have been revealed which were designed only for the Church, and which the world cannot comprehend, but the *Book of Mormon* and those testimonies therein given were to go to all the world.'

[23] "We replied, 'Yes, and we have sent that book to the Danes, the Swedes, the Spanish, the Italians, the French, the German, the Welsh, and to the islands of the sea, the book

even having been translated into Hindoostanee. So you see the Church has not been idle.' To this he made no reply. In parting with him, he said 'This may be the last time I shall ever see you in the flesh, so fare-well.'

[24] "This ended our interview with the last remaining witness who saw the plates of the *Book of Mormon*, yet not the last witness of its truth, for now such witnesses are multiplied into tens of thousands."[1]

David Whitmer never denied his testimony of the *Book of Mormon*. During 1838 embattlements between the Saints and the Missourians he had become disenchanted with Joseph Smith's leadership, and split with the Saints, but then started his own church in the 1870s. At the age of 83 he would die (January 25, 1888) as a prosperous, respected member of the Richmond, Missouri community, despite steadfastly affirming his testimony of the truthfulness of the *Book of Mormon*.

# A P P E N D I X J

# Yellow Journalism and the New York Press

(REFERENCED IN CHAPTERS 23 AND 37)

The hallmarks of *yellow journalism* were sensational headlines (often reckless with the facts) to grab buyers' attention and boost sales, along with news articles exhibiting blatant bias by reporters and editors. The term originally applied to 2 New York City newspapers 66 years after the first attacks on the *Book of Mormon*.

But in 1829 smaller western New York papers practiced their own version of yellow journalism. They reported on Joseph with salacious, false coverage, no different in style than the 2 big city papers to which the phrase was first applied in 1898 by Erwin Wardman, editor of the *New York Press*. (Others had made use of the label but he was the first to publish the term.)

This term was coined to define the policies of 2 of his competitors—Joseph Pulitzer's *New York World* and William Randolph Hearst's *New York Journal*, first headed by the 2 men in 1883 and 1895 respectively. (Both had previous newspaper success—Pulitzer in St. Louis and Hearst in San Francisco.) The newspaper war between the two had its heyday from 1895 to 1899. At that time both sought to outdo the other for increased circulation, in order to charge higher advertising rates and make more revenues.

The history of yellow journalism is intriguing. Especially in how it was launched.

Hearst's *Journal* competed in the marketplace by selling his paper for one cent—half the price of Pulitzer's *World*. So Pulitzer, too, lowered his to a penny. Hearst retaliated by hiring away Pulitzer's staff in 1896—or most of it—which was not a difficult feat since Pulitzer was short-tempered and abusive to his employees. So they willingly jumped ship.

Meanwhile, both introduced the first color comic strips. From this specifically came the term "yellow journalism," as both, interestingly enough, carried a Sunday strip featuring "The Yellow Kid," a bald, wide-mouthed, smiling kid in a neck-to-foot, yellow nightshirt. (The bright yellow nightshirt occurred from a color press foreman's experiment to develop a yellow ink that would finally work, since, heretofore, yellow ink would not work in color printing, as it was too slow drying, so the experiment on that one nightshirt caused the character to be "stuck" forever in yellow, which made him iconic among New York City newspaper readers.)

Pulitzter's *World* ran the strip first in 1896, but Hearst hired away the cartoonist, Richard F. Outcault. So Pulitzer sued. The outcome allowed only Pulitzer's *World* to retain the original comic strip name, "Down in Hogan's Alley." But since the cartoonist Outcault had created the characters, he was allowed to take them to his new newspaper—Hearst's *Journal*, under a different comic strip name, "McFadden's Row of Flats." Both strips eventually used "The Yellow Kid" name above the title of their actual strips' titles, since it was the Yellow Kid character that made the strips famous. (Parenthetically, Pulitzer, upon learning he got to keep the strip's name, went ahead and hired a replacement artist—George Luks—to do his own version of the comic strip, using the Yellow Kid.)

Further noteworthy, R. F. Outcault is widely considered the inventor of the comic strip. He was at least among the first, if not the very first one, to use the same cast of characters in an ongoing series. He hailed from Cincinatti and studied art in Paris. His "Yellow Kid" strip also launched the first comic merchandising in history.

Competing newspapers in New York City lambasted the *World* and the *Journal* as "the Yellow Kid papers," and from that the term "yellow journalism" was born, since both newspapers also had one other common trait—sensationalizing the news. (For example, both papers helped mold public opinion in New York City against the Spanish in hopes the U.S. would enter the Spanish-American War. Washington policy-makers soon did enter that war, probably outside the influence of these 2 papers [although Hearst took credit for it]).

Understanding the tactics of these papers is significant, because their attempts at molding public opinion parallel those of earlier western New York newspapers in rallying readers against Joseph's people.

Another similarity was their propensity for disregarding the truth and discarding the facts in order to make a sensationalistic story, which would sell more papers than otherwise.

An interesting side note is that cartoonist Outcault would, the year after the "Yellow Kid" strip died out at both papers, launch his most successful comic series ever—the nationally syndicated "Buster Brown" comic strip, from 1902 to 1921, whose merchandising spin-offs would become the first comic strip phenomenon, creating Buster Brown shoes (still in existence today, over a century later, which were launched at the 1904 St. Louis World's Fair); a 1905 Broadway play, a 1943 radio show (when radio was king), and a TV series from 1951–1955 (4 seasons). It had the first talking or thinking pet in American comics, predating Charlie Brown's Snoopy by half a century (Snoopy was introduced in October 1950 and began communicating his thoughts in May 1952).

The "Buster Brown" strip first ran in James Gordon Bennett junior's *New York Herald* beginning May 4, 1902.

As another side note, Bennett's was the first large metropolitan paper to investigate Joseph's people. (Bennett senior started the paper in 1835 after several failed attempts to start one, and turned it over to his son in 1866, when it was the highest-circulation newspaper in the United States, before he died in 1872.)

Amazingly, Hearst again hired Outcault away from a competitor—James Gordon Bennett junior—and in 1906 came another court battle, with a similar result to the Pulitzer battle: Bennett's *Herald* could retain exclusive use of the "Buster Brown" strip name (which other artists would draw), while Outcault could continue using the "Buster Brown" cast of characters at his new place of work—Hearst's *World*; however, this time—oddly—with no title.

Lastly, in this obscure historical footnote of a paper that was the first of its kind to write about Joseph Smith, is the interesting life of Bennett's son, James Gordon Bennett junior.

After Bennett senior hired Henry Morton Stanley exclusively to write for him, Bennett junior financed his famous 1871 expedition to Africa in search of the world-renowned missing explorer David Livingstone. From that, H. M. Stanley coined his iconic quote—deep in the African jungle on November 10, 1871, as he came upon the first white man he had seen in 8 months—"Dr. Livingstone, I presume?" (Less famous is the equally stuffy, amusingly typical British reply: "Yes, and I feel thankful that I am here to welcome you.") The account was published in Bennett's *Herald*, since Bennett had scored an "exclusive," having financed the expedition.

Bennett also volunteered his yacht during the Civil War as part of the fleet that captured an outpost in Florida, a yacht which he captained, bringing him a bit more renown. Four years later he won the first trans-oceanic yacht race from Sandy Hook, New Jersey, to The Needles of the Isle of Wight in the U.K., in an amazing period of 13 days and 22 hours, less 5 minutes, unheard of in the days of immigrant sailing ships.

In 1877 he practically fled New York for Europe after royally embarrassing himself at an engagement party thrown by his socialite fiancée's family, which put the skids to his engagement: he showed up late. And worse: drunk. And even worse: right there in the family mansion, in full view of all the guests, he urinated into the grand piano.[1]

Later, returning to the U.S., he launched the first polo match in the U.S. and founded America's first polo club. In 1906 he funded the Gordon Bennett Cup for ballooning, which continues today. He finally married at age 73 and died 4 years later in France.

(Possibly his life would have gone down a different path had he and his father embraced the religion that his father was the first to report about in their New York City newspaper decades earlier, although, obviously, any of his adventures could have occurred even so, minus, perhaps, the alcohol-induced attack on the grand piano.)

These unusual anecdotes paint a fuller picture than what most people know of the intriguing world within New York City newspapers at the turn of the 20th century. The bottom line is that cutthroat competition induced "yellow journalism," although 7 decades earlier it was clearly being practiced already by small-town newspapers in western New York targeting Joseph Smith.

A P P  N D I X

# Attacking the Great White God

(REFERENCED IN CHAPTER 23)

Despite all the accounts of a great white god (summarized in Chapter 23), some scholars attempt to discount the idea, and sometimes even strain at the notion, inventing interesting interpretations, such as one specific opposing theory[1] that declares the only reason the Aztecs bowed before Cortés was because it was their way of asserting themselves and showing "superiority." The weakness in this argument is that, while perchance the Aztecs did bow to show their "superiority," simply too many other native nations greeted the conquistadors with the same reverence or friendliness—and certainly the others had no tradition of bowing to invaders to show "superiority". The Hopi, Hawaiians, Mayans, and especially the Caribs had other traditions—ambushing with spears and blowguns—rather than bowing to invaders and strangers. Unless, of course, they perceived their invaders as long-anticipated, returning Deity, which in fact was the case, proclaim *Book of Mormon* proponents.

Further, the Franciscans, whom modern detractors wish to blame for inventing the great white god concept, were not even around in northern Canada to put their alleged spin on the Canadian tribal legends which declared the existence of the great white god that far north.

However, others disagree with the Quetzalcoatl theory of that figure being a white god such as Jesus Christ, seeing it merely as a symbol of a legend having nothing to do with Christian Deity. They have their arguments and, as with the archaeological factions—neither side can convince the other. Apparently not only archaeologists but scholars of legends are in a seemingly never-ending dance of stalemate.

In this dance, some modern scholars discount all the white God legends by claiming they are based on "pseudoscience."[2]

Their seeming arrogance, claim Latter-day Saints, lies in the supposition that only their science is "pure," while everyone else's is "pseudoscience."

For example, one scholar claimed that during the Spanish Conquest, Catholic priests conjured up the great white god scenario, claiming they wanted to tie in the natives' beliefs to Christianity, so that the natives would appear less savage.

This same theory claims that, over time, Quetzalcoatl's looks and clothing were retooled to fit a more Christian image.[3] On the other hand, one might argue that the priests had no reason to make the natives appear less savage, since the natives were already subjected to Spanish suppression. Also, the idea of priests traveling around re-painting the Quetzalcoatl drawings is more than a little far-fetched.

Another theory assumes that the legend of the returning white god had originated in the following manner—Cortes had "reworked" Moctezuma's welcome speech (as presented in the text). However, there is no proof that Cortes touched it. The theory apparently does not wish to give credence to legends that point to a great white god. So the theorists credit the Franciscans of 2 decades earlier for supposedly inventing and spreading the "Cortés-as-Quetzalcoatl legend" in the 1530s.[4] However, there are simply too many accounts of various tribes anticipating the return of the great white god, for the Franciscans to have conspiratorially invented them all.

The Hopi, for example, had distanced themselves very quickly from the Franciscans and everything Spanish; their traditions were pure and in no way touched up or reinvented by the Spanish. Same with the Hawaiians and others as well.

# APPENDIX L

## The Great White God Who Fell from Grace

(REFERENCED IN CHAPTER 23)

In the Hawaiian Islands, Captain James Cook and his compatriots were also welcomed as deity, thinking Cook was the returning white god Kona.

But the crewmen exploited the natives' good will, procuring the native women for wild beach partying. And it came back to bite them like a stingray in the groin. After a month of bliss with the natives, one of the crew members died, exposing the Brits as mere mortals. At that point, relations between them slid into the ocean like a rusty old anchor.

When the Brits saw the natives putting 2 and 2 together, they sailed off into the horizon in the nick of time—on February 4, 1779.

But soon rough seas damaged 1 of their 2 ships, splitting the foremast, and after a week at sea they had to find land. The only feasible place was back in Hawaii.

The Hawaiians, seeing them returning, still felt a bitter taste in the mouths from seeing their women seduced and their entire population duped.

It was obvious now why these duplicitous whites had sailed away so suddenly—they had feared exposure as white god frauds. And now these same "immortals" were returning with a broken mast and fear in their eyes.

The true god Kona was chuckling up there somewhere.

These were not only imposters, they were sitting ducks.

It was time to mob the daylights out of them.

First, Cook and his men sailed into the harbor, observing the natives lining the shore, holding spears, nobody smiling.

Doubtless, crewmen lost their sheepish grins when they saw their once-adoring women ready to chuck spears at them.

Nevertheless, some of the ever-optimistic Brits figured they could talk their way out of this, patch things up, and be on their way.

The Hawaiians clearly thought, "Not so fast."

To the crewmen that also became obvious when they saw the Hawaiians start hurling rocks at them.

Surviving the rock attack, the sailors saw the Hawaiians start swimming out to their ship. While grateful they were not attacked, they were nevertheless humiliated—Hawaiians now stole their small cutter vessel.

Cook wasn't about to let them get away with it. He rowed to shore and defiantly marched to King Kalani'opu'u's hut. Ripping off His Majesty's cutters was simply not acceptable, he told them. Being a stubborn British officer he made his demands boldly.

Not a great idea for a fraudulent Kona to do.

Yet the natives saw he would not back down—and he would not leave without the cutter.

But the cutter was rightfully theirs, they figured, a small token of revenge for having been taken advantage of. In fact, the imposters were getting off lightly.

Cook saw it differently.

Tempers flared.

Negotiations broke down.

Shots were fired.

A lesser Hawaiian chief was killed.

Cook and his men hightailed it back to shore.

A mob chased them.

The sailors jumped in their row boats.

The angry mob caught up to them.

Cook and his men thought it their right to fire on them.

Bad idea.

The Hawaiians swarmed them.

Most crewmen got away—but in the melee, as Cook tried launching his boat, he was struck on the head and fell with his face in the sand, then was stabbed to death.[1]

Hawaiians say a chief named Kanaina killed him.[2] They dragged his body to their village and held a strangely respectful burial for him, one in fact fit for a chief.

All told, in the attempt to escape shore, 4 armed British crewmen were killed with Cook and 2 others were wounded.

Another version states that Cook's final minute went like this: at the village he had tried to take the Hawaiian king hostage with his armed crewmen until the boat and other articles would be returned by the natives.[3]

If so—a horrible idea.

Horrible ideas flourished that day, as they underestimated the Hawaiians' sense of outrage. The Brits had tangled with the wrong sacred legacy—of Kona.

James Cook was killed on Valentine's Day, February 14, 1779.[4]

A few days later the surviving Englishmen aboard one of the ships retaliated by firing their cannons and muskets at the shore, killing some 30 Hawaiians. The 2 British ships, aptly named the *Resolution* and *Discovery* (they had made a Resolution to have an orgy, but their Discovery was that Hawaiians don't like white god imposters), eventually returned to England, minus their captain and the 4 crewmen.[5]

Cook's men had taken the natives' friendly reception for a ride, but there is no evidence Cook had participated. It wasn't his nature or reputation.

In 1779, when the American colonies were at war with Britain, Benjamin Franklin wrote American captains at sea, telling them to leave James Cook's vessel alone if they came in contact with it. He said to "not consider her an enemy, nor suffer any plunder to be made of the effects contained in her, nor obstruct her immediate return to England by detaining her or sending her into any other part of Europe or to America, but that you treat the said Captain Cook and his people with all civility and kindness . . . as common friends to mankind."[6]

Cook may have fallen into a trap, thinking it was better to let the natives assume he was Kona than to confess otherwise, as he needed to buy time with them while he gathered scientific specimens for his exploration. But his men certainly took advantage of the islanders' gullibility, and Cook did not put a stop to it. He may have broached the subject to his men, but finding them drooling with lust and an opportunity for a free-for-all (a difficult argument for Cook to counter—how many times in their lives would they be mistaken for deity and see hordes of women throw themselves at them, even at the ugliest, most socially backwards on board?) Thus the good captain may have feared a mutiny, so he backed away, placing the mission first while keeping peace with his men, at the expense of the natives.

Despite this mistake, Cook was a highly respected captain and person.

Sailing with him on the *Resolution*, David Samwell wrote, "He was a modest man, and rather bashful; of an agreeable, lively conversation, sensible and intelligent. In temper he was somewhat hasty, but of a disposition the most friendly, benevolent, and humane,"[7] thus, a far cry from the Spanish conquistadors.

Cook was actually a Scotsman raised in humble circumstances on a farm, who had left to make a life for himself by working hard to obtain an education, then going to sea where he would prove his worth to officers of the British Navy before becoming one himself—a captain of his own ship on 3 different voyages around the world. He was well liked by others and had not seen success handed to him on a silver platter as many captains had, those from families of wealth or royalty; yet it was his "hasty" temper that proved his undoing. Nevertheless, his accomplishments and humane treatment of others were a lasting legacy.

A Hawaiian town was later named for him, and more recently the Apollo 15 module *Endeavour*[8] and the space shuttle *Endeavour*[9] were both named after the first ship he took to the Pacific in 1768, the *HMS Endeavor.* His third and final voyage was on the *HMS Discovery* 11 years later in 1779, when he was killed.

The space shuttle *Discovery* was named after this ship.[10] The only portion of land on United States soil of which the author is aware that belongs to another country is the plot of ground in Hawaii on which Cook was killed. In 1874 a white memorial was built there on a section of land about 25 feet square, which is chained off. This parcel has been given to the United Kingdom.[11]

Numerous memorials honoring Cook are spread across the Pacific and the UK—and for good reason: he was a groundbreaking navigator, map-maker, and explorer, placing particular emphasis on science and the advancement of mankind.

# Theories Attacking the *Book of Mormon*

(REFERENCED IN CHAPTERS 23 AND 36)

The nation's press in general denounced Joseph and the *Book of Mormon*. However, the *New Yorker* in 1841 wrote with a surprisingly sympathetic view. While believing Joseph wrote the book himself rather than translating it from ancient plates, it editorialized that Joseph "shows a degree of talent and research that in an uneducated youth of twenty is almost a miracle of itself."[1] While complimentary in its own way, it was a form of detraction from Joseph's message that the book came from the ancients, revealed from the heavens.

Another detractor was Philastus Hurlbut, a former Saint who had been excommunicated for adultery. (While one's sins are considered wiped clean by baptism into the restored church, if afterward a member commits certain "grievous" sins such as murder or a felony, they are excommunicated. In the case of adultery, they are usually either disfellowshipped—a lesser disciplinary action—or excommunicated. "Disfellowshipping" a member within the Church of Jesus Christ of Latter-day Saints means they are asked not to take the sacrament on Sundays for a given period of time, or participate in church "callings," such as receiving church positions of teaching, etc, as well as not being invited to give public prayers in church for a period of time. "Excommunication" means removal from church membership records. Many, if not most, who are disciplined in either category seek full reinstatement, and with time and consistent actions are readmitted to full standing. Some, however, become enemies to the church. When this occurs, claim many Latter-day Saints, they often place themselves within 3 common categories: (1) they either feel "godly sorrow" from remorse, which leads them to repent and seek full fellowship again—sometimes succeeding on the first try, but sometimes trying and failing a number of times until they either succeed or give up trying—or, (2) they slide into apathy and don't care about the church or their condition within it, or (3) they enter a world of antagonism, by "kicking against the pricks" of their conscience—searing their conscience with continued "commandment-breaking" to where they are past feeling, then allowing bitterness to take over their soul, which, some believers say, allows spiritually dark forces to replace the light they once had in their soul, giving way to those forces to lead them in fighting against the church.)[2]

Philastus Hurlbut was one who, for whatever reason, became an enemy. He claimed the *Book of Mormon* had its origins in the "Solomon Spaulding manuscript," a novel written in 1812, whose author died 4 years later. Spaulding's brother John and his wife still had the manuscript, and Hurlbut met with them. From his interview with them, he learned that a few points about the unpublished book's contents seemed similar to the *Book of Mormon* but, when he actually read the manuscript, he was chagrined to discover very few similarities—the Spaulding manuscript was merely a weak adventure novel about pre-Columbian immigrants to America. The main similarity was that it claimed to be a translation of ancient scrolls discovered in a cave. It had no religious aspects to it and was written in an entirely different style—as a light novel of adventure with romantic notions.

At the other end of the spectrum, Joseph purports the *Book of Mormon* to be pure scripture, maintaining, "The *Book of Mormon* was the most correct of any book on earth and the keystone of our religion, and a man would get nearer to God by abiding by its precepts than by any other book."[3]

Hurlbut, in vain, then went searching for another manuscript of Spaulding's, despite the widow's claim he had written only one.

Next, Hurlbut learned that Sidney Rigdon had known the publisher who had rejected the Spaulding manuscript. From that very weak link, Hurlbut tried to tie Sidney to writing the *Book of Mormon*. His logic was . . . because Rigdon knew the publisher, he somehow got a hold of the manuscript, read it, and then wrote the *Book of Mormon* from it. But there was one rather obvious hitch—Sidney had never even heard of the *Book of Mormon* until well after it was published, making it rather difficult for him to have written it. Also, the fact that Sidney had merely known the publisher creates somewhat of a leap of logic—it means that the publisher, instead of returning the manuscript with a rejection slip to its rightful owner, Spaulding, would have instead sent it to Sidney, choosing this one weakly written manuscript out of the numerous bad manuscripts that a publisher receives and rejects each year. Publishers don't waste a friend's time by sending them bad, rejected manuscripts, nor do they take the chance of losing them, because manuscripts, even bad ones, were to their authors a particularly valuable possession in that day. Authors had spent months or years writing them in their best longhand, tediously using a feather quill pen dipped in an inkwell to slowly draw out 3 or 4 words at a time, much as an artist would, then authors would use sand to soak up excess ink on each page, as mentioned in Chapter 23. The goose feather quills weren't always plentiful, and the paper was very expensive.

The ink came from a handmade process, using black walnuts or berries. In the case of berries, they were strained so only the liquid was left, combined with about ½ teaspoon of white vinegar (for a 2.5 oz. inkwell) as a binding agent (in order to stick to the paper) plus a pinch of salt (to preserve it, or it would mold). In using black walnuts, the whole nuts were gathered into a container in order to rot, then would be soaked for days to months. At that point the rotten black husks would be smashed and combined with water, then heated, simmering for hours, and strained, while adding 5% alcohol as the preservative of choice. Gum arabic was finally added to improve ink flow. The resulting product was black ink.

The problem for people at this time was that berries and black walnuts were often needed for food just to survive, so were not always plentiful.

In Solomon Spaulding's case, a quill pen was doubtless used, since he died in 1816, 6 years before metal pens (dip pens with metal nibs) were mass-produced (as detailed in Chapter 23) by John Mitchell of Birmingham, England, which sped up writing considerably.

During Spaulding's lifetime (1761 to 1816), metal pens were available but hand-made and rare.

Even If Spaulding owned one, the highly expensive paper and often hard-to-find ink, coupled with the still-tedious process of writing with a metal pen, made manuscripts precious commodities. Thus, authors almost always wanted their manuscripts back from publishers immediately.

Publishers would not have wanted to be responsible for having them lost or damaged by sending them off to third parties, such as Sidney Rigdon, to read. But in Spaulding's case—it was all the more priceless of a possession from the probability that he used a quill pen with which to write.

For these reasons, an author's original manuscript was generally the only copy in existence, since the task of penning a second copy for security was simply too tedious, time-consuming, and expensive. Spaulding's lifetime was long before photocopy machines were available. While rare, primitive copy machines had been around since the 1600s, the first practical office photocopiers would not be available for 143 years after Spaulding died—not until 1959, when they were introduced by Xerox.

In short, authors demanded their prized manuscripts be returned directly to them, which Spaulding's obviously was, after it was rejected.

The fact that Spaulding's manuscript was of an entirely different genre than the *Book of Mormon*—of light adventure vs. a complex historical/theological narrative of rising and falling civilizations—requires another leap of logic to believe that the *Book of Mormon* had any ties to it.

Nevertheless, this highly fictitious tie-in theory was accepted by numerous if not most newspapers, and thus the general populace of the 19th century (and even some during the 20th century) accepted it, believing what they read in the newspapers. Even fairly intelligent people such as Rigdon's old partner Alexander Campbell jumped on the bandwagon—switching his belief from Joseph fabricating the book to that of Joseph using Spaulding's manuscript.

With or without the Spaulding manuscript, some have claimed Sidney wrote the *Book of Mormon*, because he was more educated than Joseph. A problem here is that the book was published half a year before not only he had heard of it, but even months before his associate Parley P. Pratt had heard of it. (Remember: it was Parley who introduced the *Book of Mormon* to Sidney.)

In an interview with retired Palmyra physician John Stafford, interviewers William H. Kelley and E. L. Kelley asked Dr. Stafford about Sidney's influence on Joseph. Stafford had been a neighbor of the Smiths in Manchester, New York, living 1 mile from their farm.

"'If young Smith was as illiterate as you said, Doctor, how do you account for the *Book of Mormon*?'

"'Well, I can't; except that Sidney Rigdon was connected with them.'

"'What makes you think he was connected with them?'

"'Because I can't account for the *Book of Mormon* any other way.'

"'Was Rigdon around there before the *Book of Mormon* was published?'

"'No, not as we could ever find out. Sidney Rigdon was never there, that Hurlbut, or Howe, or Tucker [3 enemies who published against Joseph] could find out.'"

Besides reporting useful, factual information about the Smith family, Pomeroy Tucker would also publish baseless claims about them. He would be countered by Stafford, even though Stafford never joined with the Smiths religiously.

"What Tucker said about them was false," said Stafford, "absolutely,"[4]

"'Well you have been looking out for the facts a long time, have you not, Doctor?'

"'Yes, I have been thinking and hearing about it for the last 50 years, and lived right among all their old neighbors there most of the time.'

"'And no one has ever been able to trace the acquaintance of Rigdon and Smith, until after the *Book of Mormon* was published and Rigdon was proselyted by Parley P. Pratt in Ohio?'

"'Not that I know of.'"[5]


By 1904 the Spaulding manuscript theory pretty much died out. That year Charles W. Brown wrote that unbelieving neighbors of the Smith family—those who knew them—discounted the Spaulding theory, believing the Smiths had authored it with Oliver Cowdery's help, discounting the angelic visit.[6] This was a seemingly logical explanation, since Oliver was around much of the translation period and was highly literate; but Latter-day Saints believe that most anyone who reads the book will realize that an illiterate family and one somewhat educated scribe could not possibly write such a work, especially in the few weeks of Joseph's actual time working on the manuscript, because of the book possessing numerous literary "footprints"—different styles of writing—with intricate and complex plot weaving. These intricate plot lines are especially evident among the accounts of the Nephites during their numerous conflicts with the Lamanites, and the missionary journeys and people's migrations that are detailed there as well. (Another problem with this theory of Oliver supervising its writing is that he came along only after a good portion of the book had already been written—an entire 116 pages had been written and later lost by Martin Harris before Oliver even met Joseph.)

Oliver died active in the faith, but during a large span of his life he had been disassociated from the church and, during that period, he had numerous opportunities to claim authorship or fraudulence, but never did. In fact, he said that he did try to translate part of the book at one time but could not even manage to translate one line. Further is the problem of no rewriting on the manuscript itself. It was just too perfectly crafted, with no mistakes or corrections on it except minor grammatical ones.

Later in the 20th century (1985) a writer named David Persuitte claimed Joseph formed his main idea from a Vermont Congregationalist minister in early Poultney, Vermont.

This minister was Ethan Smith, author of a book titled *View of the Hebrews*, published in 1823. One idea advanced by Ethan Smith in this book was that the Native Americans descended from the lost tribes of Israel.[7]

Joseph likely never saw *View of the Hebrews* until considerably later, and never mentioned it until 1842, when he probably first became aware of it, writing about it in *Times and Seasons*. He was actually pleased that another book could support the theory of a Jewish influence among the descendants of Native Americans, whereupon Joseph spoke of Ethan's book favorably, but that's as close as it ever got to the *Book of Mormon*, one book being entirely different from the other—Ethan's book being a treatise, with Joseph's book being a complex narrative of the rise and fall of civilizations, all the while containing hundreds of doctrinal teachings, none of them contradicting.

The plots and complexities of the *Book of Mormon*, with its multiple author "footprints," were still quite impossible for any young man to have written in only 4–8 weeks over a 3 month time span (April–June 1829—see Appendix G: "A New, Surprising Time Line for Translating the Plates"), especially with very little education, even had he learned of a specific theme from another manuscript or book. But the problem with these theories is this: there were literally dozens of themes in the

*Book of Mormon.* (See Chapter 23 for a summary and overview of just a few.)

# Analyzing Addison Everett's 1881 Letter about Joseph Smith's Escape

(REFERENCED IN CHAPTER 25)

Addison Everett wrote a letter to Oliver Boardman Huntington in 1881. Huntington used the letter, with slight alterations, when he published an article in the *Woman's Journal* at Salt Lake City in 1890 to describe Joseph and Oliver's account.

The article is rightly attributed to Huntington, as it describes Joseph Smith and Oliver Cowdery escaping the mob and receiving the Apostleship by Peter, James, and John. An editor of the *Woman's Journal* could have polished the article, but Huntington likely laid out the original draft, since it was published in November 1890, 16¼ years before his death in February 1907. He may have taken liberty in clarifying Everett's account—cleaning up the punctuation and grammar, etc., (unless the editor did) and/or perhaps he even received verbal clarification on points within the letter from Everett himself, since they were acquaintances.

While the *Woman's Journal* version of Everett's letter is quoted in the text, his undoctored letter is reproduced below:

"Joseph & Oliver went to the woods in a few rods, it being night, and they traveled until Oliver was exhausted & Joseph almost Carried him through mud and water. They traveled all night and just at the break of day Olive[r] gave out entirely and exclaimed O! Lord! How long Brother Joseph have we got to endure this thing; Brother Joseph said that at that very time Peter James & John came to them and Ordained them to the Apostleship."

The final 3 paragraphs from Everett's original letter are essentially the same as the magazine article, which are in part quoted in Chapter 25 of this book.

Everett's final 3 paragraphs *in full* are below:

"They had 16 or 17 miles to travel to get back to Mr. Hales, his father-in-law, and Oliver did not complain any more of fatigue.

"Now, brother Huntington, I have told you what I heard Bro. Joseph tell, almost the last time I ever heard him talk.

"It is a source of satisfaction and pleasure to me to have seen and heard the Prophet of God."[1]

Everett's letter gives additional information—most of which is not contained in the *Woman's Journal* article nor in the main text of this book. Some of that can be gleaned from the following sentence, which precedes the description of the escape and ordination:

"In the conversation between Joseph and Hyrum, Oliver Cowdery was spoken of—Joseph said 'Poor boy!'"

Several details can be ascertained from the above sentence of this letter: (1) Everett is here stating that Joseph is relating this experience (the escape and the ordination), to his brother Hyrum; (2) Everett, who reported the conversation, was either directly included in it or merely overheard it; (3) When Joseph uttered the words, "Poor boy," it apparently sparked the memory of the escape, which he then began detailing to Hyrum (and possibly to Everett and others); and (4) Joseph, in recalling Oliver's plight, felt sorry for Oliver on the occasion when he and Joseph were chased all night.

Another detail in the letter is the date of June 1844. Thus, this conversation between Joseph and Hyrum (perhaps including

Everett and others) occurred in Nauvoo, Illinois, 14 years after the escape. Finally, this conversation occurred just days before Joseph and Hyrum would see Nauvoo and their friends for the final time.

Although providing no additional information, one notes that at the end of Everett's letter to Huntington is a very typical, formal closing used in that day: "Your humble servant, Addison Everett."[2]

A P P E N D I X

# Other Churches' Claims to Revelations

(REFERENCED IN CHAPTER 26)

As pointed out by historian Richard Lyman Bushman, in a few other faiths some individuals have believed they received revelations, but they either failed to write them down or never claimed they were scripture. An example of these is Ann Lee, founder of the Shakers, a Quaker break-off group, who did not record her revelations. Others who did, such as Seventh-day Adventist Ellen White, wrote volumes of what she called revelations, but never claimed them as scripture. (The second-generation Shakers did compile a 400-page book they read in meetings as scripture—*A Holy, Sacred and Divine Roll and Book* (1843)—but it was discredited after a couple years.)[1]

Only Joseph's followers accomplished both—they (1) recorded them and (2) regarded them as scripture on a par with the Bible.

In 1833 they would be published as the *Book of Commandments* and later as the *Doctrine and Covenants*. The revelations were written in old English, like the Bible and *Book of Mormon*, and, in most instances, penned in the voice of God speaking, not Joseph writing.

(Thus, even when revelations were directed to him and not others, Joseph was simply an audience for those revelations, as others were when they received revelations through Joseph. The first recorded revelation actually reprimanded him for losing the 116 pages, and at other times he was chastised as well but, in every case, he was the vehicle for receiving revelations, whether they were directed to him or someone else.)

When Joseph received revelations, others were usually present. Parley P. Pratt states, "Each sentence was uttered slowly and very distinctly, and with a pause between each, sufficiently long for it to be recorded by an ordinary writer in long hand. This was the manner in which all his written revelations were dictated and written. There was never any hesitation, reviewing, or reading back, in order to keep the run of the subject; neither did any of these communications undergo revisions, interlinings, or corrections. As he dictated them, so they stood, so far as I have witnessed."[2] (Occasionally, grammar corrections or other slight modifications would later be made with Joseph's review.)

Then the revelations were copied and sent to all the local villages by Joseph's followers, says Levi Hancock,[3] until the process was made far easier in 1833, when they were finally published. (Details of their publishing are contained in Volume 2 of this biography).

# Who Compiled the Bible and When?

(REFERENCED IN CHAPTER 26)

The Bible's evolution to its current 66 books (80 among Catholic and Orthodox churches) is fraught with controversy.

In the 1st century were the original manuscripts, which became scattered. This resulted in most of today's books of the Bible existing separately, read as stand-alone texts. Then an effort began in the early, original Church of Christ, sometime before 100 A.D., to compile the books that comprise today's New Testament. And those early attempts were only marginally successful.

The New Testament's 27 books of today were finally compiled by 419 A.D., with most of them by the early to mid 200s as explained below.

Most scholars believe all the current New Testament books were written in a form of Greek called the Koine Greek language—the common tongue of the Eastern Mediterranean[1] and the "international language of the day," states author Archibald Macbride Hunter, "very much as English is today."[2]

The earliest efforts to compile the current books of the Bible may have taken place in Sinope (a city on the Black Sea in today's Turkey), from the efforts of a man known as Marcion of Sinope. He was a wealthy shipbuilder and theologian about 140 A.D., who modified the book of Luke but kept 10 of Paul's letters in his compilation. Other groups of Christians rejected Marcion's ideas of which books should be scripture. But because of his efforts, believers began putting together their own New Testament compilation.[3]

There were, however, efforts to take away most of the books that would become today's compilation, with attempts to focus on only 1 of the 4 main gospels. Then in about 180 A.D. came the first push to accept all 4 gospels of Matthew, Mark, Luke, and John—but only those 4—as true scripture.[4]

One of the principals pushing for that was Irenaeus, a bishop in today's Lyons, France, and a follower of Polycarp. The latter had known the Apostle John before John was taken out of the ministry about 101 A.D. (as explained in Appendix U, "Christianity after Christ: 17 Centuries of Conflict"). (In his fairly prolific writings, Irenaeus argued against the Gnostics, and was concerned about their influence on Christianity to such an extent that it consumed most of his writings.) The efforts of the Gnostics and others who drastically changed the pure principles of Christianity after 100 A.D. are touched upon in Appendix U.

The earliest of all versions of today's New Testament compilation may have come from the Muratorian fragment, dated sometime between 170 and the early 300s A.D., according to the *Anchor Bible Dictionary*.[5]

If this time period is correct, this would be the earliest known compilation of today's New Testament. But it was not a true compilation as we think of today; rather, it was a *proposal* to include the writings that mostly make up the 27 books of today's New Testament.[6]

Still, it defines today's books of the New Testament. The question is—how far back does it date?

Another source places this fragment at possibly 200 A.D.,[7] and, still another into the 500s (but only if the documents of the fragment are misunderstood).[8]

Sometime also in the early 200s a man named Origen (a scholar and theologian in Alexandria, Egypt) may have used the same 27 books of the current New Testament, but with disputes over 6 of the books that are now accepted as today's scripture.[9]

Even though these 27 books were later to be accepted by Christians *worldwide*, not everyone accepted them all at that time. Debate was rampant among the early Christians as to which books to accept, and which not. However, the "major writings" may have been accepted by nearly all believers throughout the Christian world by the middle 200s.[10]

In the late 300s it became settled—more or less. This was after the Catholic Church was organized in the early 300s as the official state-sponsored church of the Roman Empire under Constantine the Great (also detailed in Appendix U).

The Muratorian fragment may predate this period of the 300s in promoting today's compilation of the New Testament. But the first compilation of today's New Testament that was actually *promoted by a high-ranking church official* came from Athanasius, bishop of Alexandria, in 367 A.D., in a letter he wrote to his Egyptian churches.[11]

He was in fact the first to use the term *canon*,[12] (meaning "an accepted compilation"), stating the books were "canonized."[13]

Soon, the pope would make his own attempts to canonize the scripture. In 382 A.D. Pope Damasus I convened the Council of Rome, which may have issued a canon the same as today's for the New Testament.[14]

During this period (382–384 A.D.), Damasus requested the Bible manuscripts to be "revised" in Latin by the scholar Jerome, and they settled upon what the canon would be in 382 A.D.

That revision included changes, perhaps drastic ones, from the previous Latin texts.

Separate from these revisions to the Latin manuscripts, the original Koine Greek manuscripts had also been altered, and then the originals disappeared.

According to Latter-day Saints, this occurred because the priesthood authority of the Twelve Apostles was gone from the earth. Thus, the Twelve were no longer present to monitor changes to their epistles and other writings that would make up the future Bible.

So their manuscripts were changed—especially when they were translated into Latin.

Jerome's Latin compilation of the Bible, the Vulgate, was completed in 391 A.D.[15]

Meanwhile, there seemed to be 2 efforts on compilations running on separate but parallel tracks. On one track the pope's canon was moving forward; on the other track the canon from Bishop Athanasius was progressing, as begun by him in 367 A.D.

In 393 A.D. the first actual *council* to approve Athanasius's 367 A.D. canon was likely the Synod of Hippo Regius (in the city of Hippo Regius, currently Annaba, Algeria, a major city in North Africa). But this canon was not accepted church-wide until years later, when it evolved more into today's canon.

That church-wide acceptance took place in 397 and 419 A.D. at the Councils of Carthage. (Carthage was in today's Tunisia, North Africa, across the Mediterranean Sea and south of Rome, close to and southeast of Sicily.)[16]

Nevertheless, *most* of today's canon came a few years before the 397 and 419 councils of Carthage—from either the 382 Council of Rome (the canon that came from the pope's efforts) or the 393 Synod of Hippo Regius in North Africa (the canon proposed in the letter of 367 A.D. by Bishop Athanasius at Alexandria).

But the final canon of today's New Testament was apparently established at the 419 A.D. Council of Carthage (which was a follow-up to the 397 A.D. Third Council of Carthage). Here, in 419, the Book of Revelation was added, according to one source,[17] but another says it was added at the 397 Council.[18]

Thus, 1 of the 2 councils of Carthage basically established the canon as we know it today. So today's New Testament came about in either 397 or 419 A.D.—about 300 years after the original church of Jesus Christ, with the Twelve Apostles, disappeared from the earth. (See Appendix U.)

Taken all together, the canon is the result of an evolutionary process—not a sudden event with God handing over a complete compilation of books to the early Christians who had known Christ and calling it "the Bible," as some well-meaning souls have believed.

The canon's development is accurately described in the impressive 16-volume *Catholic Encyclopedia*: "The idea of a complete and clear-cut canon of the New Testament existing from the beginning, that is from Apostolic times, has no foundation in history. The Canon of the New Testament, like that of the Old, is the result of a development, of a process at once stimulated by disputes with doubters, both within and without the Roman Catholic Church, and regarded by certain obscurities and natural hesitations."[19]

Officially, the canon "did not reach its final term until the dogmatic definition of the Tridentine Council," adds the *Catholic Encyclopedia*. And that council took place in 1546.[20]

The reason this official canonization in 1546 occurred was because the canon was actually questioned by certain Protestants—those who challenged the "canonicity" of the Epistles of James, Jude, and the book of Revelation, in that order, through the 1500s.

Because of the Roman Catholic Church taking a stand on the canon in 1546, other churches decided to take a stand on it as well: In 1647 Calvinism made a declaration with its Westminster Confession of Faith; in 1563 the Church of England took a stand with its "Thirty-nine Articles;" and in 1672 the Greek Orthodox Church, at the Synod of Jerusalem, made its own declaration. All 4 councils agreed on the same 80 books of the Old and New Testaments.

A big change took place in 1885, however, when for some unknown reason, 14 of the 80 books, known as the Apocrypha, were removed from Protestant Bibles—although they had appeared for 351 years in printed editions.

In regard to the Old Testament, not much controversy attended its canonization. Basically, the only issue involved the above Apocrypha (which the Catholics term *deuterocanonical* books of the Old Testament).[21]

Going back to 382 A.D.: after Jerome was commissioned by Pope Damasus I to create a Latin Bible, the Vulgate became the standard Bible in western countries for over a millennium—from about 384 A.D. to 1526 A.D.[22]

Since Latin was not understood by the common people, they relied on what the priests claimed it said, if they even expounded on it.

Those portions of the Vulgate that were explained to artists influenced paintings and art for hundreds of years, although a few artists were well educated and could read Latin for themselves. In any case, their art was influenced by only one source.

But the monopoly of the Latin Vulgate ended when Martin Luther printed the German New Testament in 1522 and William Tyndale completed the first printed English New Testament in 1526.[23]

Their Old Testaments came a few years later—in 1534 and 1530, respectively, although Tyndale's Old Testament consisted of only 5 books. The first *full* Old Testament in English was the Coverdale Bible in 1535.

Soon, English Bibles, along with Martin Luther's German Bible, "took over." Noteworthy, Catholic priests made up an important segment of the Reformers when they broke from their Catholic tradition, casting aside the Latin Vulgate for what they felt were the purer scriptures of Luther and Tyndale, based on the more accurate translations from Greek by the brilliant Roman Catholic priest Erasmus Desiderius in the early 1500s (an account of whom is given in Chapter 26).

(For details of Bibles used by the Great Reformers, see Appendix T: "English Bibles that Shook the World." For a review of Martin Luther—his life and launching of the German Bible—see Appendix R, "Launching the Reformation: Prelude to the Restoration.")

# The Three Families of Bible Manuscripts

## (REFERENCED IN CHAPTER 26)

In translating the New Testament from Greek manuscripts, translators have had 3 "families of manuscripts" from which to choose since they began printing the New Testament in the 1500s. These families are called "text-types," and are given the designations Alexandrian, Western, and Byzantine:

1. *Alexandrian text-type* (also called *Minority Text*), is the first available text-type, but came decades after the original manuscripts were lost or destroyed. These are manuscripts from the 100s to 300s. This is the manuscript family claimed to be used in most modern translations of the New Testament. As the greatest translator of all time—Catholic priest Desiderius Erasmus—discovered in the early 1500s, this text-type had even more corruptions than the later ones (after 400 A.D.), causing him to choose the post-400 A.D. (Byzantine) text-types. This earlier "Alexandrian text-type" supposedly comes from the vicinity of Alexandria, Egypt.

2. *Western text-type* hails from the 200s to 900s, in which the scribes tended to paraphrase their work and thus produce other corruptions. The area from which this text-type came is

the swath of land between France and Italy to the North and North Africa to the south (below the Mediterranean Sea) and even to Syria on the east end of the sea). The translated Bible from this family is the *Vetus Latina*, in which Latin manuscripts were used. This is the term given the Bible before Jerome's Vulgate of 382 A.D.

3. *Byzantine text-type* (also called *Majority Text*) is the family of manuscripts from mostly the 400s to 1500s used by Desiderius Erasmus in the early 1500s, in helping to create *Textus Receptus*, the Greek translation of the Bible used for most Reformation-era Bible translations, including the King James Version in 1611. (The Reformation translations of the Bible include the Tyndale Bible, Coverdale Bible, Matthew-Tyndale Bible, Taverner's Bible, Great Bible, Geneva Bible, and Bishops' Bible, as well as the Orthodox Study Bible used for Eastern Orthodox churches, which came as a result of revising the King James Version (original 1611 and 1769 Baskerville editions.) This Byzantine family of manuscripts was dominant in the area of Constantinople in today's Turkey, and was used in the Byzantine-based churches from 400 on.


In regard to modern Bible translations, most claim to come from the Alexandrian text-type. Recently a theory has been advanced by scholars that manuscripts from this family were "thoughtfully supervised and controlled" when they were written.

While the spin sounds good, the reality is—the manuscripts were still changed. The only "control" was of the scribes by their supervisors.

All this means, in the nitty-gritty world of transcribing, is that the transcriber/supervisor team would simply agree on what marginal notes should be added to the text, based on their best guesses and what they themselves wanted to alter, to fit their own theological dogmas.

Thus, the fine-tuned talking points by certain scholars today promoting modern translations haven't changed the fact that the transcriptions were corrupted in the early centuries.

No matter how good the narrative of today's scholars sounds—that manuscripts were "carefully controlled" by early scribes—the accuracy of the transcription process was tenuous at best, depending, as it did, not only on the skill of the ancient transcription team but also the character and integrity of its members to refrain from rewriting and editing passages to fit their personal interpretations. In truth, the Alexandrian family of manuscripts suffered the same problems later found in the Byzantine text family and, according to Erasmus, even more.

This earlier, although corrupted, Alexandrian family of transcriptions is used by over 16 modern translations. Below is a list of them, followed by a list of today's best-selling Bibles, which reveals that most of the top 10 translations today may come from this Alexandrian text-type family:

1. (The Catholics') Douay-Rheims Bible (from the Latin Vulgate, using Alexandrian and Byzantine text-types, 1610)
2. American Standard Version (1901)
3. Emphasized Bible (1902)
4. Revised Standard Version (1952)
5. (Jehovah's Witnesses') New World Translation (1961)
6. (The Catholics') Jerusalem Bible (1966)
7. New American Bible (1970) and revised edition
8. New American Standard (1971)
9. The Living Bible (1971)
10. The Good News Bible (1976), and the gender-neutral edition (1991)
11. New International Version (1978 and 2011)
12. New Jerusalem Bible (1985)
13. New Century Version (written at a 5th-grade reading level, 1987)
14. English Standard Version (2001, 2011)
15. Today's New International Version (2005)

The Bible best-sellers, according to the CBA (Christian Bible Association) and their member bookstores, are the following for October 2013:

1. New International Version (1978)
2. King James Version (1769 Baskerville)[1]
3. English Standard Version (2011)
4. New King James Version (1982)
5. New Living Translation (revision of Living Bible, 1996, 2007)
6. Holman Christian Standard Bible (2003)
7. Common English Bible (2011)
8. New International Readers Version (simpler form of English, 1996)
9. *Reina Valera* (Spanish; 1569, 1602, 1862, 1909, 1960, 1995, 2011)[2]
10. New American Standard (1971)[3]

# Launching the Reformation:
# Prelude to the Restoration

(REFERENCED IN CHAPTER 26)

## Part 1

### Introducing the Reformation

For over 1200 years, the Roman Catholic Church had a lock on the Christian religious world in western Europe. As covered in Appendix U, "Christianity After Christ: 17 Centuries of Conflict," the church reigned from 315 A.D. to the 1500s with no significant threat to its power. But the rumblings of revolution began in 1380 A.D., when John Wycliffe launched the first notable—and "complete"—English Bible, translating it into handwritten English manuscripts and distributing them. (For details see Appendix T: "English Bibles that Shook the World.")

Because of that, Wycliffe's friends who read the manuscripts saw obvious discrepancies between the church and what the Bible taught.

From that point on the church strove to keep the fully translated Bible away from the common folk, fearful more people would read the Bible and compare it to certain church practices, discovering things somewhat amiss. In fact, wildly amiss.

With few exceptions the church had generally attempted to keep the Bible in Latin, so only the educated priests could read it; this way, congregations would depend on their priests for doctrine.

Ironically, for 700 years, the church had allowed *partial* English translations of the Bible, which seemed rather harmless, to be made by monks. But in 1380, everything changed with Wycliffe. A full Bible, even in the less accurate Latin version (as explained in Appendix T: "English Bibles that Shook the World") still shook things up for the church because of the obvious contradictions between what the Bible taught and certain church practices (described below).

Despite the effect the full English Bible had on its relatively few readers, Wycliffe was never caught and punished.[1]

But his copies continued to be distributed and had an impact. A few people began questioning certain church doctrines.

Seeing that, the Roman Catholic Church and its daughter, the Anglican Church,[2] threatened to execute anyone even owning an English Bible.

So when a follower of Wycliffe's named John Hus procured one and promoted his ideas, the church caught him and burned him at the stake in 1415, using Wycliffe's manuscript Bibles as kindling for the fire.

Later in Britain, while the Anglican church banned English Bibles, its efforts did not keep Reformers from translating and distributing them on the sly.

Big reasons for the church cover-up involved 2 main practices that church authorities feared being exposed by the Bible: (1) selling indulgences (paying money to receive forgiveness of sins) and (2) selling "expanded" indulgences for the release of deceased loved ones from "Purgatory," so they could move on to heaven.

There were other cover-ups of non-biblical practices as well—such as praying to Saints for intercession, building statues, etc. And there were cover-ups of non-biblical doctrines—such as the Eucharist—described later in Part 3 of this appendix.

As for indulgences, the church used this practice to obtain money. And it collected it by preying upon its members' fear of Purgatory—a halfway house between heaven and hell for those not worthy of going to heaven but not sinful enough to earn eternal damnation in hell. Purgatory was a place to purge one's sins by suffering in order to gain admittance to heaven. (See Appendix S, "Beliefs in the Afterlife: Catholic vs. Protestant vs. Latter-day Saint" for a description of Christianity's differences on this doctrine.)

For 1,050 years, from 517 to 1567 A.D., the Roman Catholic Church issued the selling of indulgences. Their belief was that a dead person could be released from Purgatory in 1 of 3 major ways—all including actions of their living loved ones: burning candles, praying for deceased loved ones, or making payments to the church.

Making payments to the church—indulgences—began in 517 at the Council of Epaone (a city in Burgundy of southeastern France) and took a strange turn in 1095 at the Council of Clermont (a city in central France), when Pope Urban II ruled that the murderous and brutal crusaders simply had to confess their sins to receive a complete penance.[3] (For more on the Crusades see Appendix U, "Christianity after Christ: 17 Centuries of Conflict.")

Selling indulgences then went into high gear when the infamous Commissaries from Rome sought the maximum amount of money for each indulgence they granted.[4]

Meanwhile, the professional "pardoners"[5] were sent out to collect money for specific projects—such as cathedrals—with unrestricted sales of indulgences.

Then they ramped it up even more when they began charging for not only a shorter period of suffering for loved ones in Purgatory, but the *immediate release* of loved ones who were already there.[6]

In 1517 Pope Leo X offered indulgences for those who gave money to rebuild St. Peter's Basilica in Rome. And then he came up with an ingenious new plan: he granted franchises to archbishops and rulers of various lands in order to sell "super-indulgences." This was an entirely new concept, allowing souls to completely escape from even setting foot in Purgatory—not just shorten their time there. And thus he took indulgences to the highest plane yet.

For these stepped-up indulgences the going rate ranged from 25 gold florins for kings, queens and archbishops (yes, history is replete with many a wild one) to a rate of only 3 florins for merchants and ¼ of 1 florin for the poor—a terrific deal for poor sinners.

With this franchising system, archbishops and various foreign rulers could keep half the money they obtained from selling indulgences,[7] and send the rest to Rome. It was a neat little deal for all involved and, needless to say, they had a heyday. The cathedrals shot up, the kings got richer, Rome fabulously wealthier, and the tens of millions of peasants poorer (but with clean souls).[8] (See this endnote for more historical information on selling indulgences.)

The large sums of money the church received was due to the large numbers of people in the church, which had its base in Europe. (The vast majority of Europe's population in fact were members of the church. In England and Wales alone, the population stood at 3 million, according to some estimates, nearly all of whom where in the church.)

Meanwhile, indulgences and other examples of institu-tionalized corruption ran against the grain of the Bible. Thus, readable versions of the Bible (in their languages) were kept away from the common folk.

But that would soon change.

The first key to that change was the invention of the printing press. In 1455, Johannes Gutenberg produced the first book ever printed on a "moveable type" press—the Latin Vulgate, which was the official Latin Bible of the church, when he printed it at Mainz, Germany.[9]

With this invention, the Bible could be printed *en masse*. Revolutionaries, called Reformers, felt it needed 2 things: 1st, to be translated to the languages of the people, and 2nd, to use more accurate manuscripts than the Latin versions that the church had used all these centuries. So the Reformers decided to go with Greek, as close to the original as possible, although even those manuscripts had been substantially corrupted—just not as much as the Latin ones.

These improvements in translation would have an effect on religious doctrine, they believed, yet that was the consequence of having greater accuracy. Then, once the Bible was out in the open, the Reformers realized they could have a field day. They would point out the contradictions of what the Bible said and what the priests said it said.

One German archbishop's area representative, Johann Tetzel, made the crucial mistake of venturing into the little town of Wittenberg in central eastern Germany, gleefully collecting cash from the simple peasants and farmers (and the hopeful higher class as well, equally afraid of Purgatory). He proudly proclaimed his doctrine of indulgences while stuffing his robes with cash for the archbishop and the pope.

A little background: Johann Tetzel was a friar, commissioned by the pope and sent by the archbishop within Germany to sell indulgences. The purpose of this money was to rebuild St. Peter's Basilica in Rome (while enabling the local franchisee, the local archbishop, to keep his half of collected funds). Tetzel's title was "papal commissioner." As such he allegedly said, "As soon as a coin in the coffer rings, a soul from purgatory springs."[10]

Martin Luther, a local priest, heard it and went ballistic—furious over the crazy comments of this fellow, Tetzel.[11] So

Luther went home and began penning one of the most famous documents in world history—the "95 Theses of Contention."

In 1517 he posted it on the wood door of the Castle Church (*Schloßkirche*) in Wittenberg, accusing the Roman church of crimes and heretical theology. He would make a huge issue of selling indulgences—and it was his Thesis #28 that sent Rome into a tailspin.

Tetzel was so bold as to write a defense of his view on indulgences, and even wrote, with the help of another, an antagonistic response to Luther's 95 Theses.[12]

But Luther's challenges did not stop there. In Thesis #86 he complained, "Why does the pope, whose wealth today is greater than the wealth of the richest Crassus, build the basilica of St. Peter with the money of poor believers rather than with his own money?"[13] (Marcus Crassus, a politician, was the richest man in Roman history, living between 115 and 53 B.C.)

As for injustices, Luther may not have known that, not far to the west in Coventry, England, that very same year Catholic Church authorities burned 7 people at the stake for teaching their children to say the Lord's Prayer in English, rather than Latin.[14]

Luther, who had first become a hard-working Augustine monk in 1506, arising at 3 A.D. each day for prayers and chores, had gone on to become a priest the following year, and refused to put up with injustices. Because of his stance, he was excommunicated.[15]

Then he was targeted for execution. But he would escape. His friend, Prince Frederick III, Elector of Saxony (a section in today's central Germany), also living in Wittenberg, sent a crew of fake robbers to kidnap Luther so he would not be assassinated by men sent from the church in Rome. And the plan worked—he was spirited off to safety in the nick of time. (For details see Part 2 of this appendix.)

Frederick and his brother John would later start their own church and assign Luther to draw up the worship services and doctrines.

As stated in Appendix U, "Christianity after Christ: 17 Centuries of Conflict," similar churches would be launched by the heads of state in Scandinavia and Switzerland. These statesmen sponsored other noted Reformers, including John Calvin in Geneva, Switzerland. The leaders of these countries were desperate to break away from the controlling bishops of Rome, who were acting with not only religious but political power, imposing taxes on the nations of Europe—which, these European leaders felt, was outrageous.

Five years after posting his famous 95 Theses, in 1522 Luther published his New Testament of the Bible in German. In order to produce it he used the Greek translations of an amazing Catholic priest and scholar, Desiderius Erasmus, described in the text.[16] (See this endnote for a summary of his work.)

Luther's translation and printing were highly illegal and he did his work in secret.

Then, in 1534, he would publish his complete Bible. This Bible would further help launch the Reformation, along with another being developed by an Englishman.

Meanwhile, across the continent and over the channel in England, the English Bible began its own fascinating history.

In Great Britain the Anglican Church was created in 597 A.D. as part of the Roman Catholic Church, and continued under the control of Rome for almost a thousand years.

During its first 9 centuries, only the aforementioned John Wycliffe created a Bible problem for the church by producing an English Bible in 1382—but only with handwritten copies—as this was 70 years before the invention of the printing press. Thus he had only limited distribution. And, as stated, it was translated from the less accurate Latin Vulgate manuscripts.

But now, all that was about to change.

With the invention of the printing press, a new English Bible could be pumped out by the thousands—one with far greater accuracy, using the Greek translation.

Church authorities would do every thing in their power to stop it.

But one man would get in their way.

William Tyndale.

The first man in England to fire the Reformation and start the Bible Revolution.

Martin Luther had lit the Reformation on the continent in Germany, but now Tyndale would join the cause and help turn world history upside down.

For details of Luther's efforts, see Part 2 below, followed by Tyndale's efforts in Part 3, and finally the century following Tyndale in Part 4.

## Part 2

### Martin Luther: Kingpin of the Reformation

Born November 10, 1483, Martin Luther would lay the groundwork for nations and peoples to break away from the Roman Catholic Church.

Because of his actions, the religious and political worlds would spin practically out of their solar system.

And it would all start with Luther's upbringing.

His father wanted him to become a lawyer. He attended 3 schools to prepare for that, focusing on grammar and rhetoric. And he later would label these courses "Purgatory and Hell,"[1] terms to which millions of students can relate today.

Another course he took was logic, which actually may have helped him in his later arguments against the church.

He then enrolled in law school but quickly dropped out, saying law represented uncertainty.[2]

Soon he went into the priesthood because of an act of nature. In July 1505, while traveling from a visit home back to the university, he was on horseback during a thunderstorm, when a bolt of lightening nearly hit him. He was terrified of death and God's judgment, and he called out, "Help! Saint Anna, I will become a monk!"[3]

So in 1507 he was ordained to the priesthood and became a monk, obtaining 2 bachelor's degrees in 1508 and a Doctor of

Theology in 1512, all at the University of Wittenberg. He would remain there the rest of his career on the faculty.

Meanwhile, policies in Rome began shooting meteoric showers that would affect Luther's view of the universe forever.

One of those with the greatest impact came when the church decided to use a representative in Germany to sell *indulgences*, in order to raise money to rebuild St. Peter's Basilica in Rome.

(Selling indulgences was the practice of the church charging money to its members for forgiveness of sins, as explained in Part 1 of this appendix and Appendix U, "Christianity After Christ: 17 Centuries of Conflict.") It also extended to paying the church for dead loved ones to get out of Purgatory.)

This representative to collect money was Johann Tetzel. Luther was appalled by the policy, and soon found himself not only at odds with Tetzel but locked into a seemingly galactic battle with Rome.

In 1517 Luther wrote a letter to his archbishop, Albert of Mainz, that would turn the course of history.

In it he argued against the sale of indulgences. With it he enclosed his "Ninety-five Theses," which was really called, "Disputation of Martin Luther on the Power and Efficacy of Indulgences." He reportedly nailed it to the wooden door of the Wittenberg church, an iconic moment in history, as it represents one courageous soul standing up to the prevailing powers.

Some claim he may not have actually posted them so bravely on the church door, since the account of the door was a story based on notes from Philipp Melanchthon, who possibly was not in Wittenberg at the time. However, Melanchthon was a close associate of Luther's, so although some may attempt to debunk this as a myth, the two were close enough that Luther would certainly have reported the details to him. (Of course the critics could conceivably be correct in this case—but some scholars take pot shots whenever they can at events involving heroism in religious history.)

The following year, 1518, Luther's friends translated the Latin letter into German, then used the printing press to distribute it. This became one of the first-ever wake-up calls to a sleeping populace over the issue of religion, using the printing press.

Luther's 95 Theses now set off a firestorm.

Archbishop Albrecht did not write him back, but he went on the warpath. He had Luther's 95 points checked for heresy, then sent his findings to Rome in December 1517. Albrecht frankly didn't want to believe Luther's arguments—he was dependent on the sale of indulgences to pay the pope for his tenure!

Luther could see right through it. He later wrote a scathing rebuke of both the archbishop and the world catholic leader: "The pope had a finger in the pie as well, because one half was to go to the building of St. Peter's Church in Rome."

His comment was dead-on: the system of indulgences had been in place for centuries, but now, an interesting incentive scheme was in place—one half of all money that was collected for indulgences was to be paid to the pope as a "franchise fee," while the other half was to be kept by the local promoter of indulgences as a commission fee. Thus, half the money would stay in the archbishop's pocket.

Pope Leo X, to his credit, was slow to assess the situation and did not jump the gun: he spent 3 years sending envoys and theologians to Luther, trying to convince him of his "error," but that backfired. Luther became even more convinced of the church's errors.

One of the church theologians wrote a heresy case against Luther, so the pope sent for Luther to be examined in Rome.

However, as the heat began to rise, a local political power, the elector Frederick, came to the rescue. He talked the pope into allowing Luther to be examined at nearby Augsburg, which probably saved his life.

There, in October 1815, Luther castigated church officials, claiming the pope was not part of the biblical church. One of Luther's reasons lay in his interpretation of Bible prophecy. He came to the conclusion that the pope was actually the Antichrist(!) Then the 2 sides debated about the Antichrist, and the hearing became a shouting match. It ended in chaos.

From it, of course, Luther was labeled an enemy to the pope.

Cjetan, the pope's emissary, had been told to arrest Luther if he refused to rescind his 95 Theses.

But Luther would not rescind them.

Yet he could not be arrested, because he had been promised protection by the elector Frederick.

Nevertheless, Cjetan broke the promise and tried. But Frederick helped him escape one night before Cjetan could nab him.

Wanting to publicly expose Luther, a theologian named Johann Maier von Eck held a public meeting to challenge Luther's assertions in June–July 1519.

Luther was bold enough to show up and respond. There, he made more claims against the church, stating that Matthew 16:18 gives no exclusive right to the pope to interpret scripture, and that the church councils as well as the pope were not infallible.

Eck was incensed. He claimed Luther was another Jan Hus—a Czech reformation leader who had been burned at the stake in 1415 for heresy. So Eck now made it his mission to take Luther down.

Then the pope issued a warning. In June 1520 he demanded Luther to take back his writings or be excommunicated.

He had 60 days.

Eck then went about various towns reading the pope's ultimatum.

But then the pope backtracked. He wanted to win Luther over. Still. He sent an emissary named Karl von Miltitz to help the 2 parties reach a compromise.

But Luther was not about to compromise. He burned the pope's edict at Wittenberg on December 10, 1520.

The pope decided he had only one course left—to excommunicate him—which he did on January 2, 1521, through an edict (called a "bull," specifically, a "papal bull," meaning one issued from the pope). It was entitled *Decet Romanum Pontificem*.

Then it fell to the political arena to punish Luther, as the political world was rife with Catholic civil authorities. Luther was ordered to the town of Worms (pronounced "Vorms") to a hearing called the Diet of Worms. (A *diet* was a formal general assembly of the Roman Empire.)

There, he showed up on April 18, 1523. No one less than Holy Roman Emperor Charles V presided. But Luther had his friend, the local German prince Frederick III, run interference for him, providing protection by obtaining a promise for safety of going to and from the hearing.

At the hearing at Worms, Johann Eck, still determined to bring Luther to his knees, dramatically laid out Luther's writings on a table and asked if they were his, and if he stood by their contents. Luther admitted he had written them but decided to think about whether or not he stood by them, perhaps figuring a trap was in the works. He prayed, talked to friends, and the next day gave his answer:

"I do not trust in the pope or in councils alone, since it is well known that they have often erred and contradicted themselves. I am bound by the Scriptures I have quoted, and my conscience is captive to the Word of God. I cannot and will not recant anything, since it is neither safe nor right to go against conscience. May God help me."[4]

Eck branded him a heretic.

Luther again refused to recant. "Here I stand. I can do no other."[5]

For the next 5 days men deliberated over his fate. Finally the Emperor wrote up his final draft of the final decision— announcing Luther's fate before the Diet of Worms, dated May 25, 1521:

"We want him to be apprehended and punished as a notorious heretic."[6] He was declared not only a heretic but an outlaw.

So, he was to be burned at the stake. Even his writings were banned. It was also declared a crime for anyone in Germany to give him shelter or food, and the edict authorized *anyone* to kill him without legal ramifications. In short, he was "wanted dead or alive."

But he was allowed by a previous promise to return home to Wittenberg, where he would be officially arrested.

Yet the civil authorities planned to arrest him on the way home anyway and break their promise.

To foil their plan, Frederick III plotted for some men to meet Luther in a forest near Wittenberg, posing as armed highwaymen (robbers), who were in fact robbers—they robbed the civil authorities of the opportunity to arrest and execute Luther. These "robbers" took off with him through the woods to the safety of the Warburg Castle at Eisenach.

There Luther translated his New Testament from Erasmus's Greek text but, emotionally, he felt exiled, labeling this period "my Patmos."[7]

In the summer of 1521 he condemned pilgrimages (taking trips to special "holy" spots and leaving gifts or money) and indulgences. In November he wrote a document assuring monks and nuns they could break their vows of not marrying, declaring that it would not be a sin because vows of not marrying were a vain attempt to win salvation.[8]

He then returned stealthily to Wittenberg in March 1522 and discovered a new opposition tearing up his town:

His following there had been "influenced" by Satan, while he had been holed up in the castle for protection. He realized he could only take care of this problem in person, so he decided to stay—but he did so longer than was wise. Yet he made the most of his visit: he preached 8 sermons in 8 days, teaching against a course that some Reformers proclaimed—of violence. These lectures of Luther were the "Invocavit Sermons" that taught basic Christian values.

Because of these sermons he was now in conflict with both the Roman Catholic Church and the radical Reformers who sought violence—and he was caught in the middle!

He was successful at Wittenberg, but he could not dissuade the radicals, those who wanted war.

Because of his pamphlets, the radicals thought he was their ally. After all, in writing he had attacked the upper classes.[9]

Feeling they had his support, they started conflicts in 3 areas of Germany in 1524, and even many nobles joined in, frustrated that they were in debt and wanting a way out from paying their wealthy debtors. Successful revolts were then launched by talented radical leaders in Thurinia and Tyrol.

And this led to all-out war.

But Luther tried putting the brakes on their efforts.

While he agreed with some of the peasants' points, he pushed for them to obey the civil authorities.[10]

But they disregarded him and launched the German Peasants War of 1524–1525.

This revolt by peasants was nothing new. In the 1400s peasants had launched smaller revolts.

But he was shocked to see a large number of monasteries, convents, bishops' palaces, and libraries burned when he visited Thuringia. As a result, he condemned the violence as the Devil's work.

Then, he was mortified when he heard that atrocities were being committed in his name!

He returned to Wittenberg and wrote a treatise, "Against the Murderous, Thieving Hordes of Peasants." And he urged the nobles to crush them. A big reason was not just the peasants' call for violence, but their political philosophy—he hated their demands for the distribution of wealth. In short, the peasants sought pure socialism. "Nothing can be more poisonous, hurtful, or devilish than a rebel," writes Luther, "for baptism does not make men free in body and property, but in soul; and the gospel does not make goods common, except in the case of those who, of their own free will, do what the apostles and disciples did in Acts 4. They [the apostles] did not demand, as do our insane peasants in their raging, that the goods of others . . . should be common. . . . I think there is not a devil left in hell; they have all gone into the peasants. Their raving has gone beyond all measure."[11]

The peasants were soon surprised that they did not have his backing. And once he clarified his position, many stopped fighting. Then, one of the rebel leaders, Thomas Muntzer, was captured and executed, and the revolution stopped cold.

Meanwhile, Luther's domestic world was a mess.

He lived on a mildewed bed, not made up for months at a time, and ate very plain food.[12]

In 1524 he wrote, "I shall never take a wife, as I felt at present. Not that I am insensible to my flesh or sex (for I am neither wood nor stone), but my mind is averse to wedlock because I daily expect the death of a heretic."[13]

But his life made a sudden upswing.

Soon he mused, "Suddenly, and while I was occupied with far different thoughts, the Lord has plunged me into marriage."[14] He married Katharina von Bora, one of the dozen nuns he had helped to escape the convent in 1523![15]

She was 26; he was 41.

And with this act he set the standard for Protestant ministers to marry. First, they had to break from Catholicism, as it was and forever would be against Catholic church policy.

Before Luther, other former priests and monks had left the order and married as well. (Although, secretly and not so secretly, popes and cardinals had for centuries held a bevy of mistresses and were also often married, which ended in 1585. For details and documentation, see Appendix U, "Christianity After Christ: 17 Centuries of Conflict.")

Luther had long opposed vows of celibacy on biblical grounds, and he soon became the chief figurehead of this movement. Soon others left their vows and married, following his example.

Nevertheless, his friend Melanchthon labeled his marriage "reckless."

His wedding present from the new elector was a new home— he and his wife moved into a former monastery, where they were happy, though often low on funds. They had 6 children together, but 2 of them died—1 within months and the other at age 13, causing an emotional trial to them. His wife, meanwhile, helped him farm their land and they took in boarders.

Soon Luther's religious reformation took on a life of its own under the protection of certain local governments.

As a result, he and his associates began a new church.

White he got government leaders to financially support it, it had few assets. And this became a trial for Luther.

He also acted as an advisor to the churches in new territories.

From 1525 to 1529 he organized a leadership for their church, established a new form of worship service in 1527, and wrote a summary of the new faith in 2 catechisms—one for the members and a more detailed one for the priests. They were simplified instructions on the Ten Commandments, baptism, the Lord's Prayer, the Lord's Supper, and a revised creed.

In that creed Luther defined the Trinity—the Father, Son, and Holy Ghost—as people to learn to know, not as concepts (similar to Joseph Smith's teachings). And he defined the 3 members of the Godhead as having a divine unity but with separate personalities and roles (also similar)—a departure from the Nicene Creed of the Catholic and Anglican churches.

When Reformer Johannes Agricola challenged his views on faith, Luther shot back that his challenger was wrong to teach that faith is separate from works.[16]

(Joseph however taught that faith is separate yet inspires good works, and that both are necessary, quoting the apostle James: "Faith without works is dead." [James 2:20])

In time Luther would mollify some religious positions, including that faith alone was necessary for salvation. He would later also approve a treatise that said repentance was necessary,[17] another similarity to Joseph's later teachings.

Luther was known for taking a stand on what he believed.

He did not believe in Purgatory.

He was against the Crusades, including the current battles against the Turks on religious grounds "as though our people were an army of Christians against the Turks, who were enemies of Christ. This is absolutely contrary to Christ's doctrine and name."[18]

In 1529 he did urge Emperor Charles V and the German people to fight against the Turks—but only in a secular war.

Luther also taught that the life of the Savior is mainly an example of the Ten Commandments, which a Christian should embody in his own daily life, and to avoid war and conflict when possible—additional similarities to Joseph's teachings.

As a Bible scholar, he received one of his bachelor's degrees in the Bible. His title on the faculty was Doctor in Bible.

Then came Luther's revolutionary work on the Bible.

Significantly, he saw shortcomings in the Latin Vulgate. So he decided to make a more accurate version of the Bible. His German translation of the New Testament came in 1522 from Erasmus's Greek text. From that he also worked with Englishman William Tyndale, who was in exile and came to visit him. (Tyndale would soon launch the *English* Bible revolution.)

Luther and his associates then finished the Old Testament 12 years later, in 1534, completing the whole Bible, and published it that year.[19]

His Bible made a significant impact on developing the German language and its literature, and it spurred on the standardizing of the German language.

William Tyndale, meanwhile, published the 1st *English* New Testament based on the same Greek translations of Erasmus that Luther used—the 3rd edition by Erasmus in 1522. (See Endnote 16 for details of Erasmus's various editions.)

As Luther's Bible would affect the German language, so Tyndale's Bible would standardize the English language.

(For a review of Tyndale's life and work, see Part 3 of this appendix.)

But unexpected problems arose for Martin Luther.

The result would shake up the political world so dramatically that the Catholic Church would lose its grip over Europe. And it all started at the Imperial Diet of Augsburg in 1530.

Here's how it went down . . .

---

Charles V, the new Holy Roman Emperor, strove to unite his empire against the Turks. But first he sought to resolve the religious problems and controversies in his territory, even "considering with love and kindness the views of everybody."[20] But, given the quagmire of people and problems he had to deal with, that quickly went out the window.

So he asked Martin Luther for a statement regarding religious problems. And Luther provided him one. His document was called the Augsburg Confession. Luther was afraid, however, to deliver it himself to the emperor, who resided in Germany at this point. The reason—Luther was still in hot water and there was no guarantee for his safety. So he feared 2 things—arrest and assassination—as he was still under the "imperial ban."

Ironically, the Reformation was under protection of many local governments in Germany. But, empire-wide, Luther was in danger of being waylaid. So he stayed behind at the Coburg fortress and sent his soon-to-be famous document with the elector's party.

The document was free from contentious language and had no attacks on the pope. It was read to the emperor and diet—the assembly—on June 25, 1530. But the diet rejected it on September 22. They demanded the Reformers recant their position and denounce heresy. They also demanded that Luther and his followers submit to the church by April or face the imperial army!

Thus the new Holy Roman Empire that ruled Germany was at odds with the local German governments in protecting the Protestant Reformation. And the Augsburg Confession became a statement of faith for Luther. Like Luther in every other aspect, this document took a stand.

This bold stand caused the Lutheran princes to band together and make their own stand—against the new Holy Roman Empire.

They decided to form a military alliance.

So Germany was now ripe for revolution. And Luther supported it.

Nevertheless, he was cautious in supporting the alliance against the empire, as he hated war over religion.

His next big controversy involved polygamy. But not for himself. He agreed with Philip I, who read of the Old Testament prophets being polygamists. Philip I desired to take a second wife. Similar to Joseph Smith's view on it centuries later (as covered in Volumes 2 and 3 of this biography), Luther told Philip to go ahead, but secretly.[21]

This was in December 1539, and Philip's targeted second spouse was his current wife's "lady in waiting." He married her, but word got out, and Luther was implicated because of his advice. Two other church reformers—Melanchthon and Bucer—were also in hot water.

Luther told Philip: "Tell a good, strong lie" and deny the marriage exists.

He did, but this created a second public controversy.[22]

Problems exploded for Luther for this advice when the truth caught up to him. And, predictably, his reputation was damaged. But his remarkable legacy lived on.

As to what happened to the stalwart old Catholic Wittenberg "Castle Church" where Martin Luther posted his 95 Theses,[23] it became a Lutheran church at last, and, after he died, Luther was actually buried under the building, with his tomb near the pulpit!

Centuries later, in 1877, Latter-day Saint President Wilford Woodruff would report a visitation from Martin Luther, as well as from theologian John Wesley and others in the St. George, Utah, Temple, requesting their temple work be done for them, as noted in Chapter 26 of the text.

All in all, his life was an inspiration to many, and he truly earned the distinction of the "First and Greatest Great Reformer."

## Part 3

## William Tyndale: A Humble Priest Outsmarts the English Crown and Creates the Bible Revolution

William Tyndale was the protagonist most noted for putting the English Bible in print. But he did much more—he set the stage for the collapse of the Catholic stranglehold over England, and thus became a key player in the Reformation.

A brilliant scholar and Catholic priest, he learned 8 languages fluently and graduated from both Oxford and Cambridge Universities. At Oxford he discovered the writings of Martin Luther and became fascinated with the ideas of John Wycliffe. He decided from his readings that the church had become completely corrupt.

Tyndale was born between 1490 and 1496 (the most current scholarship puts it at 1494) in the village of Slimbridge, Gloucestershire, of Southwest England.

At age 14, in 1508, he went to Oxford.[1]

There he earned his B.A. degree in 1512, his M.A. in 1515, and from 1517 to 1521 he left Oxford to attend Cambridge University.

While Tyndale was at Cambridge, one Thomas Bilney attended the university, graduating in 1519 during the middle of Tyndale's 4 year course work. Bilney could not find spiritual peace, so he broke the university's rules and slipped out of his room one night to secretly buy a Bible.

From reading it he was converted, then shared it in a confession at church to one Hugh Latimer. Latimer had the reputation of being the top preaching minister in England, and was a conservative Catholic with close ties to the pope. But he was secretly converted to the Reformation. Other students from the various colleges at Cambridge began meeting together and learning of the Reformation taking place in Germany—and they also felt the need for it in England. These future-thinking students would meet after classes in a room of the White Horse Inn, made famous by their secret meetings.

Soon, Tyndale finished his studies for the ministry, choosing to return to Gloucestershire where he was employed as a tutor and chaplain to the house of Sir John and Lady Anne Walsh of Little Sodbury in 1521.

Tyndale would also visit St. Austin's monastery near Bristol, where, on the "green" at the entrance, he would preach in English. This was unusual, because until now all church services in England were only in Latin, which the common folk could not understand. At this green many heard the Gospel for the first time, as it was in English.

The Walshes, a sociable couple, invited clergymen to their home for dinners, and they would include Tyndale. These dinners became somewhat of an embarrassment to the clergy—because he would reveal his knowledge of the scriptures so much better than they that he would literally "rout" them. They were, by and by, offended and stopped coming to the Walshes.[2]

Consequently, these priests "bare a secret grudge in their hearts against him," writes contemporary historian John Foxe, who interviewed those who knew Tyndale, for his monumental work, *Foxe's Book of Martyrs.*

"As this grew on, the priests of the country, clustering together, began to grudge and storm against Tyndale, railing against him in alehouses and other places, affirming that his sayings were heresy, and accus[ing] him secretly to the chancellor and others of the bishop's officers."[3]

This jealousy of the priests escalated. They started a rumor, saying Tyndale gained his biblical knowledge through Satan!

They wanted him silenced.

Upon hearing the news about Tyndale in league with Satan, the Chancellor called him in.

Before the actual hearing, when alone, he "cried in his mind heartily to God, to give him strength fast to stand in the truth of His Word," states Foxe. "When the time came for his appearance before the chancellor, he threatened him [Tyndale] grievously, reviling and railing him as though he had been a dog."[4]

When the Walshes heard about this they were concerned that they were employing an enemy to the church. So Tyndale wrote a treatise, *Enchiridion, Handbook of the Christian*. It won the Walshes over. And the chancellor also allowed him to remain a priest.

He now received a warning from a former servant of the pope, whom many believe was William Latimer himself—the above-mentioned priest who had held high positions in the church but was now retired from active ministry. He enlightened Tyndale to the fact that his life was at risk, and he needed to be careful about opposing the clergy.

As for the pope, whom Latimer had known as his personal aide, Latimer confided in Tyndale, labeling him the "Antichrist."[5] Whatever he thought of him, his opinion came from working with him closer than anyone else.

(The inner workings of some of the highest-ranking cardinals and popes are reviewed in Appendix U, "Christianity after Christ: 17 Centuries of Conflict," much of it from Catholic historical sources.)

Meanwhile, being a tutor at Gloucestershire probably left Tyndale time to pursue his own studies, those that would assist him in his future mission.

While continuing his ministry in Gloucestershire, Tyndale remained at odds with other priests on policies not in harmony with the Bible—namely, the practice of prayer to saints[6] and paying for indulgences. He even launched into a heated argument with one "learned" clergyman and in this skirmish said, "I defy the Pope and all his laws, and if God spares my life, ere [before] many years, I will cause the boy that driveth the plow to know more of the Scriptures than thou dost."[7]

Tyndale became consumed by a passion to fulfill that promise—to cause "the boy that driveth the plow" to know more of the scriptures than a priest—and at that point dedicated his life to translating the Bible into English.

Latter-day Saints see Joseph Smith as the quintessential plowboy who would know more of the scriptures than any clergyman had in 1,700 years, credited much to Tyndale's direct and indirect efforts. Robert D. Hales, of the Quorum of the Twelve Apostles, stated in the October 2005 LDS General

Conference—considered modern day scripture—that Tyndale's work "would find its way to a new land and be read by a 14-year-old plowboy named Joseph Smith."[8]

To make Tyndale's prophecy apply to *any* plowboy, he would write hundreds of powerful idioms into his translation that we know today. These would later make their way to the most-used English Bible of all time—the King James Version—of the following century.

Since Tyndale wanted the Bible to relate to every plowboy he also wrote using short sentences. It would be the most powerful translation imaginable—relating it to commoners, and from that he would start a revolution, far surpassing the accomplishments of that one "learned" clergyman he confronted, when he promised to "cause the boy that driveth the plow to know more of the Scriptures than thou dost." The plowboy in fact would know more than all the clergymen of England and Europe combined.

It was 1522 when Tyndale sought to make his mandate a reality.[9]

The priests meanwhile had another mandate—"They never ceased barking and rating [ranting] at him . . . saying that he was a heretic," writes Foxe.[10]

So Tyndale left for London, hoping to get permission and patronage for translating the Bible.

Doubtless he was armed with letters of introduction from the Walshes and others, a tradition at that time. He also took with him an English translation of a poem by Isocrates, the Greek rhetorician, to show how smoothly he could translate Greek.

But now, in London, Tyndale had to be careful whom he approached.[11]

In his state of innocence and "simplicity," as 2 men would later describe his attitude,[12] he went to the very worst person he could possibly have gone to—straight to the top, to a man who hated heretics, the Bishop of London himself, Cuthbert Tunstall.

Meeting Tunstall was actually an ordeal. Tyndale first had to meet with Sir Harry Guildford, keeper of the house, who politely received him and said he would speak to Tunstall in his behalf. Impatient to hear back from Guildford, Tyndale wrote a letter and carried it to Tunstall's home at St. Paul's cathedral. There, he gave it to Tunstall's servant, William Hebblethwaite, and asked to see the Bishop himself, "for an interview." In this manner Tyndale finally saw Bishop Tunstall, naively asking to live in his palace to translate the scriptures. Tunstall rejected his proposal. Rejected it flat. Saying his house was full already and he had no room for him.[13]

Apparently he advised Tyndale to seek a ministerial position in London in order to support himself. All this occurred most likely in September 1523.

But Tunstall wasn't finished with Tyndale. He had been alerted by his outright announcement to translate the Bible into English, and this put Tyndale at the very top of the bishop's "watch list."

Then Tunstall made certain all the important doors of London would be closed to him. An English Bible, he proclaimed, was heresy.

Needing to support himself, Tyndale became a minister at Saint Dunstan's church in London. There he felt the need to teach the Gospel in its simplicity, and at that church "he preached a while, as he had done in the country," writes Foxe.[14]

At St. Dunstan's he met a man so taken by him that he invited Tyndale into his home to stay. He was also from Gloucestershire and his name was Humphrey Monmouth—a successful merchant and alderman at church. And more importantly for Tyndale, he was a member of a highly important group of investors who would be vital to Tyndale's future—the Merchant Adventurers' Company. This group consisted of other men from Gloucestershire, the capital of English wool producers and Tyndale's home. These men traded with weavers in Belgium, where their wool was woven into cloth, and they had built a strong alliance with the weavers and wool trade dealers in Europe.

Monmouth stated that Tyndale studied both day and night, and that he ate simply, staying at his home almost a year.

Meanwhile, in London, Tyndale got to see "the demeanor of the preachers, how they boasted themselves, and set up their authority," says Foxe, who adds, they "greatly disliked him."[15]

Tyndale criticized these London priests for, according to Foxe, "juggling with the text, expounding it in such a sense as it were impossible to gather [sense] of the text, if the right meaning thereof were seen." Foxe describes how the priests would also create confusion for the masses "with apparent reasons of sophistry and tradition of their own making, founded without ground of scriptures."[16]

He adds, "Tyndale considered this only, or most chiefly, to be the cause of all mischief in the church, that the scriptures of God were hidden from the people's eyes," and that, "wresting the scripture unto their own purpose, contrary unto the meaning of the text, they would so delude the unlearned lay people, that . . . they [the lay people] could not solve their subtle riddles." So, Tyndale "was stirred up of God to translate the scripture into his mother tongue, for the profit of the simple people of the country."[17]

Tyndale next decided to find a publisher. But there he ran against another roadblock. Doubtless because of Tunstall.

No printers would touch his project with a 10-foot pole.

With this writing on the wall, he decided to make a life-altering change. It was time to skip town. Skip the whole country, in fact, and simply move out of England.

But first he had to raise money. He found his investors at the Merchant Adventurers' Company—the contacts he had made through Humphrey Monmouth, with whom he lived. These men immediately caught his vision and paid his passage.

With a fire in his soul he sailed off to Germany in 1524, soon to learn what it was like to be a hunted man on the church's blacklist.


On this journey Tyndale possibly went first to Hamburg, in north central Germany on the river Elbe.[18] (But where he actually went first is debatable. See this endnote for details.)

From there he sailed to Luther's home at Wittenberg in central east Germany. There he studied Greek more and translated the New Testament even more accurately, inspiring his new friend, Martin Luther, along the way.

Both Tyndale and Luther were inspired by the Greek New Testament texts of Desiderius Erasmus. Specifically, Luther had been hit by the impact of what he had read from Erasmus's 2nd edition, the *Novum Testamentum*, when he had been an Augustinian monk.

Both men—Tyndale and Luther—now used the 3rd edition published in 1522 for their New Testament translations, which were far more accurate than the Latin text of the Catholic-used Vulgate.

(Tyndale may have used the 1522 3rd edition of Erasmus while still in London, before coming to Germany, or he may have translated his New Testament in London using an earlier edition of Erasmus, then perhaps revised it after he arrived in Germany, using the newer edition. If he did in fact revise his translation in Germany, that means his first translation he had completed in London was not really ready for printing, as he had supposed when he lived there. In that scenario it was fortuitous that he was not able to print it in England.)

In an amazing historical twist, Greek was now available to study for the first time in centuries, so the timing couldn't have been better for both men.

Tyndale lived in Wittenberg a year, and the next year his manuscript was ready. So he moved across country to Cologne, where life-and-death adventures would now begin for him. Cologne was a city in west central Germany on the Rhine River, known for its printing presses. In that sense it was the perfect place for him to be.

On the other hand, it was a city staunchly Catholic. The bishop there kept a close eye on all new publications and especially on the city's printers. Yet Tyndale found one willing to print his New Testament. And through his connections with the Merchant Adventurers, he secured investors in England willing to pay for the printing.

By coincidence, a loyal Catholic scholar, John Dobneck, was in town, ready to wreak havoc. He wanted to gain favor with Henry VIII, the Catholic king of England, and had even written numerous attacks against Luther. (Dobneck, however, was bitter with the king for never having been given recognition for criticizing Luther. So he was always on the lookout for something bigger and better to expose with the Reformation in order to make a name for himself. His alias meant "the snail"—Cochlaeus. He was, by coincidence, in Cologne, Germany, to see the work of Rupert of Deutz printed [Rupert was an abbot—the leader of an abbey of monks—in a nearby monastery from over 400 years earlier, whom Dobneck believed had writings that applied to the current state of the Catholic Church.] And by chance he chose the *same printer as Tyndale*, Peter Quentel. Dobneck may have actually been assigned by Tunstall to obtain these printings, adding to the bizarre coincidence.[19])

Learning of Tyndale's connection to the print shop, Dobneck befriended the printer's workmen. Unfortunately for Tyndale, they got drunk one night and spilled the beans, bragging to Dobneck that all of England would soon be Lutheran, and explained why—they were printing 3,000 copies of an English New Testament to be secretly shipped to England! They further disclosed they were going fast with it and were already far into the book of Mark.[20]

Here was Dobneck's big chance, to turn his moniker from snail to rat. He went to a city senator, Hermann Rinck, who was friends to both Henry VIII and the Holy Roman Emperor living in Germany. Now he could let Henry VIII really see him shine—so he ratted on Tyndale.

When authorities raided the shop the next day, they found Tyndale had fled the coop, tipped off by the printers upon awaking from their hangover. But the authorities seized what had been printed and destroyed it.

Dobneck was furious—he had failed to capture Tyndale. How could the king be impressed with this?

He wasn't.[21]

Tyndale next shot "upriver"—southward.[22]

He went south from Cologne about 110 miles to Worms, a city in southwest Germany, also on the Rhine. This was a free city for free thinkers, and it was about to discard Catholicism and adopt Lutheranism.[23] Here, Tyndale hoped for safety and some kind of success.

He arranged for printing again, but had by now learned to constantly look over his shoulder to see if he might be stopped again. Seeing the pathway clear, he proceeded to print his New Testament in the late fall of 1525, possibly using up all his investors' money for this one final shot after the Cologne disaster, and hoping and praying to get through it without trouble.

He did. And finished printing it in about March 1526 at the shop of Peter Schoeffer. There, he possibly printed and bound 6,000 copies (or 3,000, according to most scholars).[24]

So now he finally had his New Testament in print.

The next step was getting the books to England. However, since the raid on the print shop, he knew they were on to him.

So he concocted a brilliant plan. He decided to smuggle them in cotton bales and flour sacks. Other copies were sneaked in wine cases falsely labeled, while still others went off in bales of wool and containers of cloth, with yet others inserted inside *other books.*

His tie-in to the Merchant Adventurers Company paid off and made this happen. They were willing to not only finance his operation but assist in smuggling his Bibles into England!

His Bibles, thus concealed, made their way on boats across the English Channel, up the Thames River, and to the port of London, where they were unloaded at a pier next to the steel yard where Germans worked, in fact where all goods came from Germany.

Customs officials inspected the cargo but found nothing suspicious. The German, pro-Luther workers there unpacked the precious cargo from falsely labeled containers and gave them to Bible distributors and salesmen, called colporteurs. Of particular irony, they were unloaded just 100 yards from St. Paul's Cathedral, the church headquarters where the high-ranking authorities were waging their war against Tyndale!

Meanwhile, Cuthbert Tunstall, Bishop of London, got wind of what was happening and in late May or early June 1526 heard about a shipment arriving. With plenty of time to intercept it, he sent spies to the docks. Having been tipped off, they discovered copies in various crates, but many copies got past them.

However, in October they confiscated a huge shipment and decided to hold a celebration at a special church service at Saint Paul's Cathedral.

On October 26, 1526, Tunstall preached his most famous sermon, attacking Tyndale and his Bible, saying no one should have an English Bible and that it was filled with strange doctrines. (He also lied through his teeth, saying it had 2,000 errors; then he ordered all copies to be taken outside and burned.)

This completely backfired on church authorities. While commoners had supported the monarchy vs. the Reformers, when they now saw the Bibles going up in flames, it was "too much" for them.

The line had been crossed.[25]

And at this point the common folk turned against the authorities. They were now open to Tyndale's Bible and what it might say.

Thus, the New Testament could no longer be controlled, as hard as the authorities tried.

Buying this Bible cost 2½ weeks of a servant's wages, yet it became an immediate best-seller. People sacrificed hard for this little book. It was designed to be small for easy smuggling, only 6 by 4 inches and 1.5 inches thick.[26]

In it, Tyndale packed a punch. Part of its success lay in its language—stripping away the Roman church's "hierarchy language," even changing the word "church," because of all it implied, and replacing it with "congregation." He also stripped away the word "priest" and all the hierarchy tradition it implied, using the term "elder" instead. By doing that, he seemed to throw the language into the faces of the authorities.

When word of the burning got back to Tyndale, he was convinced the church was now his ultimate *enemy*.

So he began to attack the clergy in print.

---

King Henry VIII had a cohort who was up for the challenge. His name was Thomas More.

As close personal friend and advisor to Henry VIII, he was the liaison between the king and Cardinal Wolsey. Wolsey was the second highest in command politically who ruled much in Henry's place, and the highest-ranking Catholic church leader in England—in fact it was he who had ordered Bishop Tunstall to burn the Bibles to begin with.

Thomas More was now on the ground floor of the war room developing strategies against Tyndale.[27]

Knowing Tyndale was the nation's number one enemy right now, he was determined to cut him off at the knees.

More had a mansion in Chelsea, an affluent area in central London, bordering the River Thames on the south. From there he and Tyndale would write against each other, starting in 1531. His biggest reason—More had a crushing conviction the Catholic church in England was being undermined by Tyndale. He feared that if the people would rise up against the church, they would also throw out the monarchy. So More viewed Tyndale's Bible as *an invitation to anarchy—to bring down both the church and the state.* So he now issued the ultimate threat against Tyndale—he said he would follow him to the ends of the earth.[28]

Soon, the authorities made a checklist.

Their first item of business?

Take it a step higher than just *confiscating* his Bible.

Actually *outlaw* the Bible.

And they did.

But this backfired also. It caused the English public to become even more intrigued by the whole Bible thing.

So the Bishop issued a new threat—a death warrant *to anyone found even possessing a forbidden Tyndale Bible.*

More excitement, more interest in the forbidden book.

Tyndale was winning.

Even across the English Channel in Europe the people got to witness the endless lengths to which Catholic bishops would go to stop Tyndale . . .

The English ambassador to the low countries, John Hackett—by order of Cardinal Wolsey—hunted down and burned Tyndale's books at Antwerp and Bergen op Zoom.

But for every book they found, many more got through to England and were sold for English-reading consumption, with profits going to Tyndale that financed future editions.

The high point of irony came when Bishop Tunstall went to Antwerp, Belgium, himself on assignment from Henry VIII, with a plot to purchase as many English New Testaments as possible and send them to England to be burned. He was aware Tyndale had made this city his hideout, so he began snooping around, asking where he could buy a large load of Bibles.

Word of his request reached Augustine Packington, a friend of Tyndale's, who was an Englishman and member of the Merchant Adventurers. So Packington tracked down Tunstall and asked him how many Bibles he wanted. The bishop told him, "All they could sell."[29] Packington told him he'd get back to him.

Packington then went to Tyndale and asked what he wanted to do.

Tyndale answered—he would sell all he had!

So the bishop bought them all, figuring he had outsmarted Tyndale. He left for London with his Bibles, smiling all the way. Victory was his.

But not so fast.

From the profits of his sale, Tyndale could now print 3 times more copies, and escalate his Bible distribution all through England, proving the bishop's men working the case were, in essence, idiots.[30]

With those profits Tyndale now not only printed more copies but had the luxury of revising and improving the New Testament into a 2nd edition several years later.

For now and for a long while he would keep the print shop of Martin de Keyser busy.[31]

After perhaps a year at Worms, Germany, Tyndale moved to Antwerp, Belgium, in 1529 or early 1530 for several significant reasons:

1. He was ready to print the first 5 books of the Old Testament into English, but needed a safe haven from which to plan.

2. The Merchant Adventurers set him up at the Merchant Adventurers House in Antwerp (where he would stay for years). This manor provided him security, since those who lived there enjoyed diplomatic immunity and could not be arrested.

3. Those sneaking his books into England also stayed at the House, using it as their smuggling headquarters. They furthermore used it as their base of operations for their business of exporting wool, which they had contracted for weaving in Antwerp and surrounding areas.

4. The city of Antwerp had no cathedral and thus no bishop to breathe down the necks of dissenters like Tyndale. (Bishops made cathedrals their headquarters and homes.)

5. The city had no university with a theological faculty, who were central to sniffing out heretics.

6. Antwerp was closer to England, so he could sneak his Bibles there quicker and easier.

7. It had nearly 60 print shops, with some among them willing to print heretical books like his, even though such books were outlawed. The law of averages favored him. Everyone lived and died by profit,[32] so some would take their chances.

Tyndale had come to Germany knowing Greek to translate the New Testament. But he did not know Hebrew. So, upon finishing the New Testament, he learned Hebrew to translate the Old Testament.

He now translated some of the first books of the Pentateuch, the first 5 books of Moses of the Old Testament, and then sailed from Antwerp to Hamburg to print part of them.

Perhaps he feared the king's men were keeping an eye on the Antwerp print shops, and that's why he wished to go to Hamburg. In any case he passed on printing in Antwerp for now.

Then disaster struck.

He was shipwrecked on the coast of Holland, "by which he lost all his books, writings, and copies, his money, and his time, and so was compelled to begin all again," writes Foxe.[33]

Tyndale then either returned to Antwerp and boarded another ship for Hamburg, or he boarded a ship at the shipwreck site, bound directly for Hamburg.

Arriving there he met Myles Coverdale by appointment. This man would figure prominently in the next major English Bible translation. (In that book, called the Coverdale Bible, Myles Coverdale would keep Tyndale's New Testament and his 6 soon-to-be-printed Old Testament books—the first 5 books plus Jonah.)

He and Tyndale now worked together in translating (or re-translating) the first 5 books of the Old Testament that had been lost from the shipwreck, "from Easter until December, in the house of a worshipful widow, Mistress Margaret Van Emmerson," says Foxe.[34] This was in Hamburg.

Thus, Tyndale's 6 books of the Old Testament that he re-translated were completed by year's end. He likely returned to Antwerp in early January 1530 in order to print them there, at the press of Johannes Hoochstraten.[35]

One reason to not stay in Hamburg was a plague sweeping the city. He likely wished to escape Hamburg as soon as he finished his translation with Coverdale. One can speculate additional factors: perhaps he received an "all's clear" message from the Merchant Adventurer's House about the king's men no longer guarding the Antwerp print shops, or possibly the authorities knew he was out of the country and had let up on their surveillance of the print shops, or perhaps Tyndale simply wanted to "chance it" back in Antwerp, still fearful of the king's men, but less so than of the sickness overtaking Hamburg.

Fortunately for him, whether he would stay longer in Hamburg or return to Antwerp, he had friends at both cities. At Hamburg was the widow who let him board there, as well as Myles Coverdale, while at Antwerp he had the advantages of protection and security from the Merchant Adventurers

House—with free room and food—plus a port from which to more closely ship his Bibles to England. Only the guarded print shops in Antwerp were a liability.

Whichever town he resided in now, he printed the first 5 books of the Old Testament in 1530 and also printed more New Testaments, exporting them on the sly to England and Scotland, sending out more copies than ever. He also now put most of his attention toward translating the majority of the Old Testament, which he would never print—although Myles Coverdale would. (See Appendix T: "English Bibles that Shook the World.")

The next year, 1531, the winds of change began to stiffen. Thomas More became more determined than ever to bring him down. For some unknown reason More began writing angry letters to him.

Tyndale became equally vitriolic, and they soon were launching salvos at each other, calling each other heretics.

Perhaps because of the letters, Thomas More became even more determined to win at all costs.

As a result, he instigated a sophisticated surveillance scheme to target Tyndale, pitting the nation's detective forces against him in order to figure out everything they could about him.

Reports Foxe: "The bishops and Sir Thomas More having before them [certain witnesses or spies] such as had been at Antwerp, most studiously would search and examine all things belonging to Tyndale, where and with whom he hosted [visited], whereabouts stood the house [of the guests he visited], what was his stature [what he looked like], in what apparel he went [how he was dressed, and] what resort he had [what house he lived in] in order to capture him."[36]

Then More decided to step up his war against Tyndale and show him what happens to those who cross him . . . he decided to capture a close friend of Tyndale's and kill him.

But the plot did not go down easily . . .

John Frith had been a student at Cambridge, then Oxford. He was personally picked by Cardinal Wolsey to enroll in a new college at Oxford called Cardinal College (Christ Church College today). But Frith and several other scholars turned on the church,[37] becoming secret Reformers.

But they were caught. As a punishment they were tossed into a salt cellar under a university building, where several of the young men died from the cold—"exposure"—and a bad diet. Frith was one who survived his time in the dungeon and left England immediately. He then met up with Tyndale at Antwerp and befriended him, telling him of the persecution at Oxford and of the deaths of his friends.

He and Tyndale had actually met years earlier, probably at either Cambridge or in London when Tyndale was a priest. Others believe they first met at Antwerp.

In any case, after seeing Tyndale for a time, Frith made the fatal mistake of visiting London, apparently to help a monk escape or travel to Europe. (This monk was the "prior" of the Reading Monastery, at Reading, England, in southern England.)

Whether Frith brought on his own problems by appearing to be a vagabond because he did not secure proper lodging, or whether he did conduct himself properly but was merely targeted by authorities, he was arrested.

He was later released, but word got out to the Catholic clerics that he was in England, and they had the ports closed to him—with spies sent to carefully watch for him.

He was caught again, arrested, and placed in the Tower of London—and there, he was tricked into writing his position on the Eucharist (taking "Holy Communion," also called "the Sacrament" in LDS circles). This trickery was a plot devised by William Holt, who in essence was a traitor to him.

This position paper was, unknown to him, a litmus test to determine if he would fall into the trap of showing he was a heretic or not. If he denied the actual presence of Christ in the Eucharist or if he disagreed with the church's belief in transubstantiation, he would be considered a heretic.

He and other Reformers did not believe in transubstantiation—the doctrine that the bread and wine physically turn into the body and blood of Christ during Communion—so he was labeled a heretic.

The written answers were then taken by Holt, who had talked him into answering the questions, without saying what they were for, and given to Thomas More.

More read the paper and immediately condemned Frith to death, knowing that would mentally torture Tyndale at Antwerp. Others were occasionally caught and likewise tricked into giving answers that led to their condemnation.

News about Frith was slow getting to Tyndale. When he finally got word that Firth had been arrested, he immediately wrote him, warning him not to talk or write about the Eucharist, because it would seal his fate.

But Frith had already given his answer by the time he got his advice from Tyndale.[38]

Meanwhile, Frith proved himself a man of unusual integrity. Even the jailor would let him leave the tower on occasion, because he promised he would return, which he always did.

Then Tyndale got the horrific news that Firth had been condemned to death by Thomas More. Tyndale wrote a second letter to Frith in prison, encouraging him to stay faithful to his beliefs till the end.

More knew he was victorious—making Tyndale squirm because Frith was scheduled to be tortured to death.

John Frith was burned at the stake in 1533.

Tyndale was predictably crushed.

Meanwhile, Thomas More drank a toast to the event. Especially since he knew he had gotten into Tyndale's head, mentally torturing his close friend.

The next few months saw Tyndale depressed. His hope of ever succeeding with a free England to read the English Bible seemed increasingly hopeless.

But he continued revising the New Testament while working on the Old Testament. Adding to his depression, a number of the last New Testament cases printed at Worms were confiscated.

Then, certain events would keep him from finishing the final 22 books of the Old Testament.

Tyndale was still in the safety of the Merchant Adventurer's House, owned by Thomas Pointz.

But across the channel, the King of England stepped up his attack on the Reformers. If anyone was caught smuggling the Bible into England, they would not just be executed but *burned at the stake*. Bishop Tunstall also warned the booksellers of the same fate.[39]

Then, events in England took a weird and remarkable twist.

Henry VIII fell in love with a new woman—a Protestant—Anne Boleyn. And this would turn the whole Tyndale chapter into a different and unexpected story.

Henry VIII had apparently fallen for Anne in 1527, and since their relationship had become steamy, he now wanted to do something about it. But he had a slight obstacle.

He was already married.

Enter Tyndale.

In 1528 Tyndale wrote a book, *Obedience of a Christian Man*, which would now play into some bizarre plot twists with the king of England.[40]

Tyndale had brought it out quickly in order to refute the arguments of the establishment—that the German Reformers were responsible for the Peasants' War that had torn through Germany, causing tens of thousands of deaths. Because of that war, the Reformation was under attack now for "producing anarchy," which the anti-Bible Catholics used as justification for outlawing the Bible.

Sir Thomas More also accused Tyndale for inspiring those peasants—but Tyndale's book laid out the facts to refute him—making this Tyndale's most important book to date, after the Bible. Tyndale's answer to More was, in fact, masterful. In

*Obedience of a Christian Man* Tyndale explains in a several-page section how obedience comes from God.

The next portion of his book, the major one, then discusses how to obey and respect the various classes of society—including those "above" them—which is a far cry from advocating anarchy. Tyndale then turned More's argument on its head, saying the Bible was preventive medicine against anarchy, and without it, people would be inclined to produce anarchy.[41]

King Henry VIII obtained a copy of Tyndale's book in a strange, roundabout way—from Anne Boleyn, who had lent the book to her assistant, Anne Gainsford, from whom it had been taken by Gainsford's fiancé, in jest, then discovered by the dean of their royal chapel, who had sent it on to Cardinal Wolsey, England's lead Catholic and Lord Chancellor. Wolsey controlled most matters as the king's chief advisor. He was considered an *alter rex*—another king. And of course he saw the book as heretical.

When Anne Boleyn learned about its circuitous disappearance, she was not angry, but casually commented that it was "the dearest book that ever dean or cardinal took away."[42] In her low-keyed approach she complained to the king about the book being confiscated by the cardinal, whereupon Henry VIII ordered its return.

Then Anne persuaded Henry "most tenderly" to read the book himself. Which he did, with this report: "This book is for me and all kings to read."[43] Tyndale's book denounced the pope's power in all civil matters, calling for secular rulers in government, rather than church rulers.

So Tyndale now had a new fan—the king of England.

(Ironically, Henry would use the book's concepts to break the Church of England away from the Roman Catholic Church in 1534.)[44]

Meanwhile, Anne Boleyn's background was intriguing. She had been courted by Henry VIII for about 7 years, but she maintained she kept her chastity during that period.[45] She had not wanted to be like her sister Mary, who had had an affair with him, probably from 1521 to 1524 (as well as with other notables over the years, mostly in France) while married to another man in France.

Anne then became involved with Henry VIII a year or two later, in 1525 or 1526, but only on an emotional, non-physical basis, according to her.

Then she and Henry had a secret marriage that was considered illegal. After that she became pregnant.[46]

But they were remarried to make certain, on January 25, 1533. Even that marriage did not count in the eyes of some traditionalists, however, since Henry VIII would not technically be annulled from Catherine until May 1533. Thus, some argue, Anne's marriage before May was an "affair," which, to them, defined her as his mistress. However, in the eyes of many, they had been married in January—thus they had no affair. She then gave birth to her only child, Elizabeth I, the future queen of England, on September 7, 1533, who was conceived after their first, secret marriage.

Five years earlier Tyndale had published the above book that so affected Henry VIII and Anne Boleyn. Then he published another book in 1530—*The Practyse of Prelates*—cutting down the king for planning to annul his marriage so that he could marry Anne. (At this point he was married to Catherine of Aragon, his brother's widow.) In that book Tyndale quoted a scripture from Leviticus to back up his opposition to marrying Anne.

Henry VIII went on a rampage.

He went from adoring Tyndale to calling for his arrest.

Then Henry realized something that scared him.

Tyndale's Bible was a threat.

Others could read the same passage in Leviticus and clearly see that the logic for his divorce was a house built of sand.

He was so fearful in fact of the Bible getting out to the commoners, that he is reputed to have said, "Even a pot boy would have an opinion."

Terrified, he saw Tyndale's Bible as an attack on Catholic Tudor England itself.

And he was right.

Henry VIII determined to stop Tyndale's Bible before it stopped him and caused a revolution. And maybe even dethrone him for heresy.

Even the king's guards could not hold back a million-member mob, anxious to oust him. So he didn't want to take the chance. He had to distance himself from Tyndale, and keep those blasted Bibles out of England.

But within weeks came another twist.

Henry VIII made Tyndale a startling offer—*to return to the court and work for him.* He wanted to put him in charge of communications, guaranteeing safe passage and a high salary. After all, he was, deep down, actually impressed with his writings, and by employing this strategy he could practice the old adage firsthand: "Keep your friends close and your enemies closer."

If Tyndale lived in the king's court, there would be little time for Bible mischief. So his next step was, in a roundabout way, to send an agent to meet Tyndale in Europe. (How this was roundabout is that it was actually a plan hatched by independent evangelicals to have the king bring Tyndale home unpunished.[47] These evangelicals even hired an agent, Stephan Vaughn, to find Tyndale and offer him good terms for surrendering and coming home. And their strategy was authorized by the king. Several of his letters in fact still exist.)

It was now 1531. Tyndale had been in hiding 6 years at this point and, for the first time in that period, he broke his cover and agreed to meet. He left his hideaway at Antwerp, trudged outside the city gate, and walked in a field to meet the agent, Vaughn, whose allegiance may have been, for all Tyndale knew, to the king even more than to the evangelicals.

As the most wanted man in Europe now, Tyndale was more than a bit nervous. He knew he could easily be snared.

Soon, seeing Vaughn ahead of him, he approached him and stopped. Then listened to what the king's agent had to say.[48]

He offered Tyndale a deal.

Tyndale, after hearing all the details, turned him down.

The reason? Tyndale wanted to keep spreading his Bibles across England. If he accepted employment from the king, Bibles would come screeching to a stop.

They parted and he walked back to his hideaway.

Vaughn was relentless. He began sending communications with the same request—to come to England and work for the king.

Tyndale heard from him several times over the next 6 months. But he could not take the tempting offer.

Still, Vaughn would not give up. He even visited Tyndale once again in person.

This time, Tyndale counter-proposed. He decided to risk capture to return, knowing the king might not actually employ him, but rather submit him to an agonizing death; nevertheless, he was willing to make the deal *if the king would release a Bible in English*. Tyndale was a trusting, innocent man, and likely never doubted the king would keep his word about releasing the Bible in English if they reached such an agreement, even if he gave up his own life in the process. The agent said he'd return with an answer in 2 days.

When Henry VIII heard Tyndale's counter-offer, he refused. He even tore the written proposal in pieces. This was his reason:

Henry held onto Catholic beliefs and traditions—all of them: penance, Purgatory, praying to the saints, the works. He only refused to pay allegiance to the pope. He was even committed to the Latin Vulgate. Thus, he refused to deal with Tyndale's offer. Certainly, if he accepted Tyndale's counter-proposal, it would run counter to his own paramount desire to keep the English Bible out of people's hands—and most specifically that scripture in Leviticus—which crushed his hopes for an annulment. This may have been his primary reason for clutching the Vulgate so tightly to his bosom. The commoners would never know from Leviticus that he should not ditch his wife to marry Anne Boleyn.

So, with only a Latin Bible for the commoners (to not read) he could keep his dirty little secret, secret.

Bottom line . . . he would have no part of Tyndale's Bibles in England to expose his fraudulent annulment.

———————

Seeing the deal off the table, Thomas More saw Tyndale as fair game to go after again.

He determined to resume full warfare against him—but this time with an outrageous letter-writing campaign that would personally attack him over and over and over. And it seemed to hit Tyndale right in the sweet spot of vulnerability.

He wrote back. He defended his position over and over in hundreds of pages—lashing out at More, the torturer of his friend Frith, and now his avowed enemy.

He and More were now both filled with fury, obsessed with refuting each other.[49] And the debate would consume over three-quarters of a million words (with writing coming painstakingly slow, at 2–3 words per minute, using a quill pen, per the process described in Appendix M: "Theories Attacking the *Book of Mormon*").

Thomas More decided to raise it a step. He plotted to capture and personally interrogate *other Tyndale supporters in England.* And he executed them all horribly as well—burning them at the stake, just as he had Frith, until their blood boiled and their hearts stopped.

Tyndale heard of these deaths and, instead of getting depressed this time, stepped up his end of the war. He exported more Bibles!

He was out to take on not only the Catholic church but the entire English dynasty.

Thomas More was a dedicated, loyal, self-righteous hench-man of Henry VIII. He viewed anyone disagreeing with him as an insect. His arrogance knew no bounds. Burning Reformers at the stake till they took their last agonizing breath was no less of a chore to him than lighting a roach on fire before stepping on it.

He did show one admirable trait—of loyalty to the king, the pope, and Catholicism, unwilling to support the king's marriage to Anne Boleyn as it went against his principals, as portrayed in the hit stage play and movie, *A Man for All Seasons.* But with that admirable loyalty came the fine line of stubbornness.

Tyndale was up against the most powerful, stubborn, and cruelest rulers on the planet—Thomas More and Henry VIII.

Tyndale was also a man of principle, and he was determined to expose Henry VIII as a tyrant and hypocrite.

And his physically small Bible he printed was about to destabilize an entire nation. When Thomas More met with the king and gave him the news of even more Tyndale Bibles coming into England, he got so riled up that he threw a royal tantrum.

Seeing Tyndale not backing down made the king absolutely furious.

He was determined now to extradite him to England and stop him and all this Bible madness. He pressed the Holy Roman Emperor Charles V to have him arrested in Antwerp and returned under terms of the Treaty of Cambrai. But Charles V said they needed hard evidence.

So Charles refused to arrest him.[50]

This made Henry VIII exponentially angrier.

Tyndale, meanwhile, kept marching forward, literally dotting the English landscape with his Bible—smuggling 18,000 across the channel into the British isles.

He was now declared a bona fide outlaw. A 3-way outlaw in fact—to the king of England, to the Holy Roman Empire, and to the Roman Catholic Church itself.

The authorities went "hog wild" now. They decided it was time for a full-blown manhunt.

Bounty hunters were recruited, and they went after him with all the power of the English throne.

But they failed. Tyndale hid in the confines of the Merchant Adventurers' manor.

Then things took another twist.

Henry VIII decided to go ahead and *marry* Anne Boleyn. But the pope refused to grant him an annulment.

So Henry VIII started his own church—the Church of England, in 1534, and made himself the head of it, assigning his designated church leaders to grant him an annulment.

In this decision to break away, he was inspired by Tyndale's writings—those from 1528 about secular powers being above the pope.

This link of Tyndale to the king, in fact, contributed to a major impact on world history. King Henry VIII was now excommunicated by the pope in Rome and, as stated in the text, this opened Pandora's box, releasing an entire explosion of Reformation events that would pour across the globe.

It was now 1534, and Tyndale's 2nd-edition New Testament was printed—a vast improvement over the first edition—with 4,000 changes, of which 50% corresponded more to the Greek texts he used.[51]

But a new enemy now appeared.

"Pirate printers."

Hurting Tyndale and his investors were pirated editions of the New Testament, printed by certain Dutch printers—an entirely unexpected "enemy."

The 1st pirated edition was by Christoffel van Puremund, who had printed and shipped to England a badly proofread version he had ripped off from Tyndale's Bible in November 1526.

More recently, in 1531, he had printed a 3rd pirated edition. But it seemed these rip-offs had come to an end when van Puremund was caught, imprisoned, and executed at London for smuggling them into England. Yet the icing on the cake came 3 years later in 1534 when one of Tyndale's assistants from years earlier at Cologne, George Joye, made an unexpected visit to van Puremund's widow and talked her into printing a 4th pirated edition, with his own unauthorized changes to Tyndale's version!

Tyndale was livid. He saw Joye's so-called corrections were all wrong. Worse, he had not even given Joye permission. Adding insult to injury, he released it as a "Tyndale Bible" and, on top of all that, Joye kept the profits for himself!

He did this, in fact, knowing Tyndale was preparing his own corrected 2nd edition.

Tyndale called him on the carpet in the "second forward" to his 2nd edition in 1534, saying how bad Joye's corrections were. He also chewed him out for passing off that edition as Tyndale's work, and for not putting his—Joye's—name on it.

Separate from all that, in 1534 Tyndale released a 2nd edition of the Pentateuch—the first 5 books of the Old Testament—revising only the book of Genesis. In this edition he added a prologue to each of the 5 books, outlining what it taught.[52]

Tyndale also translated and printed the book of Jonah sometime in the early 1530s—perhaps 1531.

(Of fascination to some, no copies of the Pentateuch of the Old Testament and Jonah were available for 327 years, but in 1861 one was discovered in a volume of tracts by the Bishop of Wells and Bath, in Somerset, England, in a compiled volume of tracts. Details on the unusual publishing history of this source, which ties directly to Mark Twain, is contained in this endnote, which also describes, as an interest to some, Twain's publishing company and its unusual rise and fall.)[53]


Aside from the pirated editions, Tyndale and his allies moved forward, translating, perfecting, and printing his Bible. In the 4 years leading up to 1534, Tyndale apparently translated much more of the Old Testament, eventually completing a total of 17 of its 39 books (although publishing only 6 himself).[54]

But Tyndale's tie-in to the Tudors of England was not over. King Henry VIII's Protestant wife, Anne Boleyn, was a beautiful, sweet, manipulative woman. She steered his emotions and then his ideas her way, and thus Thomas More fell from grace.

Henry VIII had Thomas More arrested.

The reason—More would not deny supremacy of the pope, which was treason. (And perhaps, say some, because he refused to attend the king's wedding—so the couple felt snubbed.)

On April 17, 1534, More was imprisoned in the Tower of London. From there he watched the landscape of life in England change, seeing what he had feared most—the demise of Catholicism in his beloved England.

And now, Henry VIII absolutely dismantled it.[55] He marched on 825 monasteries plus hundreds of Catholic churches in England, Wales, and Ireland, and took them all by force,[56] hammering a new sign above them all—"property of the Church of England."

They were now all part of his very own church. Stolen fair and square.

Meanwhile, William Tyndale saw his greatest enemy, Thomas More, also out of the way, now locked up in the Tower of London.

So Tyndale hoped things would ease up.

But they didn't. In the "what goes around, comes around" department of Tudor English history, Anne Boleyn began losing favor with the king. Why? She could not bear him a son.

As a result, things turned worse for Tyndale in Europe. Perhaps local European Catholics felt Henry VIII would no longer intervene in behalf of Protestants, since Anne was sky-diving from grace.

So local Catholics in Antwerp petitioned the Holy Roman Emperor, Charles V, to purge the city of heretics. The heretic-hunting now went full bore, and Tyndale was in his greatest danger yet.

Worse, Thomas More, still imprisoned at the Tower of London, would not give up his fight to the death with Tyndale. So he decided to have a meeting with one Henry Philips.

Antwerp seemed like a safe haven for Tyndale, even with the heretic-hunting. Or so he thought. Many times he was invited to dinner and given support by merchants, states Foxe,[57] likely those involved with the Merchant Adventurers Company. He had his favorite café and lived safely as a guest still under diplomatic immunity at the manor of Thomas Pointz, an Englishman and member of the Merchant Adventurers, who sought to protect

Tyndale. The home was part of a large estate, and had an interesting entrance—a long narrow, private walkway leading up to the manor.

In 1535 Henry Philips arrived at Antwerp and befriended Tyndale. They shared many interests. Philips was a fellow Oxford grad who seemed well off, and was agreeable to Tyndale's beliefs. They met several times and he earned Tyndale's trust. Tyndale brought him to the manor once or twice for dinner and supper, and Philips even spent a night in the house. Tyndale proudly introduced him to Pointz. Schmoozing up to the manor's owner, Philips showed off his books and studies to Pointz, wanting him to feel he was good company for Tyndale.

But Pointz became suspicious. He asked Tyndale how he got to know this fellow. Tyndale answered, "He was an honest man, handsomely learned, and very comfortable [financially independent]."[58]

To impress Pointz further, Philips convinced him to walk around the city and show him the points of interest, in which they spoke of "divers things,"[59] and even talked about Henry VIII.[60] It was a long walk—Antwerp was no village.

Finally, Pointz no longer suspected him. But when Pointz went out of town for a few days, something went terribly wrong.

Philips proved himself far different than what he appeared.

He had actually attended a strict Catholic university (perhaps in addition to Oxford, which was a shared interest he had with Tyndale)—but, unknown to anyone there, he held an interesting little secret:

He was still a loyal Catholic.

And began plotting with the imperial court in Brussels to give hard evidence to the Western Roman Emperor Charles V in order to nab Tyndale.

Philips, in fact, was a plant.

Sent by Thomas More.

Together they had met in the Tower of London, and figured out how to bring Tyndale down.

However, unexpectedly to More, Charles V was not about to extradite Tyndale to England. He would take care of it himself. He assigned his attorney to accompany Philips to visit Tyndale. And the plan was, once they got Tyndale off the estate, they would nab him. It would have to be an illegal act—a kidnapping—since Tyndale still had diplomatic immunity, living with Pointz.

So Philips gathered the emperor's attorney with other officers and brought them all to the manor where Tyndale lived.[60]

And now they were all poised for the betrayal.

Philips left them in the street and then went alone through the long narrow courtyard to get Tyndale. He knocked on the door and someone invited him in. There, Philips told Tyndale he needed to borrow 40 shillings. "I lost my purse this morning," he told him.[61]

So Tyndale lent him the money. To show his gratitude, Philips invited him to dinner. But Tyndale countered, inviting him to dinner instead, requesting him to "be my guest," at a place "where you shall be welcome."[62] Evidently they had certain cafés in town that welcomed guests more warmly if their regular customers brought them.

Later, at the appointed dinner time, Tyndale went with Philips. They left the manor on "a long narrow entry, so that two could not go in front," says Foxe.[63] Philips insisted Tyndale walk in front of him. Thus, Philips, "a tall, comely person, followed behind him."[64]

Philips, meanwhile, had set his officers on either side of the outside gate, elevated on chairs to see who was coming down the long entry from the manor.

Seeing his compatriots at the gate, Philips lifted his long arm over Tyndale's head and pointed down to him. That was the sign.

Tyndale walked out of the gate, and the authorities nabbed him. It was May 23, 1535.

They later said they pitied his simplicity when they took him. Tyndale was a simple, humble man, and apparently came across as trusting and gullible.

They took him to the state castle prison of Vilvorde, 18 miles from Antwerp, and tossed him into a dark, dank dungeon—so small he would call it a "vault."[65]

Thomas More, Tyndale's arch-nemesis, sitting in his own cell at the Tower of London the past 15 months, smiled victoriously. He had only one thing left in his life that he wanted to see—Tyndale killed.

But Thomas More could not gloat for long. Just 5 weeks later, on July 1, 1535, he himself was sentenced to death.

Then, 5 days later, on July 6, he was taken from his Tower to be executed. He had actually been sentenced to be hung, then, while still alive, cut down, castrated, cut open, and have his bowels burned over a fire. But Henry VIII decided, because of their long friendship, to merely behead him, a much more merciful ending.

More's severed head was then boiled until black and placed on a spike above the London Bridge, where traitors' heads were displayed for a month, before being tossed into the River Thames below.

(More's daughter claimed that when she was in a boat beneath the bridge, she prayed for the head to fall down, and it did, right into her boat—although some speculate her answered prayer had some assistance from a man she had hired to pull it off the spike and toss it to her.)

Inexplicably, centuries later in 1980, Thomas More was declared a "martyr" by the Church of England and,[66] even more curious, despite all the torturous deaths at his hands, he was declared a patron saint by Pope Paul II in 2000, officially declared the "heavenly Patron of Statesmen and Politicians" on October 31, 2000.[67] (At least, to those who saw the irony, Halloween seemed an appropriate day to be sainted.)

His new title, Saint Thomas More, perhaps didn't have the same ring to it for all those who had been tortured to death at his orders. But one wishes him well in his sainthood.


As for sainthood, in Catholic theology this is the veneration of a person who is determined by the pope, as recommended by a committee of cardinals, to have a person sainted, choosing one who lived a holy life sufficient to guarantee him or her a place in heaven—a doctrine respected, but not subscribed to, by Latter-day Saints. The closest that Latter-day Saint doctrine comes to that theology is when a person has his "calling and election made sure," guaranteeing them a place in the highest degree of heaven. (Such persons however are not revered by others, as Catholic saints are, nor are they prayed to for intercession to God, nor are statues and small statuettes that hang from automobile mirrors made for their veneration.)

As for the Latter-day Saint doctrine on the afterlife, while it is explained in more detail in Appendix S, "Beliefs in the Afterlife: Catholic vs. Protestant vs. Latter-day Saint," an additional note is appropriate here.

Those people who had willfully broken God's commandments, especially those who had done so the worst, will be in the lowest kingdom of heaven. But those who had lived their best and kept His commandments—whether receiving them on earth or in the Spirit World—will go to the highest. That's a simplified explanation, and there are caveats, but the "Plan of Happiness," as Latter-day Saints call it, is outlined in the scriptures.

So, according to Latter-day Saints, at some point in the eternities Thomas More and those like him will eventually end up in some degree of heaven.

(In a general sense those who are abusers and torturers would start their eternal journey in Spirit Prison, where they would first suffer for their sins based on the degree to which they sinned, for anywhere from perhaps a short period to centuries—although man cannot judge who or for how long—until they repent and accept Christ's Atonement, after which they will, upon leaving Spirit Prison, be resurrected and then qualify for 1 of the 3 main degrees of heaven, spoken of by Paul to the Corinthians in the New Testament. Emphasis should be made that only God is the judge in these matters, according to Latter-day Saint theology.)

---

In the end, Thomas More never got to witness William Tyndale's execution. After Tyndale had been in prison for only 6 weeks and 2 days, More was beheaded.

Tyndale would then suffer through another 456 days (of his 500-day imprisonment) in his dungeon. While doing this time, he turned down the offer of a legal representative, wishing to represent himself, always innocent to the wiles of the world and sophisticated enemies.

But while serving time in prison, he preached with success to the men in charge. Eventually he would convert his keeper, his keeper's daughter, and others of the keeper's household.

At length his trial was held in Augsburg, where he was "condemned by virtue of the emperor's decree, made in the assembly," records John Foxe.[68]

While living in prison, Tyndale wrote a letter requesting items to keep him warm and sane. "I beseech you my lordship to send me from my goods in his keeping a warmer cap, for I suffer greatly from cold in the head being troubled with a continual catarrh [excessive build-up of mucous in the nose or throat], which is aggravated in this prison vault. A warmer coat also, for that which I have is very thin. . . . I ask for leave to use a lamp in the evening, for it is tiresome to sit alone in the dark. But above all I beg and entreat your clemency to allow me the use of my Hebrew Bible, Hebrew grammar, and Hebrew lexicon, that I might employ my time with that study."[69]

No one knows the outcome of that request.[70]

Tyndale stayed there the full 500 days, perhaps not knowing how long he would be there, which in itself would be a cruel punishment.

Doubtless, he tried getting help from those in power—the most influential of whom were sympathetic to the Reformers—Thomas Cromwell and Anne Boleyn. But Anne was still struggling to keep her marriage afloat, incapable of providing Henry VIII a son.

Cromwell, the most powerful man in England next to Henry VIII, acted as chief minister from 1532–1540, and sought to release Tyndale.

But Tyndale's betrayer, Henry Philips, still in Belgium, acted on behalf of the emperor's authorities and blocked all of Cromwell's efforts.

Thus, Thomas Cromwell was unable to change the emperor's mind. Eventually, in 1540, Cromwell himself would be executed for treason. (Another Cromwell of note, Oliver Cromwell, would be the great-great-grandson of his sister, Katherine Williams, and is discussed in Part 4 of this appendix.) Of Thomas Cromwell, Henry VIII would later feel remorseful for leaving him to twist in the wind, as it were, and later accused his own ministers of false charges that produced Cromwell's death. Afterward, French Ambassador Charles de Marillac would write a letter saying the king declared "he had put to death the most faithful servant he ever had."[71]

Henry VIII had a propensity for killing his most loyal companions—Thomas More had actually been extremely faithful to him, only refusing to support his annulment to wife Catherine and marriage to Anne Boleyn.

Soon, Anne would be pushed away as well, just as Henry VIII had ditched his loving wife Catherine, whom he had banished to a castle prison until she died of cancer.

Still in prison at this point, Tyndale's only chance for a reprieve now lay with the soon-to-be estranged wife of the king, Anne Boleyn.

But, about 350 days into Tyndale's 500-day imprisonment, Henry VIII had his wife Anne arrested on trumped-up charges— and several days later, on May 19, 1536, had her executed.

Tyndale's last chance for a reprieve had gone the way of the guillotine.

Worthy of note, Henry VIII would end up having had 6 wives and killing 2 of them—Anne and his 5th wife, the flirtatious Kathryn Howard. (Interestingly, still another he married sight unseen—Anne of Cleve—who he realized at first glance was not as comely as her painting had portrayed her to be. He found her, in fact, so repulsive and ill-mannered that, after the marriage, he refused to even consummate it. Then he had her tossed out and the marriage annulled. Henry VIII himself, ironically at this point, was no spring chicken—old, ugly, and obese.) All in all, he was an egotistical tyrant, moody and cold-hearted. Yet a likeable chap in some ways. Nevertheless, much of England's future came from his decisions, including the birth of the Church of England and today's Anglican Communion (consisting of the Church of England today, the Episcopal Church U.S.A., and 42 other churches throughout the world, totaling 80+ million members in 160 countries worldwide). All of that, in some measure, came about from the influence of William Tyndale on Henry VIII.

Predictably, 4½ months later, on October 6, 1536, Tyndale was led from his cell, marched out of the castle prison, and tied to a stake. He saw firewood brought before him and laid at his feet.

But suddenly, mercifully, rather than watching the wood go up in flames and feeling the pain of the fire, the executioner came up behind him, placed a cord around his neck, and strangled him. It was from someone's request that he die comparatively quickly, less painfully.

Unfortunately, this didn't kill him. He partially revived, aware he was being burned. In this state of consciousness he reportedly died in a quiet, stoic manner, until his final words, according to John Foxe, which were spoken "with a fervent zeal and a loud voice:" "Lord! Open the King of England's Eyes."[72]

---

William Tyndale's Bible gave more than a spark to the Reformation. In addition to waking up people spiritually, it also united them culturally by literally saving the English language.

English had become a broken form of communication with many variations. French and Latin words had filtered in and were taking over. Different regions of the country, in fact, were splitting the language apart.

But Tyndale's Bible served as a rallying point. It unified English speakers. Ironically, while only a minor language in the early 1500s, English now became a solid, united language after the publication of Tyndale's Bible, and English spread over the next 5 centuries to become the dominant language of the world, used by over 2 billion of the 7 billion people on the planet today.[73]

William Tyndale's remarkable life was another in the realm of Reformers who, like Martin Luther, provided inspiration to hundreds of millions eventually, and also prepared the world for the later work of young Joseph Smith in the United States.


## Part 4

## The Centuries following Tyndale:
## Twists and Turns of the Reformation

After William Tyndale, his Bibles lived on, inspiring other Reformers to pick up the torch and continue the marathon. During the next 33 years, 5 more English Bibles would be published by independent Reformers and 3 more by Anglican Church authorities who used the Reformer's translations![1] (See Appendix T: "English Bibles that Shook the World" for details.")

Henry VIII was not done, however. Now out on his own, with his own church, and still angry at Rome, he thumbed his nose at the pope by making his church's first item of business *the printing of the English Bible*. A direct answer to Tyndale's dying wish.

A final irony between William Tyndale and Henry VIII was this: the new English Bible authorized by Henry VIII *would use mostly Tyndale's words*.

This sanctioned Bible was published in 1539—just 3 years after Tyndale's death. It was the first "authorized" English Bible for public use, and was called the Great Bible, with its name coming from its huge size—over 14 inches high.

Of this edition, 8,500 copies would be printed and supplied to every parish in England.

And soon thereafter another edition would be published by the Church of England, called the Bishops' Bible, trying to keep up with the Reformers' editions. These would be interspersed with independent Reformers' Bibles. The last of those would be the 1560 Geneva Bible. Then 51 years would pass before the most revered Bible of all time would go to press—the King James Version—which would use 83% of Tyndale's New Testament text and 76% of his Old Testament (of what he translated). The King James Bible would become, in fact, the biggest-selling book in the history of the English language. (Ironically, it would use portions of all 5 of the post-Tyndale independent Reformers' Bibles, each of which used nearly all of Tyndale's words! Thus, Tyndale's fingerprints have practically been stamped on every page of these Bibles for hundreds of years.)

After Tyndale, English Bibles became unstoppable, and the Reformers were now in high gear, breaking away millions of people from Catholicism into other forms of Christianity.

In summary, Henry VIII had proven an interesting husband and an even more interesting church leader. But when he died in 1547, another tumultuous period began:

His 9-year-old son, Edward VI, took power. He was a sickly little king, and died of disease at age 15, having ruled only 6 years.

Then 16-year-old Lady Jane Grey was ushered in. For all of 9 days.

Her reign would have been longer, but sitting in the wings was another relative, a woman seething with jealousy, who happened to be the daughter of Henry VIII and his first wife, Catherine. Envious and lustful for power, she designed a conspiracy, gathered some forces, and entered London with more power than Lady Jane ever expected. Then sent her off to the Tower of London, where Lady Jane was executed the following year.

This powerful woman was none other than Queen Mary I—a.k.a. "Bloody Mary," so named for her mass execution of Reformers and Protestants.

Immediately she tried reuniting England with Rome,[2] so the Reformers in England ran for their lives.

But not in time for many of them. She massacred hundreds.

Mary reigned only 5 years—1553–1558—and because of her anti-Protestant efforts, refuges fled *en masse*. The painful part was, as they left England's shores, they figured they would never see their family or friends again, and wept upon the ships. This mass exodus was termed the "Marian Exile."

As she wielded sword and guillotine against her Protestant enemies, the Reformation built up steam while in exile.

Those who escaped included Myles Coverdale and John Foxe, author of *Foxe's Book of Martyrs*, who lived through the purge and recorded it all. These 2 men fled to Geneva, Switzerland in the 1550s, which was one of the few safe havens for Reformers. And there they joined with John Calvin and others to start the Church of Geneva.[3]

Another leader who joined them was John Knox, the Great Reformer of the Scottish Church, making this congregation a veritable Who's Who of Great Reformers.

It was an exciting time for truth-seekers in exile from Queen Mary and the pope.

These Reformers at the Church of Geneva were now de-termined to produce a Bible that would educate their families and their followers while they remained in exile. It was the above-mentioned Geneva Bible—a truly amazing effort—that used almost the entire Tyndale Bible text. It was also the first mass-produced Bible for the public. (The 3 previous independent English Bibles had been printed in far lower quantities of a few thousand each.)

Geneva would be the first Bible taken to America and would become the Bible of choice for the Pilgrims and Puritans. Unknown to many, America was founded on this Bible and its Judeo-Christian principles—not upon the King James Version, as some suppose, which would come out later. In England, William Shakespeare used hundreds of quotes in his plays from this Bible, and John Milton wrote *Paradise Lost* from it. It became the standard Bible for English speakers for over a century, including half a century after the King James Version came out!

But, eventually, the King James Version would catch up and replace it.[4]

Meanwhile, many Englishmen resisted Queen Mary. So she had them slaughtered like hogs—and worse—burned at the stake. She burned hundreds to death for the crime of being Protestant.

She had a long memory of those who had opposed the Catholic cause, and her husband, Philip II from Catholic Spain, did not oppose her efforts.

From 1553, when she took power, till 1558, she showered the nation with unrelenting brutality. She even burned Archbishop Thomas Cranmer and John Rogers at the stake in 1555, those who had been appointed by Henry VIII to publish the Great Bible. Rogers was also the man behind the Matthew-Tyndale Bible of 20 years earlier, as covered in Appendix T: "English Bibles that Shook the World."

When Queen Mary I died, the next ruler took over—her half sister Elizabeth I, daughter of Henry VIII and Anne Boleyn. This new queen returned England to Protestantism and broke all ties with Rome.

With Bloody Mary gone and Elizabeth I taking over the reins, the Reformation flourished—and the folks once again had access to Bibles. Rome began pulling out its hair.

Meanwhile, across much of western Europe, people could read the Scriptures now and begin adding up 2 plus 2 of what was taught in the Bible vs. what the church at Rome was getting away with. And the Roman stranglehold began loosing its grip.

In England, after Mary's turbulent reign of terror, Queen Elizabeth swung the terror pendulum the other direction. She prevented Catholics from civilized necessities—voting, educating their children, holding public office, and becoming members of professions.[5]

Then the genocide began. Catholics were executed, possibly in even greater numbers than the Protestants had been under Mary. (One main reason is that she reigned for so much longer than Catholic Queen Mary.)[6]

The executions of Catholics would continue under new kings and queens in England.[7]

But a fantastic irony arose. As described in Appendix T: "English Bibles that Shook the World," Elizabeth and her Church of England officials decided that while it was okay to kill Catholics, they did not want to "offend" Rome. Perhaps placating the more conservative Protestants in their circle—those who missed the good old days when they were Catholics and felt they had ties back to the Apostolic church of the 1st century, she and the English church leaders decided they would now be considered "part Catholic/part Protestant."

At this point they became as oppressive to independent Reformers as they were to Catholics—highlighted by executions, torture and exiling galore, causing many to flee to the freedom of America's shores.

This would also be true with other tyrannical kings England would cultivate, with the Tudor reign ending and the Stewart line now launching forth.

The first of the Stewarts was a father-son pair consisting of the next 2 kings who would succeed Elizabeth I after her long reign would end in 1603: James I and his son Charles I, both power-hungry Royals who seemed to find particular joy in oppressing independent Separatists.

James I had one notable good deed—he was responsible for authorizing the King James Bible—but he brutalized his opposition during his 22-year reign from 1603 to 1625.

His son Charles I continued to oppress the Separatists for his 24-year reign from 1625 to 1649—2 years longer than his father.

His son, Charles II, would one day take power, but not without a remarkable 11½–year interval with the rise of one Oliver Cromwell during the English Civil War, in which England would become a constitutional republic.

Cromwell's fascinating story, as an example of both courage and intolerance, took on a new form—with the persecuted becoming the persecutors . . .

In 1642 the English Civil War erupted.

In the movie *Cromwell* (1970), the opening scene depicts a man walking into a Separatist church in England. The congregation turns and gasps—they see his ears had just been cropped, his punishment for being a Separatist, and at that point the actor Richard Harris, as Oliver Cromwell, calls out a profanity about the king.

In real life and in the movie, Cromwell soon organized forces to take out King Charles I, and they launched the English Civil War, pitting Parliament against the king.

For Cromwell it was both personal and political. The king's persecution of independent Protestants infuriated Cromwell on a personal basis, but in the political arena he saw other outrages by the king—throwing a fit over not getting funding he wanted and thus disbanding Parliament!

Both Charles and his father, King James, had been outrageously arrogant, believing in the "divine right of kings." Because they were kings, God wanted them to be kings, they figured, and the only ones in charge.

On the other hand, Oliver, a Puritan, believed God would help the freedom-loving underdogs, and with this confidence he went after the monarchy.

In the movie, as a member of Parliament, he stood in its chambers and railed against the king. (But historically he railed against the Church of England bishops.) Soon he joined forces with others discontented with the monarchy. (Inaccurately in the movie, it was always Cromwell leading them to oppose the monarchy.)

This resulted in Cromwell going into battle with his ragtag army of angry farmers, pitting pitchforks against the firearms of the disciplined British regiments, getting routed in their first battle. At this point they began training as citizen soldiers, with Cromwell at their lead. (In reality he was only one of a number of commanders.)

Then the tide turned.

And the commoners won.

A major upset by the underdogs.

In the movie, Oliver Cromwell led all the major battle scenes, but in reality he was prominent in only 2—at Marston Moor in July 1644 and Nasebuy 11 months later, neither of which he actually led, but he was a leading officer engaged in combat.

On one occasion only was he the chief commander—during a short-lived Second English Civil War at Preston, England, in which he led 9,000 men against Scottish allies to the king, as they wanted to put Charles I back in power. (Charles and his father, King James, had actually hailed from Scotland before receiving the English throne—James had actually ruled there 29 years as James VI, king of Scotland, before taking over England's crown) These allies had armies twice the size of Oliver's—but Oliver's troops won.

While the movie had some historical inaccuracies, the overall depiction of Cromwell's motives and successes was essentially accurate, giving most viewers a decent sense of it.

In the end, Cromwell's side won, and for it, they got their freedom. Parliament's troops marched on the monarchy's manor and arrested King Charles I. Oliver pushed for the death penalty, as in the movie, trying to persuade a reluctant Parliament—no English king had ever been executed. (In reality Cromwell was only one of several protagonists who pushed for the king's execution.) But Parliament finally gave in, and they beheaded King Charles I.

Then, ironically, Cromwell soon got fed up with Parliament and, like the king, disbanded it. However, unlike the king, Cromwell did not do it for revenge; rather, he saw the misuse of privileges by men in Parliament, so he marched his army into the House of Commons and sent it packing.

Cromwell then set up a free republic, and was made "Lord Protector of the Commonwealth."

He was offered the position of king, but declined, wanting his new assembly—the Barebones Parliament—to rule the nation instead. Thus, he sacrificed the highest of personal honors so his country could have a constitutional republic.

In all, Oliver Cromwell had served as Lord Protectorate of the Commonwealth for 4 years and 10 months—December 1653 till his death in September 1658. But, like his Catholic and Church of England predecessors, his legacy is obscured by controversy, which also illustrates the in-kind Separatist persecution of Catholics and mainstream Protestants after the Catholics and Protestants had persecuted each other and the Separatists.

Cromwell instigated massacres in Ireland for military purposes to put Ireland in line, but his underlings went far beyond that, attacking and killing thousands of soldiers and civilians, with one of his generals burning crops, causing the starvation of 600,000 of the 1.4 million Irish inhabitants. Because of that, although Oliver was not directly responsible for their starvation, he is often linked to it; and hated in Ireland to this day because of it and because he was actually tied to other massacres there, which he felt were necessary. His reasoning was that Ireland was predominantly Catholic. He was a Puritan and hated Catholic sympathizers, having learned of Catholic abuses of Reformers in Europe. But he obviously did not go about his opposition of Catholicism in the proper manner.

Cromwell died in 1658. His son Richard took over briefly. But in 1660 Richard lost the confidence of Parliament.

So Charles II returned his family to power, pulling the country back into a monarchy with himself as king—not just for England, but Scotland, Ireland, and Wales—as the first ruler of "Great Britain" (although his grandfather, James I, called himself the first king of Great Britain). And he grabbed up all this power in time for his 30th birthday. He would rule a quarter of a century—somewhat longer than his father or grandfather—until 1685.

Seems it simply was not time for England to have a free republic.

Despite their remarkably positive contributions and foresight, Oliver Cromwell and his allies became the 3rd of a 3-legged "tyranny" (if one factors in the Irish massacres) that had been part of 3 major religious movements: the Catholics had been first, for 12 centuries, then mainstream Anglican Protestants for 1 century thus far, and now the Separatist Protestants for 11½ years.

Such were also the ups and downs of English rule during the 1500s and 1600s—the first centuries of the Reformation.


During the 2 centuries following the Reformation, the Pilgrims would land in America in 1620, seeking religious liberty. Other colonists would arrive, including Roger Williams, founder of the Baptist church in America and founder and governor of Rhode Island. (He was also the first abolitionist in North America, and attempted to prohibit slavery in all 13 original colonies.) Unbeknownst to most people, as this part is not taught in school textbooks, Roger Williams sought for the true church of Jesus Christ through his lifetime. He eventually stepped down from leading the Baptist church, stating, "There is no regularly constituted church of Christ on earth, nor any person qualified to administer any church ordinances; nor can there be until new Apostles were sent by the great Head of the church, for whose coming I am seeking."[8]

Williams also stated, "The apostasy . . . hath so far corrupted all, that there can be no recovery out of that apostasy until Christ shall send forth new apostles to plant churches anew."[9]

John Wesley, founder of Methodism, similarly states, "It does not appear that these extraordinary gifts of the Holy Spirit were common in the church for more than 2 or 3 centuries. We seldom hear of them after that fatal period which the emperor Constantine called himself a Christian, and from a vain imagination of promoting the Christian cause thereby, heaped riches and power and honor upon Christians in general, but in particular upon the Christian clergy."[10]

(Details of those centuries following Christ and the emperor Constantine are contained in Appendix U, "Christianity after Christ: 17 Centuries of Conflict.")

Thomas Jefferson, an insightful student of Christianity, wrote a letter on June 26, 1822, to Benjamin Waterhouse, criticizing the intrusion of Greek philosophy on primitive Christianity[11] (also discussed in Appendix U). Jefferson followed up a month later in another letter: "Happy in the prospect of a restoration of primitive Christianity, I must leave to younger athletes to encounter and lop off the false branches which have been grafted into it by the mythologists of the middle and modern ages."[12] (The myths are also discussed in Appendix U.)

The Reformation became the key component in preparing the world for the full Restoration under Joseph Smith, when God the Father, his son Jesus Christ, and angels would bring forth the full Church of Jesus Christ and its priesthood authority, just as it was in the 1st century under the reign of Christ and his Twelve Apostles. This is all part of the mandate and bold claim of the Church of Jesus Christ of Latter-day Saints.

APPE S NDIX

# Beliefs in the Afterlife:
# Catholic vs. Protestant vs. Latter-day Saint

(REFERENCED IN APPENDIX R)

In the Catholic, Protestant, and Latter-day Saint views of the Afterlife, both similarities and stark differences exist. The traditional Protestant stance is that a person goes to either heaven or hell—period. To born-again and many other Protestants, accepting Jesus Christ as one's savior, despite the degree of sinning one continues to engage in, qualifies him for heaven. To many Protestants, even if a person never heard of Christ, such as in the farthest reaches of Africa, when he dies, he is thrust down to hell. For those believing in these strictest interpretations, believing in Jesus Christ is the only thing keeping people out of hell—no matter what their works.

To the Catholics, there is heaven and hell as well. But there is also a grace period of sorts (if one considers suffering grace) called Purgatory. Hell, to the Catholics, is a permanent place, much lower than Purgatory, as the final landing spot for the wicked, and by ancient tradition is believed to be located in the "bowels of the earth," deep under the ground, similar in fact to the visual imagery of the 1970 movie, *Scrooge* (the musical adaptation of Charles Dickens' *A Christmas Carol*, starring Albert Finney). This movie includes a fairly graphic scene in which Ebenezer Scrooge sees the future—his own funeral, followed by being thrust down into the bowels of the earth for his earthly deeds of greed and selfishness, primarily for not helping his fellow man, there to live in the pits of the inferno, where his old business partner, Jacob Marley, introduces his heavy chain to him, for Scrooge to carry about for eternity.

When the movie was released for its first television network showing years later, program directors chose not to include this scene, perhaps fearing it was too frightening for some (or perhaps they found it too out of harmony with progressive sectarian beliefs that no consequences exist in the hereafter for what one does in this life).

Hell in the Catholic tradition is for those who cannot obtain forgiveness. For these souls, no amount of suffering in Purgatory can release them into heaven. They simply go to hell and stay.

The Latter-day Saints' view of heaven and hell are revolutionary, yet grounded in the Bible, and considerably more upbeat.

They believe that when a person dies he goes to the Spirit World, a temporary place before the Resurrection. This Spirit World is divided in two—Paradise (for the honest and honorable, even if they never heard of Christ) and Spirit Prison (for those who knowingly broke God's commandments and were dishonest and dishonorable).

Catholics' Purgatory is akin to the Latter-day Saints' Spirit Prison—which is a *temporary* place for the sinful immediately after death. But to Latter-day Saints, Spirit Prison is for those who have known right from wrong, yet willfully sinned, and rejected repentance.

According to the Atonement doctrine, Latter-day Saints believe that Christ already went through suffering at both Gethsemane and on the cross to pay for the sins of all. Nevertheless, Christ's suffering only goes into effect for those souls who repent and utilize His Atonement, allowing them to not have to suffer in the next life *if* they repent in this life.

In Latter-day Saint scripture, the *Doctrine and Covenants*, is a revelation given to Joseph Smith in March 1830 at Manchester, New York, quoting the Savior, Jesus Christ:

"I command you to repent . . . lest . . . your sufferings [in Spirit Prison] be sore—how sore you know not, how exquisite you know not, yea, how hard to bear you know not.

"For behold, I, God, have suffered these things for all, that they might not suffer if they would repent:

"But if they would not repent they must suffer even as I;

"Which suffering caused myself, even God, the greatest of all, to tremble because of pain, and to bleed at every pore, and to suffer both body and spirit—and would that I might not drink the bitter cup, and shrink—

"Nevertheless, glory be to the Father, and I partook and finished my preparations unto the children of men.

"Wherefore, I command you again to repent, lest I humble you with my almighty power; and that you confess your sins, lest you suffer these punishments of which I have spoken." (D&C 19:15–18).[1]

In summary, for those who do not repent, the designated place for suffering is Spirit Prison, which, to Latter-day Saints, is hell. But it is temporary. Until one's sins are paid for or until they repent. As a place, it has an end, after which all souls are released.

Thus, after a person dies, and after they spend time in the Spirit World (Paradise or Spirit Prison), they are resurrected. Then they face the Final Judgment before God. There they are assigned to 1 of 3 degrees of heaven, which the Apostle Paul writes about in Corinthians of the New Testament—comparing the highest degree of heaven to the brightness of the sun and the lowest degree of heaven to the brightness of the stars, and a middle degree of heaven to the brightness of the moon—a visual concept for early Christians to easily grasp.

Since the Catholic doctrine of hell is defined as forever, it is a far cry from the LDS view of punishment in the Afterlife. The LDS doctrine holds an ultimately optimistic view—of even those who suffer in Spirit Prison (hell) eventually being admitted to the various degrees of heaven that all mankind will eventually attain. (The one exception, for a comparatively few people who qualify for it on this earth, is "perdition," which would be similar to the Catholic "hell;" however, Latter-day Saints believe it is not located per early Catholic doctrine in the bowels of the earth, and that an extremely small number of individuals qualify for it).

One additional aspect of Christ's mission on earth was to pay the price necessary for all mankind to be resurrected, to receive their mortal bodies in a perfected state, after each person has first died and gone to the Spirit World. That Resurrection will take place in steps, Latter-day Saints believe, with the most righteous being resurrected first.

The doctrines of Catholic, Protestant, and Latter-day Saints contain some common denominators, but also remarkable contrasts, and one of the primary messages of LDS missionaries is an explanation of why they believe as they do.

A P P E N D I X

# English Bibles That Shook the World

(REFERENCED IN CHAPTER 26)

Centuries before the Great Reformers translated and printed their Bibles, early attempts were made to translate the Bible to English. These English translations were not related directly to the Reformation and, in fact, were the work of monks whose translations may have been on the sly, or perhaps were closely monitored by the Roman Catholic Church, but it simply didn't care.

At that time (600–1200 A.D.), there were no challenges to the church, based on those translations. Thus, having a few hand-written English Bible portions around provided no apparent concerns to anyone. But these works inspired others later to translate complete editions of the Bible, instigating a veritable firestorm: those later translators would call the church on the carpet for various doctrines and practices not in harmony with the Bible, which eventually lead to the Reformation. (See Appendix R, "Launching the Reformation: Prelude to the Restoration".)

The early English versions, however, were especially innocuous, in part because they included very little scripture and mostly personal commentary. This early period lasted about 7 centuries, from the late 600s to the late 1300s.

Noteworthy is the fact that they were written mostly in the era of *Old English*, with only a handful of words per paragraph that would be recognizable to today's readers, as analyzed by the author and illustrated in the outline below. This outline delineates the 3 eras of English from which English Bible translators hailed:

1. *Old English* (approx. 450 to 1154 A.D.). If today's average English reader were to look at it, they would understand about 8%—1 in 12 words—from a sample of an unnamed 867 A.D. Anglo-Saxon chronicle analyzed by the author.

2. *Middle English* (approx. 1154–1470 A.D.) has between 33% and 50% of words that are both recognizable and understandable to today's readers. For this analysis, the author used the Wycliffe Bible (from 1384 A.D.), which has about 33% of words that are understandable, and Chaucer's *Canterbury Tales* (from 1390 A.D.), which has about 50% of words that are understandable.

3. *Early Modern English* (approx. 1470–1650 A.D.) has, in the author's estimation, about 97% of words that are understandable. This is evidenced by an example of one of William Shakespeare's 154 sonnets—"From Fairest Creatures We Desire Increase" (published in or before 1599)—as well as from the King James Version of the Bible (published in 1611). However, the earliest portion of the Early Modern English period, which is 140 years earlier at about 1470 A.D., has less recognizable words— considerably greater than 50% but less than 97%.

Of the 7 centuries that primitive English Bible translations were written, 5 centuries were in *Old English* and 2 were in *Middle English*.

Following is a brief breakdown of the first English translations of the Bible:

First, in the late 600s, was a translation by Venerable Bede (a monk at Monkwearmouth in northeast England).[1]

Then came a few other *Old English* translations between the 600s and 1000s:

One Old English writer named Aldhelm (a monk at Malmsbury, Wiltshire in southwest England), translated sizeable segments of various books of today's Bible plus the complete Book of Psalms in the second half of the 600s.

In the 900s came an *Old English* translation of the 4 gospels (Matthew, Mark, Luke, and John) known as the "Lindisfarne Gospels," written between the lines of the Latin text by Aldred the Scribe (a monk at Chester-le-Street, a town in Durham County of northeast England). This is the oldest *existing* translation of that part of the New Testament in any form of English.

In about 990 A.D. came the Wessex Gospels, the first translation of the 4 gospels without the accompanying Latin text and supposedly written by Ælfric of Bath (a monk in Bath, Sommerset, of southwest England).

In the 1000s Ælfric of Eynsham (a monk, teacher, and scholar in Winchester, of south-central England), translated most of the Old Testament into *Old English*, but included little biblical text and presented mostly his own commentary, which was still the style of early English translators.

In about the year 1154 came *Middle English*, as shown in the chart above. This was a period lasting until about 1470. In the first century of Middle English—the 1100s—another sketchy Bible text with mostly personal opinions was produced, called the *Ormulum*, written by Orm (a monk in Borne, Lincolnshire, of central eastern England).

Later came other works in *Middle English*:

In the first half of the 1300s Richard Rolle de Hampole (a monk, writer, and hermit in Yorkshire, of northern England) wrote an English Psalter.[2]

But in the second half of that same century—the 1300s—the world seemed to take a spin in a different direction.

The English Bible revolution was launched.

Until then, English translations had been written by the monks of the church per the above, with excerpts from the Bible that bothered no one.

But that era came crashing to an end. With the Wycliffe Bible.

In 1380 John Wycliffe was the first person to translate the complete English Bible with all 80 books, handwriting the entire manuscript.[3]

Unfortunately, his source documents were faulty—they had been edited and changed over the centuries from the original manuscripts. And this would be true of every single Bible translation in coming centuries, as well as all previous centuries (except for the long-lost original manuscripts of the 1st century).

Nevertheless, with this much material from which to work, Wycliffe and other forerunners to the Reformation could see discrepancies in what they were translating vs. what the church was practicing.

Blatantly, Wycliffe and his followers began to *oppose Roman church doctrine.*

Wycliffe was soon branded a heretic by church authorities. But his work was just beginning.

After translating the Bible from Latin, he began grinding out additional copies, all by hand, plugging along at 2–3 words per minute, taking 8 months per copy, even with the apparent use of scribes. This was 70 years before the invention of the printing press.

(For details on the process of how only 2–3 words at a time could be written with a quill pen, see Appendix M: "Theories Attacking the *Book of Mormon*.")

Wycliffe's efforts to get the scripture into the hands of others required remarkable determination and grit.

Because of the ripple effect in having a full Bible—complete with followers that could challenge the church—the institution took retribution against him. Some 44 years after he died, he was targeted for revenge by the pope, who ordered Wycliffe's bones dug up, crushed, burned, and tossed into the River Swift.[4]

(Latter-day Saints would place this in perspective—aside from a hateful desecration of his grave, he was obviously unharmed, untouched, and pain-free, while of course off-limits to the reach of the church and safe in the Spirit World, perhaps even chuckling at his would-be persecutors trying to nail him.)

But Wycliffe's limited distribution of his handwritten Bible copies was a prelude to the Great Reformers. They were the men soon to be born who would carve up the Catholic Church in Europe, stripping it of its power over numerous countries when local dukes and princes would ally themselves with these Bible translator/Reformers and their followers—and tear themselves away from Rome.

In the 1500s—142 years after Wycliffe's Bible—the Reformation was officially launched.

In March 1522 Martin Luther released his New Testament in German. It was the first Bible ever printed outside of the Latin Vulgate, and 3 presses were used to publish his first edition. Twelve years later he released his Old Testament.

Soon, a plethora of English translations hit the scene—all written in the style above termed *Early Modern English*, the period of 1470–1650. More significant than the style of English is the fact they revealed a vast difference in the doctrines taught in the 1st century by Christ's apostles vs. doctrines now being taught by the pope's cardinals at Rome.

These are all the major English Bible editions during the Reformation:

1. William Tyndale's Bible. After Wycliffe's handmade copies in 1380, fearless Reformer William Tyndale took it to the next step: he used a more accurate, Greek-based source than the Latin sources that Wycliffe had used, and he launched the first English Bible to come from *a printing press*—the New Testament in 1526 and the first 5 books of the Old Testament in 1530. (He never printed more than these 5 books of the Old Testament, however, although he *translated* 15 of the 39 Old Testament books.)

The Greek-based source he used—which Martin Luther also used—was a translation by Desiderius Erasmus, the revolutionary Roman Catholic priest who had translated the New Testament into Greek as early as 1516,[5] using more accurate Greek manuscripts than those from which the Latin Vulgate had been translated 11¼ centuries earlier (see Appendix Q: "The Three Families of Bible Manuscripts"), and who had translated with considerably more talent.

His work from existing Greek manuscripts provided a considerably more accurate rendition of the Bible than the Latin manuscripts used for the Vulgate, according to Latter-day Saint theology, by using deductive reasoning, as Joseph Smith would later claim the Martin Luther translation was the most accurate Bible he had seen, even more accurate than the King James Version,[6] the official English version used by the LDS faith, as reviewed in the text.

Tyndale's version in English, using the same Greek-based translation by Erasmus that Luther used, was very much a breakthrough in English Bible versions. (See Appendix R, "Launching the Reformation: Prelude to the Restoration" for a review of Tyndale's life story and how German authorities stopped the presses. The result was Tyndale's first attempt at printing being sabotaged, resulting in only a small portion of his first edition getting printed in 1525.)

The following year, 1526, he pulled off publishing his 2nd edition—the first full English New Testament ever printed.

Nine years later came the next Bible . . .

2.  The Coverdale Bible, in 1535, was *the 1st complete printed Bible in English*, using Martin Luther's German text (and thus the Greek text of Desiderius Erasmus, since Luther used Erasmus as his Greek source for translations).

Only 2 years later came the next . . .

3.  The Matthew-Tyndale Bible of 1537 was the 2nd complete Bible printed in English. It used Tyndale's New Testament translation and part of his Old Testament—but only as much as he had been able to translate before his capture and execution. Myles Coverdale translated the rest of the Old Testament (and the Apocrypha) from German and Latin sources. This Bible was actually the work of 3 men in at least 5 languages. John Rogers

used the name Thomas Matthew and was its editor as well as translator for some parts. For his efforts Rogers was burned at the stake in 1555 at Smithfield (now northwest London), England, the first Reformer victim of the brutal Queen Mary.[7] (More on her in Appendix R as well.)

Two years later came the next version . . .

4.  Taverner's Bible of 1539. Considered in some circles a "minor Bible," this was a revised version of the Matthew-Tyndale Bible, revised by Richard Taverner, who used words of local origin—those of "pure Saxon ancestry"[8] instead of foreign words that were hard to understand. He also utilized easily understood, powerful expressions.

That same year another Bible was released . . .

5.  The Great Bible of 1539. King Henry VIII granted a royal license to print this version, so this was the first "authorized Bible," 6 decades before King James would issue his world-famous Authorized Version. Ironically, until the Great Bible was completed, Henry VIII granted use of the Matthew-Tyndale Bible for a short time—a Bible of revolutionary Protestants! This was especially ironic in that Henry VIII had spent years of his life and thrown many a tirade, and even had ordered death warrants against William Tyndale and others connected with the English Bible revolution. Yet here he was, for a time, using their Bible!

The Great Bible got its name from its large size, with pages coming in at a commanding 15 by 10 inches. But it had "great" similarities to the Matthew-Tyndale Bible. (A more appropriate, albeit tongue-in-cheek nickname for it could have been the "Great Similarities" Bible.) It was prepared by Myles Coverdale, rather than John Rogers. And it is like the Matthew-Tyndale Bible in these 2 respects: (1) the New Testament is fully Tyndale's, while (2) the Old Testament is partially Tyndale's, with Myles Coverdale finishing it.[9]

A huge difference in the Great Bible vs. the Matthew-Tyndale Bible is that a large portion of the Great Bible includes the Latin Vulgate in italics sandwiched between Tyndale's verses. These additions were probably to appease the more conservative Englishmen who could view only the Vulgate as legitimate. Another major difference was that this Bible had portions of Tyndale's work removed—those which were deemed objectionable by certain bishops chosen by King Henry VIII to review it.

Twenty-one tumultuous years passed until the next version . . .

6.   The Geneva Bible of 1557 (as the New Testament) and 1560 (as the complete Bible). This work has a fascinating history. It was in English, but published in Switzerland and for a reason. The Reformers were on the run from England. (See Appendix R, "Launching the Reformation: Prelude to the Restoration" for details.) Worthy of note, the Geneva Bible retains over 90% of Tyndale's original English translation.

It was the first Bible to have numbered verses added and was considered the first English study Bible, complete with commentary, marginal notes, and references. But some marginal notes were wondrously controversial. So controversial, in fact, that it led to the next major edition.

Eleven years later . . .

7.   The Bishops' Bible was launched in 1568 under authority of Queen Elizabeth. (Thus it was the 2nd "authorized Bible.") It's purpose? To replace the incendiary Geneva Bible, which had those controversial marginal notes angering Church of England officials. How did it anger them? It attacked the church at Rome. Why would English officials care? By now, Queen Elizabeth sought to appease both camps—the Catholics and Protestants in her country—and this was her reason: the Church of England now saw itself as *both Protestant and Catholic!* It wanted to tie itself back to the original apostolic church, but without recognizing the pope in Rome. So, on somewhat of a public relations tightrope, the church mandated changes to fit their new narrative: marginal notes in the Geneva Bible, which called the pope "Antichrist," had to be replaced. Thus, the Church of England came up with its own Bible. But it didn't catch on. Nobody, in fact, wanted it. Except for some stuffy old Church of England readers who liked their theology dry.

Figuring it could be improved and made more sellable, it was substantially revised 4 years later, in 1572. But even that one didn't sell. Adding dryness to dryness rarely does.

8.   Next came the Catholics' answer to the hog-wild printing projects of the Protestants—the first Roman Catholic Bible in English—published in 1609: the Douay-Rheims Version, from the towns of Douay and Rheims, France. The 1582 New Testament was released first, from Rheims, France, then came the 2-volume Old Testament in 1609–1610, from the University of Douai (different spelling than the town) at Douay, France. Understandably, they were influenced by the Latin Vulgate.

Meanwhile, *another Bible in Latin* was being revised and completed by the Catholics in 1590, called the Sistine Vulgate. (The 1590 Sistine Vulgate was prepared in hurry-up mode and published with numerous errors, its publishers wanting to get it out to compete with the plethora of Protestant versions taking over the Bible publishing world of the 1500s. Because of its errors, this 1590 version was revised and published as the Clementine Vulgate just 2 years later, in 1592—and it would become the standard Latin Bible for the next 387 years, until 1979, when the *Nova Vulgata* would be released.)

Back to the English translations . . .

9.   Several more tumultuous decades after the previous English Bible of 1568 came the granddaddy of them all—the widest read of all translations: the King James Version of 1611, which would become the most printed book in history among free countries. Unknown to many, this was actually the 3rd authorized English Bible (after the Great Bible and Bishops' Bible, mentioned above).

But the King James Version ("KJV") was slow to catch on. The independent Protestant groups were still in love with the Geneva Bible of 1557/1560, and it would remain that way another 50 years after the KJV was released! Thus, the Geneva Bible was the most popular Bible on earth for a hundred years—half of that before the KJV was published and half after. Even those sailing on the Mayflower to America, the Jamestown colonists, and most other settlers in America bonded to the Geneva Bible.

This was the Bible for true Protestants escaping England for religious liberty as well as those remaining behind, choosing not to be affiliated with either the Church of England or the Roman Catholic Church.

Protestants seemed to want an independent Bible because of the way they looked askance at the Anglicans, due in large measure to the aforementioned *Catholic-Protestant two-edged sword* wielded by the Church of England—which included years of persecuting those who had broken away from them.

John Bunyan, for example, author of *The Pilgrim's Progress from This World to That Which Is to Come* (published in 1677 and later translated to over 200 languages), wrote his world-famous work in prison from 1660 to 1672—a 12-year stint for the crime of *preaching*,[10] placed there by complaints from the Church of England.[11]

His is one isolated example of hundreds of Protestants persecuted by the Archbishop of Canterbury and other leaders of the Church of England.

But at some point the Church of England ceased its persecutions of independent Protestants.

Even after that, understandably, it took many decades for the independent Protestant world to include the Church of England as part of the Protestant "fold."

The result was the Church of England's King James Version not being trusted for decades by true Protestants, who were quite happy, thank you, with their beloved Geneva Bible.

But it finally got accepted, then outlasted all others for hundreds of years.

As for how the King James Version got launched . . .

Upon the death of Queen Elizabeth I, a new ruler took over—King James I of England, who had been Prince James VI of Scotland. The Anglican clergy approached this new king in 1604 and announced their desire for a new translation to replace the Bishops' Bible. The reason: they knew the Geneva Bible was still the Bible of choice among Reformist readers, as it was much more popular than Queen Elizabeth's comparatively stuffy Bishops' Bible.

So Church of England authorities, feeling a competitive streak similar to the church at Rome, feared being left in the dust by Protestant publishers and their beloved Geneva Bible. They wanted something "better." Yet something less incendiary. After all, the Geneva Bible's controversial marginal notes about the pope being the Antichrist still wasn't sitting well with Anglican Church authorities who, wishing to look dignified, wanted to distance themselves from those blasted anti-Catholic notes.

With this as the backstory, the King James Bible proponents got the green light and proceeded to hire 47 scholars to make it all happen. They wished to create the "translation to end all translations.

And here's what they did . . .

When the King James scholars translated, they used the Tyndale New Testament, his incomplete Old Testament, the Coverdale Bible, the Matthew-Tyndale Bible, Taverner's Bible (a few phrases can be traced to it), the Great Bible, the Geneva Bible, and the Rheims New Testament.

Remarkably, the KJV used 83% of Tyndale's text for the New Testament and 76% of his Old Testament, according to one study,[12] while another states it used 84% of Tyndale for the New Testament and 75.8% for the Old Testament.[13]

Thus, Tyndale had more influence on it than all the other work by the 47 scholars combined!

Ironically, according to one source, the KJV is also *95% the same as the Geneva Bible.*[14]

Yet the Geneva is not influenced by the Roman church's Rheim's New Testament, which the King James translators did incorporate into the KJV somewhat. Nevertheless, despite the qualms some Protestants today have with the KJV because of its partial use of the Catholic Rheim's, the First Presidency of the LDS Church endorses the KJV as the most accurate of all English Bibles, as explained in the text.

The KJV also had some influence from the Latin Vulgate, but the real basis—the most important influence on the KJV (and all other printed English Bibles during that first, remarkable 85-year period from 1526 to 1611) was a Greek text known as

*Textus Receptus*, compiled by the aforementioned Desiderius Erasmus, as well as the later Theodore Beza.

(An interesting aside: Desiderius Erasmus began work on his Greek and Latin New Testament in 1512, collecting all the Latin Vulgate manuscripts possible—which had by now gone through a 1,134-year stretch of altered manuscripts—in order to compare it to his Greek.)

Despite the challenge of comparing all the above English Bibles, the 47 King James translators had another formidable task: to decipher fragments of Greek and Hebrew manuscripts—2,000 in all. But they, like Erasmus's and Beza's source documents, were copies of copies *ad infinitum*, leaving the translators a huge pile of papers with confusing marginal glosses to sift through and guess at.

The 47 scholars began their work in 1605 and spent 2 years in private research among themselves.

In 1607 they assembled their work, which was a complete and impressive process. Nevertheless, they did lack the original, unaltered manuscripts from the 1st century A.D., just as John Wycliffe, William Tyndale, and all others had earlier.

In 1610 the book went to press. And in 1611 it was released as the 1611 King James Bible. It was huge—16 inches high—meant for pulpit use initially and chained to every pulpit in England.

Then printing began for the normal-sized copies to be read by individuals. Despite all that effort, the Geneva Bible still reigned supreme, as described above for another half century after the KJV was released.

In short, the King James Version was meant to compete with the Protestant's Geneva Bible, but it had a formidable task in front of it. Slowly the Protestant world did come to accept the KJV as stated, with sales of it finally outpacing the Geneva Bible 50 years later.

10. After the King James Version was published in 1611, 158 years passed until an unusual edition was published—which includes this *little-known fact*: the KJV was revised in 1769 as the 1769 Baskerville revision. All editions since include the spelling and wording revisions of the 1769 Baskerville, *but with*

*no mention of it being revised anywhere in the pages of the KJV,
even until today.* The Baskerville edition includes the original
1611 preface, adding to the "cover-up." Perhaps the publishers
were fearful it might hurt sales if they marketed it as something
other than a "true 1611 King James Version," according to analyst
John L. Jeffcoat III.[15]

Because of this Bible-translating revolution, the Reformation
was solidly underway. Its effect would be indelibly imprinted
upon the history of European nations and their peoples—and
what was yet to come . . . in America.

For now, that included the English Civil War, when Oliver
Cromwell helped dispose of King James's son, Charles I, and
helped launch a Protestant-led constitutional republic. This was
far ahead of its time, of course, and would last only 18 years.
(See Appendix R, "Launching the Reformation: Prelude to the
Restoration" for details.) Yet the Reformers grew in confidence
from this, and many began setting their sights on America,
laying the groundwork for their descendants to fully implement
a lasting constitutional republic inspired by the American
Revolution of 1776—just over a century away.

The "stepping stone centuries" that led to the First Amendment
in America—of freedom of religion—along with the religious
freedoms in Europe and much of the free world, were the
1500s and 1600s. These were the centuries in which the Great
Reformers and their Bibles blazed the trail in the theological
wilderness, shedding good blood to establish future freedoms,
setting the stage for a people with religious liberty under the
rule of law. All of which was a prelude to the Restoration of the
Church of Jesus Christ in the latter days.

# APPENDIX U

# Christianity after Christ:
# 17 Centuries of Conflict

## REFERENCED IN CHAPTER 26

The era in world history from about 100 A.D. until 1830 is known as the Great Apostasy. This period, according to Latter-day Saints, no longer had Christ's original church upon the earth. These 17 centuries also lacked His priesthood authority on the planet. Also known as the spiritual dark ages, it was followed by a restoration of Christ's original church 17 centuries later, simply termed *The Restoration*, as foretold by prophets at various places in the original King James Bible, such as Isaiah 29:13:

"Wherefore the Lord said, Forasmuch as this people draw near me with their mouth, and with their lips do honor me, but have removed their heart far from me, and their fear toward me is taught by the precept of men:

"Therefore, behold, I will proceed to do a marvellous work among this people, even a marvellous work and a wonder: for the wisdom of their wise men shall perish, and the understanding of their prudent men shall be hid."[1]

Although Christian believers remained on the earth to continue a belief in Christ after 100 A.D., from that time forward Christianity lacked Christ's simple teachings as well as the proper keys to maintaining His organization.

In a nutshell, the Savior lived from 4 or 5 B.C. to perhaps 30 A.D. While alive He established His church with twelve apostles at the foundation, and was Himself the chief cornerstone. After He died, the Apostles continued their ministry for about 70 more years, keeping the church intact, until one by one they were killed, and the foundation of the church crumbled.

At that point the original Christian church that the Savior organized became fragmented and, when the last apostle, John, withdrew from his ministry in about 100 A.D., the authority to administer the church in the name of Jesus Christ was also withdrawn from the earth—as well as the keys to running the church.

According to early and even ancient historical sources cited below, this is how it happened . . .


The New Testament reveals that when an Apostle would die or be killed, he would be replaced in order to keep the number exactly at 12.[2] (See this endnote for examples of Apostles being replaced.)

This was doable but difficult for the Twelve, because their assignment required them to go "into all the world" to preach. Meanwhile, they depended on local church government to keep the church intact at each city and village where congregations of the church were organized. To do so, they appointed local officers—bishops over larger congregations and presiding elders over smaller ones.[3]

Apostles were men of general authority or jurisdiction. They had overall supervision of the entire church, as well as the keys to keeping the church going forward.

But from the get-go, the Apostles and others were targeted by their enemies—the Jews and later the Romans. And one by one the Apostles were killed. Specifically:

James the Greater was killed by Herod Agrippa with a sword in 27 A.D.[4]

James the Lesser was thrown off the top of the Jerusalem temple, 100 feet down, then stoned and beaten to death in about 49 A.D.[5]

Mark was dragged by a horse through the city streets of Alexandria, Egypt, till he was killed in 50 A.D.[6]

Philip was crucified in 54 A.D., Barnabus was stoned to death in 62 A.D., Paul was beheaded by Nero in 67 A.D., Matthew was beheaded in 60–70 A.D., Andrew was hanged on an olive tree in 70 A.D., Thomas was speared, tortured with hot plates, and burned to death in 70 A.D. Nathanael was flayed, then crucified in 70 A.D., Matthias was stoned while on a cross in 70 A.D., Judas Thaddeus was beaten with sticks by pagan priests in 72 A.D., Simon was crucified in 74 A.D., and Luke was hanged in about 84 A.D. Most of these details come from Eusebius, the first great Christian church historian, in his *Ecclesiastical History*,[7] as well as from Josephus and Jerome.[8]

After each Apostle was executed, the surviving members of the Twelve were so persecuted they could not even meet to replace the ones killed.

Finally only one Apostle was left—John—who was banished by the civil authorities to the isle of Patmos in the Mediterranean Sea, where he stayed until the death of the Roman Emperor Domitian in 96 A.D.[9]

His ministry ended, with nothing more heard about him after about 100 A.D. (probably 101 A.D.), and the keys to keeping the church and priesthood alive were taken from the earth.

The reason?

Wickedness had become rampant inside the church. Ordinances and beliefs had been changed by regular members without the authority to do so, and whole congregations began ignoring their leaders.

How do we know this? The Apostles wrote letters that lasted a few years and were re-copied before the originals decayed or were lost. These letters, which became part of the New Testament, report the Twelve visiting local branches of the church to help local leaders with problems. They also wrote these branch leaders about problems. These were the epistles of Paul, Peter, James, John, and Jude in the New Testament. (Paul's letters alone comprise 13 of the 27 books and 31.57% of the actual text of the New Testament.)[10]

Yet the problems in the Christian church seemed to only get worse. Some members began denying the Savior. Others were discounting the resurrection.

After wickedness had rooted itself in the church sufficiently, the Lord stopped replacing His Apostles.

Hence, John was the last Apostle.

Many remaining Christians were executed by the Romans. In public arenas, Roman citizens cheered lions tearing apart the believers unless they denied their faith. But some believers stayed valiant. Thus, some of the basic *teachings* of Christ survived, but the *authority* to administer the ordinances disappeared. And at this point, the church went into a tailspin.

Greek philosophies, pagan rites, and pre-Christian Jewish doctrine began filtering in. False, impure doctrines of all types creeped in as well, changing nearly everything about it. In summary, man-made philosophies blended in to Christianity, including *Gnosticism* (shunning the material world while seeking the secrets of the universe)[11] and *Neo-Platonism* (pursuing cosmology—a study of the origins and fate of the universe) as developed by Ammonius Saccas from Alexandria, Egypt.[12]

These philosophies skewed Christianity's simple teachings.

Outside beliefs, from various regions, also began to be absorbed into Christianity. From Egypt came the emphasis on adoring Christ's mother, Mary. From Phrygia (in today's western Turkey), in about 325 A.D., came the *actual worship* of the "great mother" (as described below).

Then, dramatic rituals outside the church began pouring in.

Will Durant, author of *Caesar and Christ: The Story of Civilization, Vol. III*, from Simon and Schuster, writes, "Christianity did not destroy paganism; it adopted it."[13]

"Greek mysteries," he states, were "passed down into the impressive mystery of the mass," with the Greek language becoming "the vehicle of Christian literature and ritual," after "having reigned for centuries over philosophy."[14]

Thus, with the authority to receive revelation for directing the church now gone—with the last apostle gone—the priesthood authority to act in Christ's name was also gone, as was the authority to baptize and confirm others and give them the Gift of the Holy Ghost. Thus, Christianity was left without revelation and without the Gift of the Holy Ghost.

The church became divided, adding problem on top of problem. Disputes over doctrine arose, including debates over the nature of God.

Physical brawls even erupted. Some of them over the doctrine of baptism, resulting in the start of baptizing babies for the first time. Bishops went head to head on other issues, resulting in bitterness and actual bloodshed.

By now, the Church of Christ had truly gone amok.

And the surviving Christians had no inspired leadership to continue.

The Great Apostasy was in full swing.

The often-asked question is, "What about Peter?" Many churches today claim to have their authority from Peter, based on Matthew 16:15–19, where the Savior says, "Thou art Peter, and upon this rock I will build my church; and the gates of hell shall not prevail against it."[15]

But Latter-day Saints maintain that popular passage is taken out of context. Christ is not referring to Peter as the rock; rather, Christ is referring to *the rock of revelation, the subject upon which Christ was already speaking*, a rock upon which Peter would depend. (This is described in the previous 2 verses when Peter says to Christ: "Thou are the Christ, the Son of the living God," and the Savior responds, "Blessed art thou, Simon Barjona: for flesh and blood hath not *revealed* it unto thee, but my Father which is in heaven."[16] And thus, "upon this rock [of revelation] I will build my church.")

When Peter was killed—between 64 and 67 A.D.[17]—the church continued, yet not by Peter appointing others (since he was not the rock), but rather by *the remaining members* of the Quorum of Twelve Apostles appointing others, using "the rock" of revelation.

This revelation came from God, which they were entitled to receive because of their priesthood authority, as recorded in the New Testament.

(Another example of priesthood authority is comparing it to modern organizations ranging from real estate to the military. In real estate, an agent cannot list or sell a person's home without both his broker's authority and the owner's authorization, even though the agent may be licensed by the state to sell real estate.

Similarly, when soldiers in the military are faced with rescuing hostages, they cannot proceed as rogue soldiers deciding who among them will lead and what they should do. They must have authority given them by their chain of command. This chain is comprised of individuals ranging from the commander-in-chief at the top to their own commanding officers, including an authorized battle plan—not one from other commanding officers, nor by another military, nor by a group of well-meaning patriots who want to help—but only by those who are duly authorized, who possess the proper "keys."

As these examples illustrate how authority works, the original church of Christ actually had Christ's priesthood authority given to His Apostles, but in time that authority—the keys—were taken from the earth.)

After the new Christian church took on pagan practices and Greek philosophies, a turnaround came.

It started to become popular. People *enjoyed* the rituals and changes, and actually began to find the church attractive.

Lions no longer dined on Christians. Christians instead were invited to dine with Roman citizens. Even given seats of honor at the dinner table. They had become popular.

But the popularity came with a price.

Church standards were lowered.

Because of this, the government stopped persecuting them.

And as a result, the church grew in numbers.

———————

Soon, along came Constantine I, Emperor of Rome. In 312 A.D. he saw Christianity as not only popular but the wave of the future.[18]

And this is why:

The Roman Empire had just been embroiled in a long civil war, and he needed something to unify his people. Religion was just the ticket. Not just any religion, but one that the masses could take to. His eyes went instantly to the new Christianity— complete with its pagan symbols and Greek-merged philosophies and mysteries of the mass. He thought of a few other things he could add to it as well. So he decided to make Christianity his state religion. He did this with a government edict in 313 A.D. called the "Edict of Milan," legalizing it as a department of civil government.[19]

Christianity was now reorganized as a government agency with the *Emperor himself ultimately in charge*—an agency alongside other departments of government, such as road-building and the military. And this is how the church became officially organized under his reign . . .

But he did not do this as an Apostle, nor as any kind of representative of Christ. He did this as the new Emperor of the Roman Empire.

Then, in order to promote Christianity, he brought in even more pagan traditions.

According to records, after he organized the church as a state agency, he was not even a Christian himself for another 25 years. And he was perhaps not the best example for the head of a church, being guilty of murder in his family.

In North Africa, a difficulty soon cropped up. A bitter division arose.[20]

Being sick of civil wars, he jumped into the fray—*even though it was a church matter*—and, as the Emperor of the Roman Empire, straightened it out.

Then he began to solidify church doctrines and essentially control the church by appointing bishops who agreed with him.

In the original church of Christ, each bishop had been equal to other bishops and could only preside over his own congregation, with no intention of taking control of another's.[21] Each also had only a single congregation. But now, under Constantine, significant changes were introduced.

In the early 300s, it was changed to *priests* overseeing a single congregation, or *parish*, while *bishops* would oversee a group of parishes, or *diocese*.

Years afterward larger houses of worship would be built, considered more significant than churches, called *cathedrals*, the headquarters of a diocese. These changes would alter what had been established by Christ, and there would be many more.

Constantine saw other problems he wanted to fix. First, he wanted to straighten out church members' beliefs. Disputes were now coming to his attention—so he decided to call councils to interpret doctrine and make it binding.[22]

At Arles (in today's France near the Mediterranean Sea) his politically appointed bishops made decisions on baptism.

But some bishops voiced objections.

Constantine hated dissent, so he swept his army through the council, leaving many lying in their gore. Those who escaped were banished.

Then, using his political authority only, he appointed other bishops to replace them.

This continued the precedent he had set of civil rulers picking bishops.[23]

Another dispute arose over the nature of God. In 325 A.D. Constantine called the Nicene Council to determine what God's nature was and to set it in a creed that people could repeat and make their mantra.

To come up with the best one, he listened to 2 bishops debate. He first liked one, then the other, changing his mind over and over, according to the persuasions of his associates. He ultimately chose the arguments of Athanasius, bishop of Alexandria, Egypt, who pushed for the Trinity: 3 Gods—the Father, Son, and Holy Ghost—in the same being. And thus he rejected Arius, a priest also from Alexandria, who pushed for

Christ as separate and distinct from, as well as subordinate to, the Father, which was more in line with New Testament teachings. (See, for example, Stephen's stoning in Acts 7:55–56 of the King James Version New Testament, showing 3 distinct beings *after* Christ's death—in addition to obviously during His life.[24]) According to non-Trinity Christian believers, such as the 1st-century Christians, the 4th-century Arius, and the 19th–21st century Latter-day Saints, the Bible passages saying Christ and the Father were one meant they were one in *purpose*, not one and the same being.

Nowhere in the Bible is the "Trinity" even mentioned, and the first writer to actually use the word "Trinity" was Tertullian, born 126 years after Christ (and about 25 years after the church fell away). Tertullian used the term "Trinity" in his works published in *Patrologia Latin*, Volumes 1–2.[25]).

But in the 300s Arius's logical explanations were overridden by the Emperor. So, with Athanasius's argument, in 325 A.D. Constantine "simplified" Christian beliefs into the Nicene Creed, which was modified somewhat 56 years later at the First Council of Constantinople, and is used today in numerous churches, where congregations recite aloud what they believe—which all goes back to this bishops' council of Constantine's political appointees.

Churches today using a form fairly close to this revised Creed of First Council of Constantinople are the Roman Catholic, Eastern Orthodox, Church of the East, Oriental Orthodox Church, African Communion, and many Protestant churches, including the Anglican Communion. (The Anglican Communion consists of 44 international denominations, autonomous but tied together through the Church of England, including the Episcopal Church U.S.A. and other Anglican churches throughout the world.[26])

With variations, this is the famous creed that begins, "I believe in one God, maker of heaven and earth, God of God, light of light, very God of very God, begotten not made . . ." (This recitation is actually from the author's memory, recited from his childhood and teen years as an "acolyte," when all the congregation would recite it together.)

However, what Constantine thought was a great idea back-fired. It led to a schism.

Those opposing the Creed were the Arians. Constantine banished them and appointed new bishops in their stead. He even had all of Arius's original writings burned.

Nevertheless, from this point on, Arianism grew and prospered, especially in outlying areas of the empire.[27]

Then Constantine's mainline church decided in 325 A.D. to promote Mary, the mother of Jesus, as a prominent figure to worship, a concept from Phrygia, as stated above. Constantine promoted this to make his church appear *different* from that of the Arians.

But this led to more schisms.[28]

And then came more changes to the church.

Clergy was now given *status* in the empire. And to show it, they began wearing the robes of royalty.[29]

By contrast, the early church leaders and, in fact, all those before the time of Constantine had worn regular clothes, according to *The Catholic Encyclopedia*:

"[In] the era before Constantine . . . priestly dress did not yet differ from the secular costume in form and ornament. The dress of daily life was worn at the offices of the Church. . . . From about the 4th to the 9th centuries [300s to 800s] . . . is the most important epoch in the history of liturgical vestments, the epoch in which not merely a priestly denim in a special sense was created, but one which at the same time determined the chief vestments of the present liturgical dress."

Thus, current priestly dress was created during Constantine's reign. And over the coming centuries—300 to 800 A.D.—It would evolve into what it is today.[30] But priestly robes were not part of the original church of Christ.

The political realm meanwhile continued to permeate everything church-related. In fact, according to *A Concise History of the Catholic Church* by Thomas Bokenkotter (Doubleday) the political world in Rome *made laws for the Church's beliefs and practices.*[31]

But Constantine had another problem on his hands. About half the Christian church did not belong to his main church; rather, they had split off into various break-off sects,[32] including Arianism. According to research by Henry Chadwick and published by Oxford University Press, as well as Eamon Duffy, published by Yale University Press, Constantine did not like the disunity, and marshaled the military to massacre some of the competing sects. He also used courts to coerce the citizens into rejecting other sects and joining his politically organized church.

To make the mainline church grow, he gifted land and money to it and granted it legal favors.[33]

Because of that, the church would become the largest landowner in the West by the 500s,[34] with an all-but-guaranteed dominance over its rival Christian sects and breakaway groups for the coming centuries.

Why Constantine went to such pains for a predominant religion is simple . . .

He hated disunity. And this is why:

Exactly 27 years before his reign, in 285 A.D., the empire had divided between east and west because of his predecessor, the emperor Diocletian.

So when Constantine came to power, he was determined to see unity. And he became obsessed with his version of Christianity outshining the others. He wanted one unified church, just as he wanted one unified empire. This is why he used compromises, creeds, and pagan rituals to popularize his church to the masses.

Ironically, he allowed some other Christian sects but did fight against those he disliked most, even using his armies to attack and crush them.

(Outlawing *all* competing Christian sects would come later, by another Roman ruler, per below.)

Constantine's final significant contribution was to found the city of Constantinople from 324 to 330 A.D. at the spot of the ancient Greek city Byzantium. He also transferred the main capital of his Roman Empire there, leaving Rome to be headquarters for only the church. Displaying his ego, he even named the newly founded city after himself.

(It would later become Europe's largest city, from 1453 to 1825, until it would be replaced by London. On 4 separate occasions it would also become the *world's* largest city in the years 340–570,[35] 1127–1145, 1153–1170,[36] and 1650–1710 A.D.[37])

In 1923, when the Republic of Turkey was created, the city of Constantinople changed its name to Istanbul, and it remains one of Europe's largest cities today.


In 337 A.D. Constantine died, ending a 25-year reign. Other Roman emperors would take over the church and keep it the official government church as well. Like him, these emperors would choose the clergy and dismiss those they disagreed with.

Additionally, "The emperors claimed for themselves the right of convoking councils," states historian Auguste Boulenger in *Historia de la Iglesia.*

"It was also the emperor who confirmed the decision of the [church] council and gave them the force of law for the whole empire."[38]

The reason?

It was still a department of the Roman government.


Then came more winds of change.

In 380 A.D. the Roman Emperor Theodosius issued a decree called the Edict of Thessalonica,[39] making Nicene Christianity the *only* church allowed in the Roman Empire.

This gave "mainstream" Christianity a monopoly.[40]

The Edict of Milan from 67 years earlier had merely legalized it—creating it as an organized church and branch of government, with emperors like Constantine attacking other churches and using courts to coerce citizens into it based on their own whims—but this new edict defined it as the only *lawful* church. All others were outlawed.

Additionally, the emperors now assumed even more power.

Whereas Constantine had presided at councils he had convened and had allowed bishops to argue, Emperor Theodosius *solely* determined church doctrine. (He liked the doctrines of 2 church leaders—Demascus I in Rome and Peter II in Alexandria—and made those doctrines the state's official religion.)

Theodosius was the last emperor to rule over the entire Roman Empire. Before dying in 395 A.D., he divided it in half between his 2 sons, with the Western Roman Empire being headquartered in Rome and the Eastern Roman Empire staying in Constantinople,[41] where it had been headquarters over the entire empire for 65 years.

Eventually, the Western Roman Empire would fall, collapsing under its own weight from a bloated bureaucracy and citizens' dependence upon it.

The most powerful nation on earth could not stay afloat anymore—it was dragged down by unmanageably high taxes caused by politicians buying votes from the non-tax-paying populace—bribing it with increased welfare in order to remain in power. It also sank from leaders not following the constitution, government excess, and devaluing the currency by dropping the silver content in coins from 100% silver to 1/5000th by 300 A.D. This occurred during the rule of Diocletian, who, in 301 A.D., 11 years before Constantine, condemned those who "are always eager to turn their own profit, even the blessings of God." He saw profits as evil, and wanted the populace to depend upon the welfare state.[42]

He succeeded.

In order to keep up with spending, the government minted more money.

Inflation ran rampant, shooting from 8 Roman dollars to buy 1 bushel of wheat in 200 A.D. to 120,000 Roman dollars to buy 1 bushel of wheat in 300 A.D., during Diocletian's rule.

Right after Diocletian came Constantine, who introduced the individual income tax. His adherence to a totalitarian state was manifest in 332 A.D. when he lashed out against people wanting a free market system. To those wishing to leave their occupations for another, he threatened them, saying they "may be bound with chains and reduced to a servile condition."[43]

Society, meanwhile, became increasingly permissive, and the moral fabric began to tear with state-sponsored orgies in the last throes of the Roman Empire. Additionally, entertainment became increasingly violent.

Once the Roman Empire was ripe, the Germanic tribes—especially the Vandals (from whom the term "vandalize" comes) and the Goths—conquered the Roman Empire's provinces in Western Europe.

Soon, Rome itself, the once-powerful city, was so ripe that it came crashing down like an ill-supported circus tent.

The 1st strike was unexpected—it was sacked by the Visigoths in 410 A.D. The 2nd strike came from the Vandals in 455 A.D.[44] (This endnote summarizes all 5 sackings after the birth of Christ.) Rome, and the entire Western Roman Empire, struggled to hold on, but, teetering under the rot of its corruption, completely collapsed in 476 A.D.

Then a German soldier came marching in to clean up.

Flavius Odoacer appointed himself the first king of Italy and officially ended the Western Roman Empire. Just 4 years later, in 480, the Byzantine Emperor Zeno also abolished it.

So with the political government of the Western Roman Empire at Rome gone, only the Eastern Roman Empire at Constantinople (which was also called the Byzantine Empire) was left. (That Eastern Roman Empire would last a thousand more years, but collapse in 1453 A.D. to the Ottoman Turks and bring an end to the 1500-year total reign of the Roman Empire,[45] as well as mark the end of the Middle Ages.[46])

The church, meanwhile, did more than survive—it grew like gangbusters. Still headquartered in Rome, it ironically thrived even with the apparent setback of not having the Western Roman Empire around to force it upon its population.[47]

Then the church gained power from another source—an unexpected one.

In 496 A.D.—20 years after the Western Roman Empire fell—a pagan king began sweeping through Western Europe, becoming the first king to unite all the tribes under one ruler.[48] And more importantly, he converted to Christianity through his wife on Christmas Day, 496 A.D., and began spreading his new religion among his conquered territories.[49] His name was Clovis I.

Now the church swept like wildfire in Western Europe, even though it was based a bit farther east, in Rome.

But it was about to be led by a Byzantine Emperor (in Constantinople), even farther east, by, once again, a political figure.

There, in 533 A.D. Emperor Justinian I decided to attack the Germans, who now controlled Italy and other western provinces from his distant headquarters. His armies initially won, but soon lost most of their gains except Rome, which they would hold onto for 200 years (till 751 A.D.). Now that Justinian ("the Great") controlled Rome, he personally took over the church.[50]

As its ruler, he ended the right of "common consent" in local church affairs. He told the clergy that they could not disagree with *anything* he proclaimed—they were allowed to only accept and ratify his acts—including on all religious matters. In 1914, at Philadelphia, ecclesiastical history professor John Cullen Ayer recorded that Justinian the Great believed "he had the right and duty of regulating by his laws the minutest details of worship and discipline and also of dictating the theological opinions to be held in the Church."[51]

The punishment for those not complying with Justinian's decree and believing different doctrines than those he set forth? Banishment.[52]

Justinian ruled the church with an iron fist for nearly 40 years—from 527 to 565 A.D. Once again this was far out of alignment with the order of the church set forth by Christ in the 1st century.

By 590 A.D., the church "had become closely linked" with the state, writes historian Earle E. Cairns.[53] It was a recurring theme.

---

Despite this setback of dictators micromanaging the church and dictating doctrine, the church continued to grow.

The next significant coup for Christianity, after the conversion of Western Europe, came almost a century later.

England, Wales, and Ireland were converted.

In 597 A.D., a monk named Augustine was sent from Rome with a group of missionaries to the Anglo-Saxons. This group arrived at Kent in southeast England, where they established the Anglican Church as a subsidiary to the church in Rome, and converted thousands of people, including the king.

The Christian church then hit another growth spurt.

A number of missionaries from Rome went to northern Europe, including Scotland, and to the Germanic and Slavic peoples, then, later, to the Vikings and other Scandinavians.[54]

But all was not well on the home front. Another emperor went meddling into church affairs in the early 600s. A Byzantine emperor, Flavius Phocas, ruled 602 to 610 A.D. and decided to fire the head of the church at Constantinople—a bishop named Cyriacus—and allow Boniface III in Rome to assume his duties, all at Boniface's request. Emperors taking sides in church matters was still an ongoing theme.

More turmoil on the home front. It was now the 700s, and with it came battles over religious icons. These icons included crosses and crucifixes, plus statues of saints and of the Mother and Christ. Most leaders opposed such additions to the church.

Including at Constantinople, with Byzantine emperor Leo III in the 730s.[55]

But in the West at Rome, church leader Gregory III disagreed with him,[56] and liked them.[57]

As usual, the Emperor won the debate.

Yet the church leader's desires prevailed 5 decades later. And this is how:

After emperor Leo III died in 741 A.D., Empress Irene of Athens reigned through various titles from 775–802 A.D. from Constantinople, and she was passionate about the veneration of icons.

But she had a royal battle on her hands.

(In defining the "veneration of icons," *The Merriam-Webster Dictionary* gives the word *veneration* as meaning "to honor (as an icon or a relic) with a ritual act of devotion."[58] The icons in question were statues, crosses, and crucifixes. [The history of word meaning and its evolution relate to a side story about dictionaries that the author has compiled in this endnote.[59]])

Despite her passionate interest in icon adoration, in 776 A.D. Empress Irene's proposal to local church leaders was shot down.

So she decided to take the fight to a church-wide council of bishops. For this, as a *political leader*, she called a *church-wide religious council* to vote on what she demanded. This was the Second Council of Nicaea in 787 A.D.,[60] where 300 bishops, led by a new church leader in Rome, passed it.

Statues and icons at church became official.[61] However, if using the 1st-century standards of the church of Christ, a decree by a political emperor or empress to change church policy would have been out of the question.

Perhaps the best known of all icons is the cross itself, which has its own extraordinary history. It came into use several decades after Christ—actually in the early 100s, according to Tertullian, in his writings during the late 100s and early 200s.[62]

However, extensive use of it as a symbol did not arise till the 300s.[63]

Graydon F. Snyder, in his book *Ante Pacem: Archaeological Evidence of Church Life Before Constantine*, states, "Most scholars now agree that the cross as an artistic reference to the passion even cannot be found prior to the time of Constantine," adding that there was "a striking lack of crosses in early Christian remains."[64]

A reason for this is explained by the *New Catholic Encyclopedia*. The early Christians "were reluctant to depict even the instrument of the Lord's passion,"[65] which coincides with Latter-day Saint policy today—of focusing on Christ's resurrection and not on the instrument of his torturous death.

While no icons are used by Latter-day Saints, they do display various paintings of inspiring scenes from the Savior's life in hallways of chapels, temples, and members' homes. They are open-minded about other Christians today using crosses and other icons, and view them as positive symbols to enhance one's faith, although they do not use icons themselves, since they were not part of the original church of Christ and mostly came into use by political powers centuries later.

The cross meanwhile had made its way somewhat into Christianity even before Empress Irene had pressed for its veneration as official policy.

This is how . . .

A number of pagans converted to Christianity, but wanted to keep their own symbols, according to *Vine's Expository Dictionary of New Testament Words* (HarperCollins/Thomas Nelson).[66]

As a result, they brought one of their favorite symbols— the "Tau cross," and used the lowered crosspiece to represent the cross of Christ. Thus, the cross was accepted culturally to appease the growing number of pagan converts, so they would feel more comfortable in the new religion. Empress Irene merely pushed for its full use in the church.

The adoption of numerous pagan practices into the church is admitted by Cardinal John Henry Newman in his book, *An Essay on the Development of Christian Doctrine*: "Constantine, in order to recommend the new religion to the heathen, transferred into it the outward ornaments to which they had been accustomed in their own [tradition]."[67] Outward ornaments included the cross.

The bottom line: Constantine liked the cross and Irene later made it official. But in the intervening centuries, it leapt onto a different stage. In Rome, during the 400s, it evolved into the crucifix—a cross with an image attached to it. And, surprisingly, the first rendering of any image on it was not the Christ—but a lamb.

Two hundred years later, in 629 A.D., the Council of Constantinople replaced the lamb with Christ on the cross.

Nine hundred years after that, in the 1500s, would come the Reformation. Most who joined this movement rejected religious images, including the crucifix, seeing it as a form of "idolatry." They felt the crucifix itself was being worshipped. Perhaps that was not the intention of some in mainline Christianity, but these Reformers noticed as much emphasis on the actual crucifix as Christ in the heavens. Similarly, many Reformers rejected the simpler "cross symbol," even without an image on it, because to them it represented something negative.

And here's why:

During the Inquisition (detailed further below), those believing differently were hunted down as "heretics." When caught they were punished—often with death. One such group were the Cathars. These rebels challenged the dominant church in northern Spain, northern Italy, and southern France, and were forced to display their "heresy" by wearing a yellow cross on their outdoor clothes. They were also ordered to live separately from members of the mainline church during a period of penitence, but could later rejoin them—if they shunned their rebellious ways. Most, however (hundreds, in fact) refused to recant and were burned at the stake or hanged.[68]

Thus, the cross has direct ties to the infamous Inquisition, which began in 1234 A.D.[69]

The church spent most of the 1200s trying to uproot the Cathars by hunting them down, killing them, and burning their texts. The last of the Cathars were found and executed in 1321.[70]

But the church was just beginning to search out and destroy heretics.

The image of the cross shifted to other violent causes. Over 150 years after the Inquisition ended in the early 1700s, it came into negative use again with the launch of the Ku Klux Klan in the United States.

The Klan was actually organized during a span of 6 years from 1865 through 1871. The 1st Ku Klux Klan was started by disenchanted southern Protestants feeling resentful of northern politicians' vengeful acts against the South.

Those attacks started when droves of "carpetbaggers"— northerners who traveled with bags made of carpet—swarmed the South to exploit the white people after the Civil War during the Reconstruction of 1865–1877. They were notorious for meddling in local politics, buying up plantations at fire-sale prices, and literally plundering the population, while opportunistic Republican politicians, also referred to as carpetbaggers, exercised outrageous policies over the defeated white population and incurred their hatred. All this started after Abraham Lincoln was killed and could not stop these unfair practices of exploitation.

Fed up with being punished, but completely misguided in their efforts to stop it, the Klan dressed in unusual costumes, wearing masks, conical shaped hats, and a cross on their robes, as they murdered hundreds of black people and dozens of white Republican carpetbaggers. Federal lawmakers struck back and, in 1871, enacted the Force Acts—legislation targeting the group—imprisoning and fining hundreds of Klansmen. So the 1st Klan was substantially destroyed in 1874, whereupon it quickly faded out until smaller, like-minded terrorist groups sprang up a few decades down the road.

A 2nd Klan would arise later, in 1915, with far fewer acts of violence, although it would claim up to 15% of the adult white male population among its adherents (3 to 6 million members)— far greater than the number of Klansmen in the 1st organization, whose number has never been revealed but was likely in the low thousands. While based on similar principles, but committing far fewer crimes than the 1st Klan, this 2nd version would once again use the cross on their robes as a symbol of hatred, but would also begin the tradition of burning a wooden cross and leaving it at the scene of those they wished to intimidate. Thus, the cross came to be seen by many as an icon of intimidation and negativity.

(This 2nd Klan would flourish in the early 1920s but mostly die out by 1930, the year after the Great Depression hit, with its membership plummeting from millions in 1925 to only 30,000 by 1930. It would completely fade out during the 1940s.

A 3rd Klan would arise in the 1950s, which still exists, and with occasional acts of violence, but on a far smaller scale than the original Klan, yet likely with similar membership numbers, averaging between 5,000 and 8,000 members.)

Despite these negative connotations of the cross, from the Cathars to the Klan, many Protestant churches slowly came to accept this icon, but they never did accept the crucifix—apparently fearing its use as a "graven image."

(However, a few Protestants did accept the crucifix and still make the "sign of the cross"—mainly among the "high church" divisions of the Anglican Communion [Episcopal Church USA and the Church of England, etc.], as well as some Lutheran churches. While a comparatively few Presbyterian priests wear a crucifix, it is even rarer to find it in a house of worship. Thus, the vast majority of Protestant churches completely reject the crucifix—Baptists, Methodists, Church of Christ, Assembly of God, Pentecostal, Seventh-day Adventists, and most in the Anglican Communion, etc.

As for the "sign of the cross," generally only the above "high church" congregations within the Anglican Communion and a few Lutherans practice it within the Protestant community.)

The "sign of the cross" is making a motion of a cross with one's hand. It had begun as a motion only on the forehead in about 200 A.D. at Carthage (modern Tunisia, Africa), and was practiced by Tertullian, who wrote of it in his book, *De Corona* in 204 A.D.[71]

But in the 300s it expanded to other parts of the body, when it finally became popular in mainline Christianity under Constantine.

These icons and the cross sign all came after the last Apostle, John, was no longer in his ministry, leaving the church susceptible to new practices.

---

Another practice came into the church. The veneration of *saints*. Yet it was struck down twice before being accepted.

Through the centuries many in the mainline Christian church taught not to pray directly to saints, as if they were God, but to seek their intercession and to pray *with* them, for God's assistance. But many believers in the church blurred the line in practice and actually prayed to the saints.

Historically, prayer involving saints evolved in this manner.

According to the *New Catholic Encyclopedia*, intercession by saints has no biblical foundation: "nothing on the subject is explicitly mentioned" in the Bible. In fact, invoking saints was "expressly condemned by the Council of Laodicea (481 A.D.) and by the early fathers."[72]

The *Cyclopedia of Biblical, Theological, and Ecclesiastical Literature* adds, "It must be remembered that they are only unscriptural additions, and that they originated after the infusion into the church system of Alexandrian Neoplatonism and Oriental Magianism, which left its traces even in the most orthodox form of Christian worship, and creed also, up to the 4th and 5th centuries, a period in the history of the Christian Church when heresies were, to use a common phrase, almost the order of the day."[73]

Many of the early Christian saints were actually pagan gods. These gods were re-imaged into saints when their pagan followers were semi-converted or forced into the church. That way, the pagans could keep their own gods, while being Christian at the same time

For example, *St. Bridgit* of Ireland was originally a pagan goddess.

At Kildare, Ireland, is a sanctuary dedicated to St. Bridgit, which, before it was a Christian sanctuary, was a pagan temple dedicated to the Celtic goddess Brigid. The priestesses of the goddess Brigid and the nuns in the order of St. Bridgit have both kept an "eternal flame" in the sanctuary for centuries, which both pagans and Christians consider sacred.

Additionally, a number of "sacred wells" were dedicated to the Celtic goddess Brigid that are now associated with the Catholic St. Bridgit.

Many still believe that saints have certain areas of interest or virtues that a living person can relate to, and are thus chosen as special guardians over specific areas of life. Specific-interest saints are "patron saints"—such as Francis of Assisi, who loved nature, so he is a patron saint of ecologists. Similarly, Francis de Sales was a writer, so he is a patron saint of writers and journalists.

Many have asked saints to pray for them in times of trouble. Since saints were supposed to have led holy lives, they are thought to be close to God, so their prayers "are particularly effective," states one traditional Christian fact site.[74]

Over 10,000 saints have been named, but there is no definitive head count. "Canonization," states one modern Catholic researcher, is "the process the church uses to name a saint [and] has only been used since the 10th century. For hundreds of years [before that] . . . saints were chosen by public acclaim."[75] Thus, popularity contests of sorts chose saints.

Although canonization began in the 10th century—the 900s—it was still apparently rather casual because a formal method of choosing saints did not begin until the 1400s. Then in 1969 it was methodized even more, with cardinals and the pope becoming involved in the choice.

Also, in 1969, the church undid the sainthood of many, *as church leaders figured many saints were simply legends and not real people.* (Potentially hundreds of millions of people had invoked fictional characters in prayer through the centuries.)

Despite these bumps in the road—major and minor—the Bible backs up belief in saints. Specifically, biblical references are made to saints praying in behalf of others. Therefore, to Catholics, saints are real. (For example, Revelations 8:3–4 in the New Testament states, "And another angel came and stood at the altar, having a golden censer, and there was given unto him much incense, and that he should offer [it] with the *prayers of all saints* upon the golden altar which was before the throne, and . . . the *prayers of the saints* ascended up before God out of the angel's hand."[76]

As Latter-day Saints see it, *saints*, as mentioned in the Bible, were simply *members* of the church, and biblical references to them were as regular church members. Thus, Latter-day Saints do not recognize saints as anyone higher than or above anyone else. With the veneration of saints beginning in the 300s (and actually condemned by the Catholic Church in 481 A.D., before Empress Irene made it official in 787 A.D.), the concept has lost some credibility to some, especially with the 1969 admission that many saints over the years were fictional, with thousands chosen out of popularity.

As for naming one's children after the apostles and martyrs, that practice began in the mainline church "as early as the fourth century," states the same Catholic source.[77]

To Latter-day Saints this is a prime example of a practice that, while not based on Bible doctrine, is a fine tradition for many, and certainly has no negative side effects, but it came centuries after the original Church of Christ was on the earth.

Some new additions to the church, however, would have negative side effects.

Beginning in 476 A.D. bishops stepped in where the former emperors had left off, as the Western Roman Empire collapsed. And the bishops began assuming political power.

By 800 A.D. the church had so much power that its leader, Leo III, crowned Charlemagne as the "Emperor of the Romans."[78] This meant that for the first time ever, *the church chose an emperor.*

Thus, authority had flip-flopped. Instead of Emperors choosing church leaders, church leaders chose Emperors.

It also meant that for the first time in 324 years, there was a Roman Empire of the West. (It would last a millennium, till 1806). But it was *different* now. And it was named differently also—the *Holy Roman Empire.* Roman institutions and traditions were actually gone. (After 924 A.D. it even had only a fraction of the old Western Roman Empire's territory. It was now primarily a Germanic empire, but included the Kingdom of Italy and a number of smaller territories around it, such as Burgundy and Bohemia.[79])

This flip-flopping of power would flip again later, back to the power of kings and emperors on rare occasions, so much so that once they actually chose a pope and another time even executed one (as described below). But overall the church would grow in power over the centuries.

And for now, the church grew and changed in other ways.

Monasteries began spreading across the West. Unfortunately, they were controlled by feudal lords appointing political leaders to run them. However, in 910 A.D. the church in Rome got fed up with this and wrested its monasteries away from the lords—a good move because they could now tone down the widespread corruption taking place in monasteries. This move also caused a leap forward in building new ones.[80] (In the 3 neighboring countries of England, Wales, and Ireland, for example, a whopping 825 monasteries would be in place by 1536 A.D.[81])

But the pendulum swung too far. The church gained so much control that it began telling the states what to do. And even making the feudal lords its puppets.

And with this new power came unimaginable corruption.


Then, horror knocked on the palaces at Rome. Especially when one powerful man marched into the city.

Known for his insatiable appetite for women, he had a high-flying lifestyle. He ordered massacres of innocent civilians and launched senseless wars seldom seen on such a selfish scale.

His reign began in 955 A.D., when he inflicted suffering on thousands while ruling with indescribable brutality.

Historian James S. Packer writes, "He would torture his followers by castration, blinding, hacking off fingers or hands, or cutting out tongues."[82]

But he would eventually meet his end—a husband would catch him red-handed with his wife during a sexual encounter and beat him senseless,[83] leaving him powerless and paralyzed.

And he would die 8 days later.[84]

His name was Pope John XII.

Here's his backstory . . .

Bishop Liudprand of Cremona in northern Italy goes into horrific details about John XII,[85] reporting that "Benedict, a Cardinal deacon, with other co-deacons and priests, said [at the Synod of Rome] they knew that he [John XII] had been paid for ordaining bishops, specifically, that he had ordained a ten year old bishop in the city of Todi [in Perugia, central Italy]." They also charged he had fornicated with various widows, and "with Stephana, his father's concubine . . . and with his own niece, and he had made the sacred palace into a whorehouse." The sacred palace was the main residence of popes from the early 300s to the 1300s.

These Cardinal deacons added, "He had blinded his confessor Benedict, and thereafter Benedict had died, that he had killed John, cardinal subdeacon, after castrating him." Finally they state, "All clerics, as well as laymen, declared that he had toasted to the devil with wine. They said when playing at dice, he invoked Jupiter, Venus, and other demons."[86]

Liudprand, the bishop who reported this, held a relatively important position as the leader of a diocese over numerous parishes. Bishops also held the "seat" at a cathedral.

Another who reported on Pope John XII was the former Presiding Bishop of Rome—Ratherius of Verona. He specifically reported on the pope's immorality.[87] (He also condemned the immorality of the Italian bishops, in general, while criticizing all the social ranks of the period.[88])

A chronicler who exposed John XII was Flodoard, who wrote for the monk Benedict at Mount Soracte, 22 miles north of Rome,[89] and whose works are highly regarded by the *Catholic Encyclopedia* for his "painstaking accuracy." Flodoard adds of John XII, "He liked to have a collection of women."[90]

And he reportedly raped female pilgrims in St. Peter's Basilica.

While some modern apologists of the medieval church have tried to discount Bishop Liudprand's reports and support John XII, others have thrown up their hands, admitting to the pope's lawlessness.

In 1910 Horace K. Mann, a papal apologist, summarizes, "There cannot be a doubt that John XII was anything but what a Pope, the chief pastor of Christendom, should have been."[91]

In the original 1st-century Church of Christ, the New Testament reveals that holders of the priesthood were married, despite the Apostle Paul's personal opinions about the drawbacks of marriage. The concept of clergy abstaining from marriage did not become church doctrine till the early 300s under Constantine—another change from the original church—and one that was unnecessarily difficult for the clergy.

Meanwhile, immorality was always shunned through the centuries, including all pre-marital or extra-marital sexual relationships.

During the 900s, 2 more memorable leaders came to the forefront . . .

Sergius III, reigning 904–911 A.D., was the only pope known to have ordered the murder of another pope (2 of them, actually— Leo V and Christopher). And he was the only pope known to have fathered an illegitimate son who became pope (John XI in 931–935). (This endnote references a collection of works about Catholic popes written by the church itself.[92])

Giving birth to this illegitimate child of Sergius III was his mistress, Marozia. (Her own mother was a Roman harlot named Theodora, who pushed for their relationship.)

From Sergius III in 904 through Benedict IX in 1048, a combined 8 popes were practically controlled by the Theophylact family and their relatives—all aristocrats at Latium, Italy, 12 miles southeast of Rome. Historical sources reveal their power-brokering and corruption.

---

John X, who reigned over the Christian world from 914 to 928 A.D., was another standout of the 900s. He had a *ménage a trois* with the same 2 women—Theodora and her daughter Marozia,[93] who, as a somewhat conniving lass, also had him murdered.[94]

Before his murder, her mother, Theodora, "exercised power on the Roman citizenry," adds Bishop Liudprand. And, according to John Foxe, she plotted for John X to overthrow his father, then helped set him up in his father's palace.[95]

Another historian, Vicente de Corminen, writes that John X was "more occupied with his lusts and debauchery than with the affairs of Christendom . . . and sacrificed everything to his passions."[96]

(Two other popes from the 900s are not included in this appendix but are relegated to this endnote, because their corruptions are unsubstantiated.[97])

In the next century, the 1000s, came even more intrigue:

Benedict IX was one of the most interesting and corrupt church leaders. He reigned 3 times between 1032 and 1048, and was guilty of "many vile adulteries and murders," claims Bishop Benno of Piacenza in northwest Italy.[98]

Other credible sources wrote of Benedict IX, including another pope, Victor III, who recorded that Benedict IX engaged in "rapes, murders, and other unspeakable acts," adding, "His life as a pope was so vile, so foul, so execrable, that I shudder to think of it."[99]

Another credible source was a church saint and later "Doctor of the Church"—a title given to only 35 men in history as the "greatest" of the church—Cardinal Peter Damian, who records in his book, *Liber Gomorrhianus*, that Benedict IX was a man "feasting on immorality" and "a demon in hell in the disguise of a priest,"[100] who routinely engaged in bestiality (sex with animals), sodomy, and sponsoring orgies.[101]

Benedict IX was reportedly the first actively homosexual pope.[102]

(It is one thing to have same-sex tendencies, and no one should be faulted on that, but quite another to act upon them and break God's laws of chastity—whether heterosexual or homosexual. This view is taken by active Latter-day Saints, who believe God's laws of marriage should only include heterosexual relationships—of one woman and one man—and that marriage should extend to the priesthood as well. In the Catholic priesthood, of course, priests are forbidden to marry. This policy held true during these medieval centuries as well, despite the lifestyles of many.)

The noted 16-volume *Catholic Encyclopedia* concludes that Benedict IX was "a disgrace to the Chair of Peter."[103]

He was appointed pope at age 11 or 12, because of connections to the powerful Theophylact family.

He was also the only pope to ever sell the papacy. He resigned his position as pope for a bribe from his godfather, John Gratian, who became the new pope, Gregory VI.

But Benedict felt seller's remorse. So he demanded his throne back.

Yet the new pope would not surrender it.

So they went to war.

Both sides slaughtered the other, and finally, German Emperor Henry III came down and removed them both, choosing a new leader of Christendom—another prime example of a political leader choosing who would lead the Christian church.

One might question if these methods—and if even the lifestyles of the church leaders—were in harmony with the original 1st-century church.

Latter-day Saints maintain that the church was far out of sync by now from the church established by Christ, a church managed by humble fishermen who obeyed the commandments of God, and that Christianity now was in stark contrast to Christianity before 100 A.D.

Then, in October 1047, the pope who had been chosen by Emperor Henry III died.[104]

So Benedict IX seized the papal palace by force and became pope again. But he was driven out by German troops in July 1048.

At that point, Benedict IX's days of power ended. He was excommunicated.

Pope Damasus II was then elected, and he was accepted universally. But Benedict IX refused to yield, and refused to face charges for "simony"—trafficking in money for spiritual things, such as selling and buying ordinations. This, in fact, is what officially caused his excommunication.

The abbot—the lead monk—at the abbey of Grottaferrata later claimed Benedict IX became penitent at some point before he died, and was buried by the abbot in 1056. But he died with a flood of blood on his hands—of hundreds, if not thousands of people, from the battles he had instigated in order to gain power.[105]

While popes and problems came to light at home, all across the church's growing empire another change arose—bishops in high population centers were feeling they should have more authority than those in smaller areas.[106]

This launched the practice of bigger-city bishops usurping power over smaller-town bishops, with absolutely no authority to, and ending the equality among congregations that had been established in the original, 1st-century Church of Christ. This could be termed "Battle One" of the "Bishops' Power War." But Battle Two got even uglier. The big-city bishops turned on *each other.*

Five were in the fray, but it narrowed to 2—the bishops of Rome and Constantinople. Defeated and dropping out were the bishops at Jerusalem (in Israel), Alexandria (Egypt), and Antioch (Turkey), who saw their churches weakened by this rivalry and eventually decimated by attacking Arabs.

The only 2 bishops left standing could not stand each other, so they excommunicated one another. (A seemingly small matter, it arose over a debate whether Rome or Constantinople had authority for the church in Sicily.[107])

So in 1054 they split into 2 churches—the Western (or Latin) church headquartered in Rome, and the Eastern (or Orthodox) church centered in Constantinople[108]—similar, geographically, to the earlier split of the Roman Empire. (The Western Roman Empire in Rome and the Eastern Roman Empire in Constantinople.)

Both churches viewed the other as heretic and declared themselves the right universal ("catholic") church.

(The Western [or Latin] Church, based at Rome, was not given the name *Roman Catholic Church* until the early 1600s, when English-speaking Catholics coined the term. According to some Catholics its true name is *One, Holy, Catholic, and Apostolic Church*, but throughout the 1900s the Vatican has on a number of occasions referred to itself as the *Catholic Church* and *Roman Catholic Church*, using the terms to also include both Eastern and Western churches, even though the Eastern [Orthodox] Church is separate from them. However, rank-and-file Catholics generally use the terms to differentiate themselves from the Eastern Church.)

Still in the 1000s came more intrigue—in the form of major political battles.

The players?

No less than the Roman emperor and the pope.

Both wanted to make appointments for the church, as both saw themselves superior to and dominant over the other.

The pope won the battle.

But then he faced new political foes.

Italian families.

They were actually torn because they wanted to be loyal to the pope, but they also wanted the power they felt was theirs by birthright. But since the church would not share it with them, they decided to go head to head with the pope.

These families and certain states seeking power were called "factions."

The church fought back, but was weakened by the fight.

It was also weakened by the conflicts resulting from having no set method for choosing popes. But in 1059 the church came up with a solution—cardinals began picking popes. Nicholas II, in fact, chose certain cardinals to pick the popes, setting a precedent that has continued till today. Yet the damage had been done—the church was weak from all this infighting.

But that was the least of its problems now.

Corruption in high places was about to light both ends of a bulging, dangerous, ecclesiastical stick of dynamite.

In 1088 came Pope Urban II, a man who was angry that many priests were married. He considered marriage unchaste. But rather than doing what most consider the Christian thing to do by altering the doctrine of celibacy (since it had no biblical foundation anyway) or by releasing those who were married, he instead gathered up all the married priests he could find and threw them into prison with life sentences. Then sold their wives and children into slavery.

Next, he launched that fascinating era of brutality known as the Crusades.

This came about when he heard of Muslim attacks against Christians who were making a pilgrimage through Muslim lands, on their way to visit Jerusalem.[109]

Furious and vengeful, he announced bold plans in 1095 A.D.,[110] and sent his forces off to slaughter the Muslims in 1096—the first of 9 major Crusades.[111]

In this first Crusade the army sought to wrestle the Holy Land away from the Muslims—with both sides committing atrocities, creating bad blood to this day. Ironically, no one even won in the end.[112]

Bitter resentment arose from the First Crusade alone, when they killed up to 100,000 Muslims.

So the Muslims retaliated . . . and the Crusaders fought back. Both sides massacred multitudes of the other.

Then the Muslims got serious. They decided to attack Constantinople—headquarters for half of Christianity, the Orthodox Church.

Learning of the plot, the Orthodox leaders in Constantinople begged the Catholics to come protect them from the invading Muslims. And this actually launched the Fourth Crusade.

But something went horribly wrong. In 1204 the Catholic Crusaders went there, all right, but *sacked Constantinople*—and the very people who had asked for their help. This left the Orthodox people angry and bitter at their cousin Catholics for centuries.

(Perhaps better late than never, however, in 2004 Pope John Paul II apologized to the living 300 million Orthodox Christians for this event.[113])

But when it happened in 1204, the papacy—badly in need of a course on diplomacy—supported this Crusade, thinking it would *force* the reunion of the Eastern and Western churches.[114] (A differing viewpoint is presented in this endnote.[115]) Since then, some individual Eastern churches have rejoined the Roman Catholic Church.[116]

Yet, as a whole, the Catholic and Orthodox churches have remained separate. Their animosity has decreased, however, at least officially. The "excommunicating" of each other was lifted by both parties in 1965.[117]


Aside from the Crusades of the 1100s and 1200s, a new form of brutality reared its ugly head—the "Inquisitions." This was a policy of the church hunting down and punishing heretics (such as the Cathars, above).

The Inquisition could be divided into 3 versions.

The first began with Pope Lucias III's *papal bull* (a pope's decree),[118] written at Verona in north-central Italy in 1184, with milder punishments.

Those found guilty were excommunicated and deprived of certain rights, such as holding public office, the right to have a will, to have a trial, and cancellation of their inherited offices and fiefs (properties granted to those who maintained them for serving their "lords").

But it set in motion the wheels of seeking out heretics—by commanding bishops to make rounds 2 or 3 times per year in their dioceses, questioning people they suspected as heretics, as well as searching out suspicious locations where they might live. Those not found in strict compliance with the church were given the above punishments.

But the punishments would turn psychopathically cruel the following century.

In the 1200s came the launch of the full-blown Inquisitions. Other atrocities occurred as well.

Noted historian Issac Milner reports: "Some noblemen in Alsace [in today's France along the northeast border] had dared to reprehend the conduct of Innocent III, the pope during 1198–1216, particularly his imposition of celibacy on the clergy. The bishops of that country had influence enough to oppress these innovators [the noblemen], and in one day they burnt in the flames a hundred of their associates."[119]

Thus, Pope Innocent III and his bishops were not so innocent when it came to torturing people to death. Their purpose was to not just ban celibacy but to enforce it with violence among the clergy—another far cry from the doctrines of Christ and His apostles during the 1st century.

While clerical celibacy had begun during the days of Emperor Constantine, it was now in full swing. Not just full swing, but full force. If you even questioned it you were burned at the stake.

And the bishops enforced it by burning these 100 noblemen—the allies of the priests who had seen through the ban on marriage as a man-made doctrine, because it had no biblical foundation.

But outdistancing that atrocity was the full-blown cruelty mode the church now adopted for the upgraded Inquisitions.

This was launched by Pope Gregory IV (1227–1241) and was markedly crueler on those found guilty of heresy. But it was taken to even a higher level—a 3rd version—by Pope Boniface VIII, reigning 1294–1303. He was the first to approve the use of torture to extract confessions from innocent people merely *accused* of heresy.

This reign of terror—the "Inquisition"—would become a hallmark of the spiritual dark ages and last nearly 500 years, till the early 1700s. And would be carried out by a group of institutions within the judicial framework of the church.

Heretic-hunters would also seek out those reading the Bible—especially those translating it into English. From John Wycliffe in 1380 to William Tyndale and others in the mid 1500s, elaborate games of cat and mouse would be played against the establishment church by those putting their lives on the line to get the Bible out to the masses, as covered in Appendix R: "Launching the Reformation: Prelude to the Restoration," and Appendix T: "English Bibles that Shook the World."

One example of the Inquisition's cruel stupidity was its treatment of the brilliant scientist Galileo Galilei, who would be investigated for heresy and placed under house arrest for life in 1633, just for saying the earth revolved around the sun.

(Although his was a comparatively spacious, 2-story, several-windowed house, 5 miles from Florence, he was truly trapped. The very next year he developed a highly painful hernia and requested Rome for permission to visit a physician, but they turned him down and threatened that if he ever asked again he would be imprisoned. In January 1642 he died, having spent the final 8 years and 1 month of his life confined there, with 7 of those years in pain from his condition.)

This instigator of "Version 3" of the Inquisition, Boniface VIII, became pope in this manner: in 1294 A.D. he persuaded the elderly Pope Celestine V to retire, so he could take over. But soon he perceived the retired pope as a threat, and captured the old man, throwing him into prison for the remainder of his life—10 months.

Boniface VIII's 9-year reign was tumultuous—he was almost constantly in conflict with various Italian states. In a remarkable power play, he picked a fight with Philip IV, King of France, and declared the king was subordinate to him, then excommunicated him.

King Philip IV was not about to take these shenanigans, so he sent an army to Italy and ordered his soldiers to beat the pope to a pulp.

Which they did. He died 3 days later. Some say by suicide.[120]


Newsworthy events of the 1200s were not over.

Church doctrines took another twist—perhaps the biggest one yet.

Noted historian and dean of Queen's College at Cambridge University, the aforementioned Isaac Milner, reports that a "growing celebrity of the Aristotlelian philosophy" began to prevail at this time. So Greek philosophies began not just influencing church doctrine (as it had for centuries)—but actually taking it over.[121]


With the 1200s finally over, the 1300s brought a new level of intrigue.

Urban VI, reigning 1378–1388, was, according to his contemporaries, not only immoral but outrageously arrogant. The account below of him is equivalent to a chapter of text in detail, outlining how remarkably askew the Christian church had become since the original 1st-century church. His story also reveals how dark the Dark Ages had truly become, especially within the Christian church.

Those who lived during his time and reported of him include John Froissart (Frenchman and chronicler for England and France), Leonardo Bruni ("the first modern historian," statesman, and secretary to 4 popes,[122] Tomaso de Acemo (bishop of Lucera, historical expert and author of *De creatione Urbani VI opusculum*),[123] and St. Antoninus of Florence (archbishop of Florence, Italy, who was venerated as a saint).[124]

Now, Urban VI's story:

The previous pope, Gregory XI, reigned 1370–1378, but the Roman populace was more than a little peeved that he was a Frenchman. One day he suddenly died of poisoning. So now was the perfect time to have a Roman pope, they figured. And they mobbed the papal headquarters to demand one.

But the cardinals didn't deliver. They elected a pope from Naples, in today's northern Italy.

Urban VI.

Realizing the mob would be furious, the cardinals who selected him fled before the mob got wind of it.

The mob, predictably, became impassioned and boiled over with new threats, but soon disappeared.

But the new pope would soon face a far worse foe than mobs . . .

Rivals appeared on the landscape.

Rivals who wanted his throne.

So Urban VI hired mercenary soldiers and attacked them, killing scores and driving the rest into the countryside.

He then appointed his nephew, Francesco Moricotte Prignani, as the Cardinal of Tuscany in central Italy, also appointing him governor of Campagna in southern Italy[125]—giving him both ecclesiastical and political governing positions. But it was made worse by the fact this nephew was both immoral and incompetent—in fact a complete political and ecclesiastical clod.

The French cardinals who had helped select Urban VI quickly had buyer's remorse. Especially when they saw almost immediately his character flaws.

Dietrich of Nieheim, holding the important office of papal notary and *Abbreviator et Scriptor* under several popes,[126] reported that the cardinals saw his elevation to pope as, in essence, an over-the-top flop.[127]

They wanted him out.

So they began to conspire against him.

Meanwhile, King Charles V of France, wanting to keep the church intact, demanded he step down and return to Avignon in southeast France.[128]

But the pope refused to step down. He used his paid militia to seize various cardinals, bishops, and lower nobles who did not want him to stay in Rome, and had them slowly tortured to death.

In addition to being power-hungry, he was vengeful and sadistic.

Furious, and needing to get rid of him, the French cardinals elected their own pope—"Anti-Pope" Clement VII (reigning 1378–1394)—who was secretly supported by the French king, Charles V.[129] (However, this choice was not much better. Before becoming pope, Clement VII had—under his former name of Robert of Geneva—commanded the papal army and earned himself the nickname "butcher of Cesena," massacring 4,000 unarmed civilians at Cesena, a coastal city in northeast Italy. [Note that his title, Clement VII—in some circles "Anti-Pope Clement VII"—is not to be confused with another pope, "Clement VII," 2 centuries later.][130]) One can imagine the feelings of the surviving families in Cesena, seeing the lead slaughterer being made pope.

Urban VI was then excommunicated from the church by the new French Anti-Pope Clement VII, who also designated Urban as the Antichrist—an ironic label coming from the commander at Cesena who had wiped out thousands of innocent people.

Urban VI was incensed that this upstart pope would do that to him.

So the battle was on.

Urban hired an even bigger mercenary army and confiscated the property of wealthy nobles.

Needing money, he also sold the office of bishop to 37 wealthy men.

He then sought to terrorize the populace to keep them in line, so he gathered up numerous citizens and tortured them. (Strangely, he reportedly loved to recite his breviary—prayers, psalms, and hymns from a book—in a loud voice in order to drown out the moans of the many he tortured in front of him, while his children jeered them.)

But then he started an intrigue in Naples that came back to bite him in the proverbial buttocks.

He crowned a new king in Naples in 1382, Charles of Durazzo, also called Charles III of Naples (not to be confused with Charles V, king of France, also living at the time).

But becoming king came with a catch. Urban VI expected Charles of Durazzo to kill his cousin, Joan I of Naples. The reason: Urban was angry at her for no longer financially supporting him. Making matters worse, she had switched her loyalty to the new French Anti-Pope, Clement VII, "the slaughterer."

Urban first excommunicated her, then issued his order for her assassination.

Charles of Durazzo kept his promise and murdered her—his own cousin.

(He already had the reputation of being "crafty and ambitious,"[131] but now had a new label on his resume—"murderer.")

Urban VI expected one other favor from his obsequious political appointee—to give up 5 cities in Naples, Italy, to his nephew, the aforementioned incompetent Cardinal Prignani.

But Urban went too far and did something that turned even Charles of Durazzo off . . .

Urban, still jealous there was another pope floating about, decided to overthrow the French Anti-Pope, Clement VII. But he had no army. So he offered English soldiers and nobles Indulgences to heaven—free passes to heaven for sinners— if they would take up arms against Anti-Pope Clement VII. ("Indulgences" are mentioned earlier and explained in Appendix R: "Launching the Reformation: Prelude to the Restoration.")

Charles of Durazzo was appalled by Urban's order to kill someone he considered the real pope, so he turned on Urban— the very man who had crowned him king—and sent an army to oust him as pope.

But when Charles of Durazzo's forces advanced on Rome, even to St. Peter's Basilica to take him out, Urban saw them coming and ran across the top of the Vatican wall to the castle. (This walkway atop the wall was fortified, so he was protected from arrows fired from below. It actually connected St. Peter's

Basilica to Castel Sant'Angelo). At the end of this 875-yard aerial corridor he hopped over the back wall and ran off, leaving his men fighting and dying for him. And he escaped undetected.[132]

Through the countryside he traveled, determined to find and face Charles of Durazzo and demand answers: why the devil did he invade him? And why didn't he follow through on the deal to give his nephew-cardinal the 5 cities?

Charles of Durazzo was so disgusted by this pathetic excuse for a pope standing before him now that he didn't even answer—he had him arrested and tossed into the village of Nocera, a prison camp of sorts, 13 miles southeast.

Several cardinals were shut up in Nocera with him, and saw what he was like. In a letter they begged him to check his indecent displays of temper.[133]

Furious at their criticism, Urban imprisoned all 6 of them in a dungeon at the castle of Nocera, in the village where he himself was a prisoner, and had them tortured.

Chronicler Egidio de Viterbo stated this was "a crime unheard of through the centuries."[134]

To the men he had assigned to conduct the tortures he complained he didn't hear enough screaming.[135]

Only one cardinal eventually lived to tell about it—Englishman Adam Easton. His account alone is almost worth another appendix, but in summary he had become a cardinal through the request of King Henry III of England (thus, Easton was another church appointee by a king) and was assigned to help with the papal disputes. So he joined other cardinals to deal with Urban VI and found himself at Nocera. There, he was confined to the Castle of Nocera on January 11, 1385, by Urban VI.

Still held captive in Nocera, Urban threw a tantrum. He excommunicated Charles of Durazzo and cut off from the church all his captors.

Charles heard about it, was angry, and set a price on his head.

Before anyone could nail Urban, however, he was rescued by 2 barons from Naples. Joining them was a supporter in Genoa, who sent 6 ships to help him get away. They sailed with him from the southwest coast of today's Italy (Naples) to the northwest coast (Genoa)—a distance of 392 miles along the coast, where he landed safely in the hands of allies.[136]

After being tortured, the cardinals went to Genoa, either forcibly taken there by Urban, or they unwisely followed him there, still wanting to straighten him out. Once at Genoa, 5 of the cardinals were executed on Urban's orders.

But Easton was not executed, due to the intercession of King Richard II of England.[137] He was returned to the castle at Nocera (or had been left there to begin with).

Easton was released from the castle nearly a year later by Charles of Durazzo and ordered to live in a Benedictine monastery as a simple monk. Three years later, on December 13, 1309, he was restored to the office of cardinal by Pope Boniface IX and went back to England.[138]

Meanwhile, Urban VI's power took a nosedive when his money dried up.

With no army to back him now, he went from town to town with his sons, trying to raise cash to launch a crusade against Charles of Durazzo and to attack Naples—the city that had been promised to him but which he had never received. Unfortunately, at every town, his sons would commit vices, causing both his sons and himself to be expelled.

Then Charles of Durazzo died.

With his chief antagonist gone now, Urban VI saw a way to regain power.

He convinced others the city was up for grabs, so he raised money for an army and went there. But unfortunately found the city somewhat of a mess. Others were also fighting for it—the son of the deceased king and a Frenchman. He forged ahead anyway and, with perfect timing, seized the Kingdom of Naples for his loser nephew.

With that success, he found others willing to invest in his dreams. He managed to raise enough money to hire a huge papal army. So he marched on Rome to take the church back.

But, 2 years later, in August 1388, while leading thousands of troops from Perugia, he fell off his mule.

From the near-fatal injury, he recovered in Rome, and there he ousted those in power at church headquarters. Feeling certain he could finally take control of the church, with nothing left to get in his way now, and with complete victory in the palm of his hands . . .

. . . came the best laid plans of mice and men.

He died.

Some say from falling off that mule. Others say he was poisoned.[139]

The story of Urban's VI's life exemplifies the intrigues of the papal palace in medieval centuries, and thus has been included here in some detail.

But the intrigues were just beginning . . .

In the 1400s came Paul II, reigning 1464–1471, who purportedly died while engaging in sodomy, rather than the official reason stated for his death—overeating melons that caused indigestion.[140]

Whatever liquid got stuck in his throat caused him to choke and collapse. Sadly, he was the first leader of Christianity to qualify for the Darwin Award, as he died in the process . . .

With numerous followers not buying the melon theory.

Incompetence at its worst.

Sixtus IV, reigning 1471–1484, was by contrast a brilliant man.

Aside from his money-making abilities, he showed remarkable generosity, which, unfortunately, was limited to his numerous relatives, to whom he gave titles.

Always on the lookout for clever new ways to raise revenue, he sold licenses for brothels in Rome and began charging a tax to priests who had a mistress. He also raised money by coming up with a fascinating new scheme—expanding the sale of indulgences to people who wanted their dead loved ones out of Purgatory.

As defined in Appendix R, Purgatory, by Catholic belief, is a halfway house between heaven and hell, where souls go to suffer for their sins, then, once purified of them, can move on to heaven. Until this point, the sale of indulgences had involved only the living, guaranteeing them less time in Purgatory once they died and hit the Afterlife. But now, Sixtus IV extended indulgences to include one's dead relatives; if you paid the right price, you could free your dead loved ones from Purgatory with an early out.

Pope Sixtus also gave gifts to his court favorites for sex—with males. And reportedly made Giovanni Sclafenate a cardinal, for "ingeniousness, loyalty . . . and his other gifts of soul and body," states the papal epitaph on his tomb.[141]

Early writer Stefano Infessura described him as a "lover of boys and sodomites,"[142] also suggesting that he sold for sex the office of bishop, while nominating numerous young men as cardinals—including his own nephew. Elsewhere, in a history written in 1679, he was accused of setting up an innovative brothel—one for both sexes.[143]

He was perhaps the most financially gifted and inventive of all medieval church leaders.

The next leader in line had fewer substantiated reports about him and is thus mentioned only in this endnote.[144]

The following leader however had a well-documented life and received such notoriety that in recent years he has earned a movie and 3 television series depicting his ingenious conspiracies.

Alexander VI.

Beginning his reign the year Columbus "discovered" America, in 1492, he plotted against his enemies with sheer brilliance. A later pope, Leo X, described him thus: "Now we are in the power of a wolf, the most rapacious perhaps that this world has ever seen. And if we do not flee, he will inevitably devour us all."[145]

Alexander was depicted rather accurately in the television series, *The Borgias*. (The title comes from his name before he was pope—Cardinal Borgia of Spain.) Holding such sellable cinematic themes as sex, violence, and conspiracies, his story was made most recently into *Showtime*'s 29-episode series from 2011–2013 starring Academy Award-winning actor Jeremy Irons.[146] (This endnote summarizes all 3 television series and the movie about him.)

Alexander was apparently the most devious designer of dark plots among all Christian leaders. He made his family wealthy and put his children in high positions, all while having a mistress and manufacturing inventive schemes against his enemies. He even set up a network of secret informers to search out his political enemies.[147] (This is separate from the "Inquisition" against religious heretics, which he also furthered, hunting out and torturing numerous innocent people). He also arranged with wild abandon for the murders of rivals, including cardinals who were in his way or whose money he wanted.

Alexander VI took power over much of Italy by force with the help of his son, Cesare, who waged warfare using the papal armies, killing thousands of innocent people.

Rumors were rampant that his daughter Lucrezia had an incestuous affair with her brother Cesare (and it was "generally believed," says historian William Rosco, that Lucrezia may have had a racy relationship with her father as well,[148] although "generally believed" is certainly not conclusive evidence.)

But there was actually evidence Alexander pawned her off to powerful families 3 different times in order to form strategic alliances. Supposedly, 2 of her husbands she hated, but one she loved. However, since he no longer served Alexander's purpose, Alexander had him assassinated—taken out by a knife-wielding, medieval hit man.

William Rosco, an apologist for the church, chose to discount the negative reports while accentuating the positive—such as Alexander's promotion of the arts and literature and enlarging the palace at the Vatican.[149] He believed those accomplishments offset the negatives, but did acknowledge what Italian historians recorded about Alexander:

"Inordinate in his ambition, insatiable in his avarice and his lust, inexorable in his cruelty, and boundless in his rapacity; almost every crime that can disgrace humanity is attributed to him without hesitation by writers whose works are published under the sanction of the Roman church."[150]

His longest-lasting love affair among many mistresses was Vannozza (Giovanna) del Cattani, who bore him 4 children of the 7 he had, as a result of breaking his vows.

One of his favorite pastimes was throwing monstrous orgies that included little boys, naked, jumping out of giant cakes to the delight of deviant revelers.

Finally, after a life of wine, women, and song—and over a dozen murders thrown in for good measure (actually thousands, counting the massacres)—he succumbed to death. Which likely came in 1 of 3 ways:

First, historians of this period report that he and his son Cesare prepared poison for several cardinals, in order to steal their estates, but the poison, says Rosco, "by the error of an attendant, was incautiously administered to themselves." (Another Darwin Award, apparently hiring a doltish attendant.)

The father took it, the son didn't, and the father died. (Rosco believes if Alexander was poisoned, however, it came from "some of those numerous enemies whom his rapacity and violence had incited to this deed of revenge," which is the 2nd possibility of how he died.)[151] The 3rd was that he may have died from a fever.[152]

Thus his reign ended after 9 years—in 1503—leaving a legacy of murder, conspiracy, and debauchery.

His forcing his daughter into political marriages, his orders to a brutal son to invade villages and wipe out thousands, his wild and deviant orgies, his unending mistresses, his plots against cardinals, and his alliances to overthrow everyone in his way—all while setting up a network of secret informers—helped to create the story of a "wolf from hell." Hence the 3 televisions series and movie about him.

The 1500s produced the most intrigue yet.

The first controversial church leader of that century was apparently accused of inappropriate behavior by the Conciliabulum of Piza, which sought his removal. But no solid proof, in this author's view, was ever presented. So it is merely relegated to this endnote[153] and not detailed here in the text. However, the *Catholic Encyclopedia* does admit to his fathering an illegitimate daughter before his papacy.[154]

Next came Leo X, reigning 1513–1521. He became infamous for granting Indulgences to rebuild St. Peter's Basilica in Rome (as covered in Appendix R, "Launching the Reformation: Prelude to the Restoration")

His legacy goes further, however. He spent $\frac{1}{7}$ of the church's cash on a single party(!). Upon his election as pope he reportedly told his brother Giuliano, "Since God has given us the papacy, let us enjoy it!"[155]

Being a spendthrift, he was a patron of the arts, as many have been in government with other people's money. His government, of course, was the church.

He apparently had a one-sided infatuation for Marcantonio Flaminio, a flamboyant young male with whom he had an affair.[156]

Those who lived in his day and wrote of his breaking vows include Francesco Guicciardini, an Italian statesman and historian who was also a major political writer of the Renaissance (1483–1540). His masterpiece was *Storia d'Italia* (*The History of Italy*),[157] a detailed political account of 1490–1534 and a pioneering achievement for writing history, using government sources to support his positions while including a realistic analysis of the people of his time.[158]

Guicciardini writes that he was "exceedingly devoted—and every day with less and less shame—to that kind of pleasure that for honor's sake may not be named."[159]

Bishop Paolo Giovio, who was the bishop of Nocera de Pagani (covering 5 municipalities around Naples in southeast Italy) was also a noted historian and biographer, as well as personal physician to the future Pope Clement VII, and was later knighted by the pope. With these credentials he wrote of Leo X, reporting that he had "an improper love for some of his chamberlains"[160]—his male assistants.

Leo X also had a love for luxury. Strangely, he had a pet elephant named Hanno—an example of his indulgence for any and every thing bizarre that entertained him. He was a man consumed with extraordinary extravagance in a city teeming with poor. In just 2 years he spent every cent of all the hard-earned savings of his predecessor, Julius II, launching a major financial crisis for the church.

To deal with it, he borrowed huge sums from princes and bankers. After he spent that, he pawned the palace furniture, jewels, and statues of the Apostles. As a result of his reckless spending, several banks and individual creditors were ruined.

In order to come up with more money, he invented a fascinating scheme.

He claimed Cardinal Alfonso Petrucci of Siena and friends were planning to assassinate him. Upon "learning" about these conspirators, he had them followed. Days later they died of "food poisoning."

Some felt Leo X used these assassinations as a way to raise money. After the cardinals were killed, he levied fines against other wealthy cardinals that he detested, and they readily paid up, also fearing "food poisoning.'"

To keep his spendthrift ways going, he came up with his final scheme—to license brothels.

Not a contender to win popularity contests, he has been described as "fat, sweaty, and effeminate."[161]


Clement VII found politics was not his strong suit. When he reigned as pope from 1523 to 1534, he began power-brokering with France, Spain, and Germany, but stepped neck deep into a pit of political manure he created—ending up sinking his whole city into it. He inadvertently got Rome sacked in 1527 by Charles V, who invaded Italy when he lost patience with Clement's incompetent manipulations of countries. This was 1100 years after the 3 sackings of Rome discussed earlier; but, unlike them, this was not a total collapse, yet a horrendous event for those who lived through it.

The people of Rome blamed him for the attack and hated him. They never, in fact, forgave him. Thus, he died with little power and fewer friends.

Next in line was Paul III, who made one of the most wondrous goofs in world history. He inadvertently stumbled into starting the Church of England. This move would, over time, take dozens of millions of people away from the Vatican, and compete with his church for the souls of additional millions. Reigning 1534–1549, his claim to fame was excommunicating English King Henry VIII for ditching his wife Catherine in order to marry his new love, Anne Boleyn. So Henry VIII started his own church.

What made Paul's position outrageously weak was that he had a mistress himself, named Guilia, but refused to let Henry VIII split with his wife, Cathryn, in order to marry Anne. Evidently Paul saw no wrong in having a mistress, but viewed annulments as evil.

In return for Guilia's sexual favors Paul III made her brother, also named Paul, a cardinal. Who later became a pope. And he made his 14- and 16-year-old grandsons cardinals as part of the deal.

Paul III had romps with other women as well, but it was his intransigence on the marriage issue that so riled up the English King, causing a whole new church to spin off. Pope Clement VII, above, had mostly tussled with the English king, refusing him an annulment during a 7-year spat between 1527 and 1534, put Paul III was the pope who actually gave the order to excommunicate the king in 1535. And that was the final straw for the king. He took his toys and went off to play with his other friends. Either pope could arguably be given the most credit, but Paul III is substantially responsible for losing all 825 monasteries and hundreds of churches in England, Ireland, and Wales, along with the aforesaid tens of millions of people, eventually, to this new church—the Church of England. (Henry VIII had a lot of toys and friends. See Appendix R, "Launching the Reformation: Prelude to the Restoration" for details.)

After Paul III came another leader, whose story is relegated to this endnote because of the lack of credible sources.[162]

These were all examples of breaking vows of chastity for centuries, while engaging in political intrigue, power-grabbing, assassinations, selling titles, appointing young boys and mistresses' relatives to high church positions, and instigating wars that resulted in the deaths of thousands, all while financing their operations through church titles sold to the rich and indulgences pawned off on the poor, the ignorant masses in fear of Purgatory, who depended upon these leaders for guidance and sacrificed every penny possible to do what they were told was necessary.

Some Catholic apologists discount certain historical sources, including high-ranking bishops, yet in the end admit to a "handful of evil popes."[163]

But even "a handful of evil popes" indicates a red flag to ongoing priesthood authority, especially when it is compared to the purity of leadership within Christ's original church of the 1st century.

Latter-day Saints would contend that whatever historical allegations are true—whether some, most, or all the reports here—would back up the claim of a Great Apostasy and break in the chain of apostolic succession. That "falling away," they reiterate, happened when the last apostle was withdrawn from the ministry in about 100 A.D., taking with him all true priesthood authority from the earth.

A summarizing statement comes from historian Louis-Marie de Cormenin in 1859, criticizing "the pride of popes and their insatiable ambition found in absolute monarchs [the popes themselves], [and in their] powerful and frequently docile auxiliaries [the cardinals and other assistants], in imposing upon the people their execrable wishes, in overwhelming the weak, in aggrandizing their estates, and at length in reaching so great a height of audacity, that they called themselves the representatives of God upon earth, and arrogated the right of giving away kingdoms, deposing princes, and dividing the world.

"The shades of ignorance then obscured the mind . . . [with] ages of misfortune, massacres, incendiarism, and famine!"[164]


The worst brutalities were yet to come, however.

These came from the Spanish conquistadors abusing Native Americans, beginning with Italian-born but Spanish-financed Christopher Columbus in 1492, who took slaves, but otherwise accomplished great work in his life, feeling led by the hand of God. Later, other conquistadors in the 1500s took their power to the extreme, not only enslaving but massacring thousands, and forcing them into their brand of Christianity (see Chapter 23). The results today have left Latin America at about 70% Catholic.

(*Foreign Affairs* magazine, published by the Council on Foreign Relations, reports in its March 2013 issue a current crisis in the Catholic Church within Latin America, with the 2 largest Catholic nations, Mexico and Brazil, rapidly declining in that faith. Within Brazil, in just 40 years [1970 to 2010], the Catholic population has dropped from over 90% to 65%. Mexico, meanwhile, has also taken a plunge in just 10 years: from 2000 to 2010 it dropped 5%—from 88% to 83%[165]—which, on the surface, does not appear that dramatic, but at second look does, as it equates to a 50% drop per century. [Meanwhile, among the fastest-growing churches in these 2 countries is the Church of Jesus Christ of Latter-day Saints.])

So, as conquistadors were spreading the faith while conquering South America, another fight was raging in Europe—another of church authorities vs. rebels.

The Reformation.

This was a new twist in world history, and it swept Europe.

Putting it in perspective, the groundwork was laid with Roman bishops gaining power in 476 A.D., when the Western Roman Empire fell and the emperors lost their clout. So the bishops stepped in and became the new power brokers.

During the next 11 centuries they retained their power, even after a new form of the Roman Empire came along in 800 A.D. (a strange form of it, actually, with mostly German territories and rulers, conceitedly called the "Holy Roman Empire," and sarcastically described by French philosopher Voltaire as being "neither holy, nor Roman, nor an empire.")[166] At times emperors would re-exert their power. (As covered, one German emperor replaced a pope, and a French king killed another pope.) But as the centuries sped along, the bishops gained more and more control of the European chessboard.

The bishops, in fact, brazenly told princes and kings what to do, and *even collected taxes from them.*

This caused many rulers, especially in Western Europe, to be resentful. So much so that they were completely fed up.

So in the 1500s, when Martin Luther and other Reformers came along, the princes and kings were biting at the bits to break away from Roman bishops. And they were more than a little willing to help rebels like Luther.

Martin Luther was the kingpin of the Reformation, and went toe to toe with the Roman church, as detailed in Appendix R, "Launching the Reformation: Prelude to the Restoration."

A Catholic priest by profession, Luther bravely posted his 95 Theses on the Castle Church door at Wittenberg, with his biggest gripe being the sale of "indulgences"—the church charging money for shortening the time people would have to spend in Purgatory once they died.

For his opposition Luther was branded a heretic and was threatened to back down or be arrested. He refused. He was excommunicated and targeted for execution. But a local prince protected him—Prince Frederick the Wise, elector of Saxony. Frederick soon died, however (in 1525), and his brother John stepped in to replace him as ruler.[167]

John, also sick of Roman power brokers meddling in his state's business, liked Luther's teachings and felt they were a good fit. So Prince John organized a church that was Europe's first break-off from Catholicism—the Lutheran Church. He then appointed Luther and his friend Philipp Melanchthon to establish the church government and worship services, the points of belief, and the duties and salaries of the clergy. Thus, the church was sponsored by Prince John of Saxony, a political figure.

Soon, the frustrated kings of Scandinavia also went head to head with Catholic bishops and stripped them of their power, setting up various Protestant churches and creating state religions as well, which most people accepted.

All such churches were appointed by political authority.[168]

In Switzerland the civil government took over the religious authority of the Catholic bishop and launched the Church of Geneva. John Calvin and Guillaume Farel were the chief architects of that faith, under their political rulers.[169]

The distinguished, 14-volume *Cambridge Modern History* series from Cambridge University, planned and coordinated by Lord Acton (Senior Professor of History at Cambridge and Fellow at Oxford University), includes an insightful section by Andrew Martin Fairbairn: "The change, though disguised in a religious habit, was yet essentially political. For the Council [of Geneva], which abolished the bishop, had made itself heir to his faculties and functions." He concludes, "Because of the change, the civil authority became ecclesiastical."[170]

The theme continued.

The Church of Geneva was like other state-sponsored churches in Europe,[171] all breaking off from the original state-sponsored church in Rome, established by Constantine in 313 A.D. with the Edict of Milan.

In England King Henry VIII broke away for personal reasons, as detailed in Appendix R, and started the Church of England.

The Catholic Church had managed to accomplish the unheard-of feat of stifling any significant dissent from within its ranks for over a thousand years—mostly by mercilessly snuffing it out as soon as it reared its head. But once Reformers at the beginning of the 1500s, like Martin Luther in Germany and William Tyndale in England, succeeded in gaining a toehold, it was as though Pandora's box had been opened. In rapid succession, splinter groups broke off from the mother church or from each other over points of doctrine, organization, and mode of worship, spawning over the next 3 centuries a host of Christian sects—Lutherans, Anglicans, Anabaptists, Separatists, Nonconformists, Calvinists, Puritans, Congregationalists, Episcopalians, Methodists, Presbyterians, Baptists, Quakers, Mennonites, and so forth.

Once the Reformation got rolling, conflicts among the various sects and the mother church tended to be violent, at least in the first 2 centuries, resulting in boatloads of devout believers fleeing to the "new land" of America in hopes of being able to practice their religion unmolested by popes and potentates and the bigotry of neighbors who did not share their beliefs. In fact, one of Joseph Smith's ancestors (and of several other famous Americans, including presidents) was John Lathrop, an early settler of Massachusetts who, as a Congregationalist minister, had been imprisoned and eventually banished to America for refusal to swear allegiance to the Church of England.

After a while, a degree of tolerance prevailed, enough for state-sponsored churches to go on the decline. But, religiously, nothing fundamental changed from the time of the Reformation until Joseph Smith's day: all the Christian sects were off-shoots of the mother church with, according to Joseph, no true divine authority on the earth.

So with the Reformation that had taken place in the 1500s came a proliferation of sects over the next few centuries. And this naturally carried over to the American colonies, setting up the environment of sectarian strife that so baffled Joseph Smith as a lad. In fact, an intense religious fervor and vying for converts, dubbed the (First) Great Awakening, had gripped his stomping grounds of New England just a few decades before his birth, as ministers adopted new methods of winning converts—camp meetings, tent revivals, and the like—on the American frontier.

The efforts of Reformers over the course of 3 centuries had clearly not brought about the unity of faith referred to by the Apostle Paul in Ephesians 4:11–14 when he wrote about the organization of Christ's church. One key component had been missing: revelation from God. Until Joseph Smith arrived on the scene and went into a grove of trees in New York to pray and inquire which church was right, the time, the place, and the person to lead the Restoration had not yet been right.


Latter-day Saints believe, as did Joseph Smith, that the Reformers were inspired of God. Ironically, these Reformers never pretended to have revelations or even divine authority. Most felt the heavens were sealed—there was no more revelation or prophets. Nor would there be for a time. (Some of the noted men of the day believed Christ's original church had fallen away—Roger Williams, founder of the Baptist church in America; John Wesley, founder of the Methodists; and founding father Thomas Jefferson all identified the existing churches as incomplete and waited for the day there would be a Restoration—with God's full authority once again on the earth. (See Appendix R, Part 4, for their full comments.)

In essence, the Christian churches after 100 A.D. were not organized of God, but came from those in political authority. Separate from these, Bible study groups became churches and formed on their own.

Both types of organizations, however, lacked divine authority, according to restorationists—those who believed in a coming Restoration.

And then there's the Bible.

The biblical position is that men must be commissioned by God to perform ordinances. Otherwise He does not recognize those ordinances—He rejects as invalid the ordinances performed by unauthorized pastors (See I Samuel 13:8–15, I Chronicles 13:9–10, Matthew 7:21–29, Acts 19:1–6, Acts 19:13–16 for biblical backup.)

Furthermore, the book of Hebrews in the New Testament states, "And no man taketh this honor unto himself, but he that is called of God as was Aaron."[172] Thus, no man can minister in the Lord's priesthood unless he is called as Aaron was. And this is how Aaron was called: God instructed Moses, *a prophet, to call and ordain others*—in this case, Aaron—to the priesthood.

Latter-day Saints cite the Bible in saying that God requires mankind to maintain 3 vehicles for a valid priesthood authority on the earth—a prophet, a prophet's representatives, and *current revelation.* From those 3 vehicles men are called to the priesthood to act in God's behalf.

Those who focus only on atrocities and intrigue—which have been committed by members of many faiths—may miss the point. Other issues must be considered.


Through the centuries, much good has come from the Roman Catholic Church, despite its historical abuses and a number of disingenuous church leaders in the latter half of the medieval period and the first two-thirds of the Renaissance. (The medieval years were the 300s to the mid 1300s, while the Renaissance was from the mid 1300s to the late 1600s.)

Renaissance, a French word, in English means "rebirth," a phenomenon that came about with diplomacy in politics, educational reform, increasingly accurate science based on observation, knowledge disseminated by the printing press, more realistic art, and a general optimism in life resulting from the end of the Black Death in 1350 A.D., a plague that had wiped out a quarter of the earth's 450 million population and 30% to 60% of Europe's.

In the Catholic Church the term "renaissance" would also apply. Since the late Renaissance, in 1585, no pope is documented to have been married or to have broken their vows by engaging in any sexual activities with harlots, mistresses, or with males before or after their election to pope, as they had for a number of centuries prior.

As for the excellent contributions of the Catholic Church through the centuries, monasteries alone have taught millions of people how to grow new crops, improve their manufacturing, and develop the science of metallurgy. They have also invented musical notation and taught mankind how to create and preserve literature.[173]

Monasteries, cathedrals, and convents for nuns spread through Europe by the thousands and provided additional good—they built and ran libraries, and often acted as banks, issuing credit to promote economic growth.[174] (They also accumulated profits in the process, and certainly power, but that does not detract from the good they did.)

Monasteries, cathedrals, and convents have also engaged in teaching arts, crafts, and establishing schools.[175]

The evolution of these schools is particularly interesting. After 1088 A.D. some of the older cathedral schools split into higher grammar schools and lower grammar schools. The higher grammar schools were for more advanced studies, giving birth to universities,[176] 1st in Bologna (Italy) in 1088, as the world's oldest continuously operating university, with the 2nd one at Oxford (in England) in 1096, then Cambridge (in England) in 1209, Salamanca (Spain) in 1218, Padua (Italy) in 1222, Naples (Italy) in 1224 (as the first public university), Toulouse (France) in 1229, and 8 others before 1300 (3 in Spain, 2 in Italy, 2 in France, and 1 in Portugal) for a total of 15 before 1300 A.D.[177]—a rich heritage indeed.

Members of the Catholic Church are rightly proud of their membership, despite the hits it has taken from the secularist media. (Some of these hits have been justified, such as when priests have been caught engaging in pedophilia, with resulting cover-ups by higher church officials, but that has occurred in nearly every large organization—including churches; yet the percentage of those church officials engaged in such activities has, by comparison, been relatively small.)

The majority of media attacks have been unjustified cheap shots to make the church look bad.

Meanwhile, the same media have mostly overlooked Catholic world charities and contributions to education, as they have Latter-day Saint charities, which donate dozens of millions of dollars and millions of volunteer man-hours in relief and welfare annually as one of the premier relief efforts in the world.

With regard to LDS relief efforts between 2005 and 2011 alone: LDS relief trucks were on the scene at Hurricane Katrina in 2005 before the National Guard even allowed humanitarian services through; and the church airlifted food, supplies and tents to the 2007 oil spill victims in South Korea, the 2010 earthquake victims in Haiti and Chili, the 2011 tsunami and earthquake victims in Japan and elsewhere, while providing on-the-ground volunteer support by hundreds of church members. In 2011 alone, 7 million LDS member volunteer hours were donated to welfare services.

A study published by the University of Pennsylvania in 2012, "Called to Serve: The Prosocial Behavior of Active Latter-day Saints," analyzed data from 2,664 church-attending LDS people around the U.S. and concluded that they "volunteer and donate significantly more than the average American and are even more generous in time and money than the upper quintile [top 20%] of religious people in America," donating on average, per person, 427.9 hours annually to charitable causes, 43% of that to non-religious causes, and 150 hours in welfare and humanitarian aid programs, plus 34 hours annually to social causes.[178]

Meanwhile, the 1.2-billion-member Roman Catholic Church is the world's largest charitable organization, still providing much-needed services and medical/humanitarian relief, although its per-member volunteer hours, on average, are not as high as among the Latter-day Saints. Nevertheless, the good they do is immeasurable in relieving suffering, providing as an institution more than anyone. And they continue to provide educational service to millions on a level quantitatively higher than public schools.

Yet neither church—Catholic nor LDS—seeks attention by advertising its humanitarian deeds.

As for the commendable work that non-Catholic Christian churches do, mankind has benefited remarkably from their humanitarian aid as well, and their followers also generally lead better lives because of them.

The question, however, is not about historical abuses—nor about the splendid charities and educational efforts of these churches—but rather authority from Jesus Christ.

The most significant question may come down to whether the authority and priesthood of Christ's original church continued through the channels of traditional Christianity or withdrew from the earth about 100 A.D., per the LDS claim. Therefore, the most important issue is authority from Jesus Christ per New Testament standards, rather than from the state, believe Latter-day Saints.

The strength of the Latter-day Saint position is emphasized by a Roman Catholic theologian, John M. Reiner, Ph.D., LL.D.,[179] a former Lutheran minister who converted to Catholicism,[180] and who visited Salt Lake City in 1898. He spoke at the Salt Lake Tabernacle to a near-capacity crowd of 7,000 on January 16,[181] and later wrote a series of letters to LDS General Authority B. H. Roberts, which were published in the *Improvement Era* magazine that same year.[182]

(Some in the LDS community have misunderstood Reiner's background, assuming he was a Catholic priest. A few others, from the Catholic community, have tried to dismiss him as not a "noted" theologian. Actually no one, certainly with any authority in the LDS community, has ever claimed he was "a noted" theologian—but some Catholic critics have misstated the LDS position on him).

Nevertheless, a Catholic theologian he was. The Merriam-Webster dictionary defines theology as "the study of religious faith, practice, and experience."[183]

And for that he was more than qualified. (He received his 4-year bachelor's plus his 4-year Master of Divinity degree,[184] then he engaged in further years of study while converting to Catholicism—obtaining both a Ph.D. and an LL.D. [a doctor's degree and a law degree], emphasizing historical and philosophical research, then becoming an author on religious controversy and ecclesiastical history. On these subjects he was an editorial contributor to several New York City newspapers. He was also a professor at Villanova University, a well-known Catholic university outside Philadelphia.[185] These disciplines add up to more than the necessary qualifications of a theologian, considering Merriam-Webster's definition of theology.)

So, his widely published statement below should certainly be respected by open-minded members of all faiths.

When he arrived in Salt Lake City 3 weeks before his lecture, he began a thorough investigation of LDS claims and visited many towns, making numerous friends among church authorities along the way, according to the *Deseret News* in 1898.[186]

One of these friends became General Authority Orson F. Whitney, who spoke with him privately and published a portion of their conversation in 1921, reporting a candid account of their visit:

"Many years ago I had an interesting conversation with a man who was a member of the Roman Catholic Church. He was a great scholar; he must have had a dozen languages at his tongue's end, and seemed to know all about history, science, law, philosophy. . . . We were frank and friendly with each other, and one day he said to me:

"'You "Mormons" are all ignoramuses. You don't even know the strength of your own position. It is so strong that there is only one other position tenable in the whole Christian world, and that is the position of the Roman Catholic church. The issue is between "Mormonism" and Catholicism. If you are right, we are wrong. If we are right, you are wrong, and that's all there is to it. These Protestant sects haven't a leg to stand on; for if we are right, we cut them off long ago, as apostates; and if we are wrong, they are wrong with us, for they were a part of us and came out of us.

"'If we do not have the apostolic succession, then such a man as Joseph Smith was necessary, and "Mormonism's" position is the only consistent one. It is either the perpetuation of the Gospel from ancient times or the restoration of the Gospel in the latter days.'"[187]

The power of his statement lies in its pure and simple logic.

Some may try to frame Reiner's comment as no longer relevant, because it came 64 years before a seemingly more inclusive position was made about the Protestant priesthood at Vatican II, held from 1962–1965, in which more liberal elements within the church interpreted the pope's views as accepting Protestant authority.

However, the position taken by the Catholic Church in 2007 reflects Reiner's attitude—that Protestantism is cut off from Catholicism, and that Rome has the only true church with the only valid priesthood authority.[188]

That view was officially reinstated by Pope Benedict XVI that year, declaring other Christian denominations not true churches because they lack apostolic succession. (See this endnote for details on the Vatican's position of the Protestant priesthood, clarifying that it does not accept it.)[189]

(In the next endnote the author examines comparisons in structure between the Roman Catholic Church and The Church of Jesus Christ of Latter-day Saints, including definitions and statistics of Catholic parishes and cathedrals compared to the LDS equivalents, as well as the officers and their duties in both churches.[190])

The 2007 clarification substantiates the position of John M. Reiner—that Catholics see themselves as possessing the one linear priesthood authority since Christ—while the Latter-day Saints see that chain as a broken one, with a need for a

Restoration, which they claim occurred in 1830 through the instrumentality of Joseph Smith.

Despite their theological differences, leaders of both churches, as well as a number of conservative Protestant churches, have made successful efforts in working together on common grounds—social and moral issues, charity, and humanitarian assistance.

On the theological front, a lingering question could be, "Why would Christ have set up His church, only to have it disappear decades later—by 100 A.D.?"

Latter-day Saints answer:

It was a pattern reoccurring through thousands of years—with God's priesthood on earth ending through either persecution or apostasy and needing to be restored.

Joseph Smith teaches that the restoration accomplished through him is the *final restoration*, before the Second Coming of Christ, and that the church will last until that Second Coming, not to be destroyed again. This, Latter-day Saints feel, is due in part to a free people set up in a free country, away from tyrannical rulers such as the early Christians faced. This time, there would be a divinely inspired Constitution in the land, which had been fought for by men inspired to found the nation and thus allow the restored church and other churches to be protected and even flourish.

The late Latter-day Saint Apostle Mark E. Peterson made a clear declaration of the church's position in 1957:

"In 1830 the Almighty restored his Church to earth again. He has raised up modern prophets and Apostles to direct the work. Under the guidance of heaven they organized his Church according to the pattern of ancient times. The powers of the priesthood have been brought back to earth by the ministry of angels. All the gifts and powers of former days have been restored. They did not come from any existing organization. They did not come from any man-made society, nor from any political unit. They came from heaven. Holy angels brought them to earth.

"This restored Church is known as The Church of Jesus Christ of Latter-day Saints, with headquarters in Salt Lake City. Its organization meets all of the specifications of the scripture. It possesses the divine priesthood of God. It is headed by prophets and Apostles as was the Church in the days of Peter and Paul."[191]

# The Missing Books of the Bible

## (REFERENCED IN CHAPTER 26)

The 14 missing books from the Bible that are mentioned in the King James Version are:

1. The book of the Wars of the Lord (Numbers 21:14)
2. The book of Jasher (Joshua 10:13, 2 Samuel 1:18)
3. The book of the acts of Solomon (1 Kings 11:41)
4. The book of Samuel the Seer (1 Chronicles 29:29)
5. The book of Nathan the prophet (1 Chronicles 29:29, 2 Chronicles 9:29)
6. The prophecy of Ahijah (2 Chronicles 9:29
7. The visions of Iddo the seer (2 Chronicles 9:29; 12:15; 13:22)
8. The book of Shemaiah (2 Chronicles 12:15)
9. The book of Jehu (2 Chronicles 20:34)
10. The sayings of the seers (2 Chronicles 33:19)
11. An early epistle of Paul to the Corinthians, earlier than current 1 Corinthians (1 Corinthians 5:9)
12. An early epistle of Paul to the Ephesians (possibly; Ephesians 3:3)

13. An epistle to the church at Laodicea (Colossians 4:16)
14. The prophecies of Enoch (Jude 1:14)

Another 3 books referenced in the Bible are either missing from the Bible entirely or are used in the Bible under a different name:

1. The book of the covenant (Exodus 24:7)
2. The manner of the kingdom, written by Samuel (1 Samuel 10:25)
3. The rest of the acts of Uzziah, written by Isaiah (2 Chronicles 26:22)[1]

# Notes on the Apocrypha

(REFERENCED IN CHAPTER 26)

The first Bible to include the term *Apocrypha* was Martin Luther's first full Bible, published in 1534, which he had translated in the early 1500s.

The Apocrypha consisted of 14 books—or portions of canonical books—not contained in the Hebrew Old Testament, but which were contained in the Greek Old Testament. (The most authoritative Greek version was the Septuagint.)

For his translation Luther cited Jerome of the 5th century, who had viewed the Hebrew and Greek Old Testaments and had noticed the difference in their contents. When Jerome finished the Vulgate in 405 A.D. he did not utilize these 14 books, electing to go with what was contained in the Hebrew Old Testament.

Even in his day there was debate about these books, but in medieval times they began to catch on—Roman and other Orthodox churches, such as Greek, Russian, and Egyptian, began to view the books that comprise the Apocrypha as fully canonical.

Hundreds of years later, in 1546, the church at Rome officially canonized their Bible at the Council of Trent, and included the Apocrypha as part of the Old Testament.[1] The books had been in use in the Roman church for centuries, and are still considered canonical today by Catholics.

While many scholars still did not accept these books as canonical, Luther claims they should have been.[2]

Luther's was the first major edition to have the Apocrypha in a separate section. He placed it between the Old and New Testaments, which gave birth to an often-used term, "inter-testamental books."[3]

All the English-language Bibles of the 1500s followed Luther's lead by including the Apocrypha, either as a section between the 2 testaments or as an appendix. These include the Coverdale Bible of 1535 (the first full Bible in English), the Matthew-Tyndale Bible of 1537, Taverner's Bible of 1539, the Great Bible of 1539, the Geneva Bible of 1560, the Bishops' Bible of 1568, and the Douay-Rheims Bible of 1582–1609. (See Appendix T: "English Bibles that Shook the World" for details of each.)

When the most accepted of all Protestant Bibles was published in 1611—the King James Version—it followed Luther's lead on 3 fronts: (1) using the name, "Apocrypha," (2) including all 14 books, and (3) placing them between the Old and New Testaments.

English Protestants at the Westminster Confession of Faith in 1647 shook the Bible world with a rather startling change— they deleted the Apocrypha from the canon, dismissing them as "human writings."[4] The rumblings for this had begun when Protestants separated themselves from the Church of England during the English Civil War of 1641–1651 and decided among themselves the Apocrypha was not scripture.

This short-term revolution would not hold. The Apocrypha continued to be included in *all* King James Version Bibles until 1666.[5]

After 1666 *most* King James Version Bibles would continue to include it for another 219 years.

Meanwhile, in the 1700s the revised Catholic Douay-Rheims Bible would drop the Apocrypha.

In 1826 a new Bible revolution was launched, and this one would last. The British and Foreign Bible Society determined they would not pay for the printing of any more Bibles that included the Apocrypha,[6] which set a new tradition among most Protestants. Despite that mandate, most editions of the King James Version would include the Apocrypha for another 59 years (until 1885).

Since 1885, the revolution has taken hold. Most re-printings of the King James Version and even modern versions of the Bible do not include the Apocrypha, even though the British and Foreign Bible Society lifted restrictions on publishing Bibles with the Apocrypha in 1966, and the American Bible Society did so in 1964. However, the tradition of the Protestant Bible-reading public since 1826 had ingrained itself so deeply since the revolution that they have never gotten back on track with it.

The text in Chapter 26 includes Joseph Smith's revelation from God about the Apocrypha—essentially that some of it is inspired and some isn't.

The final part of that revelation reads:

"Verily, I say unto you, that it is not needful that the Apocrypha should be translated. Therefore, whoso readeth it, let him understand, for the Spirit manifesteth truth; and whoso is enlightened by the Spirit shall obtain benefit therefrom."[7]

Thus, the Apocrypha is not included in the published canon, known as the "Standard Works" of the Church of Jesus Christ of Latter-day Saints.

# Harvest at the Isaac Morley Farm

(REFERENCED IN CHAPTER 32)

Details of the missionaries' journey to Ohio highlight a remark-able adventure:

At Mentor, Ohio, Oliver Cowdery and Parley P. Pratt arrived. Their only goal was to visit Sidney Rigdon. Parley reflects on their plans to see him: "At length [we] called on Mr. Rigdon, my former friend and instructor in the Reformation Baptist Society."[1] Their exploits are recounted in the main text of this volume.

After Oliver and Parley finished their initial work at Mentor, they shot off to find the other two, Ziba Peterson and Peter Whitmer Jr., at Euclid. There they had an eventful meeting.

Meanwhile, Scottish Reformer Walter Scott rode over 100 miles to spy on these newcomers at Euclid. He would later report 5 converts being made by the young men on one of their first nights,[2] and would keep a close eye on these New York youngsters calling themselves missionaries.

But the four found Euclid more interesting than they had probably ever imagined.

On November 2, 1830, a 15-year-old girl named Lucy Diantha Morley worked for a neighbor living a mile north, doing housework. When the missionaries knocked at the door, her boss invited them inside. "Three well dressed, nice-looking gentlemen came in [just older than her, in their early 20s,] I arose from my seat [and] sat them [in] some chairs. [I] took their hats and, when they were seated, they began to talk to us about the gospel as had been revealed in these last days—how an angel had appeared to one Joseph Smith and had given them authority to preach this gospel to all the world."

Because of this, "the lady of the house turned on her loom bench [weaving machine], shuttle in hand, which she shook in their faces, [and] told them to leave her house, as she would not have her children polluted with any such doctrine."

The missionaries were practically starving and asked for food, but the woman taunted them, saying she had food but not for them.

"I had been sitting there all this time listening to her foul tongue[.] I could stand it no longer, for I felt that they were the servants of God as they said they were. I said, 'Gentlemen, my father lives one mile from here. He never turns anyone hungry from his door. Go there and you will be fed and cared for.' I gave them their hats and then showed them the road that led to my father's house, and they were soon out of sight."[3] Her boss scolded her but, when Diantha finished her work, she raced home to hear what the missionaries had to say.[4]

The 4 missionaries arrived at her father's. His name was Issac Morley. He presided over a large farm of 331 acres. He had been raised a Congregationalist and had converted to the Disciples of Christ (also called Reformed Baptists) in Kirtland 2½ years earlier. He was so intensely committed to living the gospel of Christ as taught in Acts of the New Testament that he presided over a large communal order on their farm that housed many families.

Before arriving there, the missionaries had prophesied they would find a place to stay that would bear much fruit, according to a letter Oliver would write 8 days later.[5]

Isaac was the perfect contact—in fact, better than they had ever dreamed of finding.

When the missionaries arrived at Isaac's farm, they found one Lyman Wight loading up a wagon, heading for Mayfield, 8 miles southwest of Kirtland, on the road to Cleveland. Wight reports: "I desired they would hold on till I got away, as my business was of vital importance, and I did not wish to be troubled with romances nor idle speculators. Nothing daunted, they were not to be put off, but were as good-natured as you please. Curiosity got uppermost, and I concluded to stop for a short time."[6] That short time turned into a long time. He wanted to hear more and more. The missionaries put their message above eating, though extremely hungry, and continued their visit as long as Wight wanted.

Wight left with only an hour of light remaining in the sky, upon which the missionaries finally ate, then spoke with others after dinner, all the way till these strapping young New Yorkers left at 11 P.M., states young Lucy Diantha. It was a late hour for early-rising farm communities.[7]

Another person present, John Riggs, reports that the missionaries spoke to all who would listen that night. He says the young missionary Oliver declared that an angel had visited Joseph Smith, and that the boy received gold plates and translated them.[8] A simple but powerful presentation. Two other messages from the missionaries were that Jesus Christ had visited the ancient Americas, and that they—the missionaries—held the authority to act in God's name. The nearby *Painesville Telegraph* quoted Oliver's claim to that authority.[9]

Isaac Morley's communal order, "the Family," would all be converted, states Jesse Jasper Moss, a member of it,[10] with Isaac himself as the kingpin.

The reason was simple. When others began hearing about the mass conversion to the New York faith, other local residents on Morley's farm became intrigued and listened. Ann Whitney states that after "Brother Morley had received them into his house and had united himself to their faith, I felt an earnest desire to hear their principles proclaimed, and to judge for myself."[11] She joined as well. They had a domino effect on others.

Walter Scott, meanwhile, was appalled. He went searching for those who had left his faith to join the Saints and try to persuade them[12] to "return to Christ," unaware they felt closer to Christ now than ever before.

The 2 folds near Cleveland, Ohio—the Sidney Rigdon congregation at Kirtland and the Isaac Morley farm community a mile east of Kirtland—were becoming a bumper-crop harvest the missionaries would not soon forget, as they continued their missionary journey westward to seek out the Lamanites.

# Notes

# PREFACE

1.  Joseph Smith, *History of the Church of Jesus Christ of Latter-day Saints*, edited by B. H. Roberts, 7 volumes (Salt Lake City: Deseret Book, Second Revised Edition 1971), vol. 6, p. 317.

    **Note 1: This quote in the Preface of no man knowing Joseph's history was the final statement of Joseph Smith's April 7, 1844, remarks known as the King Follett Discourse. The next day he spoke a few minutes to finish his sermon, which was actually an address at the funeral of a faithful Latter-day Saint named King Follett, killed during construction of the Nauvoo, Illinois, temple.**

    **Note 2: In these notes, references to *History of the Church* are to the official 7-volume history of the Church of Jesus Christ of Latter-day Saints, also commonly called the *Documentary History of the Church*, edited and with an introduction by B. H. Roberts. The first 6 volumes are from the combined personal history and official church history that Joseph Smith himself dictated to various scribes and engaged them in maintaining, beginning in 1838; the 7th volume was prepared from the manuscript history of Brigham Young and other documents. Volume 8 is the index.**

2.  Joseph Smith, Letter (to William W. Phelps, November 27, 1832), in Joseph Smith's first letterbook, *The Joseph Smith Papers, Documents, Volume 2*, edited by Matthew C. Godfrey, Mark Ashurst McGee, Grant Underwood, Robert J. Woodford, and William G. Hartley (Salt Lake City: The Church Historian's Press, 2013), in multiple-volume series, *The Joseph Smith*

*Papers*, edited by Dean C. Jessee, Ronald K. Esplin, and Richard Lyman Bushman (Salt Lake City: The Church Historian's Press, 2008–).

3. Note: This quote was given by Tom Anderson in his writings and speeches, which I personally heard when invited by a friend to a lecture given by Anderson in Chattanooga, Tennessee. Editor of *Farm and Ranch* magazine, Anderson had a syndicated column that was published nationwide in 375 newspapers. He lived from 1910 to 2002.

   In this quote he changed the words of Ronald Reagan, who used it on October 27, 1964, in a nationally televised, paid political speech entitled, "A Time for Choosing," in behalf of presidential candidate Barry Goldwater. Reagan was more political in his version of the quote, saying, "Well, the trouble with our liberal friends is not that they're ignorant. It's just that they know so much that isn't so." Reagan likely borrowed it from 19th-century humorist Henry Wheeler Shaw, who wrote under the pen name Josh Billings and was second only to Mark Twain in his reputation as a humor writer and lecturer known for folksy common-sense wit and wisdom. Billings lived from 1818 to 1885. His original version of the quote, which is also used as the Prologue of this book, is, "It ain't ignorance causes so much trouble; it's folks knowing so much that ain't so." [Ralph Keyes, *The Quote Verifier: Who Said What, Where, and When* (New York City: Macmillan/St. Martin's Griffin, First Edition eBook 2010.] One of my favorite quotes also comes from Billings: "Consider the postage stamp, son. It secures success through its ability to stick to one thing till it gets done." (Needless to say, I found it apropos for getting through this decade-plus project.)

4. Note: The shortest distance from the Salt Lake Temple to the Great Salt Lake as the birds fly is about 6 miles northwest; however, if one wished to travel from the temple to the Great Salt Lake, they would, for over 150 years, including today, have to travel by foot and somehow navigate over fences, farmlands, and marshes en route to the lake in a northwesterly route. Because of these obstacles, people have instead traveled directly westward, which, by using paths and roads then and now, makes the journey about 15 miles.

   This rumor of girls kidnapped to the Salt Lake Temple has been circulating for over a century, including in the UK where I first heard it from a man in southwest England, purporting the tunnel's entrance is in Liverpool. Since then, I have heard variations of the rumor, with the tunnel's entrance supposedly In London or in various other cities in Europe.

5. Note: This poll was conducted by Public Policy Polling, based in Raleigh, North Carolina, sponsored by Fordham University of Bronx, New York.

As to this polling organization's accuracy, it was ranked first among 28 polling organizations in its final national pre-election estimate, according to *Politico*, on November 7, 2012. The poll involving alien amphibian conspiracy was conducted on April 2, 2013 and reported on *Fox News*, to display the cluelessness of people.

Equally frightening, and actually supporting that hypothesis, is another number reported in that poll: 5% of registered voters in the United States believe exhaust seen in the sky behind airplanes is actually chemicals sprayed by the government for sinister reasons.

The alien conspiracy theory revolves around the work of British writer David Icke, who purports that 5- to 12-foot-tall, shape-shifting reptilian humanoids drink blood and now hide in underground bases, with plans to emerge and take over the world. He believes most of the world's leaders are related to them. (I have spoken with two people in Los Angeles believing this theory.) Icke has influenced tens of millions of people in the 47 countries where he has supporters. Opinion-makers—lecturers, writers, and promoters—can and have influenced millions of people, including the invention and spreading of rumors about Latter-day Saints, no matter how off-base and outlandish their reports and theories.

6. Note: Philo T. Farnsworth (1906-1971), a Latter-day Saint, is considered the inventor of the first fully functional, complete television system, including camera and receiver, and the first fully functional all-electronic TV picture tube, the primary component of a television set. He was also the first to demonstrate it to the public. He held 165 patents, primarily in radio and TV, but also pioneered other breakthrough technologies—a defense early warning signal, the PPI projector (forerunner to today's air traffic control systems), a penetrating beam in fog for ships and airplanes, an infrared telescope and other night vision devices, radar, including calibration equipment, submarine detection devices, the baby incubator, the electron microscope, the gastroscope, an astronomical telescope, and nuclear fusion research.

His best-known work however was television. When working as a farm boy, he observed the back and forth motion used to plow a field, and this inspired him to develop the video scanning of an image as a series of lines.

His family lived in a small log cabin near Beaver, Utah, when he was born. At his next home in Rigby, Idaho, he discovered in the attic a large cache of technology magazines, which got his head to spinning. Afterwards he attended Brigham Young University, then the Naval Academy in Annapolis. There, he feared the government would own his patents he was developing if he remained at the academy. However, his decision to leave did not come until he learned he was needed to return to Utah to help support his mother, so he got an honorable discharge.

He then received a grant and moved to San Francisco, where, on September 7, 1927, his camera tube transmitted its first image to a nearby room, which surprised his staff. In the awed silence he exclaimed, "There you are—electronic television!" [Frank Lovece, "Zwory Kin vs. Farnsworth, Part II: TV's Founding Father Family Meet—in the lab," *Video* (magazine), September 1985, p. 97.]

In 1928 he unveiled it to the press, then to the public in 1934. Meanwhile, in 1928 he obtained a patent for color transmission. In 1929, at the age of 22, the television system that he had envisioned for 8 years was launched—it had no mechanical parts, and he transmitted the first 5 human images, including a 3½-inch high image of his wife with her eyes squinting shut in the bright light that was required.

He moved to the east and became employed by Philco and ITT. In 1934 RCA sued him, but he countersued, and won in 1935, receiving only modest royalties the remainder of his life. In 1965, while engaged in fusion research, his employer, ITT, canceled the project. As a result he spiraled into a stressed-induced depression, and was retired for medical reasons.

In 1967 he moved back to Utah to continue nuclear fusion research at Brigham Young University. There he was given offices and an underground bunker, but independent financing for staff salaries (those he had brought with him from ITT) and for his rented equipment, stalled. So in late December 1970 he sold all his stock and cashed in his insurance policy to keep the project going, but banks called in their outstanding loans and everything was repossessed, with the final straw coming from the IRS locking the laboratory door until all back taxes were paid. Three months later he incurred pneumonia and died.

However, his legacy was unsurpassed. In 1957 he appeared as a guest on the national TV hit show, *I've Got A Secret*, for inventing television. Stumping the panel, he received $80 and a carton of Winston cigarettes. [Elma G. Farnsworth, *Distant Vision: Romance and Discovery of an Invisible Frontier* (Salt Lake City: Pemberly Kent Publishers, Inc., 1990), p. 37.]

On the show he summed up his television work well: "There had been attempts to devise a television system using mechanical disks and rotating mirrors and vibrating mirrors—all mechanical. My contribution was to take out the moving parts and make the thing entirely electronic, and that was the concept that I had when I was just a freshman in high school in the spring of 1921 at age 14." ["Philo Farnsworth on I've Got A Secret," 1957, YouTube, https://www.youtube.com/watch?v=pKM4MNrB25o.]

On the same show he introduced concepts of high-definition TV: "We think we can eventually get in excess of 2000 lines [they would actually use pixels] instead of 525 . . . which will make for a much sharper picture. We believe in the picture-frame type of a picture, where the visual display will be just a screen. And we hope for a memory, so that the picture will be just as though it's pasted on there." [Ibid.] He was indeed a visionary.

A fitting tribute was paid to him in his early years by *Collier's Weekly*, one of America's major magazines with over 2 million circulation in its October 3, 1936, issue: "Electricity scanned television that seems destined to reach your home next year was largely given to the world by a nineteen year old boy from Utah. Today, barely thirty years old, he is setting the specialized world of science on its edge." [*Collier's Weekly* (Springfield, Ohio), October 3, 1936.]

In 1999 he was also paid a tribute by *Time* magazine in "Time 100: The Most Important People of the Century." [Neil Postman, "The *Time* 100: Scientists & Thinkers: Philo Farnsworth," *Time* (New York City), March 29, 1999.]

In 2006 he was posthumously awarded the Eagle Scout when people realized he had earned it but never been presented it. His wife Pem received it, then died 4 months later, at age 98.

Farnsworth was inducted into the Television Academy Hall of Fame in 2013, and since 2003 the Academy of Television Arts and Sciences has awarded the Philo T. Farnsworth Corporate Achievement Award to those significantly affecting broadcasting and television engineering on a long-term basis.

7. Note: Since 1982 LDS church–owned Brigham Young University has annually won the NDCA title of United States National Formation Dance Champions. The BYU Ballroom Dance Company has won the U.S. Standard Dance Championship 17 straight years, and since 1971 it has competed in the highly prestigious British Open ballroom competition every 3 years, usually placing first in both Standard formation and Latin. They are the first Americans to win the prestigious British Formation Championships—with 14 first-place trophies on their shelves. They also have sellout performances in 30-plus countries,

with the dance teams touring twice per year. [Kellene Ricks Adams, "Amazing Grace," *BYU Magazine* (Provo, Utah), Winter 1998.]

BYU was also the first university to offer dance as a class. Brian McDonald, president of the National Dance Council of America, which governs dance competitions in the U.S., states, "And now BYU is, without question, the most influential school in the nation in terms of identifying dance as both a sport and a respected curriculum." [Ibid.] The university's first offering of dance for physical education/sports classes came in 1953, and has mushroomed into the most comprehensive collegiate study of ballroom dancing in the world. ["U.S. National Amateur DanceSport Championships," *BYU Arts* (Provo, Utah), http://arts.byu.edu/events/2645/.] In March 2014 it hosted the largest amateur DanceSport event in the country in over 30 different divisions, with national amateur dance titles awarded. [Ibid.]

"Dance at BYU," states Kellene Ricks Adams in her article, "Amazing Grace," "is steeped in a tradition older than the university itself." She quotes Lee Wakefield, artistic director of the BYU Ballroom Dance Company: "The Church has a rich history of dance. The pioneers danced across the plains, the Church held dance festivals for years, and until fairly recently, annual Gold and Green Balls were a highlight in many wards and stakes around the world." [Kellene Ricks Adams, "Amazing Grace," *BYU Magazine* (Provo, Utah), Winter 1998.]

Adams adds, "BYU's teams also attract attention for their commitment to wholesome performances and modest costumes." She illuminates why, quoting Lisa Wakefield, dance company co-director and costumer director: "The company's primary goal is to spread the gospel through dance. We have to be constantly aware of the things that we do—our actions, movements, steps, and motions. We strive to be sensitive and selective in our choreography, costuming, and conduct."

Adams continues, "That sensitivity has made an impact on others In the dance field." Brian McDonald, president of the National Dance Council of America, defines the impact in Adams's article: "BYU's program and its team have been so helpful, so influential to the industry as a whole. The university's standards and its ideals motivate others to a higher performance."

The pièce de résistance came in this manner, according to Adams:

"Recently when the National Dance Council considered adopting dress standards for certain dance competitions, it turned to Lee Wakefield for help. Implementing parts of the BYU dress code, he wrote costume guidelines that were eventually implemented. 'What we do, what we wear, what we've accomplished is respected; we are making a difference,' says Wakefield.

"McDonald doesn't mince words In explaining how much of a difference. 'Let me explain it this way: We in America would be at a terrible loss If we did not have the involvement of Brigham Young University and the standards and curriculum they have set for ballroom dance. They're an example to the whole country.'" [Ibid.]

Meanwhile, in the world of hip-hop dancing, BYU's precision dance team, the Cougarettes, has won 10 consecutive National Collegiate Cheer and Dance Championship Division I titles in hip-hop. In 2014 it won its 10th title at Daytona Beach, with a nearly perfect score of 9.984. (In over 30 years a perfect score has never been awarded by a judge, until 2014 when a judge did give them a perfect 10 across the board.)

In Team Dance competition they were champions in 1997–1999, 2001, 2005–2007, and 2010–2011. In 2014 they came in second behind Penn State by less than 1/100th of a point, with the championships broadcast on the CBS Sports Network.

The Cougarettes perform at BYU football and basketball events and stage their own concerts, highly proficient in hip-hop, contemporary, jazz, lyrical, pom-pom, and character dance. ["BYU Cougarettes again National Dance Champion in Hip-Hop: Championships to be broadcast April 29, May 6 [2014] on CBS Sports Network," BYU News Release (Provo, Utah), April 17, 2012), http://news.byu.edu/archive12-apr-cougs.aspx.]

Note that a 1:40 video clip of their 2014 1st-place hip-hop performance is at this site: http://news.byu.edu/archive12-apr-cougs.aspx.

8.  Robin Williams, "Wernher von Braun (1912–1977)," (Washington, D.C.: NASA, Earth Observatory), nasa.gov/Features/von Braun/.

9.  Kathryn Dill, "The Most and Least Educated Cities in America," *Forbes*, September 16, 2014, http://www.forbes.com/sites/kathryndill/2014/09/16/the-most-and-least-educated-cities-in-america/.

Note 1: In this article about the most educated cities in America, Kathryn Dill describes how they made the list: "To determine the 'Most and Least Educated Cities in America,' financial site WalletHub took a look at the 150 largest metros in the U.S. and ranked them according to 9 weighted metrics, including percentage of adult residents with a high school diploma, associate's degree, graduate or professional degree, or above; number of doctors per capita; percentage of workers with jobs in 'computer, engineering, and sciences fields,' quality of

public schools and universities; and the number of students enrolled
in the top 200 universities in the U.S., per capita."

Note 2: Utah is also ranked in the Top 9 of the 50 states with the highest
percentage of high school graduates. ["List of U.S. States by educational
attainment," sub-headlined "2009 percentage of population 25 years old
with a High School diploma," etc.), Wikipedia, http://en.wikipedia.9org/
wiki/List_of_U.S._states_by_educational_attaintment.]

Note 3: For those with bachelors' and advanced college degrees,
Utah's rating among states is 19th and 26th respectively, but these
figures for advanced education are skewed, because a large number
of Latter-day Saints obtain these degrees after age 25 (the survey was
for 25 and under). The reason for the higher age of college graduates
among Utahans is the fact a high number of Latter-day Saints go on
church missions—2 years for men and 18 months for women, delaying
their college education and often working after their missions to earn
money for college as well. Also many residents marry under the age
of 25, as Utah is the youngest average state in the nation for marrying.
["The States Where People Marry the Youngest," http://efinisty.comcast.
net/slideshow/news-youngoldmarry/5/.] After church missions and/
or marrying, a substantial number of young people then work for a
while before pursuing or resuming college, delaying their completion
of bachelor's and post-graduate degrees until somewhat after age 25.
Were the age limit in the census article higher than 25, the rankings
for Utah would likely be higher, perhaps significantly.

10.  Joseph Smith, Letter (to John Wentworth, editor of *Chicago Democrat*),
     published in *Times and Seasons* (Nauvoo, Illinois), March 1, 1842.

11.  The Bible, King James Version, New Testament, Revelation 22:18.

12.  John Adams, "Arguments in Defense of the Soldiers in the Boston Massacre
     Trials," December 1770, The Legal Papers of John Adams, No. 64, Rex vs.
     Wemms. Summation of John Adams, next-to-last paragraph, http://law2.
     umke.edu/faculty/projects/ftrials/bostonmassacre/adamssummation.
     html.

     "The Defense delivered by Mr. Adams in the trial of William Weems, James
     Hartigan, and others, soldiers in His Majesty's Twenty-ninth Regiment,
     for the murder of Crispus Attacks, Samuel Grey, and others, on Monday
     evening, the fifth of March, 1770," http://democraticthinker.wordpress.
     com/2011/09/13/john-adams-defense-of-the-british-soldiers—i/.

     Note: As noted in the above 2 sources, when John Adams defended the
     British soldiers who fired upon the Colonists at the Boston Massacre,
     he presented his summation with a well-crafted, concise statement,

which is quoted in my Preface, but he explains it more fully in the complete sentence: "Facts are stubborn things; and whatsoever may be our wishes, our inclinations, or the dictates of our passion, they cannot alter the state of fact and evidence."

Adams made this summation at the trial in December 1770, which was 9 months after the Boston Massacre of March 5, 1770.

# CHAPTER 1

1. National Council of Churches, *Yearbook of American and Canadian Churches* (Nashville, Tennessee: Abingdon Press, 2012).

Note 1: The leading 25 Christian churches in the United States, as of 2014 and reported for 2012, are reported in the list below.

1. Roman Catholic Church. 68.2 million members. Down 0.44%.
2. Southern Baptist Convention. 16.1 million. Down 0.15%.
3. The United Methodist Church. 7.7 million. Down 1.22%.
4. The Church of Jesus Christ of Latter-day Saints. 6.2 million. Up. 1.62%.
5. Church of God in Christ. 5.5 million. No update reported.
6. National Baptist Convention, U.S.A. 5.2 million. Up 3.95%.
7. Evangelical Lutheran Church in America. 4.3 million. Down 5.9%.
8. National Baptist Convention of America. 3.5 million. No update.
9. Assemblies of God. 3 million. Up 3.99%.
10. Presbyterian Church (U.S.A.). 2.7 million. Down 3.42%.
11. African Methodist Episcopal Church. 2.5 million. No update.
12. National Missionary Baptist Convention of America. 2.5 million. No update.
13. The Lutheran Church—Missouri Synod. 2.3 million. Down 1.45%.
14. The Episcopal Church. 2 million. Down 2.71%.
15. Pentecostal Assemblies of the World. 1.8 million. Up 20%.

16. Churches of Christ. 1.6 million. No update.

17. Greek Orthodox Archdiocese of America. 1.5 million.
No update.

18. The African Methodist Episcopal Zion Church. 1.4 million.
No update.

19. American Baptist Churches in the U.S.A. 1.3 million.
Down 0.19%.

20. Jehovah's Witnesses. 1.2 million. Down 0.19%.

21. Church of God (Cleveland, Tennessee). 1.1 million.
Down 0.21%.

22. Christian Churches and Churches of Christ. 1.1 million. Up. 1.61%.

23. Seventh-day Adventist Church. 1.1 million. Up 1.61%.

24. United Church of Christ. 1.1 million. Up 2.02%.

25. Progressive National Baptist Convention. 1 million. No update.

Total Membership in Top 25: 145.7 million. Down 1.15%.

Note 2: Defenders and detractors of the Church of Jesus Christ of
Latter-day Saints disagree over the definition of Christianity, with
detractors taking the position that the church does not follow Jesus
Christ, while Latter-day Saints claim it does follow Christ. The National
Council of Churches (NCC) chooses to include the Church of Jesus
Christ of Latter-day Saints as a Christian church in the above list.

2. Daniel H. Ludlow, editor, *Encyclopedia of Mormonism* (New York City:
Macmillan, 1992), vol. 3, p. 1348.

3. "Joseph Smith Jr. Letter Books, 1829–1835," manuscript, Church Archives,
The Church of Jesus Christ of Latter-day Saints, Salt Lake City.

4. Lucy Mack Smith, *History of Joseph Smith by His Mother: The Unabridged
Original Version* (Arlington, Virginia and Provo, Utah: Stratford Books,
Revised Second Edition 2006), p. 71.

5. Ibid.

6. Ibid., p. 73.

7. Note: In analyzing this business failure of Joseph Smith senior, his
1st mistake was buying goods on credit; his 2nd was selling inventory
to customers on promise of payment instead of hard cash; and his
3rd was even agreeing to accept farm commodities in place of cash.
Parenthetically, his Boston distributor would never have taken the

commodities in lieu of cash, so he was apparently banking on his ability to sell the commodities for cash, allowing him to pay off the distributor. All in all, he was relying too heavily on the honesty of his customers, probably projecting upon them his own honesty. Chronologically, his 4th and most significant mistake was in not taking the cash offer on the table for the ginseng.

8. Lucy Mack Smith, *Biographical Sketches of Joseph Smith the Prophet and His Progenitors for Many Generations* (Liverpool, England: S. W. Richards, 1853), p. 51.

9. Lucy Mack Smith, *History of Joseph Smith by His Mother: The Unabridged Original Version* (Arlington, Virginia and Provo, Utah: Stratford Books, Revised Second Edition 2006), p. 83.

10. Larry C. Porter, *A Study of the Origins of the Church of Jesus Christ of Latter-day Saints in the States of New York and Pennsylvania, 1816–1831* (Ph.D. dissertation, Brigham Young University, 1971; published at Provo, Utah: Joseph Fielding Smith Institute for Latter-day Saint History and *BYU Studies*, 2000), p. 7.

Note: *BYU Studies* was first named *Brigham Young University Studies* when it was established in January 1959 at Brigham Young University in Provo, Utah. Since April 2012 it has been known as *BYU Studies Quarterly*. In this book it is referenced as merely *BYU Studies*. It has always been an academic journal covering a myriad of topics related to the Church of Jesus Christ of Latter-day Saints and is still published quarterly by the university.

11. Lucy Mack Smith, *History of Joseph Smith by His Mother: The Unabridged Original Version* (Arlington, Virginia and Provo, Utah: Stratford Books, Revised Second Edition 2006), p. 83.

12. Ibid., p. 50.

13. Lucy Mack Smith, Preliminary Manuscript [1844–1845], Church Archives, The Church of Jesus Christ of Latter-day Saints, Salt Lake City.

Also displayed in Lucy Mack Smith, *Lucy's Book: A Critical Edition of Lucy Mack Smith's Family Memoir,* edited by Lavina Fielding Anderson (Salt Lake City: Signature Books, 2001), pp. 299–300.

14. Lucy Mack Smith, *History of Joseph Smith by His Mother: The Unabridged Original Version* (Arlington, Virginia and Provo, Utah: Stratford Books, Revised Second Edition 2006), p. 85.

15. Ibid., pp. 89–90.

16. Frederick Chase, *A History of Dartmouth College and the Town of Hanover, New Hampshire*, edited by John P. Lord, 2 volumes (Cambridge, Massachusetts: John Wilson and Son, 1891), vol. 1, pp. 634–635.

17. Lucy Mack Smith, *History of Joseph Smith by His Mother: The Unabridged Original Version* (Arlington, Virginia and Provo, Utah: Stratford Books, Revised Second Edition 2006), p. 90.

18. Ibid., p. 91.

# CHAPTER 2

1. Lucy Mack Smith, *History of Joseph Smith by His Mother: The Unabridged Original Version* (Arlington, Virginia and Provo, Utah: Stratford Books, Revised Second Edition 2006), p. 93.

2. Ibid., p. 94.

3. Joseph Smith, Manuscript History of the Church, Book A-1, Church Historian's Office, Church Archives, The Church of Jesus Christ of Latter-day Saints, Salt Lake City, pp. 131–132.

4. Lucy Mack Smith, *History of Joseph Smith by His Mother: The Unabridged Original Version* (Arlington, Virginia and Provo, Utah: Stratford Books, Revised Second Edition 2006), p. 94.

5. Ibid.

6. Ibid.

7. Ibid., p. 95.

8. Ibid.

9. Ibid.

10. Ibid.

11. Ibid.

   **Note: In R. Vernon Ingleton's Stratford Books edition, Lucy's rough draft is set apart in a separate type font from the rest of her 1853 published book, making it easy to differentiate between her published book and her rough draft.**

12. Joseph Smith, Manuscript History of the Church, Book A-1, Church Historian's Office, Church Archives, The Church of Jesus Christ of Latter-day Saints, Salt Lake City, pp. 131–132.

13. Lucy Mack Smith, *History of Joseph Smith by His Mother: The Unabridged Original Version* (Arlington, Virginia and Provo, Utah: Stratford Books, Revised Second Edition 2006), p. 96.

14. Joseph Smith, Manuscript History of the Church, Book A-1, Church Historian's Office, Church Archives, The Church of Jesus Christ of Latter-day Saints, Salt Lake City, pp. 131–132.

15. Lucy Mack Smith, *History of Joseph Smith by His Mother: The Unabridged Original Version* (Arlington, Virginia and Provo, Utah: Stratford Books, Revised Second Edition 2006), p. 95.

16. Ibid.

17. Ibid.

18. Leroy S. Wirthlin, "Joseph Smith's Boyhood Operation: An 1813 Surgical Success," *BYU Studies*, vol. 21, no. 2 (1981), pp. 131–154.

    Leroy S. Wirthlin, "Nathan Smith (1762–1828): Surgical Consultant to Joseph Smith," *BYU Studies*, vol. 17, no. 3 (1977), pp. 319–337.

19. Lucy Mack Smith, *History of Joseph Smith by His Mother: The Unabridged Original Version* (Arlington, Virginia and Provo, Utah: Stratford Books, Revised Second Edition 2006), p. 97.

    **Note: The final sentence of this quote is contained only in Lucy's rough draft.**

20. Ibid.

21. Ibid.

22. Ibid., p. 98.

23. Ibid.

24. Joseph Smith, Manuscript History of the Church, Book A-1, Church Historian's Office, Church Archives, The Church of Jesus Christ of Latter-day Saints, Salt Lake City, pp. 131–132.

25. Ibid.

26. Ibid.

27. Lucy Mack Smith, *History of Joseph Smith by His Mother: The Unabridged Original Version* (Arlington, Virginia and Provo, Utah: Stratford Books, Revised Second Edition 2006), p. 98.

28. Ibid., p. 99.

29. Ibid.

30. Ibid., p. 100.

31. Ibid.

32. Ibid.

33. John D. Post, *The Last Great Subsistence Crisis in the Western World* (Baltimore: John Hopkins University Press, 1977), pp. 1–5.

34. Noel L. Griese, "The Bible vs. Mao: A 'Best Guess' of the Top 25 Bestselling Books of All Time," *Publishing Perspectives* (New York City, 2010), publishingperspectives.com/2010/09/top-25-bestseling-books-of-all-time/.

Note 1: Expanding the list to include Chinese government-backed printing and distribution, the list of all-time best-selling books becomes the following:

(1)  The Bible, 2.5–6 billion copies

(2)  *Quotations from Chairman Mao* (*The Little Red Book*), Mao Zedong (Chinese, 1964), 800–900 million

(3)  Qur'an, (Arabic; Muslim scripture), 800+ million

(4)  *Xinhua Dictionary* (Wei Jiangong, primary editor; Chinese, 1957), 400+ million

(5)  *Chairman Mao's Poems*, Mao Zedong (Chinese, 1966), 400 million copies

(6)  *Selected Articles of Mao Zedong*, Mao Zedong (Chinese, 1966), 252.5 million copies

(7)  *A Tale of Two Cities*, Charles Dickens, (English, 1859), 200 million copies

(8)  (tie) The *Book of Mormon*, multiple authors, translated by Joseph Smith Jr. (religious text published in 1830), over 150 million copies worldwide

(8)  (tie) *Scouting for Boys: A Handbook for Instruction in good Citizenship*, Robert Baden-Powell (English, 1980), 150 million

(8)  (tie) *The Lord of the Rings*, J. R. R. Tolkien (English, 1954–1955), 150 million copies

Note 2: Noel Griese is the compiler of this list for *Publishing Perspectives*, a project of the Frankfort Book Fair. He is also the editor of the magazine, *The Southern Review of Books*.

*Publishing Perspectives* is an e-mail news journal of international publishing containing news and reviews, released Monday through Friday by e-mail to its subscribers, and is based out of New York City. It publishes a daily newspaper for the Frankfort Book Fair (the largest book fair in the world) each year during the run of the fair.

*The Southern Review of Books*, based out of Atlanta, Georgia, is a monthly e-newsletter edited by Noel Griese, author of 17 books and former newspaper reporter and editor, as well as journalism and English teacher at the University of Wisconsin and University of Georgia. The newsletter publishes articles on the state of publishing, current statistics, and publishing news.

Note 3: The list's compiler, Noel Griese, places *The Book of Mormon*, *Scouting for Boys*, and *Lord of the Rings* at a 3-way tie at 150 million, yet admits *The Book of Mormon* is the only 1 of the 3 with over 150 million copies worldwide. The missionaries for the Church of Jesus Christ of Latter-day Saints (LDS) are the main distributors for the book, and after this list was compiled, the church's missionary force increased substantially (by 23% in a 10 month period between October 2012 and August 2013, because of the age limit being lowered by 1 year for boys and 2 years for girls—at 18 and 19, respectively). Because of this influx of new missionaries, *The Book of Mormon* may possibly pass *A Tale of Two Cities* within a few years to land in the 3rd spot of the all-time best-sellers (not counting Chinese government-sponsored books).

35. Lucy Mack Smith, *History of Joseph Smith by His Mother: The Unabridged Original Version* (Arlington, Virginia and Provo, Utah: Stratford Books, Revised Second Edition 2006), p. 100.

# CHAPTER 3

1. Lucy Mack Smith, *History of Joseph Smith by His Mother: The Unabridged Original Version* (Arlington, Virginia and Provo, Utah: Stratford Books, Revised Second Edition 2006), p. 102.

2. Ibid., p. 101.

3. Ibid.

4. Ibid., p. 102.

5. Ibid.

6. Ibid.

7. Ibid., pp. 102–103.

8. Ibid., p. 103.

9. Joseph Smith, Manuscript History of the Church, Book A-1, Church Historian's Office, Church Archives, The Church of Jesus Christ of Latter-day Saints, Salt Lake City, pp. 131-132.

10. Lucy Mack Smith, *History of Joseph Smith by His Mother: The Unabridged Original Version* (Arlington, Virginia and Provo, Utah: Stratford Books, Revised Second Edition 2006), p. 102.

    **Note: The portion used comes from Lucy's rough draft.**

11. Joseph Smith, Manuscript History of the Church, Book A-1, Church Historian's Office, Church Archives, The Church of Jesus Christ of Latter-day Saints, Salt Lake City, pp. 131-132.

12. Lucy Mack Smith, *History of Joseph Smith by His Mother: The Unabridged Original Version* (Arlington, Virginia and Provo, Utah: Stratford Books, 2006), p. 103,

13. Ibid.

14. **Note: Joseph Jr. and his mother Lucy differ on details of the trip: she says she paid Howard.** [Lucy Mack Smith, *History of Joseph Smith by His Mother: The Unabridged Original Version* (Arlington, Virginia and Provo, Utah: Stratford Books, Revised Second Edition 2006), p. 101 (from Lucy's rough draft).] **But Joseph says his father paid him.** [Joseph Smith, Manuscript History of the Church, Book A-1, Church Historian's Office, Church Archives, The Church of Jesus Christ of Latter-day Saints, Salt Lake City.] **Joseph also reports his mother Lucy having the confrontation with Howard over stealing their wagon in Utica** [Ibid.], **but Lucy says it happened 20 miles west of Utica.** [Lucy Mack Smith, *History of Joseph Smith by His Mother: The Unabridged Original Version* (Arlington, Virginia: Stratford Books, Revised Second Edition 2006), p. 103 (from Lucy's rough draft).] **Her sense of details was probably greater than her son's, since her mind for facts over the decades proved to be like a steel trap and, at the time, Joseph was only 11.**

15. Joseph Smith, Manuscript History of the Church, Book A-1, Historian's Office, Church Archives, The Church of Jesus Christ of Latter-day Saints, Salt Lake City, pp. 131–132.

16. Ibid.

17. Joseph Smith, Manuscript History of the Church, Book A-1, Historian's Office, Church Archives, The Church of Jesus Christ of Latter-day Saints, Salt Lake City.

   Also found in Joseph Smith, *The Papers of Joseph Smith*, edited by Dean C. Jessee, 2 volumes (Salt Lake City: Deseret Book, 1989–1992), vol. 1, pp. 268–269.

   Also found in Joseph Smith, *The Joseph Smith Papers*, edited by Dean C. Jessee, Ronald K. Esplin, and Richard Lyman Bushman (Salt Lake City: The Church Historian's Press, 2008–), multiple-volume series.

18. Lucy Mack Smith, *History of Joseph Smith by His Mother: The Unabridged Original Version* (Arlington, Virginia and Provo, Utah: Stratford Books, Revised Second Edition 2006), p. 104.

   **Note 1: The portion used comes from Lucy's rough draft.**

   **Note 2: Richard Lyman Bushman says Lucy and her family arrived at Palmyra, New York, with few possessions and only 9 cents.** [*Joseph Smith: Rough Stone Rolling* (New York City: Alfred A. Knopf / Borzoi Books, 2005), p. 29.]

19. Lucy Mack Smith, *History of Joseph Smith by His Mother: The Unabridged Original Version* (Arlington, Virginia and Provo, Utah: Stratford Books, Revised Second Edition 2006), p. 104.

   **Note: The portion used comes from Lucy's rough draft.**

20. Ibid.

21. **Note: Technically, Palmyra, New York was a "township" during this period, just as it is today, although it now has a population of 3,536 according to the 2010 census, with a net gain of only 46 from the previous decade's census.**

22. Lucy Mack Smith, *History of Joseph Smith by His Mother: The Unabridged Original Version* (Arlington, Virginia and Provo, Utah: Stratford Books, Revised Second Edition 2006), pp. 104–105.

   **Note: The portion used comes from Lucy's rough draft.**

23. Ibid., p. 105.

24. Pomeroy Tucker, *Origin, Rise, and Progress of Mormonism* (New York City: D. Appleton and Co., 1867), p. 12.

   **Note 1: Besides including some pertinent and useful information about the Smith family, Pomeroy Tucker also reports baseless gossip in his book. In regards to that, he is countered by another neighbor, John Stafford, a retired physician, who knew the Smith family well.**

**Stafford never joined with the Smiths theologically, yet refuted Tucker's spurious claims: "What Tucker said about them was false, absolutely"** [John Stafford, quoted in William H. Kelley and E. L. Kelley, "Interview with Orlando Saunders and Dr. John Stafford, March, 1881," *The Saints' Herald* (Plano, Illinois), vol. 28, no. 11 (June 1, 1881), p. 165.]

**Note 2: *The Saints' Herald*, cited here in 1881, has a varied and interesting history. It was launched at Cincinnati, Ohio, in January 1860, 3 months before the Civil War, by the Reorganized Church of Jesus Christ of Latter Day Saints (now Community of Christ). At that time, the first name this newspaper went by—for 17 years—was *The True Latter Day Saints' Herald*. After three years at Cincinnati the paper moved in March 1863 to Plano, Illinois, where it remained for 18 years. Then it moved to Lamoni, Iowa, in November 1881, and finally to its current location at Independence, Missouri, in 1921.**

**Meanwhile, it underwent 4 name shortenings. In 1877 (at its third home—in Plano, Iowa) it changed its name to *The Saints' Herald*, which it kept for 77 years, until 1954, when it shortened its name to *Saints' Herald* (losing the "The"), which it kept for 18 years. In 1973 it shortened its name even more, ever so slightly, knocking out the apostrophe, to simply *Saints Herald*, which it kept another 18 years. Then in 2001 it shortened it even more—to its current name, the *Herald*.**

25.  Thomas L. Cook, *Palmyra and Vicinity* (New York: Palmyra Courier-Journal Press, 1930), pp. 12, 14, referenced in Mark Lyman Staker, *Hearken O Ye People: The Historical Setting of Joseph Smith's Ohio Revelations* (Draper, Utah: Greg Kofford Books, 2009), pp. 120, 140.

26.  William Smith, Notes (ca 1875) in *Early Mormon Documents*, edited by Dan Vogel, 5 volumes (Salt Lake City: Signature Books, 1996–2003), vol 1, p. 489.

27.  Benjamin Saunders, Interview (1884), in *Early Mormon Documents*, edited by Dan Vogel, 5 volumes (Salt Lake City: Signature Books, 1996–2003), vol. 2, p. 137.

28.  Thomas L. Cook, *Palmyra and Vicinity*, (New York City: Palmyra Courier-Journal Press, 1930), pp. 12, 14, referenced in Mark Lyman Staker, *Hearken O Ye People: The Historical Setting for Joseph Smith's Ohio Revelations* (Salt Lake City: Greg Kofford Books, 2009), pp. 251–252.

29.  William Smith, Interview by J. W. Peterson, "William B. Smith's Last Statement," *Zion's Ensign* (Independence, Missouri), vol. 5, no. 3 (1894), p. 6.

Note: *Zion's Ensign* was the main missionary magazine of the Reorganized Church of Jesus Christ of Latter Day Saints (now Community of Christ), published at Independence, Missouri, from January 3, 1891 to 1932. It was a weekly publication first edited by John A. Robinson and Frederick G. Pitt. The paper began as a 4-page weekly in 6 columns, then 3 weeks later doubled its length to 8 pages, and in January 1917 it doubled again to 16 pages.

30. Milton V. Backman, *Joseph Smith's First Vision: The First Vision in Its Historical Context* (Salt Lake City: Bookcraft, 1971), p. 44.

31. Note: The 100-acre parcel of land the Smith family secured was 2 miles south of Palmyra and part of a large tract first owned by investors from Massachusetts 28 years earlier, in 1788. In those 28 years since, that same parcel had gone through several owners. The last one was Nicholas Evertson, who had died 9 years before the Smiths obtained it. The Evertson family had then secured a land agent, Zechariah Seymour, in 1820, with whom the Smiths contracted to buy the land at a cost of somewhere between $600 and $700 for 100 acres. [Larry C. Porter, *A Study of the Origins of the Church of Jesus Christ of Latter-day Saints in the States of New York and Pennsylvania, 1816–1831* (Ph.D. dissertation, BYU, 1971; published at Provo, Utah: Joseph Fielding Smith Institute for LDS History and *BYU Studies*, 2000), pp. 139-140;

Milton V. Backman, *Joseph Smith's First Vision: The First Vision in Its Historical Context* (Salt Lake City: Bookcraft, 1971), pp. 41, 43.]

32. Ibid., Larry C. Porter, *A Study of the Origins*, pp. 16–17.

Note 1: This source puts the Smiths' move to Manchester, New York, in 1818.

Note 2: The Smiths built their log house before the Evertson family appointed a land agent.

33. Ibid.

Pomeroy Tucker, *Origin, Rise, and Progress of Mormonism* (New York City: D. Appleton and Co., 1867), p. 13.

34. Lucy Mack Smith, *History of Joseph Smith by His Mother: The Unabridged Original Version* (Arlington, Virginia and Provo, Utah: Stratford Books, 2006), p. 105.

35. William Smith, Interview by J. W. Peterson, "William B. Smith's Last Statement," *Zion's Ensign* (Independence, Missouri), vol. 5, no. 3 (1894), p. 6.

36. William Smith, Notes [ca 1875] in *Early Mormon Documents*, edited by Dan Vogel, 5 volumes (Salt Lake City: Signature Books, 1996–2003), vol. 1, p. 489.

37. William Smith, *William Smith on Mormonism: A True Account of the Origin of the Book of Mormon* (Lamoni, Iowa: Herald Stream Book and Job Office, 1883), pp. 9–10, 12.

38. Lucy Mack Smith, *History of Joseph Smith by His Mother: The Unabridged Original Version* (Arlington, Virginia and Provo, Utah: Stratford Books, Revised Second Edition 2006), p. 109.

    **Note: The portion used comes from Lucy's rough draft.**

39. William Smith, Interview by J. W. Peterson, "William B. Smith's Last Statement," *Zion's Ensign* (Independence, Missouri), vol. 5, no. 3 (1894), p. 6.

40. Ibid.

41. Donna Hill, *Joseph Smith: The First Mormon* (Garden City, New York: Doubleday, 1977), p. 43.

    **Note: When using Doubleday throughout this volume, I list the location where this publisher was located at the time it released the cited book. For the purposes of clarification, the reader may note that the other books cited herein published by Doubleday after 1986 are listed with the publishing location as New York City, where it moved its headquarters in 1986, and before that, Garden City, New York.**

    **With a fairly unusual history, and as a prime example of how American book publishing has changed since the 1800s, Doubleday provides an interesting case study. The company began in 1897, founded by Frank Nelson Doubleday, and after 13 years moved to Garden City, New York, where the company remained for 73 years. In this small town executives built mansions and the company bought much property, even building a train station. By 1947 Doubleday became the world's largest publisher, with 30 million books published. In 1980 it bought the New York Mets baseball team, and in 1986 sold out to a German publisher, Bertelsmann, which began in 1835. While still owned by the German publisher, in 1988 Doubleday broke up, with portions of the company becoming part of Bertelsmann-owned Bantam Doubleday Dell Publishing Group, and with that conglomeration becoming part of Random House in 1998. Its current name is Knopf Doubleday Publishing Group, a division of Random House, with all the above still owned by Bertelsmann.**

42. Lucy Mack Smith, *History of Joseph Smith by His Mother: The Unabridged Original Version* (Arlington, Virginia and Provo, Utah: Stratford Books, Revised Second Edition 2006), p. 109.

**Note: The portion used comes from Lucy's rough draft.**

43. Ibid.

Joseph Smith, Manuscript History of the Church, Book A-1, Historian's Office, Church Archives, The Church of Jesus Christ of Latter-day Saints, Salt Lake City, pp. 131–132.

44. Mrs. M.C.R. Smith, Statement, in *Naked Truths About Mormonism: Also a Journal for Important, Newly Apprehended Truths, and Miscellany*, newspaper edited and published by A. B. Deming (Oakland, California), vol. 1 no. 2 (April 1888), Harold B. Lee Library, Brigham Young University, Provo, Utah.

**Note: *Naked Truths About Mormonism* was a bizarre name for a newspaper intended to be a monthly periodical. It was published in Oakland, California, and came from the collected anti-Mormon research of its editor, A. B. Deming. But it lasted only 2 issues—4 months apart—in January 1888 and April 1888, as Deming had difficulty selling subscriptions to his newspaper and thus ran into financial troubles. When the railroad finally refused to continue selling individual issues of it, no more editions could be printed. Deming had wanted to make it a book, but fell back to "option 2," which was cheaper and easier—making it as a newspaper.**

**Ironically, Deming was the son of Minor R. Deming, the fair-minded and protective sheriff of the Mormons in Hancock County, Illinois, the county seat of nearby Nauvoo, Illinois, from 1844 to 1845. Sheriff Deming had tried to stop the mobs from attacking the Saints in outlying areas of the county, where they had recently been burning several farms each night. But Deming contracted a fever and, hearing the howling mobs outside his Carthage residence as they planned more destruction of Mormon farms, his anxiety heightened, as well as his fever, and he died on September 10, 1845, having served as sheriff 13 months. His son, A. B. Deming, in his anger and adolescent frustration, blamed the Mormons for his father's death, because his father was so concerned for the Saints' welfare, and he turned his life into a crusade against them.**

45. Elizabeth D. E. Roundy, Letter ("Porter Rockwell"), *Jenson's Biographical Manuscripts*, unpublished, Church Archives, The Church of Jesus Christ of Latter-day Saints, Salt Lake City.

*Deseret News* (Salt Lake City), August 31, 1935.

Note: *Deseret News* is Utah's oldest daily newspaper, begun on June 15, 1850, with its presses and type brought to the territory by ox-drawn wagons from the Midwest, beginning in April 1849 and arriving August 7, 1849. Its first issue was 8 pages and its editor was Willard Richards. The paper was published on Saturdays each week. However, paper shortages forced it to publish every other week at times and, during one stretch of 1851, it could not be published for 3 months. Various attempts were made to manufacture paper locally, and after several decades it finally solved its paper problem with efficient local paper manufacturing.

On May 5, 1858, it was moved to Fillmore and Parowan, Utah, in the central and southern parts of the state for 4 months, because of the Utah War. (This war is covered in my book, *Porter Rockwell: A Biography.*) The presses returned to Salt Lake City in September 1858.

The first issue in 1850 had included among other local items of interest an outside news article that was 6 months old. But in 1860 the Pony Express began bringing faster news to the paper, and in October 1861 came the revolutionary First Transcontinental Telegraph, making news comparatively instantaneous. In 1926 it hooked into the Associated Press's teletype system for even more efficient news.

On October 8, 1865, it went from weekly, more or less, to twice per week. Just 2 years later, on November 21, 1867, it launched its first daily edition.

In the 1920s it doubled in circulation to nearly 40,000. Its numbers increased over the decades somewhat, to over 50,000, but now is back to just over the 1920s circulation for printed copies. However, adding to the 40,700+ printed copies now are 98,300+ digital copies, and 109,000+ Sunday printed copies as well as 98,000+ Sunday digital copies, as of May 2014.

Its name has ranged from *Deseret News* to *Deseret Evening News* to *Deseret Morning News* (from 2003 to 2008), then back to its current title of *Deseret News*, with high emphasis on Internet circulation (boasting the 22nd-largest circulation in the country of online editions). It has a national edition (for readers only outside of Utah) that is even higher than its Utah daily edition (with over 107,000 readers). Also, it emphasizes news sections that report LDS news and LDS news for outside the state of Utah. It currently has an impressive board of 14 distinguished advisors from various walks of life, including professors and presidents of universities, successful business executives, and civic and church leaders, including those who are not LDS.

# CHAPTER 4

1. U.S. Department of Commerce, *Historical Statistics of the United States: Colonial Times to 1970* (Washington D.C.: U. S. Bureau of the Census, 1975), p. 209.

2. "Joseph Smith Jr. Letter Books, 1829–1835," manuscript, Church Archives, The Church of Jesus Christ of Latter-day Saints, Salt Lake City, p. 1.

   Joseph Smith, History [1832], Church Archives, The Church of Jesus Christ of Latter-day Saints, Salt Lake City.

   **Note 1: Joseph Smith's lack of formal education with apparently no interest in books makes it all the more unlikely that he would be influenced by outside reading materials, which some of his later critics claimed were the source of his writings.**

   **Note 2: As for Joseph Smith's lack of education, historian Donna Hill utilizes statistics from the U.S. Bureau of Census in her analysis: "The educational attainments of the Smith family should be viewed in the context of their times. In 1870, when the U.S. Office of Education began issuing reports, the average number of days spent in school per year was only 78.4 and only 2 percent of those over age 17 graduated from high school." She also notes, "20 percent of the population over age ten were illiterate."** [U.S. Bureau of Census, Historical Statistics of the United States, Colonial Times to 1970, Bicentennial Edition, part (Washington, D.C.: U.S. Bureau of Census, 1975), pp. 376, 379, 382; cited in Donna Hill, *Joseph Smith: The First Mormon* (Garden City, New York: Doubleday, 1977), p. 457.] **Placing this into perspective of where this fits into the modern era, it may be surprising to some that these statistics were 5 years after the end of the Civil War, and only 33 years before the Wright brothers began flying aircraft (1903), and only 38 years before the first mass-produced automobiles came off the assembly line—Henry Ford's Model T by the Ford Motor Company (1908). Thus, education for the masses is a relatively new attainment in the United States.**

3. John Stafford, quoted in William H. Kelley and E. L. Kelley, "Interview with Orlando Saunders and Dr. John Stafford, March, 1881," *The Saints' Herald* (Plano, Illinois), vol. 28, no. 11 (June 1, 1881), p. 165.

4. Ibid.

5. Ibid.

6. Ibid.

7. Lucy Mack Smith, *History of Joseph Smith by His Mother: The Unabridged Original Version* (Arlington, Virginia and Provo, Utah: Stratford Books, Revised Second Edition 2006), pp. 107–109.

   **Note: The portion used comes from Lucy's rough draft.**

8. Ibid., pp. 106–107.

9. Ibid., p. 107.

10. Ibid.

11. Ibid., p. 111.

12. Ibid., pp. 84–88, 105–106, 110–111, 114.

13. Ibid., pp. 84–85.

14. Ibid., pp. 87–88.

15. "Notes written on Chambers' life of Joseph Smith," (Chambers' Miscellany), typescript, Church Archives, The Church of Jesus Christ of Latter-day Saints, Salt Lake City, p. 18.

16. William Smith, *William Smith on Mormonism: A True Account of the Origin of the Book of Mormon* (Lamoni, Iowa: Herald Stream Book and Job Office, 1883), pp. 6–7.

   **Note: In discussing their mother's concern for her children seeking their souls' salvation, William Smith also keys in on the term *importance*: "My mother continued her importunities and exertions to interest us in the importance of our immortal souls."**

17. Joseph Smith Jr., *History of the Church of Jesus Christ of Latter-day Saints*, edited by B. H. Roberts, 7 volumes (Salt Lake City: The Church of Jesus Christ of Latter-day Saints and *Deseret News*, Revised Second Edition 1948), vol. 7, p. 470.

18. Orlando Saunders, quoted in William H. Kelley and E. L. Kelley, "Interview with Orlando Saunders and Dr. John Stafford, March, 1881," *The Saints' Herald* (Plano, Illinois), vol. 28, no. 11 (June 1, 1881), p. 165.

19. Ibid.

20. Ibid.

21. "Stories from the Notebook of Martha Cox, Grandmother of Fern Cox Anderson," manuscript, Church Archives, The Church of Jesus Christ of Latter-day Saints, Salt Lake City.

   Lee C. LaFayette, "Recollections of Joseph Smith," manuscript, Church Archives, The Church of Jesus Christ of Latter-day Saints, Salt Lake City.

22. Richard Lyman Bushman, *Joseph Smith: Rough Stone Rolling* (New York City: Alfred A. Knopf / Borzoi Books, 2005), p. 37.

23. *Deseret Evening News* (Salt Lake City), January 20, 1894, p. 11.

24. Ibid.

25. Lucy Mack Smith, *Biographical Sketches of Joseph Smith the Prophet and His Progenitors for Many Generations* (Liverpool, England: S. W. Richards, 1853), pp. 51, 73, 84.

26. Joseph Smith, *History of the Church of Jesus Christ of Latter-day Saints*, edited by B. H. Roberts, 7 volumes (Salt Lake City: Deseret Book, Second Revised Edition 1948), vol. 1, pp. 2–3.

27. Joseph Smith, Manuscript History of the Church, A-1, Historian's Office, Church Archives, The Church of Jesus Christ of Latter-day Saints, Salt Lake City.

   Joseph Smith, History [1832], Church Archives, The Church of Jesus Christ of Latter-day Saints, Salt Lake City.

28. Ibid.

29. Ibid.

30. Milton V. Backman, *Joseph Smith's First Vision: The First Vision in Its Historical Context* (Salt Lake City: Bookcraft, 1971), pp. 61–71.

# CHAPTER 5

1. Lucy Mack Smith, *Biographical Sketches of Joseph Smith the Prophet and His Progenitors for Many Generations* (Liverpool, England: S. W. Richards, 1853), p. 54.

**Note: Although Joseph Smith senior's father Asael was a proponent of Thomas Paine's writings, much of the American public felt at odds with Paine for having written his book *The Age of Reason*, which had a strongly anti-Christian tone to it. Universalists, of course, had no qualms with it, since their beliefs coincided with Payne's and did not line up with traditional Christianity as taught by the mainstream churches.**

2. Ibid., pp. 37, 48, 54.

3. Ibid., pp. 45–48.

4. Ibid.

5. *Palmyra Register* (Palmyra, New York), June 7, August 16, and September 13, 1820.

   Milton V. Backman Jr., "Awakenings in the Burned-over District: New Light on the Historical Setting of the First Vision," *BYU Studies* (Provo, Utah), vol. 9, no. 3 (Spring 1969), p. 316.

6. Ibid., Milton V. Backman Jr., p. 317.

7. Alexander Neibaur journal, 1841–1862, entry of May 24, 1844, manuscript, Church Archives, The Church of Jesus Christ of Latter-day Saints, Salt Lake City, p. 7.

8. Orsamus Turner, *History of the Pioneer Settlement of Phelps and Gorham's Purchase and Morris' Reserve* (Rochester, New York: William Allington, 1851), p. 213.

9. Pomeroy Tucker, *Origin, Rise, and Progress of Mormonism* (New York City: D. Appleton and Co., 1867), p. 18.

10. Joseph Smith Jr., *History of the Church of Jesus Christ of Latter-day Saints*, edited by B. H. Roberts, 7 volumes (Salt Lake City: The Church of Jesus Christ of Latter-day Saints and *Deseret News*, Revised Second Edition 1948), vol. 1, p. 3.

11. Orsamus Turner, *History of the Pioneer Settlement of Phelps and Gorham's Purchase and Morris' Reserve* (Rochester, New York: William Allington, 1851), p. 214.

12. *Latter Day Saints' Messenger and Advocate* (Kirtland, Ohio), vol. 1, no. 5 (February 18, 1835), p. 78.

**Note: The *Latter Day Saints' Messenger and Advocate* newspaper was published monthly in Kirtland, Ohio, for exactly 3 years—from October 1834 to September 1837. It replaced the *The Evening and the Morning Star* (which was the church's first newspaper, edited by W. W. Phelps and published at Independence, Missouri, while the church's headquarters remained in Kirtland, Ohio). The Missouri paper (*The Evening and the Morning Star*) lasted from June 1832 to July 1833, until it was destroyed by a mob on July 20, 1833. Issues were later edited and reprinted at Kirtland, Ohio, as a sort of phoenix publication, titled more simply, *Evening and Morning Star*.**

**The *Latter Day Saints' Messenger and Advocate*'s first editor was Oliver Cowdery, until he was replaced in May 1835, just 6 months into his work, by John Whitmer and W. W. Phelps. Oliver returned as editor however in March 1836 when Whitmer and Phelps went back to Missouri. When Oliver was editor the second time, he may have**

allowed Warren Cowdery, his brother, to do most of the work—at least that was Warren's claim.

In February 1837 Warren Cowdery was made the official editor, but that ended 7 months later when he was basically fired by the church's leaders, who were displeased with his work. At that point the paper shut down. It was replaced by the *Elders' Journal*, but due to the tumultuous events in Kirtland during late 1837, they only got 2 issues printed before the press was taken over by Warren Parrish's group of dissenters.

So, the *Elders' Journal* was relocated to the church's new headquarters at Far West, Missouri, to where Joseph Smith and other church leaders escaped in early 1838, per the text of Vol. 2 of this biography. Once there, the *Elders' Journal* was published in 1837 and 1838, with only 2 issues released (making 4 total, counting the 2 Ohio issues). At Far West it was edited by Joseph Smith's brother, Don Carlos Smith, until publication ceased due to the start of the Mormon Wars in Missouri. The wars culminated in Joseph's followers being driven from the state as part of the "Exterminating Order" by Governor Lilburn W. Boggs, also detailed in Vol. 2 of this biography.

13. Joseph Smith, History [1832], Historian's Office, Church Archives, The Church of Jesus Christ of Latter-day Saints, Salt Lake City.

   Also found in Joseph Smith, *The Papers of Joseph Smith*, edited by Dean C. Jessee, 2 volumes (Salt Lake City: Deseret Book, 1989–1992), vol. 1, p. 6.

   Also found in Joseph Smith, *The Joseph Smith Papers*, edited by Dean C. Jessee, Ronald K. Esplin, and Richard Lyman Bushman (Salt Lake City: The Church Historian's Press, 2008–), multiple-volume series.

14. Ibid.

15. "Notes from Oral History Conducted February 13, 1974, of Allen Wesley Coates by Gordon C. Thomasson, in Shortsville, New York," L. Tom Perry Special Collections, Harold B. Lee Library, Brigham Young University, Provo, Utah.

16. Ibid.

17. "The Old Soldier's Testimony," *The Saints' Herald* (Lamoni, Iowa), vol. 31, no. 40 (October 4, 1884), p. 643.

18. "Another Testimony," *Deseret Evening News* (Salt Lake City), January 20, 1891.

19. William Smith, *William Smith on Mormonism: A True Account of the Origin of the Book of Mormon* (Lamoni, Iowa: Herald Stream Book and Job Office, 1883), pp. 6–7.

20. "Another Testimony," *Deseret Evening News* (Salt Lake City), January 20, 1891.

21. The Bible, King James Version, New Testament, James 1:5–7.

    Joseph Smith, Manuscript History of the Church, Book A-1, Historian's Office, Church Archives, The Church of Jesus Christ of Latter-day Saints, Salt Lake City.

    Also found in Joseph Smith, *The Papers of Joseph Smith*, edited by Dean C. Jessee, 2 volumes (Salt Lake City: Deseret Book, 1989–1992), vol. 1, p. 271.

    Also found in Joseph Smith, *The Joseph Smith Papers*, edited by Dean C. Jessee, Ronald K. Esplin, and Richard Lyman Bushman (Salt Lake City: The Church Historian's Press, 2008–), multiple-volume series.

22. "Joseph Smith—History," *The Pearl of Great Price* (Salt Lake City: The Church of Jesus Christ of Latter-day Saints, 1979), pp. 10–15.

23. "Another Testimony," *Deseret Evening News* (Salt Lake City), January 20, 1891.

24. "Joseph Smith—History," *The Pearl of Great Price* (Salt Lake City: The Church of Jesus Christ of Latter-day Saints, 1979), p. 15.

    Joseph Smith Jr., *History of the Church of Jesus Christ of Latter-day Saints*, edited by B. H. Roberts, 7 volumes (Salt Lake City: The Church of Jesus Christ of Latter-day Saints and *Deseret News*, Revised Second Edition 1948), vol. 1, chapters 1–5.

25. Joseph Smith, Journal, November 9, 1835, in Joseph Smith, *The Papers of Joseph Smith*, edited by Dean C. Jessee, 2 volumes (Salt Lake City: Deseret Book, 1989–1992), vol. 2, pp. 68–69.

    "Joseph Smith Jr. Letter Books, 1829–1835," manuscript, Church Archives, The Church of Jesus Christ of Latter-day Saints, Salt Lake City, pp. 2–3 (the 1835 account).

    Also found in Joseph Smith, *The Joseph Smith Papers*, edited by Dean C. Jessee, Ronald K. Esplin, and Richard Lyman Bushman (Salt Lake City: The Church Historian's Press, 2008–), multiple-volume series.

    Dean C. Jessee, "The Early Accounts of Joseph Smith's First Vision," *BYU Studies* (Provo, Utah), vol. 9, no. 3 (Spring 1969), pp. 275–294.

26. "Joseph Smith—History," *The Pearl of Great Price* (Salt Lake City: The Church of Jesus Christ of Latter-day Saints, 1979), verses 15–17.

27. *Journal of Discourses*, edited by George D. Watt, et al., 26 volumes (Liverpool, England: Franklin D. Richards and Sons, 1854–1886), vol. 14, p. 141.

Note: The *Journal of Discourses* holds some historical relevance, but is not considered altogether accurate, as the transcribing techniques were not foolproof. It contains 1438 sermons by 55 leaders—290 given by Brigham Young between 1851 and 1877, and 513 given by 4 other chief speakers—John Taylor (162), Orson Pratt (127), Heber C. Kimball (113), and George Q. Cannon (111). Twenty-two other leaders each gave only one lecture contained in the series, while the rest are made up by the other 28 leaders.

George D. Watt , the first Latter-day Saint convert in the British Isles, performed the most important work of the 12 reporters (or more) who took notes of the lectures that comprise the *Journal of Discourses*. Watt was the first, who learned Pittman shorthand upon coming to America after converting to the church in Great Britain in 1837. He alone recorded all lectures for the first 4 volumes, and contributed to at least volumes 5–12, of the 26-volume set. The other 11 people who reported the speeches that comprise the *Journal of Discourses* include another major reporter, George F. Gibbs, as well as Julia Young, daughter of Brigham, who recorded one speech. From 1867–1876 Watt's main replacement was David W. Evans.

The imperfection of the transcribing process resulted from these individuals simply trying to keep up with note-taking by hand when church sermons were given. Thus, mistakes did occur, causing some comments by church leaders to not be accurately reported, and on other occasions, when, for example, displaying humor, especially dry wit, their comments have been misinterpreted and thus misunderstood, creating some confusion over the years from certain remarks that were made. But it was the only system they had. Despite the imperfect note-taking process, much valuable information has been passed down.

28. "The Old Soldier's Testimony," *The Saints' Herald* (Lamoni, Iowa), vol. 31, no. 40 (October 4, 1884), p. 643.

29. Ibid.

Note: When William Smith related his account of his brother Joseph becoming unconscious from the First Vision, he did so in an interview in 1884—64 years after the fact—which was published in a newspaper article that year.

30. Charles Lowell Walker, *The Diary of Charles Lowell Walker, edited by A. Karl Larson and Katherine Miles Larson*, 2 volumes (Logan, Utah: Utah State University Press, 1980), vol. 1, pp. 755–756.

31. Ibid.

Note: Historian Mark L. McConkie notes that, when John Alger heard Joseph Smith Jr. make the declaration that God touched his eye before the First Vision, Alger would have been at least 10½ years of age. This is because he was in Joseph Smith senior's house in Kirtland, Ohio, when he heard it. (Alger was born November 11, 1820, and Joseph Smith senior had moved to Kirtland in mid-May 1831.) Alger described himself as "a small boy" when he heard it, according to Charles Lowell Walker, so it probably occurred soon after Smith senior had moved to Kirtland. Since Smith senior would move away from Kirtland 7 years later, the oldest that John Alger could have been was 18. Thus, Alger had to have been between 10½ and 18 years of age when he heard Joseph Jr. report this incident, if in fact he heard it accurately.

McConkie also notes that the idea that the Father appeared first, and then the Son, coincides with Joseph Smith's own account of the First Vision in 1835. [Mark L. McConkie, *Remembering Joseph* (Salt Lake City: Deseret Book, 2003), p. 313.]

32. "Joseph Smith—History," *The Pearl of Great Price* (Salt Lake City: The Church of Jesus Christ of Latter-day Saints, 1979), verses 15–17.

# CHAPTER 6

1. Joseph Smith Jr., *History of the Church of Jesus Christ of Latter-day Saints*, edited by B. H. Roberts, 7 volumes (Salt Lake City: The Church of Jesus Christ of Latter-day Saints and *Deseret News*, Revised Second Edition 1948), vol. 1, pp. 5–8.

   "Joseph Smith—History," *The Pearl of Great Price* (Salt Lake City: The Church of Jesus Christ of Latter-day Saints, 1979), verses 18–26.

2. "Joseph Smith Jr. Letter Books, 1829–1835," manuscript, Church Archives, The Church of Jesus Christ of Latter-day Saints, Salt Lake City, pp. 2–3.

3. Lucy Mack Smith, Preliminary Manuscript [1844–1845], p. 343, Church Archives, The Church of Jesus Christ of Latter-day Saints, Salt Lake City.

Also displayed in Lucy Mack Smith, *Lucy's Book: A Critical Edition of Lucy Mack Smith's Family Memoir*, edited by Lavina Fielding Anderson (Salt Lake City: Signature Books, 2001).

4. *Deseret Evening News* (Salt Lake City), January 20, 1894, p. 11.

5. Thomas H. Taylor, quoted in William H. Kelley and E. L. Kelley, "Interview with Orlando Saunders and Dr. John Stafford, March 1881," *The Saints' Herald* (Plano, Illinois), vol. 28, no. 11 (June 1, 1881), p. 167.

Also displayed in *Juvenile Instructor* (Salt Lake City), vol. 17, no. 19 (October 1, 1882), pp. 299–302.

**Note: The *Juvenile Instructor* began as a private publication for Latter-day Saints in 1866 by George Q. Cannon of the church's Quorum of the Twelve, who served as its first editor. His family kept the magazine going, then sold it to the church, which published it as an official organ for the Sunday School from 1901 to 1929. Its readers were youth and children, mostly in the church, and it contained articles, stories, illustrations, and teachings. It was the first magazine for children published in the United States west of the Mississippi River.**

6. Thomas H. Taylor, quoted in William H. Kelley and E. L. Kelley, "Interview with Orlando Saunders and Dr. John Stafford, March 1881," *The Saints' Herald* (Plano, Illinois), vol. 28, no. 11 (June 1, 1881), p. 166.

**Note: John H. Gilbert set type for the book that Joseph Smith would translate. Gilbert worked at the E. B. Grandin print shop in Palmyra, New York.**

7. *Wayne Sentinel* (Palmyra, New York), September 30, 1824.

**Note: This weekly Palmyra-based newspaper, the *Wayne Sentinel*, lasted for at least 40 years, from 1823 to 1863 or later. It was owned and published by E. B. Grandin, and was the first newspaper to ever publish news about Joseph Smith.**

Joseph Smith, Manuscript History of the Church, Book A-1, Historian's Office, Church Archives, The Church of Jesus Christ of Latter-day Saints, Salt Lake City.

8. Eliza R. Snow, *Biography and Family Record of Lorenzo Snow* (Salt Lake City: Deseret News Co. Printers, 1884), p. 243.

9. *Journal of Discourses*, edited by George D. Watt, et al., 26 volumes (Liverpool, England: Franklin D. Richards and Sons, 1854–1886), vol. 7, pp. 289–290.

10. "Records of the Session of the Presbyterian Church in Palmyra," Western Presbyterian Church, records still located at this church, vol. 2 (1828–1848).

   **Note: In 1793 Palmyra's Presbyterian Church was formed at East Palmyra, New York. On February 26, 1817, 56 members living on the west side of town separated and founded the Western Presbyterian Church of Palmyra, according to its historian. However, the "Guide" to the records of the across-town Presbyterian Church on the east side, contained in the Cornell University Library at Ithaca, New York, states that the Presbyterian church of Palmyra merely has its roots in 1783, when it began at the school house as a Congregational church. Then, in 1807, it became a Presbyterian church. No mention is made in the Cornell University Guide of the break-off.** ["Guide to the First Presbyterian Church of East Palmyra Records, 1817–1900," Division of Rare and Manuscript Collections, Cornell University Library, Ithaca, New York.] **Nonetheless, the break-off occurred with the Western Presbyterian Church starting 10 years later. (Separate from but to some extent similar to the west-side church's records, the east-side records consist of 2 volumes comprising session minutes and membership information, revival information and church issues. Volume 1 covers 1817–1834 and Volume 2 covers 1834–1900, both of which are at Cornell University. The records prior to 1817 were lost.)**

11. Joseph Smith Jr., *History of the Church of Jesus Christ of Latter-day Saints*, edited by B. H. Roberts, 7 volumes (Salt Lake City: The Church of Jesus Christ of Latter-day Saints and *Deseret News*, Revised Second Edition 1948), vol. 1, p. 6.

   Lucy Mack Smith, *Biographical Sketches of Joseph Smith the Prophet and His Progenitors for Many Generations* (Liverpool, England: S. W. Richards, 1853), p. 90.

12. *The Doctrine and Covenants of the Church of Jesus Christ of Latter-day Saints: Containing Revelations given to Joseph Smith, the Prophet, with Some Additions by His Successors in the Presidency of the Church* (Salt Lake City: The Church of Jesus Christ of Latter-day Saints, 1981), 20:5 (section 20, verse 5).

   **Note: This current version of the *Doctrine and Covenants* used by the Church of Jesus Christ of Latter-day Saints is based on the First Edition at Kirtland, Ohio, titled *Doctrine and Covenants of the Church of the Latter Day Saints: Carefully Selected from the Revelations of God*, published in 1835.**

   **This book of scripture was a compilation of mostly revelations, later termed "sections," for church members, and the book evolved through**

the years for Latter-day Saints. The 1844 Edition had 8 new sections added. In 1873 an additional 26 sections were included and the order was changed to a mostly chronological order, rather than by subject matter. The 1876 Edition also had 1 section removed—changing the church's position on polygamy. In 1921 the "Lectures on Faith" were removed with the explanation that they "were never presented to nor accepted by the Church as being otherwise than theological lectures or lessons." [Introduction, 1921 edition of the *Doctrine and Covenants*.] The Community of Christ and other churches believing in Joseph Smith have different versions of the *Doctrine and Covenants*, mostly based on the 1844 Edition at Nauvoo, Illinois.

As for the name of this book changing since the 1835 Edition, the reason is this: The church that Joseph was instrumental in founding went through several name changes in its first 8 years; initially it was the Church of Christ (when established in 1830); later it was referred to by members and church leaders as the Church of Jesus Christ, as well as the Church of God [Joseph Smith Jr., *History of the Church of Jesus Christ of Latter-day Saints*, edited by B. H. Roberts, 7 volumes (Salt Lake City: The Church of Jesus Christ of Latter-day Saints and *Deseret News*, Revised Second Edition 1948), vol. 3, p. 24, footnote]. In 1834 a resolution called for the name of the church to be Church of the Latter Day Saints, based on church meeting minutes of 1832. ["Minutes of Conference," *The Evening and the Morning Star* (Independence, Missouri), vol. 2, no. 20 (1832), p. 160.] That, in fact, was the name of the church when the first *Doctrine and Covenants* was published; therefore, that name is part of the book's title in the 1835 First Edition. In 1838 came the final name for the organization, by revelation, according to Joseph: the Church of Jesus Christ of Latter-day Saints. [Joseph Smith, Manuscript History of the Church, Church Historian's Office, Church Archives, The Church of Jesus Christ of Latter-day Saints, Salt Lake City, Book A-1, p. 37.]

13. Joseph Smith, History [1832], Historian's Office, Church Archives, The Church of Jesus Christ of Latter-day Saints, Salt Lake City.

14. Patriarchal Blessings, Book A, Church Archives, The Church of Jesus Christ of Latter-day Saints, Salt Lake City, pp. 1–2.

15. Ibid.

16. Ibid.

17. Richard Lyman Bushman, *Joseph Smith: Rough Stone Rolling* (New York City: Alfred A. Knopf / Borzoi Books, 2005), p. 42.

18. Lucy Mack Smith, *History of Joseph Smith by His Mother: The Unabridged Original Version* (Arlington, Virginia and Provo, Utah: Stratford Books, Revised Second Edition 2006), pp. 113–114.

   **Note: Lucy writes on these pages that the gunshot incident, in which someone fired at but missed Joseph, while he was crossing his yard, "alarmed us much." She says they knew not the cause of the attack because Joseph was a "remarkably quiet, well-disposed child;" thus, they did not suspect "anyone had ought against him." He was 14 at the time.**

19. Joseph Smith Jr., *History of the Church of Jesus Christ of Latter-day Saints*, edited by B. H. Roberts, 7 volumes, (Salt Lake City: The Church of Jesus Christ of Latter-day Saints and *Deseret News*, Revised Second Edition 1948), vol. 1, p. 9.

20. *The Doctrine and Covenants of the Church of Jesus Christ of Latter-day Saints: Containing Revelations given to Joseph Smith, the Prophet, with Some Additions by His Successors in the Presidency of the Church* (Salt Lake City: The Church of Jesus Christ of Latter-day Saints, 1981), 1:9.

21. Report of Ezra Pierce in William H. Kelley, *A Defense of Monogamic Marriage* (Independence, Missouri: Reorganized Church of Jesus Christ of Latter-day Saints, no date), p. 163.

22. *The Saints' Herald* (Plano, Illinois), June 1, 1881, p. 165.

23. Mark Ashurst-McGee, "The Josiah Stowell Jr. - John S. Fullmer Correspondence," *BYU Studies* (Provo, Utah), vol. 38, no. 3 (1999), p. 113.

24. John Stafford, quoted in William H. Kelley and E. L. Kelley, "Interview with Orlando Saunders and Dr. John Stafford, March 1881," *The Saints' Herald* (Plano, Illinois), vol. 28, no. 11 (June 1, 1881).

   **Note: This incident of Joseph Smith "scuffling" with other young men while drinking occurred after he had been married several years. When he came inside, reports John Stafford, "his wife felt bad about it, and when they went home, she put her shawl on him."**

25. Cragun Cox, "Reminiscences of Joseph Smith by Cragun Cox," manuscript, Utah State Historical Society, Salt Lake City.

26. Ibid.

27. Joseph Smith, History [1832], Historian's Office, Church Archives, The Church of Jesus Christ of Latter-day Saints, Salt Lake City.

28. Joseph Smith, Letter (to Oliver Cowdery), *Latter Day Saints' Messenger and Advocate* (Kirtland, Ohio), vol. 1, no. 3 (December 1834).

29. Ibid.

30. John Stafford, quoted in William H. Kelley and E. L. Kelley, "Interview with Orlando Saunders and Dr. John Stafford, March 1881," *The Saints' Herald* (Plano, Illinois), vol. 28, no. 11 (June 1, 1881).

31. *The Doctrine and Covenants of the Church of Jesus Christ of Latter-day Saints: Containing Revelations given to Joseph Smith, the Prophet, with Some Additions by His Successors in the Presidency of the Church* (Salt Lake City: The Church of Jesus Christ of Latter-day Saints, 1981), 1:9–10.

32. Lucy Mack Smith, *History of Joseph Smith by His Mother: The Unabridged Original Version* (Arlington, Virginia and Provo, Utah: Stratford Books, Revised Second Edition 2006), p. 122.

   **Note: The 3 portions in quotes are from Lucy's rough draft.**

33. "Joseph Smith—History," *The Pearl of Great Price* (Salt Lake City: The Church of Jesus Christ of Latter-day Saints, 1979), verse 29.

34. Ibid., verse 30.

35. Joseph Smith Jr., *History of the Church of Jesus Christ of Latter-day Saints*, edited by B. H. Roberts, 7 volumes (Salt Lake City: The Church of Jesus Christ of Latter-day Saints and *Deseret News*, Revised Second Edition 1948), vol. 1, pp. 11–14.

   Lucy Mack Smith, *History of Joseph Smith by His Mother: The Unabridged Original Version* (Arlington, Virginia and Provo, Utah: Stratford Books, Revised Second Edition 2006), pp. 122–124.

36. Ibid., Joseph Smith Jr., *History of the Church*, vol. 1, p. 13.

37. Ibid.

38. Lucy Mack Smith, *History of Joseph Smith by His Mother: The Unabridged Original Version* (Arlington, Virginia and Provo, Utah: Stratford Books, Revised Second Edition 2006), pp. 122.

39. Ibid. p. 129.

# CHAPTER 7

1. Lucy Mack Smith, *History of Joseph Smith by His Mother: The Unabridged Original Version* (Arlington, Virginia and Provo, Utah: Stratford Books, Revised Second Edition 2006), pp. 129–130.

2. Ibid.

3.  Joseph Knight Sr., 5-page manuscript, #183301847, Historical Department, The Church of Jesus Christ of Latter-day Saints, Salt Lake City.

**Note 1: Joseph Knight Sr. wrote his short manuscript sometime between 1833 and 1847.**

Also displayed in Joseph Knight Sr., "Joseph Knight's Recollection of Early Mormon History," edited by Dean C. Jessee. *BYU Studies* (Provo, Utah), vol. 17, no. 1 (Autumn 1976).

**Note 2: Joseph Knight's report of Joseph Smith's first 2 visits to the hill where young Joseph Smith actually saw the plates is reported properly, but in Knight's 1st paragraph he mistakenly merges the facts of the 1823 visit with the 1824 one. He begins with the 1823 visit to the hill, then relates the 1824 visit to the hill as if it were in 1823, and finally returns to the 1823 account about Joseph needing to bring his oldest brother. In his next paragraph Knight correctly chronicles the 1824 facts.**

4.  **Note: Joseph Smith's mother mistakenly records that Moroni told Joseph the name of the hill before the plates were attempted to be translated. In fact, she makes the same mistake at two places in her history. First, she describes in the rough draft of her book the angel Moroni's first visit to Joseph in their Manchester farmhouse, whereupon she quotes Joseph quoting Moroni: "'The record is on a side hill on the hill of Cumorah, three miles from this place. Remove the grass and moss, and you will find a large, flat stone. Pry that up, and you will find the record under it, lying on four pillars of cement.' Then the angel left him."** [Lucy Mack Smith, *History of Joseph Smith by His Mother: The Unabridged Original Version* (Arlington, Virginia and Provo, Utah: Stratford Books, Revised Second Edition 2006), p. 122.] **Parenthetically, she—not Joseph—adds the details of the stone box's description, since Joseph says only this: "While he [Moroni] was conversing with me about the plates, the vision was opened to my mind that I could see the place where the plates were deposited."** [Joseph Smith Jr., *History of the Church of Jesus Christ of Latter-day Saints*, edited by B. H. Roberts, 7 volumes (Salt Lake City: The Church of Jesus Christ of Latter-day Saints and *Deseret News*, Revised Second Edition 1948), vol. 1, p. 13.] **However, Joseph could have related to his family more details than what he actually recorded, which is certainly true regarding his later efforts to obtain the plates. But other facts he learned from the angel (which were presented by Lucy in her rough draft—such as naming the hill, etc.) probably did not come to him from the angel at that time, so her presenting them at this point in her chronicle—even in her rough draft—was an easy trap to fall into. By the time she wrote her book (in 1845–1846, although it was not**

published until 1853) it was common knowledge what the hill was named, since the plates had long been translated. Thirty-seven pages later in her history she makes the same gaffe, quoting Joseph saying, "As I passed by the Hill Cumorah . . . ." [Lucy Mack Smith, *History of Joseph Smith by His Mother: The Unabridged Original Version* (Arlington, Virginia and Provo, Utah: Stratford Books, Revised Second Edition 2006), p. 159.] **If David Whitmer's account is accurate per Appendix G: "A New, Surprising Time Line for Translating the Plates," Joseph would have learned the hill's name only after most of the plates were translated in June 1829, and certainly not in these preliminary events of trying to obtain the plates.**

5. *Times and Seasons* (Nauvoo, Illinois), vol. 3, p. 729 (March 15, 1842).

   Note: *Times and Seasons* **newspaper was published at Nauvoo, Illinois, by Joseph Smith's followers from November 1839 to February 1846, replacing the** *Elders' Journal*, **and was the last LDS paper published in the United States during Joseph Smith's lifetime.**

   **Before being used for this newspaper, its press and type were buried at Far West, Missouri, during the "Missouri War" of 1837–1838. In April 1839 they were secretly recovered and taken to Nauvoo, where Joseph Smith's brother, Don Carlos Smith, and Ebenezer Robinson served as its first editors. Joseph Smith took it over as director in January 1842, and listed himself as editor in its issues, but others actually edited it—John Taylor and Wilford Woodruff. In 1844 it was sold to Taylor, who took over the newspaper. As a trusted supporter of Joseph Smith, and one Joseph considered doctrinally sound and loyal to God and the church, Taylor enjoyed the prophet's complete confidence in the newspaper's direction.**

6. Ibid.

7. "Joseph Smith Jr. Letter Books, 1829–1835," manuscript, Church Archives, The Church of Jesus Christ of Latter-day Saints, Salt Lake City, p. 4.

8. Lucy Mack Smith, Preliminary Manuscript [1844–1845], Church Archives, The Church of Jesus Christ of Latter-day Saints, Salt Lake City.

   Also displayed in Lucy Mack Smith, *Lucy's Book: A Critical Edition of Lucy Mack Smith's Family Memoir*, edited by Lavina Fielding Anderson (Salt Lake City: Signature Books, 2001), p. 346.

9. Lucy Mack Smith, *History of Joseph Smith by His Mother: The Unabridged Original Version* (Arlington, Virginia and Provo, Utah: Stratford Books, Revised Second Edition 2006), p. 131.

10. Joseph Knight Sr., 5-page manuscript, #183301847, Historical Department, The Church of Jesus Christ of Latter-day Saints, Salt Lake City.

11. Joseph Smith Jr., *History of the Church of Jesus Christ of Latter-day Saints*, edited by B. H. Roberts, 7 volumes (Salt Lake City: The Church of Jesus Christ of Latter-day Saints and *Deseret News*, Revised Second Edition 1948), vol. 1, p. 16.

12. Lucy Mack Smith, *History of Joseph Smith by His Mother: The Unabridged Original Version* (Arlington, Virginia and Provo, Utah: Stratford Books, Revised Second Edition 2006), pp. 131–132.

13. Ibid., p. 132.

14. William Smith, *William Smith on Mormonism: A True Account of the Origin of the Book of Mormon* (Lamoni, Iowa: Herald Stream Book and Job Office, 1883), pp. 9–10.

15. Lucy Mack Smith, *History of Joseph Smith by His Mother: The Unabridged Original Version* (Arlington, Virginia and Provo, Utah: Stratford Books, Revised Second Edition 2006), p. 133.

16. Ibid., pp. 133–134.

17. Ibid.

18. Ibid.

19. Ibid.

20. Wandle Mace, "Autobiography," manuscript, ca. 1890, L. Tom Perry Special Collections, Harold B. Lee Library, Brigham Young University, Provo, Utah.

21. Ibid.

**Note: Italics are author's emphasis.**

22. Joseph Knight Jr., Autobiographical Sketch, 1862, p. 1, Church Archives, The Church of Jesus Christ of Latter-day Saints, Salt Lake City.

23. The Bible, King James Version, New Testament, 2 Timothy 3:12.

24. Elizabeth D. E. Roundy, Letter ("to President Spencer Clawson, President, Semi Centennial Jubilee Committee"), no date, Mormon Biography File, Church Archives, The Church of Jesus Christ of Latter-day Saints, Salt Lake City, n.d. (no date).

**Note: This letter from Elizabeth Roundy refers to Porter Rockwell's visit to her, stating that this information came to her "in 1875 when he came to me to write the history of his life," and that it was "from his own statement made to me." This "statement" may be the full**

**extent of what he told her as the history of his life, or it could merely be an excerpt from a longer, more complete history of his life, which is lost. He would die 3 years later at age 65.**

Also contained in Jenson's Biographical Manuscripts, Church Historical Department, Salt Lake City, unpublished, with excerpts published in "Church Section," *Deseret News* (Salt Lake City), August 31, 1935.

25. Richard Lloyd Dewey, *Porter Rockwell: A Biography* (New York City: Paramount Books, Ninth Revised Edition 2006), p. 6.

26. Parley P. Pratt, "Discourse by Parley P. Pratt (of September 7, 1856)," *Deseret News* (Salt Lake City), December 24, 1856.

   **Note: In this account of Parley P. Pratt first meeting Porter Rockwell's mother at Hyrum Smith's home in 1830, one may conclude that the 2 families—the Smiths and the Rockwells—were still friends. This was a decade after they had first met and become friends in Palmyra, New York.**

27. William Smith, *William Smith on Mormonism: A True Account of the Origin of the Book of Mormon* (Lamoni, Iowa: Herald Stream Book and Job Office, 1883), pp. 9–10.

   Lucy Mack Smith, Preliminary Manuscript [1844–1845], p. 344, Church Archives, The Church of Jesus Christ of Latter-day Saints, Salt Lake City.

28. Lucy Mack Smith, *History of Joseph Smith by His Mother: The Unabridged Original Version* (Arlington, Virginia and Provo, Utah: Stratford Books, Revised Second Edition 2006), p. 137.

29. Ibid.

30. Ibid., p. 140.

31. Ibid., pp. 141–142.

32. Ibid., p. 142.

33. Ibid., p. 143.

34. Ibid.

35. C. M. Stafford report, in *Naked Truths About Mormonism: Also a Journal for Important, Newly Apprehended Truths, and Miscellany*, newspaper edited and published by A. B. Deming (Oakland, California), vol. 1, no. 2 (April 1888), L. Tom Perry Special Collections, Harold B. Lee Library, Brigham Young University, Provo, Utah.

36. Joseph Smith, journal, recorded by Willard Richards, January 9, 1843, Church Archives, The Church of Jesus Christ of Latter-day Saints, Salt Lake City.

37. Joseph Smith Jr., *History of the Church of Jesus Christ of Latter-day Saints*, edited by B. H. Roberts, 7 volumes (Salt Lake City: The Church of Jesus Christ of Latter-day Saints and *Deseret News*, Revised Second Edition 1948), vol. 5, p. 247.

38. Ibid., p. 126.

39. Joseph Knight Sr., 5-page manuscript, #183301847, Historical Department, The Church of Jesus Christ of Latter-day Saints, Salt Lake City.

40. Lucy Mack Smith, *History of Joseph Smith by His Mother: The Unabridged Original Version* (Arlington, Virginia and Provo, Utah: Stratford Books, Revised Second Edition 2006), p. 135.

41. Joseph Knight Sr., 5-page manuscript, #183301847, Historical Department, The Church of Jesus Christ of Latter-day Saints, Salt Lake City.

42. Lucy Mack Smith, *History of Joseph Smith by His Mother: The Unabridged Original Version* (Arlington, Virginia and Provo, Utah: Stratford Books, Revised Second Edition 2006), p. 135.

43. Joseph Knight Sr., 5-page manuscript, #183301847, Historical Department, The Church of Jesus Christ of Latter-day Saints, Salt Lake City.

44. Lucy Mack Smith, *History of Joseph Smith by His Mother: The Unabridged Original Version* (Arlington, Virginia and Provo, Utah: Stratford Books, Revised Second Edition 2006), p. 135.

45. Ibid.

46. Joseph Knight Sr., 5-page manuscript, #183301847, Historical Department, The Church of Jesus Christ of Latter-day Saints, Salt Lake City.

47. Lucy Mack Smith, *History of Joseph Smith by His Mother: The Unabridged Original Version* (Arlington, Virginia and Provo, Utah: Stratford Books, Revised Second Edition 2006), p. 135.

48. Ibid.

49. Joseph Knight Sr., 5-page manuscript, #183301847, Historical Department, The Church of Jesus Christ of Latter-day Saints, Salt Lake City.

50. Joseph Smith, History [1832], Historian's Office, Church Archives, The Church of Jesus Christ of Latter-day Saints, Salt Lake City.

Also found in Joseph Smith, *The Papers of Joseph Smith*, edited by Dean C. Jessee, 2 volumes (Salt Lake City: Deseret Book, 1989–1992), vol. 1, pp. 6–8.

Also found in Joseph Smith, *The Joseph Smith Papers*, edited by Dean C. Jessee, Ronald K. Esplin, and Richard Lyman Bushman (Salt Lake City: The Church Historian's Press, 2008–), multiple-volume series.

51. Lucy Mack Smith, *History of Joseph Smith by His Mother: The Unabridged Original Version* (Arlington, Virginia and Provo, Utah: Stratford Books, Revised Second Edition 2006), pp. 135–136.

52. Ibid., p. 136.

53. *Latter Day Saints' Messenger and Advocate* (Kirtland, Ohio), vol. 2, no. 1 (October 1835), pp. 197–198.

Richard Lyman Bushman, *Joseph Smith: Rough Stone Rolling* (New York City: Alfred A. Knopf / Borzoi Books, 2005), p. 45.

54. Lucy Mack Smith, *History of Joseph Smith by His Mother: The Unabridged Original Version* (Arlington, Virginia and Provo, Utah: Stratford Books, Revised Second Edition 2006), p. 136.

55. Richard Lyman Bushman, *Joseph Smith: Rough Stone Rolling* (New York City: Alfred A. Knopf / Borzoi Books, 2005), p. 45.

56. *Letters by Oliver Cowdery to W. W. Phelps on the Origin of the Book of Mormon, and the Rise of the Church of Jesus Christ of Latter-day Saints* (Liverpool, England: Thomas Ward, 1844), p. 33.

57. Joseph Knight Sr., 5-page manuscript, #183301847, Historical Department, The Church of Jesus Christ of Latter-day Saints, Salt Lake City.

58. Lucy Mack Smith, *History of Joseph Smith by His Mother: The Unabridged Original Version* (Arlington, Virginia and Provo, Utah: Stratford Books, Revised Second Edition 2006), p. 135.

59. Ibid., p. 136.

60. Ibid., p. 137.

61. **Note: Regarding the prophecy by Joseph Smith of a local farmer dying, and of Deacon Jessup taking the last cow from his poor widow and orphans a year later, the 1853 published edition of Lucy's history uses the term "Joseph's supposition," but the fair-copy manuscript uses the term "Joseph's prophecy."**

62. Lucy Mack Smith, *History of Joseph Smith by His Mother: The Unabridged Original Version* (Arlington, Virginia and Provo, Utah: Stratford Books, Revised Second Edition 2006), pp. 145–146.

63. **Note: This analysis—of Joseph's mother and 3 of his siblings joining the Presbyterians out of having a convenient meeting place to attend church—is from Richard Lyman Bushman in *Joseph Smith: Rough Stone Rolling.***

64. Richard Lyman Bushman, *Joseph Smith: Rough Stone Rolling* (New York City: Alfred A. Knopf / Borzoi Books, 2005), p. 25.

65. William Smith, Interview (1893) in *Early Mormon Documents*, edited by Dan Vogel, 5 volumes (Salt Lake City: Signature Books, 1996–2003), vol. 1, pp. 512–513.

    Richard Lyman Bushman, *Joseph Smith: Rough Stone Rolling* (New York City: Alfred A. Knopf / Borzoi Books, 2005), p. 110.

66. *Wayne Sentinel* (Palmyra, New York), September 25, 1824.

67. Joseph Knight Sr., "Joseph Knight's Recollection of Early Mormon History," edited by Dean C. Jessee, *BYU Studies* (Provo, Utah), vol. 17, no. 1 (Autumn 1976), p. 31.

68. **Note: As detailed earlier in this chapter, family friend Joseph Knight Sr. indicates that Alvin Smith was supposed to accompany his brother Joseph to the plates when Joseph could finally obtain them, but because Alvin was now dead, plans changed; thus, Joseph was to take Emma Hale to the hill instead, when the time was right.** [Joseph Knight Sr., "Joseph Knight's Recollection," edited by Dean C. Jessee, *BYU Studies* (Provo, Utah), vol. 17, no. 1 (Autumn 1976), p. 31.]

# CHAPTER 8

1. "Stories from the Notebook of Martha Cox, Grandmother of Fern Cox Anderson," Church Archives, The Church of Jesus Christ of Latter-day Saints, Salt Lake City.

2. Joseph Knight Jr., manuscript, Joseph Knight Jr. Folder, Church Archives, The Church of Jesus Christ of Latter-day Saints, Salt Lake City.

3. "Stories from the Notebook of Martha Cox, Grandmother of Fern Cox Anderson," Church Archives, The Church of Jesus Christ of Latter-day Saints, Salt Lake City.

   Lee C. LaFayette, "Recollections of Joseph Smith," Church Archives, The Church of Jesus Christ of Latter-day Saints, Salt Lake City.

4. Thomas H. Taylor, quoted in William H. Kelley and E. L. Kelley, "Interview with Orlando Saunders and Dr. John Stafford, March 1881," *The Saints' Herald* (Plano, Illinois), vol. 28, no. 11 (June 1, 1881), p. 165.

   *Juvenile Instructor* (Salt Lake City), vol. 17, no. 19 (October 1, 1882), pp. 299–302.

5. Lucy Mack Smith, *History of Joseph Smith by His Mother: The Unabridged Original Version* (Arlington, Virginia and Provo, Utah: Stratford Books, Revised Second Edition 2006), pp. 152–153.

6. Ibid., p. 154.

7. Ibid., pp. 152–153.

8. Ibid., pp. 154–155.

9. Ibid., pp. 156–157.

# CHAPTER 9

1. Lucy Mack Smith, *History of Joseph Smith by His Mother: The Unabridged Original Version* (Arlington, Virginia and Provo, Utah: Stratford Books, Revised Second Edition 2006), pp. 156–157.

2. Joseph Smith Jr., *History of the Church of Jesus Christ of Latter-day Saints*, edited by B. H. Roberts, 7 volumes (Salt Lake City: The Church of Jesus Christ of Latter-day Saints and *Deseret News*, Revised Second Edition, 1948), vol. 3, p. 29.

3. *Tiffany's Monthly* (New York City), August 1859, p. 164.

   **Note 1: This article is comprised of an interview with Martin Harris. Interestingly, *Tiffany's Monthly* was a "spiritualist" magazine that for some reason took an interest in him. The reader will note from Appendix H: "What Happened to the Three Witnesses?" that Harris had gone off to other religious paths from 1838–1870, before settling with the mainstream Latter-day Saint fold. At one point during this period before 1870, he did apparently consult with a Mrs. Fox, who was a medium.**

   **Note 2: The full name of this magazine was *Tiffany's Monthly: Devoted to Investigation of Spiritual Science*. It was founded and published in New York City by Joel Tiffany, who lived 1811–1893. The magazine existed from 1856 to the early 1860s, and in the course of publishing it, Tiffany was decidedly anti-Mormon. He wrote a 3-part**

article titled, "Mormonism," but it lacked sufficient details to make it credible. His interview with Martin Harris was the one and only substantive contribution to the article, consisting of 17 pages over the course of 3 issues: Part 1A was published in the May 1859 issue on pages 46–51, Part 1B was published in the July 1859 issue on pages 119–121, and Part 2 was published in the August 1859 issue on pages 163–170. The magazine was either published (and sponsored) by Partridge & Brittan, which was a New York publishing house, or Partridge & Brittan merely typeset and printed it for Joel Tiffany.

4. Larry C. Porter, *A Study of the Origins of the Church of Jesus Christ of Latter-day Saints in the States of New York and Pennsylvania, 1816–1831* (Ph.D. dissertation, Brigham Young University, 1971; published at Provo, Utah: Joseph Fielding Smith Institute for Latter-day Saint History and *BYU Studies*, 2000), p. 77.

5. *Young Woman's Journal* (Salt Lake City), vol. 16, no. 12 (December 1905), pp. 549–550.

   Note: *Young Woman's Journal* was an official publication of the Church of Jesus Christ of Latter-day Saints, issued monthly from 1897 to 1929. It included articles on religion, literature, hygiene, housekeeping, and marriage, and included recipes, patterns for sewing, lesson guides, and poetry. In 1929 it merged with the existing *Improvement Era* magazine to serve both young women and young men.

6. James V. Palmer, "Reminiscences," Church Archives, The Church of Jesus Christ of Latter-day Saints, Salt Lake City, pp. 69–70.

7. *Utah Genealogical and Historical Magazine* (Salt Lake City), vol. 6 (July 1915), pp. 147–148.

   Note: *Utah Genealogical and Historical Magazine* was a quarterly publication by the Genealogical Society of Utah, from 1910 to 1940. It was a magazine covering early church members, research techniques, articles on early settlers, and extracts from British records. Its headquarters was in Salt Lake City. Today the family history arm of the LDS church has 4600 local family history sites across the world.

8. Brigham H. Roberts, *A Comprehensive History of the Church of Jesus Christ of Latter-day Saints*, 6 volumes (Salt Lake City: Deseret News Press, 1930), vol. 2, p. 350.

9. *The Juvenile Instructor* (Salt Lake City), vol. 27 (June 1, 1892), pp. 344–345.

   *Young Woman's Journal* (Salt Lake City), vol. 16, no. 12 (December 1905), pp. 549–550.

"Reminiscences of Bathsheba W. Smith," pp. 5–11, Church Archives, The Church of Jesus Christ of Latter-day Saints, Salt Lake City.

10. James Palmer, "Reminiscences and Journal," pp. 69, 73–76, original manuscript, Church Archives, The Church of Jesus Christ of Latter-day Saints, Salt Lake City.

11. Thomas Ford, *A History of Illinois from its Commencement as a State in 1814 to 1847* (Chicago: S. C. Griggs and Co., 1854), pp. 354–355.

12. Thomas Gregg, *The Prophet of Palmyra* (New York City: John B. Alden, 1890), p. 36.

13. *St. Louis Weekly Gazette* (St. Louis), June 1844.

   **Note: The *St. Louis Weekly Gazette* began publication in 1843.**

14. Ibid.

15. *Improvement Era* (Salt Lake City), vol. 32, no. 7 (May 1929), p. 54.

   **Note: The *Improvement Era* was an official, monthly Latter-day Saint magazine published from 1897 to 1970. It replaced the earlier, unofficial church members' magazine, *The Contributor* (1879–1896) and the official church magazine for young females, *Young Woman's Journal* (1897–1929). The *Improvement Era* was in turn replaced by the *Ensign* and *New Era* magazines in January 1971.**

16. *Salt Lake Herald* (Salt Lake City), January 12, 1895.

   **Note: *The Salt Lake Herald* was published from 1870 to 1909. It was first named the *The Salt Lake Daily Herald* and lasted from 1870 to 1889. Its sister publication, *The Sunday Herald*, lasted from 1889 to 1895. It was neutral but supportive of the Latter-day Saints, and was owned by 2 church members. One, named Sloan, became a convert to the LDS church in his adult life. Their paper was a 4-page daily. In 1920 stiff competition for scarce advertising dollars caused it to go under. In its lifetime it found those competitors to be the church-owned *Deseret News*, which had to be more careful in what it published than the *The Salt Lake Herald*, and 2 anti-Mormon newspapers—*The Salt Lake Tribune* (1870 to present) and the *Salt Lake Democrat* (1885–1887). In 1898 a Democratic senator from Montana bought the *Herald* and caused its revenues to increase three-fold. In 1909 he sold it to Utah Republicans, who changed its name to the *The Salt Lake Herald-Republican*, which it remained until its demise in 1920.**

17. Richard Steckel, "New Light on the 'Dark Ages': The Remarkably Tall Stature of Northern European Men during the Medieval Era," *Social*

*Science History* (Durham, North Carolina), vol. 28, no. 2 (Summer 2004), pp. 211–229.

**Note 1: *Social Science History* is a quarterly academic journal that began in 1976 and is still publishing at Durham, North Carolina. It is the official publication of the Social Science History Association, published by Duke University Press, and its chief purpose is to focus on historical explanation.**

Richard Steckel, *The Journal of Economic Literature* (Pittsburgh, Pennsylvania), vol. 31, no. 1 (Spring 2007), pp. 1–34.

**Note 2: Research on the height of men was part of a comprehensive study by the Global History of Health Project and was funded by the National Science Foundation, conducted by Richard Steckel and his staff, based on skeletal data from 30 previous studies.**

**Note 3: The *Journal of Economic Literature* was begun as the *Journal of Economic Abstracts* in 1963 and underwent a name change in 1969 to its current title. Published quarterly at Pittsburgh, Pennsylvania, by the American Economics Association, the magazine's purpose it to help economists keep current on economic literature. It includes book reviews, an index of dissertations in North American universities, a bibliography of new books, articles of economic theories, and essays of current economic theories. One of the major contributions of this journal was its invention of a much-used system to classify economics publications.**

18. **Note: Appendix A in this book, "The Height of Men through History," analyzes the surprisingly cyclical pattern of mankind's height.**

19. *New York Herald* (New York City), February 19, 1842.

**Note: *The New York Herald*, as explained in Appendix J of this biography—"Yellow Journalism and the New York Press"—has a fascinating history. The paper lasted from 1835 to 1924 and was started by James Gordon Bennett senior. It was the most popular daily newspaper in the United States. Boldly stating his intent, Bennett said the purpose of the newspaper "is not to instruct but to startle." [Carl Sandburg, *Storm Over the Land* (New York City: Harcourt Brace and Company, 1942), p. 87.] In 1887 he launched the European edition, the *Paris Herald*, which later became the *International Herald Tribune*. Bennett junior moved to Paris and tried to manage the paper from there by telegram but found it difficult, so the paper struggled. In 1918 he died.**

**At this point new owners came aboard, and some interesting intrigue lay in store. After Bennett junior's death, "serial-publisher" Frank Munsey bought it, a man had who started many magazines and**

newspapers, then sold it and the *Paris Herald* in 1924 to the *New York Tribune*. At this point the U.S. papers combined and were renamed the *New York Herald Tribune*, while the European edition was renamed the *Paris Herald Tribune*.

In 1959 a new owner—movie, magazine, and newspaper venture capitalist John Whitney—took over both papers. But in 1966 the New York newspaper died—the one whose beginning under James Gordon Bennett senior went back to 1835. This left only the Paris newspaper. And the Whitney family kept it going.

In December 1966 the *Washington Post* became a joint owner. In May 1967 *The New York Times* came aboard also. That year the combined, three-way ownership renamed this Paris paper the *International Herald Tribune*. By 1991 both papers solely owned it, with the Whitney family out.

On December 30, 2002, *The New York Times* made a power play. It devised a plan to take it over by telling the *Washington Post* it was going to start its own European paper. In consequence, the *Post* now felt the fear of competition and also knew it was incapable of running a foreign newspaper alone. It decided its only way out was to sell its share of the *International Herald Tribune*—which it did—to the *Times*. So the Paris edition continued with only one owner now—*The New York Times*.

It is currently printed at 35 sites in the world and, on October 15, 2013, it was renamed *The New York Times International Edition*, published in LaDefense, France, with a circulation of 242,000.

20. *St. Louis Weekly Gazette* (St. Louis), June 1844.

21. *Deseret News* (Salt Lake City), August 16, 1878, p. 2.

22. *Relief Society Magazine* (Salt Lake City), vol. 31 (March 1944), p. 136.

Note: The *Relief Society Magazine* was an official organ of the Church of Jesus Christ of Latter-day Saints from 1915 to December 1970, replacing the privately published *Woman's Exponent* that was published from 1872 to 1915. The *Relief Society Magazine* was managed by women editors. It was a significant publication that helped Utah women, and its founding editor was Susa Young Gates, who edited it for 7 years—from 1915 to 1922. The magazine was replaced by the *Ensign* in January 1971.

23. *Young Woman's Journal* (Salt Lake City), vol. 17, no. 12 (December 1906), p. 556.

24. Parley P. Pratt, *Autobiography of Parley P. Pratt* (Arlington, Virginia and Provo, Utah: Stratford Books, 2005), pp. 24–25.

25. Parley P. Pratt, *The Autobiography of Parley Parker Pratt: One of the Twelve Apostles of the Church of Jesus Christ of Latter-day Saints, Embracing His Life, Ministry and Travels, with Extracts, in Prose and Verse, from his Miscellaneous Writings*, edited by his son, Parley P. Pratt (New York City: Russell Brothers, 1874), pp. 45–46.

26. *St. Louis Weekly Gazette* (St. Louis), June 1844.

27. *The Juvenile Instructor* (Salt Lake City), vol. 27 (June 1, 1892), pp. 344–345.

   *Young Woman's Journal* (Salt Lake City), vol. 16, no. 12 (December 1905), pp. 549–550.

   "Reminiscences of Bathsheba W. Smith," Church Archives, The Church of Jesus Christ of Latter-day Saints, Salt Lake City, pp. 5–11.

28. *Young Woman's Journal* (Salt Lake City), vol. 17, no. 12 (December 1906), p. 544.

29. Joseph Smith Jr., *History of the Church of Jesus Christ of Latter-day Saints*, edited by B. H. Roberts, 7 volumes (Salt Lake City: The Church of Jesus Christ of Latter-day Saints and Deseret News, Revised Second Edition 1948), vol. 5, p. 411.

30. Mercy Rachel, "Autobiographical Sketch," no date, Church Archives, The Church of Jesus Christ of Latter-day Saints, 1892.

   "Recollections of the Prophet Joseph Smith," *The Juvenile Instructor* (Salt Lake City), vol. 27, no. 13 (July 1, 1892), pp. 398–400.

31. "Reminiscences of Bathsheba W. Smith," pp. 5–11, Church Archives, The Church of Jesus Christ of Latter-day Saints, Salt Lake City.

   "Recollections of the Prophet Joseph Smith," *The Juvenile Instructor* (Salt Lake City), vol. 27 (June 1, 1892), pp. 344–345.

   *Young Woman's Journal* (Salt Lake City), vol. 16, no. 12 (December 1905), pp. 549–550.

   **Note: Bathsheba W. Smith included this description of Joseph in her interview—he "looked the soul and honor of integrity."**

32. William Taylor account in "Joseph Smith, the Prophet," *Young Woman's Journal* (Salt Lake City), vol. 17, no. 12 (December 1906), pp. 547–548.

33. Helen D. O'Connor, as quoted in "Jacob Jones—Biography of a Pioneer," no date, Church Archives, The Church of Jesus Christ of Latter-day Saints, Salt Lake City.

34. *Juvenile Instructor* (Salt Lake City), vol. 27, no. 1 (January 15, 1892), pp. 56–57.

35. E. Dale LeBaron, *Benjamin Franklin Johnson: Friend to the Prophets* (Provo, Utah: Benjamin F. Johnson Family Organization, 1997), p. 221.

36. "Newel Knight Journal," *Scraps of Biography: Tenth Book of the Faith Promoting Series* (Salt Lake City: Juvenile Instructor Office, 1883), p. 47.

37. Peter H. Burnett, *An Old California Pioneer* (Oakland, California: Biobooks, 1946), p. 40.

38. Wandle Mace, "Autobiography," manuscript, ca. 1890, L. Tom Perry Special Collections, Harold B. Lee Library, Brigham Young University, Provo, Utah.

39. *Juvenile Instructor* (Salt Lake City), vol. 27, no. 13 (July 1, 1892), pp. 398–400.

40. *BYU Studies* (Provo, Utah), vol. 40, no. 2 (2001), p. 171.

41. Emma Smith Bidamon, Interview by Joseph Smith III, "Last Testimony of Sister Emma," *The Saints' Herald* (Plano, Illinois), vol. 26, no. 19 (October 1, 1879), pp. 289–290.

   **Note: This interview of Emma was conducted by her son, Joseph Smith III, between February 4 and 10, 1879, and published 8 months later.**

42. Issac Hale, Affidavit (1834), in Eber D. Howe, *Mormonism Unvailed* [sic]: *Or, A Faithful Account of that Singular Imposition and Delusion* (Painesville, Ohio: published by the author, 1834), p. 263.

43. Ibid.

44. Ibid.

45. Brigham Young discourse, *Journal of Discourses*, edited by George D. Watt, et al., 26 volumes (Liverpool, England: Franklin D. Richards and Sons, 1854–1886), vol. 19, p. 37 (June 17, 1877).

   **Note: The discourse here cited about Porter Rockwell seeing treasure was given by Brigham Young two months and two days before his final address that was recorded for the *Journal of Discourses*. His final one for the book series was given August 19, 1877. He would die 10 days later.**

   Donna Hill, *Joseph Smith: The First Mormon* (Garden City, New York: Doubleday, 1977), p. 63.

46. Martin Harris, Interview by Ole A. Jensen, July 1875, quoted in Grant Ivins, "Notes on the Trial of Joseph Smith," manuscript, Church Archives, The Church of Jesus Christ of Latter-day Saints, Salt Lake City.

47. Lucy Mack Smith, *History of Joseph Smith by His Mother: The Unabridged Original Version* (Arlington, Virginia and Provo, Utah: Stratford Books, Revised Second Edition 2006), p. 148.

48. W. D. Purple, *Chenango Union* (Chenango County, New York), May 3, 1877.

   **Note: This long-lasting weekly newspaper, the *Chenango Union*, was published at Norwich, New York, 148 miles west of New York City and 95 miles east of Palmyra, from 1847–1975.**

49. Mrs. M. C. R. Smith, Statement, in *Naked Truths About Mormonism: Also a Journal for Important, Newly Apprehended Truths, and Miscellany*, newspaper edited and published by A. B. Deming (Oakland, California), vol. 1, no. 2 (April 1888), L. Tom Perry Special Collections, Harold B. Lee Library, Brigham Young University, Provo, Utah.

50. *Wayne Sentinel* (Palmyra, New York), February 16, 1825.

51. *A Book of Commandments for the Government of the Church of Christ, Organized According to Law, on the 6th of April, 1830* (Zion [Independence, Missouri]: W. W. Phelps & Co., 1833; reprinted at Independence, Missouri: Board of Publication, Church of Christ Temple Lot, 1960), p. 15.

# CHAPTER 10

1. Emily M. Austin, *Mormonism: Or, Life among the Mormons* (Madison, Wisconsin: M. J. Cantwell, 1882), p. 32.

2. Lucy Mack Smith, *History of Joseph Smith by His Mother: The Unabridged Original Version* (Arlington, Virginia and Provo, Utah: Stratford Books, Revised Second Edition 2006), p. 148.

3. Larry C. Porter, *A Study of the Origins of the Church of Jesus Christ of Latter-day Saints in the States of New York and Pennsylvania, 1816–1831* (Ph.D. dissertation, Brigham Young University, 1971; published at Provo, Utah: Joseph Fielding Smith Institute for Latter-day Saint History and *BYU Studies*, 2000), pp. 69, 73.

4. "A. W. B. Letter to the editor," *Evangelical Magazine and Gospel Advocate* (Utica, New York), vol. 2 (April 9, 1831).

**Note:** *Evangelical Magazine and Gospel Advocate* **was published and edited at Utica, New York, by one Reverend Dolphius Skinner (who wisely went by D. Skinner). His publication lasted from 1830 to 1850 and his writings were unabashedly anti-Mormon.**

5. *Latter Day Saints' Messenger and Advocate* (Kirtland, Ohio), vol. 2, no. 1 (October 1835), p. 201.

**Note: This description of Joseph Smith's accuser at his trial in Bainbridge, New York—as being "officious"—came from Oliver Cowdery, who later learned of the incident firsthand from Joseph. According to the *Merriam-Webster Dictionary*, *officious* is an adjective "used to describe an annoying person who tries to tell other people what to do in a way that is not wanted or needed." Joseph, unfortunately, had a bevy of enemies through his life who were, at a minimum, officious.**

6. Joseph Knight Sr., 5-page manuscript, #183301847, Historical Department, The Church of Jesus Christ of Latter-day Saints, Salt Lake City.

   Also found in Joseph Knight Sr., "Joseph Knight's Recollection of Early Mormon History," edited by Dean C. Jessee, *BYU Studies* (Provo, Utah), vol. 17, no. 1 (Autumn 1976).

7. Ibid.

8. Lucy Mack Smith, *History of Joseph Smith by His Mother: The Unabridged Original Version* (Arlington, Virginia and Provo, Utah: Stratford Books, Revised Second Edition 2006), p. 149.

9. Joseph Smith, Manuscript History of the Church, Book A-1, Historian's Office, Church Archives, The Church of Jesus Christ of Latter-day Saints, Salt Lake City.

   Also found in Joseph Smith, *The Papers of Joseph Smith*, edited by Dean C. Jessee, 2 volumes (Salt Lake City: Deseret Book, 1989-1992), vol. 1, pp. 313–314.

   Also found in Joseph Smith, *The Joseph Smith Papers*, edited by Dean C. Jessee, Ronald K. Esplin, and Richard Lyman Bushman (Salt Lake City: The Church Historian's Press, 2008–), multiple-volume series.

10. Lucy Mack Smith, *History of Joseph Smith by His Mother: The Unabridged Original Version* (Arlington, Virginia and Provo, Utah: Stratford Books, Revised Second Edition 2006), p. 151.

11. Lucy Mack Smith, Preliminary Manuscript [1844–1845], Church Archives, The Church of Jesus Christ of Latter-day Saints, Salt Lake City.

Also displayed in Lucy Mack Smith, *Lucy's Book: A Critical Edition of Lucy Mack Smith's Family Memoir*, edited by Lavina Fielding Anderson (Salt Lake City: Signature Books, 2001), pp. 365–366.

# CHAPTER 11

1. Issac Hale, Affidavit (1834), in Eber D. Howe, *Mormonism Unvailed* [sic]: *Or, A Faithful Account of that Singular Imposition and Delusion* (Painesville, Ohio: published by the author, 1834), p. 264.

2. Joseph Smith III, "The Last Testimony of Sister Emma," *The Saints' Herald* (Plano, Illinois), vol. 26, no. 19 (October 1, 1879), pp. 289–290.

3. Donna Hill, *Joseph Smith: The First Mormon* (Garden City, New York: Doubleday, 1977), p. 69.

4. Joseph Smith III, "The Last Testimony of Sister Emma," *The Saints' Herald* (Plano, Illinois), vol. 26, no. 19 (October 1, 1879), pp. 289–290.

5. **Note: In this source the interviewer, Joseph Smith III, misspelled Zechariah's last name as Tarbell. Others misspelled it as Tarbill. The correct spelling is Tarble.**

6. Issac Hale, Affidavit (1834), in Eber D. Howe, *Mormonism Unvailed* [sic]: *Or, A Faithful Account of that Singular Imposition and Delusion* (Painesville, Ohio: published by the author, 1834), p. 263.

7. Joseph Smith III, "The Last Testimony of Sister Emma," *The Saints' Herald* (Plano, Illinois), vol. 26, no. 19 (October 1, 1879), pp. 289–290.

**Note: Regarding her marriage date, Emma Smith states in her 1879 interview with son Joseph Smith III, "I think the date [is] correct [January 18, 1827]. My certificate of marriage was lost many years ago, in some of the marches we were forced to make." [Joseph Smith III, "The Last Testimony of Sister Emma," *The Saints' Herald* (Plano, Illinois), vol. 26, no. 19 (October 1, 1879), pp. 289–290.] Interesting is the fact a woman who went through as many hardships for nearly two decades with her husband could not precisely recall her anniversary. One can conjecture on the theory that hardships and stress, coupled with tragedy—as well as "moving on" for decades in another marriage— can erase even the most significant memories, given time. But in her case, perhaps not. Emma may have been "holding back," given the framework of her interview—with her son asking these questions— and in the presence of her new husband.**

8. Issac Hale, Affidavit (1834), in Eber D. Howe, *Mormonism Unvailed* [sic]: *Or, A Faithful Account of that Singular Imposition and Delusion* (Painesville, Ohio: published by the author, 1834), p. 264.

9. Ibid.

10. Joseph Smith, Manuscript History of the Church, Book A-1, Historian's Office, Church Archives, The Church of Jesus Christ of Latter-day Saints, Salt Lake City.

   Also found in *Joseph Smith, The Papers of Joseph Smith*, edited by Dean C. Jessee, 2 volumes (Salt Lake City: Deseret Book, 1989–1992), vol. 1, pp. 282–283.

   Also found in *The Joseph Smith Papers*, edited by Dean C. Jessee, Ronald K. Esplin, and Richard Lyman Bushman (Salt Lake City: The Church Historian's Press, 2008–), multiple-volume series.

   Peter Ingersol, Affidavit (1833), in Eber D. Howe, *Mormonism Unvailed* [sic]: *Or, A Faithful Account of that Singular Imposition and Delusion* (Painesville, Ohio: published by the author, 1834), p. 235.

   Issac Hale, Affidavit (1834), in Eber D. Howe, *Mormonism Unvailed* [sic]: *Or, A Faithful Account of that Singular Imposition and Delusion* (Painesville, Ohio: published by the author, 1834), pp. 263–264.

11. Ibid., Peter Ingersol.

12. Ibid.

   *Susquehanna Register* (Montrose, Pennsylvania), May 1, 1834.

   **Note: The *Susquehanna Register*, published at Montrose, Pennsylvania, began in 1834 and closed its doors in 1849. It was released weekly by publishers James Chapman and B. H. Mills.**

13. Joseph Smith Jr., *History of the Church of Jesus Christ of Latter-day Saints*, edited by B. H. Roberts, 7 volumes (Salt Lake City: The Church of Jesus Christ of Latter-day Saints and *Deseret News*, Revised Second Edition 1948), vol. 1, p. 16.

14. Joseph Knight Sr., 5-page manuscript, #183301847, Historical Department, The Church of Jesus Christ of Latter-day Saints, Salt Lake City.

15. Lucy Mack Smith, *History of Joseph Smith by His Mother: The Unabridged Original Version* (Arlington, Virginia and Provo, Utah: Stratford Books, Revised Second Edition 2006), pp. 164–165.

16. Ibid., p. 158.

17. Ibid.

18. Ibid., p. 159.

19. Ibid.

20. Ibid.

21. Joseph Knight Sr., 5-page manuscript, #183301847, Historical Department, The Church of Jesus Christ of Latter-day Saints, Salt Lake City.

22. Joseph Knight Sr., "Joseph Knight's Recollection of Early Mormon History," edited by Dean C. Jessee, *BYU Studies* (Provo, Utah), vol. 17, no. 1 (Autumn 1976), p. 33.

23. Lucy Mack Smith, *History of Joseph Smith by His Mother: The Unabridged Original Version* (Arlington, Virginia and Provo, Utah: Stratford Books, Revised Second Edition 2006), p. 161.

24. Ibid., p. 162.

25. Ibid.

26. Ibid., p. 163.

27. Ibid.

28. Ibid.

29. Ibid.

30. Ibid.

31. Ibid., pp. 163–164.

32. Ibid., p. 164.

33. Joseph Knight Sr., 5-page manuscript, #183301847, Historical Department, The Church of Jesus Christ of Latter-day Saints, Salt Lake City.

34. Lucy Mack Smith, *History of Joseph Smith by His Mother: The Unabridged Original Version* (Arlington, Virginia and Provo, Utah: Stratford Books, Revised Second Edition 2006), p. 168.

35. *Tiffany's Monthly* (New York City), August 1859, p. 166.

36. Ibid.

37. Lucy Mack Smith, *History of Joseph Smith by His Mother: The Unabridged Original Version* (Arlington, Virginia and Provo, Utah: Stratford Books, Revised Second Edition 2006), p. 168.

38. Ibid.

39. Ibid., p. 164.

40. **Note: Macedon, New York, was originally part of Palmyra, but had broken away in 1823, 4 years earlier than this point in Joseph's narrative (1827). This was probably due to the fact that Macedon was becoming economically independent, being right on the canal itself. The canal was nearing completion and Palmyra's portion of it had actually been completed a year earlier in 1822, with the whole of it to be finished in 1825. This was giving Macedon's residents the economic confidence it needed to declare its separation from Palmrya. Macedon was originally settled just 24 years prior to breaking away—1789— when Palmyra was formed.** ["Brief History of Macedonia"—Office of the Wayne County, New York Historian, Wayne County, New York.]

41. Lucy Mack Smith, *History of Joseph Smith by His Mother: The Unabridged Original Version* (Arlington, Virginia and Provo, Utah: Stratford Books, Revised Second Edition 2006), p. 164.

42. Ibid.

43. Ibid.

44. Ibid., p. 165.

45. *Journal of Discourses*, edited by George D. Watt, et al., 26 volumes (Liverpool, England: Franklin D. Richards and Sons, 1854–1886), vol. 2, pp. 180–181 (February 18, 1852).

46. Lucy Mack Smith, *History of Joseph Smith by His Mother: The Unabridged Original Version* (Arlington, Virginia and Provo, Utah: Stratford Books, Revised Second Edition 2006), p. 165.

47. Ibid.

48. Ibid., pp. 165–166.

49. Ibid.

50. Ibid., p. 166.

51. Ibid.

52. Ibid.

53. Ibid., p. 167.

54. Ibid.

55. Ibid.

Lucy Mack Smith, *Biographical Sketches of Joseph Smith the Prophet and His Progenitors for Many Generations* (Liverpool, England: S. W. Richards, 1853), pp. 102–104.

Lucy Mack Smith, Preliminary Manuscript [1844–1845], pp. 381–384, Church Archives, The Church of Jesus Christ of Latter-day Saints, Salt Lake City.

56. Ibid.

57. *Tiffany's Monthly* (New York City), August 1859, p. 166.

58. Willard Chase, Affidavit (1833), in Eber D. Howe, *Mormonism Unvailed* [sic]*: Or, A Faithful Account of that Singular Imposition and Delusion* (Painesville, Ohio: published by the author, 1834).

59. "Another Testimony," *Deseret Evening News* (Salt Lake City), January 20, 1891.

60. Lucy Mack Smith, *History of Joseph Smith by His Mother: The Unabridged Original Version* (Arlington, Virginia and Provo, Utah: Stratford Books, Revised Second Edition 2006), p. 168.

# CHAPTER 12

1. Brigham Young discourse, *Journal of Discourses*, edited by George D. Watt, et al., 26 volumes (Liverpool, England: Franklin D. Richards and Sons, 1854–1886), vol. 5, p. 55.

2. *Kansas City Times* (Kansas City, Missouri), April 11, 1895.

   **Note: This was a morning newspaper that was published for a remarkably long 133 years—from 1867 to 1990.**

   Lucy Mack Smith, *History of Joseph Smith by His Mother: The Unabridged Original Version* (Arlington, Virginia and Provo, Utah: Stratford Books, Revised Second Edition 2006), p. 168.

   Lucy Mack Smith, *Biographical Sketches of Joseph Smith the Prophet and His Progenitors for Many Generations* (Liverpool, England: S. W. Richards, 1853), pp. 102–104.

3. Ibid., Lucy Mack Smith, *History.*

4. Ibid., p. 169.

5. Ibid.

6. Ibid.

7. Ibid., p. 170.

8. Ibid.

9. Ibid.

10. Ibid.

11. *The Saints' Herald* (Lamoni, Iowa), vol. 31 (1884), pp. 643–644.

12. Joseph Knight Sr., 5-page manuscript, #183301847, Historical Department, The Church of Jesus Christ of Latter-day Saints, Salt Lake City.

Joseph Knight Sr., "Joseph Knight's Recollection of Early Mormon History," edited by Dean C. Jessee, *BYU Studies* (Provo, Utah), vol. 17, no. 1 (Autumn 1976), pp. 33–34.

13. "Another Testimony," *Deseret Evening News* (Salt Lake City), January 20, 1891.

14. Ibid.

15. Ibid.

16. Ibid.

17. Ibid.

18. **Note: When William Smith is referring to Joseph fearing to transgress and lose the plates, a casual observer might think William is referring to Joseph suffering from losing the 116 page manuscript. But that event would not happen until later, after a portion of the plates would be translated. At this point in Joseph's chronology, he had not even begun translating. His concerns and those of his family were solely on survival of the plates. If however William is referring to the loss of the 116 pages and is stating that Joseph is fearing to "lose them again," he likely has the chronology confused.**

    **Since the interview is taking place 63 years later, in 1891, William may have in his mind transposed the two events (plate survival vs. losing the 116 pages). As a side note: not that he ever claimed it, but it is doubtful William ever saw Joseph translate. The translation would not begin until Joseph would move away to Pennsylvania, and though most of the translating would take place when Joseph moved back to New York, at Fayette, it was far enough away from Manchester—where William lived—that William likely never saw his brother translate. Yet he apparently saw the plates wrapped in Joseph's frock, as stated in Chapter 12, soon after Joseph retrieved them from the hill.**

19. "Another Testimony," *Deseret Evening News* (Salt Lake City), January 20, 1891.

20. Joseph Smith III, "Last Testimony of Sister Emma," *The Saints' Herald* (Plano, Illinois), vol. 26, no. 19 (October 1, 1879), pp. 289–290.

Lucy Mack Smith, *Biographical Sketches of Joseph Smith the Prophet and His Progenitors for Many Generations* (Liverpool, England: S. W. Richards, 1853), p. 124.

21. Ibid., Joseph Smith III.

22. Lucy Mack Smith, *History of Joseph Smith by His Mother: The Unabridged Original Version* (Arlington, Virginia: Stratford Books, Revised Second Edition 2006), p. 173.

23. Ibid., pp. 173–174.

24. Ibid., p. 174.

25. *Tiffany's Monthly* (New York City), August 1859, pp. 164–165.

26. Lucy Mack Smith, *History of Joseph Smith by His Mother: The Unabridged Original Version* (Arlington, Virginia and Provo, Utah: Stratford Books, Revised Second Edition 2006), p. 171.

27. Ibid.

28. Ibid., p. 174.

   Joseph Knight Sr., "Joseph Knight's Recollection of Early Mormon History," edited by Dean C. Jessee. *BYU Studies* (Provo, Utah), vol. 17, no. 1 (Autumn 1976), pp. 33–34.

29. Ibid., both Lucy Mack Smith and Joseph Knight Sr.

30. "A Journal or Diary of Joseph Bates Noble. 1810–1834," Typescript copy, L. Tom Perry Special Collections, Harold B. Lee Library, Brigham Young University, Provo, Utah.

   **Note: Alva Beaman was one of the men with Joseph Smith when Joseph had earlier been hired by Josiah Stowell to search for the silver mine.**

31. Ibid., p. 10.

32. Lucy Mack Smith, *History of Joseph Smith by His Mother: The Unabridged Original Version* (Arlington, Virginia and Provo, Utah: Stratford Books, Revised Second Edition 2006), p. 174.

33. Ibid., p. 175.

34. Ibid.

   Joseph Knight Sr., "Joseph Knight's Recollection of Early Mormon History," edited by Dean C. Jessee, *BYU Studies* (Provo, Utah), vol. 17, no. 1 (Autumn 1976), pp. 33–34.

35. Lucy Mack Smith, *History of Joseph Smith by His Mother: The Unabridged Original Version* (Arlington, Virginia: Stratford Books and Provo, Utah, Revised Second Edition 2006), p. 175.

36. Joseph Knight Sr., 5-page manuscript, #183301847, Historical Department, The Church of Jesus Christ of Latter-day Saints, Salt Lake City.

37. Lucy Mack Smith, *History of Joseph Smith by His Mother: The Unabridged Original Version* (Arlington, Virginia: Stratford Books and Provo, Utah, Revised Second Edition 2006), p. 170.

38. *Journal of Discourses*, edited by George D. Watt, et al., 26 volumes (Liverpool, England: Franklin D. Richards and Sons, 1854–1886), vol. 2, pp. 180–181 (February 18, 1855).

39. David Whitmer, Interview (1878), in Orson Pratt, "Report of Elders Orson Pratt and Joseph F. Smith," *The Latter-day Saints' Millennial Star* (London), vol. 40, no. 49 (December 9, 1878), pp. 771–774.

Note: *The Latter-day Saints' Millennial Star*, commonly shortened to *Millennial Star* by those who reference it, was the longest-standing magazine in Latter-day Saint church history, beginning with its first issue at Manchester, England, in May 1840, edited by Parley P. Pratt, and ending in 1970 when all LDS church magazines were consolidated and coordinated at church headquarters in Salt Lake City. After its release at Manchester it was published in Liverpool beginning in April 1842 and later at London at the Latter-day Saints' Book Depot, 30 Florence St., Islington. In the course of its editors, 5 future church presidents were at the helm—Wilford Woodruff, Joseph Fielding Smith, Heber J. Grant, George Albert Smith, and David O. McKay. In its 130-year history it was published at times weekly, semi-monthly, and monthly.

40. *Tiffany's Monthly* (New York City), August 1859, p. 164.

41. Joseph Knight Sr., "Joseph Knight's Recollection of Early Mormon History," edited by Dean C. Jessee, *BYU Studies* (Provo, Utah), vol. 17, no. 1 (Autumn 1976), pp. 33–34.

42. Lucy Mack Smith, *History of Joseph Smith by His Mother: The Unabridged Original Version* (Arlington, Virginia and Provo, Utah: Stratford Books, Revised Second Edition 2006), p. 174.

43. Joseph Knight Sr., "Joseph Knight's Recollection of Early Mormon History," edited by Dean C. Jessee, *BYU Studies* (Provo, Utah), vol. 17, no. 1 (Autumn 1976), pp. 33–34.

44. Lucy Mack Smith, *Lucy's Book: A Critical Edition of Lucy Mack Smith's Family Memoir*, edited by Lavina Fielding Anderson (Salt Lake City: Signature Books, 2001), p. 800.

45. **Note: Alva Beaman would serve as Elders Quorum President in Kirtland, Ohio, and in the High Council at Independence, Missouri. He would die at Kirtland in 1837, presumably active in the faith, and his wife would die at Nauvoo, Illinois, also probably active, in 1840. The 3 youngest of their 8 children would join the Latter-day Saints.**

46. Lucy Mack Smith, *History of Joseph Smith by His Mother: The Unabridged Original Version* (Arlington, Virginia and Provo, Utah: Stratford Books, Revised Second Edition 2006), p. 175.

47. Ibid.

48. Ibid.

49. **Note: Joseph Knight records that after Alva Beaman and Samuel Lawrence came searching for the plates at the Smiths' residence—with Beaman holding up the rods that pointed to the fireplace—"They [the Smith family] had to guard the house until some time in November."** [Joseph Knight Sr., 5-page manuscript, #183301847, Historical Department, The Church of Jesus Christ of Latter-day Saints, Salt Lake City.]

50. Lucy Mack Smith, *History of Joseph Smith by His Mother: The Unabridged Original Version* (Arlington, Virginia and Provo, Utah: Stratford Books, Revised Second Edition 2006), p. 175.

51. Ibid., p. 176.

    Lucy Mack Smith, *Biographical Sketches of Joseph Smith the Prophet and His Progenitors for Many Generations* (Liverpool, England: S. W. Richards, 1853), p. 109.

52. Mrs. M. C. R. Smith, Statement, in *Naked Truths About Mormonism: Also a Journal for Important, Newly Apprehended Truths, and Miscellany*, newspaper edited and published by A. B. Deming (Oakland, California), vol. 1 no. 2 (April 1888), L. Tom Perry Special Collections, Harold B. Lee Library, Brigham Young University, Provo, Utah.

53. John Stafford, quoted in William H. Kelley and E. L. Kelley, "Interview with Orlando Saunders and Dr. John Stafford, March 1881," *The Saints' Herald* (Plano, Illinois), vol. 28, no. 11 (June 1, 1881), p. 165.

54. Lucy Mack Smith, *History of Joseph Smith by His Mother: The Unabridged Original Version* (Arlington, Virginia and Provo, Utah: Stratford Books, Revised Second Edition 2006), p. 176.

**Note: The final 4 words are from Lucy's rough draft.**

55. Ibid., p. 175.

56. Ibid., p. 176.

57. Ibid., p. 175.

58. Ibid., p. 176.

59. *Tiffany's Monthly* (New York City), August 1859, p. 167.

60. Lucy Mack Smith, *History of Joseph Smith by His Mother: The Unabridged Original Version* (Arlington, Virginia and Provo, Utah: Stratford Books, Revised Second Edition 2006), p. 176.

61. **Note: Lucy leaves out the confrontation of Joseph with Alva Beaman and Samuel Lawrence, and makes no mention of the rods incident, detailing only the mob attack that was thwarted by the Smith boys, followed by her account of the brother-sister team of Willard Chase and Sally Chase leading a mob attack on the cooper shop.**

    **It is possible the incident of Beaman and his rods occurred after that of the Chases. If Sally Chase did conduct her search before Beaman did, this would have necessitated Joseph burying the plates in the hearth, then taking them to the cooper shop (which he did) and then taking them back to the hearth and burying them there a second time. This is an unlikely scenario since the shop loft had already proven itself a successful spot to hide the plates.**

    **Also making this scenario of the Beaman rods incident occurring after the Chase incident an unlikely one is the fact that Beaman had helped Joseph bury the plates in the hearth the first time and thus Beaman knew the hearth was a likely hiding place. Thus, Joseph probably did not hide them under the hearth a second time after the Chases' attack. I feel it, therefore, more likely that the Beaman rods incident occurred before the Chases came with a mob, as chronicled in the text.**

# CHAPTER 13

1. *Kansas City Daily Journal* (Kansas City, Missouri), June 5, 1881.

    **Note: This paper, the *Kansas City Daily Journal*, reported the Latter-day Saints period in Jackson County, Missouri, perpetuating the misinformation about them for 64 years (until its demise in 1897).**

Their editorializing ("reporting") would affect several generations of the general population there, even after the Saints had been expelled from the county by mobs. Those reading the paper and believing its falsehoods included my mother's parents and their parents in the mid-to-late 1800s.

A similar scenario would be played out in other areas where the Saints lived, as newspapers would affect 2 or 3 generations of readers.

For techno-enthusiasts and genealogists who rely on old newspapers, the following details may be helpful:

The *Kansas City Journal* was published in Missouri from 1854 to 1942, the city's oldest newspaper by 1942. In 1854 it began 1 year after the city was founded and was published under a different name, *The Kansas City Enterprise.* The *U.S. Newspaper Directory, 1690–Present,* lists the paper as starting in 1858 rather than 1854, with its first name the *Kansas City Daily Western Journal of Commerce,* until it became the *Kansas City Daily Journal* in 1878.

Thus, according to what seem to be conflicting sources, the *Kansas City Journal* began in either 1854 or 1858, then in 1878 changed its name to *Kansas City Daily Journal.* Its purpose was to cover the news of the country, yet it focused primarily on Jackson County, Missouri. For the next 18 years it would alternate its name between *Kansas City Journal* and *Kansas City Daily Journal,* until 1897, when it decided to keep only the name *Kansas City Journal.* (In 1891–1892 it went by *Kansas City Journal,* but returned to the *Kansas City Daily Journal* from 1892–1897, its final 6 years of publication.)

2. Willard Chase, Affidavit (1833), in *Eber D. Howe, Mormonism Unvailed [sic] Or, A Faithful Account of that Singular Imposition and Delusion* (Painesville, Ohio: published by the author, 1834), p. 245.

3. Knight Sr., 5-page manuscript, #183301847, Historical Department, The Church of Jesus Christ of Latter-day Saints, Salt Lake City.

4. Thomas H. Taylor, quoted in William H. Kelley and E. L. Kelley, "Interview with Orlando Saunders and Dr. John Stafford, March 1881," *The Saints' Herald* (Plano, Illinois), vol. 28, no. 11 (June 1, 1881), p. 167.

5. William W. Campbell, *The Life and Writings of DeWitt Clinton* (New York City: Baker and Scribner, 1849), p. 150.

6. *Wayne Sentinel* (Palmyra, New York), June 26, 1829.

7. *Rochester Advertiser and Telegraph* (Rochester, New York), August 31, 1829.

Note: The *Rochester Advertiser* existed only 3 years, from 1826 to 1829, and was published by Luther Tucker. The only extant (still existing) issue is December 12, 1826. Its name was lengthened to include "*and Telegraph*" sometime between 1827 and 1829. Meanwhile the *Rochester Telegraph* had a longer lifespan, from 1818 to 1830, with its last 2 or 3 years with the *Advertiser*. The oldest extant issue of any paper from Monroe County is the *Rochester Telegraph* of July 7, 1818.

8. *Rochester Gem* (Rochester, New York), September 5, 1829.

Note: The *Rochester Gem* was published from about 1829 to 1843. Incidentally, the very first Monroe County newspaper had been the *Rochester Gazette*, which was published from 1816 to 1821.

9. Lucy Mack Smith, *History of Joseph Smith by His Mother: The Unabridged Original Version* (Arlington, Virginia and Provo, Utah: Stratford Books, Revised Second Edition 2006), p. 177.

10. Donna Hill, *Joseph Smith: The First Mormon* (Garden City, New York: Doubleday, 1977), p. 75.

11. Lucy Harris, Statement (1833), in Eber D. Howe, *Mormonism Unvailed [sic] Or, A Faithful Account of that Singular Imposition and Delusion* (Painesville, Ohio: published by the author, 1834).

12. Lucy Mack Smith, *History of Joseph Smith by His Mother: The Unabridged Original Version* (Arlington, Virginia and Provo, Utah: Stratford Books, Revised Second Edition 2006), p. 178.

13. Ibid., p. 177.

14. Ibid., p. 179.

15. Ibid.

16. Ibid.

17. Ibid.

18. Ibid.

19. Ibid.

20. Ibid., pp. 179–80.

21. *Tiffany's Monthly* (New York City), August 1859, p. 168.

22. Ibid., p. 167.

23. Ibid., pp. 168–170.

24. Ibid.

25. Ibid.

26. Lucy Mack Smith, *History of Joseph Smith by His Mother: The Unabridged Original Version* (Arlington, Virginia and Provo, Utah: Stratford Books, Revised Second Edition 2006), p. 180.

27. Ibid.

28. Joseph Knight Sr., 5-page manuscript, #183301847, Historical Department, The Church of Jesus Christ of Latter-day Saints, Salt Lake City.

    Also displayed in Joseph Knight Sr., "Joseph Knight's Recollection of Early Mormon History," edited by Dean C. Jessee, *BYU Studies* (Provo, Utah), vol. 17, no. 1 (Autumn 1976).

29. Lucy Mack Smith, *History of Joseph Smith by His Mother: The Unabridged Original Version* (Arlington, Virginia and Provo, Utah: Stratford Books, Revised Second Edition 2006), p. 180.

30. Ibid., p. 181.

31. Elizabeth D. E. Roundy, Letter ("to President Spencer Clawson, President, Semi Centennial Jubilee Committee," not dated), Mormon Biography File, Church Archives, The Church of Jesus Christ of Latter-day Saints, Salt Lake City.

32. Ibid.

33. Lucy Mack Smith, *History of Joseph Smith by His Mother: The Unabridged Original Version* (Arlington, Virginia and Provo, Utah: Stratford Books, Revised Second Edition 2006), p. 181.

34. Ibid.

35. *Tiffany's Monthly* (New York City), August 1859, pp. 168–170.

36. Lucy Mack Smith, *History of Joseph Smith by His Mother: The Unabridged Original Version* (Arlington, Virginia and Provo, Utah: Stratford Books, Revised Second Edition 2006), p. 181.

37. Lucy Mack Smith, *Biographical Sketches of Joseph Smith the Prophet and His Progenitors for Many Generations* (Liverpool, England: S. W. Richards, 1853), p. 119.

    *Tiffany's Monthly* (New York City), August 1859, p. 170.

38. Issac Hale, Affidavit (1834), in Eber D. Howe, *Mormonism Unvailed [sic]: Or, A Faithful Account of that Singular Imposition and Delusion* (Painesville, Ohio: published by the author, 1834), p. 264.

39. Ibid.

Joseph Knight Sr., "Joseph Knight's Recollection of Early Mormon History," edited by Dean C. Jessee, *BYU Studies* (Provo, Utah), vol. 17, no. 1 (Autumn 1976), p. 34.

40. Joseph Knight Sr., 5-page manuscript, #183301847, Historical Department, The Church of Jesus Christ of Latter-day Saints, Salt Lake City.

41. Issac Hale, Affidavit (1834), in Eber D. Howe, *Mormonism Unvailed [sic]: Or, A Faithful Account of that Singular Imposition and Delusion* (Painesville, Ohio: published by the author, 1834), p. 264.

42. Joseph Smith III, "Last Testimony of Sister Emma," *The Saints' Herald* (Plano, Illinois), vol. 26, no. 19 (October 1, 1879), pp. 289–290.

43. Joseph Knight Sr., 5-page manuscript, #183301847, Historical Department, The Church of Jesus Christ of Latter-day Saints, Salt Lake City.

44. Joseph Smith III, "Last Testimony of Sister Emma," *The Saints' Herald* (Plano, Illinois), vol. 26, no. 19 (October 1, 1879), pp. 289–290.

45. Lucy Mack Smith, *History of Joseph Smith by His Mother: The Unabridged Original Version* (Arlington, Virginia and Provo, Utah: Stratford Books, Revised Second Edition 2006), p. 176.

46. Emma Smith Bidamon, Letter (to Mrs. Pilgrim, March 27, 1870), Emma Bidamon letters, Library-Archives, History Commission, Community of Christ, The Auditorium, Independence, Missouri.

47. Ibid.

48. Joseph Knight Sr., "Joseph Knight's Recollection of Early Mormon History," edited by Dean C. Jessee, *BYU Studies* (Provo, Utah), vol. 17, no. 1 (Autumn 1976), p. 35.

49. James E. Lancaster, "'By the Gift and Power of God': The Method of Translation of the Book of Mormon," *Saints' Herald* (Independence, Missouri), vol. 109 (November 15, 1962), pp. 14–23.

50. Royal Skousen, editor, "Critical Methodology and the Text of the Book of Mormon," *Review of Books on the Book of Mormon*, vol. 6, no. 1 (1994), pp. 121–144.

Royal Skousen, editor, *The Original Manuscript of the Book of Mormon: Typographical Facsimile of the Extant Text* (Provo, Utah: FARMS, Brigham Young University, 2001).

Royal Skousen, editor, *The Printer's Manuscript of the Book of Mormon: Typographical Facsimile of the Entire Text in Two Parts* (Provo, Utah: FARMS, Brigham Young University, 2001).

**Note: This analysis by Royal Skousen of Joseph Smith's method of translating covers the period of Oliver Cowdery as his scribe.**

51. Ibid.

52. Ibid.

53. *The Saints' Herald* (Plano, Illinois), October 1, 1879, pp. 289–290.

**Note 1: This quote by Emma Smith about Joseph Smith translating with his face in a hat comes from an interview by Joseph Smith III with his mother Emma on February 4–10, 1879.**

**Note 2: See Note 19 in Chapter 1 regarding the changed locations and name alterations of *The Saints' Herald*.**

54. Ibid., p. 290.

    "Last Testimony of Sister Emma," *Saints' Advocate* (Plano, Illinois), October 1, 1879, pp. 49–52, 290.

    **Note: This publication, the *Saints' Advocate*, was a sister publication of *The Saints' Herald*, also located in Plano, Illinois, and it lasted from 1878 to 1886.**

55. Ibid.

56. Ibid.

57. Joseph Smith, Letter (to John Wentworth, editor of Chicago Democrat), published in *Times and Seasons* (Nauvoo, Illinois), p. 708 (March 1, 1842).

58. "Last Testimony of Sister Emma," *Saints' Advocate* (Plano, Illinois), October 1, 1879, pp. 49–52, 290.

    *The Saints' Herald* (Plano, Illinois), no. 26 (October 1, 1879), p. 290.

59. Joseph Knight Sr., 5-page manuscript, #183301847, Historical Department, The Church of Jesus Christ of Latter-day Saints, Salt Lake City.

60. Ibid.

61. *The Saints' Herald* (Plano, Illinois), vol. 26 (October 1, 1879), p. 290.

    "Last Testimony of Sister Emma," *Saints' Advocate* (Plano, Illinois), October 1879, pp. 49–52, 290.

62. Joseph Knight Sr., "Joseph Knight's Recollection of Early Mormon History," edited by Dean C. Jessee, *BYU Studies* (Provo, Utah), vol. 17, no. 1 (Autumn 1976).

63. **Note: This trip of Joseph senior and Samuel Smith with Joseph Knight Sr. to Harmony, Pennsylvania, is not mentioned in Lucy's history.**

64. Joseph Knight Sr., 5-page manuscript, #183301847, Historical Department, The Church of Jesus Christ of Latter-day Saints, Salt Lake City.

65. Ibid.

**Note: On the last page of his 5-page manuscript Joseph Knight Sr. says of his wife's death: "She Died the Seventh Day of August [1831]."**

66. Joseph Smith, History [1832], Church Archives, The Church of Jesus Christ of Latter-day Saints, Salt Lake City.

Also found in Joseph Smith, *The Papers of Joseph Smith*, edited by Dean C. Jessee, 2 volumes (Salt Lake City: Deseret Book, 1989–1992), vol. 1, p. 9.

Also found in Joseph Smith, *The Joseph Smith Papers*, edited by Dean C. Jessee, Ronald K. Esplin, and Richard Lyman Bushman (Salt Lake City: The Church Historian's Press, 2008–), multiple-volume series.

67. Lucy Mack Smith, *History of Joseph Smith by His Mother: The Unabridged Original Version* (Arlington, Virginia and Provo, Utah: Stratford Books, Revised Second Edition 2006), p. 182.

68. Joseph Smith, History [1832], Church Archives, The Church of Jesus Christ of Latter-day Saints, Salt Lake City.

Also found in Joseph Smith, *The Papers of Joseph Smith*, edited by Dean C. Jessee, 2 volumes (Salt Lake City: Deseret Book, 1989–1992), vol. 1, p. 9.

Also found in Joseph Smith, *The Joseph Smith Papers*, edited by Dean C. Jessee, Ronald K. Esplin, and Richard Lyman Bushman (Salt Lake City: The Church Historian's Press, 2008–), multiple-volume series.

69. Lucy Mack Smith, *Biographical Sketches of Joseph Smith the Prophet and His Progenitors for Many Generations* (Liverpool, England: S. W. Richards, 1853), pp. 113–114.

70. Joseph Smith, History [1832], Church Archives, The Church of Jesus Christ of Latter-day Saints, Salt Lake City.

Also found in Joseph Smith, *The Papers of Joseph Smith*, edited by Dean C. Jessee, 2 volumes (Salt Lake City: Deseret Book, 1989–1992), vol. 1, p. 9.

Also found in Joseph Smith, *The Joseph Smith Papers*, edited by Dean C. Jessee, Ronald K. Esplin, and Richard Lyman Bushman (Salt Lake City: The Church Historian's Press, 2008–), multiple-volume series.

71. Lucy Mack Smith, *History of Joseph Smith by His Mother: The Unabridged Original Version* (Arlington, Virginia and Provo, Utah: Stratford Books, Revised Second Edition 2006), pp. 182–183.

# CHAPTER 14

1. John A. Clark, *Gleanings by the Way* (Philadelphia: W. J. and J. K. Simon; and New York City: Robert Carter, 1842) pp. 222, 229.

2. "The Anthon Transcript: People, Primary Sources, and Problems," *BYU Studies* (Provo, Utah), vol. 10, no. 3 (Spring 1970), pp. 328–330.

3. **Note: The 5 scholars on Martin Harris' list to visit, who were noted for their studies on Egyptology, were Charles Anthon of Columbia, George Ticknor and T. D. Wolsey of Yale, and Edward Everett and Edward Robinson of Harvard.**

4. **Note: "The big city" is the accurate designation for New York City for this period in American history. The later-used term, "The Big Apple," would not be coined for another 81 years—until 1909. Edward Martin, author of *The Wayfarer*, referred to New York City with that term, but it would be another 12 years, in 1921, before it would be regularly used, when sportswriter John Joseph Fitz Gerald of the *New York Morning Telegraph* would make the term more widely known as he wrote about horse racing. While he would continue using it through the rest of the 1920s, jazz musicians would pick up and run with the term through the 1930s and '40s. Nevertheless, "The Big Apple" was still somewhat of an underground name—most Americans still did not know it. The label in fact all but disappeared until the 1970s when the New York Convention Visitors' Bureau made the term a household word. It launched the term to attract tourists—wanting to give the city a wholesome, all-American feel after years of turbulence with Democratic Mayor John Lindsay leading through years of street crime, riots, union-led strikes, and blackouts. (Lindsay had the gall to label it "the Fun City." It didn't stick. "The Big Apple" did.)**

5. Joseph Smith Jr., *History of the Church of Jesus Christ of Latter-day Saints*, edited by B. H. Roberts, 7 volumes (Salt Lake City: The Church of Jesus Christ of Latter-day Saints and *Deseret News*, Revised Second Edition 1948), vol. 1, p. 20.

6. Ibid.

7. Joseph Knight Sr., 5-page manuscript, #183301847, Historical Department, The Church of Jesus Christ of Latter-day Saints, Salt Lake City.

8. Joseph Smith, History [1832], Church Archives, The Church of Jesus Christ of Latter-day Saints, Salt Lake City.

Also found in Joseph Smith, *The Papers of Joseph Smith*, edited by Dean C. Jessee, 2 volumes (Salt Lake City: Deseret Book, 1989–1992), vol. 1, p. 9.

Also found in Joseph Smith, *The Joseph Smith Papers*, edited by Dean C. Jessee, Ronald K. Esplin, and Richard Lyman Bushman (Salt Lake City: The Church Historian's Press, 2008–), multiple-volume series.

9. The Bible, King James Version, Old Testament, Isaiah 29:11.

10. Anthony Metcalf, *Ten Years Before the Mast: Shipwrecks and Adventures at Sea! Religious Customs of the People of India and Burmah's Empire. How I Became a Mormon and why I Became an Infidel!* (Milad, Idaho: published by the author, 1888) p. 71.

11. *Journal of Discourses*, edited by George D. Watt, et al., 26 volumes (Liverpool, England: Franklin D. Richards and Sons, 1854–1886), vol. 2, p. 288 (January 7, 1855).

12. Richard B. Parkinson, *The Rosetta Stone* (London: British Museum Objects in Focus, British Museum Press, 2005), p. 20.

E. A. Wallis Budge, *The Rosetta Stone in the British Museum: The Greek, Demotic and Hieroglyphic Texts of the Decree Inscribed on the Rosetta Stone Conferring Additional Honours on Ptolemy V. Epiphanes (203–181 B.C.) with English Translations and a Short History of the Decipherment of the Egyptian Hieroglyphs, and an Appendix Containing Translations of the Stelae of Sân (Tanis) and Tall al-Maskhûṭah* (London: The Religious Tract Society, 1929), p. 2.

Carol Andrews, *The British Museum Book of the Rosetta Stone* (London: British Museum Press: 1985), p. 12.

13. Anthon Harris, Letter (1834), in Eber D. Howe, *Mormonism Unvailed [sic]: Or, A Faithful Account of that Singular Imposition and Delusion* (Painesville, Ohio: published by the author, 1840), pp. 269–272.

14. Anthon Harris, Letter (1841), in John A. Clark, *Gleanings by the Way* (Philadelphia: W. J. and J. K. Simon; and New York City: Robert Carter, 1842), pp. 233–238.

15. Charles Anthon, Statement, in Thomas Gregg, *The Prophet of Palmyra* (New York City: John B. Alden, 1890), pp. 57–59.

16. Ibid., pp. 60–62.

17. John A. Clark, *Gleanings by the Way* (Philadelphia: W. J. and J. K. Simon; and New York City: Robert Carter, 1842), p. 229.

18. James Gordon Bennett, "James Gordon Bennett's 1831 Report on 'The Mormonites,'" edited by Leonard J. Arrington, *BYU Studies* (Provo, Utah), vol. 10, no. 3 (Spring 1970), p. 362.

19. "Memorandum of John Gilbert, Esq.," September 8, 1892, typescript. Church Archives, The Church of Jesus Christ of Latter-day Saints, Salt Lake City, p. 4.

20. "The Prophet" (anonymously written and published placard), New York City, December 21, 1844.

Note: This placard, entitled "The Prophet," likely was an issue or special issue of the Latter-day Saint weekly newspaper, *The Prophet*, begun by eastern church leader G. T. Leach in New York City with the first issue released on May 14, 1844. Leach edited the first few issues, until the fall of that year, when Samuel Brannan, a young convert from near Kirtland, took over as publisher, and began editing it with the November 23, 1844 issue. The last issue was May 24, 1845. Brannan then launched a new newspaper for eastern Latter-day Saints as a successor to and continuation of *The Prophet*, entitled *New-York Messenger*, which launched July 5, 1845.

Brannan would later lead a ship of 238 poor LDS emigrants on the ship *Brooklyn* for a 6-month, 24,000-mile journey to California by way of Cape Hope and Hawaii.

A little more info about Brannan: In San Francisco he became highly successful, so much so that he refused to leave his financial kingdom to join the main body of Saints in Salt Lake Valley, so he left the church. In California he established newspapers, cities, and highly successful retail stores for gold miners, becoming even wealthier, but was wiped out by a divorce, moved to San Diego, and died a pauper, his body held for a year in a receiving vault, unknown who it was, until finally discovered and then buried with a simple stake to mark his grave.

21. Joseph Knight, Sr., "Joseph Knight's Recollection of Early Mormon History," edited by Dean C. Jessee, *BYU Studies* (Provo, Utah), vol. 17, no. 1 (Autumn 1976), p. 34.

22. *The Book of Mormon* (Salt Lake City: The Church of Jesus Christ of Latter-day Saints, 1981), Mormon 9:32 (chapter 9, verse 32).

23. Lucy Mack Smith, *History of Joseph Smith by His Mother: The Unabridged Original Version* (Arlington, Virginia and Provo, Utah: Stratford Books, Revised Second Edition 2006), p. 183.

24. Ibid.

25. Ibid.

26. Ibid., pp. 183–184.

27. Ibid., p. 184.

28. Ibid.

29. Ibid.

30. Ibid.

31. Ibid., pp. 184–185.

32. Ibid., p. 185.

# CHAPTER 15

1. Lucy Mack Smith, *History of Joseph Smith by His Mother: The Unabridged Original Version* (Arlington, Virginia and Provo, Utah: Stratford Books, Revised Second Edition 2006), p. 185.

2. Ibid.

3. Ibid.

4. Ibid.

5. Ibid., pp. 185–186.

6. Ibid., p. 189.

7. Ibid., p. 192.

8. Ibid.

9. Ibid., pp. 193–194.

10. Ibid., p. 194.

11. Ibid., p. 195.

12. Ibid., p. 197.

13. Ibid., p. 198.

14. Ibid.

15. Ibid.

16. Ibid.

17. Ibid., pp. 198–199.

18. Ibid., p. 199.

19. Ibid.

20. Ibid., p. 195.

21. **Note: In this reference from Lucy Mack Smith about Joseph Smith fearing to tell his wife Emma about the lost 116-page manuscript, the last 6 words quote the 1853 original edition of Lucy Mack Smith's book. But the 1903 Preston Nibley Edition changes her words to clarify her obvious meaning by stating "it" should kill her at once, not "I" should kill her at once.**

22. Lucy Mack Smith, *History of Joseph Smith by His Mother: The Unabridged Original Version* (Arlington, Virginia and Provo, Utah: Stratford Books, Revised Second Edition 2006), p. 195.

23. Ibid., p. 196.

    **Note: Includes material from Lucy's rough draft.**

## CHAPTER 16

1. Donna Hill, *Joseph Smith: The First Mormon* (Garden City, New York, Doubleday, 1977), pp. 82–83.

2. Ibid., p. 83.

3. *The Doctrine and Covenants of the Church of Jesus Christ of Latter-day Saints: Containing Revelations given to Joseph Smith, the Prophet, with Some Additions by His Successors in the Presidency of the Church* (Salt Lake City: The Church of Jesus Christ of Latter-day Saints, 1981), 10:10.

4. Lucy Mack Smith, *History of Joseph Smith by His Mother: The Unabridged Original Version* (Arlington, Virginia and Provo, Utah: Stratford Books, Revised Second Edition 2006), p. 199.

5. **Note: In the *Book of Mormon* the religious history was taken from the "small plates of Nephi," while the mostly secular history was taken from the "Book of Lehi," which was part of the "larger plates." The**

term "Book of Lehi" was used by Joseph Smith in the Preface of the 1830 Edition of the *Book of Mormon.*

6. Lucy Mack Smith, *History of Joseph Smith by His Mother: The Unabridged Original Version* (Arlington, Virginia and Provo, Utah: Stratford Books, Revised Second Edition 2006), p. 199.

7. **Note: The first U.S. statistics for divorce began 59 years after Martin and Dolly Harris's separation, when, in 1890, it listed only 3.0 couples per 1,000 as divorced,** ["100 Years of Marriage and Divorce Statistics, United States, 1867-1967," Data from the National Vital Statistics System Series, volumes 21, 24 (Washington, D.C.: Superintendent of Documents, United States Government Printing Office), p. 9] **although a higher number of couples were likely separated than divorced.**

8. Lucy Mack Smith, *History of Joseph Smith by His Mother: The Unabridged Original Version* (Arlington, Virginia and Provo, Utah: Stratford Books, Revised Second Edition 2006), p. 202.

9. Ibid.

10. Ibid., p. 203.

11. Ibid., p. 204.

12. George Q. Cannon, *Life of Joseph Smith the Prophet* (Arlington, Virginia and Provo, Utah: Stratford Books, 2005), p. 28.

13. Ibid.

14. Joseph Lewis and Hiel Lewis, Statement (1879), in *Early Mormon Documents*, edited by Dan Vogel, 5 volumes (Salt Lake City: Signature Books, 1996–2003), vol 1. pp. 305–306; cited in Richard Lyman Bushman, *Joseph Smith: Rough Stone Rolling* (New York City: Alfred A. Knopf / Borzoi Books, 2005), p. 578 n 45.

15. Lucy Mack Smith, *History of Joseph Smith by His Mother: The Unabridged Original Version* (Arlington, Virginia and Provo, Utah: Stratford Books, Revised Second Edition 2006), p. 201.

16. Ibid., pp. 201–202.

17. Ibid., p. 206.

18. Ibid.

19. *The Doctrine and Covenants of the Church of Jesus Christ of Latter-day Saints: Containing Revelations given to Joseph Smith, the Prophet, with Some Additions by His Successors in the Presidency of the Church* (Salt Lake City: The Church of Jesus Christ of Latter-day Saints, 1981), 4:1–3.

20. Lucy Mack Smith, *History of Joseph Smith by His Mother: The Unabridged Original Version* (Arlington, Virginia and Provo, Utah: Stratford Books, Revised Second Edition 2006), p. 212.

21. *The Doctrine and Covenants of the Church of Jesus Christ of Latter-day Saints: Containing Revelations given to Joseph Smith, the Prophet, with Some Additions by His Successors in the Presidency of the Church* (Salt Lake City: The Church of Jesus Christ of Latter-day Saints, 1981), 5:29.

22. Ibid., 5:34.

# CHAPTER 17

1. Richard Lloyd Anderson, "The Second Witness of Priesthood Restoration," *Improvement Era* (Salt Lake City), vol. 71 (September 1968), pp. 15–24.

2. Lucy Mack Smith, *History of Joseph Smith by His Mother: The Unabridged Original Version* (Arlington, Virginia and Provo, Utah: Stratford Books, Revised Second Edition 2006), pp. 207-208.

3. Richard Lloyd Anderson, "The Second Witness of Priesthood Restoration," *Improvement Era* (Salt Lake City), vol. 71 (September 1968), pp. 15–24.

4. Lucy Mack Smith, *History of Joseph Smith by His Mother: The Unabridged Original Version* (Arlington, Virginia and Provo, Utah: Stratford Books, Revised Second Edition 2006), p. 208.

5. Ibid.

6. Ibid.

7. Ibid., pp. 208–209.

8. Ibid., p. 209.

9. Ibid.

10. Ibid., pp. 208–209.

11. Ibid., pp. 210–211.

12. Ibid., p. 211.

13. Ibid.

14. Lucy Mack Smith, *Biographical Sketches of Joseph Smith the Prophet and His Progenitors for Many Generations* (Liverpool, England: S. W. Richards, 1853), pp. 128–130.

15. Lucy Mack Smith, *History of Joseph Smith by His Mother: The Unabridged Original Version* (Arlington, Virginia and Provo, Utah: Stratford Books, Revised Second Edition 2006), p. 212.

16. Ibid.

17. Richard Lyman Bushman, *Joseph Smith: Rough Stone Rolling* (New York City: Alfred A. Knopf / Borzoi Books, 2005), p. 71.

18. R. B. Neal, *Oliver Cowdery's Defence and Renunciation* (Ashland, Kentucky: Ashland Independent, 1906), p. 6.

19. Emma Smith Bidamon, Interview by Joseph Smith III, "Last Testimony of Sister Emma." *The Saints' Herald* (Plano, Illinois), vol. 26, no. 19 (October 1, 1879), pp. 289–290.

20. Richard Lyman Bushman, *Joseph Smith: Rough Stone Rolling* (New York City: Alfred A. Knopf / Borzoi Books, 2005), p. 71.

21. *Latter Day Saints' Messenger and Advocate* (Kirtland, Ohio), vol. 1, no. 1 (October 1834), p. 14.

22. Emma Smith Bidamon, Interview by Joseph Smith III, "Last Testimony of Sister Emma." *The Saints' Herald* (Plano, Illinois), vol. 26, no. 19 (October 1, 1879), pp. 289–290.

23. Ibid.

24. Elizabeth Ann Whitney, Affidavit (1870), in *Early Mormon Documents*, edited by Dan Vogel, 5 volumes (Salt Lake City: Signature Books, 1996–2003), vol 5, p. 260.

    **Note: Later in Fayette, New York, Joseph Smith's scribes would be Oliver Cowdery and 3 of Elizabeth Ann Whitmer's siblings—the Whitmer brothers. With Joseph living in their house and by having three of Elizabeth Ann's brothers assisting him, she was in a better situation than most to see the inner workings of the translation process on a regular basis.**

25. Joseph Knight, 5-page manuscript, #183301847, Historical Department, The Church of Jesus Christ of Latter-day Saints, Salt Lake City.

26. Lucy Mack Smith, *Biographical Sketches of Joseph Smith the Prophet and His Progenitors for Many Generations* (Liverpool, England: S. W. Richards, 1853), pp. 91–92.

27. Abel Chase, Interview (1881) in *Early Mormon Documents*, edited by Dan Vogel, 5 volumes (Salt Lake City: Signature Books, 1996–2003), vol. 2, p. 85.

Willard Chase, Affidavit (1833) in Eber D. Howe, *Mormonism Unvailed [sic]: Or, A Faithful Account of that Singular Imposition and Delusion* (Painesville, Ohio: published by the author, 1834), pp. 240–241.

Pomeroy Tucker, *Origin, Rise, and Progress of Mormonism* (New York City: D. Appleton and Co., 1867), p. 19.

28. Alva Hale, Statement (1834), in Eber D. Howe, *Mormonism Unvailed [sic]: Or, A Faithful Account of that Singular Imposition and Delusion* (Painesville, Ohio: published by the author, 1834), pp. 263, 268.

29. Mark Ashurst-McGee, "A Pathway to Prophethood: Joseph Smith Junior as Rodsman, Village Seer, and Judeo-Christian Prophet" (master's thesis, Logan Utah: Utah State University, 2000), chapter 4.

   Richard Lyman Bushman, *Joseph Smith: Rough Stone Rolling* (New York City: Alfred A. Knopf / Borzoi Books, 2005), p. 49.

30. Ibid.

31. Court Record of Bainbridge, New York, March 20, 1886, in *Early Mormon Documents*, edited by Dan Vogel, 5 volumes (Salt Lake City: Signature Books, 1996–2003), vol 4, p. 253.

32. Mark Ashurst-McGee, "A Pathway to Prophethood: Joseph Smith Junior as Rodsman, Village Seer, and Judeo-Christian Prophet" (master's thesis, Logan Utah: Utah State University, 2000), chapter 4.

33. Richard S. Van Wagoner and Steven Walker, "Joseph Smith: 'The Gift of Seeing,'" *Dialogue: A Journal of Mormon Thought* (Salt Lake City), vol. 15 (1982), no. 2, pp. 48–68.

34. Alva Hale, Statement (1834), in Eber D. Howe, *Mormonism Unvailed [sic]: Or, A Faithful Account of that Singular Imposition and Delusion* (Painesville, Ohio: published by the author, 1834), pp. 263, 268.

35. Ibid.

36. Dean C. Jessee, "The Original Book of Mormon Manuscript," *BYU Studies* (Provo, Utah), vol. 10, no. 3 (Spring 1970), pp. 259–278.

   Richard Lyman Bushman, *Joseph Smith: Rough Stone Rolling* (New York City: Alfred A. Knopf / Borzoi Books, 2005), p. 579, n. 63.

37. *The Doctrine and Covenants of the Church of Jesus Christ of Latter-day Saints: Containing Revelations given to Joseph Smith, the Prophet, with Some Additions by His Successors in the Presidency of the Church* (Salt Lake City: The Church of Jesus Christ of Latter-day Saints, 1981), 10: 38–47.

38. Ibid.

39. Joseph Smith, Manuscript History of the Church, Book A-1, Historian's Office, Church Archives, The Church of Jesus Christ of Latter-day Saints, Salt Lake City.

    Also found in Joseph Smith, *The Papers of Joseph Smith*, edited by Dean C. Jessee, 2 volumes (Salt Lake City: Deseret Book, 1989–1992), vol. 1, p. 289.

    Also found in Joseph Smith, *The Joseph Smith Papers*, edited by Dean C. Jessee, Ronald K. Esplin, and Richard Lyman Bushman (Salt Lake City: The Church Historian's Press, 2008–), multiple-volume series.

    *Latter Day Saints' Messenger and Advocate* (Kirtland, Ohio), vol. 1, no. 1 (October 1834), pp. 14–15.

40. Ibid., *Latter Day Saints' Messenger and Advocate*, p. 14.

    **Note: The italics are Oliver Cowdery's emphasis.**

41. Joseph Knight Sr., 5-page manuscript, #183301847, Historical Department, The Church of Jesus Christ of Latter-day Saints, Salt Lake City.

    Also displayed in Joseph Knight Sr., "Joseph Knight's Recollection of Early Mormon History," edited by Dean C. Jessee, *BYU Studies* (Provo, Utah), vol. 17 (Autumn 1976), no. 1, p. 36.

    Joseph Smith, Manuscript History of the Church, Book A-1, Historian's Office, Church Archives, The Church of Jesus Christ of Latter-day Saints, Salt Lake City.

    Also found in Joseph Smith, *The Papers of Joseph Smith*, edited by Dean C. Jessee, 2 volumes (Salt Lake City: Deseret Book, 1989–1992), vol. 1, pp. 292–293.

    Also found in Joseph Smith, *The Joseph Smith Papers*, edited by Dean C. Jessee, Ronald K. Esplin, and Richard Lyman Bushman (Salt Lake City: The Church Historian's Press, 2008–), multiple-volume series.

42. **Note: All 4 people at the Smith household in Harmony, Pennsylvania, at the time were hungry and probably worried about when they would see their next meal.**

43. Joseph Knight Sr., 5-page manuscript, #183301847, Historical Department, The Church of Jesus Christ of Latter-day Saints, Salt Lake City.

44. *The Doctrine and Covenants of the Church of Jesus Christ of Latter-day Saints: Containing Revelations given to Joseph Smith, the Prophet, with Some Additions by His Successors in the Presidency of the Church* (Salt Lake City: The Church of Jesus Christ of Latter-day Saints, 1981), 6:22–23.

45. David Whitmer, Interview (1878), in Orson Pratt, "Report of Elders
    Orson Pratt and Joseph F. Smith," *The Latter-day Saints' Millennial Star*
    (London), vol. 40, no. 49 (December 9, 1878), pp. 771–774.

46. Brigham H. Roberts, *A Comprehensive History of the Church of Jesus
    Christ of Latter-day Saints*, 6 volumes (Salt Lake City: Deseret News Press,
    1930), vol. 1, p. 123.

47. *The Doctrine and Covenants of the Church of Jesus Christ of Latter-day
    Saints: Containing Revelations given to Joseph Smith, the Prophet, with
    Some Additions by His Successors in the Presidency of the Church* (Salt
    Lake City: The Church of Jesus Christ of Latter-day Saints, 1981), 6:14.

48. Ibid. 9:7–8.

49. *Latter Day Saints' Messenger and Advocate* (Kirtland, Ohio), vol. 1, no. 1
    (October 1834), pp. 14–15.

50. R. Scott Lloyd, "LDS Film, Historic Site in the Works," *Deseret News* (Salt
    Lake City), September 30, 2014, p. B5.

    **Note: R. Scott Lloyd's September 30, 2014, article in the *Deseret News*
    quotes Stephen B. Allen of the LDS Church missionary department
    and Reid Neilson, LDS Church history department managing director
    about Joseph Smith and Oliver Cowdery meeting John the Baptist on
    a hillside, rather than down by the river, a new concept that breaks
    away from tradition.**

    **Lloyd writes, "Research for the site development has brought about a
    change in traditional understanding about the priesthood restoration
    narrative. Previously it was believed the angel came to the two men on
    the riverbank, followed immediately by the baptisms. Now, historians
    have concluded that the visitation happened on a hillside near the
    Smith and Hale homes in the 'sugar maple bush,' a grove where sap
    was tapped for making sugar."**

    **Lloyd quotes Reid Neilson: "We looked at some of the records of
    Oliver Cowdery, and we thought about what he was really trying to
    say about where the priesthood restoration took place."**

    **An Interesting side note is how busy the river traffic was at that time.
    "In addition," states Neilson, "we were able to look at old newspapers
    and find out how many boats were going up and down the river and
    about how busy the site was."**

    **According to Lloyd's article, Neilson also states that researchers have
    concluded river flooding in May 1829 would have made the river bank
    an unlikely spot for the angel's visitation, although that location has
    been the traditional understanding for people in the church, adding,**

"It changed our understanding of what went on. So Joseph and Oliver went up the hillside, received the Aaronic Priesthood and went back down where the water was to do the baptizing."

Stephen B. Allen adds, "That will be news to many people. They will be surprised to see that the priesthood restoration took place up in the sugar grove."

In a personal note, Allen states, "I walked that grove this summer, just before we started building the visitors center, and I can tell you this site is every bit as pristine and beautiful—and has a spirit about it—as the Sacred Grove." The Sacred Grove is where Joseph Smith received the "First Vision," where he saw the Father and Jesus Christ, His Son, as Latter-day Saints believe, and is located In Palmyra, New York.

51. *Latter Day Saints' Messenger and Advocate* (Kirtland, Ohio), vol. 1, no. 1 (October 1834), p. 15.

52. Ibid.

Note: In his description of the angel appearing "in a cloud of light," Oliver Cowdery also refers to this visitor as an "angel of God" and a "messenger from heaven."

# CHAPTER 18

1. Oliver Cowdery, Letter (to Phinehas Young, March 23, 1846), Church Archives, The Church of Jesus Christ of Latter-day Saints, Salt Lake City.

2. Joseph Smith Jr., *History of the Church of Jesus Christ of Latter-day Saints*, edited by B. H. Roberts, 7 volumes (Salt Lake City: The Church of Jesus Christ of Latter-day Saints and *Deseret News*, Revised Second Edition 1948), vol. 1, pp. 39–41.

3. Reuben Miller, journal, October 21, 1848, p. 14, Church Archives, The Church of Jesus Christ of Latter-day Saints, Salt Lake City.

4. Joseph Smith, Manuscript History of the Church, Book A-1, Historian's Office, Church Archives, The Church of Jesus Christ of Latter-day Saints, Salt Lake City.

Also found in Joseph Smith, *The Papers of Joseph Smith*, edited by Dean C. Jessee, 2 volumes (Salt Lake City: Deseret Book, 1989–1992), vol. 1, p. 291.

Also found in Joseph Smith, *The Joseph Smith Papers*, edited by Dean C. Jessee, Ronald K. Esplin, and Richard Lyman Bushman (Salt Lake City: The Church Historian's Press, 2008–), multiple-volume series.

5. Joseph Smith Jr., *History of the Church of Jesus Christ of Latter-day Saints*, edited by B. H. Roberts, 7 volumes (Salt Lake City: The Church of Jesus Christ of Latter-day Saints and *Deseret News*, Revised Second Edition 1948), vol. 1, p. 42.

6. *Latter Day Saints' Messenger and Advocate* (Kirtland, Ohio), vol. 1, no.1 (October 1834), pp. 15–16.

7. Ibid.

8. Joseph Smith Jr., *History of the Church of Jesus Christ of Latter-day Saints*, edited by B. H. Roberts, 7 volumes (Salt Lake City: The Church of Jesus Christ of Latter-day Saints and *Deseret News*, Revised Second Edition 1948), vol. 1, p. 42.

**Note: Lucy Mack Smith describes the event of Joseph Smith and Oliver Cowdery's baptism a bit differently, and certainly more succinctly: "One morning they sat down to their work as usual, and the first thing which presented itself through the Urim and Thummim was a commandment for Joseph and Oliver to repair to the water and attend to the ordinance of baptism."** [Lucy Mack Smith, *History of Joseph Smith by His Mother: The Unabridged Original Version* (Arlington, Virginia and Provo, Utah: Stratford Books, Revised Second Edition 2006), p. 212.] **Her rough draft adds they "immediately went down to the Susquehanna River."** [Ibid., p. 212 (includes Lucy's rough draft after the first 3 words).]

9. Lucy Mack Smith, *History of Joseph Smith by His Mother: The Unabridged Original Version* (Arlington, Virginia and Provo, Utah: Stratford Books, Revised Second Edition 2006), pp. 212–213.

10. Joseph Smith, Manuscript History of the Church, Book A-1, Historian's Office, Church Archives, The Church of Jesus Christ of Latter-day Saints, Salt Lake City.

Also found in Joseph Smith, *The Papers of Joseph Smith*, edited by Dean C. Jessee, 2 volumes (Salt Lake City: Deseret Book, 1989–1992), vol. 1, p. 291.

Also found in Joseph Smith, *The Joseph Smith Papers*, edited by Dean C. Jessee, Ronald K. Esplin, and Richard Lyman Bushman (Salt Lake City: The Church Historian's Press, 2008–), multiple-volume series.

11. Larry C. Porter, "The Restoration of the Aaronic and Melchizedek Priesthoods," *Ensign* (Salt Lake City), vol. 26 (December 1996), pp. 30–47.

Note: The *Ensign* magazine is an official publication of the Church of Jesus Christ of Latter-day Saints, which includes stories, sermons, and faith-promoting articles. It began publication in January 1971 and is still being published today. Two other official church publications launched that month as well—*New Era* (for youth) and *Friend* (for children)—which replaced 4 former magazines of long standing:

(1) *Improvement Era* (from 1897 to 1970, which in turn replaced the independent, unofficial magazine, *The Contributor*, published from 1879 to 1896);

(2) *Relief Society Magazine* (for women, published from 1915 to 1970, which replaced the independent, unofficial church publication, *Woman's Exponent*, which had been published from 1872 to 1914);

(3) *The Instructor* (from 1930 to 1970, the official Sunday School magazine that replaced *The Juvenile Instructor*, an unofficial church publication from 1866 to 1900 that became an official church publication from 1901 to 1929); and

(4) *The Latter-day Saints' Millennial Star* (in England, from 1840 to 1970, which varied publication from weekly to monthly during that 130-year period).

Except for *Millennial Star*'s varied release times, all magazines have been monthly.

12. Joseph Smith Jr., *History of the Church of Jesus Christ of Latter-day Saints*, edited by B. H. Roberts, 7 volumes (Salt Lake City: The Church of Jesus Christ of Latter-day Saints and Deseret News, Revised Second Edition 1948), vol. 1, pp. 40–43 n.

13. Oliver Cowdery, Letter (to Phinehas Young, March 23, 1846), Church Archives, The Church of Jesus Christ of Latter-day Saints, Salt Lake City.

14. Lucy Mack Smith, Preliminary Manuscript [1844–1845], Church Archives, The Church of Jesus Christ of Latter-day Saints, Salt Lake City.

Also found in Lucy Mack Smith, *Lucy's Book: A Critical Edition of Lucy Mack Smith's Family Memoir*, edited by Lavina Fielding Anderson (Salt Lake City: Signature Books, 2001), p. 343.

Note 1: The portion used comes from Lucy's rough draft.

Note 2: Some have interpreted one passage of Latter-day Saint scripture (D&C 128:21) to mean that the higher (Melchizedek) Priesthood was restored to David Whitmer. This comes from one unexplained statement, "the voice of God in the chamber of old Father Whitmer," which details that the voice was heard there (in his chamber) as well as other places through the trials of the church. Then the verse lists prophets and angels declaring their rights and that information comes "line upon line," to church members, giving them hope.

In the previous verse, 20, it states, "The voice of Peter, James, and John in the wilderness between Harmony, Susquehanna county, and Colesville, Broome county, on the Susquehanna river, declaring themselves as possessing the keys of the kingdom, and of the dispensation of the fullness of times!" Some have apparently interpreted that as a tie-in to the next verse about "the voice of God in the chamber of old Father Whitmer." However, mainstream Latter-day Saints believe the subject is changed between the 2 verses—20 and 21—and that in any case the verse is obscurely worded. Thus, they believe the Melchizedek Priesthood was not restored through David Whitmer, though some outside the mainstream church have believed it was, because of these two verses.

By contrast, Oliver Cowdery asserts on more than one occasion that the ancient Apostle Peter restored the Melchizedek Priesthood to him and Joseph alone. For example, in one letter in which he wrote Phinehas Young in 1846, Oliver states that he stood with Joseph in the presence of John [the Baptist] "to receive the lesser priesthood, and in the presence of [the Apostle] Peter, to receive the greater." [Oliver Cowdery, Letter (to Phinehas Young, March 23, 1846), Church Archives, The Church of Jesus Christ of Latter-day Saints, Salt Lake City.] Also, in 1904 Joseph Fielding Smith quotes Oliver Cowdery making this statement in 1848: "I was also present with Joseph when the higher or Melchizedek priesthood was conferred by the holy angel from on high." [Joseph Fielding Smith, "Restoration of the Melchizedek Priesthood," *Improvement Era*, vol. 7, no. 12 (October 1904), pp. 941–942.]

As for the two men—Joseph and Oliver—keeping this event of receiving the priesthood to themselves, historian Richard Lyman Bushman [*Joseph Smith: Rough Stone Rolling* (New York City: Alfred A. Knopf / Borzoi Books, 2005), p. 75] outlines the following interesting facts:

(1) that in 1830 Joseph never mentioned the event of them receiving the priesthood in a key statement Joseph made—still, it does not take away from the importance of the event;

(2) that the first compilation of revelations, which was in 1833, also left out Joseph and Oliver receiving the priesthood;

(3) that David Whitmer never heard about John the Baptist (who restored the lesser priesthood first) until 1834; [David Whitmer, Interview (1883, by Zenas H. Gurley) in *Early Mormon Documents*, edited

by Dan Vogel, 5 volumes (Salt Lake City: Signature Books, 1996–2003), vol. 5, pp. 136–137, 329);

William E. McLellin, Letter (to Joseph Smith III, 1872), in Ibid.]

**(4) and that Joseph's first mention of receiving the priesthood was in his 1832 history (not published until years later), referring to receiving the Priesthood "by the ministering of angels" but not mentioning John the Baptist by name;** [Joseph Smith, History (1832), Church Archives, The Church of Jesus Christ of Latter-day Saints, Salt Lake City]

**(5) however, unlike David Whitmer, Oliver Cowdery did maintain he received authority from angels before 1830, according to an 1830 newspaper report of what he claimed.** [*Painesville Telegraph* (Painesville, Ohio), November 16, 1830.]

15. *The Doctrine and Covenants of the Church of Jesus Christ of Latter-day Saints: Containing Revelations given to Joseph Smith, the Prophet, with Some Additions by His Successors in the Presidency of the Church* (Salt Lake City: The Church of Jesus Christ of Latter-day Saints, 1981), 4:1.

16. Joseph Smith Jr., *History of the Church of Jesus Christ of Latter-day Saints*, edited by B. H. Roberts, 7 volumes (Salt Lake City: The Church of Jesus Christ of Latter-day Saints and *Deseret News*, Revised Second Edition 1948), vol. 1, pp. 44–46.

    *The Doctrine and Covenants of the Church of Jesus Christ of Latter-day Saints: Containing Revelations given to Joseph Smith, the Prophet, with Some Additions by His Successors in the Presidency of the Church* (Salt Lake City: The Church of Jesus Christ of Latter-day Saints, 1981), 11:6, 8.

17. Lucy Mack Smith, *History of Joseph Smith by His Mother: The Unabridged Original Version* (Arlington, Virginia and Provo, Utah: Stratford Books, Revised Second Edition 2006), p. 215.

18. Ibid.

19. Ibid.

20. Ibid., p. 216.

21. Ibid.

22. Ibid., p. 217.

23. Ibid.

24. Ibid., pp. 217–219.

25. Ibid.

    **Note: Only the portion from Lucy's rough draft is used.**

26. *Journal of Discourses*, edited by George D. Watt, et al., 26 volumes (Liverpool, England: Franklin D. Richards and Sons, 1854–1886), vol. 2, p. 213.

    **Note: This incident of Joseph Smith being charged and found guilty of exorcising evil spirits in New York, then being acquitted, was told to George A. Smith by Patriarch Emer Harris. This was the older brother of Martin Harris, who received Martin's first copy of the *Book of Mormon*, read it, and was baptized by Hyrum Smith in February, 1831. He would serve missions and work on both the Ohio and Nauvoo temples, then move to Utah in 1850 and remain faithful to the LDS church until his death at age 78.**

27. Joseph Knight Jr., manuscript, Joseph Knight Jr. Folder, Church Archives, The Church of Jesus Christ of Latter-day Saints, Salt Lake City.

28. Ibid.

    **Note: Joseph Smith also received a revelation for the father of Joseph Knight Jr. to keep the Lord's commandments and to help establish Zion.**

29. Lucy Mack Smith, *History of Joseph Smith by His Mother: The Unabridged Original Version* (Arlington, Virginia and Provo, Utah: Stratford Books, Revised Second Edition 2006), p. 221.

30. Ibid.

31. **Note: Fayette, New York, was equidistant from Harmony and Palmyra—28 miles from Harmony and 27 miles from Palmyra.**

32. Orson Pratt, "Report of Elders Orson Pratt and Joseph F. Smith," *The Latter-day Saints' Millennial Star* (London), vol. 40, no. 49 (December 9, 1878), pp. 771–774.

# CHAPTER 19

1. Lucy Mack Smith, *History of Joseph Smith by His Mother: The Unabridged Original Version* (Arlington, Virginia and Provo, Utah: Stratford Books, Revised Second Edition 2006), p. 222.

2. David Whitmer, Interview (1878), in Orson Pratt, "Report of Elders Orson Pratt and Joseph F. Smith," *The Latter-day Saints' Millennial Star* (London), vol. 40, no. 49 (December 9, 1878), pp. 771–774.

3. Ibid.

4. Lucy Mack Smith, *History of Joseph Smith by His Mother: The Unabridged Original Version* (Arlington, Virginia and Provo, Utah: Stratford Books, Revised Second Edition 2006), p. 222.

**Note: In regards to David Whitmer seeing the miracle of his fields getting harrowed quickly so that he could go to Harmony to help Joseph and Oliver travel to Fayette, Lucy is either adding new information to Whitmer's account, or she is reporting the same event differently.**

**Her version states that by noon David was surprised to see he had harrowed (plowed) half the wheat, and by evening he was done with it all—in 1 day.**

**His version is that before he started, 5–7 acres of the 20-acre plot had been mysteriously done already by someone else.**

**Neither account can be dismissed as less factual than the other: the reality could have been a merging of the two—with her merely adding details of how surprised he was to see how much acreage he had plowed, perhaps after the 5–7 acres had been mysteriously plowed by someone else already, which was all he talked about. If there is a discrepancy, it is difficult to determine who is more accurate: on the one hand his report is in the first person; on the other, hers was recorded a third of a century before his (1845 vs. 1878), and her overall track record for accuracy of details is almost beyond remarkable.**

5. Ibid., pp. 222–223.

**Note: In regards to David Whitmer having his fields plowed early, which convinced him to go help Joseph Smith, this entire quote by Lucy about this is in her published 1853 text. However, the final 15 words that end at this endnote number in the text are from only her rough draft. Similarly, another 2 portions of this quote that are from only her rough draft are noted in the 2 endnotes (nos. 6 and 7 below), pp. 222–223.**

6. Ibid., p. 223.

**Note: The 13-word sentence ending at this endnote number is from Lucy's rough draft.**

7. Ibid.

   **Note: The last 10 words ending at this endnote number are from Lucy's rough draft.**

8. Ibid., non–rough draft material.

   **Note: Regarding David Whitmer's trip to Pennsylvania for the purpose of giving Joseph Smith a ride to Fayette, Lucy places the mileage from Fayette, New York, to Harmony, Pennsylvania as 135 miles. On modern roads today the distance is 106 miles. The route at that time could have been more circuitous than today's, in which case her 135 mile figure may be accurate. However, if the route then was similar to today's, she was up to 29 miles off. While roads, of course, have drastically improved and changed since then, the actual routes often have not. The more direct state highways and interstate highways have made it a point to bypass towns, in which case those routes today are shorter. Between smaller towns, however, many routes have not changed much over the years.**

9. Lyndon W. Cook, editor, *David Whitmer Interviews: A Restoration Witness* (Orem Utah,: Grandin Book Co., 1991), p. 123.

10. David Whitmer, Interview, in Orson Pratt, "Report of Elders Orson Pratt and Joseph F. Smith," *The Latter-day Saints' Millennial Star* (London), vol. 40, no. 49 (December 9, 1878), pp. 771–774.

    **Note: The additional miracle of David Whitmer being met "some distance from the house" by Joseph and Oliver—because Joseph had prophesied exactly when Whitmer would arrive—is a segment I italicized for emphasis.**

11. *Lucy Mack Smith, History of Joseph Smith by His Mother: The Unabridged Original Version* (Arlington, Virginia and Provo, Utah: Stratford Books, Revised Second Edition 2006), p. 224.

    **Note: When David Whitmer arrived at Harmony, Pennsylvania, to give Joseph Smith and Oliver Cowdery a ride to his home in Fayette, New York, it was Joseph and David's first meeting. However, according to historian Richard Bushman, Joseph had met David's father, Peter Whitmer Sr., shortly after translation had commenced. [Richard Lyman Bushman, *Joseph Smith: Rough Stone Rolling* (New York City: Alfred A. Knopf / Borzoi Books, 2005), p. 76.] On another occasion, according to Lucy, Joseph's parents had met David's parents on their way to visit Joseph in Harmony.**

12. Ibid.

13. Ibid.

14. David Whitmer, Interview, in Orson Pratt, "Report of Elders Orson Pratt and Joseph F. Smith," *The Latter-day Saints' Millennial Star* (London), vol. 40, no. 49 (December 9, 1878), pp. 771–774.

**Note: This account of the roadside stranger continues, as David Whitmer reports of it in his interview with Orson Pratt and Joseph F. Smith in 1878 at Richmond, Missouri:**

**Question by Joseph F. Smith: "Did you notice his appearance?"**

**Response by David Whitmer: "I should think I did. He was I should think, about 5 feet 8 or 9 inches tall and heavy set, about such a man as James Vancleave there, but heavier; his face was as large, he was dressed in a suit of brown woolen clothes, his hair and beard were white, like Brother Pratt's, but his beard was not so heavy. I also remember that he had on his back a sort of knapsack with something in [it], shaped like a book. It was the messenger who had the plates, who had taken them from Joseph just prior to our starting from Harmony. Soon after our arrival home, I saw something which led me to the belief that the plates were placed or concealed in my father's barn. I frankly asked Joseph if my supposition was right, he told me it was."**

15. Edward Stevenson, Journal, December 23, 1877; cited in Richard L. Anderson, *Investigating the Book of Mormon Witnesses* (Salt Lake City: Deseret Book, 1981), pp. 30–31.

Edward Stevenson, Interview (December 22–23, 1877), Richmond, Missouri, Diary of Edward Stevenson, Church Archives, The Church of Jesus Christ of Latter-day Saints, Salt Lake City, in Lyndon W. Cook, editor, *David Whitmer Interviews: A Restoration Witness* (Orem, Utah: Grandin Book Co., 1991), p. 13.

**Note: Edward Stevenson's journal entry about the incident of the roadside stranger was possibly not as accurate as the Orson Pratt-Joseph F. Smith account, because both Pratt and Smith had been present for their interview and could likely recall more information than if only one had been present. Ostensibly in both interviews notes were taken, but having two men reviewing the notes (the Pratt-Smith team) and making clarifications may have resulted in a more accurate report.**

**Edward Stevenson reported another interview with David Whitmer 9 years later, in 1886, [*Juvenile Instructor* (Salt Lake City), vol. 22 (1887), p. 55] which I will label account #3. (The first 2 accounts are in the text at Chapter 19.)**

Account #3: "While on the return journey from Palmyra, David noticed a somewhat aged-looking man who approached them on the road. He had a very pleasant face, about which, however, there seemed something peculiar, and he carried a knapsack on his back fastened with straps which crossed his breast. David asked him to take a ride, but he declined, saying: 'I am going over to Cumorah,' and then disappeared very suddenly, though there was no chance for him to secrete himself in the open country through which the party was then passing. All felt very strange concerning this personage and the Prophet was besought to inquire of the Lord concerning him. Shortly afterwards, David relates, the Prophet looked very white but with a heavenly appearance and said their visitor was one of the three Nephites to whom the Savior gave the promise of life on earth until He should come in power. After arriving home [at their Fayette farm], David again saw this personage."

One other source for this account gets farther away from the time it happened, which may cause it to lose some credibility. I will label it account #4, and it comes from Joseph F. Smith of the Pratt-Smith team 40 years *after* their interview of Whitmer. This is Joseph F. Smith's journal entry from April 25, 1918:

Account #4: "When they started for New York, Joseph and Emma were on the hind seat (of the wagon) [actually Emma was probably still at Harmony] and Oliver and David on the front seat. In the middle of the prairie, all of the sudden, there appeared a man walking along the road, and David said he raised his hat and rubbed his brow as if he were a little warm, and said good morning to them and they said good morning. Oliver and David looked at each other and began to marvel and wonder: Where did he come from, and what does this mean? And Joseph said, 'Ask him to ride.' So David, who was teamster, asked him if he would get in and ride with them. He said, 'No, I'm just going over to Cumorah.' David said, 'Cumorah? Cumorah? What does that mean?' He had never heard of Cumorah, and he said, 'I thought I knew this country all around here, but I never heard of Cumorah,' and he inquired about it. While he was looking around and trying to ascertain what the mystery was, the man was gone, and when he looked back he did not see him anymore. Then he demanded, 'What does it mean?' Joseph informed him that the man was Moroni [labeling him Moroni is likely speculation, coupled with a memory lapse, on the part of Joseph F. Smith, as described in the following analysis] and that the bundle on his back contained plates which Joseph had delivered to him before they departed from Harmony, Susquehanna County, and that he was taking them for safety, and would return them when he (Joseph) reached father Whitmer's home. There was a

**long talk about this."** [Joseph F. Smith, Diaries, entry of April 25, 1815, Church Archives, The Church of Jesus Christ of Latter-day Saints, Salt Lake City.]

**The reason I believe it was not Moroni is at least two-fold:**

**(1) This 2nd account of Joseph F. Smith was 40 years after the 1st report he was a part of—in which he and Pratt both reported the roadside stranger was one of the three Nephites. In that 40-years-earlier interview both Pratt and Smith worked on both the interview and on polishing their report—so both men together likely got the facts straight. In the process, the Pratt-Smith team had most likely written up their report from their notes and memory immediately following the interview, as it was considered a highly important gathering of information for the church. By contrast, Joseph F. Smith, on his own, is writing this account 4 decades later.**

**(2) Numerous accounts have described the three Nephites as older-looking bearded gentlemen in the common clothes of mortals, as their mission upon earth has been to blend in with and assist mankind to prepare it for the Restored Gospel (with numerous folkloristic reports of them saving mortals as well, dressed as "common men" ofttimes). Moroni has never been thus described.**

**(3) As a side note, another person—David Whitmer's mother—would soon see the stranger and refer to him as "Brother Nephi," but likely this was an inaccurate label, perhaps stemming from the fact she heard he was "one of the Nephites," per Endnote 17 below.**

**The most important aspects to Stevenson's 1877 account presented in Chapter 19 are the corroborating details to Whitmer's account presented in 1878 to Orson Pratt and Joseph F. Smith, plus a few new, interesting details not contained in the Pratt-Smith report.**

**The 1877 Stevenson account of the roadside stranger differs in these details:**

**(1)  His height. (It differed by 1 to 2 inches from the Pratt-Smith report that stated he was "about 5 feet 8 or 9 inches", while Stevenson's account says he was "about 5 feet 10.")**

**(2) His knapsack. (The Pratt-Smith report states "he has on his back a sort of knapsack with something in [it], shaped like a book," but in the 1877 Stevenson account Whitmer describes it as "an old fashioned army knapsack strapped over his shoulders and something square in it.")**

(3) His walk. (An interesting detail in the 1877 Stevenson account is that "he [the stranger] walked alongside of the wagon.")

(4) His perspiration. (He "wiped the sweat off his face.")

(5) His expression. (The 1877 Stevenson account states he was "smiling very pleasant").

(6) His reference to Cumorah. (The 1877 Stevenson account says, "I am going across to the Hill Cumorah.")

Thus, 6 additional details of this incident are contained in the Stevenson report of 1877.

Likewise, the Pratt-Smith interview provides details not evident in the 1877 Stevenson interview—13 in fact—including the stunning account of David Whitmer's mother, Mary Elsa, encountering the stranger who actually showed her the plates because her faith, as covered below in Note 17.

16. *The Book of Mormon* (Palmyra, New York: Printed by E. B. Grandin for the Author, 1830), Mormon 6:6.

Note: In the *Book of Mormon* the first references to the term Cumorah are in 3 of the previous 4 verses to this citation of Moroni 6:6: Mormon 6:2–5.

17. David Whitmer, Interview (1878), in Orson Pratt, "Report of Elders Orson Pratt and Joseph F. Smith," *The Latter-day Saints' Millennial Star* (London), vol. 40, no. 49 (December 9, 1878), pp. 771–774.

Note 1: David Whitmer states here in the text that Emma Smith was at his family home in Fayette, New York, yet he does not mention her going on the trip there from Harmony with him, Joseph, and Oliver in May 1829. He describes their reactions to seeing the roadside stranger, but never mentions her reaction nor even being present in the wagon with them in his various interviews. Yet both he and his nephew (as stated below in Note 2) mention her being in Fayette with them later. She possibly traveled north to Fayette separately, several days later, after tying up loose ends at her Harmony farm, a task for which she may not have had time before Joseph and Oliver hurried up to Fayette to finish the translation. In that case, someone among the Whitmer clan or her own family could have taken her to Fayette. An outside possibility is that both David Whitmer and his nephew are simply mistaken on the chronology of Emma's visit: she may not have gone to Fayette in May 1829 (although this is unlikely, because not only did Whitmer and his nephew recall her being there as among those listed for additional work for Mary Whitmer, but

David Whitmer recalls Emma assisting in the translation at Fayette). Emma did actually move to Fayette a year later with Joseph, and that may be the only time she went there, but by then the translation had been finished for about 11 months. So it is very likely Emma did go to Fayette in the spring of 1829 to be with her husband; the main question is when and how.

Note 2: Although Danish convert Andrew Jenson would become the Assistant Church Historian in 1897 (and later briefly become an acting Church Historian for 1 year, 1899–1900, with another man named John Jaques), he first served as a part-time assistant to the Church Historian's office in 1886, traveling and interviewing people while paid a small stipend. Two years after beginning that work, in 1888, he wrote a report from an interview he had with David Whitmer's nephew, David C. Whitmer, which he had that year. The focus of it is David C.'s grandmother (the mother of David Whitmer of the Three Witnesses). This is Andrew Jenson's report:

"Her son, David Whitmer, before his death, testified on several occasions that his mother had seen the plates, and when Elders Edward Stevenson and Andrew Jenson [Jenson was writing this] visited Richmond, Missouri, in 1888, John C. Whitmer, a grandson of the lady in question, testified in the following language:

"'I have heard my grandmother [David Whitmer's mother, Mary Musselman Whitmer] say on several occasions that she was shown the plates of the *Book of Mormon* by a holy angel, whom she always called Brother Nephi.'"

Andrew Jenson then interjects a comment, based on church tradition— that only Moroni had held possession of the plates, since he had originally buried them centuries earlier and recently revealed them to Joseph—but in my opinion Moroni certainly could have delegated one of the three Nephites to take the plates from Joseph at Harmony and return them to him a few days later at Fayette, especially when considering both the physical descriptions of the stranger and the fact he was earlier labeled as one of the three Nephites by the Pratt-Smith team in their official church interview with David Whitmer, per Endnote 15 above. Jenson now adds this comment in parenthesis, one which I believe is inaccurate in relation to who the stranger was: "(She undoubtedly refers to Moroni, the angel who had the plates in charge.)"

"It was at this time, she said, when the translation was going on at the house of the elder Peter Whitmer, her husband [Peter Whitmer Sr.], Joseph Smith with his wife and Oliver Cowdery, whom David Whitmer had short time previous had brought up from Harmony, Pennsylvania, were all boarding with the Whitmers, and my grandmother in having so many extra persons to care for, when her own large household was often overloaded with work to such extent that she felt it to be quite a burden. One evening, when (after having done her usual day's work in the house) she went to the barn to milk the cows, she met a stranger carrying something on his back that looked like a knapsack. At first she was a little afraid of him, but when he spoke to her in a kind, friendly tone and began to explain to her the nature of the work which was going on in her house, she was filled with inexpressible joy and satisfaction. He then untied the knapsack and showed her a bundle of plates, which in size and appearance corresponded with the description subsequently given the witnesses to the *Book of Mormon*. This strange person turned the leaves of the book of plates over, leaf after leaf, and also showed her the engravings upon them; after which he told her to be patient and faithful in bearing her burden a little longer, promising that if she would do so, she should be blessed; and her reward would be sure, if she proved faithful until the end. The personage then suddenly vanished with the plates, and where he went she could not tell. From that moment my grandmother was enabled to perform her household duties with comparative ease, and she felt no more inclination to murmur because her lot was hard." [David C. Whitmer, Interview, in Andrew Jenson, *LDS Biographical Encyclopedia*, 4 volumes (Salt Lake City: Andrew Jenson History Company, 1901–1936, vol. 1: 1901), vol. 1, p. 283.]

In a more philosophical note about heavenly messengers, David Whitmer himself was asked a question about another event, the one which made him one of the Three Witnesses being shown the plates by an angel. In an 1883 interview he was asked by John Hart, "Did the personage or angel who showed you the plates tell you his name?"

"No, he did not. The idea has obtained ground that it was Moroni, the last of the Nephite prophets. It may have been Moroni, or it may have been one of the three Nephite Apostles who were promised that they should not taste of death. It is not important who he was, but I know that he was a messenger from God." [David Whitmer, Interview by James H. Hart, dispatch sent from Seneca, Newton County, Missouri, August 23, 1883, published in *Deseret News*, September 4, 1883.] **This is not saying that the messenger who showed Oliver and David the plates when they became two of the Three Witnesses in about June 1829 was the same as the roadside stranger of May 1829. They were probably separate, in fact, because, had he been the same personage, the two men likely would have made mention somewhere in their**

**interviews over the years that he was the same being they had just seen weeks later.**

18. Lucy Mack Smith, *History of Joseph Smith by His Mother: The Unabridged Original Version* (Arlington, Virginia and Provo, Utah: Stratford Books, Revised Second Edition 2006), p. 224.

19. David Whitmer, *An Address to All Believers in Christ* (Richmond, Missouri: published by the author, 1887), p. 30.

    **Note 1: The subtitle to this book, *An Address to All Believers in Christ*, is "by a Witness to the Divine Authenticity of the Book of Mormon."**

    **Note 2: In addition to 3 Whitmer sons helping Joseph Smith as scribes when he translated the plates at their family home in Fayette, New York, as stated in Note 17 above, David Whitmer remembers Emma Smith taking a turn as scribe there as well.**

20. Joseph Smith, Manuscript History of the Church, Book A-1, Historian's Office, Church Archives, The Church of Jesus Christ of Latter-day Saints, Salt Lake City.

    Also found in Joseph Smith, *The Papers of Joseph Smith*, edited by Dean C. Jesse, 2 volumes (Salt Lake City: Deseret Book, 1989–1992), vol. 1, p. 293.

    Also found in Joseph Smith, *The Joseph Smith Papers*, edited by Dean C. Jessee, Ronald K. Esplin, and Richard Lyman Bushman (Salt Lake City: The Church Historian's Press, 2008–), multiple-volume series.

21. Ibid., Joseph Smith, Manuscript History.

22. **Note: Of the 8 Whitney children, only 2 would die still active in the mainstream faith: Christian (age 37, in 1835) and Peter Jr. (age 26, 5 days short of turning 27, in 1836).**

23. David Whitmer, *An Address to All Believers in Christ* (Richmond, Missouri: published by the author, 1887), p. 30.

24. Larry C. Porter, *A Study of the Origins of the Church of Jesus Christ of Latter-day Saints in the States of New York and Pennsylvania, 1816–1831* (Ph.D. dissertation, Brigham Young University, 1971; published at Provo, Utah: Joseph Fielding Smith Institute for Latter-day Saint History and *BYU Studies*, 2000), pp. 61, 91–95.

25. David Whitmer, *An Address to All Believers in Christ* (Richmond, Missouri: published by the author, 1887).

26. David Whitmer, *David Whitmer Interviews: A Restoration Witness*, edited by Lyndon W. Cook (Orem, Utah: Grandin Book, 1991), p. 86.

27. Ibid., p. 62.

   *Kansas City Journal* (Kansas City, Missouri), June 5, 1881.

28. Lucy Mack Smith, *History of Joseph Smith by His Mother: The Unabridged Original Version* (Arlington, Virginia and Provo, Utah: Stratford Books, Revised Second Edition 2006), pp. 225–226.

29. Ibid., p. 225.

   **Note: As elsewhere in her book, Lucy refers to Fayette, New York, as "Waterloo."**

30. Ibid., p. 226.

   **Note: In Chapter 19 where Lucy states, "The next morning after attending to the usual services, namely, reading, singing, and praying," I have clarified the statement by adding this in editor's parentheses: "[daily Smith family]" before the word** *services.* **One could interpret her wording,** *the usual services,* **to mean all the New Believers did this, or she could have meant it was a habit of the Whitmer family; however, due to her son William's earlier comments about his parents holding Smith family** *services* **of prayers on a regular basis,** ["Notes written on Chambers' life of Joseph Smith," Chambers' Miscellany, typescript, Church Archives, The Church of Jesus Christ of Latter-day Saints, Salt Lake City, p. 18;

   William Smith, *William Smith on Mormonism: A True Account of the Origin of the Book of Mormon* (Lamoni, Iowa: Herald Stream Book and Job Office, 1883), pp. 6–7] **I assume she meant her family observed this ritual.**

31. Joseph Smith Jr., *History of the Church of Jesus Christ of Latter-day Saints*, edited by B. H. Roberts, 7 volumes (Salt Lake City: The Church of Jesus Christ of Latter-day Saints and *Deseret News*, Revised Second Edition 1948), vol. 1, p. 54.

32. Martin Harris, Interview by Ole A. Jensen, July 1875, in "Testimony of Martin Harris (One of the Witnesses to the *Book of Mormon*)," Special Collections, Harold B. Lee Library, Provo, Utah, pp. 1–6.

33. Joseph Smith Jr., *History of the Church of Jesus Christ of Latter-day Saints*, edited by B. H. Roberts, 7 volumes (Salt Lake City: The Church of Jesus Christ of Latter-day Saints and *Deseret News*, Revised Second Edition 1948), vol. 1, pp. 54–55.

34. William H. Kelley, Letter ("Letter from Elder W. H. Kelley"), *The Saints' Herald* (Lamoni, Iowa), vol. 29 (March 1, 1882), pp. 68–69.

35. Reuben Miller, Diaries, 1848–1849, October 21, 1848, Church Archives, The Church of Jesus Christ of Latter-day Saints, Salt Lake City.

36. Joseph Smith Jr., *History of the Church of Jesus Christ of Latter-day Saints*, edited by B. H. Roberts, 7 volumes (Salt Lake City: The Church of Jesus Christ of Latter-day Saints and *Deseret News*, Revised Second Edition 1948), vol. 1, pp. 54–55.

37. David Whitmer, Interview (1878), in Orson Pratt, "Report of Elders Orson Pratt and Joseph F. Smith," *The Latter-day Saints' Millennial Star* (London), vol. 40, no. 49 (December 9, 1878), pp. 771–774.

38. Joseph Smith Jr., *History of the Church of Jesus Christ of Latter-day Saints*, edited by B. H. Roberts, 7 volumes (Salt Lake City: The Church of Jesus Christ of Latter-day Saints and *Deseret News*, Revised Second Edition 1948), vol. 1, p. 55.

# CHAPTER 20

1. Martin Harris, Interview by Ole A. Jensen (July 1875), in "Testimony of Martin Harris (One of the Witnesses to the *Book of Mormon*)," pp. 1–6, L. Tom Perry Special Collections, Harold B. Lee Library, Brigham Young University, Provo, Utah.

2. Joseph Smith, Manuscript History of the Church, Book A-1, Historian's Office, Church Archives, The Church of Jesus Christ of Latter-day Saints, Salt Lake City.

   Also found in Joseph Smith, *The Papers of Joseph Smith*, edited by Dean C. Jesse, 2 volumes (Salt Lake City: Deseret Book, 1989–1992), vol. 1, pp. 296–298.

   Also found in Joseph Smith, *The Joseph Smith Papers*, edited by Dean C. Jessee, Ronald K. Esplin, and Richard Lyman Bushman (Salt Lake City: The Church Historian's Press, 2008–), multiple-volume series.

   Joseph Smith Jr., *History of the Church of Jesus Christ of Latter-day Saints*, edited by B. H. Roberts, 7 volumes (Salt Lake City: The Church of Jesus Christ of Latter-day Saints and *Deseret News*, Revised Second Edition 1948), vol. 1, p. 55.

   **Note: The 7-volume *History of the Church* has Joseph quoting Martin Harris's reaction a bit differently: "'Tis enough: 'tis enough; mine eyes have beheld; mine eyes have beheld." There, Joseph next states,**

**"and jumping up, he shouted, 'Hosanna,' blessing God, and otherwise rejoicing exceedingly."** [Ibid., pp. 54–55.]

3. Ibid.

4. Lucy Mack Smith, *History of Joseph Smith by His Mother: The Unabridged Original Version* (Arlington, Virginia and Provo, Utah: Stratford Books, Revised Second Edition 2006), pp. 226–227.

5. Ibid., pp. 227–228.

6. Ibid., p. 228.

7. Ibid., pp. 228–229.

8. Lucy, p. 229.

9. *Journal of Discourses*, edited by George D. Watt, et al., 26 volumes (Liverpool, England: Franklin D. Richards and Sons, 1854–1886), vol. 19, p. 37 (June 17, 1877).

10. Ibid.

11. Ibid.

12. Ibid.

13. "And Also the Testimony of Eight Witnesses," *The Book of Mormon* (Palmyra, New York: Printed by E. B. Grandin for the Author, 1830), p. 590 (final printed page).

    Lucy Mack Smith, *History of Joseph Smith by His Mother: The Unabridged Original Version* (Arlington, Virginia and Provo, Utah: Stratford Books, Revised Second Edition 2006), pp. 229–230.

14. Ibid., p. 230.

15. John Whitmer, "Address to the Patrons of the Latter Day Saints' Messenger and Advocate," *Latter Day Saints' Messenger and Advocate* (Kirtland, Ohio), vol. 2, no. 6 (March 1836), p. 286.

    **Note: Myron Bond, a woman in Cadillac, Michigan, wrote a letter August 2, 1878, saying, "John Whitmer told me last winter . . . [he] 'saw and handled' [the plates and] . . . helped to copy [the *Book of Mormon*] as the words fell from Joseph Smith's lips by supernatural or almighty power."** [Myron Bond, Letter (from Cadillac, Michigan, August 2, 1878), to *The Saints' Herald* (Plano, Illinois), August 15, 1878.] **It was a topical subject at the time, as John Whitmer had died just 3 weeks earlier, on July 11, 1878.**

16. *The Ensign of Liberty of the Church of Christ* (Kirtland, Ohio: The Church of Christ, 1847–1849), vol. 1 (January 1848).

Note: *The Ensign of Liberty of the Church of Christ* was a magazine published by the Church of Christ at Kirtland, Ohio. It lasted for 2 years, from 1847 to 1849, and was published with 7 volumes (designated as issues). It was edited by William E. McLellin, who pushed David Whitmer to organize a church, believing Whitmer had the authority. Whitmer did organize a church, calling it the Church of Christ, recruiting such notables as Oliver Cowdery, Martin Harris, John Whitmer, and Hiram Page, but David Whitmer never joined his group in Kirtland for any significant length of time and, feeling a lack of leadership, the group died out. However in the 1870s he reorganized it, then he died in 1888. The last of his followers was his grandniece, John C. Whitmer's daughter, who died in 1961.

17. Joseph Smith, Manuscript History of the Church, Book A-1, Historian's Office, Church Archives, The Church of Jesus Christ of Latter-day Saints, Salt Lake City.

    Also found in Joseph Smith, *The Papers of Joseph Smith*, edited by Dean C. Jesse, 2 volumes (Salt Lake City: Deseret Book, 1989–1992), vol. 2, pp. 299–300.

    Also found in Joseph Smith, *The Joseph Smith Papers*, edited by Dean C. Jessee, Ronald K. Esplin, and Richard Lyman Bushman (Salt Lake City: The Church Historian's Press, 2008–), multiple-volume series.

    *Times and Seasons* (Nauvoo, Illinois), October 1, 1842.

# CHAPTER 21

1. Lucy Mack Smith, *History of Joseph Smith by His Mother: The Unabridged Original Version* (Arlington, Virginia and Provo, Utah: Stratford Books, Revised Second Edition 2006), p. 230.

2. Blake McKelvey, *Rochester: The Water-Power City, 1812–1854* (Cambridge, Massachusetts: Harvard University Press, 1945), p. 151.

3. Pomeroy Tucker, *Origin, Rise, and Progress of Mormonism* (New York City: D. Appleton and Co., 1867), pp. 51–53.

4. Lucy Mack Smith, *History of Joseph Smith by His Mother: The Unabridged Original Version* (Arlington, Virginia and Provo, Utah: Stratford Books, Revised Second Edition 2006), pp. 231–232.

5. Ibid., p. 232.

6. Tom's Inflation Calculator. www.halfhill.com/inflation.html.

 Note: This is the most reliable inflation calculator I have found.

7. David Whitmer, *An Address to All Believers in Christ* (Richmond, Missouri: published by the author, 1887), p. 75.

8. Ibid.

9. Ibid.

10. Ibid.

11. Note: Later in Utah, Stephen Harding would deal cordially with Latter-day Saint church leaders until he would become critical of them and their religious practices, causing them to petition to have him removed. Harding would then become Chief Justice of the Colorado State Supreme Court, until he would be removed for incompetency and immorality.

12. Lucy Mack Smith, *History of Joseph Smith by His Mother: The Unabridged Original Version* (Arlington, Virginia and Provo, Utah: Stratford Books, Revised Second Edition 2006), p. 232.

 Note: Peter Whitmer's involvement as a guard to the manuscript of the translated plates was pointed out only in Lucy's rough draft, in which she does not designate if it was Peter senior or junior. Likely it was junior, who was one of the Eight Witnesses and, as pointed out earlier, was 1 of only 2 of the 10-member Whitmer family to "endure to the end" in church activity among the mainstream Latter-day Saints, dying 7 years later in 1836.

13. Dean C. Jessee, "The Original Book of Mormon Manuscript," *BYU Studies* (Provo, Utah), vol. 10, no. 3 (Spring 1970), pp. 259–278.

14. Pomeroy Tucker, *Origin, Rise, and Progress of Mormonism* (New York City: D. Appleton and Co., 1867), p. 53.

15. John H. Gilbert, Letter (to James T. Cobb, February 10, 1879), in Larry C. Porter, *A Study of the Origins of the Church of Jesus Christ of Latter-day Saints in the States of New York and Pennsylvania, 1816–1831* (Ph.D. dissertation, Brigham Young University, 1971; published at Provo, Utah: Joseph Fielding Smith Institute for Latter-day Saint History and *BYU Studies*, 2000), pp. 30, 32.

16. Oliver Cowdery, Letter (to Joseph Smith, December 28, 1829), Joseph Smith Jr. Collection, 1805–1844, Church Archives, The Church of Jesus Christ of Latter-day Saints, Salt Lake City.

17. Thomas Gregg, *The Prophet of Palmyra* (New York City: J. B. Alden, 1890), pp. 38–39.

18. Pomeroy Tucker, *Origin, Rise, and Progress of Mormonism* (New York City: D. Appleton and Co., 1867) p. 56.

19. Richard Lyman Bushman, *Joseph Smith: Rough Stone Rolling* (New York City: Alfred A. Knopf / Borzoi Books, 2005), p. 80.

20. Joseph Smith, *The Joseph Smith Papers*, edited by Dean C. Jessee, Ronald K. Esplin, and Richard Lyman Bushman (Salt Lake City: The Church Historian's Press, 2008–), multiple-volume series.

   Also found in Joseph Smith, Letter (to Oliver Cowdery, October 22, 1829), in Joseph Smith, *Personal Writings of Joseph Smith*, edited by Dean C. Jessee (Provo, Utah: Brigham Young University Press, Revised Edition 2002), pp. 251–252.

21. Lucy Mack Smith, *Biographical Sketches of Joseph Smith the Prophet and His Progenitors for Many Generations* (Liverpool, England: S. W. Richards, 1853), p. 142.

22. Lucy Mack Smith, *History of Joseph Smith by His Mother: The Unabridged Original Version* (Arlington, Virginia and Provo, Utah: Stratford Books, Revised Second Edition 2006), pp. 235–237.

23. Ibid., p. 236.

   **Note: The final 5 words are only from Lucy's rough draft.**

24. Ibid., pp. 235–237.

25. Ibid., pp. 240–242.

26. Ibid., p. 242.

27. Ibid., pp. 242–243.

28. Milton V. Backman and James B. Allen, "Membership of Certain of Joseph Smith's Family in the Western Presbyterian Church of Palmyra," *BYU Studies* (Provo, Utah), vol. 10, no. 4 (Summer 1970), pp. 482–484.

# CHAPTER 22

1. Lucy Mack Smith, *History of Joseph Smith by His Mother: The Unabridged Original Version* (Arlington, Virginia and Provo, Utah: Stratford Books, Revised Second Edition 2006), p. 245.

2. Ibid., p. 246.

3. Ibid.

4. Ibid.

5. Ibid., p. 247.

6. Lucy Mack Smith, *Biographical Sketches of Joseph Smith the Prophet and His Progenitors for Many Generations* (Liverpool, England: S. W. Richards, 1853), p. 149.

7. Lucy Mack Smith, *History of Joseph Smith by His Mother: The Unabridged Original Version* (Arlington, Virginia and Provo, Utah: Stratford Books, Revised Second Edition 2006), pp. 247–248.

8. *The Reflector* (Palmyra, New York), January 13, 22, 1830.

   **Note: *The Reflector* was a short-lived newspaper published from 1829 to early 1830 in Palmyra, New York. It was edited and owned by Abner Cole.**

9. Lucy Mack Smith, *History of Joseph Smith by His Mother: The Unabridged Original Version* (Arlington, Virginia and Provo, Utah: Stratford Books, Revised Second Edition 2006), p. 251.

   **Note: The portion used comes from Lucy's rough draft.**

10. Donna Hill, *Joseph Smith: The First Mormon* (Garden City, New York: Doubleday, 1977), p. 97.

11. *Wayne Sentinel* (Palmyra, New York), March 19, 1820.

12. Ibid., March 26, 1820.

13. **Note: A DNA analysis performed in 1997 by Scott Woodward, a researcher at the time with Brigham Young University, showed that the leather used for all three First Edition copies of the *Book of Mormon*, which he and his team analyzed, was calfskin and not sheepskin. In addition to the interview with this professor, I learned from a book restoration artist, Ethan Ensign of Scrub Oak Bindery in Salt Lake City, that the characteristics of all two dozen copies of the original First Edition that he has restored are those of calfskin, "and definitely not sheepskin." Based on the characteristics pointed out by him, it is clear that calfskin was used on another three copies that my crew and I inspected and measured with instruments of our own (including the use of our digital micrometer) to measure the thickness of the paper and leather to within 5/100,000 of an inch. All analyses point to the use of calfskin by the original binder, and not sheepskin, as was the apparent initial intention of the binder.**

14. E. B. Grandin, Diary, January 1831–1841, located at Albany Public Library, Albany, New York.

15. Joseph Knight Sr., 5-page manuscript, #183301847, Historical Department, The Church of Jesus Christ of Latter-day Saints, Salt Lake City.

   **Note: Joseph Knight adds that, in contrast to Martin Harris leaving for home, frustrated that the *Book of Mormon* copies would not sell, he stayed a few days "waiting for some books to be bound"—another indication that the books were not bound the same week as they came off the press, as many have assumed. In actuality, the binding was part of an 18-month project after the books were printed.**

16. Joseph Knight Sr., "Joseph Knight's Recollection of Early Mormon History," edited by Dean C. Jessee, *BYU Studies* (Provo, Utah), vol. 17, no. 1 (Autumn 1976), pp. 36–37.

17. *The Doctrine and Covenants of the Church of Jesus Christ of Latter-day Saints: Containing Revelations given to Joseph Smith, the Prophet, with Some Additions by His Successors in the Presidency of the Church* (Salt Lake City: The Church of Jesus Christ of Latter-day Saints, 1981), 19:26, 35.

18. Lucy Mack Smith, *Biographical Sketches of Joseph Smith the Prophet and His Progenitors for Many Generations* (Liverpool, England: S. W. Richards, 1853), p. 151.

19. Wayne Cutler Gunnell, "Martin Harris—Witness and Benefactor to the Book of Mormon" (master's thesis, Provo Utah: Brigham Young University, 1955), p. 38.

20. Ibid.

21. Thomas L. Cook, *Palmyra and Vicinity* (Interlaken, New York: Heart of the Lakes Publishing, 1980), p. 205.

22. Wayne Cutler Gunnell, "Martin Harris—Witness and Benefactor to the Book of Mormon" (master's thesis, Provo Utah: Brigham Young University, 1955), pp. 37–38.

23. Pomeroy Tucker, *Origin, Rise, and Progress of Mormonism* (New York City: D. Appleton and Co., 1867), pp. 50–55.

   Larry C. Porter, *A Study of the Origins of the Church of Jesus Christ of Latter-day Saints in the States of New York and Pennsylvania, 1816–1831* (Ph.D. dissertation, Brigham Young University, 1971; published at Provo, Utah: Joseph Fielding Smith Institute for Latter-day Saint History and *BYU Studies*, 2000), p. 30.

24. Joseph Smith Sr. File, Historical Department, The Church of Jesus Christ of Latter-day Saints, Salt Lake City.

   **Note: The signed contract between Martin Harris and Joseph Smith on January 16, 1830, for repaying the cost of printing the *Book of Mormon*, is contained in this file at the church's Historical Department.**

25. **Martin Harris's $3,000 investment in August 1829, when he mortgaged his farm, is valued in today's money at $129,580.**


# CHAPTER 23

1. **Note: In launching the first American public library, Benjamin Franklin gave books to the town of Exeter (later Franklin), Massachusetts. The town's board voted November 20, 1790, to lend his collection to all its inhabitants, just 39½ years before the *Book of Mormon*'s publication and release (which is approximately where Joseph's story is being recounted in the text, at this note).**

   **This would become known as the Franklin Public Library—America's first public library.**

   **Its predecessor was a "subscription library" called the Library Company of Philadelphia, which Ben Franklin had begun in 1731. He was so proud of it that he called it the "Mother of all N. American Subscription Libraries," and even served as a librarian for it for 3 months (December 1733 – March 1734). He remained connected with the library as a secretary another 23 years, until 1757.**

2. Hugh W. Nibley, *Temple and Cosmos: The Collected Works of Hugh Nibley, Volume 12* (Salt Lake City: Deseret Book, 1993).

3. Lucy Mack Smith, *Biographical Sketches of Joseph Smith the Prophet and His Progenitors for Many Generations* (Liverpool, England: S. W. Richards, 1853), pp. 51, 73, 84.

4. Robert Paul, *BYU Studies* (Provo, Utah), vol. 22, no. 3 (Summer 1982), p. 240.

   **Note: In addition to the 1819 book auction referred to in the text, a few other book auctions were held in Palmyra, New York, later.**

5. *The Saints' Herald* (Plano, Illinois), vol. 26, no. 19 (October 1, 1879), pp. 289–290.

6. Paul Y. Hoskisson, "An Introduction to the Relevance of and a Methodology for a Study of the Proper Names of the Book of Mormon," in *By Study and Also by Faith*, edited by John M. Lundquist and Steven D. Ricks, 2 volumes (Salt Lake City: Deseret Book, 1990), vol. 2, pp. 126–135.

   **Note: Paul Y. Hoskisson points out that in the *Book of Mormon*, 21 names of animal types and residents of localities were included in and derived from the 337 proper names.**

7. *The Book of Mormon* (Palmyra, New York: Printed by E. B. Grandin for the Author, 1830), Alma 11:4–19.

8. *The Book of Mormon* (Palmyra, New York: Printed by E. B. Grandin for the Author, 1830).

9. Wilford Woodruff, Wilford Woodruff's Journal, 1834, Church Archives, The Church of Jesus Christ of Latter-day Saints, Salt Lake City.

10. Joseph Smith, Letter (to N. C. Saxton, January 4, 1833), in Joseph Smith, *Personal Writings of Joseph Smith*, edited by Dean C. Jessee (Provo, Utah: Brigham Young University Press, Revised Edition 2002), p. 297.

    Joseph Smith, History [1838], Church Archives, The Church of Jesus Christ of Latter-day Saints, Salt Lake City.

    Also found in Joseph Smith, *The Joseph Smith Papers*, edited by Dean C. Jessee, Ronald K. Esplin, and Richard Lyman Bushman (Salt Lake City: The Church Historian's Press, 2008–), multiple-volume series.

11. **Note: The Thor Heyerdahl writings were the first sources of information I obtained about ancients in America, thus paving the way to an open-minded approach toward the subject of two divergent groups once existing on the continent before one eliminated the other, before I was introduced to the *Book of Mormon*.**

12. Harold T. Wilkins, "Harold T. Wilkins Legend of a Fabulous Empire," *The Pan American: Magazine of the Americas* (New York City), vol. 7 (1946), p. 11.

    **Note: This magazine, *The Pan American: Magazine of the Americas*, concentrated many articles on Latin America and was published in New York City from 1940 to 1950 by Famous Features Syndicate.**

13. Hubert Howe Bancroft, 39 volumes, *History of the Pacific States of North America: Mexico*, Volume 5 (San Francisco: A. L. Bancroft & Co., 1874), p. 18.

    **Note: This series by Hubert Howe Bancroft, entitled *History of the Pacific States of North America*, consists of 39 volumes written and first published from 1874 to 1890, of which 35 are actual area histories**

and another 4 consist of miscellaneous information (including vol. 39 itself—about his methods of research). Bancroft wrote and published another 9 unrelated books about history and civilization from 1883 to 1917. Of those 9, 3 were released while he was still working on the 39-volume series. Of the other 6, one was published the year before he died.

Bancroft had a fascinating and unusual journey getting to his position as an historian. He was born at Granville, Ohio, on May 5, 1832, was tutored at home by his mother, realized college was too expensive, and started working—at his brother-in-law's bookstore in Buffalo, New York.

In 1852 he took a load of books on consignment to sell for his brother-in-law in California, taking advantage of the California Gold Rush of 1848–1855, in which 300,000 people flooded the territory, which quickly became a state in 1850. He learned of his brother-in-law's death, sold his books, took odd jobs, and at his sister's request returned to Buffalo. But hated it. So he returned to California in 1858 and became a printer, publisher, and bookseller in San Francisco. There he became wildly successful in business. And obsessed with history and collecting books about it. In the summer of 1862 and all of 1866 he went to Europe and collected books about the Pacific Coast. By 1867 he was rich and could have retired. But with the death of his wife, whom he had met in California on his second move there, he now decided to make something of his time, talents and wealth and put them to good use. He decided in 1869 to write the first history of the far west—in fact a history of the entire western half of North America.

In 1871 he actually started writing the history, after gathering more research and settling his affairs, and in that year he also hired a staff of researchers and writers—perhaps "rough draft" writers, which was revolutionary for the day. His staff would vary in size from 6 to 50 people.

His 1st set of the above-mentioned 39 volume series was the 5-volume *Native Races of the Pacific States* (1874).

But scholars criticized it. Nevertheless, undaunted, Bancroft forged ahead and kept writing and publishing.

As each volume within a topic would be completed, he would publish it, such as his 2nd series topic, *History of Central America*, being released from 1883 to 1887 and his 3rd series topic, *History of Mexico*, from 1883 to 1887.

The citation for this endnote is from vol. 5 of his Mexico series, which comprised volumes 9 to 14 of his major set, *History of the Pacific States of North America*.

Noteworthy, his volume 26 was *History of Utah* (1889), but one of his most important works is his 7-volume *History of California* (volumes 18–24) from 1886–1890, along with his *California Pastoral* (volume 34) in 1888 and *California inter Pocula* (Latin for "over a glass, while drinking") (volume 35) in 1888.

All 39 volumes were again published as a comprehensive edition, entitled *The Works of Hugh Howe Bancroft*, from 1882 to 1890, and it sold 6,000 sets—a remarkable achievement with intense marketing.

His reputation among scholars improved due to a change in emphasis of historical research in the U.S., such as the acceptance of hiring assistants and focusing on local histories. Still, it took 20 years to sell his library of books to the University of California, after numerous failed attempts. In 1905 he not only succeeded, but they named the library after him and made him a professor of history. In 1911 he was even elected president of the Pacific Coast branch of the American Historical Association. After a life of immense research and writing productivity, he died in 1918.

14. John W. Welch, editor, *Chiasmus in Antiquity: Structures, Analyses, Exegesis* (Hildesheim, Germany: Gerstenberg Verlag, 1981; reprinted at Provo, Utah: Maxwell Institute, 1998).

   John W. Welch, "Chiasmus in the Book of Mormon," *BYU Studies* (Provo, Utah), vol. 10, no. 1 (Autumn 1969), pp. 69–84.

15. John W. Welch, "How Much Was Known About Chiasmus in 1829 When the Book of Mormon Was Translated?" *FARMS Review* (Provo, Utah), vol. 15, no. 1 (2003), pp. 47–80.

   Note 1: This source from John W. Welch effectively counters arguments that claim Joseph, by 1825, may have had access to the knowledge of chiasmus. (Even if Joseph had this knowledge, there simply was not enough time to deconstruct and reconstruct so many sentences throughout the book in the short amount of actual time he translated it. For an analysis of just how few weeks were involved in translating, see Appendix G: "A New, Surprising Time Line for Translating the Plates").

   Note 2: *FARMS Review* was a publication of FARMS, the Foundation for Ancient Research and Mormon Studies, which had begun in 1979 as a private, non-profit organization by John W. Welch in California. The following year FARMS came to Utah when Welch accepted a position to teach at Brigham Young University. In 1997 FARMS became an actual part of BYU, at the invitation of then-church President Gordon B. Hinckley. [*Ensign* (Salt Lake City), January 1998.]

The journal's name has changed several times, and until 2012 it published scholarly commentary, book reviews, and essays that defended the LDS faith. Since then, it has taken a different direction, but still a scholarly one, as explained below. From 1990 to 1995 it was called *Review of Books on the Book of Mormon*. From 1996 to 2002 it was named *FARMS Review of Books*. From 2003 to 2010 it was *The FARMS Review*.

In 2010 the FARMS name was removed and the journal was renamed *Mormon Studies Review*, which came out with its first issue the following year, with the same strategy of aggressively defending the LDS faith with scholarly research and analysis.

Then, in 2011, BYU combined FARMS with 2 other entities—Center for the Preservation of Ancient Religious Texts and the Middle Eastern Texts Initiative, calling it the Institute for the Study and Preservation of Ancient Texts. All were under the leadership of the Neal A. Maxwell Institute for Religious Scholarship.

In 2012, at *Mormon Studies Review*, FARMS' co-founder and editor for 23 years, Daniel C. Peterson, was replaced, so the journal could (1) adopt a more secular viewpoint, (2) become more public-relations friendly, and (3) cater to those of various faiths. Peterson and some of his associates felt the new course was a mistake—they indicated the journal should remain proactive in defending the church from critics by aggressively setting the record straight with scholarly articles and books, rather than focusing on the new, secular approach, which the new editorial staff had for years wished to implement. [Peggy Fletcher Stack, "Shake-up hits BYU's Mormon studies Institute," *The Salt Lake Tribune* (Salt Lake City), June 26, 2012.] **Peterson's point was well taken, as even non-LDS critics conceded that the scholarly efforts of FARMS were superior to the claims of non-Mormon scholarly critics. Specifically, 2 evangelical scholars, Paul Owen and Carl Mosser, examined FARMS' works and reported at the April 25, 1997 Far West Annual Meeting of the Evangelical Theological Society, praising FARM's high quality scholarship and claiming that their fellow evangelicals had lost the scholarly, apologetic battle against the Mormons due to their high-grade research and publishing.** [Paul Owen and Carl Mosser, "Mormon Scholarship, Apologetics, and Evangelical Neglect: Losing the Battle and Not Knowing it?" *Trinity Journal* (Deersfield, Illinois), vol. 19, no. 2, new series (Fall 1998), pp. 179–205.]

**Roman Catholic scholar Massimo Introvigne came up with the same conclusion on his own.** [Massimo Introvigne, "The Book of Mormon Wars: A Non-Mormon Perspective," *Journal of Book of Mormon Studies* (Provo, Utah), vol. 5, no. 2 (1996), pp. 1–25.]

**After the change of guard in 2012, Peterson immediately became editor of the Middle Eastern Text Initiative.**

**Note 3: *Trinity Journal* is published at Deersfield, Illinois, by the faculty of Trinity Evangelical Divinity School of Trinity Christian University, established in 1897. The journal began in 1980 and is published twice yearly. It includes reviews and essays on historical, theological, and biblical topics, many of which are geared to pastors as well as "informed evangelicals."**

**Note 4: Note: *Journal of Book of Mormon Studies*, renamed *Journal of the Book of Mormon and Other Restoration Scripture* in 2008, is published by the Neal A. Maxwell Institute for Religious Scholarship on the Brigham Young University campus at Provo, Utah, and is supported by the Laura F. Willes Center for Book of Mormon Studies. It was first published in 1992, with only one issue; since then it has been published twice per year. It is a peer-reviewed journal that publishes articles on history and the significance of scriptures that came through Joseph Smith.**

16. Richard Lyman Bushman, *Joseph Smith: Rough Stone Rolling* (New York City: Alfred A. Knopf / Borzoi Books, 2005), p. 93.

17. Ibid.

18. Ibid.

19. Warren P. Aston, "Newly Found Altars from Nahom," *Journal of Book of Mormon Studies* (Provo, Utah), vol. 10, no. 2 (2001), pp. 56–61.

20. Richard Lyman Bushman, *Joseph Smith: Rough Stone Rolling* (New York City: Alfred A. Knopf / Borzoi Books, 2005), p. 93.

21. Krister Stendahl, "The Sermon on the Mount and Third Nephi," in *Reflections on Mormonism: Judaeo-Christian Parallels*, edited by Truman G. Madsen (Provo, Utah: Religious Studies Center, Brigham Young University, 1978), pp. 139–154.

    James H. Charlesworth, "Messianism in the Pseudepigrapha and the Book of Mormon," in *Reflections on Mormonism: Judaeo-Christian Parallels*, edited by Truman G. Madsen (Provo, Utah: Religious Studies Center, Brigham Young University, 1978), pp. 99–137; cited in Richard Lyman Bushman, *Joseph Smith: Rough Stone Rolling* (New York City: Alfred A. Knopf / Borzoi Books, 2005), pp. 94, 583 n 40.

22. Cyrus H. Gordon, "Foreword," in Alexander von Wuthenau, *Unexpected Faces in Ancient America, 1500 B.C. – A.D. 1500: The Historical Testimony of the Pre-Columbian Artists* (New York City: Crown, 1975), pp. xi-xiii; cited in Richard Lyman Bushman, *Joseph Smith: Rough Stone Rolling* (New York City: Alfred A. Knopf / Borzoi Books, 2005), pp. 94, 583 n 39.

23. Richard H. Popkin, "The Rise and Fall of the Jewish Indian Theory," in *Menasseh Ben Israel and His World*, edited by Yosef Kaplan, Henry Mechoulan, and Richard H. Popkin (Leiden, Holland: E. J. Brill, 1989), pp. 63–83; cited in Richard Lyman Bushman, *Joseph Smith: Rough Stone Rolling* (New York City: Alfred A. Knopf / Borzoi Books, 2005), pp. 63–82.

Daniel Clarke Sanders, *A History of the Indian Wars with the first Settlers of the United States to the Commencement of the Late War; Together with an Appendix, Not before Added to this History, Containing Interesting Accounts of the Battles Fought by Gen. Andrew Jackson* (Rochester, New York: Edwin Scrantom, 1828), p. 119.

24. Richard Lyman Bushman, *Joseph Smith: Rough Stone Rolling* (New York City: Alfred A. Knopf / Borzoi Books, 2005), p. 96.

25. Diane E. Wirth, 2002, "Quetzalcoatl, the Maya Maise God, and Jesus Christ," maxwellinstitute.byu.edu/publications, *Journal of Book of Mormon Studies* (Provo, Utah: Maxwell Institute, 2002), vol. 11, no. 1 (2002), pp. 4–15.

26. David Hatcher Chidress, *Lost Cities of North & Central America* (Kempton, Illinois: Adventures Unlimited Press, 1992).

**Note: The white deity attributes of Viracocha were first reported by Pedro Cieza de Leon (1553) and later by Pedro Sarmiento de Gamboa (1907).** [Pedro Samiento de Gamboa, translated by Clement Markham, *History of the Incas* (Cambridge, England: The Hakluyt Society, 1907), pp. 28–50.]

27. Donald A. MacKensie, *Myths of Pre-Columbian America* (London: The Gresham Publishing Co., First Edition, 1924), pp. 268–270.

28. "Viracocha," *Bloomsbury Dictionary of Myth* (London: Bloomsbury Publishing, Ltd., 1996).

29. Colonel Alexander Braghine, *The Shadow of Atlantis* (Kempton, Illinois: Adventures Unlimited Press, 1997), p. 34.

**Note: Cusco, Peru, at a remarkably high elevation of two miles, was the capital of the Inca Empire. The Incas had first occupied the area after 1200 A.D. Then Spanish explorers arrived there in 1533, and Francisco Pizarro 4 months later, in 1534. Unfortunately, the Spanish destroyed many Inca palaces, temples, and buildings, and Pizarro**

sacked much of the city in 1535. Meanwhile, many of the Incas who weren't outright killed by the Spanish succumbed to smallpox, inadvertently brought by the explorers.

30. Ibid.

31. Donald A. MacKensie, *Myths of Pre-Columbian America* (London: The Gresham Publishing Co., First Edition, 1924), pp. 269–270.

32. Ibid., p. 270.

33. Hubert Howe Bancroft, *History of the Pacific States of North America: Volume 5: Mexico* (San Francisco: A. L. Bancroft & Co., 1874), pp. 23–24, notes 53–58.

34. John Taylor, *An Examination Into and an Elucidation of the Great Principle of the Mediation and Atonement of Our Lord and Savior Jesus Christ* (Salt Lake City: Deseret News Company, 1882), p. 201.

35. Matthew Restall, *Seven Myths of the Spanish Conquest* (Oxford, England and New York City: Oxford University Press, 2003).

Matthew Restall, "Topiltzin Quetzalcoatl: The Once and Future Lord of the Toltecs" (book review), in *Hispanic American Historical Review* (Durham, North Carolina), vol. 83, No. 4 (November 2003), pp. 750–751.

**Note 1: Matthew Restall wrote this article while on the staff of Pennsylvania State University.**

**Note 2: *Hispanic American Historical Review* is published quarterly by Duke University Press in Durham, North Carolina. Published since 1918 in cooperation with the Conference on Latin American History and the American Historical Association, it covers book reviews, essays and all facets of scholarship on Latin American culture and history, and is published.**

36. David Carrasco, *Quetzalcoatl and the Irony of Empire: Myths and Prophecies in the Aztec Tradition* (Chicago: University of Chicago Press, 1982).

H. B. Nicholson, *Topiltzin Quetzalcoatl: the Once and Future Lord of the Toltecs*, in the 35-volume series, *Mesoamerican Worlds: From the Olmec to the Danzantes*, edited by David Carrasco (of Harvard University) and Eduarto Matos Moctezuma (of El Colegio Nacional, Mexico), series general editors (Boulder, Colorado: University Press at Colorado, 2000).

H. B. Nicholson, *The "Return of Quetzalcoatl": Did it play a role in the conquest of Mexico?* (Lancaster, California: Labyrinthos, 2001).

37. Lucile Taylor Hansen, "Lucile Taylor Hansen and the Katezahl Legend: An Autobiographical Memoir," transcribed and edited by Kathy Doore,

from the original handwritten journal of L. Taylor Hansen, in possession of Ms. Doore.

38. **Note: The Mayans traded cacao (cocoa beans), jade, and obsidian with other cultures. They also fought back against the Spaniards, who found them more difficult to conquer than some other tribes, especially since the Mayans had no controlling central government to take over. Thus, the Spaniards had to take on each municipality. However, the Mayans eventually succumbed.**

39. **Note 1: Five islands are the most viable candidates for the one upon which Christopher Columbus first landed (which he named "San Salvador Island"). They stretch from Rum Cay (once called Santa Maria de la Concepcion, 342 miles southeast of Miami and 182 miles southeast of Nassau) to an island today called San Salvador Island (360 miles southeast of Miami and 200 miles southeast of Nassau) to Samana Cay to Plana Cay to the candidate farthest away from Miami—Grand Turk Island (653 miles from the U.S. city). Grand Turk is among the 40-island group "Turks and Caicos Islands," which are today politically distinct from but are geographically a part of the Bahamas.**

    **Thus Columbus landed on an island somewhere in this 311-mile stretch of islands in the Bahamas. Notably, over 3,000 islands make up the Bahamas, so it is rather remarkable that the list has been narrowed by researchers to only 5 most likely candidates.**

    **Six less-likely candidates—but still candidates—are Lignum Vitae Cay, East Caicos, Egg Island, Cat Island, Conception Island, and Mayaguana. They are all part of the Caribbean's Greater Antilles, which are the northern islands of the Caribbean.**

40. John Cummins, *The Voyage of Christopher Columbus: Columbus' Own Journal of Discovery (Newly Restored and Translated)* (New York City: St. Martin's Press, 1972), p. 241.

41. Letter from Christopher Columbus to King Ferdinand of Spain, February 15, 1493, in Martin Fernandez de Navarrete, *Coleccion de los viages y descubrimietos que hicieron por mar los espanoles desde fines del siglo XV: con varios documentos Ineditos concernientes a la historia de la marina castellana y de los establecimientos espanoles en Indias*, 4 volumes (Madrid: Imprensa Real), vol. 1 (1825), p. 167.

    **Note 1: As one of the world's most famous and important collections of correspondence, Christopher Columbus's letters, which detail his first trip to the Caribbean, written on his return trip to Spain while in the Canary Islands, is dated February 15, 1493. But they are clouded**

in mystery. He addressed at least one letter to Lucis de Santangel, who was an official with the title, "Escribano de Racion," and was like a finance minister to the king of Spain, Ferdinand II.

Joseph Adler, "Christopher Columbus' Voyage of Discovery: Jewish and New Christian Elements," *Midstream*, November 25, 1998, http://www. saudades.org/ccolumbusvoyage.html).]

**Santangel was Columbus's most important proponent—he was the one who had persuaded Queen Isabella to finance the voyage 8 months earlier. Columbus, in his now-famous letter, asked for more money for a second voyage—so the letter naturally went to Santangel first.**

**The best-known part of this letter announces his discovery of islands on the edge of the Indian Ocean in Asia, calling their inhabitants "Indians." He had no idea at the time that he had "merely" discovered the Caribbean islands off the coast of America. Beyond this initial letter, his other letters are apparently copies of this one-and-only original letter sent from sea.**

**Columbus apparently sent 2 copies of the same letter to other notables—one to Gabriel Sanchez, the treasurer of Aragon, perhaps at Santangel's request due to complicated political reasons, and a second one to the Catholic monarchs. That one especially may have had important ramifications, noted below.**

**As for the second manuscript copy sent to Catholic monarchs, it has only recently appeared, in 1985, remaining unprinted for about 500 years, but is now finally in print and, like the Sanchez letter, is only slightly different from the original manuscript letter sent to Santangel, likely due to copying and translating discrepancies.**

**However, Christopher Columbus's son, Ferdinand Columbus, once stated that Columbus wrote two letters to the Catholic monarchs during a storm near the Azores on February 14, 1493, then placed them in waterproof casks, throwing one overboard and tying the other to the stern, so if the ship sank, at least one copy would make it to shore safely.** [Ferdinand Columbus, *Historia del almirante Don Cristobal Colon en la cual se da particular y verdadera relacion de su vida y de sus hechos, y del descubrimiento de las Indias Occidentales, Llamadas Nuevo-mundo*, 2 volumes (Madrid: Minnesa, 1892), vol. 1, pp. 162–163;

Christopher Columbus, translated by Clements Robert Markham, *The Journal of Christopher Columbus (During His First Voyage, 1492-93) and Documents Relating the Voyages of John Cabot and Gaspar Corte Real* (London: Hakluyt Society, First Edition 1893; reprinted at Charleston,

South Carolina: Nabu Pess, 2013), Columbus's journal portion: Lib. 1, chapters 35 to 75.]

**His report is corroborated by Franciscan Bartolome de las Casas.** [Bartholome de las Casas, *Historia de las Indias, 1875–1876* (Madrid: Ginesta, 1875, vol. 1, p. 447.]

**As for these 2 "storm" letters sent by Christopher Columbus to the Catholic monarchs, his son Ferdinand Columbus does not say if they were a copy of the same letter the Catholic monarchs did receive (which is a copy of the one sent by his father to the finance minister Santangel) or if the storm letters were entirely different letters altogether.**

**In all, between 1493 and 1497, a total of 17 editions of the letter were published,** [Matthew S. Edney, "The Columbus Letter: The Diffusion of Columbus' Letter through Europe, 1493–1497" (online article, 1996, revised 2009: http://shelf3d.com/i/Columbus's%20Letter%20on%20 the%20First%20Voyage] **making it a best-seller for the day with over 3,000 copies printed. (The copy sent to Gabriel Sanchez may be the origin of the numerous Latin editions of his letter,** [Andres Benaldez, translated by Cecil Jane, *The Voyages of Christopher Columbus: Being the Journals of his First and Third, and the Letters Concerning his First and Last Voyages, to Which is Added the Account of His Second Voyage Written by Andres Benaldez* (London: Argonaut Press, 1930, pp. 39–40; Steven Anzovin, *Famous First Facts* (New York City: H. W. Wilson Company, 2000), p. 109] **while the original sent to Santangel was the origin for a number of printed Spanish editions of the letter).**

**As for the effect Columbus's letter may have had, Pope Alexander VI—an interesting fellow in his own right, as discussed in Appendix U, "Christianity After Christ: 17 Centuries of Conflict"—issued a papal bull (a pope's decree) dated September 26, 1493, giving Spain claim over all land discovered by its westward exploration parties, which presumably included India, China, and Africa. (The decree would be true for other countries as well, such as Portugal, but for now Spain was way ahead of the game on everyone, because of Columbus.)**

**Columbus's financiers, the rulers of Spain, possibly had heard of the coming decree by the pope, but even had they not, they were "sold" on Columbus's request for more money, because the day before the pope's decree was issued giving Spain a virtual monopoly of the world, Columbus launched his second voyage with 17 ships and a crew of 1,500! The financing had obviously been in place for months, along with months of preparations. Due to his insight, inspiration,**

and persistence, Columbus had a head start on the whole of Europe in staking claim to what would be the New World.

Note 2: A significant source for information about Columbus's discovery of the islands off America—the Caribbean islands—is Martin Fernandez de Navarrete, a Spanish sailor and historian who lived from 1765 to 1844 and who rediscovered Las Casas' abstract of the log that Columbus had made on his first voyage. After being a sailor at the Great Siege of Gibraltar and successfully fighting Algerine pirates, Navarrete fell ill, sending him into early sailor-retirement, but in 1789 he was assigned by the crown to study the national archives regarding Spain's navy. In his collecting and writing he came upon the treasure of treasures—Columbus's sailing journal—and published it in his set of 4 historical maritime volumes that were released from 1825 to 1837.

Note 3: Various sources provide fascinating information about Columbus and the complicated political intrigues that resulted in financing for his voyage. (One outstanding source for information about Santangel, the finance minister, is Joseph Adler, whose work was published in *Midstream*, an "intellectual Zionist journal" published at New York City. (A side note about this journal: *Midstream* has been a substantial publication, at first issued quarterly in 1955, then monthly since 1965. It offers opinions on religious, political, and social subjects for Jewish communities.)

42. Note: In regards to the overall island area known as the Lesser Antilles, where the reportedly ferocious Carib tribe lived, this group of Caribbean islands stretched as far as the Virgin Islands to the north, Trinidad to the south, and Aruba to the far west.

43. Colonel Alexander Braghine, *The Shadow of Atlantis: The Temple Church and the Temple* (New York City: E. P. Dutton, 1940) p. 34.

Note: The Caribs also lived on the mainland in South America—including Venezuela and the Guianas (3 territories in northeast South America: French Guiana, Guyana, and Suriname)—as far south as the Amazon River.

44. Note: In regards to early Latin American civilizations degenerating into a state of less-civilized practices after a loss of their forefathers' Christian beliefs, the Caribs are an interesting example. However, the now-living Carib descendants deny their ancestors practiced all-out cannibalism, and at worst used it only for occasional rituals where a small part of an enemy's corpse was thrown into a stew pot and symbolically eaten for courage; they also deny the Caribs actually went on hunting sprees to devour their enemies. The subject

has been a controversial one for years. Christopher Columbus was the first white man to report about the Caribs, when he discovered them in the "West Indies," which is the Caribbean. In his letters he called them cannibals, as did other Spanish chroniclers who claimed the Caribs gobbled their way up the chain of islands, consuming one peaceful Arawak islander after another until they would move to the next island. Modern research indicates this is likely false; some say the Caribs attacked the "Arawaks" (who, as the text points out, were in fact the Locono) but with only occasional ritualistic practices of cannibalism (which is still cannibalism), and others say the Caribs did not even attack the "Arawaks" that often. Columbus's first encounter with natives, as mentioned in the text, was with the so-called "Arawak people." The Spanish would define the area as having two main tribes—the more docile group of "Arawaks" and the more ferocious Caribs; however, more recent research also indicates they could have been the same tribe but perhaps distant cousins and possibly not even that much at war with one another. Centuries ago the Spanish reported that for years the Caribs invaded the islands of the "Arawaks," viciously attacking and killing the men while taking the "Arawak" women as slaves. But modern writers (and especially the descendants of the Caribs) generally claim those Spanish reports were incorrect.

45.  Ken Sekaquaptewa, Interview by Vance Hawkins (March 27, 2013), Orem, Utah.

Note 1: A copy of Hawkins's notes is in the my possession and is used by permission of those involved in the interview.

Note 2: When the Spanish first learned of the Hopi, General Francisco Vasquez de Coronado was at the Zuni villages. He immediately sent Pedro de Tovar to find the Hopi tribe. [J. O. Brew, "Hopi Prehistory and History to 1850," in *Southwest* (vol. 9 of book series), volume editor is Alonso Ortiz, general editor is William C. Sturtevant, *Handbook of North American Indians* (Washington, D.C.: Smithsonian Institution, 1979), vol. 9, pp. 514–523.]

46.  Ibid., Interview of Ken Sekaquaptewa.

47.  Frank Waters, *The Book of the Hopi* (New York City: Viking Press, 1963), p. 252.

48.  Ibid.

49.  J. O. Brew, "Hopi Prehistory and History to 1850," in *Southwest*, vol. 9, edited by Alonso Ortiz, volume editor, in William C. Sturtevant,

general editor, *Handbook of North American Indians* (Washington, D.C.: Smithsonian Institution, 1979), pp. 514–523.

50. Ibid.

51. **Note: Several years after Pedro de Tovar misinterpreted the handshake from the Hopi people, Spanish explorer Garcia Lopez de Cardenas explored the Rio Grande and met other Hopi, who received him warmly and helped him on his journey.** [ibid., J. O. Brew.] **Apparently this occurred sometime before the village was destroyed, when the Spaniards were still on good terms with the Hopi.**

52. The Bible, King James Version, New Testament, Revelation 9:13.

53. Harold Courlander, *The Fourth World of the Hopis: The Hopi Indians as Preserved in Their Legends and Traditions* (New York City: Outlet Book Publishing, 1971), p. 31.

   **Note 1: Another tradition related to burials is that the traditional Hopi woman's wedding gown is a white blouse that is draped over one shoulder and has a white skirt with a white sash (with a bit of red on the end). When she dies, she is buried with that gown on the other shoulder.** [Ken Sekaquaptewa, Interview by Vance Hawkins (March 27, 2013), Orem, Utah.]

   **Note 2: A copy of Hawkins's notes is in the my possession and is used by permission of those involved in the interview.**

54. Jacob Hamblin, *Jacob Hamblin: His Life in His Own Words* (Provo, Utah: Stratford Books, softcover 2001, eBook 2012).

55. Lucile Taylor Hansen, "Lucile Taylor Hansen and the Katezahl Legend: An Autobiographical Memoir," transcribed and edited by Kathy Doore, from the original handwritten journal of L. Taylor Hansen, in possession of Ms. Doore.)

56. The Bible, King James Version, New Testament, John 10:16.

   **Note: The remainder of the verse in John 10:16 reads, "and there shall be one fold, and one shepherd."**

57. Hubert Howe Bancroft, *History of the Pacific States of North America: Volume 5: Mexico* (San Francisco: A. L. Bancroft & Co., 1874), pp. 23–24, notes 53–58.

58. Robert F. Marx with Jenifer G. Marx, *In Quest of the Great White Gods: Contact Between the Old and New World from the Dawn of History* (New York City: Crown Publishers, 1992).

59. T. J. O'Brien, *Fair Gods and Feathered Serpents: A Search for Ancient America's Bearded White God* (Bountiful, Utah: Horizon Publishers, 1997), p. 219.

**Note: As stated in Appendix K, anti-Christian skeptics are quick to dismiss any reports reflecting ancient American Christianity, and in doing so they attack the intellectual honesty of the Franciscans, who of course are no longer around to defend themselves. But the genuine native Mayan terms contained in the Franciscans' report cannot be disputed, and they lend credence to the account, proving it was not all "simply made up." My opinion is that the burden of proof actually lies with the skeptics, since portions of the report, using genuine native Mayan terms, exist.**

60. Ibid.

61. The Bible, King James Version, Old Testament, Genesis, chapter 11.

62. *The Book of Mormon* (Palmyra, New York: Printed by E. B. Grandin for the Author, 1830), 4 Nephi 1:16.

63. Ibid., 3 Nephi 5:11–13, 16–18.

64. Ibid., Mormon 8:35.

65. Ibid., Moroni 10:4. ،

66. Ibid., Moroni 10:34.

67. Joseph Knight Jr., manuscript, Joseph Knight Jr. Folder, Church Archives, The Church of Jesus Christ of Latter-day Saints, Salt Lake City.


# CHAPTER 24

1. **Note 1: Joseph Smith would write in 1838 that the church was organized at the Whitmer house in Fayette, New York.** [Joseph Smith, Manuscript History of the Church, Book A-1, Historian's Office, Church Archives, The Church of Jesus Christ of Latter-day Saints, Salt Lake City;

also found in Joseph Smith, *The Papers of Joseph Smith*, edited by Dean C. Jessee, 2 volumes (Salt Lake City: Deseret Book, 1989–1992), vol. 1, p. 302;

also found in Joseph Smith, *The Joseph Smith Papers*, edited by Dean C. Jessee, Ronald K. Esplin, and Richard Lyman Bushman (Salt Lake City: The Church Historian's Press, 2008-), multiple-volume series.] **In 1842 he would write that it was Manchester, New York.** [Joseph

Smith, Letter (to John Wentworth, editor, *Chicago Democrat*), published in *Times and Seasons* (Nauvoo, Illinois), p. 708 (March 1, 1842).] **The simple confusion is due to the fact there were two meetings—the one serving as the actual organizational meeting was held at Fayette, but another important meeting in Manchester was held afterward.**

**Note 2: Young John Wentworth was a huge man. He stood 6 foot 6 inches and weighed 300 pounds. But his intellect and ambition made things happen. He had just graduated from Dartmouth College in 1836 and moved to the booming town of Chicago, population 2,500, to practice law, and quickly became a partner in an investment firm. Running in high-end circles, and at the time a dedicated Democrat, he was in the right place at the right time when a new opportunity hit.**

**The city's only newspaper, *The Chicago Democrat*, had just started 3 years earlier by a Jacksonian Democrat, John Calhoun. Pursuing other ventures, Calhoun now handed the paper over to fellow Democrats in his party, and they in turn hired John Wentworth within 1 month of his arriving in Chicago to edit it. Within 3 years, by 1839, he bought the *Democrat* for himself.**

**At age 26, in 1842, Wentworth wrote Joseph Smith for a "sketch of the rise, progress, persecution and faith of the Latter-day Saints" for a friend in New Hampshire, George Barstow, who was writing a history of New Hampshire. George did not use Joseph's response in his history, nor did Wentworth in his paper, but the good that came out of the exercise would become immeasurable, believe Latter-day Saints, because, simply put, it would become Latter-day scripture.**

**It would also become the best, most concise summary of Latter-day Saint beliefs, and was tabbed the Articles of Faith. Later it would be included in the smallest book of LDS scripture, *The Pearl of Great Price*, as the smallest section, consisting of just 13 sentences—now 13 verses.**

**Joseph first published the Articles of Faith in the March 1, 1842, issue of *Times and Seasons*.** [*Times and Seasons* (Nauvoo, Illinois), vol. 3, no. 9, pp. 706–710 (March 1, 1842).]

**As for Wentworth's story—his was a sterling example of success and problems in a booming America—where for ambitious young men the sky was the limit. He used his paper to promote himself, which assisted his already innate abilities to get ahead. At age 28, in 1843, he was elected U.S. Congressman—the youngest member of the House of Representatives, and served 5 times as a Democrat in Washington, D.C.**

In 1857 at a fairly young age of 42 he was elected mayor of Chicago and was re-elected. He would also become the city's police commissioner, determined to shut down the city's brothels, and he also served on the state board of education. Meanwhile he was the biggest property owner in all of Cook County. He re-entered Congress in the late 1850s, this time as a converted Republican, due in part to its anti-slavery position, and thus served a sixth term.

With all this success he was hit with growing trials in his life. He had spread himself too thin. Was on too many paths. The job as mayor zapped the energy right out of him. His newspaper began to flounder.

Besides no longer having the tremendous mental and physical stamina it took to run a newspaper and simultaneously be mayor, investment banker, and property mogul, he faced other trials. For years he was watching his rival newspapers grow and even take over what had once been his monopoly—especially from the *Chicago Tribune*, which had started in 1847 and grown bigger by the day.

Then he faced the stress of knowing that, to stay competitive, he would have to spend a fortune on sending reporters to cover the anticipated Civil War that was about to start.

All the while he saw his printing equipment becoming more antiquated with each passing year—needing more and more repairs, bringing him more and more headaches; so he would have to modernize to stay in business and especially to be competitive with the fresh young newspapers in town. But the cost to upgrade—and just thinking about it—gave him more stress. So he put the plan on hold.

Finally he was hit with a lawsuit. J. Young Scammon served papers against his paper for depicting him in a political cartoon as a "wild cat banker."

Serving as a politician was hard enough—local stressful matters as mayor and then national stressful matters as a returning congressman (plus the worries of investment banking and property ownership.) But the set of problems from his newspaper was the final straw.

It was time to change direction. He closed the doors to his beloved paper, the *Democrat*, just weeks before the Civil War started in the spring of 1861 and handed over his subscription list to the *Tribune* (which persuaded Scammon to drop the lawsuit).

All newspaper publishers hope their paper will serve as a legacy and local history for future generations. But most issues of the *Democrat* would burn in the Chicago Fire of 1871—although some still exist today in Chicago's museums and libraries.

John Wentworth went on with his life probably completely unaware that his long-distance ties to Joseph Smith had ended up in a book of modern scripture, a book of writings by a young prophet with the stamp of approval by God himself, believe Latter-day Saints. All from a simple request from the admirably ambitious Mr. John Wentworth.

2. *A Book of Commandments for the Government of the Church of Christ, Organized According to Law, on the 6th of April, 1830* (Zion [Independence, Missouri]: W. W. Phelps & Co., 1833; reprinted at Independence, Missouri: Board of Publications, Church of Christ Temple Lot, 1960); cited in Richard Lyman Bushman, *Joseph Smith: Rough Stone Rolling* (New York City: Alfred A. Knopf / Borzoi Books, 2005), p. 111.

3. Joseph Smith, History [1838], Church Archives, The Church of Jesus Christ of Latter-day Saints, Salt Lake City.

   Also found in Joseph Smith, *The Papers of Joseph Smith*, edited by Dean C. Jessee, 2 volumes (Salt Lake City: Deseret Book, 1989–1992), vol. 1, pp. 241.

   Also found in Joseph Smith, *The Joseph Smith Papers*, edited by Dean C. Jessee, Ronald K. Esplin, and Richard Lyman Bushman (Salt Lake City: The Church Historian's Press, 2008–), multiple-volume series.

4. David Whitmer, *David Whitmer Interviews: A Restoration Witness*, edited by Lyndon W. Cook (Orem, Utah: Grandin Book, 1991), p. 11.

   David Whitmer, *An Address to All Believers in Christ* (Richmond, Missouri: published by the author, 1887), p. 32.

5. David Lewis, "Testimony Taken in the Presence of Andrew Jensen, Hiram B. Clawson, Martin S. Lindsay, Stokey Anderson, and M. Minerva Jenson, Historian's Office, September 10, 1908," Mormon Biography File, Church Archives, The Church of Jesus Christ of Latter-day Saints, Salt Lake City.

6. Joseph Smith Jr., *History of the Church of Jesus Christ of Latter-day Saints*, edited by B. H. Roberts, 7 volumes (Salt Lake City: The Church of Jesus Christ of Latter-day Saints and *Deseret News*, Revised Second Edition 1948), vol. 1, pp. 74–78.

7. Note: In regards to the first men in the church receiving the office of "elder," in 1881 David Whitmer recalled that they had become elders 8 months before the organizational meeting of April 6, 1830, more than a half century earlier. In Whitmer's recollection he and at least 5 others were ordained by August 1829: Joseph, Hyrum, Samuel Smith, Oliver Cowdery, and Peter Whitmer. [David Whitmer, *An Address to All Believers in Christ* (Richmond, Missouri: published

by the author, 1887), p. 32.] **However, Whitmer's report of the season and year—the summer of 1829—is accurate for only when Joseph and Oliver heard that they would one day receive the office of Elder: in fact they received a revelation in April 1829 stating that one day they would receive the office. In the intervening 5 decades Whitmer apparently confused the time line as to when they first heard they would receive the office vs. when they were actually ordained to it.**

8.  Joseph Smith Jr., *History of the Church of Jesus Christ of Latter-day Saints*, edited by B. H. Roberts, 7 volumes (Salt Lake City: The Church of Jesus Christ of Latter-day Saints and *Deseret News*, Revised Second Edition 1948), vol. 1, p. 78.

9.  Joseph Knight Sr., 5-page manuscript, #183301847, Historical Department, The Church of Jesus Christ of Latter-day Saints, Salt Lake City.

10. Joseph Smith, Manuscript History of the Church, Book A–1, Historian's Office, Church Archives, The Church of Jesus Christ of Latter-day Saints, Salt Lake City.

    Also found in Joseph Smith, *The Papers of Joseph Smith*, edited by Dean C. Jessee, 2 volumes (Salt Lake City: Deseret Book, 1989–1992), vol. 1, pp. 302–303.

    Also found in Joseph Smith, *The Joseph Smith Papers*, edited by Dean C. Jessee, Ronald K. Esplin, and Richard Lyman Bushman (Salt Lake City: The Church Historian's Press, 2008–), multiple-volume series.

11. Lucy Mack Smith, Preliminary Manuscript [1844–1845], Church Archives, The Church of Jesus Christ of Latter-day Saints, Salt Lake City.

    Also displayed in Lucy Mack Smith, *Lucy's Book: A Critical Edition of Lucy Mack Smith's Family Memoir*, edited by Lavina Fielding Anderson (Salt Lake City: Signature Books, 2001), p. 477.

12. Joseph Smith, History [1838], Church Archives, The Church of Jesus Christ of Latter-day Saints, Salt Lake City.

    Also found in Joseph Smith, *The Papers of Joseph Smith*, edited by Dean C. Jessee, 2 volumes (Salt Lake City: Deseret Book, 1989–1992), vol. 1, pp. 244.

    Also found in Joseph Smith, *The Joseph Smith Papers*, edited by Dean C. Jessee, Ronald K. Esplin, and Richard Lyman Bushman (Salt Lake City: The Church Historian's Press, 2008–), multiple-volume series.

13. *The Doctrine and Covenants of the Church of Jesus Christ of Latter-day Saints: Containing Revelations given to Joseph Smith, the Prophet, with*

*Some Additions by His Successors in the Presidency of the Church* (Salt Lake City: The Church of Jesus Christ of Latter-day Saints, 1981), 21:1.

**Note: Joseph Smith was designated these 5 titles—seer, translator, prophet, apostle of Jesus Christ, and elder—described in the text at this April 6, 1830, organizational meeting, but he would actually "grow" into these callings. For example, he was probably about three months away from receiving the keys of apostleship, as outlined in Chapter 25.**

14. Ibid.

15. Lucy Mack Smith, *History of Joseph Smith by His Mother: The Unabridged Original Version* (Arlington, Virginia and Provo, Utah: Stratford Books, Revised Second Edition 2006), Lucy's published text, p. 251.

16. Ibid., p. 251.

    **Note: The portion used comes from Lucy's rough draft.**

17. Ibid., Lucy's published text, p. 251.

    Lucy Mack Smith, Preliminary Manuscript [1844–1845], Church Archives, The Church of Jesus Christ of Latter-day Saints, Salt Lake City.

    Also displayed in Lucy Mack Smith, *Lucy's Book: A Critical Edition of Lucy Mack Smith's Family Memoir*, edited by Lavina Fielding Anderson (Salt Lake City: Signature Books, 2001), p. 477.

18. Joseph Smith, Manuscript History of the Church, Book A–1, Historian's Office, Church Archives, The Church of Jesus Christ of Latter-day Saints, Salt Lake City.

    Also found in Joseph Smith, *The Papers of Joseph Smith*, edited by Dean C. Jessee, 2 volumes (Salt Lake City: Deseret Book, 1989–1992), vol. 1, p. 303.

    Also found in Joseph Smith, *The Joseph Smith Papers*, edited by Dean C. Jessee, Ronald K. Esplin, and Richard Lyman Bushman (Salt Lake City: The Church Historian's Press, 2008–), multiple-volume series.

19. Joseph Knight Sr., 5-page manuscript, #183301847, Historical Department, The Church of Jesus Christ of Latter-day Saints, Salt Lake City.

    Joseph Knight Sr., "Joseph Knight's Recollection of Early Mormon History," edited by Dean C. Jessee, *BYU Studies* (Provo, Utah), vol. 17, no. 1 (Autumn 1976), p. 37.

20. Joseph Knight Sr., 5-page manuscript, #183301847, Historical Department, The Church of Jesus Christ of Latter-day Saints, Salt Lake City.

21. Ibid.

22. Ibid.

23. *The Doctrine and Covenants of the Church of Jesus Christ of Latter-day Saints: Containing Revelations given to Joseph Smith, the Prophet, with Some Additions by His Successors in the Presidency of the Church* (Salt Lake City: The Church of Jesus Christ of Latter-day Saints, 1981), 18:28, 37.

24. David Lewis, "Testimony Taken in the Presence of Andrew Jensen, Hiram B. Clawson, Martin S. Lindsay, Stokey Anderson, and M. Minerva Jenson, Historian's Office, September 10, 1908," Mormon Biography File, Church Archives, The Church of Jesus Christ of Latter-day Saints, Salt Lake City.

25. David Whitmer, *An Address to All Believers in Christ* (Richmond, Missouri: published by the author, 1887), p. 32.

26. Richard H. Broadhead, "Prophets, Publics, and Publication: The Case of John Brown," *Proceedings of the American Antiquarian Society*, vol. 3, part 2 (2001), p. 535.

27. Joseph Smith, Letter (to N. C. Saxton, January 4, 1833), in Joseph Smith, *Personal Writings of Joseph Smith*, edited by Dean C. Jessee (Provo, Utah: Brigham Young University Press, Revised Edition 2002), p. 296.

28. *Deseret Evening News* (Salt Lake City), January 20, 1894.

    William Smith, "William B. Smith's Last Statement," Interview by J. W. Peterson, *Zion's Ensign* (Independence, Missouri), vol. 5, no. 3 (1894), p. 6.

29. Katherine Smith (Katherine Smith Salisbury Younger), *Kansas City Times* (Kansas City, Missouri), April 11, 1893.

30. Joseph Smith, Manuscript History of the Church, Book A-1, Historian's Office, Church Archives, The Church of Jesus Christ of Latter-day Saints, Salt Lake City.

    Also found in Joseph Smith, *The Papers of Joseph Smith*, edited by Dean C. Jessee, 2 volumes (Salt Lake City: Deseret Book, 1989–1992), vol. 1, p. 305.

    Also found in Joseph Smith, *The Joseph Smith Papers*, edited by Dean C. Jessee, Ronald K. Esplin, and Richard Lyman Bushman (Salt Lake City: The Church Historian's Press, 2008–), multiple-volume series.

31. Joseph Smith Jr., *History of the Church of Jesus Christ of Latter-day Saints*, edited by B. H. Roberts, 7 volumes (Salt Lake City: The Church of Jesus

Christ of Latter-day Saints and *Deseret News*, Revised Second Edition 1948), vol. 1, pp. 82–84.

32. Ibid.

33. Ibid.

34. Newel Knight, "Autobiography and Journal of Newel Knight, 1800–1847," Church Archives, The Church of Jesus Christ of Latter-day Saints, Salt Lake City.

35. Joseph Smith Jr., *History of the Church of Jesus Christ of Latter-day Saints*, edited by B. H. Roberts, 7 volumes (Salt Lake City: The Church of Jesus Christ of Latter-day Saints and *Deseret News*, Revised Second Edition 1948), vol. 1, p. 83.

36. Joseph Smith, Manuscript History of the Church, Book A-1, Historian's Office, Church Archives, The Church of Jesus Christ of Latter-day Saints, Salt Lake City.

Also found in Joseph Smith, *The Papers of Joseph Smith*, edited by Dean C. Jessee, 2 volumes (Salt Lake City: Deseret Book, 1989–1992), vol. 1, pp. 306–307.

Also found in Joseph Smith, *The Joseph Smith Papers*, edited by Dean C. Jessee, Ronald K. Esplin, and Richard Lyman Bushman (Salt Lake City: The Church Historian's Press, 2008–), multiple-volume series.

Newel Knight, "Autobiography and Journal of Newel Knight, 1800–1847," Church Archives, The Church of Jesus Christ of Latter-day Saints, Salt Lake City.

**Note: The higher (Melchizedek) priesthood, which is generally associated with the power of exorcism—to free people from evil spirits—was probably restored between mid and late May 1829, almost a year before this incident of exorcising an evil spirit from Newel Knight as described in the text. Using faith alone, people have apparently assisted others in becoming free from such spirits, but if the actual priesthood is used—such as probably in this instance—that priesthood would have been the Melchizedek Priesthood. This account of Newel Knight lacks details explaining if Joseph used merely faith or if he used the priesthood for this exorcism, but most Latter-day Saints assume it was probably the priesthood, since it was now back upon the earth.**

37. Joseph Smith, Manuscript History of the Church, Book A-1, Historian's Office, Church Archives, The Church of Jesus Christ of Latter-day Saints, Salt Lake City.

Also found in Joseph Smith, *The Papers of Joseph Smith*, edited by Dean C. Jessee, 2 volumes (Salt Lake City: Deseret Book, 1989–1992), vol. 1, pp. 307–309.

Also found in Joseph Smith, *The Joseph Smith Papers*, edited by Dean C. Jessee, Ronald K. Esplin, and Richard Lyman Bushman (Salt Lake City: The Church Historian's Press, 2008–), multiple-volume series.

38. Journal History, June 9, 1830, Church Archives, The Church of Jesus Christ of Latter-day Saints, Salt Lake City.

   **Note: Journal History is a daily history of the church from 1830 to the present. It is compiled from mostly newspapers and includes diary entries and meetings minutes. A copy is on the north wall of the Church History Library and is arranged by date. Page numbers start over with each date.** ["Journal History of the Church," The Church of Jesus Christ of Latter-day Saints, Salt Lake City, October 6, 2011, www. http://history.lds.org/article/chi-journal-history?lang=eng.] **The Journal History has been accurately coined by Utah historiographer Gary Topping as "an immense scrapbook compilation consisting of several hundred volumes of various historical records."** [Gary Topping, *Utah Historians and the Reconstruction of Western History* (Norman, Oklahoma: University of Oklahoma Press, 2003).]

   *Far West Record: Minutes of the Church of Jesus Christ of Latter-day Saints, 1830–1844*, edited by Donald Q. Cannon and Lyndon W. Cook (Salt Lake City: Deseret Book, 1983), June 9, 1830, pp. 1–2.

39. Donald Q. Cannon, "Licensing in the Early Church," *BYU Studies* (Provo, Utah), vol. 22, no. 1 (Winter 1982), p. 97.

40. *Far West Record: Minutes of the Church of Jesus Christ of Latter-day Saints, 1830–1844*, edited by Donald Q. Cannon and Lyndon W. Cook (Salt Lake City: Deseret Book, 1983), June 9, 1830, pp. 1–2.

41. Joseph Smith, Manuscript History of the Church, Book A-1, Historian's Office, Church Archives, The Church of Jesus Christ of Latter-day Saints, Salt Lake City.

   Also found in Joseph Smith, *The Papers of Joseph Smith*, edited by Dean C. Jessee, 2 volumes (Salt Lake City: Deseret Book, 1989–1992), vol. 1, pp. 307–309.

   Also found in Joseph Smith, *The Joseph Smith Papers*, edited by Dean C. Jessee, Ronald K. Esplin, and Richard Lyman Bushman (Salt Lake City: The Church Historian's Press, 2008–), multiple-volume series.

42. Ibid.

43. "Newel Knight Journal," *Scraps of Biography: Tenth Book of the Faith Promoting Series* (Salt Lake City: Juvenile Instructor Office, 1883), pp. 47–65.

    Joseph Smith, Manuscript History of the Church, Book A-1, Historian's Office, Church Archives, The Church of Jesus Christ of Latter-day Saints, Salt Lake City.

    Also found in Joseph Smith, *The Papers of Joseph Smith*, edited by Dean C. Jessee, 2 volumes (Salt Lake City: Deseret Book, 1989–1992), vol. 1, p. 250.

    Also found in Joseph Smith, *The Joseph Smith Papers*, edited by Dean C. Jessee, Ronald K. Esplin, and Richard Lyman Bushman (Salt Lake City: The Church Historian's Press, 2008–), multiple-volume series.

44. "Newel Knight Journal," *Scraps of Biography: Tenth Book of the Faith Promoting Series* (Salt Lake City: Juvenile Instructor Office, 1883), p. 54.

45. **Note: Among the group of New Believers was the Joseph and Polly Knight family, of which 13 were baptized on June 28, 1830. They immediately became an anchor to the group. This was almost 3 months after the church was organized and, although modest in numbers, this growing community of converts in Fayette would prove to be a major second community of the fledgling church.**

46. "Newel Knight Journal," *Scraps of Biography: Tenth Book of the Faith Promoting Series* (Salt Lake City: Juvenile Instructor Office, 1883), pp. 47–65.

47. Joseph Smith, History [1838], Church Archives, The Church of Jesus Christ of Latter-day Saints, Salt Lake City.

    Also found in Joseph Smith, *The Papers of Joseph Smith*, edited by Dean C. Jessee, 2 volumes (Salt Lake City: Deseret Book, 1989–1992), vol. 1, p. 251.

    Also found in Joseph Smith, *The Joseph Smith Papers*, edited by Dean C. Jessee, Ronald K. Esplin, and Richard Lyman Bushman (Salt Lake City: The Church Historian's Press, 2008–), multiple-volume series.

48. Newel Knight, Autobiographical Sketch, manuscript, 1862, p. 2, Church Archives, The Church of Jesus Christ of Latter-day Saints, Salt Lake City.

    "Newel Knight Journal," *Scraps of Biography: Tenth Book of the Faith Promoting Series* (Salt Lake City: Juvenile Instructor Office, 1883), pp. 47–65.

49. Lucy Mack Smith, *History of Joseph Smith by His Mother: The Unabridged Original Version* (Arlington, Virginia and Provo, Utah: Stratford Books, Revised Second Edition 2006), p. 262.

# CHAPTER 25

1. Joseph Knight Sr., "Joseph Knight's Recollection of Early Mormon History," edited by Dean C. Jessee, *BYU Studies* (Provo, Utah), vol. 17, no. 1 (Autumn 1976), p. 38.

2. Ibid.

3. Joseph Smith, History [1838], Church Archives, The Church of Jesus Christ of Latter-day Saints, Salt Lake City.

   Also found in Joseph Smith, *The Joseph Smith Papers*, edited by Dean C. Jessee, Ronald K. Esplin, and Richard Lyman Bushman (Salt Lake City: The Church Historian's Press, 2008–), multiple-volume series.

4. "A. W. B. Letter to the editor," *Evangelical Magazine and Gospel Advocate* (Utica, New York), vol. 2 (April 9, 1831).

5. "Newel Knight Journal," *Scraps of Biography: Tenth Book of the Faith Promoting Series* (Salt Lake City: Juvenile Instructor Office, 1883), pp. 47–65.

6. Ibid.

7. Ibid.

8. Ibid.

9. Joseph Knight Sr., 5-page manuscript, #183301847, Historical Department, The Church of Jesus Christ of Latter-day Saints, Salt Lake City.

10. Joseph Smith, History [1838] Church Archives, The Church of Jesus Christ of Latter-day Saints, Salt Lake City.

    Also found in Joseph Smith, *The Papers of Joseph Smith*, edited by Dean C. Jessee, 2 volumes (Salt Lake City: Deseret Book, 1989–1992), vol. 1, pp. 252–253.

    Also found in Joseph Smith, *The Joseph Smith Papers*, edited by Dean C. Jessee, Ronald K. Esplin, and Richard Lyman Bushman (Salt Lake City: The Church Historian's Press, 2008–), multiple-volume series.

11. Joseph Knight Sr., 5-page manuscript, #183301847, Historical Department, The Church of Jesus Christ of Latter-day Saints, Salt Lake City.

12. *Times and Seasons* (Nauvoo, Illinois), pp. 549–550 (June 1, 1844).

Mark Ashurst-McGee, "The Josiah Stowell Jr. - John S. Fullmer Correspondence," *BYU Studies* (Provo, Utah), vol. 38, no. 3 (1999), p. 114.

13. Newel Knight, "Autobiographical Sketch," manuscript, 1862, p. 2, Church Archives, The Church of Jesus Christ of Latter-day Saints, Salt Lake City.

14. "Newel Knight Journal," *Scraps of Biography: Tenth Book of the Faith Promoting Series* (Salt Lake City: Juvenile Instructor Office, 1883), pp. 47–65.

15. Lucy Mack Smith, *History of Joseph Smith by His Mother: The Unabridged Original Version* (Arlington, Virginia and Provo, Utah: Stratford Books, Revised Second Edition 2006), p. 263.

**Note: The portion used comes from Lucy's rough draft.**

16. "Newel Knight Journal," *Scraps of Biography: Tenth Book of the Faith Promoting Series* (Salt Lake City: Juvenile Instructor Office, 1883), pp. 47–65.

17. Mark Ashurst-McGee, "The Josiah Stowell Jr. - John S. Fullmer Correspondence," *BYU Studies* (Provo, Utah), vol. 38, no. 3 (1999), p. 114.

18. Ibid.

19. "Newel Knight Journal," *Scraps of Biography: Tenth Book of the Faith Promoting Series* (Salt Lake City: Juvenile Instructor Office, 1883), pp. 47–65.

20. Ibid.

21. Joseph Knight Sr., 5-page manuscript, #183301847, Historical Department, The Church of Jesus Christ of Latter-day Saints, Salt Lake City.

22. *Times and Seasons* (Nauvoo, Illinois), pp. 549–550 (June 1, 1844).

Wesley P. Walters, "Joseph Smith's Bainbridge, New York, Court Trials," *Westminster Theological Journal* (Philadelphia, Pennsylvania), vol. 36, no. 2 (1974), pp. 123–155.

**Note: Since 1938 the *Westminster Theological Journal* has been published semiannually by the Westminster Theological Seminary. Published in Philadelphia, Pennsylvania, it focuses on Reformed and Presbyterian scholarship and all aspects of church history and theology, containing in each issue articles and book reviews by scholars, graduate students and seminary faculty. Its editors are appointed by the faculty of the Westminster Theological Seminary. Hundreds of libraries subscribe to this journal.**

23. Ibid., *Times and Seasons.*

24. Joseph Knight Sr., 5-page manuscript, #183301847, Historical Department, The Church of Jesus Christ of Latter-day Saints, Salt Lake City.

25. "Newel Knight Journal," *Scraps of Biography: Tenth Book of the Faith Promoting Series* (Salt Lake City: Juvenile Instructor Office, 1883), pp. 47–65.

26. Joseph Smith, Manuscript History of the Church, Book A-1, Historian's Office, Church Archives, The Church of Jesus Christ of Latter-day Saints, Salt Lake City.

    Also found in Joseph Smith, *The Papers of Joseph Smith*, edited by Dean C. Jessee, 2 volumes (Salt Lake City: Deseret Book, 1989–1992), vol. 1, pp. 314–315.

    Also found in Joseph Smith, *The Joseph Smith Papers*, edited by Dean C. Jessee, Ronald K. Esplin, and Richard Lyman Bushman (Salt Lake City: The Church Historian's Press, 2008–), multiple-volume series.

27. Joseph Knight Sr., 5-page manuscript, #183301847, Historical Department, The Church of Jesus Christ of Latter-day Saints, Salt Lake City.

28. "Newel Knight Journal," *Scraps of Biography: Tenth Book of the Faith Promoting Series* (Salt Lake City: Juvenile Instructor Office, 1883), pp. 52–61.

29. Ibid.

30. Ibid.

31. Ibid.

32. Ibid.

33. Ibid.

34. Lucy Mack Smith, *History of Joseph Smith by His Mother: The Unabridged Original Version* (Arlington, Virginia and Provo, Utah: Stratford Books, Revised Second Edition 2006), p. 263.

35. Joseph Smith Jr., *History of the Church of Jesus Christ of Latter-day Saints*, edited by B. H. Roberts, 7 volumes (Salt Lake City: The Church of Jesus Christ of Latter-day Saints and *Deseret News*, Revised Second Edition 1948), vol. 1, p. 97.

36. "A. W. B. Letter to the editor," *Evangelical Magazine and Gospel Advocate* (Utica, New York), vol. 2 (April 9, 1831).

37. Joseph Smith Jr., *History of the Church of Jesus Christ of Latter-day Saints*, edited by B. H. Roberts, 7 volumes (Salt Lake City: The Church of Jesus

Christ of Latter-day Saints and *Deseret News*, Revised Second Edition 1948), vol. 1, p. 93.

38. Joseph Knight Sr., 5-page manuscript, #183301847, Historical Department, The Church of Jesus Christ of Latter-day Saints, Salt Lake City.

39. "Newel Knight Journal," *Scraps of Biography: Tenth Book of the Faith Promoting Series* (Salt Lake City: Juvenile Instructor Office, 1883), pp. 55–61.

40. Addison Everett, quoted in Oliver Boardman Huntington, "Words and Incidents of the Prophet Joseph's Life," *Young Woman's Journal* (Salt Lake City), vol. 2, no. 2 (November 1890), pp. 75–76.

**Note: Regarding this court incident at Colesville, Broome County, New York, when Joseph Smith was on trial facing charges leveled by those who disagreed with his religious beliefs, Addison Everett wrote a description of it to Oliver Boardman Huntington in 1881 describing the activities of John Reid. It is more succinct than the account I use in the text: "In court he stated that the first miracle done was to create this earth. About that time his attorney [Reid] told the court that he wanted to see Mr. Smith alone a few moments. When alone Mr. Reid said that there was a mob in front of the house and hosting [hoisting] the window, Joseph and Oliver went to the woods."** [Addison Everett, Letter (to Oliver B. Huntington, St. George, Utah), February 17, 1881, recorded in "Oliver Boardman Huntington, Journal #14 [under back-date of] 31 Jan. 1881," L. Tom Perry Special Collections, Harold B. Lee Library, Brigham Young University, Provo, Utah.] **This 1881 letter from Addison Everett to Oliver Boardman Huntington, both of whom resided at St. George, Utah, at the time, would be fleshed out by Huntington for an article he would write 9 years later for the *Young Woman's Journal*.** [Addison Everett, Letter (to Oliver B. Huntington, St. George, Utah, February 17, 1881), *Young Woman's Journal* (Salt Lake City), vol. 2 (November, 1890), pp. 76–77.] **He possibly received the additional details of the court scenes, which are not contained in the letter, from Addison Everett himself, since they were friends.** [For the same letter with several additional details, see Oliver B. Huntington Diary #15, February 18, 1883, pp. 44–47, L. Tom Perry Special Collections, Harold B. Lee Library, Brigham Young University, Provo, Utah.]

41. Addison Everett, Letter (to Oliver B. Huntington, St. George, Utah), February 17, 1881, recorded in "Oliver Boardman Huntington, Journal #14 [under back-date of] 31 Jan. 1881," L. Tom Perry Special Collections, Harold B. Lee Library, Brigham Young University, Provo, Utah.

42. John Reid, Statement, in Lucy Mack Smith, *History of Joseph Smith by His Mother: The Unabridged Original Version* (Arlington, Virginia and Provo, Utah: Stratford Books, Revised Second Edition 2006), pp. 263–264.

43. **Note: Despite John Reid and Addison Everett claiming Joseph and Oliver left the courtroom with Reid, Newel Knight claims Joseph and Oliver left with the constable;** ["Newel Knight Journal," *Scraps of Biography: Tenth Book of the Faith Promoting Series* (Salt Lake City: Juvenile Instructor Office, 1883), pp. 52–61] **but the result was the same—they escaped the mob, into the woods.**

44. Lucy Mack Smith, *History of Joseph Smith by His Mother: The Unabridged Original Version* (Arlington, Virginia and Provo, Utah: Stratford Books, Revised Second Edition 2006), p. 263.

    **Note: The portion used comes from Lucy's rough draft.**

45. Ibid., pp. 263–264.

46. "Newel Knight Journal," *Scraps of Biography: Tenth Book of the Faith Promoting Series* (Salt Lake City: Juvenile Instructor Office, 1883), p. 61.

47. Oliver B. Huntington, "Words and Incidents of the Prophet Joseph's Life," *Young Woman's Journal* (Salt Lake City), vol. 2, no. 2 (November 1890), pp. 75–76.

    **Note: Addison Everett finished his 1881 letter to Oliver Boardman Huntington with this: "Now Brother Huntington I have told you what I heard Brother Joseph tell, almost the only time I ever heard him talk. It is a source of satisfaction and pleasure to me to have seen and heard the Prophet of God."**

48. Addison Everett, Letter (to Joseph F. Smith, St. George, Utah), January 16, 1882, Joseph F. Smith Collection, Personal Papers, MS 1325, Church Archives, The Church of Jesus Christ of Latter-day Saints, Salt Lake City.

    **Note: Addison Everett's letter to Joseph Fielding Smith contains a final paragraph, presented below in its exact, original form with notations in manuscript-publishing format. It relates to the mob escape and ordination scenes:**

    > **"But as the Mob spirit had not abated when they returned [to Harmony,] they had to remove to Father Whitmores <at Fatet[te] Seneca Co> to finish the Translation. I should <jud[g]e> it to <Be> the Latter part of August."**

    **In this paragraph Everett estimates this event occurring in "the Latter part of August." But he is somewhat off in his time line of events, a forgivable mistake considering he is looking back 51 years. He**

is correct, however, in stating Joseph and Emma moved the latter part of August 1830 from Harmony because of the mob spirit there, and he is correct in stating they moved to Fayette, New York, to the Whitmers. As detailed in the text, the reason for this 1830 move was not to work on the translation but to escape to safety, since Emma's father would no longer protect them from increasing persecution in Harmony, Pennsylvania. (Note that Oliver would move to Fayette first, then Joseph and Emma, and they would all stay at "Father Whitmer's," which was the home of Peter Whitmer senior.)

Everett is also correct in stating they had moved to Fayette to finish the translation; however, that was a year earlier, when they had moved there for only 1 month, on about June 1, 1829, to be free from temporal challenges while Joseph finished translating.

So he is correct on his facts, just off on his dates. The translation would have been finished about July 1, 1829, exactly 1 year prior to this escape scene of about July 1, 1830.

49. *Journal of Discourses*, edited by George D. Watt, et al., 26 volumes (Liverpool, England: Franklin D. Richards and Sons, 1854–1886), vol. 23, p. 183 (May 6, 1882).

Note: Historian Larry C. Porter introduces the possibility that Erastus Snow was influenced by Addison Everett when Snow made this comment of Joseph and Oliver being pursued by enemies when the three ancient apostles, Peter, James, and John, appeared to them and conferred the Apostleship to Joseph and Oliver. The reason that Snow could have been influenced is because both men happened to later settle in the same community of St. George, Utah, before writing about it; still, they may have arrived at their facts independently, but "in any instance," says Porter, "it is evident that Elder Snow thought the account was true." [Larry C. Porter, "Dating the Restoration of the Melchizedek Priesthood," *Ensign* (Salt Lake City), June 1979.]

50. Wesley P. Walters, "Joseph Smith's Bainbridge, New York, Court Trials," *Westminster Theological Journal* (Philadelphia, Pennsylvania), vol. 36, no. 2 (1974), p. 124.

Joseph Smith, History [1838] Church Archives, The Church of Jesus Christ of Latter-day Saints, Salt Lake City.

Also found in Joseph Smith, *The Papers of Joseph Smith*, edited by Dean C. Jessee, 2 volumes (Salt Lake City: Deseret Book, 1989–1992), vol. 1, pp. 252–253.

Also found in Joseph Smith, *The Joseph Smith Papers*, edited by Dean C. Jessee, Ronald K. Esplin, and Richard Lyman Bushman (Salt Lake City: The Church Historian's Press, 2008–), multiple-volume series.

51. **Note: Now that they held the higher priesthood, on April 6, 1830, Joseph and Oliver ordained some of the other men to priesthood offices and confirmed still others members of the church and gave them the Gift of the Holy Ghost.** [Joseph Smith, Manuscript History of the Church, Book A-1, Historian's Office, Church Archives, The Church of Jesus Christ of Latter-day Saints, Salt Lake City;

Joseph Smith, *The Papers of Joseph Smith*, edited by Dean C. Jessee, 2 volumes (Salt Lake City: Deseret Book, 1989–1992), vol. 1, p. 302;

Joseph Smith, *The Joseph Smith Papers*, edited by Dean C. Jessee, Ronald K. Esplin, and Richard Lyman Bushman, multiple-volume series (Salt Lake City: The Church Historian's Press, 2008–);

*Times and Seasons* (Nauvoo, Illinois), p. 708 (March 1, 1842);

Edward Stevenson, Diary, December 22–23, 1877, in David Whitmer, *David Whitmer Interviews: A Restoration Witness*, edited by Lyndon W. Cook (Orem, Utah: Grandin Book, 1991), p. 11).]

**Further, according to Joseph Knight, at that first organizational church meeting held April 6, 1830, Joseph gave instructions on how to build up the church—which were all responsibilities of the higher priesthood.** [Joseph Knight Sr., 5-page manuscript, #183301847, Historical Department, The Church of Jesus Christ of Latter-day Saints, Salt Lake City;

Joseph Knight Sr., "Joseph Knight's Recollection of Early Mormon History," edited by Dean C. Jessee, *BYU Studies* (Provo, Utah), vol. 17, no. 1 (Autumn 1976), p. 37.]

# CHAPTER 26

1. Joseph Smith Jr., *History of the Church of Jesus Christ of Latter-day Saints*, edited by B. H. Roberts, 7 volumes (Salt Lake City: The Church of Jesus Christ of Latter-day Saints and *Deseret News*, Revised Second Edition 1948), vol. 1, p. 101.

2. Lucy Mack Smith, *History of Joseph Smith by His Mother: The Unabridged Original Version* (Arlington, Virginia and Provo, Utah: Stratford Books, Revised Second Edition 2006), p. 264.

3. Ibid.

4. Joseph Smith Jr., *History of the Church of Jesus Christ of Latter-day Saints*, edited by B. H. Roberts, 7 volumes (Salt Lake City: The Church of Jesus Christ of Latter-day Saints and *Deseret News*, Revised Second Edition 1948), vol. 1, p. 96.

5. Addison Everett, Letter (to Joseph F. Smith, St. George, Utah), January 16, 1882, Joseph F. Smith Collection, Personal Papers, MS 1325, Church Archives, The Church of Jesus Christ of Latter-day Saints, Salt Lake City.

6. Joseph Knight Jr., manuscript, Joseph Knight Jr. Folder, Church Archives, The Church of Jesus Christ of Latter-day Saints, Salt Lake City.

   Also contained in "Joseph Knight Jr.," in Hyrum L. Andrus and Helen Mae Andrus, *They Knew the Prophet* (Salt Lake City: Bookcraft, 1974), p. 6.

7. Joseph Smith, History [1838] Church Archives, The Church of Jesus Christ of Latter-day Saints, Salt Lake City.

   Also found in Joseph Smith, *The Papers of Joseph Smith*, edited by Dean C. Jessee, 2 volumes (Salt Lake City: Deseret Book, 1989–1992), vol. 2, p. 258.

   Also found in Joseph Smith, *The Joseph Smith Papers*, edited by Dean C. Jessee, Ronald K. Esplin, and Richard Lyman Bushman (Salt Lake City: The Church Historian's Press, 2008–), multiple-volume series.

   Joseph Smith Jr., *History of the Church of Jesus Christ of Latter-day Saints*, edited by B. H. Roberts, 7 volumes (Salt Lake City: The Church of Jesus Christ of Latter-day Saints and *Deseret News*, Revised Second Edition 1948), vol. 1, p. 97.

   Newel Knight, Autobiographical Sketch, manuscript, 1862, p. 2, Church Archives, The Church of Jesus Christ of Latter-day Saints, Salt Lake City.

8. Joseph Smith, Manuscript History of the Church, Book A-1, Historian's Office, Church Archives, The Church of Jesus Christ of Latter-day Saints, Salt Lake City.

   Also found in Joseph Smith, *The Papers of Joseph Smith*, edited by Dean C. Jessee, 2 volumes (Salt Lake City: Deseret Book, 1989–1992), vol. 1, p. 318.

   Also found in Joseph Smith, *The Joseph Smith Papers*, edited by Dean C. Jessee, Ronald K. Esplin, and Richard Lyman Bushman (Salt Lake City: The Church Historian's Press, 2008–), multiple-volume series.

For a similar report, see "Newel Knight Journal," *Scraps of Biography: Tenth Book of the Faith Promoting Series* (Salt Lake City: Juvenile Instructor Office, 1883), p. 61.

9. Joseph Smith Jr., Statement (February 16, 1832), in *Teachings of the Prophet Joseph Smith*, edited by Joseph Fielding Smith (Salt Lake City: Deseret Book, 1938), pp. 9–10.

   **Note: I added the italics.**

   Joseph Smith Jr., *History of the Church of Jesus Christ of Latter-day Saints*, edited by B. H. Roberts, 7 volumes (Salt Lake City: The Church of Jesus Christ of Latter-day Saints and *Deseret News*, Revised Second Edition 1948), vol. 6, p. 57.

   **Note: This quote from Joseph Smith about believing in the Bible in its proper form continues with the following explanation: "I believe the Bible as it read when it came from the pen of the original writers."**

10. *The Doctrine and Covenants of the Church of Jesus Christ of Latter-day Saints: Containing Revelations given to Joseph Smith, the Prophet, with Some Additions by His Successors in the Presidency of the Church* (Salt Lake City: The Church of Jesus Christ of Latter-day Saints, 1981), 21:1.

    Joseph Smith Jr., *History of the Church of Jesus Christ of Latter-day Saints*, edited by B. H. Roberts, 7 volumes (Salt Lake City: The Church of Jesus Christ of Latter-day Saints and *Deseret News*, Revised Second Edition 1948), vol. 1, p. 78.

    **Note 1: This description of Joseph's callings as a seer, a translator, and a prophet, was from a revelation given him at Fayette, New York, on April 6, 1830, the day the church was organized.**

    **Note 2: On January 19, 1841, this description of his callings would be phrased, "a prophet and a seer, and a revelator."** [*The Doctrine and Covenants of the Church of Jesus Christ of Latter-day Saints: Containing Revelations given to Joseph Smith, the Prophet, with Some Additions by His Successors in the Presidency of the Church* (Salt Lake City: The Church of Jesus Christ of Latter-day Saints, 1981), 124:94.]

11. **Note: In Joseph's revision of the Bible, he would keep exactly 89.05% of the Bible's verses unrevised.**

12. *The Book of Mormon* (Palmyra, New York: Printed by E. B. Grandin for the Author, 1830), 1 Nephi 13:29.

13. Keith Elliott and Ian Moir, *Manuscripts and the Text of the New Testament: An Introduction for English Readers* (London: Continuum International Publishing Group, Imprint: T & T Clark., 2000), p. 9.

**Note: Some say the biblical autographs (the original manuscripts) written by the apostles and prophets ended up in thousands of fragmented documents and either disappeared or dissolved into dust.**

14. D. W. Outlaw, *God: Trail of Evidence: His Name is Jesus: The Quest for the Truth* (Bloomington, Indiana: iUniverse Publishing, July 11, 2011), p. 152.

15. "Epistle 337" in *Collected Works of Erasmus*, translated by R. A. B. Mynors and D. F. S. Thomson; annotated by Wallace K. Ferguson, 89 volumes (Toronto: University of Toronto Press, 1976), vol. 3, p. 134.

16. Joseph Smith Jr., *History of the Church of Jesus Christ of Latter-day Saints*, edited by B. H. Roberts, 7 volumes (Salt Lake City: The Church of Jesus Christ of Latter-day Saints and *Deseret News*, Revised Second Edition 1948), vol. 6, p. 57.

17. Ibid.

18. Ibid., vol. 1, p. 245.

19. **Note: In fairness, probably many priests, monks, and scholars who transcribed early Bible manuscripts had pure intent, so honest mistakes were made along the way. But the worst damage came from those who sabotaged accurate renderings by intentionally inserting their own religious dogmas into the manuscripts when transcribing—including deletions—which apparently were more than a few.**

20. M. M. Parvis, *Interpreter's Dictionary of the Bible*, 5 volumes (Nashville: Abingdon Press, 2009), vol. 4, pp. 594–595.

21. **Note: Appendix P: "Who Compiled the Bible," lists three prominent cities in North Africa in which the Bible canon was determined— Alexandria (Egypt), Hippo Regius (Algeria), and Carthage (Tunisia).**

22. Alexander Campbell, editor, *The Sacred Writings of the Apostles and Evangelists of Jesus Christ, Commonly Styled The New Testament, Translated from the Original Greek, by George Campbell, James MacKnight, and Phillip Doddridge, Doctors of the Church of Scotland. With Prefaces to the Historical and Epistolary Books; and an Appendix, Containing Critical Notes and Various Translations of Difficult Passages* (Buffaloe, Virginia [now Bethany, West Virginia]: published by Alexander Campbell, 4 editions: 1826, 1828, 1832, 1835).

23. Noah Webster, editor, *The Holy Bible, Containing the Old and New Testaments, in the Common Version. With amendments of the Language* (New Haven, Connecticut: Durrie and Peck, 1833).

24. John G. Palfrey, *The New Testament in the Common Version, Conformed to Griesbach's Standard Greek Text* (Boston: *Boston Daily Advertiser*, 1828).

    **Note: This translation of the New Testament by John G. Palfrey reveals his Unitarian doctrinal concepts.**

25. Thomas Belsham, et al., *The New Testament, in an Improved Version, upon the Basis of Archbishop Newcome's New Translation: with a Corrected Text, and Notes Critical and Explanatory* (London: Richard Taylor & Co., 1808; American Edition published at Boston: William Wells, 1809; and Fourth London Edition with corrections and additions published at London: Richard and Arthur Taylor, 1817).

    **Note: This translation of the New Testament by Thomas Belcham was published to promote his Unitarian beliefs.**

26. Abner Kneeland, *The New Testament: Being the English only of the Greek and English Testament* (Philadelphia: William Fry, First Edition 1823).

    **Note: This translation of the New Testament by Abner Kneeland reveals Kneeland's Unitarian doctrinal concepts.**

27. David Bernard, *The Holy Bible; Being the English Version of the Old and New Testaments, Made by Order of King James I. Carefully Revised and Amended, the meaning of the sacred original being given, in accordance with the best translations and most approved Hebrew and Greek lexicographers: By Several Biblical Scholars* (Philadelphia: J. B. Lippincott, 1842).

    **Note: David Bernard's translation of the Bible was influenced by his Baptist beliefs.**

28. **Note: These figures for the number of English Bible translations—22 during Joseph's lifetime, 75 during the entire 19th century, and 322 total—are synthesized from various reports I've studied. As a start, I recommend Laurence M. Vance, *A Brief History of English Bible Translations*. [Auburn, Alabama: Vance Publications, 1993.] Vance has compiled a remarkable list of English translations of the Bible, amounting to 290 between 1611 and 1993. He did miss about a dozen, however, since 1993, when another 20 or so translations have cropped up, bringing the total count to about (or probably just over) 322, which includes New Testaments only, Old Testaments only, and combinations of both.**

29. Kent P. Jackson, "The King James Bible in the Days of Joseph Smith," in *The King James Bible and the Restoration*, edited by Kent P. Jackson (Provo, Utah: Religious Studies Center, Brigham Young University, 2011), pp. 138–161.

30. Ibid.

31. Note: This bishop who persecuted John Lathrop, English reformer and ancestor to Joseph Smith, was William Laud, Archbishop of Canterbury. He was eventually imprisoned and beheaded for his abuse and torture of reformers. In 1637 he had Henry Burton, William Prynne, and John Bastwick branded on their cheeks with an *SE* ("Seditious Libeller"), and he also cut off their ears. Laud ruled with an iron fist during King Charles I's reign, which, among other factors, helped to spark Oliver Cromwell and others to lead the English Revolution. (Cromwell's exploits fighting the king are covered in Appendix R, "Launching the Reformation: Prelude to the Restoration," Part 4, 2nd half.) Inexplicably, Laud is remembered each January 10 with a commemoration from both the Church of England and the Episcopal Church of the United States, and is buried at St. John's College, Oxford, England (though many of his victims' descendants would likely prefer his remains to be ceremoniously tossed into a volcanic pit).

32. Kent P. Jackson, "The King James Bible in the Days of Joseph Smith," in *The King James Bible and the Restoration*, edited by Kent P. Jackson (Provo, Utah: Religious Studies Center, Brigham Young University, 2011), pp. 138–161.

33. Note: Under Queen "Bloody" Mary I's short reign of 1555–1558, in which she tried to return control of the Church of England to Rome, Reformation leaders all across Europe were hunted down and executed or imprisoned by both Roman and Anglican Church leaders. In fact, not just Reformation leaders, but hundreds of rank-and-file Protestants were burned at the stake.

34. Charles Dickens, *A Tale of Two Cities* (New York City: Barnes and Noble Classics, 2004), p. 1.

35. Wilford Woodruff, Journal, vol. 7, pp. 367–369, Church Archives, the Church of Jesus Christ of Latter-day Saints, Salt Lake City.

Wilford Woodruff, *Wilford Woodruff's Journal: 1833–1898 Typescript*, edited by Scott Kenny, 9 volumes (Salt Lake City: Signature Books, 1984).

Vicki Jo Anderson, *The Other Eminent Men of Wilford Woodruff* (Cottonwood, Arizona: Zichron, 1994).

Note 1: Wilford Woodruff served as an apostle from 1839 to 1889 and as President of the Church of Jesus Christ of Latter-day Saints from 1889 to 1898. While serving as an apostle he was the first president of the St. George, Utah, Temple from 1877 to 1884. In 1898 he gave details of an experience there years earlier:

"Every one of those men that signed the Declaration of Independence, with General Washington, called upon me, as an Apostle of the Lord Jesus Christ, in the Temple at St. George, two consecutive nights, and demanded at my hands that I should go forth and attend to the ordinances of the House of God for them. . . . I told these brethren [his staff at the temple] that it was their duty to go into the Temple and labor until they had got endowments for all of them. They did it. Would those spirits have called upon me, as an Elder in Israel to perform that work if they had not been noble spirits before God? They would not." [Wilford Woodruff, *Conference Report* (Salt Lake City: The Church of Jesus Christ of Latter-day Saints, 1898), pp. 89–90.]

In 1877 Woodruff declared, "I will here say that two weeks before I left St. George, the spirits of the dead gathered around me, wanting to know why we did not redeem them. Said they, 'You have had the use of the Endowment House for a number of years, and yet nothing has ever been done for us. We laid the foundation of the government you now enjoy and we never apostatized from it, but we remained true to it and were faithful to God. These were the signers of the Declaration of Independence, and they waited on me for two days and two nights. I thought it very singular, that notwithstanding so much work had been done, and yet nothing had been done for them. The thought never entered my heart, from the fact, I suppose, that heretofore our minds were reaching after our more immediate friends and relatives. I straightway went into the baptismal font and called upon Brother McAllister [his first assistant at the temple] to baptize me for the signers of the Declaration of Independence, and fifty other eminent men, making one hundred in all, including John Wesley, Columbus, and others. I then was baptized for every president of the United States except three; and when their cause is just, somebody will do the work for them." [*Journal of Discourses*, edited by George D. Watt, et al., 26 volumes (Liverpool, England: Franklin D. Richards and Sons, 1854–1886), vol. 19, p. 229 (September 16, 1877).]

Note that Woodruff ironically used the term "when their cause is just," turning that phrase on its head, since it was the same phrase that had been used against the Saints by 1 of these 3 presidents—Martin van Buren. When living, van Buren had learned from Joseph Smith at the White House about their numerous persecutions and murders in Missouri (as detailed in Volume 2). At that time Joseph requested justice and compensation for their hundreds of stolen farms. Van Buren replied by saying their "cause was just," but he could do nothing for him, because if he did, in the elections he would lose the whole state of Missouri.

Wilford Woodruff's journal adds that he baptized J. D. T. McAllister for 21 departed spirits, including George Washington and his forefathers, plus all the presidents of the U.S. except three—Buchanan, Van Buren, and Grant. At the temple that day, Lucy Bigelow Young was baptized for Martha Washington and her family, and 70 eminent women of the world. Woodruff records, "There were baptized in all today 682." [Wilford Woodruff Journal, Church Archives, The Church of Jesus Christ of Latter-day Saints, Salt Lake City, vol. 7, pp. 367–369.]

Years later, on the night of March 19, 1894, Woodruff had a dream in which Benjamin Franklin appeared to him. Woodruff writes, "I spent some time with him and we talked over our Temple ordinances which had been administered for Franklin and others. He wanted more work done for him than had already been done. I promised him it should be done. I awoke and then made up my mind to receive further blessings for Benjamin Franklin and George Washington." [Wilford Woodruff, *Wilford Woodruff's Journal: 1833–1898 Typescript*, edited by Scott Kenny, 9 volumes (Salt Lake City: Signature Books, 1984);

Wilford Woodruff, quoted in Matthias E. Cowley, *Wilford Woodruff: History of His Life and Labors* (Salt Lake City: Bookcraft, 1975), pp. 585–589.]

The "further blessings" for those two men were likely those described by Ezra Taft Benson, who would write that both men, along with John Wesley and Christopher Columbus, were ordained high priests. [Ezra Taft Benson, *Teachings of Ezra Taft Benson* (Salt Lake City: Bookcraft, 1988), pp. 603–604.]

While Columbus has his critics, Ezra Taft Benson puts his mistakes into perspective: "Notwithstanding the mistakes he made in his life and the human faults he had, Christopher Columbus was a man of notable spiritual sensitivity. Given the powers of repentance and forgiveness. It should come as no surprise that President Wilford Woodruff vicariously had his endowments done and ordained him a High Priest three days after he was baptized for him." [Ezra Taft Benson, quoted in Arnold K. Garr, *Christopher Columbus: A Latter-day Saint Perspective* (Provo, Utah: Religious Studies Center Specialized Monograph Series, Volume 8, 1992).]

Brigham Young's clerk, James G. Bleak, adds, "I was also present in the St. George Temple and witnessed the appearance of the Spirits of the Signers. . . . the spirits of the Presidents . . . And also others, such as Martin Luther and John Wesley . . . who came to Wilford Woodruff and demanded that their baptism and endowments be done. Wilford

Woodruff was baptized for all of them. While I and Brothers J. D. T. McAllister and David H. Cannon (who were witnesses to the request) were endowed for them. These men . . . laid the foundation of this American Gov., and signed the Declaration of Independence and were the best spirits the God of Heaven could find on the face of the earth to perform this work. Martin Luther and John Wesley helped to release the people from religious bondage that held them during the dark ages. They also prepared the people's hearts so they would be ready to receive the restored gospel when the Lord sent it again to men on the earth." [James Gordon Bleak, Personal journal of James Godson Bleak, The James Godson Bleak Papers, 1864–1895, A Register of the Collection at the Utah State Historical Society, 4 boxes, Salt Lake City.]

An unheralded star among early Latter-day Saint pioneers was James Godson Bleak. He was born in England and converted at age 21 with his wife. They emigrated to America and were 2 of the survivors of the Martin Handcart Company (135 of the 575 perished en route). His second wife actually attended one of the Lincoln-Douglas debates and personally spoke with Abraham Lincoln about it afterward at a banquet. In 1861, from north Ogden, he was called by Brigham Young to help settle the St. George area. There, he helped build the temple. At age 43, as a married man with two wives, he was called to England on a mission and edited *The Latter-day Saints' Millennial Star.* Upon returning, he helped finish building the temple at St. George and became the Temple Historian there. This gave him access to the records and personal experiences involving the eminent spirits of which Wilford Woodruff writes.

As for the 56 signers of the Declaration of Independence, all had their work done for them except 2—John Hancock and William Floyd—who apparently were not ready at the time. Thus, 54 had their temple work performed for them.

Of the 18 presidents of the U.S. who had served until that time, 15 had their temple work done for them, excepting the above 3 listed— Buchanan, Van Buren, and Grant, the 3 who, during their terms of office as president of the United States, had demonstrated hostility toward the Saints or callous indifference to their plight.

Worthy of note, many *baptisms* by proxy for the dead for the nation's founders and signers had been performed earlier in Nauvoo, Illinois, and later at the Endowment House in Salt Lake City. But their *endowments* were done in the St. George Temple. [Brian H. Stuy, "Wilford Woodruff's Vision of the Signers of the Declaration of

Independence," in Stephen C. Taysom, *Dimensions of Faith: A Mormon Studies Reader* (Salt Lake City: Signature Books, 2011), pp. 83–111.]

**Note 2: One little-known fact is that on November 18, 1861, Abraham Lincoln checked out the *Book of Mormon* from the Library of Congress for 8 months, returning it on July 29, 1862.** [Ledgers, Library of Congress, Washington, D.C., November 18, 1861, and July 29, 1862.)

36. **Note: For the Joseph Smith Translation of the Bible, there is one unusually long "translated" section—the first 5 chapters of the book of Genesis plus part of Chapter 6, comprising 356 verses that Joseph Smith wrote by revelation, calling it the book of Moses, the longest revised section of his "translation" of the Bible.**

37. Kent P. Jackson, "Joseph Smith's Cooperstown Bible: The Historical Context of the Bible Used in the Joseph Smith Translation," *BYU Studies* (Provo, Utah), vol. 40, no. 1 (2001), pp. 41–70.

38. **Note: The 4 pages that Joseph Smith wrote were Old Manuscript 2, pages 81–83 and 86. The 7 pages he fixed were: Old Manuscript 1, page 7; New Testament Manuscript 2, folio 2, page 9; and folio 4, pages 109–110, 114, 146–147.** [Kent P. Jackson, "New Discoveries in the Joseph Smith Translation of the Bible," in *By Study and by Faith: Selections from the Religious Educator*, edited by Richard Neitzel Holzapfel and Kent P. Jackson (Provo, Utah: Religious Studies Center, Brigham Young University, 2009), pp. 169–181.]

39. **Note: The scribes who assisted Joseph Smith in writing his dictations when he revised passages of the Bible were: first, Oliver Cowdery, then John Whitmer, Emma Smith, Sidney Rigdon, and finally Frederick G. Williams, along with, at some point, Jesse Gause, the mysterious soul who had been invited into the First Presidency and, after a few months, apparently left the church and disappeared, perhaps even unannounced.**

40. Joseph Smith, Sidney Rigdon, and Frederick Williams, Letter (to the Brethren in Zion, July 2, 1833), Joseph Smith Collection, Church History Library, Salt Lake City.

Joseph Smith Jr., *History of the Church of Jesus Christ of Latter-day Saints*, edited by B. H. Roberts, 7 volumes (Salt Lake City: The Church of Jesus Christ of Latter-day Saints and *Deseret News*, Revised Second Edition 1948), vol. 1, p. 368.

Joseph Smith, *The Joseph Smith Papers*, edited by Dean C. Jessee, Ronald K. Esplin, and Richard Lyman Bushman (Salt Lake City: The Church Historian's Press, 2008–), multiple-volume series.

41. Ibid., Joseph Smith, *History of the Church of Jesus Christ of Latter-day Saints.*

    Ibid., Joseph Smith, *The Joseph Smith Papers.*

42. Thomas E. Sherry and W. Jeffrey Marsh, "Precious Truths Restored: Joseph Smith Translation Changes Not Included in Our Bible," *The Religious Educator* (Provo, Utah), vol. 5 (2004), no. 2. pp. 57–74.

    **Note: In 1974 when this article was published, Thomas E. Sherry was the Institute Director at Corvallis, Oregon, and W. Jeffrey Marsh was Associate Professor of Ancient Scripture at Brigham Young University.**

    **In the article cited above, they state in note 23, p. 74: "For other reasons why the Prophet may not have made all possible revisions, see Robert L. Millet, 'Joseph Smith's Translation of the Bible: A Historical Overview,' in *The Joseph Smith Translation*, pp. 33–35." The full name of the book (and publishing details) to which they refer is: *The Joseph Smith Translation: The Restoration of Plain and Precious Truths*, edited by Monte S. Nyman and Robert L. Millet (Provo, Utah: Religious Studies Center, Brigham Young University: 1985), pp. 33–35.**

43. Kent P. Jackson, "Joseph Smith's Cooperstown Bible: The Historical Context of the Bible Used in the Joseph Smith Translation," *BYU Studies* (Provo, Utah), vol. 40, no. 1 (2001), pp. 41–70.

44. *The Doctrine and Covenants of the Church of Jesus Christ of Latter-day Saints: Containing Revelations given to Joseph Smith, the Prophet, with Some Additions by His Successors in the Presidency of the Church* (Salt Lake City: The Church of Jesus Christ of Latter-day Saints, 1981), 42:56–58.

45. Robert J. Matthews, *A Bible! A Bible!* (Salt Lake City: Bookcraft, 1990), pp. 133–143.

46. Robert J. Matthews, "Joseph Smith Translation (JST) of the Bible," in Daniel H. Ludlow, editor, *Encyclopedia of Mormonism*, 4 volumes (New York City: Macmillan Publishing Company, 1992) vol. 1.

47. "Bible Dictionary," in Appendix, The Holy Bible, Containing the Old and New Testaments, Translated out of the Original Tongues: And with the Former Translations Diligently Compared and Revised, By His Majesty's Special Command: Authorized King James Version with Explanatory Notes and Cross References to the Standard Works of the Church of Jesus Christ of Latter-day Saints (Salt Lake City: The Church of Jesus Christ of Latter-day Saints, 1979), Appendix, pp. 725–726.

48. **Note: Latter-day Saint Apostle Dallin H. Oaks states, "Scores of JST excerpts too lengthy for inclusion in footnotes are included in their entire text following the Bible Dictionary." These lengthy excerpts**

constitute the JST appendix. [Dallin H. Oaks, "Scripture Reading, Revelation, and the JST," in *Plain and Precious Truths Restored: The Doctrinal and Historical Significance of the Joseph Smith Translation*, edited by Robert L. Millet and Robert J. Matthews (Salt Lake City: Bookcraft, 1995), p. 11.]

49. Note: The Church of Jesus Christ of Latter-day Saints uses just over ⅓ of Joseph Smith's revised verses. They consist of the 411 verses placed in the *Pearl of Great Price* in 1851 plus the 800 or so added to the King James Bible as footnotes plus appendix in 1979. The approximately 1200 verses combined are among the most important revised Bible verses, and so far, to Latter-day Saints, they are the only canonized revised verses of the 3,410 he revised.

50. Note: This short book of LDS scripture, the *Pearl of Great Price*, comprises 5 sections. Two of these sections are from the 411 revised verses noted above: (1) The Book of Moses—derived from Genesis Chapters 1–5 and 6:1–13 of the King James Version of the Bible, and (2) Joseph Smith–Matthew—derived from and expanded upon the original text of the KJV found in Matthew 23:39 and Chapter 24. The *Pearl of Great Price* was first organized and published as a pamphlet by Franklin D. Richards in Liverpool, England in 1851. It contained today's Joseph Smith–Matthew and parts of The Book of Moses. In 1878 more of The Book of Moses was added, then both books were canonized 2 years later, in 1880. The Book of Moses consists of 356 verses while Joseph Smith–Matthew consists of 55 verses, bringing the total to 411 verses.

51. Thomas E. Sherry and W. Jeffrey Marsh, "Precious Truths Restored: Joseph Smith Translation Changes Not Included in Our Bible," *The Religious Educator* (Provo, Utah), vol. 5 (2004), no. 2.

    Note: *The Religious Educator* is an academic journal about Latter-day Saint history and scriptures. Published since 2000 in Provo, Utah, at the Religious Studies Center, it focuses on inspirational and informative articles. Some are about research, others are for gospel teachers. It is published three times per year with dynamic photography instituted into its graphic art covers.

52. First Presidency Statement on the King James Version of the Bible, "News of the Church," *Ensign* (Salt Lake City), August 1992, p. 80.

53. Joseph Smith, quoted in Joseph Fielding Smith, compiler, *Teachings of the Prophet Joseph Smith* (Salt Lake City: Deseret Book Company, First Edition 1938), p. 349.

54. Emma Smith Bidamon, Letter (to Joseph Smith III, December 2, 1867), Emma Smith Papers, Community of Christ Archives, Independence, Missouri.

55. **Note: According to historian Robert J. Matthews, "In 1944 a 'New Corrected Edition' [of Joseph Smith's Translation] was published by the RLDS Church in which at least 352 verses were amended to correct typographical and judgment errors in the 1867 Edition."** [Robert J. Matthews, "Joseph Smith Translation (JST) of the Bible," in *Encyclopedia of Mormonism*, edited by Daniel H. Ludlow (New York City: Macmillan Publishing, 1992).]

   **The second-largest group having its roots with Joseph Smith—the Missouri-based Community of Christ (formerly Reorganized Church of Jesus Christ of Latter Day Saints [RLDS])—placed all 3,410 changed verses into its regular text of the Bible, so its text is somewhat of a departure from the King James Version; whereas the LDS Church has kept the King James Version without changes to the text, placing the "more important" corrected-by-Joseph verses in footnotes and an appendix.**

56. Robert J. Matthews, "A Plainer Translation," *Joseph Smith's Translation of the Bible—A History and Commentary* (Provo, Utah: Brigham Young University Press, 1975); cited in Kent P. Jackson, "New Discoveries in the Joseph Smith Translation of the Bible," in *By Study and by Faith: Selections from the Religious Educator*, edited by Richard Neitzel Holzapfel and Kent P. Jackson (Provo, Utah: Religious Studies Center, Brigham Young University, 2009).

57. Kent P. Jackson, "Joseph Smith's Cooperstown Bible: The Historical Context of the Bible Used in the Joseph Smith Translation," *BYU Studies* (Provo, Utah), vol. 40, no. 1 (2001), pp. 41–70.

58. "New Discoveries in the Joseph Smith Translation of the Bible," in *By Study and by Faith: Selections from the Religious Educator*, edited by Richard Neitzel Holzapfel and Kent P. Jackson (Provo, Utah: Religious Studies Center, Brigham Young University, 2009), pp. 169–181.

   Scott H. Faulring, Kent P. Jackson, and Robert J. Matthews, editors, *Joseph Smith's New Translation of the Bible: Original Manuscripts* (Provo, Utah: Religious Studies Center, Brigham Young University, 2004).

59. John L. Jeffcoat III, "English Bible History Article & Timeline," 2012, WWW. GREATSITE.COM.

60. *The Doctrine and Covenants of the Church of Jesus Christ of Latter-day Saints: Containing Revelations given to Joseph Smith, the Prophet, with*

*Some Additions by His Successors in the Presidency of the Church* (Salt Lake City: The Church of Jesus Christ of Latter-day Saints, 1981), 91:1–2.

**Note: Regarding the Apocrypha, the remainder of this revelation to Joseph Smith reads: "Verily, I say unto you, that it is not needful that the Apocrypha should be translated. Therefore, whoso readeth it, let him understand, for the Spirit manifesteth truth; And whoso is enlightened by the Spirit shall obtain benefit therefrom; And whoso receiveth not by the Spirit, cannot be benefited. Therefore it is not needful that it should be translated. Amen." This revelation was given to Joseph Smith at Kirtland, Ohio, on March 9, 1833, when Joseph came to the Apocrypha section of his Bible and reportedly prayed about it, as recorded in D&C 91:3–6.**

61. Lucy Mack Smith, *History of Joseph Smith by His Mother: The Unabridged Original Version* (Arlington, Virginia and Provo, Utah: Stratford Books, Revised Second Edition 2006), pp. 252–253.

62. Ibid., pp. 253–254.

63. Ibid., pp. 254–255.

64. *The Doctrine and Covenants of the Church of Jesus Christ of Latter-day Saints: Containing Revelations given to Joseph Smith, the Prophet, with Some Additions by His Successors in the Presidency of the Church* (Salt Lake City: The Church of Jesus Christ of Latter-day Saints, 1981), 25:4.

65. Ibid., 25:5.

66. Ibid., 25:6.

67. Ibid., 25:7.

68. Ibid., 25:11.

    *A Book of Commandments for the Government of the Church of Christ, Organized According to Law, on the 6th of April, 1830* (Zion [Independence, Missouri]: W. W. Phelps & Co., 1833; reprinted at Independence, Missouri: Board of Publications, Church of Christ Temple Lot, 1960), 26:11.

69. *The Doctrine and Covenants of the Church of Jesus Christ of Latter-day Saints: Containing Revelations given to Joseph Smith, the Prophet, with Some Additions by His Successors in the Presidency of the Church* (Salt Lake City: The Church of Jesus Christ of Latter-day Saints, 1981), 25:8.

70. Ibid., 25:10.

71. Ibid., 25:3.

72. Ibid., 25:13.

73. Ibid., 25:14.

74. "Newel Knight Journal," *Scraps of Biography: Tenth Book of the Faith Promoting Series* (Salt Lake City: Juvenile Instructor Office, 1883), pp. 47–65.

75. Ibid.

76. "The Missionaries of the Church of Jesus Christ of Latter-day Saints, Set Apart Since 1830," microfilm, Church Archives, The Church of Jesus Christ of Latter-day Saints, Salt Lake City.

## CHAPTER 27

1. *Lucy Mack Smith, Biographical Sketches of Joseph Smith the Prophet and His Progenitors for Many Generations* (Liverpool, England: S. W. Richards, 1853), p. 155.

2. Lucy Mack Smith, *History of Joseph Smith by His Mother: The Unabridged Original Version* (Arlington, Virginia and Provo, Utah: Stratford Books, Revised Second Edition 2006), p. 258.

3. Ibid., pp. 258–259.

4. Ibid., pp. 259–261.

   **Note: This report of Joseph Smith senior's brother, John Smith, is included in Lucy Mack Smith's history of her son Joseph.**

5. Lucy Mack Smith, *Biographical Sketches of Joseph Smith the Prophet and His Progenitors for Many Generations* (Liverpool, England: S. W. Richards, 1853), pp. 155–156.

6. Joseph Smith Jr., *History of the Church of Jesus Christ of Latter-day Saints*, edited by B. H. Roberts, 7 volumes (Salt Lake City: The Church of Jesus Christ of Latter-day Saints and *Deseret News*, Revised Second Edition 1948), vol. 2, pp. 441–442.

7. "Joseph Smith Jr., Letter Books, 1829–1835," manuscript, Church Archives, The Church of Jesus Christ of Latter-day Saints, Salt Lake City.

8. Joseph Smith Jr., *History of the Church of Jesus Christ of Latter-day Saints*, edited by B. H. Roberts, 7 volumes (Salt Lake City: The Church of Jesus Christ of Latter-day Saints and *Deseret News*, Revised Second Edition 1948), vol. 1, pp. 108–109.

9. Ibid.

10. Ibid., p. 109.

11. Ibid.

12. *The Doctrine and Covenants of the Church of Jesus Christ of Latter-day Saints: Containing Revelations given to Joseph Smith, the Prophet, with Some Additions by His Successors in the Presidency of the Church* (Salt Lake City: The Church of Jesus Christ of Latter-day Saints, 1981), 24:3.

13. Joseph Smith Jr., *History of the Church of Jesus Christ of Latter-day Saints*, edited by B. H. Roberts, 7 volumes (Salt Lake City: The Church of Jesus Christ of Latter-day Saints and *Deseret News*, Revised Second Edition 1948), vol. 1, p. 108.

14. Donna Hill, *Joseph Smith: The First Mormon* (Garden City, New York: Doubleday, 1977), p. 115.

15. Ibid.

16. **Note: Joseph and Emma Smith actually stayed at Harmony, Pennsylvania, the entire 2⅔-year period they called it their residence, except for travels to New York on church business. The longest period away from Harmony was from about June 1, 1829, through much of the summer and early fall of that year. The month of June itself was spent at the Whitmers' home in order to finish translating the *Book of Mormon* with less temporal obstacles.**

17. Contract between Joseph Smith and Isaac Hale, in *Early Mormon Documents*, edited by Dan Vogel, 5 volumes (Salt Lake City: Signature Books, 1996–2003), vol 4, pp. 427–435.

# CHAPTER 28

1. **Note: Joseph Smith's revelation that caused his first controversy with Oliver Cowdery had to do with the subject of baptism. Specifically, what irked Oliver was the wording that described the qualification necessary for baptism—that candidates must "truly manifest by their works that they have received of the Spirit of Christ unto a remission of their sins."** [Joseph Smith, History [1838] Church Archives, The Church of Jesus Christ of Latter-day Saints, Salt Lake City;

also found in Joseph Smith, *The Papers of Joseph Smith*, edited by Dean C. Jessee, 2 volumes (Salt Lake City: Deseret Book, 1989–1992), vol. 1, pp. 259–260;

also found in Joseph Smith, *The Joseph Smith Papers*, edited by Dean
C. Jessee, Ronald K. Esplin, and Richard Lyman Bushman (Salt Lake
City: The Church Historian's Press, 2008–), multiple-volume series.]
**Oliver thought this passage gave priesthood leaders too much power
to determine if a candidate for baptism had "truly manifest by their
works" if they were ready or not.** [Ibid.]

2.  Ibid., all 3 sources but with different page numbers than the above
    citations, including Joseph Smith, *The Papers of Joseph Smith*, vol. 1,
    p. 260.

3.  Ibid., all 3 sources but with different page numbers than the above
    citations, including Joseph Smith, *The Papers of Joseph Smith*, vol. 1,
    pp. 261–262.

4.  Joseph Smith Jr., *History of the Church of Jesus Christ of Latter-day Saints*,
    edited by B. H. Roberts, 7 volumes (Salt Lake City: The Church of Jesus
    Christ of Latter-day Saints and *Deseret News*, Revised Second Edition
    1948), vol. 1, p. 109.

5.  Ibid.

6.  **Note: Oliver Cowdery and Elizabeth Ann Whitmer would marry
    December 18, 1832. She was born January 22, 1815, making her
    16 years and 11 months old when they married. Oliver was born
    October 3, 1806, making him 26 years and 2 months old—about 9
    years difference, which was not an extraordinary age difference for
    the day.**

7.  Joseph Smith, History [1838] Church Archives, The Church of Jesus
    Christ of Latter-day Saints, Salt Lake City.

    Also found in Joseph Smith, *The Papers of Joseph Smith*, edited by Dean
    C. Jessee, 2 volumes (Salt Lake City: Deseret Book, 1989–1992), vol. 1,
    p. 260.

    Also found in Joseph Smith, *The Joseph Smith Papers*, edited by Dean C.
    Jessee, Ronald K. Esplin, and Richard Lyman Bushman (Salt Lake City:
    The Church Historian's Press, 2008–), multiple-volume series.

8.  Ibid., all 3 sources but with different page numbers than the above
    citations, including Joseph Smith, *The Papers of Joseph Smith*, vol. 1,
    p. 370.

9.  Ibid.

    **Note: With regards to the Whitmers and Oliver Cowdery wanting
    to change the wording of Joseph's revelation about a candidate's
    qualifications for baptism, all of them were eventually swayed to**

Joseph's viewpoint, says Joseph, which means Oliver must have been convinced by Joseph as well, since he was part of the group.

10. **Note: Joseph placed the problem of Oliver and the Whitmer clan's rebelling on pride. He writes, "From the experience, they were all to learn the necessity of humility and meekness before the Lord, that he might teach us of his ways." Another part of the problem, he says, was "presumption and rash judgment."** [Joseph Smith, History [1838] Church Archives, The Church of Jesus Christ of Latter-day Saints, Salt Lake City;

   also found in Joseph Smith, *The Papers of Joseph Smith*, edited by Dean C. Jessee, 2 volumes (Salt Lake City: Deseret Book, 1989–1992), vol. 1, p. 260;

   also found in Joseph Smith, *The Joseph Smith Papers*, edited by Dean C. Jessee, Ronald K. Esplin, and Richard Lyman Bushman (Salt Lake City: The Church Historian's Press, 2008–), multiple-volume series.]

11. **Note: No time elements are given as to when Hiram Page was receiving revelations from a stone and convincing church members of their "veracity," but Joseph Smith learned of this problem sometime between his arriving at Fayette in late August 1830 and before the September 26, 1830, general conference.**

12. "Newel Knight Journal," *Scraps of Biography: Tenth Book of the Faith Promoting Series* (Salt Lake City: Juvenile Instructor Office, 1883), pp. 64–65.

13. Ibid., pp. 47–65.

14. Ibid. pp. 64–65.

15. *The Doctrine and Covenants of the Church of Jesus Christ of Latter-day Saints: Containing Revelations given to Joseph Smith, the Prophet, with Some Additions by His Successors in the Presidency of the Church* (Salt Lake City: The Church of Jesus Christ of Latter-day Saints, 1981), 28:2.

   Journal History, September 26, 1830, Church Archives, The Church of Jesus Christ of Latter-day Saints, Salt Lake City.

16. *The Doctrine and Covenants of the Church of Jesus Christ of Latter-day Saints: Containing Revelations given to Joseph Smith, the Prophet, with Some Additions by His Successors in the Presidency of the Church* (Salt Lake City: The Church of Jesus Christ of Latter-day Saints, 1981), 28:11.

17. Journal History, September 26, 1830, Church Archives, The Church of Jesus Christ of Latter-day Saints, Salt Lake City.

18. *The Doctrine and Covenants of the Church of Jesus Christ of Latter-day Saints: Containing Revelations given to Joseph Smith, the Prophet, with Some Additions by His Successors in the Presidency of the Church* (Salt Lake City: The Church of Jesus Christ of Latter-day Saints, 1981), 28:1–2.

19. Ibid., 28:3.

20. Ibid., 28:6.

21. Ibid., 28:13.

22. David Whitmer, *An Address to All Believers in Christ* (Richmond, Missouri: published by the author, 1887), pp. 31–58.

23. Ibid.

# CHAPTER 29

1. Joseph Smith, Manuscript History of the Church, Book A-1, Historian's Office, Church Archives, The Church of Jesus Christ of Latter-day Saints, Salt Lake City.

   Also found in Joseph Smith, *The Papers of Joseph Smith*, edited by Dean C. Jessee, 2 volumes (Salt Lake City: Deseret Book, 1989–1992), vol. 1, p. 323.

   Also found in Joseph Smith, *The Joseph Smith Papers*, edited by Dean C. Jessee, Ronald K. Esplin, and Richard Lyman Bushman (Salt Lake City: The Church Historian's Press, 2008–), multiple-volume series.

2. "Newel Knight Journal," *Scraps of Biography: Tenth Book of the Faith Promoting Series* (Salt Lake City: Juvenile Instructor Office, 1883), pp. 64–65.

3. Ibid., pp. 47–65.

4. *The Doctrine and Covenants of the Church of Jesus Christ of Latter-day Saints: Containing Revelations given to Joseph Smith, the Prophet, with Some Additions by His Successors in the Presidency of the Church* (Salt Lake City: The Church of Jesus Christ of Latter-day Saints, 1981), 29:7-8.

5. **Note: Lucy writes that Joseph and Emma went directly from Harmony to Manchester.** [Lucy Mack Smith, *History of Joseph Smith by His Mother: The Unabridged Original Version* (Arlington, Virginia and Provo, Utah: Stratford Books, Revised Second Edition 2006), p. 264.] **But Joseph's history states he went straight to Fayette,** [Joseph Smith Jr., *History of the Church of Jesus Christ of Latter-day Saints*, edited by B. H. Roberts,

7 volumes (Salt Lake City: The Church of Jesus Christ of Latter-day Saints and *Deseret News*, Revised Second Edition 1948), vol. 1, p. 109] **apparently to deal with the rebellion.**

6.  Lucy Mack Smith, *History of Joseph Smith by His Mother: The Unabridged Original Version* (Arlington, Virginia and Provo, Utah: Stratford Books, Revised Second Edition 2006), p. 264.

7.  Ibid., pp. 264–265.

8.  Ibid., p. 265.

9.  Ibid., pp. 265, 279.

10. Ibid., p. 279.

11. Ibid.

**Note: Lucy says Waterloo but apparently means Fayette, New York, throughout her history.**

12. Ibid., p. 269.


# CHAPTER 30

1.  Lucy Mack Smith, *History of Joseph Smith by His Mother: The Unabridged Original Version* (Arlington, Virginia and Provo, Utah: Stratford Books, Revised Second Edition 2006), p. 269.

2.  Ibid., pp. 269–270.

3.  Ibid., pp. 270–273.

4.  Ibid., pp. 273–274.

5.  Ibid., p. 277.

6.  Ibid., p. 276.

7.  Ibid.

8.  Ibid., p. 276.

    **Note: The portion used comes from Lucy's rough draft.**

9.  Ibid., p. 276, published text.

10. Ibid., p. 276, published text.

11. Ibid., pp. 277–280.

## CHAPTER 31

1. Donna Hill, *Joseph Smith: The First Mormon* (Garden City, New York: Doubleday, 1977), p. 120.

2. Lucy Mack Smith, *History of Joseph Smith by His Mother: The Unabridged Original Version* (Arlington, Virginia and Provo, Utah: Stratford Books, Revised Second Edition 2006), p. 262.

3. Ibid.

4. Ibid.

5. **Note: The following dates are the birthdays of the 4 young men who were called on missions to the Lamanites: Parley P. Pratt, April 12, 1807; Oliver Cowdery, October 3, 1806; Ziba Peterson, ca. 1810; and Peter Whitmer Jr., September 27, 1809.**

6. Ibid., p. 279.

7. Ibid., pp. 279–280.

8. Ibid., p. 279.

9. Parley P. Pratt, *The Autobiography of Parley Parker Pratt: One of the Twelve Apostles of the Church of Jesus Christ of Latter-day Saints, Embracing His Life, Ministry and Travels, with Extracts, in Prose and Verse, from his Miscellaneous Writings, edited by his son, Parley P. Pratt* (New York City: Russell Brothers, 1874), p. 59.

10. Ibid., p. 6.

    **Note: Historian Mark L. Staker quotes E. B. Grandin later saying that it took Grandin 4 days to travel from Palmyra, New York, to Kirtland, Ohio. Lucy, traversing the same routes, took twice as long (8 days), but she was delayed by weather. Her journey is discussed in Chapters 39 and 40.**

11. James Stuart, *Three Years in North America*, (Edinburgh: Robert Cadell and Company, 1833), p. 138; cited in Mark Lyman Staker, *Hearken, O Ye People: The Historical Setting for Joseph Smith's Ohio Revelations* (Salt Lake City: Greg Kofford Books, 2009), p. 50.

12. Parley P. Pratt, *The Autobiography of Parley Parker Pratt: One of the Twelve Apostles of the Church of Jesus Christ of Latter-day Saints, Embracing His Life, Ministry and Travels, with Extracts, in Prose and Verse, from his Miscellaneous Writings, edited by his son, Parley P. Pratt* (New York City: Russell Brothers, 1874), p. 28.

13. James Boardman (attributed to him, but cited for author as "a Citizen of the World"), *America and the Americans* (London: Longman, Rees, Orme, Brown, Green, & Longman, 1833), pp. 157–165.

14. Mark Lyman Staker, *Hearken, O Ye People: The Historical Setting for Joseph Smith's Ohio Revelations* (Salt Lake City: Greg Kofford Books, 2009), p. 51.

15. Oliver Cowdery, Letter (from "Kirtland, Ohio, to Our Beloved Brethren [in Fayette, New York], November 12, 1830"), holograph copy in Newel Knight, "Autobiography," typescript, MS 2737, Box 56, Folder 5, Church Historical Library, The Church of Jesus Christ of Latter-day Saints, Salt Lake City.

16. Parley P. Pratt, *The Autobiography of Parley Parker Pratt: One of the Twelve Apostles of the Church of Jesus Christ of Latter-day Saints, Embracing His Life, Ministry and Travels, with Extracts, in Prose and Verse, from his Miscellaneous Writings, edited by his son, Parley P. Pratt* (New York City: Russell Brothers, 1874), p. 28.

17. Ibid.

18. Mark Lyman Staker, *Hearken O Ye People: The Historical Setting of Joseph Smith's Ohio Revelations* (Draper, Utah: Greg Kofford Books, 2009), p. 51.

19. Oliver Cowdery, Letter (from "Kirtland, Ohio, to Our Beloved Brethren [in Fayette, New York], November 12, 1830"), holograph copy in Newel Knight, "Autobiography," typescript, MS 2737, Box 56, Folder 5, Church Historical Library, The Church of Jesus Christ of Latter-day Saints, Salt Lake City.

# CHAPTER 32

1. Milton V. Backman, *The Heavens Resound: A History of the Latter-day Saints in Ohio, 1830–1838* (Salt Lake City: Deseret Book, 1983), pp. 13–14.

2. David Whitmer, *An Address to All Believers in Christ* (Richmond, Missouri: published by the author, 1887), p. 35.

3. Reuben P. Harmon, "Having Been Duly Sworn, Testifies as Follows," in *Public Discussion of the Issues between the Reorganized Church of Jesus Christ of Latter Day Saints and the Church of Christ (Disciples), Held in Kirtland, Ohio, Beginning February 12, and Closing Mar. 8, 1884, Between E. L. Kelley, Reorganized Church of Jesus Christ of Latter Day Saints, and*

*Clark Braden, of the Church of Christ* . . . , edited by Edmund Levi Kelley
and Clark Braden (St. Louis: Clark Braden, 1884), p. 393.

4.  "We observe in the New Harmony Gazette," *Painesville Telegraph*
    (Painesville, Ohio), vol. 5, no. 7 (August 25, 1826), p. 3.

**Note 1: This article about communal living proposed at Robert Owen's
Independence Day speech was first published in the *New Harmony
Gazette*, a newspaper owned by Robert Owen's followers, before it
was reprinted in the *Painesville Telegraph*.**

**Note 2: The *Painesville Telegraph* was published from 1822 to 1906.
Eber D. Howe, its founder, stayed with the newspaper for 13 years,
until his final issue on January 23, 1835, then sold it to his younger
brother, Asahel Howe, who became its editor, publishing his first
issue February 6, 1835.**

5.  Ibid.

**Note 1: Three-quarters of a year after Robert Owen gave his unusual
Independence Day speech of July 4, 1826, the following occurred in
the spring of 1827—Alexander Campbell made his first public comment
about Robert Owen: "I have felt some degree of sympathy for him,
and of mortification too . . . . [I] am not yet able to form a satisfactory
opinion of the social system as advanced by him."** [Robert Owen and
Alexander Campbell, *Debate on the Evidences of Christianity, Containing
an examination of the Social System, of all the Systems of Skepticism of
Ancient and Modern Times, Held in the City of Cincinnati, Ohio, from the 13th
to the 21st of April, 1829, Between Robert Owen, of New Lanark, Scotland,
and Alexander Campbell, of Bethany, Virginia. Reported by Charles H. Sims,
Stenographer. With an Appendix, written by the Parties. Vol. 1* (Bethany,
Virginia: published by Alexander Campbell, 1829), p. 4; quoted in Mark
Lyman Staker, *Hearken O Ye People: The Historical Setting of Joseph
Smith's Ohio Revelations* (Draper, Utah: Greg Kofford Books, 2009),
p. 40. (Staker quotes a later edition with a different title: *The Evidences
of Christianity: A Debate between Robert Owen, of new Lanark, Scotland,
and Alexander Campbell, President of Bethany College, Va.*)]

**Notwithstanding Owen's comments on religion and marriage, Campbell
at one point was so optimistic for a merger between his philosophy
of communal living and Owen's that he would have actually accepted
Owen's movement had it merely *allowed* religion in it—*even if the
movement were an agnostic one*, according to a paper Campbell
wrote.** [Ibid.]

6.  Ibid., reference to note above, Robert Owen and Alexander Campbell.

7.  Ibid.

8. Mark Lyman Staker, *Hearken O Ye People: The Historical Setting of Joseph Smith's Ohio Revelations* (Draper, Utah: Greg Kofford Books, 2009), p. 40.

**Note: Sidney Rigdon's congregation at the Reuben P. Harmon barn consisted of converts who were possibly influenced by Harmon family members that were part of a communal order named the Kendal Community, established May 1, 1826 (officially as the "Friendly Association for Mutual Interests").** [Documents G-1-22 and G-1-25 In the Rotch-Wales Papers, Massillon Public Library, Massillon, Ohio; cited in Mark Lyman Staker, *Hearken O Ye People: The Historical Setting of Joseph Smith's Ohio Revelations* (Draper, Utah: Greg Kofford Books, 2009), pp. 39, 41 n 10.] **(Additionally, there was another communal order—not associated with the Kendal Community—a mile east of Kirtland at the Isaac Morley farm. Disciples there were meeting under a different minister than Sidney—likely Isaac Morley's brother-in-law. That communal group, which I call the "Morley farm order," was established in February 1830.)**

9. Ibid.

**Note: Alexander Campbell prepared for the debate with Robert Owen for a year, then faced off against him in 1829 at Cincinnati, Ohio. Meanwhile, as historian Mark L. Staker points out, a "brother minister" (probably Sidney Rigdon, whose congregations were the most exposed and vulnerable to Samuel Underhill's recruiting for the Kendal Community communal order) again asked Alexander Campbell to debate Underhill, hoping that Campbell would win the debate, which in turn would give Sidney assistance in keeping his congregations intact and not going off to join the Kendal Community that Underhill led. Despite Sidney's second request, Campbell ignored him again. In my opinion, with Campbell disregarding him, Sidney at this point felt no more allegiance to Campbell, and this action—or inaction—would come back to bite Campbell in the backside when Sidney would later leave Campbell's movement and take his congregations *en masse* with him. (As a side note, several years later, Robert Owen would eventually agree to a debate with Underhill in nearby Cleveland.)** [Richard J. Cherok, "Debating for God: Alexander Campbell's Challenge to Skepticism in Antebellum America," Ph.D. dissertation, Kent State University, 2002.]

10. Fogarty, *American Command*, p. xxiv; cited in Richard Lyman Bushman, Joseph Smith: *Rough Stone Rolling* (New York City: Alfred A. Knopf / Borzoi Books, 2005).

11. Amos Sutton Hayden, *Early History of the Disciples In the Western Reserve, Ohio* (Cincinnati: Chase and Hall, 1875), pp. 298–299.

12. Ibid.

13. Parley P. Pratt, *The Autobiography of Parley Parker Pratt: One of the Twelve Apostles of the Church of Jesus Christ of Latter-day Saints, Embracing His Life, Ministry and Travels, with Extracts, in Prose and Verse, from his Miscellaneous Writings, edited by his son, Parley P. Pratt* (New York City: Russell Brothers, 1874), p. 38.

14. John Wickliffe Rigdon, "'I Never Knew a Time When I Did Not Know Joseph Smith': A Son's Record of the Life and Testimony of Sidney Rigdon," edited by Karl Keller, *Dialogue: A Journal of Mormon Thought* (Salt Lake City), vol. 1, no. 4 (Winter 1966), pp. 15–42, especially pp. 23–24.

    **Note: This encounter of Parley P. Pratt at Sidney Rigdon's home was later told to Sidney's son, John, by John's mother and sister, according to John himself in this cited source.**

15. Ibid.

    **Note: Newspaper writer Matthew Clapp was one of Sidney Rigdon's congregational members. He wrote an article for the *Painesville Telegraph* 4 months after Sidney Rigdon had met the Latter-day Saint missionaries in October 1830.** [M. S. C. (Matthew Clapp), "Mormonism," *Painesville Telegraph* (Painesville, Ohio), vol. 2, no. 35 (February 15, 1831), p. 4.] **According to Clapp, Sidney "partly condemned" but was open to reading and even considering the *Book of Mormon*.**

16. Ibid.

17. Joseph Smith Jr., *History of the Church of Jesus Christ of Latter-day Saints*, edited by B. H. Roberts, 7 volumes, (Salt Lake City: The Church of Jesus Christ of Latter-day Saints and *Deseret News*, Second Revised Edition 1948), vol. 1, p. 124.

18. John Wickliffe Rigdon, "'I Never Knew a Time When I Did Not Know Joseph Smith': A Son's Record of the Life and Testimony of Sidney Rigdon," edited by Karl Keller, *Dialogue: A Journal of Mormon Thought* (Salt Lake City), vol. 1, no. 4 (Winter 1966), pp. 15–42, especially pp. 23–24.

    **Note: Karl Keller wrote this article for *Dialogue* magazine, giving the backdrop to John Wickliffe Rigdon's manuscript about his father, Sidney Rigdon. In so doing, Keller edited the manuscript, which is actually an unpublished lecture that John Wickliffe Rigdon occasionally (or often) presented while living in Friendship, New**

York, where his father Sidney died at age 83 in 1876. In the late 1890s, after rejoining the LDS church, John Wickliffe Rigdon also wrote a more detailed manuscript, entitled "Life Story of Sidney Rigdon," based on the lecture, containing a few incidents not contained in the lecture manuscript, with far more rambling and verbiage, then sold it in September 1900 to the LDS church in Salt Lake City while on a visit there, but the church never published it. Keller reviewed that manuscript and indicates the lecture manuscript reads far better and has the most important information. In short, the lecture manuscript is what constitutes most of the article in *Dialogue* after Keller presents the backdrop to the lecture.

19. Ibid.

20. Parley P. Pratt, *The Autobiography of Parley Parker Pratt: One of the Twelve Apostles of the Church of Jesus Christ of Latter-day Saints, Embracing His Life, Ministry and Travels, with Extracts, in Prose and Verse, from his Miscellaneous Writings, edited by his son, Parley P. Pratt* (New York City: Russell Brothers, 1874), pp. 59–60.

21. M. S. C. (Matthew Clapp), "Mormonism," *Painesville Telegraph* (Painesville, Ohio), vol 2, no. 35 (February 15, 1831), p. 3.

22. Parley P. Pratt, *The Autobiography of Parley Parker Pratt: One of the Twelve Apostles of the Church of Jesus Christ of Latter-day Saints, Embracing His Life, Ministry and Travels, with Extracts, in Prose and Verse, from his Miscellaneous Writings, edited by his son, Parley P. Pratt* (New York City: Russell Brothers, 1874), p. 47.

23. Joseph Smith Jr., *History of the Church of Jesus Christ of Latter-day Saints*, edited by B. H. Roberts, 7 volumes (Salt Lake City: The Church of Jesus Christ of Latter-day Saints and *Deseret News*, Second Revised Edition 1948), vol. 1, p. 124.

24. 1830 Federal Census, Kirtland, Ohio.

Note: This number—of 1,018 Kirtland residents—is based on the 1830 census, with most of the population being young families.

25. *Painesville Telegraph* (Painesville, Ohio), November and December issues, 1830.

26. Lucy Mack Smith, *History of Joseph Smith by His Mother: The Unabridged Original Version* (Arlington, Virginia and Provo, Utah: Stratford Books, Revised Second Edition 2006), p. 280.

Note: Lucy mentions only "twenty to thirty" converts at Kirtland whom the missionaries baptized in their first wave of Ohio conversions, but the number of new members mushroomed shortly afterward,

**especially with additional converts made outside Kirtland.** [Mark Lyman Staker, *Hearken O Ye People: The Historical Setting of Joseph Smith's Ohio Revelations* (Draper, Utah: Greg Kofford Books, 2009), pp. 52–62.]

27. Parley P. Pratt, *The Autobiography of Parley Parker Pratt: One of the Twelve Apostles of the Church of Jesus Christ of Latter-day Saints, Embracing His Life, Ministry and Travels, with Extracts, in Prose and Verse, from his Miscellaneous Writings, edited by his son, Parley P. Pratt* (New York City: Russell Brothers, 1874), p. 47.

28. Court Records of Geauga County, Ohio, 1807–1904, Court of Common Pleas, Marriage of Lewis B. Wood and Laura Cleveland, performed November 4, 1830, recorded November 11, 1830, Archives and Records Center, Chardon, Ohio.

29. Mark Lyman Staker, *Hearken O Ye People: The Historical Setting of Joseph Smith's Ohio Revelations* (Draper, Utah: Greg Kofford Books, 2009), p. 57.

30. Ibid.

31. Oliver Cowdery, Letter (from "Kirtland, Ohio, to Our Beloved Brethren [in Fayette, New York], November 12, 1830"), holograph copy in Newel Knight, "Autobiography," typescript, MS 2737, Box 56, Folder 5, Church Historical Library, The Church of Jesus Christ of Latter-day Saints, Salt Lake City.

   **Note: On that day, November 5, 1831, instead of 17 people being baptized on the Morley farm, there may have been 16 people baptized there and 1 in Mayfield, because John Murdock records in his journal that he was baptized on November 5 at Mayfield, Ohio. Nevertheless, writes researcher Mark Lyman Staker, "Cowdery implies that all 17 of the initial converts were baptized in Kirtland."** [Mark Lyman Staker, *Hearken O Ye People: The Historical Setting of Joseph Smith's Ohio Revelations* (Draper, Utah: Greg Kofford Books, 2009), p. 67.]

32. Walter Scott (attributed to), Commentary (on Josiah Jones, "History of the Mormonites"), *The Evangelist* (Pittsburgh, Pennsylvania), vol. 9 (June 1, 1831), p. 132.

   **Note: *The Evangelist* was a monthly periodical published by Walter Scott in the 1830s and early 1840s. Scott possibly launched it in early 1831, when he lived at Pittsburgh, Pennsylvania (although at least one source believes he launched it in January 1832 at Cincinnati). If he did start it in January 1832, then another owner/editor had the same paper a year earlier, or else there existed a different paper by the same name a year earlier, likely at a different location. In any**

case, the version of *The Evangelist* that existed in June 1831 as "vol. 9" is the one that published the "Commentary" on Josiah Jones, per the citation above.

As for Walter Scott, he did live at Pittsburgh in 1831, so if it was his *Evangelist* paper that published this commentary, he did so at Pittsburgh, which I took the liberty of inserting into the citation above.

Additional details for early American newspaper enthusiasts: Walter Scott began *The Evangelist* in either 1832 or early 1831. He then moved to Cincinatti in 1832 and finally to Carthage, Ohio, in 1833 for 13 years, where he continued editing *The Evangelist*. He discontinued it for a year in either 1835 or 1836 to concentrate on a book (*The Gospel Restored*, published in 1836). He also co-edited another newspaper in 1837, *The Christian* (either while his *Evangelist* paper was on a year hiatus or afterwards). (Meanwhile, he revived *The Evangelist* in either 1836 or January 1838.) When he did revive *The Evangelist* it was with a new title: *The Evangelist of the True Gospel*. In 1844 he discontinued it, then in 1845 launched another newspaper, the *Protestant Unionist*, with partner Robert Forrester, but it was comparatively short-lived.

# CHAPTER 33

1. Levi Ward Hancock, Autobiography, ca 1854, MS 5072, pp. 18–19, microfilm of holograph, Church History Library, The Church of Jesus Christ of Latter-day Saints, Salt Lake City.

2. Ibid.

3. Ibid.

4. Frederick G. Mather, "The Early Days of Mormonism," *Lippincott's Magazine of Popular Literature and Science* (Philadelphia, Pennsylvania), vol. 26 (August 1880), (entire article covers pp. 198–211), p. 206.

   Note 1: The sheriff and attorney heading to Mayfield, Ohio, were Varnem J. Card, a local attorney, and John Barr, the deputy sheriff, whom Frederick G. Mather quotes in his article for *Lippincott's Magazine of Popular Literature and Science.*

   Note 2: *Lippincott's Monthly Magazine of Popular Literature and Science* was a literary magazine published post Civil War, from 1865 to 1915, at Philadelphia. In 1915 it moved to New York City and was renamed *McBride's Magazine*, merging in 1916 with *Scribner's Magazine*.

During its 50-year history it focused on literary criticism, general articles, and original stories. Its first name was *Lippincott's Magazine of Literature, Science, and Education*. From 1871 to 1885 (when this cited article was published) it was named *Lippincott's Magazine of Popular Literature and Science*, and its third and final name, from 1885 to 1915, was *Lippincott's Monthly Magazine*.

5. Hancock, Autobiography, Levi Ward Hancock, Autobiography, ca 1854, MS 5072, p. 19, microfilm of holograph, Church History Library, The Church of Jesus Christ of Latter-day Saints, Salt Lake City.

6. Mark Lyman Staker, *Hearken O Ye People: The Historical Setting of Joseph Smith's Ohio Revelations* (Draper, Utah: Greg Kofford Books, 2009), p. 58.

7. Josiah Jones, "History of the Mormonites," *The Evangelist* (Pittsburgh, Pennsylvania), vol. 9 (June 1, 1831), pp. 132–136.

8. Parley P. Pratt, *The Autobiography of Parley Parker Pratt: One of the Twelve Apostles of the Church of Jesus Christ of Latter-day Saints, Embracing His Life, Ministry and Travels, with Extracts, in Prose and Verse, from his Miscellaneous Writings, edited by his son, Parley P. Pratt* (New York City: Russell Brothers, 1874), p. 48.

9. Levi Ward Hancock, Autobiography, ca 1854, MS 5072, p. 19, microfilm of holograph, Church History Library, The Church of Jesus Christ of Latter-day Saints, Salt Lake City.

10. Reuben P. Harmon, "Having Been Duly Sworn, Testifies as Follows," in *Public Discussions of the Issues between the Re-organized Church of Jesus Christ of Latter Day Saints and the Church of Christ (Disciples)*, edited by Clark Braden (St. Louis: Clark Braden Publisher, 1884).

   Mark Lyman Staker, *Hearken O Ye People: The Historical Setting of Joseph Smith's Ohio Revelations* (Draper, Utah: Greg Kofford Books, 2009), pp. 59–62.

   Note: This missionary meeting at Kirtland, Ohio, in which Sidney Rigdon announced his preaching days were over, was held Sunday night, November 7, 1830, at the Methodist chapel overlooking Kirtland's Flats.

11: Oliver Cowdery, Letter (from "Kirtland, Ohio, to Our Beloved Brethren [in Fayette, New York], November 12, 1830"), holograph copy in Newel Knight, "Autobiography," typescript, MS 2737, Box 56, Folder 5, Church

Historical Library, The Church of Jesus Christ of Latter-day Saints, Salt Lake City.

12. **Note: Sidney and wife Phebe were baptized Monday, November 8, 1831.** [*Painesville Telegraph* (Painesville, Ohio), vol. 2, no. 35 (February 15, 1831).] **The** *Painesville Telegraph* **reports, "The Monday following [the sermon at the Methodist chapel] he [Sidney] was baptized." Further detailing exactly when the Rigdons were baptized, Josiah Jones states that Sidney was "rebaptized" (from a Protestant to a New Believer) on a Monday, the day after he spoke at the Methodist chapel on the hill,** [Josiah Jones, "History of the Mormonites," *The Evangelist* (Pittsburgh, Pennsylvania), vol. 9 (June 1, 1831), pp. 132–136] **which definitely puts it at November 8, 1831.**

13. John Wickliffe Rigdon, "'I Never Knew a Time When I Did Not Know Joseph Smith': A Son's Record of the Life and Testimony of Sidney Rigdon," edited by Karl Keller, *Dialogue: A Journal of Mormon Thought* (Salt Lake City), vol. 1, no. 4 (Winter 1966), pp. 15–42, especially pp. 23–24.

14. Reuben P. Harmon, "Having Been Duly Sworn, Testifies as Follows," *in Public Discussions of the Issues between the Reorganized Church of Jesus Christ of Latter Day Saints and the Church of Christ (Disciples)*, edited by Clark Braden (St. Louis, Clark Braden Publisher, 1884).

15. Ibid.

16. "The Book of Mormon," *Painesville Telegraph* (Painesville, Ohio), vol. 2, no. 24 (November 30, 1830), p. 3.

17. Parley P. Pratt, *The Autobiography of Parley Parker Pratt: One of the Twelve Apostles of the Church of Jesus Christ of Latter-day Saints, Embracing His Life, Ministry and Travels, with Extracts, in Prose and Verse, from his Miscellaneous Writings, edited by his son, Parley P. Pratt* (New York City: Russell Brothers, 1874), p. 48.

18. Mark Lyman Staker, *Hearken O Ye People: The Historical Setting of Joseph Smith's Ohio Revelations* (Draper, Utah: Greg Kofford Books, 2009), p. 60.

19. John Corrill, *A Brief History of the Church of Jesus Christ of Latter Day Saints* (St. Louis, published by the author, 1839), p. 22.

20. Joel Miller, Statement, in *Naked Truths About Mormonism: Also a Journal for Important, Newly Apprehended Truths, and Miscellany*, newspaper edited and published by A. B. Deming (Oakland, California), vol. 1 no. 2 (April 1888), L. Tom Perry Special Collections, Harold B. Lee Library, Brigham Young University, Provo, Utah.

21. Parley P. Pratt, *The Autobiography of Parley Parker Pratt: One of the Twelve Apostles of the Church of Jesus Christ of Latter-day Saints, Embracing His Life, Ministry and Travels, with Extracts, in Prose and Verse, from his Miscellaneous Writings, edited by his son, Parley P. Pratt* (New York City: Russell Brothers, 1874), p. 47.

22. **Note: Sidney and Phebe Rigdon's two oldest children were 9-year-old daughter Athalia and soon-to-be-8-year-old daughter Nancy, both of whom would not be eligible age-wise to join the church for another year, in November 1831, when the age requirement would become age 8, as stated in Paragraph 3 of Chapter 34. New Believers were not getting baptized at this point until their mid-teens and older.**

23. John Murdock, Journal, ca 1830–1859, MS 11942, microfilm of holograph, Church History Library, The Church of Jesus Christ of Latter-day Saints, Salt Lake City, p. 1.

24. Ibid.

25. Ibid., pp. 1–2.

26. Ibid., p. 1.

27. Levi Ward Hancock, Autobiography, ca. 1854, MS 5072, p. 23, microfilm of holograph, Church History Library, The Church of Jesus Christ of Latter-day Saints, Salt Lake City.

28. Samuel Underhill, "Chronicles, Notes, and Maxims," no date, Stark County Historical Society, Massillon, Ohio.

29. Nancy Trowle, *Vicissitudes Illustrated, in the Experience of Nancy Trowle in Europe and America, Second Edition* (Portsmouth, New Hampshire: John Caldwell, Second Edition 1833), pp. 156–157.

    **Note: Nancy Trowle's castigations against Joseph Smith continued in melodramatic form: "Oh! Blush at such abominations! And let shame, forever, cover your face!"**

30. Ibid.

# CHAPTER 34

1. Parley P. Pratt, *The Autobiography of Parley Parker Pratt: One of the Twelve Apostles of the Church of Jesus Christ of Latter-day Saints, Embracing His Life, Ministry and Travels, with Extracts, in Prose and Verse, from his*

*Miscellaneous Writings, edited by his son, Parley P. Pratt* (New York City: Russell Brothers, 1874), p. 48.

2. Mark Lyman Staker, *Hearken O Ye People: The Historical Setting of Joseph Smith's Ohio Revelations* (Draper, Utah: Greg Kofford Books, 2009), p. 71.

3. *The Doctrine and Covenants of the Church of Jesus Christ of Latter-day Saints: Containing Revelations given to Joseph Smith, the Prophet, with Some Additions by His Successors in the Presidency of the Church* (Salt Lake City: The Church of Jesus Christ of Latter-day Saints, 1981), 68:25.

4. *The Book of Mormon* (Palmyra, New York: Printed by E. B. Grandin for the Author, 1830), Alma 45:4.

5. *The Doctrine and Covenants of the Church of Jesus Christ of Latter-day Saints: Containing Revelations given to Joseph Smith, the Prophet, with Some Additions by His Successors in the Presidency of the Church* (Salt Lake City: The Church of Jesus Christ of Latter-day Saints, 1981), 41:5.

6. Joseph Smith, Letter ("To Hyrum Smith, March 3–4, 1831"), in Joseph Smith, *Personal Writings of Joseph Smith*, edited by Dean C. Jessee (Provo, Utah: Brigham Young University Press, Revised Edition 2002), p. 256.

   Also found in Joseph Smith, *The Joseph Smith Papers*, edited by Dean C. Jessee, Ronald K. Esplin, and Richard Lyman Bushman (Salt Lake City: The Church Historian's Press, 2008–), multiple-volume series.

   Joseph Smith, Letter (to Martin Harris, February 22, 1831), Church Archives, The Church of Jesus Christ of Latter-day Saints, Salt Lake City.

7. Mark Lyman Staker, *Hearken O Ye People: The Historical Setting of Joseph Smith's Ohio Revelations* (Draper, Utah: Greg Kofford Books, 2009), p. 73.

8. Invie P. Axtell, Interview (March 1880), in E. L. Kelly, "From Painesville, Ohio," *The Saints' Herald* (Plano, Illinois), vol. 27, no. 6 (June 1880), pp. 80–85.

   **Note: Invie Axtell writes, "At that time [Joseph's group] was known as the new revelation." Axtell's father was the Painesville Baptist minister and likely knew the labels given to the Saints by the locals.**

9. "Delusion," *Painesville Gazette* (Painesville, Ohio); reprinted in *Working Man's Advocate* (New York City), vol. 2, no. 17 (December 11, 1830), p. 4.

   **Note: *Working Man's Advocate* was a weekly newspaper from 1829 to the 1840s in New York City.**

10. Abner Cole, "We Have Been Informed" *The Reflector* (Palmyra, New York), June 22, 1830, p. 46.

    Abner Cole, "The Age of Miracles Has Again Arrived," *The Reflector* (Palmyra, New York), June 30, 1830, p. 53.

    **Note: Abner Cole, in his two newspaper printings of late June 1830, used a bizarre label for Joseph's followers—"Gold Bible apostles."**

11. Abner Cole, *The Reflector* (Palmyra, New York), 1831; reprinted in *Painesville Telegraph* (Painesville, Ohio), March 1831, p. 3.

    **Note: For 2 months the *Painesville Telegraph*'s editor, Eber Dudley Howe, had been using his own term for the Saints—"Mormonites"— which was now being used in Ohio and perhaps a few other places, but it would soon catch on as their most-used nickname until the term "Mormons" would replace it.**

12. "Fanaticism," *Geauga Gazette* (Painesville, Ohio), February 1, 1831.

    **Note 1: As with other anti-Joseph articles, this one was republished in probably several newspapers, including the June 12, 1831, issue of the *Commercial Courant*.**

    **Note 2: The *Geauga Gazette* was published in Painesville, Ohio, from 1828–1833. Researcher Mark Lyman Staker points out that copies of this issue of the *Geauga Gazette* no longer exist.**

13. *The Journals of William E. McLellin, 1831–1836*, edited by Jan Shipps and John W. Welch (Provo, Utah: *BYU Studies*, 1994), pp. 122, 136 (entries for Sunday, May 19, 1833, and Sunday, August 31, 1834).

14. *Painesville Telegraph* (Painesville, Ohio), January 18, 1831).

15. Thomas Hamilton, *Men and Manners in America*, 2 volumes (Edinburgh: W. Blackwood, 1833), vol. 2, p. 310; reprinted as *Men and Manners in America (Cambridge Library Collection—North American History)*, (Cambridge, England: Cambridge University Press, 2009).

16. Joseph Smith Jr., *History of the Church of Jesus Christ of Latter-day Saints*, edited by B. H. Roberts, 7 volumes (Salt Lake City: The Church of Jesus Christ of Latter-day Saints and *Deseret News*, Revised Second Edition 1948), vol. 1, p. 125.

17. Mark Lyman Staker, *Hearken O Ye People: The Historical Setting of Joseph Smith's Ohio Revelations* (Draper, Utah: Greg Kofford Books, 2009), p. 64.

18. **Note 1: None of the Ohio converts had been instructed about their leadership duties, recalls a musing George A. Smith, 34 years afterward.**

[George A. Smith in *Journal of Discourses*, edited by George D. Watt, et al. (Liverpool: Franklin D. Richards and Sons, 1854–1886), vol. 11, p. 4 (November 15, 1864).] **This includes new converts given charge of affairs, such as Isaac Morley, but he was still the best option, due to his overall leadership experience and other talents and abilities.**

**Note 2: Mark Lyman Staker is my favorite author for the period of the Latter-day Saints in Ohio. His book, *Hearken O Ye People: The Historical Setting of Joseph Smith's Ohio Revelations* (Draper, Utah: Greg Kofford Books, 2009), is a masterpiece, and I heartily recommend the reader to obtain a copy.**

19. Lucy Mack Smith, *History of Joseph Smith by His Mother: The Unabridged Original Version* (Arlington, Virginia and Provo, Utah: Stratford Books, Revised Second Edition 2006), p. 280.

20. *Painesville Telegraph* (Painesville, Ohio), January 18, 1831.

21. **Note: As the *Painesville Telegraph* points out, John Whitmer arrived in Kirtland in mid-January 1831 to lead the church there—not 2 months earlier (November 1830), as some historians believe. Nor did the 5 missionaries wait for his arrival before proceeding to Missouri, which is also commonly believed due to an error by Lucy in her book (in all editions, plus on p. 280 of the 2006 Edition commonly cited here). Lucy is correct on one point and incorrect on another when she writes: "Joseph dispatched John Whitmer to take the presidency of the church at Kirtland and when he arrived there, those appointed to go to Missouri proceeded on their mission."** [Lucy Mack Smith, *History of Joseph Smith by His Mother: The Unabridged Original Version* (Arlington, Virginia and Provo, Utah: Stratford Books, Revised Second Edition 2006), p. 280.] **Lucy's error is the time frame, because the missionaries had already gone to Missouri 2 months earlier.**

22. **Note: The total distance of the journey from Palmyra, New York, to Independence, Missouri, was 1,500 miles, estimates Parley P. Pratt.** [Parley P. Pratt, *Autobiography of Parley P. Pratt* (Arlington, Virginia and Provo, Utah: Stratford Books, 2005), p. 32.] **Today, following their route—which is exactly the same on a portion of it (as they traveled on the Ohio and Mississippi Rivers by riverboat) and overland the remainder of the way—the total mileage is about 1,382 miles. My breakdown follows:**

**The trip today consists of 259 miles the first leg of the journey—on land from Palmyra, New York, to Kirtland, Ohio; then by land another 266 miles to Cincinnati, Ohio; then by river 616 miles from Cincinnati to St. Louis; then on land again another 241 miles from St. Louis to**

Independence, Missouri. Joseph had also traveled another 27 miles to begin his journey, from Waterloo, New York, via Palmyra.

The land distances are possibly not much different in 1831 vs. various modern-day routes. The missionaries and other New Believers would usually travel by both steamboat and land—making the total route from between 1,382 and 1,500 miles (Parley P. Pratt's estimation). The only discrepancy would have been the overland travel, as the routes were somewhat different than today on some portions of the journey, while other portions on land were similar, and the river route was the same as today.

23. Parley P. Pratt, *Autobiography of Parley P. Pratt* (Arlington, Virginia and Provo, Utah: Stratford Books, 2005), pp. 29–30.

24. Thomas K. Wharton, "From England to Ohio, 1830–1832: The Journal of Thomas K. Wharton," edited by James H. Rodebaugh, in *Ohio History* (Kent, Ohio), vol. 65, no. 1 (January 1956), p. 15.

Note: Beginning in June 1887, *Ohio History* magazine was published in Columbus, Ohio, by the Ohio Historical Society. But in 2007 it switched publishers to Kent State University Press at Kent, Ohio. The university established its press in 1965, but did not take over publishing the journal until 2007. Before that it was published by the historical society now called the Ohio History Connection. Originally it was titled Ohio State Archaeological and Historical Society, which formed in 1885, two years before it launched the magazine. The society changed its name in 1954 to Ohio Historical Society, then again on April 14, 2014, to Ohio History Connection. *Ohio History* is now published yearly or twice yearly. It includes book reviews, research notes, edited primary documents, and essays for scholars.

25. Ibid.

26. Emil Schlup, "The Wyandot Mission," *Ohio State Archaeological and Historical Quarterly* (Columbus, Ohio), vol. 15 (1906), p. 180.

Note: *The Ohio State Archaeological and Historical Quarterly* is the original name of today's *Ohio History*, as described above—which is its sixth different name since it began publishing.

27. Thomas K. Wharton, "From England to Ohio, 1830–1832: The Journal of Thomas K. Wharton," edited by James H. Rodebaugh, in *Ohio History* (Columbus, Ohio), vol. 65, no. 1 (January 1956), p. 15.

28. Parley P. Pratt, *Autobiography of Parley P. Pratt* (Arlington, Virginia and Provo, Utah: Stratford Books, 2005), p. 31.

29. Ibid.

# CHAPTER 35

1. Orson Hyde, "History of Orson Hyde," *The Latter-day Saints' Millennial Star* (London), vol. 26 (November 19, 1864), no. 47, p. 760 (full article on pp. 743–760).

2. Mark Lyman Staker, *Hearken O Ye People: The Historical Setting of Joseph Smith's Ohio Revelations* (Draper, Utah: Greg Kofford Books, 2009).

   Charles Fisk, "The First Fifty Years of Recorded Weather History in Minnesota (1820–1869): A Year-by-Year Narrative Account," 1994, research files at the Minnesota Historical Society, St. Paul, Minnesota.

3. Richard L. Evans, *A Century of "Mormonism" in Great Britain* (Salt Lake City: Deseret News Press), 1937.

4. **Note: Latter-day Saint membership in the U.K. dipped to as low as 2,600 in 1892, before climbing back to all-time high numbers there, when a temple and the first European stake were dedicated in 1958 and 1960 respectively. A relatively short 35-year period (from 1955 to 1990) saw converts shoot up to 160,000, attending services in 250 of their own chapels. In another 19 years (to 1989) members would increase to the statistics given in the text—of 186,000 in 347 congregations. Orson Hyde had both a direct and indirect effect on all those joining before 1870, and an indirect one afterward.**

5. Charles Dickens, *The Uncommercial Traveller* (London: Chapman and Hall, 1861), pp. 223–225.

6. Parley P. Pratt, *Autobiography of Parley P. Pratt* (Arlington, Virginia and Provo, Utah: Stratford Books, 2005), p. 31.

7. Ibid., p. 32.

8. "The Mormon Challenge," *Painesville Telegraph* (Painesville, Ohio), vol. 2, no. 35 (February 15, 1831), p. 2.

# CHAPTER 36

1. Joseph Smith, Manuscript History of the Church, Book A-1, Historian's Office, Church Archives, The Church of Jesus Christ of Latter-day Saints, Salt Lake City.

Also found in Joseph Smith, *The Papers of Joseph Smith*, edited by Dean C. Jessee, 2 volumes (Salt Lake City: Deseret Book, 1989–1992), vol. 1, p. 348.

Also found in Joseph Smith, *The Joseph Smith Papers*, edited by Dean C. Jessee, Ronald K. Esplin, and Richard Lyman Bushman (Salt Lake City: The Church Historian's Press, 2008–), multiple-volume series.

2. Lucy Mack Smith, *History of Joseph Smith by His Mother: The Unabridged Original Version* (Arlington, Virginia and Provo, Utah: Stratford Books, Revised Second Edition 2006), p. 281.

3. Ibid.

4. Ibid.

**Note: At the church meeting held in Joseph Smith's home at Waterloo, New York, on December 10, 1830, Sidney Rigdon and Edward Partridge entered together. Since both had come all the way from Ohio and arrived at Joseph's home together, they likely had traveled together from Ohio.**

5. Joseph Smith Jr., *History of the Church of Jesus Christ of Latter-day Saints*, edited by B. H. Roberts, 7 volumes (Salt Lake City: The Church of Jesus Christ of Latter-day Saints and *Deseret News*, Revised Second Edition 1948), vol. 1, pp. 129, 131.

6. Parley P. Pratt, *Autobiography of Parley P. Pratt* (Arlington, Virginia and Provo, Utah: Stratford Books, 2005), p. 31.

7. Ibid., p. 33.

8. Ibid.

9. Parley P. Pratt, *The Autobiography of Parley Parker Pratt: One of the Twelve Apostles of the Church of Jesus Christ of Latter-day Saints, Embracing His Life, Ministry and Travels, with Extracts, in Prose and Verse, from his Miscellaneous Writings, edited by his son, Parley P. Pratt* (New York City: Russell Brothers, 1874), pp. 54–56.

10. Ibid.

11. Oliver Cowdery, Letter (to Joseph Smith, April 8, 1831), in Joseph Smith Jr. Collection, 1805–1844, Joseph Smith Letter Books, Letter 7, Church Archives, The Church of Jesus Christ of Latter-day Saints, Salt Lake City.

12. Parley P. Pratt, *Autobiography of Parley P. Pratt* (Arlington, Virginia and Provo, Utah: Stratford Books, 2005), p. 37.

13. Ibid.

14. David Whitmer, *An Address to All Believers in Christ* (Richmond, Missouri: published by the author, 1887), p. 35.

15. Ibid.

16. Ibid.

17. Joseph Knight Sr., 5-page manuscript, #183301847, Historical Department, The Church of Jesus Christ of Latter-day Saints, Salt Lake City.

18. Larry C. Porter, *A Study of the Origins of the Church of Jesus Christ of Latter-day Saints in the States of New York and Pennsylvania, 1816–1831* (Ph.D. dissertation, Brigham Young University, 1971; published at Provo, Utah: Joseph Fielding Smith Institute for Latter-day Saint History and *BYU Studies*, 2000), pp. 116–117.

19. *The Doctrine and Covenants of the Church of Jesus Christ of Latter-day Saints: Containing Revelations given to Joseph Smith, the Prophet, with Some Additions by His Successors in the Presidency of the Church* (Salt Lake City: The Church of Jesus Christ of Latter-day Saints, 1981), 38:28.

20. Ibid., 38:31–32.

21. Larry C. Porter, *A Study of the Origins of the Church of Jesus Christ of Latter-day Saints in the States of New York and Pennsylvania, 1816–1831* (Ph.D. dissertation, Brigham Young University, 1971; published at Provo, Utah: Joseph Fielding Smith Institute for Latter-day Saint History and *BYU Studies*, 2000), p. 124.

22. David Whitmer, *An Address to All Believers in Christ* (Richmond, Missouri: published by the author, 1887) p. 71.

23. Lucy Mack Smith, *History of Joseph Smith by His Mother: The Unabridged Original Version* (Arlington, Virginia and Provo, Utah: Stratford Books, Revised Second Edition 2006), p. 280.

24. Joseph Knight Sr., 5-page manuscript, #183301847, Historical Department, The Church of Jesus Christ of Latter-day Saints, Salt Lake City.

25. **Note: Lucy lists most of those who traveled with Joseph Smith by sleigh to Kirtland, Ohio. In her book, however, she confuses the Knights, saying it was Newel Knight who accompanied them.** [Lucy Mack Smith, *History of Joseph Smith by His Mother: The Unabridged Original Version* (Arlington, Virginia and Provo, Utah: Stratford Books, Revised Second Edition 2006), p. 282.] **However, Newel would not leave New York for Ohio until spring 1831. Research indicates it was Joseph Knight Sr., instead, who accompanied Joseph and Emma to Ohio.** [Larry C. Porter, "'Ye Shall Go to the Ohio': Exodus of the New York Saints to Ohio, 1831," in *Regional Studies in Latter-day Saint Church History: Ohio*, edited by

Milton V. Backman Jr. (Provo: Brigham Young University Department of Church History and Doctrine, 1990), p. 3.]

**The senior Knight took them in his sleigh.** [Joseph Knight Sr., 5-page manuscript, #183301847, Historical Department, The Church of Jesus Christ of Latter-day Saints, Salt Lake City.]

26. Lucy Mack Smith, *History of Joseph Smith by His Mother: The Unabridged Original Version* (Arlington, Virginia and Provo, Utah: Stratford Books, Revised Second Edition 2006), p. 282.

# CHAPTER 37

1. Joseph Smith Jr., *History of the Church of Jesus Christ of Latter-day Saints*, edited by B. H. Roberts, 7 volumes (Salt Lake City: The Church of Jesus Christ of Latter-day Saints and *Deseret News*, Revised Second Edition 1948), vol. 1, p. 146.

2. James Henry Rollins, Reminiscences, 1896, p. 3, Church Archives, The Church of Jesus Christ of Latter-day Saints, Salt Lake City.

3. Linda King Newell and Valeen Tippetts Avery, *Mormon Enigma: Emma Hale Smith, Prophet's Wife, "Elect Lady," Polygamy's Foe—1804–1879* (Garden City, New York: Doubleday, 1984), pp. 37–38.

4. Horace Whitney, Letter (to Elizabeth Ann Whitney, February 6, 1870), Newel Kimball Whitney Collection, Box 6, Folder 26, L. Tom Perry Special Collections, Harold B. Lee Library, Brigham Young University, Provo, Utah.

5. Mark Lyman Staker, *Hearken O Ye People: The Historical Setting of Joseph Smith's Ohio Revelations* (Draper, Utah: Greg Kofford Books, 2009), p. 226.

6. Joseph Smith Jr., *History of the Church of Jesus Christ of Latter-day Saints*, edited by B. H. Roberts, 7 volumes (Salt Lake City: The Church of Jesus Christ of Latter-day Saints and *Deseret News*, Revised Second Edition 1948), vol. 1, p. 146.

   Milton V. Backman Jr., *The Heavens Resound: A History of the Latter-day Saints in Ohio, 1830–1838* (Salt Lake City: Deseret Book, 1983) pp. 43–45.

7. Lucy Mack Smith, *History of Joseph Smith by His Mother: The Unabridged Original Version* (Arlington, Virginia and Provo, Utah: Stratford Books, Revised Second Edition 2006), p. 282.

8. Milton V. Backman Jr., *The Heavens Resound: A History of the Latter-day Saints in Ohio, 1830–1838* (Salt Lake City: Deseret Book, 1983) p. 51.

9. Richard Lloyd Anderson, "The Impact of the First Preaching in Ohio," *BYU Studies* (Provo, Utah), vol. 11, no. 4, (Summer 1971), pp. 474–496.

   **Note: Philo Dibble actually heard his first sermon in the Kirtland, Ohio, area from Oliver Cowdery, before Oliver left Ohio for Missouri.**

10. Ibid.

11. John Whitmer, *From Historian to Dissident: The Book of John Whitmer*, edited by Bruce N. Westergren (Salt Lake City: Signature Books, 1995), pp. 42, 47.

12. Ibid.

    Davis Bitton, "Kirtland as a Center of Missionary Activity, 1830–1838," *BYU Studies* (Provo, Utah), vol. 11, no. 4 (Summer 1971), pp. 497–516.

13. Ibid., David Bitton, "Kirtland."

    John Whitmer, *From Historian to Dissident: The Book of John Whitmer*, edited by Bruce N. Westergren (Salt Lake City: Signature Books, 1995), pp. 42, 47.

# CHAPTER 38

1. *The Doctrine and Covenants of the Church of Jesus Christ of Latter-day Saints: Containing Revelations given to Joseph Smith, the Prophet, with Some Additions by His Successors in the Presidency of the Church* (Salt Lake City: The Church of Jesus Christ of Latter-day Saints, 1981), 43:3.

2. Lucy Mack Smith, *History of Joseph Smith by His Mother: The Unabridged Original Version* (Arlington, Virginia and Provo, Utah: Stratford Books, Revised Second Edition 2006), pp. 283–284.

3. The Bible, King James Version, New Testament, The Acts of the Apostles 2:44–45.

4. Ibid., Acts 4:34–35.

5. **Note: Joseph had translated the Book of Moses from mid-1830 to early 1831: Chapters 2–5 from June to October 1830, then Chapter 6 from November to December 1830, Chapter 7 in December 1830, and finally Chapter 8 two months later—in February 1831.**

6. Mark Lyman Staker, *Hearken O Ye People: The Historical Setting of Joseph Smith's Ohio Revelations* (Draper, Utah: Greg Kofford Books, 2009), p. 309.

7. Joseph Smith Jr., *History of the Church of Jesus Christ of Latter-day Saints*, edited by B. H. Roberts, 7 volumes (Salt Lake City: Deseret Book, Second Revised Edition 1948), vol. 1, p. 146.

8. Samuel F. Whitney, "Statement of Reverend S. F. Whitney on Mormonism," in *Naked Truths About Mormonism: Also a Journal for Important, Newly Apprehended Truths, and Miscellany*, newspaper edited and published by A. B. Deming (Oakland, California), vol. 1, no. 1 (January 1888), p. 3, L. Tom Perry Special Collections, Harold B. Lee Library, Brigham Young University, Provo, Utah.

9. Ibid.

10. Donna Hill, *Joseph Smith: The First Mormon* (Garden City, New York: Doubleday, 1977), p. 131.

11. **Note: In her 1879 interview Emma clarified how many children she had lost before her first child would live. She was asked by her interviewer, Joseph Smith III, who was her first surviving biological child, "How many children did you lose, Mother, before I was born?" She answered, "There were three. I buried one in Pennsylvania, and a pair of twins in Ohio."** [Emma Hale Smith, in Joseph Smith III, "Last Testimony of Sister Emma," *The Saints' Herald* (Plano, Illinois), vol. 26, no. 19 (October 1, 1879), pp. 289–290.] **Of the twins she would adopt before Joseph III was born, she states, "They were both sick when your father was mobbed [discussed in Vol. 2 of this biography]. The mob who tarred and feathered him left the door open when they went out with him; the child relapsed and died. Julia lived, though weaker than the boy."** [Ibid.] **Emma and Joseph had raised the boy for 11 months—from a period that began 10 days after his April 30, 1831, birth to 5 days after the mob attack, when he died March 29, 1832. Counting the adopted children, Emma had now lost 4 of her first 5.**

# CHAPTER 39

1. Lucy Mack Smith, *History of Joseph Smith by His Mother: The Unabridged Original Version* (Arlington, Virginia and Provo, Utah: Stratford Books, Revised Second Edition 2006), p. 285.

2. Ibid., pp. 286–287.

3. Ibid., p. 287.

4. Ibid., pp. 287–288.

5. Ibid., p. 288.

6. Ibid., pp. 286–287.

7. Ibid., p. 287.

8. Ibid., p. 289.

9. Ibid., p. 290.

10. Ibid.

11. Ibid., p. 291.

12. Ibid.

13. Ibid., pp. 291–292.

14. Ibid.

# CHAPTER 40

1. Lucy Mack Smith, *History of Joseph Smith by His Mother: The Unabridged Original Version* (Arlington, Virginia and Provo, Utah: Stratford Books, Revised Second Edition 2006), pp. 293–294.

2. Ibid., p. 295.

3. Ibid.

4. Richard Lloyd Dewey, *Porter Rockwell: A Biography* (New York City: Paramount Books, Ninth Revised Edition 2006), p. 7.

5. Lucy Mack Smith, *History of Joseph Smith by His Mother: The Unabridged Original Version* (Arlington, Virginia and Provo, Utah: Stratford Books, Revised Second Edition 2006), p. 296.

6. Ibid., pp. 296–297.

7. Ibid., p. 296.

8. Ibid., p. 298.

9. Ibid., p. 299.

10. Ibid.

11. Ibid., pp. 200–301.

12. Ibid., p. 301.

Note: As stated earlier, Lucy commonly refers to Fayette as Waterloo in her history.

13. Ibid., p. 302.

14. Milton V. Backman Jr., *The Heavens Resound: A History of the Latter-day Saints in Ohio, 1830–1838* (Salt Lake City: Deseret Book, 1983), p. 51.

# AFTERWORD

1. Jane Snyder Richards, quoted in "Joseph Smith, the Prophet," *Young Woman's Journal* (Salt Lake City), vol. 16, no. 12 (December 1905), p. 556.

2. Bathsheba W. Smith, quoted In *Juvenile Instructor* (Salt Lake City), vol. 27, no. 11 (June 1, 1892), pp. 344–345.

3. Jane Snyder Richards, quoted in "Joseph Smith, the Prophet," *Young Woman's Journal* (Salt Lake City), vol. 16, no. 12 (December 1905), p. 556.

4. William Farrington Cahoon, quoted in *Juvenile Instructor* (Salt Lake City), vol. 29, no. 16 (August 15, 1892), pp. 492–493.

5. Jesse N. Smith, Lecture, to Church History class of Professor John Henry Evans at Latter Day Saint University, Salt Lake City, April 11, 1905, recorded in "Autobiography and Journal of Jesse Nathaniel Smith 1834–1906," Church Archives, The Church of Jesus Christ of Latter-day Saints, Salt Lake City.

Note: Today's LDS Business College was known in 1905 as Latter Day Saint University. It was founded in 1886 as Salt Lake Academy. Three years later, in 1889, it was renamed Salt Lake State Academy. One year later, in 1890, it was renamed Latter-day Saints University. By 1895 it offered a 4-year degree, but has never been a fully functional university. From 1927 to 1931 it became LDS College, and in 1931 it received the name by which it is known today—LDS Business College. It offers 2-year degrees in various disciplines such as paralegal studies, accounting, business, interior design, and executive medical assistant. It first became accredited in 1976, and today has over 2,200 students, with over 76,000 alumni.

Jesse Nathaniel Smith, *Journal of Jesse Nathaniel Smith, the Life Story of a Mormon Pioneer, 1834–1906* (Salt Lake City: Jesse N. Smith Family Association, 1953), pp. 454–455.

6. Moses Wilson, quoted in *Journal of Discourses*, edited by George D. Watt, et al., 26 volumes (Liverpool, England: Franklin D. Richards and Sons, 1854–1886), vol. 17, p. 92.

7. John H. Hess, quoted in "Recollections of the Prophet Joseph Smith," *Juvenile Instructor* (Salt Lake City), vol. 27 (May 15, 1892), pp. 302–303.

8. Ibid.

9. John M. Bernhisel, Letter (to Governor Thomas Ford, June 14, 1844), John M. Bernhisel File, Church Archives, The Church of Jesus Christ of Latter-day Saints, Salt Lake City.

   Washington Franklin Anderson, "Reminiscences of John M. Bernhisel," typescript, pp. 1–4, Church Archives, The Church of Jesus Christ of Latter-day Saints, Salt Lake City.

10. Emma Smith, Letter (to Joseph Smith III, August 1, 1869), Emma Smith Papers, Library-Archives, History Commission, Community of Christ, The Auditorium, Independence, Missouri.

    **Note: The entire quote from this letter of Emma Smith to her son Joseph III about his father's popularity—of his inability to even work in the yard without being inundated by neighbors "trampling the garden"—is this: "I do not expect you can do much more in the garden than your father could, and I never wanted him to go into the garden to work, for if he did it would not be fifteen minutes before there would be three or four or sometimes a half dozen men round him and they would tramp the ground down faster than he could hoe it up."**

11. Thomas Ford, *A History of Illinois, From its Commencement as a State in 1818 to 1847* (Chicago: S. C. Griggs & Co., 1854), pp. 354–355.

12. Ezra Booth, Letter (to Edward Partridge), *Painesville Telegraph* (Painesville, Ohio), December 6, 1831, p. 1.

13. George Q. Cannon, *Life of Joseph Smith the Prophet* (Arlington, Virginia and Provo, Utah: Stratford Books, 2005), p. 24.

14. J. B. Newhull, Report, *Advertiser and Argus* (Salem, Massachusetts), 1843.

    **Note 1: This report by J. B. Newhall, about Joseph Smith being a "jolly fellow," was published in the Salem, Massachusetts, weekly newspaper, *Advertizer and Argus*. The article covers a lecture J. B.**

Newhull gave, in which he reveals details of a conversation he had with Joseph.

Note 2: J. B. Newhall, in addition to being a traveling journalist, would become the secretary to Iowa Territory Governor James Clark, who served 1845–1846. After his research, Newhall wrote and published a book with William John Peterson, entitled *Glimpse of Iowa*, published by W. D. Skillman at Burlington, Iowa, in 1846. It was reprinted by the State Historical Society of Iowa in 1957 at Des Moines, Iowa.

Note 3: For students of early American newspapers, the *Advertizer and Argus* newspaper began as *The Commercial Advertizer* in 1832. It was a semi-weekly, then sold in 1837 and changed its name to *The Salem Advertizer*. Afterwards, it published as the *Salem Advertizer and Argus* from 1841 to 1844. In 1844 the "*and Argus*" was omitted. Its last issue was in 1849. It had begun as an organ of the Democratic Party, and in its 17-year history it alternated between semi-weekly and weekly but was weekly only a total of 4½ years, including its last 6 months. It was semi-weekly when it reported this conversation with Joseph Smith in 1843.

15. Brigham Young, in *Journal of Discourses*, edited by George D. Watt, et al., 26 volumes (Liverpool, England: Franklin D. Richards and Sons, 1854–1886), vol. 4, p. 78.

16. Benjamin F. Johnson, Letter (to George S. Gibbs, 1903), manuscript, p. 4, Mormon File, Box 7, Henry E. Huntington Library and Art Gallery, San Marino, California (copy at L. Tom Perry Special Collections, Harold B. Lee Library, Brigham Young University, Provo, Utah).

17. Peter H. Burnett, *An Old California Pioneer* (Oakland, California: Biobooks, 1946), p. 40.

18. Ibid., p. 34.

19. *The Doctrine and Covenants of the Church of Jesus Christ of Latter-day Saints: Containing Revelations given to Joseph Smith, the Prophet, with Some Additions by His Successors in the Presidency of the Church* (Salt Lake City: The Church of Jesus Christ of Latter-day Saints, 1981), 3:6 (1828).

20. Ibid., 5:21 (1829).

21. Ibid. 93:47 (1833).

22. Ibid. 124:1 (1838).

23. Joseph Smith, Letter (to Emma, from Greenville, Indiana, June 6, 1832), original manuscript, Mormon Collection, Chicago Historical Society, Chicago, Illinois.

   **Note: For historical background to this letter, see:** Joseph Smith Jr., *History of the Church of Jesus Christ of Latter-day Saints*, edited by B. H. Roberts, 7 volumes (Salt Lake City: The Church of Jesus Christ of Latter-day Saints and *Deseret News*, Revised Second Edition 1948), vol. 1, pp. 271–272.

24. John Taylor, in *Journal of Discourses*, edited by George D. Watt, et al., 26 volumes (Liverpool, England: Franklin D. Richards and Sons, 1854–1886), vol. 21, pp. 94, 163; vol. 23, pp. 36–37.

25. William Clayton, Letter (from Nauvoo, Illinois to church members in Manchester, England, December 10, 1840), Church Archives, The Church of Jesus Christ of Latter-day Saints, Salt Lake City.

   **Note: In this William Clayton letter the grammar has been modernized.**

26. Howard Coray, Letter (from Sanford, Colorado to Martha Jane Lewis, August 2, 1889), Church Archives, The Church of Jesus Christ of Latter-day Saints, Salt Lake City.

27. Benjamin F. Johnson, Journal of Benjamin F. Johnson, Benjamin F. Johnson File, Church Archives, The Church of Jesus Christ of Latter-day Saints, Salt Lake City.

   Benjamin F. Johnson, "An Interesting Letter" (from Patriarch Benjamin F. Johnson to George S. Gibbs, 1903), Benjamin F. Johnson File, Church Archives, The Church of Jesus Christ of Latter-day Saints, Salt Lake City.

28. Lucy Meserve Smith, *Juvenile Instructor* (Salt Lake City), vol. 27, no. 15 (August 1, 1892), p. 470.

29. Diary of William Holmes Walker, pp. 3, 7–14, L. Tom Perry Special Collections, Harold B. Lee Library, Brigham Young University, Provo, Utah.

30. Benjamin F. Johnson, Journal of Benjamin F. Johnson, Benjamin F. Johnson File, Church Archives, The Church of Jesus Christ of Latter-day Saints, Salt Lake City.

   Benjamin F. Johnson, "An Interesting Letter" (from Patriarch Benjamin F. Johnson to George S. Gibbs, 1903), Benjamin F. Johnson File, Church Archives, The Church of Jesus Christ of Latter-day Saints, Salt Lake City.

31. John H. Hess, quoted in "Recollections of the Prophet Joseph Smith," *Juvenile Instructor* (Salt Lake City), vol. 27 (May 15, 1892), pp. 302–303.

32. Emmeline Blanche Wells, quoted in "Joseph Smith, the Prophet," *Young Woman's Journal* (Salt Lake City), vol. 17, no. 12 (December 1906), p. 556.

33. Ibid.

34. Parley P. Pratt, *Autobiography of Parley P. Pratt* (Arlington, Virginia and Provo, Utah: Stratford Books, 2005), p. 25.

35. Edward Stevenson, "The Home of My Boyhood," *Juvenile Instructor* (Salt Lake City), vol. 29, no. 14 (July 15, 1894), pp. 443–445.

36. Ibid.

37. Joseph B. Noble, "Autobiographical Sketch of Joseph Bates Noble," no date, Mormon Biography File, Church Archives, The Church of Jesus Christ of Latter-day Saints, Salt Lake City.

38. John Taylor, in *Journal of Discourses*, edited by George D. Watt, et al., 26 volumes (Liverpool, England: Franklin D. Richards and Sons, 1854–1886), vol. 21, pp. 94, 163; vol. 23, pp. 36–37.

39. The Bible, King James Version, New Testament, Revelation 14:6–7.

40. Ibid., Ephesians 4:11–14.

41. Edward Stevenson, "The Home of My Boyhood," *Juvenile Instructor* (Salt Lake City), vol. 29, no. 14 (July 15, 1894), pp. 443–445.

42. *The Book of Mormon* (Palmyra, New York: Printed by E. B. Grandin for the Author, 1830), Moroni 10:4.

# APPENDIX A

1. Joseph Smith, Manuscript History of the Church, Book C-1, Historian's Office, Church Archives, The Church of Jesus Christ of Latter-day Saints, Salt Lake City, p. 963.

2. Ibid., p. 1260.

3. *Latter Day Saints' Messenger and Advocate* (Kirtland, Ohio), vol. 1, no. 1 (October 1834), p. 13.

4. Joseph Smith, Manuscript History of the Church, Book B-1, Historian's Office, Church Archives, The Church of Jesus Christ of Latter-day Saints, Salt Lake City, p. 631.

5. Ibid., p. 105.

6. Ibid., pp. 120–122.

7. Ibid., p. 791.

8. Ibid., p. 794.

9. Joseph Smith Jr., in Reed C. Durham Jr., "Joseph Smith's Own Story of a Serious Childhood Illness," *BYU Studies* (Provo, Utah), vol. 10, no. 4 (Summer 1970), pp. 480–481.

10. Ibid., pp. 480–482.

11. James Mulholland, "Journal," Manuscript, Church Historian's Library, The Church of Jesus Christ of Latter-day Saints, Salt Lake City.

12. Joseph Smith, Manuscript History of the Church, Book C-1, Historian's Office, Church Archives, The Church of Jesus Christ of Latter-day Saints, Salt Lake City, p. 954.

13. Ibid., p. 1023.

14. **Note: In Joseph Smith's 5 journals is one especially intriguing section, from December 21, 1842, through part of June 27, 1844, which he neither wrote nor dictated. Instead, a scribe wrote it in the first person as though Joseph himself had written it (but probably with Joseph's supervision). The scribe for this section was his personal clerk, Willard Richards, who also infused some pages from others' diaries, including those of friend George Albert Smith.**

# APPENDIX B

1. Richard Steckel, *Social Science History*, "New Light on the 'Dark Ages:' The Remarkably Tall Stature of Northern European Men during the Medieval Era," vol. 28, no. 2 (summer 2004), pp. 211–229.

   Richard Steckel, *The Journal of Economic Literature*, (Published by The American Economic Association, Pittsburgh, Pennsylvania, since 1969), vol. 31, no. 1 (spring 2007), pp. 1–34.

# APPENDIX C

1. Mrs. M. C. R. Smith, Statement, in *Naked Truths About Mormonism: Also a Journal for Important, Newly Apprehended Truths, and Miscellany*, newspaper edited and published by A. B. Deming (Oakland, California),

vol. 1, no. 2 (April 1888), Harold B. Lee Library, Brigham Young University, Provo, Utah.

2. *Wayne Sentinel* (Palmyra, New York), February 16, 1825.

   **Note 1: The *Vermont Journal* article of 1825, which is reprinted here in the *Wayne Sentinel*, adds that even respectable citizens who had for years been digging for treasure in the Green Mountains believed legends of treasure "enchanted by the Devil or Robert Kidd."**

   **Note 2: The *Vermont Journal* had a remarkably long lifespan for early-to-mid 19th-century, small-town newspapers—it was published for 122 years in Windsor, Vermont, from 1844–1965.**

3. Ibid.

4. *Lyons Advertiser* (Lyons, New York), August 29, 1827.

   **Note: The *Lyons Advertiser* was a weekly newspaper published in Lyons, New York, from 1822–1828.**

5. Barnes Frisbie, *The History of Middleton, Vermont in Three Discourses* (Rutland, Vermont: Tuttle and Co., 1867), pp. 44–46.

6. *The Palmyra Reflector* (Palmyra, New York), February 1, 1831.

# APPENDIX D

1. Wandle Mace, "Autobiography of Wandle Mace," typescript, Special Collections, Harold B. Lee Library, Brigham Young University, Provo, Utah and Church Archives, The Church of Jesus Christ of Latter-day Saints, Salt Lake City (ca. 1890), pp. 48–49.

2. Lucy Mack Smith, *History of Joseph Smith by His Mother: The Unabridged Original Version* (Arlington, Virginia and Provo, Utah: Stratford Books, Revised Second Edition 2006), p. 176.

3. Mrs. M. C. R. Smith, Statement, in *Naked Truths About Mormonism: Also a Journal for Important, Newly Apprehended Truths, and Miscellany*, newspaper edited and published by A. B. Deming (Oakland, California), vol. 1, no. 2 (April 1888), Harold B. Lee Library, Brigham Young University, Provo, Utah.

4. *Tiffany's Monthly* (New York City), August 1859, p. 169.

5. William D. Purple, Reminiscence (1877), in *Early Mormon Documents*, 5 volumes, edited by Dan Vogel (Salt Lake City: Signature Books, 1996–2003), vol. 4, pp. 133–134.

6. Eber D. Howe, *Mormonism Unvailed [sic]: Or, A Faithful Account of that Singular Imposition and Delusion* (Painesville, Ohio: published by the author, 1834), pp. 240–244.

7. Pomeroy Tucker, *Origin, Rise, and Progress of Mormonism* (New York City: D. Appleton and Co., 1867), p. 19.

8. Brigham H. Roberts, *A Comprehensive History of the Church of Jesus Christ of Latter-day Saints*, 6 volumes (Salt Lake City Utah: Deseret News, 1930), vol. 1, p. 129.

9. *Tiffany's Monthly* (New York City), August 1859, p. 169).

10. Michael D. Quinn, *Early Mormonism and the Magic World View*, Second Edition, revised (Salt Lake City: Signature Books, 1998), pp. 77–79.

11. *Early Mormon Documents*, 5 volumes, edited by Dan Vogel (Salt Lake City: Signature Books, 1996–2003), vol. 4, p. 250).

12. *Tiffany's Monthly* (New York City), August 1859, p. 164.

13. **Note: After the Urim and Thummim were returned to Joseph, Emma assisted him with translating a small portion of the plates until chores consumed them both in preparing for fall and winter, 1828–1829, according to Joseph's mother.** [Lucy Mack Smith, *Biographical Sketches of Joseph Smith the Prophet and His Progenitors for Many Generations* (Liverpool, England: S. W. Richards, 1853), pp. 125–126.]

14. *Omaha Herald* (Omaha, Nebraska), October 17, 1886.

    *Kansas City Journal* (Kansas City, Missouri), June 19, 1881.

    **Note: The *Omaha Herald* was begun in 1864 by George L. Miller, a founder of the city who edited it until 1887, then sold it in 1889 to Gilbert Hitchcock, owner of the *Evening World*, to become today's highly successful *Omaha World-Herald*.**

15. Richard S. Van Wagoner and Steven Walker, "Joseph Smith: 'The Gift of Seeing,'" *Dialogue: A Journal of Mormon Thought* (Salt Lake City), vol. 15, no. 2 (1982), p. 54.

16. Bainbridge (New York) Court Record, March 20, 1886, in *Early Mormon Documents*, 5 volumes, edited by Dan Vogel (Salt Lake City: Signature Books, 1996–2003), vol. 4, p. 253.

17. Eber D. Howe, *Mormonism Unvailed [sic]: Or, A Faithful Account of that Singular Imposition and Delusion* (Painesville, Ohio: published by the author, 1834), pp. 237–238, 259.

# APPENDIX E

1. E. A. Wallis Budge, *Rosetta Stone in the British Museum: The Greek, Demotic, and Hieroglyphic texts of the Decree Inscribed on the Rosetta Stone Conferring Additional Honours on Ptolemy V. Epiphanes (203–181 B.C.) with English Translations and a Short History of the Decipherment of the Egyptian Hieroglyphs, and an Appendix Containing Translations of the Stelae of San (Tanis) and Tall al-Maskhūtah* (London: The Religious Tract Society, 1929), p. 2.

2. Jonathan Downs, *Discovery at Rosetta* (New York City: Skyhorse Publishing, 2008).

3. Carol Andrews, *The British Museum Book of the Rosetta Stone* (London: British Museum Press, 1985), p. 12.

4. "Domestic Occurrences: March 31st, 1802," *The Gentleman's Magazine, and Historical Chronicle* (London), vol. 72, Part 1, p. 270.

   **Note:** ***The Gentleman's Magazine*, based out of London, existed from 1731 to 1922, and was the first publication to use the term "magazine" in its title, based on the French word, meaning "storehouse." Thus, a magazine in its truest sense is a "storehouse" of information and news. In its nearly two-century history, this magazine had 5 variations of its name, always keeping the words "Gentleman's Magazine." For example, when the above-cited article was written in 1802, the publication was called *Gentleman's Magazine, and Historical Chronicle*, which as a moniker lasted almost a century, from 1736 to 1833. The first issue, published in May 1731, had exceptionally stunning graphics on the front page for its day, and was at that time titled *The Gentleman's Magazine: Or, Monthly Intelligencer*, which as a title lasted only its first 5 years, the shortest of the 5 variations to its name. In 1868, until its demise in 1922, it ended up with its shortest title ever, simply, *The Gentleman's Magazine*. It was a magazine in the purest sense.**

5. Matthew Raper, Stephen Weston, et al., "Rosetta Stone, brought to England in 1802: Account of, with three versions: Greek, English translation by S. Weston; Latin translation by Professor Heyne; with notes by Porson,

Taylor, Combe, Weston, and Heyne," in *Archaeologia* (London), vol. 16 (1810–1812), pp. 208–263.

Note: *Archaeologia* **was a magazine in London published by the Society of Antiquaries of London. Its early publications, including the one cited here, comprised lectures given at meetings and included engraved illustrations. Members received these as single issues, which were eventually combined into volumes for a series titled** *Vetusta Monumenta*, **published 1718–1906. Thus, volume 16 (1810–1812), here cited, was right in the middle of the two-century project.**

"Has tabulus inscriptionem . . . ad formam et modulum exemplaris inter spolia ex bello Aegyptiaco nuper reportati et in Musco Britannico asservati suo sumptu incidendas curavit Soe (Antiquar Londin, A.D. MDCCCIII" [1803]), Charles Alfred Slothard, *Vetusta Monumenta, or, Ancient Monuments illustrative of the History and Topography of Great Britain* (London: Society of Antiquities of London, 1803), vol. 4, plates 5–7.

6. Richard B. Parkinson, *The Rosetta Stone* (London: British Museum Press, 2005).

7. Budge, E. A. Wallis, *The Mummy: Chapters on Egyptian Funeral Archaeology* (Cambridge, England: Cambridge University Press, 1894), p. 109.

8. Richard B. Parkinson, W. Diffie, and R. S. Simpson, *Cracking Codes: The Rosetta Stone and Decipherment* (Berkeley: University of California Press, 1999), p. 26.

9. Simon Ager, "Ancient Egyptian scripts," *Omniglot: the online encyclopedia of writing systems & languages* (Bangor, Wales), www.omniglot.com/writing/egyptian/htm.

10. Ibid.

# APPENDIX F

1. Bainbridge (New York) Court Record (1826) in *Early Mormon Documents*, edited by Dan Vogel, 5 volumes (Salt Lake City: Signature Books, 1996–2003), vol. 4, pp. 249–250.

2. Ibid.

3. Ibid.

4. Richard Lyman Bushman, *Joseph Smith: Rough Stone Rolling* (New York City: Alfred A. Knopf / Borzoi Books, 2005), p. 51.

**Note: Regarding William Stafford's comment of Joseph senior seeking answers to questions (regarding treasure) from his son, historian Richard Lyman Bushman comes to the conclusion that Joseph senior was the one actually seeking to hunt treasure, while Joseph Jr. did not wish to join them.**

5. Dan Vogel, "The Locations of Joseph Smith's Early Treasure Quests," *Dialogue: A Journal of Mormon Thought* (Salt Lake City), vol. 27, no. 3 (1994), pp. 229–231.

6. *Deseret News* (Salt Lake City), December 25, 1852.

   *The Doctrine and Covenants of the Church of Jesus Christ of Latter-day Saints: Containing Revelations given to Joseph Smith, the Prophet, with Some Additions by His Successors In the Presidency of the Church* (Salt Lake City: The Church of Jesus Christ of Latter-day Saints, 1981), section 111.

   Fawn M. Brodie, *No Man Knows My History: The Life of Joseph Smith the Mormon Prophet* (New York City: Alfred A. Knopf, 1945), pp. 192–193.

7. Bainbridge (New York) Court Record (1826), in *Early Mormon Documents*, edited by Dan Vogel, 5 volumes (Salt Lake City: Signature Books, 1996–2003), vol. 4, p. 254.

# APPENDIX G

1. David Whitmer, Interview (1878), in Orson Pratt, "Report of Elders Orson Pratt and Joseph F. Smith," *The Latter-day Saints' Millennial Star* (London), vol. 40, no. 49 (December 9, 1878), pp. 771–774.

2. Ibid., pp. 769–774.

3. *Kansas City Daily Journal* (Kansas City, Missouri), June 5, 1881.

4. Lucy Mack Smith, *History of Joseph Smith by His Mother: The Unabridged Original Version* (Arlington, Virginia and Provo, Utah: Stratford Books, Revised Second Edition 2006), pp. 225–228.

5. Richard Lyman Bushman, *Joseph Smith: Rough Stone Rolling* (New York City: Alfred A. Knopf / Borzoi Books, 2005), p. 580, n. 84.

6. Lucy Mack Smith, *History of Joseph Smith by His Mother: The Unabridged Original Version* (Arlington, Virginia and Provo, Utah: Stratford Books, Revised Second Edition 2006), p. 224.

7. *The Book of Mormon* (Palmyra, New York: Printed by E. B. Grandin for the Author, 1830), p. 123.

8. *The Doctrine and Covenants of the Church of Jesus Christ of Latter-day Saints: Containing Revelations given to Joseph Smith, the Prophet, with Some Additions by His Successors In the Presidency of the Church* (Salt Lake City: The Church of Jesus Christ of Latter-day Saints, 1981), 10: 38–41.

9. Ibid., 10:45.

10. Richard Lyman Bushman, *Joseph Smith: Rough Stone Rolling* (New York City: Alfred A. Knopf / Borzoi Books, 2005), p. 580, n. 84.

# APPENDIX H

1. Thomas Ford, *A History of Illinois from its Commencement as a State in 1814 to 1847* (Chicago: S. C. Griggs and Co., 1854), p. 257.

2. David Whitmer, *An Address to All Believers in Christ* (Richmond, Missouri: published by the author, 1887), p. 75.

3. Ibid., pp. 8–9.

**Note: In this 75-page booklet David Whitmer also refutes another claim:**

**"To show the reader what I have had to contend with, I give you below a copy of a leaflet which I had printed and distributed in March, 1881. . . .**

**"'Unto all nations, kindreds, tongues, and people, unto whom these presents shall come:**

**"'It having been represented by one John Murphy, of Polo, Caldwell County, Missouri, that I, in a conversation with him last summer, denied my testimony as one of the Three Witnesses to the *Book of Mormon*.**

**"'To the end, therefore, that he may understand me now, if he did not then; and that the world may know the truth, I wish now, standing as it were, in the very sunset of life, and in the fear of God, once and for all to make this public statement:**

**"'That I have never at any time denied that testimony or any part thereof, which has so long since been published with that book, as one of the Three Witnesses. Those who know me best will know that**

I have always adhered to that testimony. And that no man may be misled or doubt my present views in regard to the same.'"

4. James H. Hart, Interview of David Whitmer, August 21, 1883, in Letter of James H. Hart to *Deseret News* (dispatch sent from Seneca, Newton County, Missouri), August 23, 1883, published in *Deseret News* (Salt Lake City), September 4, 1883.

Note: James H. Hart was the former stake president of the St. Louis Stake and financial agent for the LDS church. Before writing and sending his dispatch to the *Deseret News*, he first wrote details of his interview with David Whitmer in both shorthand and longhand in his journal. [James H. Hart, Journal, Special Collections and Manuscripts, Harold B. Lee Library, Brigham Young University, Provo, Utah.]

Both of Hart's complete interviews with Whitmer are contained in Lyndon W. Cook, *David Whitmer Interviews: A Restoration Witness* (Orem, Utah: Grandin Books, 1991), which we recommend the reader to obtain.

5. *Richmond Democrat* (Richmond, Missouri), vol. xvi, no. 6 (February 2, 1888), p. 1, http://chroniclingamerica.loc.gov/lccn/sn86063662/1888-02-02/ed-1/seq-1/.

Note 1: Before beginning his conversation, David Whitmer made clear to everyone present that he was in his right mind:

"Addressing himself to the attending physician, [he] said: . . .

"'Dr. Buchanan I want you to say whether or not I am in my right mind, before I give my dying testimony.'

"The doctor answered, 'Yes, you are in your right mind for I have just had a conversation with you.'"

Then the conversation proceeded per the text in this appendix.

Note 2: In quoting this article about David Whitmer's final moments, I have inverted the order of the three paragraphs from how they originally appeared in the *Richmond Democrat*, to a chronological order, so as to make more sense of it and the events leading up to his death. Other than that, the newspaper article is quoted verbatim, including grammatical errors, in both the text and this note. Interestingly enough, the majority of sources quoting this article have re-written the original sentences, departing from the original text (in an effort, presumably, to correct grammatical errors).

Note 3: The *Richmond Democrat* was a weekly, 4-page newspaper published from 1873 to 1906 at Richmond, Ray County, Missouri. Its first title was the *Ray County Chronicle*, published from 1876 to 1878 by its first owner. In 1878 it was sold to Colonel Thomas D. Bogie, who took over as editor. In 1893 he sold it to another, but he returned as publisher and editor 4 years later in 1887.

Note 4: When David Whitmer died, the *Richmond Democrat* newspaper presented a front-page article about him with the paper's main headline for the week—"THE LAST WITNESS DEAD!" An engraved portrait of him follows, and then the subheadline "David Whitmer, the aged Patriarch, Gone to His Rest," followed by a smaller headline: "His Parting Injunction to His Family and Friends. He Departs in Peace." Remarkably, the newspaper kept the tone of this article completely supportive—as if believers had written it—not questioning at all the account of Whitmer as one of the Three Witnesses. Also included in the story was his visitation from an angel who showed him the gold plates. Whitmer's reputation in Richmond was held in such high regard for honesty and integrity that his account in the newspaper concerning the *Book of Mormon* was given the highest respect. In the 6 columns that made up a newspaper page, the first $3\frac{1}{3}$ columns were devoted to him—all on the front page. (The remaining $2\frac{2}{3}$ columns consisted of several other important items: the next $\frac{2}{3}$ column covered 4 news articles plus an advertisement, followed by $1\frac{2}{3}$ columns of a reprinted sermon, finished off by $\frac{1}{3}$ of a column consisting of 4 paragraphs—2 advertisements and 2 small editorials.)

The *Richmond Democrat* closed with this final accolade:

"Notwithstanding the cold, damp weather, a large number of friends and acquaintances followed the hearse and mourning family to the new cemetery, west of the city, where the body was laid to rest and all that was mortal of one of the most memorable men, ever connected with the history of Ray county, was forever hidden from view.

"On account of the cold there were no other services at the grave. Mr. Snyder, on behalf of the family, thanked the friends of the deceased for the kindness shown them and the worthy deceased during his illness, and expressed their gratitude for all attention showing.

"A benediction was then pronounced, and the dead was left to rest in peace."

6. *Collected Discourses 1886–1898*, edited by Brian H. Stuy, 5 volumes (Burbank, California and Woodland Hills, Utah: B. H. S. Publishing, 1987–1992), vol. 2, pp. 164–165.

7. *The Saints' Herald* (Lamoni, Iowa), vol. 35 (October 13, 1888).

8. Orson Pratt, "Report of Elders Orson Pratt and Joseph F. Smith," *The Latter-day Saints' Millennial Star* (London), vol. 40, no. 49 (December 9, 1878), pp. 771–774.

9. David Whitmer, *An Address to All Believers in Christ* (Richmond, Missouri: published by the author, 1887), p. 8.

10. *Collected Discourses 1886–1898*, edited by Brian H. Stuy, 5 volumes (Burbank, California and Woodland Hills, Utah: B. H. S. Publishing, 1987–1992), vol. 2, pp. 164–165.

11. Stephen Burnett, Letter "to Brother Johnson" (April 15, 1838), Joseph Smith Jr. Letter Books, Church Archives, The Church of Jesus Christ of Latter-day Saints, Salt Lake City.

12. Anthony Metcalf, *Ten Years Before the Mast: Shipwrecks and Adventures at Sea! Religious Customs of the People of India and Burmah's Empire. How I Became a Mormon and why I Became an Infidel!* (Milad, Idaho: published by the author, 1888).

13. Martin Harris, Interview by Robert Barter, 1870, in *Early Mormon Documents*, edited by Dan Vogel, 5 volumes (Salt Lake City: Signature Books, 1996–2003), vol. 2, p. 390.

14. Martin Harris, Interview by David B. Dille, September 15, 1853, in ibid., vol. 2, pp. 296–297.

15. Martin Harris, Letter (from Smithfield, Utah Territory, to Hanna B. Emerson, January 1871), *The True Latter Day Saints' Herald* (Plano, Illinois), vol. 22 (October 15, 1875), p. 630.

**Note: In this testimony Martin Harris decries all critics who claim he denied ever seeing the plates or the administration of the angel, adding he never denied "the organization of the Church of Jesus Christ of Latter-day Saints." This confession is interesting because of his affiliation with several apostate groups before coming back to the fold. He was thus stating that despite his lack of affiliation with the mainstream church, he had never turned against it, nor had become an enemy to it.**

16. Don K. Dalling, Martin Harris Family Group Records, Martin Harris Family Organization, Murray, Utah, in possession of and cited in Dennis A. Wright, "Caroline Young Harris: The Kirtland Wife of Martin Harris," *Regional Studies in Latter-day Saint Church History: Ohio and Upper Canada*, edited by Guy L. Dorius, Craig K. Manscill, and Craig James Ostler (Provo, Utah: Religious Studies Center, Brigham Young University, 2006), pp. 111–123.

17. Dennis A. Wright, "Caroline Young Harris: The Kirtland Wife of Martin Harris," *Regional Studies in Latter-day Saint Church History: Ohio and Upper Canada*, edited by Guy L. Dorious, Craig K. Manscill, and Craig Ostler (Provo, Utah: Religious Studies Center, Brigham Young University, 2006), pp. 111–123.

18. Cyrus Wheelock, Letter (from Birmingham, England, October 31, 1845), in Orson Hyde, "Martin Harris," *The Latter-day Saints' Millennial Star* (London), vol. 8 (November 15, 1846), p. 128.

19. George Mantle, Letter (to Marietta Walker, St. Catherine, Missouri, December 26, 1888), in *Autumn Leaves: Published for the Youth of the Reorganized Church of Jesus Christ of Latter Day Saints* (Lamoni, Iowa), vol. 2 (1889), pp. 141–142.

    **Note 1: George Mantle precedes this comment in the text with the following account in his letter:**

    **"I . . . met with the brethren at a conference in Birmingham. I was then an elder and presiding over the Dudley Branch, brother John Banks being president of the district. That morning he introduced Cyrus H. Wheelock to the conference as the future president.**

    **"From that the business went on as usual, but when we met in the afternoon Wheelock seemed to be quite out of sorts! The first we knew of the cause, an elderly man asked permission to speak a few words to us. We then knew that disturbed Wheelock."**

    **Note 2: This newspaper from the Reorganized Church of Jesus Christ of Latter Day Saints was geared toward youth and lasted from 1888 to 1928—40 years. Its first editor and founder was Marietta Walker.**

20. Orson Hyde, "Martin Harris," *The Latter-day Saints' Millennial Star* (London), vol. 8 (November 15, 1846), p. 128.

    **Note: Cyrus Wheelock adds that Martin Harris was "politely informed by Elder Banks [the District President] that the season of the year had come when Martin [should seek] a more genial climate than England."**

21. Cyrus Hubbard Wheelock, Journal, entry for October 25, 1846, Church Archives, The Church of Jesus Christ of Latter-day Saints, Salt Lake City.

22. Orson Hyde, "Martin Harris," *The Latter-day Saints' Millennial Star* (London), vol. 8 (November 15, 1846), p. 128.

23. George Mantle, Letter (to Marietta Walker, St. Catherine, Missouri, December 26, 1888), in *Autumn Leaves: Published for the Youth of the*

*Reorganized Church of Jesus Christ of Latter Day Saints* (Lamoni, Iowa), vol. 2 (1889), pp. 141–142.

24. Cyrus Hubbard Wheelock, Journal, entry for October 25, 1846, Church Archives, The Church of Jesus Christ of Latter-day Saints, Salt Lake City.

Note: Cyrus Wheelock would play a role in honorably assisting Joseph Smith in June 1844 at Carthage, Illinois, as recounted in Volume 3 of this biography.

25. Orson Hyde, "Martin Harris," *The Latter-day Saints' Millennial Star* (London), vol. 8 (November 15, 1846), p. 128.

26. George Mantle, Letter (to Marietta Walker, St. Catherine, Missouri, December 26, 1888), in *Autumn Leaves: Published for the Youth of the Reorganized Church of Jesus Christ of Latter Day Saints* (Lamoni, Iowa), vol. 2 (1889), pp. 141–142.

27. "Strangism—Invitation to Imposters," *The Latter-day Saints' Millennial Star* (London), vol. 8 (November 20, 1846), p. 136.

28. Zion's Reveille (Voree, Wisconsin), vol. 1 (December 1846), p. 3.

Note: In this article, *Zion's Reveille* does not give Brooks' first name, however.

The *Reveille* was a Strangite publication that lasted from December 1846 to September 16, 1847, initially published monthly, then weekly, at Voree, Wisconsin. This newspaper was sandwiched between two others—the *Voree Herald* (January – November 1846) and the *Gospel Herald* (September 23, 1847 – June 6, 1850). They comprised 3 newspapers of the Strangite movement.

29. George Albert Smith, Letter (to Josiah Fleming, March 29, 1838), George A. Smith Letters, Church Archives, The Church of Jesus Christ of Latter-day Saints, Salt Lake City.

30. Martin Harris, Letter (presumably by Harris), in *St. Louis Luminary* (St. Louis, Missouri), February 17, 1855.

Note: This unofficial Latter-day Saint church newspaper—*St. Louis Luminary*—was edited by Erasmus Snow and published for 1 year, from 1854 to 1855 at St. Louis, Missouri. Its purpose was primarily to clean up exaggerations in Eastern newspapers and in Congress. It also published minutes of LDS church conferences in St. Louis, missionary reports, local church news, news from Salt Lake Valley, bits of wisdom, humor, poetry, and ads.

31. U. S. Census at Kirtland, Ohio, 1860.

32. "Correspondence: Letter from James McKnight to G. Q. Cannon, February 27, 1862," *The Latter-day Saints' Millennial Star* (London), vol. 24 (April 19, 1862), pp. 250–251.

33. William Harrison Homer, "The Passing of Martin Harris," *The Improvement Era* (Salt Lake City), March 29, 1926, pp. 468–472.

34. Ibid., p. 470.

   **Note: The event of connecting the entire continent by railroad—from the Atlantic to the Pacific—occurred on May 10, 1869, at Promontory Point, Utah, 53 miles northwest of Ogden via Brigham City and 32 miles west of Brigham City; it is also 66 miles northwest of Salt Lake City. Between 500 and 3,000 people attended, by various reports, including dignitaries. In this historical ceremony a "golden spike" was hammered into the last railroad ties, connecting East and West—a momentous occurrence in the development of western civilization development.**

35. "Minutes of the Harris Family Reunion, 1928," Typescript, Harold B. Lee Library, Brigham Young University, Provo, Utah.

   Also quoted in Larry D. Christiansen, "Martin Harris of Clarkston, Utah; His Last Year and His Burial Site from Mount to Memorials," Internet document, 30 pages printed, www.rootsweb.ancestry.com/-utcache/clarkston/harris (site not workable on all servers), revised January 2007.

36. **Note: George A. Smith's ties to Joseph Smith are covered in Volumes 2 and 3 of this biography.**

37. **Note: Many Latter-day Saints believe Brigham Young was prophetic in calling for wide streets in Salt Lake City decades before trolley cars, automobiles, buses, and light rail would even be invented, much less before they would run through the streets of Salt Lake City.**

38. Martin Harris, quoted in Edward Stevenson, Letter, *The Latter-day Saints' Millennial Star* (London), vol. 44, no. 5 (January 30, 1882), p. 79.

   Ibid., vol. 44, no. 6 (February 6, 1882), p. 86.

   Edward Stevenson, "Letter to Deseret News on One of the Three Witnesses," *The Latter-day Saints' Millennial Star* (London), vol. 48, no. 23 (June 7, 1886), pp. 366–367.

39. U. S. Census, 1870, Utah Territory.

40. Madge H. Tuckett and Belle H. Wilson, *Martin Harris Story* (Provo, Utah: Vintage Books, 1983), p. 85.

41. Helen Homer Parks, quoted in Ben J. Ravsten, *History of Clarkston: The Granary of Cache Valley, 1864–1964* (Logan, Utah: B. J. and E. P. Ravsten, 1966), pp. 162–163.

Cited in Larry D. Christiansen, "Martin Harris of Clarkston, Utah; His Last Year and His Burial Site from Mount to Memorials," Internet document, 30 pages printed, www.rootsweb.ancestry.com/-utcache/clarkston/harris (site not workable on all servers), revised January 2007.

42. Madge H. Tuckett and Belle H. Wilson, *Martin Harris Story* (Provo, Utah: Vintage Books, 1983), p. 85.

43. Helen Homer Parks, Letter, in Ben J. Ravsten, *History of Clarkston: The Granary of Cache Valley, 1864–1964* (Logan, Utah: B. J. and E. P. Ravsten, 1966), p. 163.

44. Ibid., pp. 162–163.

Cited in Larry D. Christiansen, "Martin Harris of Clarkston, Utah; His Last Year and His Burial Site from Mount to Memorials," Internet document, 30 pages printed, www.rootsweb.ancestry.com/-utcache/clarkston/harris (site not workable on all servers), revised January 2007.

45. Dennis A. Wright, "Caroline Young Harris: The Kirtland Wife of Martin Harris," in *Regional Studies of Latter-day Saint Church History: Ohio and Upper Canada*, edited by Guy L. Dorius, Craig K. Manscill, and Craig James Ostler (Provo, Utah: Religious Studies Center, Brigham Young University, 2006), pp. 111–123.

46. Rhett S. James, Correspondence, January 11, 1999, cited in Dennis A. Wright, "Caroline Young Harris: The Kirtland Wife of Martin Harris," in *Regional Studies of Latter-day Saint Church History: Ohio and Upper Canada*, edited by Guy L. Dorius, Craig K. Manscill, and Craig James Ostler (Provo, Utah: Religious Studies Center, Brigham Young University, 2006), pp. 111–123.

47. Dalling, Correspondence, in Scott R. Shelton, *Martin Harris in Cache Valley—Events and Influence* (master's thesis published, Logan, Utah: Utah State University, 1986), p. 30.

48. Dennis A. Wright, "Caroline Young Harris: The Kirtland Wife of Martin Harris," in *Regional Studies of Latter-day Saint Church History: Ohio and Upper Canada*, edited by Guy L. Dorius, Craig K. Manscill, and Craig James Ostler (Provo, Utah: Religious Studies Center, Brigham Young University, 2006), pp. 111–123.

**Note: This 1962 report from Dennis A. Wright also includes information of Dolly (Lucy) Harris, who was Martin Harris's first wife, as now being sealed to Martin as well.**

49. William Harrison Homer, "The Passing of Martin Harris," *The Improvement Era* (Salt Lake City), March 29, 1926, pp. 469–470.

# APPENDIX I

1. Orson Pratt, "Report of Elders Orson Pratt and Joseph F. Smith," *The Latter-day Saints' Millennial Star* (London), vol. 40, no. 49 (December 9, 1878), pp. 771–774.

# APPENDIX J

1. Davis Rains Wallace, *The Bonehunters' Revenge: Dinosaurs, Greed, and the Greatest Scientific Feud of the Gilded Age* (Boston: Houghton Mifflin, 1999), p. 5.

**Note: At the high society engagement party of James Gordon Bennett junior and his fiancée, it was the fireplace into which Bennett urinated, according to some guests,** [Eric Homberger, *Mrs. Astor's New York: Money and Social Power in a Gilded Age* (New Haven, Connecticut: Yale University Press, 2002), p. 13] **while others claimed it was the grand piano.**

# APPENDIX K

1. Matthew Restall, *Seven Myths of the Spanish Conquest* (Oxford, England and New York City: Oxford University Press, 2003).

2. Michael Shermer, "White God Legends," *The Skeptic: Encyclopedia of Pseudoscience*, 2 volumes (Santa Barbara, California: ABC-CLIO, 2007), p. 578.

   Kenneth R. Mills, William B. Taylor, and Sandra Lauderdale Graham, *Colonial Spanish America: A Documentary History* (Lanham, Maryland: Rowman and Littlefield Publishers, 1998), pp. 39–40.

3. Brant Gardner, "The Christianization of Quetzalcoatl," *Sunstone* (Salt Lake City), vol. 10, p. 11.

   **Note: *Sunstone* is an independent magazine published by the Sunstone Foundation in Salt Lake City since 1974. Published 5 times per year,**

it is traditionally an alternative magazine in the Latter-day Saint community, more liberal than most magazines of interest to Latter-day Saints. It became especially liberal on religious issues after 1993, when more conservative and moderate members of the foundation and symposiums ceased to participate and write for the magazine. But according to those at the magazine it has evened out with more balance in recent years under new leadership.

4. Matthew Restall, *Seven Myths of the Spanish Conquest* (Oxford, England and New York City: Oxford University Press, 2003), p. 114.

## APPENDIX L

1. Vanessa Collingridge, *Captain Cook: The Life, Death and Legacy of History's Greatest Explorer* (New York City: Random House: Ebury Press, 2003), p. 410.

2. Sheldon Dibble, *History of the Sandwich Islands* (Lahainaluna, Hawaii: Press of the Mission Seminary, 1843), p. 61.

3. Vanessa Collingridge, *Captain Cook: The Life, Death and Legacy of History's Greatest Explorer* (New York City: Random House: Ebury Press, 2003).

4. Note: Captain James Cook died on a historically significant day, one that had become notable not many decades before he was killed. He lived from November 7, 1728, to February 14, 1779—Valentine's Day.

Valentine's Day was named after St. Valentine, martyred in 269 A.D., but at that time his name had no association with romantic love nor would it for over a thousand years.

The first reported tie of St. Valentine to romance was within a group of friends of English poet Geoffrey Chaucer, who lived from 1343 to 1400.

The first known written valentine was penned by a French prisoner named Charles, Duke of Orleans, to his wife, from the Tower of London, in 1415.

In 1477 came the first known written English valentine. Margery Brewes wrote these words to her future husband, John Paston: "My right and well-beloved valentine." [Norman Davis, *The Paston Letters—A Selection in Modern Spelling* (New York City: Oxford University Press, 1963), pp. 233–235.]

**But February 14 took 300 years to evolve into a popular event—first in the 1700s within the English-speaking countries, and later to other countries. In England it included gifts of flowers, candy, and greeting cards—at first handmade, then later mass-produced by printers who found a ready market for mostly young men too awkward to think of ways to express their feelings to young women in writing.**

**British captain James Cook, hated by the Hawaiians, ironically met his demise on this day devoted to love.**

5. Vanessa Collingridge, *Captain Cook: The Life, Death and Legacy of History's Greatest Explorer* (New York City: Random House: Ebury Press, 2003).

6. Benjamin Franklin, *The Works of Benjamin Franklin; containing several Political and Historical Tracts not included in any former Edition, and many Letters official and private not hitherto published; with Notes and a Life of the Author* (Boston: Tappan, Whittemore, and Mason, 1847).

7. David Samwell, Ebenezer Townsend Jr., George Gilbert, Hawaiian Historical Society, Joseph Ingraham, John Meares, Bruce Cartwright, *The Death of Captain James Cook* (Paradise of the Pacific Press, 1791); newer Edition: *The Death of Captain James Cook and Other Writings* (Cardiff, Wales: University of Wales Press, 2007).

8. "Call Signs," National Aeronautics and Space Administration (NASA) (Washington, D.C.: Public Communications Office, NASA Headquarters), http://history.nasa.gov/SP-4029/Apollo_18-17_Call_Signs.htm.

9. "Space Shuttle Endeavor" (Merritt Island, Florida: John F. Kennedy Space Center), www.nasa.gov/centers/Kennedy/shuttleoperations/orbiters/orbitersend.html.

10. "Space Shuttle Endeavor" (Merritt Island, Florida: John F. Kennedy Space Center), www.nasa.gov/centers/Kennedy/shuttleoperations/orbiters/orbitersend.html.

11. John M. MacFarlane, "The Captain Cook Memorial at Kealakakua Bay Hawaii," *The Nauticapedia* (Victoria, British Columbia, Canada, 2011), www.nauticapedia.ca/Articles/Cook_Memorial.php.

# APPENDIX M

1. *New Yorker*, article reprinted in *Iowa Territorial Gazette and Advertiser* (Burlington, Iowa), February 13, 1841.

Note: The *Iowa Territorial Gazette and Advertiser* has its roots in Belmont, Wisconsin, in 1836, where it was named the *Belmont Gazette*. It moved after its first year to Burlington, Iowa—the government headquarters for the territory of Wisconsin—where the paper published under its new name for about three years. A competing paper, the *Advertiser*, also existed in Burlington, Iowa, and started probably about the same year the *Gazette* moved there—in 1837. The two papers merged in about 1841 and published articles critical of Joseph Smith and the Latter-day Saints.

2. Note: Glen L. Pace, Second counselor in the Presiding Bishopric of the Church of Jesus Christ of Latter-day Saints, stated this at the April 1989 General Conference: "It seems that history continues to teach us: you can leave the Church, but you can't leave it alone. The basic reason for this is simple. Once someone has received a witness of the Spirit and accepted it, he leaves neutral ground. One loses his testimony only by listening to the promptings of the evil one, and Satan's goal is not complete when a person leaves the Church, but when he comes out in open rebellion against it." [Glen L. Pace, 159th Annual General Conference, April 1989, *Ensign Magazine*, Salt Lake City, May 1989.]

3. Joseph Smith Jr., *History of the Church of Jesus Christ of Latter-day Saints*, edited by B. H. Roberts, 7 volumes, Second Edition, revised (Salt Lake City: The Church of Jesus Christ of Latter-day Saints and Deseret News, 1948), vol. 4, p. 461.

4. John Stafford, quoted in William H. Kelley and E. L. Kelley, "Interview with Orlando Saunders and Dr. John Stafford, March 1881," *The Saints' Herald* (Plano, Illinois), vol. 28, no. 11 (June 1, 1881).

5. Ibid.

6. Charles W. Brown, "Manchester in the Early Days," *Shortsville Enterprise* (Shortsville, New York), March 11, 1904, Manuscript File, Harold B. Lee Library, Brigham Young University, Provo, Utah.

Note 1: Charles W. Brown cites for his information "the author of the 'Phelps and Gorham Purchase.'"

Note 2: Brown is cited in Donna Hill, *Joseph Smith: The First Mormon* (Garden City, New York: Doubleday, 1977), pp. 104, 464. In that book the newspaper is misnamed the *Shortsville Enterprise Press*.

Note 2: Charles W. Brown would have certainly been in the proximity of the Smith neighbors, as the paper for which he wrote this article, the *Shortsville Enterprise*, was in the village closest to Manchester, where the Smiths lived. However, only the old-timers would have had firsthand recollections of the rumors that Oliver Cowdery was somehow tied to the book's authorship, as it was now 74 years after the rumors had first circulated when the book was published.

The newspaper itself began in 1882, which was 52 years after the publication of the *Book of Mormon* in 1830. The town of Shortsville was incorporated in 1889, actually 7 years after the paper began, and the newspaper lasted until at least 1904, when Brown wrote this article for it. The paper was published weekly on Thursdays. Sometime in the next several decades (at least by 1976), it became the *Shortsville-Manchester Enterprise*.

7. David Persuitte, *Joseph Smith and the Origins of the Book of Mormon* (Jefferson, North Carolina: McFarland), 1985.

# APPENDIX N

1. Addison Everett, Letter (to Oliver B. Huntington in St. George, Utah, Feb. 17, 1881), recorded in "Oliver Boardman Huntington, Journal #14, [under back date of] 31 Jan. 1881," Harold B. Lee Library, Brigham Young University, Provo, Utah.

   **Note: For essentially the same letter with additional details see:** O. B. Huntington Diary #15, entry for February 18, 1883, pp. 44–47, Harold B. Lee Library, Brigham Young University, Provo, Utah.

2. Ibid.

# APPENDIX O

1. Philemon Stewart, *A Holy, Sacred and Divine Roll and Book* (Lebanon, New York: United Society of Believers, 1843).

   Stephen J. Stein, *The Shaker Experience in America: A History of the United Society of Believers* (New Haven, Connecticut: Yale University Press, 1992), pp. 177–198; cited and analyzed by Richard Lyman Bushman in *Joseph Smith: Rough Stone Rolling* (New York City: Alfred A. Knopf / Borzoi Books, 2005), pp. 589–590.

2. Parley P. Pratt, *The Autobiography of Parley Parker Pratt: One of the Twelve Apostles of the Church of Jesus Christ of Latter-day Saints, Embracing His Life, Ministry and Travels, with Extracts, in Prose and Verse, from his*

*Miscellaneous Writings, edited by his son, Parley P. Pratt* (New York City: Russell Brothers, 1874), pp. 165–166.

3. Levi Hancock Diary, p. 45, L. Tom Perry Special Collections, Harold B. Lee Library, Brigham Young University, Provo, Utah; cited in Richard Lyman Bushman, *Joseph Smith: Rough Stone Rolling* (New York City: Alfred A. Knopf / Borzoi Books, 2005), p. 130.

# APPENDIX P

1. Daniel B. Wallace, *Grammar Beyond the Basics: An Exegetical Syntax of the New Testament* (Grand Rapids, Michigan and Miami, Florida: Zondervan/HarperCollins Publishers, 1997).

Jeremy Duff and David Wenham, *The Elements of New Testament Greek* (Cambridge, England: Cambridge University Press, 2005).

Friedrich Wilhelm Blass, editor, translated by Henry St. John Thackeray, *Grammar of New Testament Greek* (New York City: Macmillan and Company, 1905).

**Note: Author/researcher Christopher Rico writes, "By far the most predominant element in the language of the New Testament is the Greek of common speech which was disseminated in the East by the Macedonian conquest."** [Christopher Rico, "Chapter 4: New Testament Greek," in David E. Aune, *The Blackwell Companion to the New Testament* (Hoboken, New Jersey: Wiley-Blackwell, 2010), chapter 4.]

2. Archibald Macbride Hunter, *Introducing the New Testament: Third Revised Edition* (Louisville, Kentucky: Westminster John Knox Press, 1996), pp. 9–10.

Bruce Manning Metzger and Bart D. Ehrman, *The Text of the New Testament: Its Transmission, Corruption, and Restoration (Fourth Edition)* (New York City: Oxford University Press, USA).

**Note: On page 52n (the note on p. 52) these authors state, "The New Testament was written in Koine Greek, the Greek of daily conversation. The fact that from the first all the New Testament writings were written in Greek is conclusively demonstrated by their citations from the Old Testament."**

3. Adolf von Harnack, translated by Rev. J. R. Wilkinson, M.A., *Origin of the New Testament: and the most important consequences of the new creation*

(London: Williams and Norgate Publisher, 1925; and First Edition in German, 1914).

4. Everett Ferguson. "Factors leading to the Selection and Closure of the New Testament Canon," in *The Canon Debate*, edited by L. M. McDonald and J. A. Sanders (Peabody, Massachusetts: Hendrickson Publishers, 2002), p. 301.

   Irenaeus, Bishop of Lyons (France), *Adversus Haereses: Libre Quinque* (Charleston, South Carolina: Nabu Press/BiblioLif, 2010), 3.11.8 (book 3, chapter 11, section 8).

5. David Noel Freedman, *Anchor Bible Dictionary*, 6 volumes (New York City: Bantam Doubleday Dell Publishing Group, 1992).

6. J. J. deJonge, "The New Testament Canon," in *The Biblican Canons*, edited by J. J. deJonge and J. M. Auwers (Leuven, Belgium: Leuven University Press, 2003), p. 315.

7. Ibid.

8. F. F. Bruce, *The Canon of Scripture* (Downers Grove, Illinois: InterVarsity Press, 1988), p. 23.

9. Mark A. Noll, *Turning Points* (Ada, Michigan: Baker Academic, 1997), pp. 36–37.

10. R. R. Ackroyd and C. F. Evans, editors, *The Cambridge History of the Bible (volume 1)* (Cambridge, England: Cambridge University Press, 1970), p. 308.

11. Athanasius of Alexandria, Festal Letter 39, in Carter Lindberg, *A Brief History of Christianity* (Hoboken, New Jersey: Wiley Blackwell Publishing, 2005), p. 15.

12. F. F. Bruce, *The Canon of Scripture* (Downers Grove, Illinois: InterVarsity Press, 1988).

13. David Brakke, "Canon Formation and Social Conflict in Fourth-Century Egypt: Athanasius of Alexandria's Thirty Ninth 'Festal Letter,'" in *The Harvard Theological Review* (Cambridge, England: Cambridge University Press / for Harvard Divinity School Stable), vol. 87, no. 4 (October, 1994), pp. 395–419.

14. Carter Lindberg, *A Brief History of Christianity* (Hoboken, New Jersey: Wiley Blackwell Publishing, 2005), pp. 1, 15.

   **Note: Pope Damasus I reigned 366–384 A.D.**

15. Michael Collins and Matthew A. Price, *The Story of Christianity* (Carol Stream, Illinois: Tyndale House Publishers, 1999), pp. 61–62.

16. Note: The notes from the Synod of Hippo Regius and the details of their acts are lost; however, a summary of their acts survived and was read and accepted by the Third Council of Carthage in 419 A.D. [Lee Martin McDonald and James A. Sanders, editors, *The Canon Debate* (Peabody, Massachusetts: Hendrickson Publishers, 2002), appendix D-2, note 19.] Interestingly, Augustine presided over the Carthage councils and regarded the canon as already closed before they met. [Everet Ferguson, "Factors leading to the Selection and Closure of the New Testament Canon," in ibid., McDonald and James A. Sanders, p. 320.]

17. Ibid., Appendix D-2, p. 595, note 19.

18. Heinrich Joseph Dominicus Denzinger, *Sources of Catholic Dogma* (Fitzwilliam, New Hampshire: Loreto Publications, 2002), p. 92.

19. Charles G. Herbermann, Edward A. Pace, Conde B. Pallen, Thomas J. Shahan, John J. Wynne, editors, *The Catholic Encyclopedia: An International Work of Reference on the Constitution, Doctrine, Discipline, and History of the Catholic Church*, 16 volumes with index (New York City: The Encyclopedia Press, 1907–1914).

20. Ibid.

21. Note: Another way of stating it: The Catholics accepted the Greek Old Testament—the Septuagint—while the Protestants accepted the Hebrew Old Testament, the same books minus the Apocrypha. The word *apocrypha* means "hidden," and applies to those books in the Septuagint that are not in the Hebrew Bible.) From the early 1500s to 1885 Protestants did accept the Apocrypha, but in a separate section placed between the two testaments in their Bibles.

Some churches accept fewer apocryphal books, to varying degrees, than the standard 14, bringing the total number of biblical books for them in the 70s (compared to the Protestants' 66 and the Catholics' 80). The Ethiopian Orthodox Tweahedo Church uses even more apocryphal books than the standard 14—one more—putting its total at 81.

22. Note: By the 1200s the Latin Bible was called the *Versio Vulgata* and was the official version of the Bible in the Roman Catholic Church, eclipsing earlier Latin translations (as a group called the *Vetus Latina*).

In 1943 Pope Pius XII allowed other translations than just the Latin Vulgate for the Roman Catholic Church. Specifically, in English, he allowed the New American Bible.

23. Note: As covered in Appendix S: "English Bibles that Shook the World," William Tyndale attempted to print the New Testament in 1525, but Catholic German authorities stopped his press, so his first edition had only some pages printed. A year later he successfully printed the first complete New Testament. Then, in 1530, he printed 5 books of Moses and the book of Jonah from the Old Testament.

# APPENDIX Q

1. Note: The 1769 Baskerville Edition of the King James Version is not listed as such by the Christian Booksellers Association in its list of best-selling Bibles, but the only version of the King James Bible being sold (except for collectibles) is indeed the 1769 Baskerville Edition, which replaced the 1611 Edition of the King James Bible, as mentioned in Appendix S.

2. Note: The 1909 edition of the *Reina Valera* was used for the LDS Spanish translation of the Bible, utilizing "a very conservative update of outdated grammar and vocabulary," according to a statement in the LDS Spanish edition, which was published in September 2009.

3. "Bible Translations (October 2013 Bestsellers)," *Retailers + Resources Weekly*, November 2, 2013, cbanews.org/bibletranslations-october-2013-bestsellers/.

# APPENDIX R

## PART 1

1. William Paul, "John Wycliffe," *English Language Bible Translators* (Jefferson, North Carolina and London, England: McFarland and Company, 2003), p. 264.

2. Note: Arguably, the Anglican Church in England had general independence, but it did declare allegiance to the Roman Catholic Church's pope, so, in essence, it was still under Roman control by its acquiescence to Roman church authority. For details, see Appendix S: "English Bibles that Shook the World."

3. Enrico dal Covolo, "The Historical Origin of Indulgences" (Manassas, Virginia: Trinity Communications, 2013), CatholicCulture.org/culture/library/view.cfm?recnum+1054.

"Plenary Indulgence," in F. L. Cross, E. A. Livingstone, editors, *The Oxford Dictionary of the Christian Church* (New York City: Oxford University Press, 2005).

4. Johann Peter Kirsch, "The Reformation," in Charles G. Herbermann, Edward A. Pace, Conde B. Pallen, Thomas J. Shahan, John J. Wynne, editors, *The Catholic Encyclopedia: An International Work of Reference on the Constitution, Doctrine, Discipline, and History of the Catholic Church,* 16 volumes with index (New York City: The Encyclopedia Press, 1907–1914), vol. 12.

5. Ibid.

6. Enrico dal Covolo, "The Historical Origin of Indulgences" (Manassas, Virginia: Trinity Communications, 2013), CatholicCulture.org/culture/library/view.cfm?recnum+1054.

7. Ibid.

8. **Note: In contrast to Pope Leo X, Pope Boniface IX condemned certain religious orders who claimed they were authorized by him to forgive numerous types of sins while promising perpetual happiness in this world by taking people's money. Meanwhile, the indulgences angle seemed especially successful for the church to cash in on the more vulnerable simple-minded.** [W. H. Kent, "Indulgences," in Charles G. Herbermann, Edward A. Pace, Conde B. Pallen, Thomas J. Shahan, John J. Wynne, editors, *The Catholic Encyclopedia: An International Work of Reference on the Constitution, Doctrine, Discipline, and History of the Catholic Church*, 16 volumes with index (New York City: The Encyclopedia Press, 1907–1914).]

**Large indulgences took a leap in 1350 at Rome when it was believed that an indulgence of *14,000 years* had been granted for praying in the presence of the Imago Pietatis—"Man of Sorrows"—a pilgrimage spot where people flocked, located at the basilica of Santa Croce in Gerusalemme at Rome.** [Gertrud Schiller, English translation from German: *Iconography of Christian Art, Vol. II*, 2 volumes (London: Lund Humphries, 1971), vol. 2, pp. 199–200.]

**But in 1567 indulgences for many came to an end. Pope Pius V cancelled all grants of indulgences that involved money,** [W. H. Kent, "Indulgences," in Charles G. Herbermann, Edward A. Pace, Conde B. Pallen, Thomas J. Shahan, John J. Wynne, editors, *The Catholic Encyclopedia: An International Work of Reference on the Constitution, Doctrine, Discipline, and History of the Catholic Church*, 16 volumes with index (New York City: The Encyclopedia Press, 1907–1914);

"Myths About Indulgences," *Catholic Answers: to Explain & Defend the Faith* (San Diego, California), www.catholic.com/tracts/myths-about-indulgences] likely in response to the Reformation that had been spearheaded by Martin Luther. This was part of the "Counter-Reformation" within the Catholic Church, beginning mostly in 1563 with that monumental change (although some say the Counter-Reformation took place all during the Council of Trent [1545-1563] and even earlier).

Historically, 3½ centuries earlier, in 1215, the Fourth Lateran Council had suppressed some abuses, but they had not halted many until the Counter-Reformation at the Council of Trent ended in 1567.

The Council of Trent, held at Trento, Italy, actually started in 1545 and lasted through 3 different popes and 25 sessions. It was interrupted several times by political and religious bickering and conflicts. The major Counter-Reformation changes actually took place during the council's third period, from 1559 to 1563, under Pope Pius IV.

The council had commenced for various purposes, but the 2 most significant ones with long-lasting results were (1) to set straight the abuses that the Great Reformers were condemning, and (2) to officially set the canon of the Bible; thus, it proved to be one of the most historically significant ecumenical councils in history. [F. L. Cross, E. A. Livingstone, editors, *The Oxford Dictionary of the Christian Church* (New York: Oxford University Press, 2005), in entry, "Trent, Council of."] The Counter-Reformation ended in 1648, at the close of the Thirty Years' War, which devastated much of Europe—especially Germany and the Italian states.

Since then, reforms have taken place, all resulting perhaps directly or indirectly from the outcry of the Great Reformers of the Protestant movement.

9. Note: Johann Gutenberg's press was invented in about 1450. His first book, the Latin Vulgate, was released in either 1454 or 1455. (In March 1555 the future Pope Pius II wrote a letter saying he saw parts of the printed Bible.) It was actually surprisingly beautiful, with each leaf colorfully enhanced and hand-decorated after printing on many but not all copies.

Only wealthy church-related institutions and universities could afford this first edition, but it was the beginning of future possibilities—printing thousands of books at a time at cheaper costs with technical improvements.

Of this first, printed Latin edition—"the Gutenberg Bible"—only about 160 to 185 copies were printed. (In the same March 1455 letter by the future pope, he cited sources claiming 158 and 180 copies were printed.)

At last count, about 48 copies are accounted for today, with 13 copies in Germany, 11 in the U.S. and 8 in the U.K. The first one in the U.S. came in 1847. The last one to sell was in 1978, for $2.2 million. Their value today would allow a complete copy to sell for $25 to 35 million.

10. "Johann Tetzel," *Encyclopedia Britannica*, 32 volumes (Chicago: Encyclopedia Britannica, 2007).

11. Ibid.

12. Note: These are the "Anti-theses" in response to Luther's 95 Theses, written at least in part by Johann Tetzel's friend and former professor, Konrad Wimpina. The one in which they defended indulgences was Thesis 55 of Tetzel's One Hundred and Six Theses. [Henry Clay Vedder, *The Reformation in Germany* (New York City: Macmillan Company, 1914), p. 405.]

13. Hans J. Hillerbrand, "Martin Luther: Indulgences and Salvation," *Encyclopedia Britannica*, 32 volumes (Chicago: Encyclopedia Britannica, 2007).

14. John Foxe, *Actes and Monuments of these Latter and Perillous Days, Touching Matters of the Church* (London: John Day, First Edition [1,800 pages] 1563; Second Edition [2,300 pages] 1570), Chapter XII: "The Life and Story of the True Servant and Martyr of God."

Note 1: The burning of the 7 people at Coventry, England, for teaching their children the Lord's Prayer in English occurred in either 1517 or 1519.

Note 2: This book by John Foxe, often called *Foxe's Book of Martyrs*, is the most authoritative work to ever cite atrocities against the Protestant Reformers. In 2009 the *Encyclopaedia Britannica* noted it was "factually detailed and preserves much firsthand material on the English Reformation unobtainable elsewhere." It took years to obtain that acceptance. In the late 1800s and early 1900s it was not trusted as much as it is today. [Patrick Collinson, "John Foxe as Historian," in *TAMO: John Foxe's The Acts and Monuments Online* (Sheffield, Yorkshire, England: The University of Sheffield / Humanities Research Institute, 2011), www.johnfoxe.org/index/php?realm=more&gototype=modern &type=essay&book=essay3.]

15. Note: Martin Luther's excommunication took place 4 years after his posting of the "95 Theses" at Wittenberg, due to the pope's careful

and patient investigatory style. Some churchmen wanted him cut off right away—even executed—while others wished to gently persuade him of his "error." He was finally excommunicated at the famous Diet of Worms Council in 1521.

16. Note: In 1516 Desiderius Erasmus published his first Greek-Latin New Testament, then he published other revised editions over the next several years. In 1519 came his Second Edition, and in 1522 his Third Edition (likely used by Martin Luther for his German translation and by William Tyndale for the first-ever published English New Testament in 1525 (partially published) and 1526 (complete) as well as by Robert Stephanus in his 1550 Edition that was later used by translators (along with Tyndale's Bible) for the Geneva Bible and King James Version and others. In 1527 came Erasmus's Fourth Edition, which had parallel columns in Greek, his own Latin translation, and the Latin Vulgate, showing the remarkable inaccuracies of the Vulgate. In 1535 came his Fifth and final Edition, which left out the Vulgate. His later editions were called the *Textus Receptus*, which is often cited as the source used for 16th-century Bibles; however, in my opinion, they are often mistaken, as they generally used his earlier editions, especially the Third Edition, per above.

## PART 2

1. Martin Marty, *Martin Luther: A Penguin Life* (New York City: Viking Pilgrim, 2004), pp. 2–3.

2. Ibid., p. 5.

3. Martin Brecht, translated by James L. Schaaf, *Martin Luther: His Road to Reformation 1483–1521*, 3 volumes (Philadelphia: Fortress Press, 1985), vol. 1, p. 48.

4. Martin Brecht, translated by Wolfgang Katenz, "Luther, Martin," in Hans J. Hillerbrand, editor, *The Oxford Encyclopedia of the Reformation*, 4 volumes (New York City: Oxford University Press, 1996), vol. 1, p. 460.

5. Derek Wilson, *Out of the Storm: The Life and Legacy of Martin Luther* (New York City: St. Martin's Press, 2008), pp. 153, 170.

   Richard Marius, *Martin Luther: Christian between God and Death* (Cambridge, Massachusetts: Harvard University Press / The Belkna Press, 1999), p. 155.

   Note: Martin Luther may not have actually said these words ("Here I stand; I can do no other") which have been attributed to him, as

**eyewitnesses did not record them, but the words were included in later versions of his speech.**

6.  Dennius Bratcher, "The Diet of Worms" in *The Voice: Biblical and Theological Resources for Growing Christians* (Oklahoma City, Oklahoma: Christian Resource Institute, 2013), www.crivoice.org/creededictworms.html.

7.  Martin Luther, "Letter 82," in Jaroslav Jan Pelikan, Hilton C. Oswald and Helmut T. Lehmann, editors, *Luther's Works*, 55 volumes (Philadelphia: Fortress Press, 1999).

**Note: Martin Luther's comment—"my Patmos"—is in reference to the Apostle John, who wrote the book of Revelation in the New Testament and was exiled to the island of Patmos.**

8.  Richard Marius, *Martin Luther: Christian between God and Death* (Cambridge, Massachusetts: Harvard University Press / The Belkna Press, 1999), pp. 163–164.

9.  A. G. Dickens, *The German Nation and Martin Luther* (London: Edward Arnold, 1974), pp. 132–133.

10.  Michael Hughes, *Early Modern Germany: 1477–1806* (Philadelphia: University of Pennsylvania Press, 1992), p. 50.

11.  Jaroslav Jan Pelikan, Hilton C. Oswald, and Helmut T. Lehmann, editors, *Luther's Works*, 55 volumes (St. Louis: Concordia Publishing House and Philadelphia: Fortress Press, 1955), vol. 46, pp. 50–51.

12.  Martin Marty, *Martin Luther: A Penguin Life* (New York City: Viking Penguin, 2004), p. 109.

13.  Philip Schaff, "Luther's Marriage, 1525," *History of the Christian Church, Volume VII: Modern Christianity: The German Reformation* (New York City: Charles Scribner's Sons, 1892; reprinted at Grand Rapids, Michigan: Calvin College / Christian Classics Ethereal Library, 2005), p. 77.

14.  Ibid.

15.  Derek Wilson, *Out of the Storm: The Life and Legacy of Martin Luther* (New York City: St. Martin's Press, 2008), p. 232.

16.  Martin Brecht, translated by James L. Schaaf, *Martin Luther: His Road to Reformation 1483–1521*, 3 volumes (Philadelphia: Fortress Press, 1985), vol. 2, pp. 264–265.

17.  Michael A. Mullett, *Martin Luther* (Oxford, England: Routledge/Taylor and Francis Group, 2004), pp. 186–187.

Martin Brecht, translated by James L. Schaaf, *Martin Luther: His Road to Reformation 1483–1521*, 3 volumes (Philadelphia: Fortress Press, 1985), vol. 2, pp. 264–265, 267.

18. Martin Luther, *Vom Kriege wider die Türken* (translation: *On War against the Turk*), published in 1529, quoted in William P. Brown, *The Ten Commandments: The Reciprocity of Faithfulness* (Louisville, Kentucky: Westminster John Knox Press, 2004), p. 258.

    Bernhard Lohse, *Martin Luther: An Introduction to his Life and Work*, translated by Robert C. Schultz (Edinburgh: T & T Clark, 1987), p. 61.

19. **Note: While others had translated the Latin Vulgate into German, Martin Luther honed the Greek version (from Desiderius Erasmus's translating) to fit his doctrine, as other translators had with the Vulgate version.**

20. Eric W. Gritsch, *A History of Lutheranism* (Minneapolis: Fortress Press, First Edition 2002; Second Edition 2010), p. 45.

21. Martin Brecht, translated by James L. Schaaf, *Martin Luther: His Road to Reformation 1483–1521*, 3 volumes (Philadelphia: Fortress Press, 1985), vol. 3, p. 206.

22. Ibid., p. 212.

23. **Note: The "Castle Church" where Martin Luther posted his "Ninety-five Theses," has a phoenix-like history in more than one way. Not only did it rise from its first life as a Catholic church to a Lutheran establishment, but it literally was reduced to ashes, from which it was reborn as a new building on the same property. When Luther posted his "Ninety-five Theses," the church building had only been completed for 9 years, having been built from 1490 to 1509, a 19-year construction project.**

    **In 1760, when the church was 251 years old, the original wood doors were destroyed, as well as priceless works of art, as the church was mostly leveled by fire resulting from French cannon fire during the Seven Years' War, leaving only half the foundation.**

    **But the ruins were swept away and the church was rebuilt shortly after the war. At that time a new wooden door replaced the original door on which Luther had posted (some say engraved) his 95 theses. In 1858 a third door was built for the church—a heavy, bronze door that replaced the newer wooden door.**

    **The church was then renovated during a 9-year construction project—from 1883 to 1893—keeping the bronze door, which is still in place today.**

## PART 3

1. **Note: At Oxford University, William Tyndale attended the Magdalen School.**

2. Herbert Samworth, *Tyndale's Ploughboy: The Life of William Tyndale— Part 3, Little Sodbury Manor* (Powell, Tennessee: Reformers, 2010), www. tyndalesploughboy.org/life-of-william-tyndale-part-3.

3. John Foxe, *Actes and Monuments of these Latter and Perillous Days, Touching Matters of the Church* (London: John Day, First Edition [1,800 pages] 1563; Second Edition [2,300 pages] 1570), Chapter XII: "The Life and Story of the True Servant and Martyr of God."

4. Ibid.

5. **Note: The main source for William Tyndale's reported altercation with other priests is John Foxe, who received information from Richard Webb of Gloucestershire about the events there, and recorded them per the account in the text, as related verbatim in a summary below.**

   **When other priests would vary from Tyndale's opinions, states Foxe, "he would show them in the Book [the Latin Vulgate], and lay plainly before them the open and manifest places of the scriptures, to confute their errors and confirm his sayings. And thus continued they for a certain season, reasoning and contending together divers times until at length they waxed weary."**

   **Not much later, "there was a sitting of the bishop's chancellor appointed, and warning was given to the priests to appear, amongst whom Master Tyndale was also warned to be there."**

   **To those who knew Tyndale in later years, he was, states John Foxe, "a man of most virtuous disposition, and of life unspotted."**

   [John Foxe, *Actes and Monuments of these Latter and Perillous Days, Touching Matters of the Church* (London: John Day, First Edition [1,800 pages] 1563; Second Edition [2,300 pages] 1570), Chapter XII: "The Life and Story of the True Servant and Martyr of God."]

6. Fred R. Coulter, *A Tribute to William Tyndale: The "Father" of All English Bibles* (Hollister, California: Christian Biblical Church of God, 2011), www.churchathome.org/pdf/William_Tyndale_Tribute.pdf.

   "William Tyndale: biography" (Electric Family, 1995–2006), www. famouspeople.com/cat-william-tyndale.

7.  John Foxe, *Actes and Monuments of these Latter and Perillous Days, Touching Matters of the Church* (London: John Day, First Edition [1,800 pages] 1563; Second Edition [2,300 pages] 1570), Chapter XII: "The Life and Story of the True Servant and Martyr of God."

8.  Robert D. Hales, "Preparations for the Restoration and the Second Coming: 'My Hand Shall Be over Thee,'" Address before the October 2005 General Conference of the Church of Jesus Christ of Latter-day Saints, *Ensign* (Salt Lake City: The Church of Jesus Christ of Latter-day Saints, October Conference issue, 2005).

9.  **Note: The English translation of the Bible had been outlawed in 1408, under the direction of Thomas Arundel, Archbishop of Canterbury. This law declared that no one could own an English Bible.**

10. **Note: After opposing priests made life difficult for William Tyndale, slandering him as a heretic, John Foxe writes that Tyndale went to his master and "desired him, of his good will, that he might depart . . . [then] with the good will of his master, departed."**

11. Melvin Bragg, narrator, *The Most Dangerous Man in Tudor England, BBC Documentary*, aired on BBC 2, June 6, 2013.

12. John Foxe, *Actes and Monuments of these Latter and Perillous Days, Touching Matters of the Church* (London: John Day, First Edition [1,800 pages] 1563; Second Edition [2,300 pages] 1570), Chapter XII: "The Life and Story of the True Servant and Martyr of God."

    Josiah Pratt and John Stoughton, *The Actes and Monuments of John Foxe*, 8 volumes (London: Religious Tract Society, 1877; revising the 1563 Edition), vol. 5, pp. 121–123.

    **Note: Josiah Pratt was on the faculty of Trinity College, founded in 1546 by King Henry VIII, as part of Cambridge University.**

13. William Tyndale, preface to *Five bokes of Moses Called the Pentateuch* (possibly published at Marburg, Germany, 1530).

14. John Foxe, *Actes and Monuments of these Latter and Perillous Days, Touching Matters of the Church* (London: John Day, First Edition [1,800 pages] 1563; Second Edition [2,300 pages] 1570), Chapter XII: "The Life and Story of the True Servant and Martyr of God."

15. Ibid.

16. Ibid.

    **Note 1: John Foxe continues of these priests: "All their labor was with might and main to keep it down, so that either it should not be read**

at all, or if it were, they would darken the right sense with the mist of their sophistry."

Note 2: William Tyndale later wrote a prologue to the Old Testament books he would translate in 1530. In it he would outline the events that led him to London. Some glean from it that Little Sodbury is where he formulated his plans to translate the Bible after dealing with the difficult priests there. It was at this point he made a prediction that even the plowboy would someday know more than they. So, in this prologue he states, in part, "Which thing [the behavior of the priests] only moved me to translate the new Testament. I had perceived by experience how that it was impossible to establish the lay-people in any truth, except the scriptures were plainly laid before their eyes in their mother-tongue . . . whatsoever truth is taught them, these enemies of all truth [the priests he had dealt with] quench it again, partly with the smoke of the bottomless pit." [John F*oxe, Actes and Monuments of these Latter and Perillous Days, Touching Matters of the Church* (London: John Day, First Edition [1,800 pages] 1563; Second Edition [2,300 pages] 1570), Chapter XII: "The Life and Story of the True Servant and Martyr of God."]

17. Ibid.

18. **Note: James Frederic Mozley in his biography of William Tyndale presents evidence that Tyndale first went straight to Wittenberg, Germany, where Martin Luther lived, to work with him.** [James Frederic Mozley, *William Tyndale* (New York City: The Macmillan Company, 1937).] **Some scholars agree with him.**

    **But most, according to Dr. Herbert Samworth in *The Life of William Tyndale: Part 5, Tyndale in Germany*, believe Tyndale went to Hamburg first and stayed there with a Mrs. Emmerson, a widow believing in the Reformation.** [Herbert Samworth, *Tyndale's Ploughboy: The Life of William Tyndale—Part 5, Tyndale in Germany* (Powell, Tennessee: Reformers, 2010), www. tyndalesploughboy.org/life-of-william-tyndale-part-5.]

    **However, the majority of Tyndale scholars could be mistaken that he first stayed in Hamburg, since Martin Luther was his prime interest. Getting together with Luther at Wittenberg seemed to be his main focus—especially since they shared the same concern for translating the Bible from Greek—thus, Wittenberg could indeed have been Tyndale's first stop in Germany.**

19. Melvin Bragg, narrator, *The Most Dangerous Man in Tudor England*, BBC Documentary, aired on BBC 2, June 6, 2013.

20. Note: The printers at Cologne, Germany, who got drunk and bragged to John Dobneck that all of England would soon be Lutheran, apparently did not realize that Tyndale and Luther were not of the same religion, but merely allies; however since both were Reformers, the printers likely labeled any Reformers "Lutheran."

21. Note: True, John Dobneck's discovery stopped the presses at Cologne, Germany, but Tyndale flew the coop into the German countryside, so Henry VIII once again never gave Dobneck an ounce of praise—not even for stopping the presses. Dobneck would write Henry VIII several letters boasting about his actions, implying he had saved all of England from a spiritual downfall, but he never heard anything back, not even the slightest acknowledgment (nor especially the handsome reward he had hoped for), which only gave more cause for bitterness on Dobneck's part. He would write the king one last time, but would again hear nothing back. (Later he would write an attack on Martin Luther and mention these events.)

22. Note: The Rhine River begins 3,359 feet high in the Swiss Alps and ends at sea level 820 miles northward at the North Sea near Rotterdam, Netherlands, thus causing the water to flow northward, due to gravitational pull. The Rhine has only about 500 miles of navigable water, flowing from Basel, Switzerland, on the southern border of Germany, to near Rotterdam, the Netherlands, on the North Sea. The first 320 miles of the river coming from the Swiss Alps is not boat worthy—with water coming down the mountains in torrents and waterfalls. But after it leaves Switzerland, through the entire country of Germany, the Rhine flows smoothly. This makes Germany the country having the most use for the Rhine, although it does flow through 6 of today's nations. Of particular fascination to many, the Rhine is replete with castles and rich history, and even has modern-day cruise excursions on the river.

23. Joannes Cochlaeus, *Commentaria de Actis et Scriptis Martini Lutheri* (St. Victor [Near Mainz], Germany: Franciscus Berthem, 1549), p. 134.

24. Herbert Samworth, *Tyndale's Ploughboy: The Life of William Tyndale—Part 6, Tyndale in Worms* (Powell, Tennessee: Reformers, 2010), www.tyndalesploughboy.org/life-of-william-tyndale-part-6.

Note: If William Tyndale had printed 6,000 copies at Worms, Germany, half of that number would have been a "repeat printing" of the First Edition he had started at Cologne, before the invasion by Dobneck. (Thus, he may have attempted 3,000 copies at Cologne, which were destroyed on the press.)

25. Peter Ackroyd, *The Life of Thomas More* (New York City: Nan A. Talese / Knopf Doubleday, 1999), p. 270.

26. David Daniell, Introduction, *Tyndale's 1534 New Testament* (London: Yale University Press, 1989), p. XIV.

27. **Note: Thomas More was also Chancellor of the Duchy of Lancaster, controlling the judicial and executive concerns of much of northern England, as well as serving as speaker of the House of Commons.**

28. Melvin Bragg, narrator, *The Most Dangerous Man in Tudor England*, BBC Documentary, aired on BBC 2, June 6, 2013.

29. John Foxe, *Actes and Monuments of these Latter and Perillous Days, Touching Matters of the Church* (London: John Day, First Edition [1,800 pages] 1563; Second Edition [2,300 pages] 1570), Chapter XII: "The Life and Story of the True Servant and Martyr of God."

30. **Note: Thomas More backed up this account of Cuthbert Tunstall's blunder, claiming Tunstall had come to him and told him about the plan to buy up all of Tyndale's Bibles.**

    **However, More first learned the details of the outcome—of Tyndale's having received profits from that sale to Tunstall, which allowed him to print many more copies—from a heretic, George Constantine. More had obtained the information by promising Constantine he would free him if he would tell him where Tyndale got the money to print all the new Bibles flooding the country.**

    **Constantine was happy to tell him—he could not only get his freedom but could brag how Tyndale had outsmarted the highest church authorities in the land and tripled his profits to revise and publish even more Bibles. So with a smile on his face, George Constantine informed Thomas More that it was Tunstall, the Bishop of London, who had financed Tyndale. Thomas More was anguished. He replied to Constantine that he knew this would happen, and had even warned Bishop Tunstall "that's what would happen" if he proceeded with this crazy plan to buy up all the Bibles in Antwerp. George Constantine then sauntered away from prison a very happy heretic, leaving church authorities in his wake, shaking their fists in rage.**

31. **Note: John Foxe writes that unfair criticisms of the contents of William Tyndale's New Testament began coming from the Catholic clergy in England. "They scanned and examined every title and point . . . and so narrowly, that there was not one 'i' therein but if it lacked a prick over his head [if he did not dot the *i*] they did note it, and numbered it unto the ignorant people for a heresy." Such intellectual dishonesty rankled Tyndale.**

Foxe adds that Tyndale was equally critical of the clergy—but unlike them, his criticisms were based on honest perceptions: "The intent [of the clergy] (as Tyndale saith) [is] that the world being kept still in darkness . . . through vain superstition and false doctrine, [is] to satisfy their ambition and insatiable covetousness, and to exalt their own honor above king and emperor."

While at Worms, Germany, William Tyndale published his first tract (separate from his New Testament), titled *A Compendious introduction, prologue or preface of Paul to the Romans*, based on a tract by Martin Luther, describing the book of Romans. An enlarged version of it was placed in the prologue of Tyndale's revised New Testament of 1534. [John Foxe, *Actes and Monuments of these Latter and Perillous Days, Touching Matters of the Church* (London: John Day, First Edition [1,800 pages] 1563; Second Edition [2,300 pages] 1570), Chapter XII: "The Life and Story of the True Servant and Martyr of God."]

32. Herbert Samworth, *Tyndale's Ploughboy: The Life of William Tyndale— Part 8, The Pentateuch* (Powell, Tennessee: Reformers, 2010), www. tyndalesploughboy.org/life-of-william-tyndale-part-8.

33. John Foxe, *Actes and Monuments of these Latter and Perillous Days, Touching Matters of the Church* (London: John Day, First Edition [1,800 pages] 1563; Second Edition [2,300 pages] 1570), Chapter XII: "The Life and Story of the True Servant and Martyr of God."

34. Ibid.

35. Note: One question for historians apparently has no definitive answer: how long did William Tyndale remain in Hamburg after he translated his portion of the Old Testament?

36. John Foxe, *Actes and Monuments of these Latter and Perillous Days, Touching Matters of the Church* (London: John Day, First Edition [1,800 pages] 1563; Second Edition [2,300 pages] 1570), Chapter XII: "The Life and Story of the True Servant and Martyr of God."

37. Note: The other scholars at Oxford, along with John Frith, who turned against the church were also handpicked by Cardinal Wolsey.

38. Note: John Frith's answer to church authorities was actually quite diplomatic, saying he felt indifferent about the matter. Ironically, that indifference is what caused his demise.

39. Peter Ackroyd, *The Life of Thomas More* (London: Anchor Books, 1999), p. 270.

40. Note: At Antwerp, William Tyndale had written his 1st theological book, *The Parable of the Wicked Mammon*, based on the parable

in Luke 16. Five months later came his 2nd book, *Obedience of a Christian Man*. It was twice the length of the 1st and came from the press of Johnannes Hoochstraten in Antwerp.

41. Herbert Samworth, *Tyndale's Ploughboy: The Life of William Tyndale—Part 7, Tyndale and His Tracts* (Powell, Tennessee: Reformers, 2010), www.tyndalesploughboy.org/life-of-william-tyndale-part-7.

Note: In the beginning section of his book, *Obedience of a Christian Man*, Tyndale discusses another theme: that when people are persecuted, they should grow in their faith; and the Bible, he says, states that followers of God will suffer persecution.

42. Antonia Fraser, *The Wives of Henry VIII* (New York City: Alfred A. Knopf, 1992), p. 145.

43. Ibid.

44. David Daniell, *William Tyndale: A Biography* (New Haven, Connecticut and London: Yale University Press, 1994).

David Daniell, Interview by William H. Noah (Host, Producer), *William Tyndale: His Life, His Legacy*, video recording (London: Avalon Press, 2004).

45. Michael Graves, *Henry VIII: A Study in Kingship* (London: Pearson Longman, 2003), p. 132.

46. David Starkey, *Six Wives: The Queens of Henry VIII* (New York City: HarperCollins Publishers, 2003).

47. Herbert Samworth, Tyndale's Ploughboy: *The Life of William Tyndale—Part 9, Events After 1530* (Powell, Tennessee: Reformers, 2010), www.tyndalesploughboy.org/life-of-william-tyndale-part-9.

48. Melvin Bragg, narrator, *The Most Dangerous Man in Tudor England*, BBC Documentary, aired on BBC 2, June 6, 2013.

49. Ibid.

50. J. G. Bellamy, *The Tudor Law of Treason: An Introduction* (London: Routledge & Kegan Paul, 1979), p. 89.

51. Roland H. Worth, *Church, Monarch, and Bible in Sixteenth Century England: The Political Context of Biblical Translation* (Jefferson, North Carolina: McFarland, 2000), pp. 38–39.

Note: Today only 6 or 8 copies of Tyndale's First Edition New Testament are known to exist. The only complete copy of his First Edition New Testament is located at Stuttgart, Germany, in a museum.

52. Note: One scholar, Herbert Samworth, analyzes, "There is no definitive authority that states how many of these [Second Edition Pentateuch copies] were printed." He then speculates that William Tyndale printed the same number of Pentateuch Old Testament copies as his New Testament copies—estimating them at 3,000 each. [Herbert Samworth, *Tyndale's Ploughboy: The Life of William Tyndale—Part 8, The Pentateuch* (Powell, Tennessee: Reformers, 2010), www.tyndalesploughboy.org/ life-of-william-tyndale-part-8.]

When stating that the same number of Old Testament copies were printed as the New Testament, Samworth apparently means 3,000 copies of each New Testament Edition were printed, because in Part 6 of his book (as mentioned in Note 24 above), he advances the theory that 6,000 New Testament copies were printed at his second attempt at printing the First Edition. (By doing this, Tyndale would have averaged 3,000 copies per edition. That Second Edition was the first successfully printed edition after the disastrous first attempt by another printer at Cologne.) [Ibid., *Part 6, Tyndale in Worms.*] Other editions would come, with many more thousands of copies in all, putting the New Testament in "best seller" mode for basically illiterate England.

53. Elias Benjamin Sanford, *A Concise Cyclopedia of Religious Knowledge: Biblical, Biographical, Geographical, Historical, Practical and Theological* (Hartford, Connecticut: The S. S. Scranton Company, 1909), p. 108.

Note: This book from Elias Benjamin Sanford was first published in 1890 by Mark Twain's publishing company at New York City—Charles L. Webster & Company. This publishing house was begun by Twain (his real name was Samuel L. Clemens) and his wife's nephew, Charles L. Webster, 6 years earlier, in 1884. Twain ousted Webster because of failing health in 1888, and Webster died shortly thereafter, but the company retained its name and Twain took on another partner, Frederick J. Hall, who became its active manager, until the firm went belly-up in 1894, causing much public embarrassment to Twain. At that time he was a household name, and in that day, bankruptcies were considered shameful, as people were expected at all costs to meet their obligations.

Initially the company had launched with success, not only with his own books, but with the memoirs of Ulysses S. Grant. Then it took a financial nosedive with a failed publishing title, covering the life of Pope Leo XIII, which sold less than 200 copies.

To stay alive, the company took on an aggressive new concept.

In 1891 it launched a new line of books titled "Library of American Literature," with a $100,000 investment (in today's money: $3.3 million), including funds from the company itself. That portion of the company—the new line of books—was sold 2 years later to William Evarts Benjamin. But a year later the company completely collapsed.

When it died, it actually was running in profit mode, and had assets of $150,000–200,000 above its liabilities (which were less than $250,000). What took the company under was the interest it owed on matured loans that needed to be paid, but could not be. (The company had expected new investors to come aboard, but when they suddenly and unexpectedly backed out, it was left high and dry, unable to pay the interest on those previous obligations.)

Twain was then personally liable for the difference, but at the time could not cover the spread, [*The New York Times* (New York City), April 19, 1894] so he was financially wiped out, despite the fact he was one of the top-earning authors in the world.

But, in addition to the interest he could not pay on the loans, the deeper, underlying reason the company went under was because Mark Twain drained it of its profits, so that he could invest them in the Paige typesetting machine—a mechanical marvel at the time that unfortunately suffered from numerous breakdowns. Before it could get the design problems fixed, it was replaced by the revolutionary Linotype machine, the standard for decades thereafter. (The Linotype has its own fascinating history, invented by Ottmar Mergenthaler, a German immigrant to New York City, who invented it in 1884. The machine was used till the 1970s and 1980s until it was replaced by phototypesetting and later by computerized typesetting and composition systems.)

In the Paige typesetting machine Twain invested $300,000 (the equivalent of $9.9 million today—actually $9,911,974, not counting inflation for his investments for the first decade, from 1880 to 1889) [Tom's Inflation Calculator, www.halfhill.com/inflation.calculator.html] —which came from most of the profits from his own books, plus much of his wife's inheritance.

His partner, Hall, had actually worked hard at the company and had proven to be a tremendous asset to Twain.

But after the bankruptcy, Twain accused Hall of deception, and used that argument as a reason to not pay him back for a personal loan he owed. [J. Mark Baggett, "Hall, Fred," in J. R. LeMaster and James D. Wilson, editors, *The Mark Twain Encyclopedia* (New York City: Garland

Publishers, 1993), p. 344; later reprinted as *The Routledge Encyclopedia of Mark Twain* (Oxford, England: Routledge, 2011).]

**But Twain would rebound, and he showed personal integrity despite his attempted weaseling out of the debt to Hall: he befriended a principal in the Standard Oil Company, Henry H. Rogers. Their 15-year friendship saved the day for Twain. Rogers had him file for bankruptcy and transfer his copyrights to Twain's wife so that creditors could not seize them, then he took charge of all of Twain's money until the creditors were paid off, even though Twain was not legally responsible to pay off those creditors. Twain then embarked on a year-long global tour, although sick during much of it, until, in 1900, he earned enough to pay back all his debts.**

**Needless to say, Mark Twain's venture into mechanical marvels and the world of publishing was a flat-out failure, despite his remarkable writing success that he (and most writers) should have "stuck to."**

54. **Note: Myles Coverdale published his 1535 Bible as the first printed complete Old and New Testaments in English. It would use all of Tyndale's New Testament and the aforementioned first 5 books of the Old Testament, which he had re-translated with Tyndale after the shipwreck. It would also include the book of Jonah that they had worked on together. The remainder of the Old Testament came from his own translating. The full name of Coverdale's Bible is *The Bible, that is the Holy Scripture of the Old and New Testament, faithfully translated into English*. Then, in 1537, the next Bible would come out—the Matthew Bible from John Rogers, which would use all of Tyndale's New Testament and 15 of Tyndale's later-translated 17 Old Testament books that had never been published in Tyndale's lifetime.**

55. Melvin Bragg, narrator, *The Most Dangerous Man in Tudor England*, BBC Documentary, aired on BBC 2, June 6, 2013.

56. Simon Schama, "Burning Convictions," *A History of Britain, Volume 1: At the Edge of the World? 3500 B.C. – 1603 A.D.* (New York City: Miramax Books, 2003), pp. 309–311.

    John Vidmar, *The Catholic Church Through the Ages* (Mahwah, New Jersey: Paulist Press, 2005), p. 220.

57. John Foxe, *Actes and Monuments of these Latter and Perillous Days, Touching Matters of the Church* (London: John Day, First Edition [1,800 pages] 1563; Second Edition [2,300 pages] 1570), Chapter XII: "The Life and Story of the True Servant and Martyr of God," p. 1229.

58. Ibid.

59. Ibid.

60. Ibid.

61. Ibid.

62. Ibid.

63. Ibid.

64. Ibid.

65. **Note: The cell at Vilvorde, Belgium, where William Tyndale was imprisoned, no longer exists; another building was built on the site in the 1700s.**

66. "Holy Days," *Worship—The Calendar*, Church of England, 2001 calendar.

67. Pope Paul II, Apostolic Letter (October 31, 2000), from the Vatican.

68. John F*oxe, Actes and Monuments of these Latter and Perillous Days, Touching Matters of the Church* (London: John Day, First Edition [1,800 pages] 1563; Second Edition [2,300 pages] 1570), Chapter XII: "The Life and Story of the True Servant and Martyr of God."

69. Ibid.

70. Melvin Bragg, narrator, *The Most Dangerous Man in Tudor England*, BBC Documentary, aired on BBC 2, June 6, 2013.

71. James Gairdner, John Sherren Brewer, and Robert Henry Brodie, editors, *Letters and Papers, Foreign and Domestic, of the Reign of Henry VIII: Preserved in the Public Record Office, the British Museum, and Elsewhere in England*, 21 volumes (London: British Museum of History, 1862–1932, and New York City: Kraus Reprint Co., 1965), Volume 16 (edited by only Gairdner and Brodie), p. 284.

    **Note: When Thomas Cromwell uttered his final words before his beheading, he stated, "I die in the Catholic faith," which author John Schofield analyzed as meaning not in the Roman Catholic Church, since he leaned toward supporting Reformers to the extent he could, but the "Holy Catholic and Apostolic Church" of the New Testament.** [John Schofield, *The Rise and Fall of Thomas Cromwell: Henry VIII's Most Faithful Servant* (Charleston, South Carolina: The History Press, 2008), p. 261.]

72. John F*oxe, Actes and Monuments of these Latter and Perillous Days, Touching Matters of the Church* (London: John Day, First Edition [1,800 pages] 1563; Second Edition [2,300 pages] 1570), Chapter XII: "The Life and Story of the True Servant and Martyr of God."

73. Note: As for the number of English Bibles printed in the decades following Tyndale, some enthusiastic Protestant sources estimate that during William Shakespeare's lifetime (1564–1616), which began 28 years after Tyndale's death, 2 million English Bibles were sold through the British Isles. However, since the population probably stood at no more than 1 million in England and Wales by 1616, with many of them children and with the adults chiefly illiterate, this number of 2 million English Bibles sold in Britain during Shakespeare's lifetime is outrageously exaggerated. Still, the effect of Tyndale's work on the proliferation of Bibles throughout the British Isles cannot be overlooked.

## PART 4

1. Note: The only English Edition of the Bible during the 1500s not influenced by Tyndale's Bible was the one produced by the Roman Catholic Church and printed in France—the Douay-Rheims, with the New Testament in 1582 and the 2-volume Old Testament in 1609–1610, which were influenced by the Latin Vulgate.

2. John Vidmar, *The Catholic Church Through the Ages* (Mahwah, New Jersey: Paulist Press, 2005), pp. 225–226.

   Christopher Haigh, editor, *The English Reformation Revisited* (Cambridge, England: Cambridge University Press, 1987), p. 159.

3. Note: John Calvin was the author of the most famous theological book ever published—before or perhaps since (with the exception of the Bible and the *Book of Mormon* since)—*Calvin's Institutes of the Christian Religion.*

4. Note: At least 144 editions of the Geneva Bible were published between 1560 and 1644. After that, the favorability rating among readers gave the nod to the King James Version, as the KJV finally kicked in among English readers, even among breakaway Protestant groups that were leaving the Church of England.

5. John Vidmar, *The Catholic Church Through the Ages* (Mahwah, New Jersey: Paulist Press, 2005), pp. 225–226.

   Leo Frank Solt, *Church and State in Early Modern England, 1509–1640* (New York City: Oxford University Press, 1990), p. 149.

6. John Vidmar, *The Catholic Church Through the Ages* (Mahwah, New Jersey: Paulist Press, 2005), pp. 225–226.

7. Simon Schama, *A History of Britain, Volume 1: At the Edge of the World? 3500 B.C.–1603 A.D.* (New York City: Miramax Books, 2003), pp. 272–273.

8. William Cullen Bryan, editor, *Picturesque America; or, the Land We Live In*, 2 volumes (New York City: D. Appleton and Co., Volume 1, 1872), vol. 1, p. 502.

9. Edward B. Underhill, *Struggles and Triumphs of Religious Liberty: An historical Survey of Controversies Pertaining to the Rights of Consciences, from the English Reformation to the Settlement of New England* (New York City: Lewis Colby, 1851).

   William F. Anderson, *Apostasy or Succession, Which?* (Independence, Missouri: Board of Publications, Church of Christ [Temple Lot], 1966), pp. 238–239.

10. John Wesley, *Works*, 7 volumes (New York City: Methodist Book Concern, 1903), vol. 7, section 89, pp. 26–27.

    **Note 1: This 1903 Edition of John Wesley's Works was the first to contain his chief writings of prose. He actually compiled his first series of all his works between 1771 and 1774 at Bristol, England, in 32 volumes.**

    **Note 2: After Wesley made the comment that is contained in the text, he went on to say, "The real cause of it was the love of many, almost all Christians, so called, was waxed cold. The Christians had no more of the Spirit of Christ than the other heathens. The Son of Man, when he came to examine His Church, could hardly find faith upon the earth. This was the real cause why the extraordinary gifts of the Holy Ghost were no longer to be found in the Christian Church, because the Christians were turned heathens again, and had only a dead form left."**

11. Thomas Jefferson, Letter (to Benjamin Waterhouse, June 26, 1822), quoted in Norman Cousins, *In God We Trust: The Religious Beliefs and Ideals of the Founding Fathers* (New York City: Harper and Brothers, 1958), p. 162.

12. Thomas Jefferson, Letter (to Benjamin Waterhouse, July 26, 1822), quoted in ibid.

# APPENDIX S

1. *The Doctrine and Covenants of the Church of Jesus Christ of Latter-day Saints: Containing Revelations given to Joseph Smith, the Prophet, with Some Additions by His Successors In the Presidency of the Church* (Salt Lake City: The Church of Jesus Christ of Latter-day Saints, 1981), 19:15–18.

# APPENDIX T

1. **Note: Venerable Bede was the only English-born Catholic to ever achieve an appointment from the pope (Leo XIII) as a Doctor of the Church, which took place 12 centuries later in 1899.**

2. "Richard Rolle de Hampole," in Charles G. Herbermann, Edward A. Pace, Conde B. Pallen, Thomas J. Shahan, John J. Wynne, editors, *The Catholic Encyclopedia: An International Work of Reference on the Constitution, Doctrine, Discipline, and History of the Catholic Church*, 16 volumes with index (New York City: The Encyclopedia Press, 1907–1914).

3. William Paul, "John Wycliffe," *English Language Bible Translators* (Jefferson, North Carolina and London: McFarland and Company, 2003), p. 264.

   **Note: Of the 2 editions of Wycliffe's Bible, the 1st adhered more to the Latin order of wording in the text from which he translated, while the 2nd tried to flow more with English sentence structure.**

4. **Note: This pope who took vengeance on John Wycliffe's corpse was Martin V, who reigned from 1417 to 1431.**

5. **Note: As noted earlier (in Appendix R, Part 1, note 15), both William Tyndale and Martin Luther probably used the Third Greek Edition of the New Testament, translated by Desiderius Erasmus and published in 1522. (Erasmus's First Greek Edition was published in 1516.)**

6. Joseph Smith, quoted in Joseph Fielding Smith, compiler, *Teachings of the Prophet Joseph Smith* (Salt Lake City: Deseret Book Company, First Edition 1938), p. 349.

7. **Note: Smithfield, England, was the center of executions for religious heretics** [Larkin Dunton, *The World and Its People* (New York City, Boston, Chicago: Silver Burdett & Company, Publishers, 1896), p. 24] **and political rebels such as Scottish patriot William Wallace in 1305, as well as the Peasants' Revolt leader Wat Tyler in 1381.**

8. David Daniell, *The Bible in English* (London, England and New Haven Connecticut: Yale University Press 2003), p. 220.

9. F. F. Bruce, *The English Bible: A History of Translations* (Oxford, England: Oxford University Press, 1961).

10. John Bunyan, *The Pilgrim's Progress*, edited and introduction by Roger Sharrock (Harmonsworth: Penguin Books, Ltd), pp. 10, 59, 94, 326–327, 375.

11. **Note: The editor of this Penguin Books Edition of *The Pilgrim's Progress*, Roger Sharrock, who also wrote the introduction, is representative of newer scholarship that places the period of time that John Bunyan wrote his book as 1660–1672, during his 1st sentence in jail. Earlier belief was that it was written during his 2nd sentence in jail—when he was incarcerated for just 6 months in 1675.** [One example of this earlier belief is contained in John Brown, *John Bunyan (1628–1688): His Life, Times, and Work* (London: The Hulbert Publishing Company, First Edition 1885, revised 1928).]

12. David Daniell, *The Bible in English: Its History and Influence* (London, England; New Haven, Connecticut: Yale University Press, 2003), p. 448.

13. Brian Moynahan, *William Tyndale: If God Spare My Life* (London: Abacus, 2003), pp. 1–2.

14. John L. Jeffcoat III, "English Bible History Article & Timeline," 2012, (www.greatsite.com, Phoenix, Arizona: WWW. GREATSITE.COM).

15. Ibid.

**Note: Jeffcoat's work is utilized in this appendix. He grants permission when his website is prominently noted in capital letters per the citation above, in Endnote 14.**

# APPENDIX U

1. **Note: See the Topical Guide of the unaltered King James Version of the Bible, published by the Church of Jesus Christ of Latter-day Saints, under "Apostasy," for other biblical references. The Bible as published by the LDS Church is the standard King James Version. In this edition, no changes have been made to the actual text. However to facilitate a better understanding of it, the church's publishing arm has added footnotes, a Topical Guide, a Bible Dictionary, and maps of the Holy Land as study aids.**

2. Note: From New Testament accounts it is evident that the Savior and the Quorum of Twelve Apostles intended to continue having a constant Quorum of Twelve at the head, after Jesus was killed—and not a quorum of 11, 10 or 8. For example:

(1) They chose Matthias to replace Judas. [The Acts of the Apostles 1:15–26, King James Version of the New Testament.]

(2) The Holy Ghost led them to choose Barnabas and Saul, according to the Holy Ghost, "for the work whereunto I have called them." In Acts of the Apostles of the New Testament, this scripture states the other church leaders then "laid their hands upon them." [Acts 13:1–3.] Obviously one of them was replacing the dead Apostle James, brother of John, who had died just 1 chapter earlier. [Acts 12:2.]

(3) Acts Chapter 14 names who they are: Apostles Barnabas and Paul. [Acts 14:14.] Paul states at one point "Other of the Apostles saw I none save James the Lord's brother." [Galatians 1:19.] Thus, James (the Lord's brother), Barnabas, and Paul were three replacement apostles.

3. Pierre Battifol, *L'Eglise naissante et le catholicisme* (Paris: J. Gabalda, 1911), pp. 153, 144.

4. Ronald C. Conte Jr., "Important Dates in the Lives of Jesus and Mary" (Catholic Planet, 2007), catholicplanet.com/martyrs.htm.

Ronald C. Conte Jr. "A New Approach: The Martyrdoms of James and Mark" (Catholic Planet, 2003), www.biblicalchronology.com/martyrs. htm.

Note: Ronald C. Conte Jr. details the years for the deaths of James the Greater, James the Lesser, and Mark in relation to the reigns of the Roman rulers, then narrows down the dates to the exact months and weeks using the calendar in relation to Easter and Passover, as well as scriptural references. His work revises the traditional information provided by Jerome, Josephus, and Eusebius.

5. Ibid.

6. Ibid.

7. Isaac Boyle, translated by Christian Frederic Cruse, "Eusebius of Caesarea, Bishop of Caesarea," *The Ecclesiastical History* (New York City: T. Mason and G. Lane, for the Methodist Episcopal Church, 1839).

Modern Edition: Eusebius, *Eusebius' The Ecclesiastical History: Complete and Unabridged* (Peabody, Massachusetts: Hendrickson Publishers, 1998), vol. 3, chapter 23.

Note: Eusebius of Caesarea lived from 260 to 340 A.D.

8. Note: Flavius Josephus lived from 37 or 38 A.D. to 100 A.D. He wrote *Antiquities of the Jews*. In Book 20, Chapter 9, p. 1, he discusses the death of James, the brother of Jesus. Josephus is considered one of the primary historians of the early Christian era.

   Flavius Josephus, translated by William Whisten, *Josephus: The Complete Works* (Nashville, Tennessee: HarperCollins / Thomas Nelson, First Trade Paperback Edition, 2003).

   Note: Jerome, referred to in the text of Appendix U, lived from 347 to 419 A.D. and is noted as one of the chief early historians.

   Jerome, *The Principal Works of St. Jerome* (Seattle, Washington: Amazon Digital Services, Kindle Edition, 2010).

9. Ibid.

10. Note: This statistic of Paul's letters comprising 31.57% of the actual text of the New Testament is one that I have not verified. Also, this number does not include Paul as writing the book of Hebrews, which for centuries was inaccurately attributed to him. Counting the number of New Testament books, Paul's books comprise 48.15%. However, according to one analysis of Paul's extent of authorship, he evidently used scribes for 6 of his 13 epistles (letters) and possibly for all 13, simply adding a postscript at the end of 7 of those 13. [Lincoln H. Blumell, "Scribes and Ancient Letters: Implications for the Pauline Epistles," in *How the New Testament Came to Be: The Thirty-fifth Annual Sidney B. Sperry Symposium*, edited by Kent P. Jackson and Frank F. Judd Jr. (Provo, Utah: Religious Studies Center, Brigham Young University; and Salt Lake City: Deseret Book, 2006), pp. 208–226.]

   Understanding Paul's personality, which comes through his letters that make up the New Testament, is to realize that he would have dictated these epistles and not allowed others to write them. Writers using scribes was a common practice, and when an apostle of the church used scribes, that apostle certainly would have been serious enough about the letters' contents to not turn over actual authorship to those scribes; thus, Paul and the other apostles, holding their office as a sacred duty, would have carefully dictated all epistles they sent out.

11. Note: Gnosticism was often associated with early Christianity. Adolf von Harnack, a German Lutheran theologian and critical scholar, researched the influence of Hellenistic philosophy on early Christianity. From his studies, in 1885 he defined Gnosticism as "the acute Hellenization of Christianity." [Adolf von Harnack, "Christentum,"

in Kurt Nowak et al, editors, *Wissenschaft und Gesellschaft* (Göttingen, Germany: Vandenhoeck & Ruprecht, 2003).]

**Karen L. King believes Gnosticism was of Oriental origin.** [Karen L. King, *What is Gnosticism?* (Cambridge, Massachusetts: Harvard University Press / Belknap Press, First Edition 2003).]

12. **Note: Neo-Platonism was a revival of Plato's philosophies. Although begun by Ammonius Saccas, Neo-Paltonism was also influenced by his student Plotinus** [Mubabinge Bilolo, *Fondements Thebains de la Philosophie de Plotin l'Egyptien* (Munich, Paris, Kinshasa: Academy of African Thought & African Institute for Future Studies, 2007), section 1] **and was promulgated by the very influential Origen, another pupil of Saccas.**

13. Will Durant, *Caesar and Christ (The Story of Civilization, Vol. III)*, 11 volumes (New York City: Simon & Schuster, 1935–1975), vol. 3 (1944), p. 595.

14. Ibid.

15. The Bible, King James Version, New Testament, Matthew 16:15–19.

16. **Note: Italics are author's emphasis. The verses quoted are from the King James Version. Christ states here that Peter has received a revelation—that Christ is the Son of God.**

17. Johann Peter Kirsch, "St. Peter," in Charles G. Herbermann, Edward A. Pace, Conde B. Pallen, Thomas J. Shahan, and John J. Wynne, editors, *The Catholic Encyclopedia: An International Work of Reference on the Constitution, Doctrine, Discipline, and History of the Catholic Church*, 16 volumes with index (New York City: The Encyclopedia Press, 1907–1914).

18. Auguste Boulenger, *Historia de Iglesia* (Lyon, France: Emmanuel Vitte, 1925), p. 127.

19. Michael Collins; Matthew A. Price, *The Story of Christianity* (Carol Stream, Illinois: Tyndale House Publishers, 1999), pp. 58–59.

20. Albert de Broglie, *L'eglise et l'Empire Romain Au IVe Siecle Valentinien Et Theodose* (Paris: Les Editions Didler, 1856, vol. 1, p. 254; and newer French edition published at Ann Arbor, Michigan: University of Michigan Library, 2009).

21. Gustave Bardy, *La theologie de L'Eglise de saint Clement de Rome a saint Irenee* (Collection *Unam Sanctam*, Vol. 13). English translation: *Theology of the Church of St. Clement of Rome to St. Irenaeus* (Paris: Editions du Cerf, 1945), vol. 13, p. 14.

22. Eamon Duffy, *Saints and Sinners, a History of the Popes* (New Haven, Connecticut: Yale University Press, Third Edition 2006), p. 29.

   Diarmaid MacCulloch, *Christianity: The First Three Thousand Years* (New York City: Viking Press, 2010), pp. 199, 212.

   **Note: This title was originally published as *A History of Christianity* (London: Allen Lane, 2009).**

23. James Thomson Shotwell and Louis Ropes Loomis, *The See of Peter* (New York City: Columbia University Press, 1991), p. 451.

   **Note 1: This book, *The See of Peter*, is a collection of primary sources on the ascendancy of the early papacy within the Roman Catholic Church, covering the period up to about 400 A.D. and utilizing 3 different texts. It was originally published in 1927.**

   **Note 2: By Catholic definition, a "see" is a "seat," while "The Holy See" is the jurisdiction of the church in Rome—which is the entire Roman Catholic Church, worldwide.**

24. The Bible, King James Version, New Testament, The Acts of the Apostles, 7:55–56.

25. Tertullian, *Patrologia Latiniam*, 221 volumes (Petit Montrouge [a section of Paris]: Imprimerie Catholique, Jacques-Paul Migne, 1844–1855), Volumes 1–2.

26. **Note: The Anglican Communion includes 4 "extraprovincial churches" on the islands of Bermuda, Cuba, Ceylon, and the Falklands, plus 2 non-island extraprovincial churches—all 6 under the jurisdiction of the Church of England, plus 38 distinct church bodies loosely associated and historically originating from the Church of England.**

27. Diarmaid MacCulloch, *Christianity: The First Three Thousand Years* (New York City: Viking, 2010), pp. 199, 221.

28. Ibid., p. 199.

   Henry Chadwick, "The Early Christian Community," in John McManners, *The Oxford Illustrated History of Christianity* (New York City: Oxford University Press, 1990), p. 56.

29. Ibid., Diarmaid MacCulloch.

30. Antal Aldasy, "Vestments," in Johann Peter Kirsch, "St. Peter," in Charles G. Herbermann, Edward A. Pace, Conde B. Pallen, Thomas J. Shahan, and John J. Wynne, editors, *The Catholic Encyclopedia: An International Work of Reference on the Constitution, Doctrine, Discipline, and History*

*of the Catholic Church*, 16 volumes with index (New York City: The Encyclopedia Press, 1907–1914), vol. 15, p. 388.

**Note: Antal Aldasy, Ph.D., author of this article within *The Catholic Encyclopedia*, was the Archivist for the Library of the National Museum, Budapest, Hungary, having led the dioceses of Transylvania, Veszprem, Waitzen, Zengg-Matrus, and Zips.**

31. *Catechism of the Catholic Church* (New Hope, Kentucky: Urbi Et Orbi Communications, 1994), p. 862, quoted in August Franzen and Remigius Baumer, *Papstgeschichte* (Freiburg im Breisgau, Germany: Freiburg Herder [publisher], 1988).

   Thomas Bokenkotter, *A Concise History of the Catholic Church* (New York City: Doubleday, 2004), p. 41.

32. Ramsay McMullen, *Christianizing the Roman Empire: (A.D. 100–400)* (New Haven, Connecticut: Yale University Press, 1984), p. 93.

33. Ibid.

34. Eamon Duffy, *Saints and Sinners, a History of the Popes* (New Haven, Connecticut: Yale University Press, Third Edition, 2006), p. 64.

35. Tertius Chandler, *Four Thousand Years of Urban Growth: An Historical Census* (Lewiston, New York: The Edwin Mellen Press, 1987; Revised Edition November 1987).

36. Ibid.

37. Ibid.

38. Auguste Boulenger, *Historia de Iglesia* (Lyon, France: Emmanuel Vitte, 1925), p. 170.

39. The Edict of Thessalonica, 380 A.D., Codex Theodosianus, XVI.1.2, in Sidney Zdeneck Ehler and John B. Morrall, *Church and State Throughout the Centuries: A Collection of Historic Documents and Commentaries* (Pine Beach, New Jersey: Newman House Press, 1967; First Edition 1954), p. 6.

40. Eamon Duffy, *Saints and Sinners, a History of the Popes* (New Haven, Connecticut: Yale University Press, Third Edition 2006), p. 27.

   Henry Chadwick, "The Early Christian Community," in John McManners, editor, *The Oxford Illustrated History of Christianity* (New York City: Oxford University Press, 1990), p. 56.

   Eamon Duffy, *Saints and Sinners: A History of the Popes* (New Haven, Connecticut: Yale University Press, Third Edition 2006), p. 34.

41. **Note: Later the two Roman empires would come together when the emperor Zeno would rule over both from Constantinople.**

42. Archaeological Institute of America (author), "Diocletian's Edict, De Pretiis Rerum Venalium," *Papers of the American School of Classical Studies at Athens, Vol. V, 1886–1890,* (Boston: Damrell and Upham; and Leipzig, Germany: Harrassowitz Publishing, 1892), vol. 5, p. 240.

43. Averil Cameron and Peter Garnsey, editors, "Rural Life in the Later Roman Empire," *The Cambridge Ancient History, Vol. XIII: The Late Empire A.D. 337–425* (Cambridge, England: The Press Syndicate of the University of Cambridge, 1998, 2003), vol. 13, p. 288.

44. **Note: Rome was softened for the blow of the invading Visigoths 2 years before they attacked, when, in 408 A.D., the Visigoths laid siege to the city—not allowing any food or supplies in, thus creating starvation and disease on a grand scale. At this point the Roman Senate gave in to the Visigoths' extortionate demands for gold, silver, silk, and pepper. However, even after giving in to the Visigoths, the city was sacked by them 2 years later in 410 A.D.**

    **The Vandals then attacked Rome for its 2nd sacking (after the birth of Christ) when, in 455 A.D., the city was plundered.**

    **In the following century, Rome was sacked a 3rd time, in 546 A.D. when the Gothic King Totila ordered the attack.**

    **A 4th sacking took place in 846 A.D. by Arab plunderers.**

    **The 5th sacking took place 700 years later in 1527, performed by troops of Charles V, the Holy Roman Emperor. They were sent there by Charles V but some say the troops mutinied and sacked the city on their own.**

    **Before this series of sackings, there had been one before the birth of Christ, 800 years before the 410 A.D. Visigoth sacking, when, in 387 B.C., the Gauls had sacked the city after the Battle of Allia, which had taken place beside the Allia River.**

45. Arnaldo Momigliano and Aldo Schiavone, *Storia di Roma,* reprinted in *Journal of Roman Studies* (London: The Society for the Promotion of Roman Studies), vol. 87 (November 1997), p. xxi.

46. Roger Crowley, *Constantinople: The Last Great Siege, 1453* (London: Faber and Faber, 2013).

    **Note: Before and after the fall of the city Constantinople to the Turks of the Ottoman Empire, several intellectuals—including Greek and others—fled to Italy, helping to launch the Renaissance.**

47. **Note: During this period, the church at Rome competed with Arianism for the barbarian tribes, both parties wanting to convert them to their form of Christianity.** [Jacques Le Goff, translated by Julia Barrow, *Medieval Civilization 400–1500 A.D.* (Hoboken, New Jersey: Blackwell Publishers, First Edition 1988), pp. 5–20.]

48. **Note: Hailing from Gaul, Clovis I first took control of Belgica Secunada (now Belgium, northern France) in 486 A.D. and the territories of the Alemanni (today's northeastern France, northern Switzerland, and southwestern Germany). (Specifically, Clovis-conquered territories of Alemanni included Alsace on the northeast border of today's France, Swabia in southwest Germany, and northern Switzerland.)**

    **Then he invaded and took control of the lands of the Burgundians (in today's central eastern France) in 500 A.D. and then, in 507 A.D. he took portions of Visigothic territory (today's southwestern France, Spain, and Portugal). Yet it would be 534 A.D. before the kingdom of Burgundy would be fully merged into the Frankish kingdom. In summary, Clovis I was the first significant Christian conqueror in western Europe.**

49. Jacques Le Goff, translated by Julia Barrow, *Medieval Civilization 400–1500 A.D.* (Hoboken, New Jersey: Blackwell Publishers, First Edition 1988), p. 21.

50. **Note: Justinian I (Justinian the Great) was the Byzantine Emperor from 527 to 565 A.D., and thus was the leader of the Eastern Roman Empire. He was also the last Roman emperor to speak Latin as his first language.**

51. Joseph Cullen Ayer, editor, *A Source Book for Ancient Church History: From the Apostolic Age to the Close of the Conciliar Period* (New York City: Charles Scribner's Sons, 1913), p. 553.

    **Note: Joseph Cullen Ayer was a professor of ecclesiastical history in the Divinity School of the Protestant Episcopal Church at Philadelphia.**

52. Franz Xaver von Funk and Charles Louis Dessolavy, *Lehrbuch der Kirchengeschichte* (1886); and English Edition: Franz Xaver von Funk and Charles Louis Dessolavy, *A Manual of Church History*, 2 volumes, translated from Fifth German Edition by Luigi Cappadelta [pseudonym] (London: Kegan, Paul, Trench, Trubner & Co., 1910).

53. Earle E. Cairns, *Christianity through the Centuries: A History of the Christian Church* (Grand Rapids, Michigan: Zondervan, First Edition 1954; Third Revised Edition 1996), p. 124.

54. Michael Collins, Matthew A. Price, *The Story of Christianity* (Carol Stream, Illinois: Tyndale House Publishers, 1999), pp. 84–86.

55. Note: Leo III ruled the Byzantine Empire from 717 to 741 A.D.

56. John Vidmar, *The Catholic Church Through the Ages* (Mahwah, New Jersey: Paulist Press, 2005), p. 34.

57. **Note: Pope Gregory III reigned over the church from 731 to 741 A.D.**

58. *The Merriam-Webster Dictionary* (Springfield, Massachusetts: Merriam-Webster), online at www.Merriam-webster.com.

59. **Note: The *Merriam-Webster Dictionary* is one of the world's most respected dictionaries. In 1806 Noah Webster published his first dictionary, *A Compendious Dictionary of the English Language*, standardizing American speech. Heretofore, words and vocabularies were spelled, pronounced, and used differently in different regions of the United States.**

   **In 1807 Webster began work on his final dictionary—*An American Dictionary of the English Language*—a 33-year project. During a year abroad in 1825 he revised it in Paris and at Cambridge University, adding about 12,000 new words, upping the total to 70,000 words. He then published that in 1828, and revised it as a Second Edition in 1840 as 2 volumes.**

   **After Noah Webster died, in 1843 brothers George and Charles Merriam obtained the publishing and revision rights to Webster's last edition—of 1840—and revised it further. In 1847, they published it, keeping all the main text and adding new sections, updating it again in 1859 with illustrations. Then in 1864 they overhauled it, keeping many of Webster's definitions while changing the title to *An American Dictionary*. By 1884 it had 118,000 words, 3,000 more than any other English dictionary. ["Webster's Unabridged," *The Week: A Canadian Journal of Politics, Literature, Science and Arts* (Toronto, Canada), vol. 10 (February 11, 1884), p. 160.]**

   **In 1890 they changed its name to *Webster's International*. In 1909 and 1934 it was enlarged and renamed *Webster's New International*, with over 500,000 words. Later, the 1934 Edition, in reprints, was renamed *Webster's Second International* and *New International, Second Edition*.**

   **In 1961 it was overhauled again and expanded as *Webster's Third New International*.**

   **Then Merriam lost exclusive rights to the Webster name, which went into public domain.**

In 1964 the Merriam-Webster company was bought by Encyclopedia Britannica and became a subsidiary.

In 1983, under the name "Merriam-Webster, Incorporated," it published a new dictionary—*Webster's Ninth New Collegiate Dictionary*—the most recent at that time in a series of Collegiate Dictionaries that had begun in 1898, separate from the comprehensive dictionaries listed above.

In 1996 Merriam-Webster launched its website, giving free access to their online dictionary and thesaurus.

Since 2003 they have made available two top dictionaries: (1) the *Merriam-Webster's Collegiate Dictionary, Eleventh Edition*, on CD-ROM for personal computers (which also has apps for the iPhone, iPod touch, Android and BlackBerry—the on-line dictionary used by this author is based on this Edition); and (2) *Webster's Third New International Dictionary, Unabridged* (not online), promoting itself as the most current, complete, non-specializing dictionary of English, also with apps for iPhone, iPod touch, and Android.

Additionally, they publish handbooks and manuals for the English language such as the *Encyclopedia of Literature*, *Secretarial Handbook*, *Collegiate Thesaurus*, and compilations on geography, biography, proper names, synonyms, English usage, medical terms, sports terms, etc.

Many scholars may prefer the Oxford line of dictionaries, but the author has chosen Merriam-Webster, published by Encyclopaedia Britannica, for its clarity and style. (For actual reading enjoyment, he also uses the American Heritage Dictionary of the English Language, written in a lively, though conservative, style and adorned with illustrations, published so far in 5 editions from 1969 to 2011.)

60. Eamon Duffy, *Saints and Sinners, a History of the Popes* (Yale University Press, 1997), pp. 63, 74.

August Franzen and Remigius Baumer, *Papstgeschichte* (Freiburg im Breisgau, Germany: Freiburg Herder, 1988), quoting Thomas Bokenkotter, *A Concise History of the Catholic Church* (New York City: Doubleday, 2004), p. 35.

61. Eamon Duffy, *Saints and Sinners, a History of the Popes* (Yale University Press, 1997), pp. 63, 74.

Note: The new pope, Hadrian I, was not personally present at the Second Council of Nicaea in 787 A.D., but his representatives were, and they pushed for the veneration of icons along with the Byzantine Empress herself, Irene of Athens.

62. Cleveland Coxe, compiler and arranger of notes, *The Writings of the Fathers Down to 325: Ante-Nicene Fathers, Volume 4: Tertullian, Part Fourth: Minucius Felix,* 10 volumes (Edinburgh, Scotland: T & T Clark, 1885), vol. 4.

Note: Tertullian quotes *Octavius*, Chapters IX and XXIX, in regard to the first use of the cross as a symbol.

63. James Stranger, "Archaeological Evidence of Jewish Believers?" in Oskar Skarsaune and Reidar Hvalvik, *Jewish Believers in Jesus: The Early Centuries* (Grand Rapids, Michigan: Baker Academic, 2007), p. 715.

64. Graydon F. Snyder, *Ante Pacem: Archaeological Evidence of Church Life Before Constantine* (Macon, Georgia: Mercer University Press, 2003).

65. *New Catholic Encyclopedia,* edited by the faculty of the Catholic University of America in Washington, D.C., 15 volumes with index (Farmington Hills, Michigan: Gale Publishing, Second Edition 2002).

Note: This source, the *New Catholic Encyclopedia*, published by Gale Publishing of Farmington Hills, Michigan, in 2002, is technically the revision of a revision. The very first *Catholic Encyclopedia* was the 1907–1912 published work entitled *Catholic Encyclopedia: An International work of Reference On the Constitution, Doctrine, Discipline, And History of The Catholic Church*, published in 16 volumes plus 4 supplemental volumes from 1922 to 1958. That original work was published by Robert Appleton Company of New York City, whose name was changed in 1913 to Encyclopedia Press.

Then, 5½ decades later, in 1967, came the *New Catholic Encyclopedia*, First Edition, published by McGraw Hill of New York City in cooperation with The Catholic University of America of Washington, D.C., in 15 volumes. This work included updates and revisions of the original *Catholic Encyclopedia*, plus 4 new supplements from 1974 to 1996.

Then, 3½ decades later, in 2002, came the *New Catholic Encyclopedia*, Second Edition, referenced at the beginning of this note. It was published in 15 volumes, including an index volume, from Gale Publishing of Farmington Hills, Michigan, after an ambitious revamping of the 1967 work published by McGraw Hill. It did delete 3.5 million words from the 1967 edition and added hundreds of new articles, plus new information and numerous updates, so it is substantially different in many ways, but 4 new supplements have also come out for it—from 2009 to 2013.

Meanwhile, the original edition (original *Catholic Encyclopedia* of 1907–1914) was placed online by Kevin Knight of Denver Colorado in 1996. His website is New Advent [www.newadvent.org/cathen/]. In 2007 came another online edition of the original *Catholic Encyclopedia* of 1907–1914 from Catholic Online in Bakersfield, California [oce. catholic.com/index/php?title-home].

For access to the 1967 online edition of *New Catholic Encyclopedia, First Edition*, from McGraw Hill, and the 2002 edition of the *New Catholic Encyclopedia, Second Edition*, from Gale Publishing, I recommend contacting the publishers for their electronic versions.

For my purposes, all 3 sets are treated as different works for source material, because of the variety of information in each.

66. W. E. Vine, *Vine's Expository Dictionary of New Testament Words* (Nashville, Tennessee: HarperCollins Christian Publishing / Thomas Nelson, 2003).

67. Cardinal John Henry Newman, *An Essay on the Development of Christian Doctrine* (First Edition at London: James Toovey, 1845; and modern edition at New York City: Cambridge University Press, 2010), p. 373.

Note: Cardinal John Henry Newman adds in his book that the church "sanctified" the pagan symbols and practices that appealed to the heathens, making them "safe" for the religion, a questionable practice to critics.

68. Sean Martin, *The Cathars: The Most Successful Heresy of the Middle Ages* (Minneapolis: Chartwell Books, 2009), pp. 105–121.

69. Jonathon Sumption, *The Albigensian Crusade* (London: Faver and Faver, 1999), pp. 179–181.

70. Stephen O'Shea, *The Perfect Heresy: The Revolutionary Life and Death of the Medieval Cathars* (New York City: Walker & Company / Macmillan), pp. 239–246.

Jonathon Sumption, *The Albigensian Crusade* (London: Faver and Faver, 1999), pp. 179–181.

71. Tertullian, *De Corona*, Chapter 3, quoted in "The Cross and Crucifix," *Original Catholic Encyclopedia* (Catholic Answers, El Cajon, California), oce.catholic.com/index.php?title=home.

Note: *De Corona*, translated, means, "The Chaplet."

72. *New Catholic Encyclopedia*, edited by the faculty of the Catholic University of America in Washington, D.C., 15 volumes with index (Farmington Hills, Michigan: Gale Publishing, Second Edition 2002).

73. John M. McClintock and James Strong, *The Cyclopedia of Biblical, Theological, and Ecclesiastical Literature* (Grand Rapids, Michigan: Baker Academic, 1982; and First Edition 1867–1887).

    **Note: Baker Academic publishes both Catholic and Protestant-supportive titles.**

74. "Frequently Asked Questions about Saints" (Bakersfield, California: Catholic Online, 2013), www.catholic.org/saints.faq.php.

75. Ibid.

76. The Bible, King James Version, New Testament, Revelation 8:3–4.

77. "Frequently Asked Questions about Saints" (Bakersfield, California: Catholic Online, 2013), www.catholic.org/saints.faq.php.

78. Note: Leo III reigned over the church from 800 to 814 A.D.

79. James Bryce, *The Holy Roman Empire* (New York City: Macmillan Publishing, 1913), p. 183.

    Joachim Whaley, *Germany and the Holy Roman Empire: Volume I, Maximillian I to the Peace of Westphalia, 1493–1648*, 2 volumes (Oxford History of Early Modern Europe) (Oxford, England: Oxford University Press, 2013), vol. 1, pp. 17–20.

    Lonnie R. Johnson, *Central Europe: Enemies, Neighbors, Friends* (Oxford, England: Oxford University Press, First Edition 1996), p. 23.

80. Eamon Duffy, *Saints and Sinners, a History of the Popes* (Yale University Press, 1997), pp. 88–89.

81. Simon Schama, "Burning Convictions," *A History of Britain, Volume 1: At the Edge of the World? 3500 B.C. – 1603 A.D.* (New York City: Miramax Books, 2000), pp. 309–311.

    John Vidmar, *The Catholic Church Through the Ages* (Mahwah, New Jersey: Paulist Press, 2005), p. 220.

82. E. R. Chamberlin, *The Bad Popes* (New York City: Dial Press, 1969), Chapter 2, as cited in James S. Packer, *Saints, Sinners, and Christian History, The Contradictions of the Christian Past* (Springville, Utah: Cedar Fort, 2008), p. 1.

83. *The Popes' Rights and Wrongs* (London: Truber & Co., 1860).

    Dr. Angelo S. Rappaport, *The Love Affairs of the Vatican* (New York City: Barnes and Noble Books, First Edition 1995).

    Peter de Rosa, *Vicars of Christ: The Dark Side of the Papacy* (Dublin, Ireland: Poolbeg Press, 1988), pp. 211–215.

Huns Kung, translated by John Bowden, *The Catholic Church: A Short History* (New York City: Modern Library, 2001), p. 79.

Horace K. Mann, *The Lives of the Popes in the Early Middle Ages, Volume IV: The Popes in the Days of Feudal Anarchy, 999–1048 A.D.*, 19 volumes (London: Kegan, Paul, Trench, Trubner & Co., Ltd, 1910), vol. 4, pp. 241–272, especially p. 264.

84. **Note: The date that Pope John XII died was May 14, 964 A.D. His reign had begun December 16, 955 A.D., when he was in his late teens or 20s. His birth date, while unknown, occurred sometime between 930 and 937 A.D.**

    **Bishop Liudprand states that Satan himself smote John XII on the temple while he was in the act of adultery with a woman outside Rome, but Ferdinand Gregorovius clarifies it was her jealous husband.** [Ferdinand Gregorovius, translated from Fourth German Edition by Mrs. Gustavus W. Hamilton, *History of the City of Rome in the Middle Ages, Volume 3: A.D. 800–1002* (London: George Bell & Sons, Revised Second Edition, 1903).] **He may have instead died of apoplexy.** [Karl Joseph von Hefele, *Conciliengeschichte, vol. iv*, 9 volumes (Freiburg, Germany, 1867), vol. 4, p. 61.]

85. Liudprand of Cremona, *Antapodosis*, translated by Paolo Squatriti, cited in *The Complete Works of Liudprand of Cremona* (Washington, D.C.: Catholic University of America Press, 2007).

    **Note: Liudprand was a bishop of Cremona, living from 922 to 972 A.D. in Lombardy, northern Italy. He reported the proceedings and chronicled the charges made against John XII in 963 A.D. at the Synod of Rome in his book *Antapodosis*.**

    **The Catholic Encyclopedia states, "Liutprand's writings are a very important source for the tenth century," although they are "unfair towards his enemies." However, even though he sided with the emperor and "condemned" John XII's actions,** [Johann Peter Kirsch, "Liutprand of Cremona," in Charles G. Herbermann, Edward A. Pace, Conde B. Pallen, Thomas J. Shahan, John J. Wynne, editors, *The Catholic Encyclopedia: An International Work of Reference on the Constitution, Doctrine, Discipline, and History of the Catholic Church*, 16 volumes with index (New York City: The Encyclopedia Press, 1907–1914)] **he would not have necessarily viewed the pope as his enemy. He reported what others said of John XII at the assembly of bishops at Rome in 963 A.D.**

    **The encyclopedia article spelling is the alternate spelling of his name.**

86. Horace K. Mann, *The Lives of the Popes in the Early Middle Ages, Vol. IV: The Popes in the Days of Feudal Anarchy, 999–1048 A.D.*, 19 volumes

(London: Kegan, Paul, Trench, Trubner & Co., Ltd, 1910), vol. 4, pp. 241–272.

Note: Horace K. Mann's writings are doubted by certain Catholic Church apologists, although most Protestant historians writing of this period accept his work.

87.  Ibid., p. 242

Note: Ratherius of Verona lived from 877 to 974 A.D.

88.  Note: Ratherius of Verona wrote *Praeloquia*, a treatise about how such immorality of the clergy contrasted that of virtuous living. [Ibid., Horace K. Mann.]

The location where Ratherius wrote this treatise was in Pavia, Lombardy, Northern Italy (earlier the capital of the kingdom of the Lombards—from 568–774 A.D.).

Ratherius was later removed as the presiding bishop in Rome by Hugh Capet (Hugh the Great, the first king of the Franks, in today's France) in 935 A.D.

His writings are doubted by certain church apologists, although most Protestant historians who write of the period accept his writings, as they do for Liudprand.

89.  Note: The chronicler Flodoard, a Frenchman, lived from 894 to 966 A.D. and worked at the mountain where Benedict of Soracte lived (now Soracte, in the province of Rome that includes the only ridge in Tiber Valley), and there wrote his chronicles that report the pope's abuses. [Flodoard, Chronicles, vol. XXXVII, in *Patrologiae Latinae*, 217 volumes + a 4-volume index (Paris: Jacques-Paul Migne, 1844–1855).]

Prior to that, Flodoard was canon of the cathedral at Reims, where he was educated and shown much favor by the pope, according to *Catholic Encyclopedia*, which lauds his writing, stating of another work of his—a history of the church of Reims ("Historia Remensis ecclesiae")—"His work is of the greatest value on account of the completeness of the material as well as the truthfulness of the narration." Another major work of his is "Annales," which the *Catholic Encyclopedia* likewise praises: "With the most painstaking exactness he narrates in plain, simple language all the events that happened during these years [919–966 A.D.] and thus the work is of the utmost importance." ["Flodoard," in Charles G. Herbermann, Edward A. Pace, Conde B. Pallen, Thomas J. Shahan, John J. Wynne, editors, *The Catholic Encyclopedia: An International Work of Reference on the Constitution,*

*Doctrine, Discipline, and History of the Catholic Church*, 16 volumes with index (New York City: The Encyclopedia Press, 1907–1914).]

90. Ibid.

91. Horace K. Mann, *The Lives of the Popes in the Early Middle Ages, Vol. IV: The Popes in the Days of Feudal Anarchy, 999–1048 A.D.*, 19 volumes (London: Kegan, Paul, Trench, Trubner & Co., Ltd, 1910), vol. 4, pp. 241–242.

92. J. Busaeus, editor, *Anastasii Bibliothecani Vitae seq Gesta Romanorum Pontificum* (Mainz, Germany: unknown publisher, First Edition 1602).

**Note: This book was later re-published under the title *Liber Pontificalis* (*Book of the Popes*), which reported popes that they consider from the beginning up to the 1400s. Subsequent editions of this book have covered more recent centuries of papal rule.**

93. Liudprand of Cremona, *Antapodosis*, translated by Paolo Squatriti, included in *The Complete Works of Liudprand of Cremona* (Washington, D.C.: Catholic University of America Press, 2007).

94. Liudprand of Cremona, *Antapodosis*, quoted in Lindsay Brook, "Popes and Pornocrats: Rome in the Middle Ages," *Foundations: The Journal of the Foundation for Medieval Genealogy* (Vowchurch, Hereford, England, 2003), vol. 1, p. 1.

**Note: *Foundations: The Journal of the Foundation for Medieval Genealogy* is a magazine that was first published in 2003 and is still in circulation. Since 2012 its issues are published annually each summer. The foundation and its magazine promote scholarship on medieval research, publishing articles and reviews relating to medieval genealogy (which they define as before 1500). The foundation and its magazine are located in England at Vowchurch, Herefordshire, 50 miles northeast of Cardiff, Wales, on the Welsh border.**

Joseph McCabe, *Crisis in the History of the Papacy: A Study of Twenty Famous Popes whose Careers and whose Influence Were Important in the Development of the Church and in the History of the World* (London, New York City: G. P. Putnam's Sons, 1916).

95. John Foxe, George Townsend, Third Edition revised and corrected by Josiah Pratt, *The Acts And Monuments Of John Foxe, With A Life And Defence Of The Martyrologist, Vol. 2* (First Edition, minus Josiah Pratt, published at London: John Day, 1554; edition referenced is Third Edition, published at London: George Seeley and W. Burnside, 1870), vol. 2, p. 35.

96. Louis-Marie de la Haye, Vicente de Cormenin, *A Complete History of the Popes of Rome: From Saint Peter, the First Bishop to Pius the Ninth, the Present Pope, Including the History of Saints, Martyrs, Fathers, of the Church, Religious Orders, Cardinals, Inquisitions, Schisms, and the latest Reformers* (Philadelphia: James L. Gihon, 1859), pp. 296–298.

97. **Note: Near the end of the 900s came the 3rd memorable church leader of that century—Pope John XV, who reigned from 985 to 996 A.D. Described in less substantiated claims as loving money and "corrupt in all his acts," he may have been unpopular with the people because he supposedly split the church's finances among his relatives.**

   **The 1st pope of the 1000s, Sylvester II, reigned from 999 to 1003. His enemies claimed he studied magic and astrology at Cordoba (in south central Spain) and Seville (in southwestern Spain) and at the University of Al Karaouine in Morocco (at the most northern and western part of Africa). Legends arose he was a sorcerer "in league with Satan," but no credible sources exist, and criticisms of his reign are relegated to the files of mere rumor, in my opinion.**

98. Post multa turpia adultera homicidia manibus suis perpetrata, postremo, etc., in Ernst Ludwig Dummler, *Monumenta Germaniae Historica, Libelli de lite* (Hanover: Deutsches Institut für Erforschung des Mittelalters, 1891; later edition: 1934), p. 584.

   A. C. Black, editor, Benedictine Monks of St. Augustine's Abbey, compilers, in Ramsgate, England, *The Book of Saints, A Dictionary of Servants of God Canonized by the Catholic Church* (New York City: Macmillan Publishing, Fourth Edition 1947).

   **Note: Piacenza in northwest Italy is the "gateway to the Alps."**

99. Pope Victor III, *Dialogues, vol. 3*, in Ernst Ludwig Dummler, *Monumenta Germaniae Historica, Libelli de Lite* (Hanover: Deutsches Institut für Erforschung des Mittelalters, 1891, later edition: 1934), p. 1.

   **Note: Pope Victor III was earlier named Desiderius, the great Abbot of Monte Cassino, 81 miles southeast of Rome. He reigned as pope from 1086 to 1087.**

100. Peter Damian, *Liber Gomorrhianus* (ca. 1051 A.D.). Modern edition referenced: Peter Damian, edited by Pierre T. Payer, *Book of Gomorrah: An eleventh century treatise against clerical homosexual practice* (Waterloo, Ontario, Canada: Wilfrid Laurier University Press, 1982).

101. Ibid.

   **Note: Peter Damian was a cardinal-bishop serving at Ostia, the port city of ancient Rome, beginning in 1057.** [(Charles G. Herbermann,

Edward A. Pace, Conde B. Pallen, Thomas J. Shahan, John J. Wynne, editors, *The Catholic Encyclopedia: An International Work of Reference on the Constitution, Doctrine, Discipline, and History of the Catholic Church,* 16 volumes with index (New York City: The Encyclopedia Press, 1907–1914); and New Advent (Denver, Colorado), www.newadvent.org/cathen/11764a.htm.] **His position there ended in 1067,** [Catholic Online, www.catholic.org/saints/saint.php?saint_id=780; and Catholic News Agency, Englewood, Colorado, www.catholicnewsagency.com/saint. php?n=154] **from which he expanded his service to working directly with the papacy. He was assigned as legate (a cardinal sent as a special representative of the pope—in his case as an ambassador of sorts) to straighten out pressing matters in Milan and Florence, Italy, and to France over the next few years. Damian was born at Ravena, Italy, in 1007 and died in 1072. The *Encyclopedia Britannica* boasts of his accomplishments, saying he had "extraordinary knowledge of canon law."** [*Encyclopedia Britannica*, 32 volumes (Chicago: Encyclopedia Britannica, 2007), www.britannica.com/EBchecked/topic/453772/Saint-Peter-Damian.]

102. Lynne Yamaguchi Fletcher, *First Gay Pope and Other Records* (Boston: Alyson Books, 1992).

103. "Pope Benedict IX," in Charles G. Herbermann, Edward A. Pace, Conde B. Pallen, Thomas J. Shahan, John J. Wynne, editors, *The Catholic Encyclopedia: An International Work of Reference on the Constitution, Doctrine, Discipline, and History of the Catholic Church,* 16 volumes with index (New York City: The Encyclopedia Press, 1907–1914).

104. **Note: Holy Roman Emperor Henry III chose Pope Clement II, who died in 1047. Henry himself lived from 1017 to 1056 in Germany.**

105. Dom Greg, *De Sepulcro Benedicti IV* (Rome: Piacentini, 1747) and Tosti, *St. Benedict and Grottaferrata* (Rome, 1895) in Charles G. Herbermann, Edward A. Pace, Conde B. Pallen, Thomas J. Shahan, John J. Wynne, editors, *The Catholic Encyclopedia: An International Work of Reference on the Constitution, Doctrine, Discipline, and History of the Catholic Church,* 16 volumes with index (New York City: The Encyclopedia Press, 1907–1914).

106. Karl Joseph von Hefele, Joseph Hergenrother, Henri Leclercq, Alois Knopfler, Albert Michel, Charles de Clercq, and Pierre Richard, *Histoire des Conciles d'après les documents originaux* (Paris: Letouzey et Ane, 1907, First Edition 1858), pp. 777–778.

107. Eamon Duffy, *Saints and Sinners, a History of the Popes* (New Haven, Connecticut: Yale University Press, Third Edition, 2006), p. 91.

108. Ibid.

Michael Collins; Matthew A. Price, *The Story of Christianity* (Carol Stream, Illinois: Tyndale House Publishers, 1999), p. 103.

John Vidmar, *The Catholic Church Through the Ages* (Mahwah, New Jersey: Paulist Press, 2005), p. 104.

109. Thomas Bokenkotter, *A Concise History of the Catholic Church* (New York City: Doubleday, Revised Edition 2004), p. 155.

110. **Note: Urban II instigated the First Crusade at the Council of Clermont when the Byzantine emperor Alexus I appealed for help to fight off a Turkish invasion.** [Jonathan Riley-Smith, *The First Crusaders, 1095–1131* (Cambridge, England: Cambridge University Press, 1997), p. 8.] **By complying, Urban II thought the two factions, Orthodox and Catholic, might reconcile,** [John Vidmar, *The Catholic Church Through the Ages* (Mahwah, New Jersey: Paulist Press, 2005), pp. 130–131] **and at the very least he sought to help their Greek religious cousins.** [Thomas Bokenkotter, *A Concise History of the Catholic Church* (New York City: Doubleday, Revised Edition, 2004), p. 140.]

111. **Note: Three years after this, Urban II's reign would end—in 1099— after 11 years at the helm of the church.**

112. Jacques Le Goff, translated by Julia Barrow, *Medieval Civilization 400–1500* (Hoboken, New Jersey: Blackwell Publishing, 1991), pp. 65–67.

113. "Pope Sorrow Over Constantinople," BBC News, June 29, 2004.

114. Thomas Ashbridge, *The Crusades: The War for the Holy Land* (New York City: Simon and Schuster, 2010), pp. 531–532.

115. **Note: Presenting a different viewpoint, historian Christopher Tyerman maintains that Innocent III expressly forbade any such attack against Constantinople.** [*God's War: A New History of the Crusades* (Cambridge, Massachusetts: Harvard University / Belknap Press, 2006), pp. 525–560.] **Thus, Crusaders were to blame, he claims, not the church hierarchy.**

**Historically, 3 main attempts have been made to reunite these 2 churches—while this Fourth Crusade was the 1st attempt (by force, with or without papal authority), the 2nd and 3rd attempts occurred through diplomacy (at the Second Council of Lyon in 1274 and the Council of Florence in 1439), but all these attempts failed.** [Eamon Duffy, *Saints and Sinners, a History of the Popes* (New Haven, Connecticut: Yale University Press, Third Edition, 2006), pp. 119, 131.]

116. John Vidmar, *The Catholic Church Through the Ages* (Mahwah, New Jersey: Paulist Press, 2005), p. 104.

117. Eamon Duffy, *Saints and Sinners, a History of the Popes* (New Haven, Connecticut: Yale University Press, Third Edition, 2006), p. 278.

118. **Note: A *papal bull* is a pope's declaration issued on paper with a seal stamped on it, using softened lead to form the seal. The stamp itself is an instrument that is pressed downward into the lead, creating a design in the soft metal for the purpose of authenticating a document. The term *papal bull* comes from the Latin word *bulla*, meaning *lead seal*.**

119. Isaac Milner, *History of the Church of Christ, Volume the Fourth, Part 1: Containing the Remainder of the Thirteenth Century; also the Fourteenth, Fifteenth, and Part of the Sixteenth Century, Edited from the Manuscripts of the late Rev. Joseph Milner with Additions, Corrections, &c. By the Rev. Isaac Milner, D.D., Dean of Carlisle, and Master of Queen's College, Cambridge [University], First American Edition*, 7 volumes (Boston: Farrand, Mallory and Co., 1809; and London: Luke Hansard & Sons, for T. Cadell & W. Wavies, in the Strand, 1812), volume 4, chapter 13.

**Note: Isaac Milner was Dean of Carlisle (of the Cathedral at Carlisle in northern England) and Master of one of the colleges within Cambridge University named Queen's College. He took over writing this series from his brother, Joseph, who had completed the first 3 volumes before he died.**

120. E. R. Chamberlin, *The Bad Popes* (New York City: Dial Press, 1969), p. 153.

121. Isaac Milner, *History of the Church of Christ, Volume the Fourth, Part 1: Containing the Remainder of the Thirteenth Century; also the Fourteenth, Fifteenth, and Part of the Sixteenth Century, Edited from the Manuscripts of the late Rev. Joseph Milner with Additions, Corrections, &c. By the Rev. Isaac Milner, D.D., Dean of Carlisle, and Master of Queen's College, Cambridge [University], First American Edition*, 7 volumes (Boston: Farrand, Mallory and Co., 1809; and London: Luke Hansard & Sons, for T. Cadell & W. Wavies, in the Strand, 1812), volume 4, chapter 13.

122. Leonardo Bruni, edited and translated by James Haskins, *History of the Florentine People* (Cambridge, Massachusetts: Harvard University Press, 2001).

123. Tommaso de Acemo, *De creatione Urbani VI opusculum* (Muratoria, L.A. Rerum Italy: script), vol. 3.

**Note: de Acemo was the Bishop of Lucera in today's province of Foggia, in southeastern Italy, 150 miles southeast of Rome, a few miles from the Adriatic Sea.**

124. Ludwig Pastor, edited by Frederick Ignatius Antrobus, *The History of the Popes: From the Close of the Middle Ages, Drawn from the Secret Archives of the Vatican and other Original Sources, vol. 1,* 15 volumes (First English Edition: 1899; edition referenced published at London: Kegan Paul, Trench, Trubner & Co., 1906), vol. 1, p. 1024, notes.

**Note: Ludwig Pastor was Professor of History at University of Innsbruck (at Innsbruck, in western Austria). As a German historian and diplomat, he was elevated to nobility by the Emperor of Germany, Joseph I, in 1908. Pastor became Director of the Austrian Historical Institute in Rome. In his writings he states that when the cardinals recorded Urban's election to pope, it "turned his head"—in other words, in today's vernacular, he got a big head over it.**

125. Ibid.

126. Charles G. Herbermann, Edward A. Pace, Conde B. Pallen, Thomas J. Shahan, John J. Wynne, editors, *The Catholic Encyclopedia: An International Work of Reference on the Constitution, Doctrine, Discipline, and History of the Catholic Church,* 16 volumes with index (New York City: The Encyclopedia Press, 1907–1914), vol. 4, p. 789.

**Note: Dietrich of Nieheim hailed from Germany but was based in Avignon, France, where much of the action was about to take place.**

127. Ludwig Pastor, edited by Frederick Ignatius Antrobus, *The History of the Popes: From the Close of the Middle Ages, Drawn from the Secret Archives of the Vatican and other Original Sources, vol. 1,* 15 volumes (First English Edition: 1899; edition referenced published at London: Kegan Paul, Trench, Trubner & Co., 1906), vol. 1, p. 122.

128. **Note: Avignon, France is near the Mediterranean coast.**

129. Ludwig Pastor, edited by Frederick Ignatius Antrobus, *The History of the Popes: From the Close of the Middle Ages, Drawn from the Secret Archives of the Vatican and other Original Sources, vol. 1,* 15 volumes (First English Edition: 1899; edition referenced published at London: Kegan Paul, Trench, Trubner & Co., 1906), vol. 1, p. 127.

Walter Ullmann, *The Origins of the Great Schism: A Study in Fourteenth Century Ecclesiastical History* (London: Burnes & Oates, 1948), p. 54.

130. **Note: The other Pope Clement VII would reign 155 years later, from 1523 to 1534.**

131. Ludwig Pastor, edited by Frederick Ignatius Antrobus, *The History of the Popes: From the Close of the Middle Ages, Drawn from the Secret Archives of the Vatican and other Original Sources, vol. 1,* 15 volumes

(First English Edition: 1899; edition referenced published at London: Kegan Paul, Trench, Trubner & Co., 1906), vol. 1, p. 136.

**Note: Charles of Durazzo's family, from Albania, assisted in the building of Genoa—an independent state that existed from 1005 to 1797 and from 1814 to 1815, on the northwest Italian coast.**

132. **Note: The castle near St. Peter's Basilica was built between 130 and 137 A.D. The fortified wall connecting the two structures ("Comidore di Borgo," now called "Passeto di Borgo"), was built in 1277 and used by popes for protection in case of invasion. In 1901 the castle was turned into a museum.**

133. **Note: The 392-mile distance from Naples to Genoa along Italy's west coast is about 10% shorter than traveling by road, which is 435 miles, probably on a similar route people traveled in medieval times. (Parenthetically, a different measuring system is used on water. A "nautical mile" is 1.1508 miles, which is 15% longer than a mile on land or "statute mile." If describing this distance from Naples to Genoa in nautical miles, it would be 392 ÷ 1.1508 = 341 nautical miles, vs. 435 regular miles).**

134. Barbara Tuchman, *A Distant Mirror: The Calamitous 14th Century* (New York City: Alfred A. Knopf, 1978), pp. 330–331.

135. "Scelus nulo antea saeculo auditum," Egidio da Viterbo, *Historia viginti saeculorum,* in Ludwig Pastor, edited by Frederick Ignatius Antrobus, *The History of the Popes: From the Close of the Middle Ages, Drawn from the Secret Archives of the Vatican and other Original Sources, vol. 1,* 15 volumes (First English Edition: 1899; edition referenced published at London: Kegan Paul, Trench, Trubner & Co., 1906), vol. 1, p. 137 note.

136. E. R. Chamberlin, *The Bad Popes* (New York City: Dial Press, 1969).

137. **Note: If English cardinal Adam Easton had gone to Genoa in northern Italy with the others, he would have been given a stay of execution by Pope Urban VI and returned to the Castle of Nocera, with further imprisonment likely upon the orders of Charles of Durazzo.**

**The other alternative is that Easton never went to Genoa. In that scenario, Urban may have planned for the execution of 5 of the 6 cardinals while they were still at Nocera, but for some reason waited till he could escape and take the 5 cardinals with him to Genoa, and leave Easton behind. In either case, because of English King Richard II's intercession, Easton was not executed at Genoa and was either returned to or never left Nocera. (Note that various non-primary sources hypothesize on Easton in these scenarios, but I have not found any conclusive evidence from reliable, primary sources.)**

138. Dudley Baxter, *England's Cardinals* (London: Burns & Oates, 1903), pp. 26–27.

139. "Pope Urban VI," in Charles G. Herbermann, Edward A. Pace, Conde B. Pallen, Thomas J. Shahan, John J. Wynne, editors, *The Catholic Encyclopedia: An International Work of Reference on the Constitution, Doctrine, Discipline, and History of the Catholic Church*, 16 volumes with index (New York City: The Encyclopedia Press, 1907–1914).

140. Leonie Frieda, *The Deadly Sisterhood: A Story of Women, Power, and Intrigue in the Italian Renaissance, 1427–1527* (New York City: HarperCollins, 2013), chapter 3.

141. Stefano Infessura, *Diario della citta di Roma (1303–1494)*, English translation: *Diary of the City of Rome (1303–1494)* (Rome: Forzani e.c., 1890), pp. 155–156.

**Note: According to the apologetic *New Catholic Dictionary*, Stefano Infessura's book was a partisan historical chronicle on the events of Rome and included unsubstantiated rumors. Infessura, however, was known for being the eyes and ears of the city.**

Mano Masini and Giuseppe Portigliotti, *Attraverso il Rinascimento. Pier Luigi Farnese, vol. XXXVIII* (Italy: Archivio di antropologia criminale, 1917), vol. 38, p. 473.

142. Ibid., Stefano Infessura.

143. Anon., *A True history of the Lives of the Popes of Rome with a description of their particular vices and misdemeanors . . . with a full discovery of the cursed tenets of the Church of Rome: concerning the Popes Power (1679)* (London: unknown publisher, First Edition 1679; and Ann Arbor, Michigan: ProQuest: EEBO [Early English Editions Online], online and paperback, 2010).

144. **Note: Right after Pope Sixtus IV came Innocent VIII, reigning 1484–1492. The following allegations have been made about Innocent VIII, accepted as facts in some circles, but I have not found credible sources for them.**

**(1) Innocent VIII was the first pope to publicly admit having a mistress and illegitimate children.**

**(2) He was creative at raising revenue—he financed his dynasty by marrying off his children to wealthy families, receiving land and money in return.**

**(3) Compared to his overall record, a minor indiscretion occurred when he made his 13-year-old grandson a cardinal.**

(4) In the first year of his reign, he began torturing and burning to death those suspected of witchcraft, as part of the Inquisition.

145. James Reston, *Dogs of God* (New York City: Anchor Books, 2005), p. 287.

**Note: According to Michael E. Mallet, Pope Leo X may not have actually made this comment about Pope Alexander VI being a rapacious "wolf"; rather, he may have said this about him: "Flee, we are in the clutches of the world."** [Michael E. Mallett, *The Borgias: The Rise and Fall of a Renaissance Family* (New York City: HarperCollins / Granada Edition, 1969), p. 9.]

**Pope Leo X, before he became pope, was Giovanni de Medici.**

146. **Note: The first TV series about Alexander VI and his family, titled *The Borgias*, was released in 1981, a BBC-Italian co-production consisting of 10 episodes. Next came the 2011–2013 Showtime channel's historical drama, *The Borgias*, in 29 episodes spanning three seasons, ending the spring of 2013. Season 4 was cancelled. Finally came a French-German co-production about the Borgias lasting 3 seasons, titled *Borgia*, from 2011–2014. The one feature film about him and his family, *Los Borgias*, was produced in Spain in 2006.**

147. William Rosco, *The Life and Pontificate of Leo the Tenth, Vol. II*, 2 volumes (First Edition 1805; referenced is "Second Edition, Corrected" published at London: T. Cadell and W. Davies, Strand, 1806), vol. 2, p. 483.

148. Ibid., pp. 485–486.

149. Ibid., pp. 487–488.

150. Ibid., pp. 482–483.

151. Ibid., p. 481.

152. Ibid.

153. Louis Crampton, *Homosexuality and Civilization* (Cambridge, Massachusetts: Harvard University Press, 2006), p. 278.

153. **Julius II, reigning as pope from 1503 to 1513, was accused of immoral behavior by the Conciliabulum of Piza, and from that they attempted to dispose him in 1511, saying he was a "sodomite covered with shameful ulcers." Certainly being accused isn't solid proof, and there has not been enough evidence to indict him, in my opinion.**

154. **Note: the *Catholic Encyclopedia* states of Julius II: "Giullano [his actual name before he was pope] was a patron of the fine arts, and spent most of his superfluous money in the erection of magnificent palaces and fortresses. Still his early private life was far from stainless, as is**

sufficiently testified by the fact that before he became pope he was the
father of three daughters, the best known of whom, Felice, he gave in
marriage to Giovanni Giordana Orsini in 1506." ["Julius II," Catholic
Encyclopedia / New Advent, www.newadvent.org/cathen/08562a.htm.]

"Far from stainless" is a vague reference to the fact Felice was
illegitimate, as stated more clearly by additional credible, historical
analyses, including the excellent book from Oxford University Press
in 2005, *The Pope's Daughter: The Extraordinary Life of Felice della
Rovere*. Known as Felice della Rovere (ca. 1483–1536), she became
one of the most powerful women of the Italian Renaissance. [Caroline
Murphy, *The Pope's Daughter: The Extraordinary Life of Felice della Rovere*
(Oxford, England: Oxford University Press, 2005).]

155. William Samuel Lilly, *The Claims of Christianity* (New York City:
D. Appleton & Company, 1894), p. 191.

156. Carlo Faconi, *Leone X* (Milan, Italy: Rusconi, 1987), p. 157.

157. Francesco Guicciardini, *Storia d'Italia* (Italian First Edition at Italy:
unknown publisher, 1540; First American-published Italian Edition at
unknown city: University of California Libraries, 1836; and modern
edition in English at Princeton, New Jersey: Princeton University Press,
1984).

158. Carlo Faconi, *Leone X* (Milan, Italy: Rusconi, 1987), p. 157.

Paul Strathern, *The Medici: Godfathers of the Renaissance* (London:
Jonathan Cape, Ltd., 2003), p. 277.

159. Francesco Guicciardini, *Storia d'Italia* (Italian First Edition at Italy:
unknown publisher, 1540; First American-published Italian Edition at
unknown city: University of California Libraries, 1836; and modern
edition in English at Princeton, New Jersey: Princeton University Press,
1984).

Carlo Faconi, *Leone X* (Milan, Italy: Rusconi, 1987), p. 157.

Paul Strathern, *The Medici: Godfathers of the Renaissance* (London:
Jonathan Cape, Ltd., 2003), p. 277.

160. Joseph McCabe, *History of the Popes* (London: Watts & Co., 1939),
p. 409.

161. Note: This site is a straightforward and informal modern summary of
Leo X and is for educational and entertainment purposes. [(Pro-mom:
Religion and philosophy, 2009) Promom.hubpages.com/hub/Ten-Bad-
Popes.]

162. Francis A. Burkle-Young and Michael Leopoldo Doerrer, *The Life of Cardinal Innocenzo del Monte: A Scandal in Scarlet* (Lewiston, New York: Edwin Meller, 1997).

**Note: Pope Julius III, reigning 1550–1555, allegedly had a not-so-innocent friendship with Innocenzo Ciocchi el Monte, a cardinal with whom the Venetian ambassador claimed Julius had a long-lasting homosexual affair.**

**But at Parma in north-central Italy Julius allegedly switched partners, falling for a 17-year-old, and made him a cardinal.**

163. Will R. Huysman, *Banana Republican: Catholic Apologetics* (Bronx, New York City: Fordham University, 2009), http://thebananarepublican1.wordpress.com/2009/10/17/pope-john-xii/, 2009).

**Note: This is one Catholic apologetic source admitting to "a handful of evil popes," posted in 2009. There have been other Catholic sources making essentially the same admission.**

164. Louis-Marie de la Haye, Vicente de Cormenin, *A Complete History of the Popes of Rome: From Saint Peter, the First Bishop to Pius the Ninth, the Present Pope, Including the History of Saints, Martyrs, Fathers, of the Church, Religious Orders, Cardinals, Inquisitions, Schisms, and the latest Reformers* (Philadelphia: James L. Gihon, 1857), p. 5.

**Note: Additional commentary is presented by Vicente de Cormenin in 1859, using rather dramatic terminology, describing "the religious passions which drove men to the most horrible extremes, and caused them to resemble tigers, gorged with blood rather than human beings."**

165. *Foreign Affairs* (Tampa, Florida), March 19, 2013.

**Note: *Foreign Affairs* is a magazine published by the Council on Foreign Relations beginning in 1922. It is a bimonthly magazine of 163,000 subscribers established at New York City, with a second office in Washington, D.C. Its purpose is to influence foreign policy and to an extent economics, making recommendations to each presidential administration while interacting with (influencing) the media. Its members include senior politicians, senior media figures, and CIA directors, and it has been primarily funded by the Ford Foundation and the Rockefeller Foundation since the late 1930s,** [Thomas F. O'Brien, *The Centuries of U.S. Capitalism in Latin America* (Albuquerque, New Mexico: University of New Mexico Press), pp. 105–106] **which some political pundits claim have pursued political and social purposes above and beyond the charitable contributions for which they are mostly known.**

Considered "the most important influential think tank," [Jim Lobe, Interpress Service News Agency, August 19, 2005, who added in his article that *Foreign Affairs*' managing editor wrote a column for *The New York Times*] the Council on Foreign Relations (CFR) has included most important government officials since 1945 on its membership rolls. A survey of 502 government officials contacted from 1945 to 1972 showed just over half were members of CFR. [Peter Grose, *Continuing the Inquiry: The Council on Foreign Relations from 1921 to 1996* (New York City: Council on Foreign Relations Press, 1996).]

The Council's website boasts of its magazine, *"Foreign Affairs* is widely considered to be the most influential magazine for the analysis and debate of foreign policy and economics."

Since its inception, an impressive array of writers have contributed, including 11 Secretaries of State. With some exceptions, it has been criticized as solidly establishment while simultaneously left-leaning, apparent from its board membership and funding over the years, as well as its policy recommendations to presidential administrations. Its "establishment / left-of-center" viewpoint is exemplified by one recent-years example, Fareed Zakaria, former managing editor of *Foreign Affairs* (afterwards editor of *Newsweek International*, current columnist for the *Washington Post*, and editor-at-large for *Time* magazine).

While being technically nonpartisan in order to maintain its non-profit status, the left-leaning ideology among its most influential contributors to the magazine goes back to nearly its beginning, including the 1925 series of articles by W. E. B. Du Bois, an African-American intellectual who accomplished much good for the American civil rights movement but also had known Soviet sympathies. (He praised Stalin in a eulogy in the March 16, 1953 article, "On Stalin," in *National Guardian* magazine and, after visiting the USSR in 1926, he concluded Communism was a better vehicle to solve race problems than the American system. [David Levering Lewis, *W. E. B. Du Bois: A Biography* (New York City: Henry Holt and Company, 2009), p. 698.]

Josef Stalin, by 1953 when Du Bois wrote the eulogy, was well recognized for having killed 20–60 million fellow Russians and East Europeans, not counting another 20 million Russian soldiers and civilians killed in war during his reign, thus having several times more murder victims attributed to him than to Adolf Hitler in Nazi Germany (5.1 to 5.9 million Jews by most counts plus 5 million non-Jews, totaling 11 million aside from combat victims). ["Who Were the Five Million Non-Jewish Holocaust Victims?", http://www. holocaustforgotten.com/non-jewishvictims.htm; and "How Many Jews

Were Killed in the Holocaust?", Wiki Answers, https//wiki.answers. com/Q/How_many_Jews_were_killed_In_the_Holocaust?#slide=1.] **To Stalin is attributed this famous quote: "One death is a tragedy, one million is a statistic."** [Paraphrased from Leonard Lyons, columnist, "Loose-Leaf Notebook," *Washington Post*, January 30, 1947, p. 9; and Leonard Lyons, "Lyons Den," *Salt Lake Tribune*, January 30, 1947, p. 8, column 3.] **(This quote apparently morphed over the years to a more concise version of the one actually given by Stalin, as reported by columnist Leonard Lyons in 1947. Stalin, as Commissar of Munitions, was allegedly at a meeting of high-level commissars in which he heard a lecturer giving the death figures from a famine in the Ukraine, and, becoming impatient, interrupted the speaker, saying, "If only one man dies of hunger, that is a tragedy; if millions die, that's only statistics.")**

**Stalin forced another 9 to 11 million peasants off their lands, exiled 1 million from Moscow and Leningrad, dispatched 4 to 6 million to forced labor camps with their indescribable hardships of cold, hunger, and little sleep—prisoners rising at 4 A.M. and working till midnight— and he tortured numerous others (in addition to the 6 million he systematically starved to death from artificially created famines), while arresting yet another 1 million for "political crimes" (the first 7 years after World War II alone), according to Georgian historian Roy Aleksandrovich Medvedev in the newspaper *Argumenti I Fakti*,** [quoted in Palash R. Ghosh, *International Business Times* (published at New York City, 10 international editions in 7 languages), March 5, 2013] **putting the non-combat victim count at a conservative 20 million.**

**Meanwhile, Aleksandr Solzhenitsyn, the great Nobel Prize–winning Russian writer and historian who lived through 8 years of forced labor due to a simple criticism of Stalin in a personal letter, put the victim count closer to 60 million. Solzhenitsyn, a personal hero of mine, reformed his former beliefs, making a turnabout from former idealistic Red Army captain and state-sponsored atheist to converted Christian and anti-Soviet writer in exile, exposing the gulag system.**

**In short, Stalin clearly believed the ends justified the means in destroying individualism and promoting a totalitarian state, and ironically a number of American ideologues have looked past the tortures and murders, impressed with Stalin's vision for mankind in a socialist paradise.**

**Along with the CFR's ideological bent, which critics claim has contributed to the morass of problems in U.S. foreign polices and Keynesian economic, debt-driven strategies in recent decades, as a magazine, *Foreign Affairs* has contributed valuable information and**

facts about world affairs, such as the information I utilized for this book regarding statistics of Roman Catholic membership in Latin America.

166. Francis-Marie Arouet Voltaire, *Esssai sur histoire generale et sur les moeurs et l'espirit des nations* (translated into English its title in full is, *An Essay on Universal History, the Manners, and Spirit of Nations, from the Reign of Charlemagne to the Age of Lewis XIV* ) (1756; Farmington Hills, Michigan: Gale ECCO Print, 2014), chapter 70.

   **Note: Voltaire was a French writer and philosopher living from 1694 to 1778. His original text in French when he made this sarcastic quote was, "*Ce corps qui s'appelait et qui s'appelle encoe le saint empire romain n'etait en auune maniere ni sain, ni romain, ni empire,*" which, translated into English, reads, "The agglomeration which was called and which still calls itself the Holy Roman Empire was neither holy, nor Roman, nor an Empire."**

167. Johann Lorenz von Mosheim, *Institutionum historiae ecclesiasticae Antiquae at Recentioris libri iv*, 1726. English version: edited and translated to English by James Murdock (with additions to 1841 Edition by Henry Soames), *Institutes of Ecclesiastical History, Ancient and Modern, in Four Books, Much Corrected, Enlarged, and Improved, from the Primary Authorities*, 3 volumes (New Haven, Connecticut: A. H. Maltby, First Edition 1832), vol. 3 (containing book 4), century XVI.

   **Note: Johann Lorenz von Mosheim was a German Lutheran church historian. He was Chancellor of the University of Göttingen, writing this book originally in Latin.**

168. Ibid.

   *Isaac Milner, History of the Church of Christ, Volume the Fourth, Part 1: Containing the Remainder of the Thirteenth Century; also the Fourteenth, Fifteenth, and Part of the Sixteenth Century, Edited from the Manuscripts of the late Rev. Joseph Milner with Additions, Corrections, &c. By the Rev. Isaac Milner, D.D., Dean of Carlisle, and Master of Queen's College, Cambridge [University], First American Edition*, 7 volumes (Boston: Farrand, Mallory and Co., 1809; and London: Luke Hansard & Sons, for T. Cadell & W. Wavies, in the Strand, 1812), vol. 4.

169. **Note: While John Calvin achieved world renown as a Great Reformer, Guillaume Farel was actually a noteworthy Reformer on his own, but without the notoriety. He was in fact the man who first invited Calvin to join him in Switzerland.**

170. Andrew Martin Fairbairn, Chapter 11, in Lord Action, Stanley Leathes, Sir Adolphas William Ward, and G. W. Prothero, editors, *Cambridge*

*Modern History, Volume 2: The Reformation: The End of the Middle Ages,* 14 volumes (Cambridge, England: Cambridge University Press, 1902–1912; specifically 1903), vol. 2, p. 366.

**Note: This impressive series from Cambridge University Press covers 1450–1910.**

171. Ibid.

172. The Bible, King James Version, New Testament, Hebrews 5:4.

173. Thomas E. Woods Jr., *How the Catholic Church Built Western Civilization* (Buntingford, Hertfordshire, England: Regnery House Publishing / Regnery History, 2005), pp. 44–48.

174. Jacques Le Goff, *Medieval Civilization 400–1500* (Hoboken, New Jersey: Blackwell Publishing, First Edition 1991), pp. 80–82.

**Note 1: According to *The New York Review of Books*, "Jacques Le Goff is one of the most distinguished of the French medieval historians of his generation, a generation in which the French have consistently set the pace for medieval studies."** [Maurice Keen, book review, *The New York Review of Books* (New York City), May 18, 1989.]

**Note 2: *The New York Review of Books* is a semi-monthly magazine of literature, culture, book reviews, and current affairs, published since 1963. *Esquire* magazine calls it "the premier literary intellectual magazine in the English language."** [Matt Schedel, Obituary. "New York Review of Books' Founder Barbara Epstein," *The Washington Post* (Washington, D.C.), June 19, 2006, p. B05.]

**Note 3: *The Washington Post* was founded in 1877, has won 47 Pulitzer Prizes, and is known mostly for its political reporting on the White House and Congress. Employing 740 writers, it is one of few U.S. papers with foreign bureaus, currently with 16, but in 2009 it closed its U.S. regional bureaus in New York, Chicago, and Los Angeles. It is the 7th-largest U.S. paper, with over 474,000 weekday circulation and 838,000 on Sunday. In recent years it has made attempts to provide more balance, beefing up its stable of conservative columnists, but some conservative critics claim its editors choose news coverage that follows a more left-leaning narrative.**

Thomas E. Woods Jr., *How the Catholic Church Built Western Civilization* (Buntingford, Hertfordshire, England: Regnery House Publishing / Regnery History, 2005), p. 40.

175. August Franzen, Remigius Baumer, and Roland Frolich, *Kleine Kirchengeschichte* (Freiburg, Germany: Herder, 2001), p. 323.

176. Thomas E. Woods Jr., *How the Catholic Church Built Western Civilization* (Buntingford, Hertfordshire, England: Regnery House Publishing / Regnery History, 2005), pp. 44–48.

177. **Note: In chronological order, the next 2 universities among the first 15 ever established and which are still operating (as numbers 8 and 9 respectively) are Siena (Italy) in 1240 and Paris (France), which was established sometime between 1150 and 1250 A.D.**

   **The dates all these universities began were obtained from information provided by the universities themselves, as well as other sources.**

178. "Penn Research Shows That Mormons Are Generous and Active in Helping Others," *Penn News* (Philadelphia: University of Pennsylvania, April 17, 2012), http://www.upenn.edu/pennnews/news/penn-research-shows-mormons-are-generous-and-active-helping-others.

   **Note: This is a University of Pennsylvania study titled, "Called to Serve: The Prosocial Behavior of Active Latter-day Saints." It was sponsored by the University of Pennsylvania School of Social Policy and Practice and was conducted by Ram Cnnan, Associate Dean of Research, Professor, and Chair of the Doctoral Program in Social Welfare, along with fellow researchers Van Evans and Daniel W. Curtis. The University of Pennsylvania is a member of the Ivy League of universities.**

179. *The New York Times* (New York City), June 14, 1902.

   **Note: *The New York Times* was founded in 1851 and is the third-largest daily newspaper in the United States, after the *Wall Street Journal* and *USA Today*. Politically much farther left-of-center than the other two, it maintains an impressive 26 foreign news bureaus (and another 11 throughout the U.S. plus 10 more in New York State) with a staff of 1,150 in its news department.**

   **It was initially titled *The New York Daily Times* and switched to *The New-York Times* in 1857, then dropped the hyphen in the decade of the 1890s. Since its inception, it has been a daily paper.**

   **The author's favorite historical tidbit in relation to *The New York Times* is this—its founder and editor was Henry Raymond, who defended his newspaper business as riots broke out on July 13, 1863, just 2 years into the 4-year Civil War, when Congress passed laws to draft men into military service.**

   **On the morning of the draft's opening day, a mob of 500 attacked the draft's headquarters, lighting it on fire and burning other buildings, then it attacked the responding fire trucks, destroying the vehicles**

and killing the horses. Next, the mob cut telegraph wires so no other fire trucks could respond. Mostly of Irish descent, the rioters turned it into a race war, taking out their frustrations on blacks, whom the Irishmen and other whites feared would soon be freed and would take their jobs after the war; also they resented that blacks were the alleged cause of the war due to the slavery issue, and were thus the reason for the draft and the men in New York City being uprooted from their homes and lives to go fight an unpopular war. (In all, ironically, only 45,000 men nationwide were actually drafted to serve, of the 750,000 who were forced to register for the draft.)

In this riot the mobbers destroyed 50 buildings, including an orphanage for black children, fire stations, and two Protestant churches, since the rioters were predominantly Catholic immigrants. When the rioters came upon *The New York Times* building, founder Raymond manned a Gatling gun to hold off the mob and got his staff to join in, each manning a Gatling gun. In all about 2,000 people were injured in the riots and at least 120 killed, including 11 black men lynched. The black population mostly deserted the city during the 4-day riots.

Today *The New York Times* is controlled by Arthur Ochs Sutzburger Jr, as publisher and chairman of the company, whose family has controlled it since 1896.

180. Ibid., February 27, 1901.

181. *Deseret News* (Salt Lake City), January 22, 1898.

Note: The Salt Lake Tabernacle held 8,000 people when it was completed in 1867, after a 3-year construction period. Thirty-one years later, in 1898, it still had that seating capacity when John M. Reiner gave his lecture.

In 2007 a 2-year renovation was completed that removed seating for 1,000 people, putting the new capacity at 7,000, as leg room was increased in the pews from 9 to 14 inches.

182. "Dr. John M. Reiner on Mormonism," *Improvement Era* (Salt Lake City, 1898), vol. 1, no. 7 (May) 1898; also online at https://archive.org/details/improvementera17unse.

Note: This article in the *Improvement Era* magazine contains a letter to the magazine from John M. Reiner on March 12, 1898, dated at Elizabeth, New Jersey, with a response from B. H. Roberts, undated.

B. H. Roberts, *Collected Discourses*, 1886–1898 (Salt Lake City: Deseret Book, 2014; gospelink.com/library/contents/1235), vol. 5, p. 384.

Also cited in *Thy Servants Speak: Conference Set R: Conference Set Journal of Discourses, Collected Discourses, Conference Reports 1853 to 1922 (vol. 19)* (Salt Lake City: Eborn Books, 2012; and published online at Salt Lake City: Deseret Book, gospelink.com/library/contents/1235).

Orson F. Whitney, *Through Memory's Halls: The Life Story of Orson F. Whitney as Told by Himself* (Independence, Missouri: Zion's Printing and Publishing Company, 1930), pp. 222–223.

183. *Merriam-Webster Dictionary* (Springfield, Massachusetts, 1996), online at www.Merriam-webster.com/dictionary/theology.

184. **Note: A Lutheran's Masters of Divinity degree then and now consists of obtaining a 4-year Bachelor's Degree, followed by a 4-year Master's Degree involving 2 years of course study, a 1-year Internship acting as a pastor, and a final year of study in theology.**

185. **Note: The classes taught by John M. Reiner, Ph.D. and LL.D., at Villanova University were literary criticism and journalism, while his research, writings, and personal studies emphasized religion and religious history.**

186. *Deseret News* (Salt Lake City), January 22, 1898.

187. Orson F. Whitney, *Saturday Night Thoughts, Part 3* (7 parts in 1 volume) (Salt Lake City: Deseret News Press, 1921), pp. 63–64.

**Note 1: The first published account of Orson F. Whitney's conversation with Catholic theologian John M. Reiner came in 1917 in a pamphlet, "The Strength of the Mormon Position" (Independence, Missouri: Zion's Printing and Publishing Co., 1917), pp. 9–10. In this 58-page pamphlet Whitney does not give Reiner's name.**

**This conversation was also printed in his 1921 book** [*Saturday Night Thoughts, Part 3* (7 parts in 1 volume) (Salt Lake City: Deseret News Press, 1921), pp. 63–64] **and in his 1930 autobiography.** [*Through Memory's Halls: The Life Story of Orson F. Whitney, as Told by Himself* (Independence, Missouri: Zion's Printing and Publishing Company, 1930), pp. 222–223.] **Two years before the autobiography, on April 7, 1928, Whitney gave this same account of his conversation with Reiner in the 1928 LDS General Conference.** [Elder Orson F. Whitney, *Ninety-eighth Annual Conference of the Church of Jesus Christ of Latter-day Saints, Held In the Tabernacle and Assembly Hall, Salt Lake City, Utah, April 6, 7, and 8, 1928, With a Full Report of All the Discourses* (Salt Lake City: The Church of Jesus Christ of Latter-day Saints, 1928), pp. 60–61. Online: www.ldslearning.org./lds-general-conference-report-april-1928-cumorah.pdf.]

Note 2: This book by Orson F. Whitney, *Saturday Night Thoughts*, has a fascinating history. A majority of its contents consists of a series of 40 articles (divided into 7 parts) in Saturday issues of the *Deseret Evening News* from the last week of October 1918 to the last week of May 1919—exactly 7 months—for the purpose of inspiring the Latter-day Saint population where the paper was circulated, primarily in Utah, since the Saints were unable to attend church for several months due to a flu epidemic raging worldwide: the "Spanish flu" (so called because it received more press coverage for its epidemic in Spain, as the U.S. and other western countries sought to cover up the realities of its impact in the rest of the world in order to prevent a panic). Of the 1.8 billion people living on the planet then (compared to 7 billion today), 500 million were affected, mostly young adults rather than the usual elderly and children who are affected by influenza. Another oddity was that its worse months were in the summers, rather than the usual winters, when influenza hits hardest. It likely spread due to World War I soldiers weakened by chemical warfare, stress, and exposure from the cold and rain, without waterproof clothing, who returned home. It also spread quickly due to general enhancements and interest in worldwide travel at that time—automobile sales were exploding and people were traveling more by train as well—to the extent that between 50 and 100 million people died. That amounted to 10 to 20% of those who caught it, or 3 to 6% of the world's population, with more dying in one year than who died during the Black Death in a whole century. (However, a much smaller percentage of the population died during this period than during the Black Death, since the total number of people living on the planet was considerably higher in the early 20th century than in the 14th). The Spanish Flu lasted from January 1918 to December 1920, although, as stated, its worst effects in Utah were only during a 7-month period from October 1918 to May 1919, when public gatherings in the state were banned. Even April's General Conference had to be postponed to a later date.

Note 3: The opposition by Protestants to Catholic authority allows them to embrace historical criticisms of popes, but the irony is that while Protestant Reformers needed reasons to break away from Catholicism, their followers then and now have a fine line to walk, as many realize they need to tie into a legitimate Catholic priesthood authority that goes back to the Apostolic church, in order for them to have authority—a logical argument presented by Catholic theologian John R. Reiner at the end of this appendix.

Other Protestants believe that the only authority they need—in fact the only authority they admittedly "have"—is from their belief in the

Bible and the Gospel. The countering argument by Latter-day Saints to that logic is the following:

In civil society if a person merely had to believe in the system of laws found in the legal books in order to practice law, they could just go out and call themselves a lawyer, without taking any state bar exams that would authorize them to practice law. Their claim to practice it is that they "believe in the law books," and "the law books give them authority."

Soon, society would be chaotic, as many unqualified so-called lawyers would be interpreting the law for their clients, without any idea what they were doing. Thus, civilized society wisely authorizes certain people to practice law (those who qualify by passing a state bar exam, with or without law school to prepare for it). At that point civil society gives them its authority.

In the kingdom of heaven on earth, believe Latter-day Saints, granting authority to act in ecclesiastical matters is similar to having the authority to act in legal matters. Only with God's *authority* can one rightfully practice religious duties. The name for that authority to practice such duties is the *priesthood*.

This illustrates the concept of authority, which is separate from a mere belief in a book, such as the Bible—even though it is the word of God—because belief in a book does not give one *authority*.

These examples in this endnote tie in to the 6 pages of text in this appendix that illustrate priesthood authority being compared to the military and to real estate—and the need to have priesthood keys, in the eyes of Latter-day Saints.

188. Ronald Macaulay, "The counter-reformation of Pope John Paul II," *Cambridge Papers* (Cambridge, England: Jubilee Centre), vol. 9, no. 3 (September 2000).

189. Note 1: The table was set for when John XXIII was elected pope in 1958. (These ecumenical councils are highly important, fairly rare conferences—there have been only 21 ecumenical councils since 325 A.D.—the first one being at Nicea under Constantine's direction.) The previous ecumenical council was Vatican I in 1870.

On January 12, 1959, John XXII announced plans to convene Vatican II, which was held from 1962–1965, 92 years after Vatican I.

In Vatican II, reforms were announced that were interpreted by more liberal elements within the church to be more inclusive of Protestant viewpoints and priesthood. In June 1963 John XXII was succeeded by

Paul VI, who continued with the revolutionary changes. However, in 1978, John Paul II (1978–2005) was elected, and he showed strongly traditionalist viewpoints, while also promoting the "progressive" ones that emerged from Vatican II, thus pursuing two conflicting agendas at once through 2005, leaving a lack of clarity to many regarding the Catholic viewpoint toward the Protestant priesthood.

Then, what appeared to be conflicting doctrine got all cleared up when Pope Benedict XVI (2005–2013) approved a document in 2007, stating that other Christian denominations were not true churches because they lacked apostolic succession. This 2007 document by Pope Benedict XVI generated criticism from Protestant denominations, and it has not been overturned by the new pope, Francis, who was elected in March 2013. ["Pope: Other Christian Denominations Not True Churches," (Fox News, July 10, 2007), www.foxnews.com/story/2007/07/10/pope-other-christian-denominations-not-true-churches/; and "Pope: Only One 'True Church,'" (CBS News, July 10, 2007), www.cbsnews.com/news/pope-only-one-true-church/.]

In 2009 came this report from CBS News:

"Pope Benedict XVI has restated the universal primacy of the Roman Catholic Church, approving a document released Tuesday that says Orthodox Churches were defective and that other Christian denominations were not true churches," and "did not have the 'means of salvation.'" The report says, "The Vatican seeks to set the record straight on Vatican II's ecumenical intent, saying some contemporary theological interpretation had been 'erroneous or ambiguous' and had prompted 'confusion and doubt.' . . .

"'Christ established here on earth only one Church,' the document said. The other communities 'cannot be called "churches" in the proper sense' because they do not have apostolic succession—the ability to trace their bishops back to Christ's original apostles."

The report also states that Pope Benedict complained about "the erroneous interpretation of the council by liberals saying it was not a break from the past but rather a renewal of church tradition." [Ibid., CBS News.]

Further, on November 23, 2006 Pope Benedict XVI (2005–2013) reported about a meeting he had with Rowan Williams, head of the Anglican Communion, saying there were "serious obstacles to our ecumenical progress." [Paragraph 4 of a joint statement: "Common Declaration of Pope Benedict XVI and the Archbishop of Canterbury his grace Rowan Williams," issued "from the Vatican."]

Apparently, Pope Francis, serving since March 2013, is open to dialogue with Protestants but has not shown any willingness to change the Catholic Church's viewpoints on accepting the priesthood of other churches.

Note 2: In a nutshell, according to 2005–2009 statistics that were supplied by the Roman Catholic Church, there were 410,593 priests and 217,616 parishes worldwide (about 1.9 priests per parish). Meanwhile there were 5,065 Catholic bishops and 2,797 dioceses and archdioceses in the world, seated in 3,068 cathedrals (about 1.8 bishops per diocese/cathedral). This means that, on average worldwide, for every cathedral there were 71 parishes and thus perhaps about the same number of physical churches that house parishes. This number may vary in different parts of the world and in different eras of history.

190. Note: In comparing Roman Catholic terminology to Latter-day Saint definitions, a Catholic *parish* is the equivalent of an LDS *ward* or *branch* (a branch being smaller and less fully organized than a ward). The counterpart of a Catholic *diocese* is an LDS *stake* (so named from comparing the church, or Zion, to a tent, which has stakes holding it up, spread out from the main body of the tent). A Catholic *archdiocese* is a larger diocese with a larger geographical area and can contain other dioceses within it, especially when it is within one large city. Thus, an archdiocese is comparable to an LDS *region*, which contains several LDS stakes.

A Catholic parish meets in a parish *church* or *chapel*, while an LDS congregation meets in a *chapel* or *meetinghouse* (synonymous terms, with the slight distinction that *chapel* can refer either to the entire building or only to the main auditorium where sacrament meeting and other large worship services are held).

A Catholic *cathedral* is like an LDS *stake center* (although typically far more ornate), as both are larger than regular chapels. However, some old cathedrals in Europe, still in use today, are quite small, such as Christ Church Cathedral at Oxford, Oxfordshire, in south-central England and the Carlisle Cathedral at Carlisle, Cumbria, in northern England—the 2 smallest cathedrals in England and now part of the Church of England—as well as one at Dunkeld (later converted to the Church of Scotland). Other houses of worship that are as spacious and ornate as the typical cathedral are termed *minsters* instead. The distinction between the two is that a cathedral is associated with a bishop, while a minster is not. Both cathedrals and stake centers carry on more functions. A Catholic cathedral has numerous special functions compared to a regular Catholic parish church or chapel, as outlined below, while a Latter-day Saint stake center has only a few additional special functions over those of a regular LDS chapel.

In the Catholic cathedral, its leader, the bishop, has an office called a *chancery*. In the LDS stake center, its leader, the stake president, has an office simply called the *stake president's office*. At a cathedral is a *parish center*, where non-worship activities take place. In a stake center is a *cultural hall*, usually containing a full-size basketball gymnasium. Smaller-sized gymnasiums are also contained in many regular LDS chapels—often only ½- or ¾-size compared to the full-size gym that is typically in a stake center's cultural hall.

Parish priests live in a church-owned *rectory*, while LDS bishops live in their privately owned homes, for which they are responsible for paying.

Catholic bishops and archbishops often live in a *bishop's palace*, if they have one connected to a cathedral, whereas LDS stake presidents, like LDS bishops, live in regular houses or apartments, whatever their regular job's income can afford, since the Church of Jesus Christ of Latter-day Saints has an almost entirely lay clergy, as compared to the Catholic professional clergy.

Thus, LDS bishops and other leaders are not paid for their ecclesiastical work, and hold other jobs, generally volunteering enough hours after work for their church to equate to a part-time or even another full-time job.

In contrast to the almost entirely lay clergy of the Latter-day Saints, Catholic priests and all Catholic leaders are paid clergy and have the ministry as their sole occupation.

Ranking above Catholic bishops are *archbishops*. Within larger cities they are termed *metropolitan archbishops* or *metropolitans*. Both preside over an archdiocese. The LDS equivalent to an archbishop or a Metropolitan archbishop is an LDS *regional representative*, who oversees several stakes, which comprise the aforementioned region. Ranking above them are the LDS *general authorities*.

A few LDS general authorities hold their positions for life, but all other positions below them—regional representatives, stake presidents, and bishops—are temporary, usually for a period of up to 5 years.

Differences in the lifestyle of leaders for the two churches include not only their theological beliefs, of course, but their clothing and even their domestic lives.

Catholic priests, bishops, cardinals, and the pope take vows to never marry, whereas LDS leaders generally are married. Also, LDS leaders wear regular business clothes—suits and ties while performing their priesthood duties—while Catholic leaders wear special robes, called vestments, specific to their offices.

The higher-ranking Catholic and LDS leaders share some organizational similarities. Ranking above LDS bishops, stake presidents, and regional representatives are LDS general authorities. These high-ranking LDS leaders might be equated with the Catholic *cardinals*. The very highest LDS general authorities are the Quorum of the Twelve Apostles and the First Presidency of the Church, which include the president (also known as the prophet) and his two counselors. The closest equivalents to them perhaps are the highest-ranking cardinals, particularly those in Rome at the Vatican, working most closely with the pope.

The highest of all church leaders in the two churches are the Catholic *pope* and the Latter-day Saint church *president.*

In the LDS Church, while there is no paid clergy in local ministries, there is a living stipend given to the comparatively few of the general authorities—the highest-ranking LDS leaders—who are needed full-time, often with almost incessant travel involved.

On the congregational level, with Catholics, typically only 1 parish meets in a church (or chapel); thus, for every 71 chapels there are about 71 parishes. And for every 71 parishes on average there exists a cathedral. These averages are based on worldwide numbers, which may differ from country to country.

The average LDS stake (similar in structure to a Catholic diocese) consists of 7.1 wards.

With Latter-day Saints, up to 3 wards or branches meet in each chapel; thus, for every 2 or 3 chapels there is a stake center, which itself houses a full complement of wards or branches.

In less-developed LDS areas are *districts* instead of stakes, and *branches* instead of wards. Some branches are under the umbrella of a stake, while others are within the jurisdiction of a district. In the least developed areas of all, church organization falls under the purview of a *mission*, presided over by a *mission president*, who oversees the efforts of the all-volunteer proselyting missionaries. In the better-developed areas mission presidents and missionaries deal only with proselytizing.

Many branches meet in rented halls or even in members' homes, although a growing number have their own chapel, often in only the 1st or 2nd stage (explained below).

A 1st-stage LDS chapel consists of a simple single-story building that houses one large room sizeable enough to hold the main church meeting, called *sacrament meeting*, for an entire small congregation— up to about 75–100 people—plus it houses other, smaller rooms that contain offices, classrooms, rest rooms, and a "library" for checking out supplies.

Once a branch outgrows that building, the church constructs a 2nd-stage building and keeps that 1st-stage building. The 2nd-stage building consists of a regular, main chapel with a high ceiling, pews, and piano and organ. (Only pianos are found in 1st-stage buildings).

The 3rd stage for a chapel is the *cultural hall*, consisting of a gymnasium and stage for social and athletic events, plus a kitchen. Thus, branches and their chapels are a work in progress, and when the membership in a given area grows large enough, the chapel expands from a 1st-stage chapel to a 2nd-stage chapel, to a completed 3rd-stage chapel. During that last stage, the branch is often large enough to be designated a ward. (At times, membership grows briskly enough in an area to jump straight to a complete 3rd-stage building when starting construction.)

When branches are "upgraded" to wards, the districts to which they belong are often upgraded as well—to stakes. And in that case a stake center is built. Stake centers are also built when the church grows sufficiently large in an area to warrant a new stake, split off from the first.

The humorous side of LDS terminology has arisen when people learning about the church—as well as new converts—have been invited to an event at the "stake center," and show up, expecting a steak dinner. (The author, himself, like countless other investigators and new members, slipped into this misunderstanding at his first invitation to a stake event.)

At LDS chapels the main meeting is called *sacrament meeting*, in which bread and water are passed to members of the church in remembrance of the Savior's sacrifice. After the sacrament, members of the church—men, women, and youth—present pre-assigned talks of usually 10 or 15 minutes, which they prepare beforehand, then present at the podium to the congregation. On the stand, the bishop presides, flanked by his two counselors. Hymns are also sung and prayers open and close the meeting.

In the same 3-hour block of meetings are 2 others. First is Sunday School, for youth and adults. The 3rd meeting in this block is Priesthood Meeting (for boys over 12 and men) and Relief Society Meeting (for women over 18). For youth, this 3rd meeting is called Young Men's and Young Women's (short for Young Men's and Young Women's Mutual Improvement Association, or "Mutual"). The meeting for children aged 3 to 12 is called Primary, and for infants between the ages of 1½ and 3 there is Nursery (mainly a baby-sitting meeting, where basics such as sharing are taught).

For Catholics, the one meeting of worship is termed *Mass*, and, similarly, *communion*, where the sacrament of the Lord's Supper is served. The priest may read and expound the scriptures and leads in prayer.

In regards to Catholic cathedrals, the word itself is based on the Latin word, *cathedra*, or *seat*, for the bishop. (Catholic terminology also uses the words *chair* and *throne* for the bishop's seat.)

Cathedrals have at least 20 specific functions and features beyond those of a regular parish church. These include the following:

(1) The chair or throne for the bishop

(2) Seating for a choir

(3) A pipe organ

(4) At least 3 worship services daily plus additional services on Sunday

(5) A lectern for reading the Bible

(6) A pulpit for expounding the Bible

(7) A repository for local history

(8) Events that are held for local and national civic celebrations and even events of sadness with special services

(9) Funerals for famous people

(10) Coronation ceremonies for monarchs

(11) Burial spots or memorials for community and church leaders

(12) Announcements of significant civic news

(13) A bell or bells to announce a worship service, the start and end of a war, "peals" for weddings and other rejoicings, and deep bell soundings for disaster or death

(14) Optional clocks and chimes outside to give the time

(15) Its own school (as parish churches often do also)

(16) In many cases, offices of a mayor and council and even a local court, plus sports and service clubs

(17) Often, associated buildings like the bishop's palace and/or monastery buildings

(18) Sometimes, serving as a destination spot for pilgrimages (such as Santiago de Compostela in Spain), where people travel to venerate a saint or a holy object and where, on occasion, prayers have reportedly been answered or miracles have occurred

(19) A registry of births, marriages, and deaths (generally recorded here rather than in parish churches)

(20) Often, especially in older cathedrals, shrines, sacred relics, and/or sarcophagi (sometimes with the corpse on display behind glass) of venerated individuals

In contrast to these numerous functions and features of a cathedral, LDS stake centers simply hold offices for the stake president, the stake clerk, often a family history library, and a conference room for the stake *high council*—12 men called to assist the stake president in visiting local wards and overseeing stake business. As stated, stake centers have larger cultural halls for social and sporting events than ward buildings. They also house a baptismal font, unlike most regular chapels, for performing baptism by immersion—the necessary initiation rite or ordinance to become a member of the church.

Some few Catholic houses of worship also have a baptismal font, but this is not a common feature, since the church abandoned the practice of baptism by immersion many centuries ago.

191. Mark E. Petersen, "Which Church is Right?" (pamphlet) (Salt Lake City: The Church of Jesus Christ of Latter-day Saints, 1957).

Note 1: Mark E. Petersen presented some Apostasy and Restoration concepts and statements utilized herein.

Note 2: Based on the observations of many active Latter-day Saints, doubts seem to melt away for those church members who are grounded in their faith—those who base their convictions on the *Book of Mormon*. They cite their logic on this argument—that if the *Book of Mormon* is true—and if indeed it is a translation from prophets' writings in ancient America, then Joseph Smith was a prophet, since he translated it by divine means. And if he was a true prophet, then it stands to reason his claims to have received divine direction to establish a church are also true, along with the authority (the priesthood) to act in Christ's name, just as Christ's ancient church had, as governed by twelve apostles. The church Joseph was instrumental in founding today is also governed by twelve living apostles, which the church maintains possesses the same priesthood authority now, restored to the earth.

## APPENDIX V

1. "Bible Dictionary," in Appendix, The Holy Bible, Containing the Old and New Testaments, Translated out of the Original Tongues: And with the Former Translations Diligently Compared and Revised, By His Majesty's Special Command: Authorized King James Version with Explanatory Notes and Cross References to the Standard Works of the Church of Jesus Christ of Latter-day Saints (Salt Lake City: The Church of Jesus Christ of Latter-day Saints, 1979), pp. 725–726.

## APPENDIX W

1. J. Waterworth, translator, "The Fourth Session," *Council of Trent: The canons and decrees of the sacred and ecumenical Council of Trent* (London: Dolman, 1848), pp. 17–21.

   Note: The council of Trent's 4th session was convened on April 8, 1546.

2. "Theological Glossary," *The Jerusalem Bible: Reader's Edition* (New York City: Doubleday, First Edition 1966).

3. F. F. Bruce, *The Canon of Scripture* (Downers Grove, Illinois: IVP Academic: InterVarsity Press, 2010).

4. The Bible: Authorized King James Version with Apocrypha (Oxford, England and New York City: Oxford World's Classics/Oxford University Press, 1998).

5. Sir Fredric G. Kenyon, *Dictionary of the Bible*, edited by James Hastings (New York City: Charles Scribner's Sons, 1909).

6. Leslie Howsam, *Cheap Bibles: Nineteenth Century Publishing and the British and Foreign Bible Society* (Cambridge Studies in Publishing and

Printing History) (Cambridge, England: Cambridge University Press, 2002), p. 14.

7. *The Doctrine and Covenants of the Church of Jesus Christ of Latter-day Saints: Containing Revelations given to Joseph Smith, the Prophet, with Some Additions by His Successors In the Presidency of the Church* (Salt Lake City: The Church of Jesus Christ of Latter-day Saints, 1981), 91: 3–5.

# APPENDIX X

1. Parley P. Pratt, *Autobiography of Parley P. Pratt* (Arlington, Virginia and Provo, Utah: Stratford Books, 2005), p. 27.

2. Walter Scott (attributed), commentary [on Josiah Jones], "History of the Mormonites," *The Evangelist* (Pittsburgh, Pennsylvania), vol. 9 (June 1, 1831), pp. 132–136, cited in Mark Lyman Staker, *Hearken O Ye People: The Historical Setting of Joseph Smith's Ohio Revelations* (Draper, Utah: Greg Kofford Books, 2009), pp. 52, 66.

3. Lucy Diantha Morley Allen, "Autobiographical Sketch," unpublished, Morley Family Histories, MS 6106, holograph, Historical Library, Church Archives, The Church of Jesus Christ of Latter-day Saints, Salt Lake City.

4. Ibid.

5. Oliver Cowdery, Letter (from "Kirtland, Ohio, to Our Beloved Brethren [in Fayette, New York], November 12, 1830"), holograph copy in Newel Knight, "Autobiography," typescript, MS 2737, Box 56, Folder 5, Church Historical Library, The Church of Jesus Christ of Latter-day Saints, Salt Lake City.

6. Lyman Wight, quoted in Joseph Smith III and Heman C. Smith, *The History of the [Reorganized] Church of Jesus Christ of Latter Day Saints, 1805–1890*, 4 volumes (Lamoni, Iowa: The Reorganized Church of Jesus Christ of Latter-day Saints, 1896–1903), vol. 1, p. 154.

**Note: This historical book series was picked up and continued by F. Henry Edwards, *The History of the [Reorganized] Church of Jesus Christ of Latter Day Saints*, Volumes 5–8 (Independence, Missouri: Herald House, 1897–1903).**

7. Lucy Diantha Morley Allen, "Autobiographical Sketch," unpublished, Morley Family Histories, MS 6106, holograph, Church Historical Library,

Church Archives, The Church of Jesus Christ of Latter-day Saints, Salt Lake City.

8. John Riggs, "Autobiographical Sketch," 1880, p. 1, MS 855, microfilm of holograph, Church Historical Library, The Church of Jesus Christ of Latter-day Saints, Salt Lake City.

9. "The Book of Mormon," *Painesville Telegraph* (Painesville, Ohio), vol. 2, no. 25 (December 7, 1830), p. 3.

10. Jesse Jasper Moss, "Autobiography of a Pioneer Preacher," edited by M. M. Moss, *Christian Standard*, January 8, 1938, p. 33.

Note: The *Christian Standard* magazine was connected to the religious Restoration Movement and began publishing in 1866 at Cleveland, Ohio, about 25 miles southwest of Kirtland, becoming the most influential publication of the movement. The magazine is now published out of Cincinnati.

11. Elizabeth Ann Whitney, "A Leaf from an Autobiography," *Woman's Exponent* (Salt Lake City), vol. 7, no. 7 (September 1, 1878), p. 51.

Note 1: This fascinating magazine, *Woman's Exponent*, was published in Salt Lake City from 1872 to 1914. Its purpose was to uplift and strengthen Latter-day Saint women and to educate those not of the LDS faith about women in the church. It was not an official church organ, yet at one time approximately 10% of the LDS Relief Society members subscribed to it. (The Relief Society is one of the oldest and largest organizations for women in the world, consisting of 6 million members in over 170 countries and territories. All LDS women over the age of 18 comprise its membership, and there are no membership dues. It was and is the official organization for women in the church since its founding In 1843 at Nauvoo, Illinois.) The magazine included news, stories, poems, humor, and bits of wisdom, and was replaced by the official church publication, *Relief Society Magazine*, which was published from 1915 to 1970.

12. Philo Dibble, "Philo Dibble's Narrative," *Early Scenes in Church History* (Salt Lake City: Juvenile Instructor Office, 1882), pp. 76–77.

# *Porter Rockwell: A Biography*

by Richard Lloyd Dewey

Porter Rockwell was the bodyguard to Joseph Smith and Brigham Young. He was the only man to kill more outlaws than Wyatt Earp, Doc Holladay, and Batt Masterson combined, a man who believed if he never cut his hair he could never be killed. Famed British journalist Jules Remy wrote in 1861, "He is the stuff from which heroes are wrought."

Richard Lloyd Dewey quotes hundreds of original sources—journals, letters, and court records, some from sources never before tapped - and weaves them all together in fascinating form.

Journalistic, fast-flowing writing sweeps the reader through explosive early Mormon history with charm and style, reporting little-known events.

Considered the definitive work on Porter Rockwell, this book is impressively illustrated by renowned western artist Clark Kelley Price.

"Riveting reading, solidly researched."
—Gannett Newspapers (*USA Today*, etc.)

"The writing is slick and the pace is fast. Dewey has done his homework."
—*Deseret News*

"The best book of several written on Porter Rockwell."
—Duaine Hiatt, *This People Magazine*

Hardcover, $29.95                    ISBN: 978-0-929753-23-2

*Look for it in your favorite bookstore.*

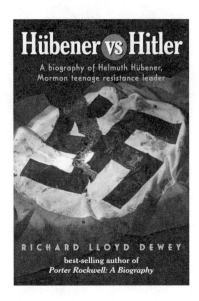

# Hübener vs Hitler

### A Biography of Helmuth Hübener,
### Mormon Teenage Resistance Leader

REVISED, SECOND EDITION

by Richard Lloyd Dewey

From Nazi Germany comes one of the most intriguing true tales of the 20th century: a group of teenage Germans who waged a war of their own against Adolf Hitler.

Nobel Laureate author Günther Grass said Hübener's life should be held up as a role model to every teen in the world.

Master biographer Richard Lloyd Dewey recounts the compelling true story of Helmuth Hübener—the bold and brilliant teenager who formed the youngest resistance group to face the Nazis.

He details how young Hübener recruited others, how his group eluded the SS, and how they played cat and mouse with the Gestapo.

This is a mesmerizing story of the entire group and presents the most comprehensive account ever of this astonishingly brave trio of young Latter-day Saints.

Softcover, $25.00                    ISBN: 978-0-929753-30-0

*Look for it in your favorite bookstore.*

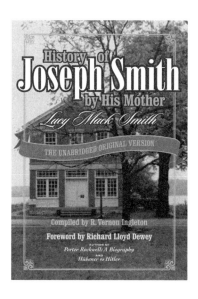

# *History of Joseph Smith by His Mother*
### THE UNABRIDGED ORIGINAL VERSION
## by Lucy Mack Smith

compiled by R. Vernon Ingleton
with foreword by Richard Lloyd Dewey

"The ***best version yet*** of Lucy's book," states biographer and historian Richard Lloyd Dewey.

3 reasons why:

1) It takes the ***original*** 1853 ***published version, unabridged***, and puts it in modern, readable type.

2) It adds her ***rough draft***, missing from the published edition, and plugs it into the right spots in a ***separate*** typeface. This easy-to-read format is innovate and flows easily for the reader.

3) It contains ***footnotes of all the changes*** made by editors and church historians over the years.

Hardcover, $27.95                    ISBN:  978-0-929753-22-5

*Look for it in your favorite bookstore.*